UTAH'S HERITAGE

UTAH'S HERITAGE

S. GEORGE ELLSWORTH

PROFESSOR OF HISTORY, UTAH STATE UNIVERSITY

Peregrine Smith, Inc.
SANTA BARBARA AND SALT LAKE CITY
1972

Manufactured in the United States of America

ISBN: 0-87905-006-3
Library of Congress
Catalog Card Number: 72-85712

S. George Ellsworth, author of *Utah's Heritage*, was born in Arizona of Utah and Arizona pioneer ancestors and reared in Utah, California, and Missouri, where he received his early schooling. He holds a bachelor's degree from Utah State Agricultural College, and master's and doctor's degrees in history from the University of California, Berkeley. He taught junior and senior high school at Bunkerville, Nevada, before serving in the United States Army during World War II. At Utah State University since 1951, he is currently professor of history and editor of the *Western Historical Quarterly*, a national journal for western historians. In 1959 he delivered the Faculty Honor Lecture and in 1965 was named Professor of the Year.

The designer for *Utah's Heritage*, Dale W. Bryner, received his B.F.A. (1962) and M.F.A. (1965) degrees from the University of Utah. He is currently Assistant Professor of Art at Weber State College, Ogden. In addition to teaching, Mr. Bryner is a practicing artist who has won numerous awards for paintings, drawings, and graphic design in both state and national competitions.

The picture editor for *Utah's Heritage*, Margaret Derrick Lester, attended Salt Lake City schools and the University of Utah. A long-time librarian with the Salt Lake Public Library system, Mrs. Lester left in 1957 to become Curator of Photographic Collections for the Utah State Historical Society. Under her guidance, the collection has developed and gained national attention.

The following is gratefully acknowledged by the publishers:

In memory of Simon P. Eggertsen of Provo, Utah, an educator who loved Utah and its heritage, a grant has been given to aid in the publication of this book. The grant was made by the S. B. Eggertsen Foundation through Dean E. Eggertsen, its Trustee.

Cover design: Dale W. Bryner.
End sheets: Navajo rug design.

PREFACE

This volume is the latest in a series of studies of Utah written for the use in the social studies program of the public schools of Utah. The books by Orson F. Whitney, Levi Edgar Young, John Henry Evans, and Milton R. Hunter have been used through the years. *Utah's Heritage* continues in the tradition set by these authors and brings the account to the present day, covering a wide range of subjects and human activities. Attention has been given to all the people who have helped to make Utah, insofar as records of their activities are available.

The book is based on primary sources wherever possible—letters, diaries, newspapers, official reports and records. The excellent studies by reliable scholars have also been used. Emphasis has been on telling and explaining the facts of the story with a minimum of comment and interpretation. The author has tried to stay out of the presentation. A list of the wide range of sources and literature for Utah's history is presented in the Teacher's Guide and constitutes, in its way, a bibliography of works used in writing the book.

The book brings under one cover a single treatment of the whole of Utah's history. New is its coverage of the twentieth century, heretofore touched only briefly by previous writers. The breadth of coverage of life in territorial Utah and the contributions of many different people to Utah are also new. The information presented on the geography and the Indians of Utah is found in specialized literature; the presentation here summarizes a large body of scientific studies.

The book may be used either as a narrative history or as a resource book. In the classroom it should be supplemented by a multitude of written materials. The text summarizes large bodies of material, easily expanded by reference to the literature. There is also a large amount of audio-visual materials available. The Teacher's Guide to classroom activities should be used with this book and as a reference tool to the large body of written material and audio-visual materials in the form of films, filmstrips, pictures, and sound presentations.

INTRODUCTION

Did you know that—

Utah has one of the largest
dinosaur graveyards in the world?

Volcanoes once erupted
on Utah's landscape?

During the ice age a large lake
covered much of western Utah,
and that Great Salt Lake, Utah Lake,
and Sevier Lake are remnants?

Utah is rich in mineral wealth
and other natural resources?

Some Utah Indians were among
the most advanced people
in the Americas?

Utah's Indians were Utah's
first explorers and farmers?

Utah has one of the most
varied landscapes of any state
in the Union?

Utah's past is just as varied and colorful. Spanish explorers were in Utah the same year the Declaration of Independence was signed. Mountain Men had been trapping beaver in Utah streams over twenty-five years before Utah was permanently settled by the Mormons.

It was the Mormon settlement of Utah that gave Utah her unique character. If it had not been for the coming of the Mormons to Utah when they did, Utah would not have been settled for years and then, most likely, Utah would have become essentially a mining and cattle state. She would not have been the agricultural state she is nor would her cities and towns be quite like they are.

The Mormon experience was one of America's most interesting social experiments. The Mormons planned to build a complete society with their own political, economic, and social system. They had a dream of reforming the world. No other state in the Union, except the original colonies, has such a background. We will learn about that experiment and how the Mormons brought thousands of convert immigrants to Utah for a unique life here. We will study that life—an attempt to establish a religious kingdom on the American frontier.

But the Mormons were not the only builders of Utah. Many other people came and made contributions. Because of the variety of people who came to Utah, our state has one of the most exciting histories of the western states.

Utah is a state rich in the variety of resources and industries. Utah is an agricultural state, a livestock state, a mining state, a manufacturing state, and a recreational and scenic state. Salt Lake City, besides being the political capital of Utah, is the religious capital of the world-wide Mormon church, and is the financial and commercial center of the Mountain West. Odgen is the railroad center of the Mountain West.

We may gain many values from our study of Utah's heritage. History is the memory of mankind. What would we do without a memory? If we lost our memories we would wander aimlessly. And if society lost its memory—its history—it too would be doomed to wander aimlessly. As we study the lives of others (or when we see a great play or show), we share the experiences of others and have a little of their experience for our own. Having had that experience, we may be able to plan our lives a little better. We may be able to avoid the mistakes they made, and imitate their ways of success.

A knowledge of history helps us see where we are, where we have been, and where we might go. The present is rooted in the past, and we can see that the future has already begun. History teaches us that change is always going on, that it cannot be stopped, nor can it be speeded up very much. History teaches us the influence of individuals, and lets us know that we can have influence in our times. Utah history also illustrates the influence of ideas and customs.

Utah's Heritage is written to be read as a story, but it is organized so it can be used as a reference book, a resource book for finding answers to many questions or problems.

The twenty-six chapters in the book are grouped into eight units. Each unit covers a major topic or period in Utah's historical development and is introduced by statements that summarize the major themes in the unit. Each chapter has an introduction to the major themes in that chapter followed by a list of the sections in the chapter. Section titles state the most important point to be learned in that section. Main topics in each section are printed in bold face type. Important points—names, places, and events supporting these main topics—are printed in italic.

The illustrations in the book have been selected with care. Maps, drawings, paintings, and photographs are used that were produced at the time of the events told. Most maps drawn by Dale Bryner are based on the author's maps which were sketched after a careful reading of the sources. Many photographs and paintings used here have not been published widely. Illustrations have been chosen to tell something important or interesting about the subject. Each picture tells a story—of the person who took it, of the place shown, of the people there, of the event recorded, and of the material culture shown such as the houses, buildings, means of transportation, tools, and clothing. By comparing photographs of the same general area, taken at different periods, we may be able to see historical development. Photographs help us have a feeling for another time and other places. Portraits help us meet and understand persons who otherwise are only names.

Our Utah heritage is more meaningful and useful to us if we know a lot about it. Many of us have learned of that heritage from our parents and grandparents. We can learn about it too from studying the record of the past presented here in these pages.

CONTENTS

THIS IS UTAH'S HERITAGE

UNIT ONE
NATURE'S GIFTS TO UTAH

Utah is a land rich in natural beauty with many resources useful for man. Utah has been called "the geologist's paradise." It is the sightseer's delight, the vacationer's picnic ground, the sportsman's hunting ground, and the photographer's ready-made outdoor studio. For its many-colored formations Utah has been called "the Rainbow Land."

Utah is filled with harsh contrasts. It is a land of wide expanses of wilderness country. It is a region of high mountains and fertile valleys bordered by forbidding deserts. Utah's high mountains are covered with forests and lined by running brooks. Her high plateaus and canyonlands are cut by muddy rivers that make deep canyons through nearly perpendicular rock walls, broken into amazing shapes of fantastic colors.

Utah is a desert land. There are extremes of hot and cold, and only small areas of rich soil with nearby water. Today Utah cities and towns appear as oases in the desert. It is human effort that has made the desert blossom. Frugality and hard work have been required at all times to keep man's hold on this oasis in the desert.

The land is the stage on which the drama of human history takes place. The natural environment limits man in some of the things he is able to do. Utah is poor in agricultural lands suitable for crops, compared to the great population centers of the earth. Without transportation to bring in essential goods for her people, Utah would always be next to poverty. Yet there are small valleys where land and water come together to make possible thriving human settlements. Located at "the crossroads of the West," Utah receives much from other communities in the nation, and contributes much to her neighbors and the nation.

THE FORMATION OF THE LAND

Utah has one of the most varied landscapes of all the states in the Union. There are mountains covered with forests and filled with cold, pure streams. There are high plateaus cut by muddy rivers exposing rock formations of amazing shapes and colors. Utah has the largest body of salt water in the western hemisphere—the Great Salt Lake. In the western part of the state are deserts and near-barren mountains. On the other hand, the high Wasatch Mountain peaks are often topped with snow until the middle of summer. Some of Utah's canyons are of gigantic proportions, some are small and delicate, sculptured by wind and rain. Utah is a beautiful land with a great variety of scenery. How did these wonders of nature come to be? A study of the historical geology of Utah, which is the study of the development of the land, will help us with the answers.

IN THIS CHAPTER WE WILL LEARN

1. Utah is as old as creation.

2. Through most of Utah's earth history, ancient seaways covered Utah.

3. Dinosaurs roamed Utah's marshes during the Age of Reptiles.

4. How Utah's landscape of mountains, valleys, and plateaus was formed.

5. During the Ice Age, Lake Bonneville covered much of western Utah.

6. The forces of nature are still shaping the land of Utah.

In some areas of Utah it is possible to see how the land may have looked before the coming of man. This view shows the area of Zion National Park.

Erosion in these rocks reveals layers of strata laid down by ancient seaways.

Shallow seaways covered most of Utah during prehistoric times.

1. UTAH IS AS OLD AS CREATION

There is no better place in the world to see the development and changes of the earth than in the rugged canyons and lofty mountains of Utah. The story of the long creation of the earth is shown in many places. The canyons and some of the uplifted mountains show us rocks that were once the sediments (mud and sand) of ancient seaways. Utah is one of the best places in the world to find the remains of dinosaurs which lived long ago in swampy regions that covered eastern portions of the state. The remains of volcanoes and of glaciers can be seen in several places.

The landscape has been changed only a little by man. However, the forces of nature have changed the landscape in many places.

2. THROUGH MOST OF UTAH'S EARTH HISTORY, ANCIENT SEAWAYS COVERED UTAH

The ancient seaway of North America. From the earliest times until fairly recent geologic times, a long, narrow, shallow, seaway that covered most of Utah extended over much of western North America. Shifts in the earth's crust changed the shoreline of the ancient seaway from time to time. Sometimes the depth of the water changed. When it became very shallow, land appeared in places.

The ancient seaway laid down sediment and preserved fossils. Rivers and streams washed soils from the surrounding land to the bottom of the sea where they formed *sediment*. Dead plants and animals were buried in the layers of accumulating earth. In time the sediments were compressed into hard rocks. The remains of plants and animals were also pressed thin but left their traces in the layers of rock. These remains are called *fossils*. As long periods of time passed, additional layers of sediments were laid. These layers are shown in the rocks that formed from them. In these layers are to be found the fossil remains of the plant and animal life of those periods of time in Utah.

Earth eruptions gave Utah volcanoes and igneous rocks. Sedimentary rocks are not the only kind found in Utah. Thousands of feet beneath the earth's surface, generally in the area covered by the sea, molten, or melted, material was formed. When this material hardened beneath the earth's surface, it formed rocks such as granite. When the molten material was forced through the earth's surface, it came in the form of lava, creating volcanoes. Rocks produced from such a fiery origin are called *igneous* rocks. *Extinct volcanoes* may be seen today in several places in Utah. Southwest of Fillmore in the Black Rock Desert of Millard County are several extinct volcanoes. In Washington County, north of Santa Clara, and in the great cliffs region of Kane County, good examples may be seen of past fiery eruptions. In southeastern Utah, in the Canyonlands section of the Colorado Plateau, are domal mountains which are igneous in origin—they are nearly volcanoes but did not erupt to the surface.

There are other reminders of the time of volcanoes. *Hot springs* are often associated with volcanic activity or lava flow and are caused by water flowing near the heated rocks on its way to the surface, dissolving minerals on the way. Among the noted hot springs of Utah are the iron springs at Ogden and springs at Salt Lake City, Castilla, Grantsville, Lehi, Sevier Desert, Midway Hot Pots, Monroe, Milford, and the Virgin River.

Rocks of all geologic ages are to be seen in Utah. Traveling throughout the state, one

This aerial view looks down into the crater of one of Utah's extinct volcanoes west of Fillmore. Notice the extent of lava flow.

This fossil trilobite from Marjum Pass, House Range, Utah, lived about five hundred million years ago.

can see rocks of every geologic age. One can also see the fossil remains of plant and animal life: corals, trilobites, cephalopods, insects, fish, amphibians, reptiles, musk oxen, horses, camels, deer, mountain sheep, and mammoths. There are excellent remains of petrified wood, too. However, Utah is especially famous for its fossil reptiles.

This view shows tilting and erosion of the earth's crust at the southeast end of the Uinta Mountains. Some of the rocks exposed here contain dinosaur bones.

A technician puts the finishing touches on a spectacular mass of fossil bones at Dinosaur National Monument.

This skeletal reconstruction of a diplodocus dinosaur is from remains found in Utah.

More important for man today is the fact that during long periods of the earth's history the materials which formed Utah's rich store of metals, minerals, coal beds, natural gas, and oil were laid. In Utah these materials generally represent the younger or more recent geologic times.

3. DINOSAURS ROAMED UTAH'S MARSHES DURING THE AGE OF REPTILES

Utah in the Age of Reptiles. One of the most interesting geologic ages for Utah is the time of the reptiles. For a very long time, during the later ages of the Mesozoic ("middle life") Era, creatures—some of gigantic size—roamed over most of the earth. The ancient seaway bordered the region of eastern Utah then, and rivers and swamplands were everywhere. Such places were favorite haunts of the dinosaurs and other reptiles. Dinosaurs became trapped in sandbars and swamps, where they died and were buried. Their bones finally became part of the formation that was laid as succeeding layers of sediment.

The Morrison Formation is a graveyard of dinosaur bones. The sedimentary rock known as the Morrison Formation is world famous as a "graveyard" of dinosaur bones. The world's most complete dinosaur skeleton was found in this formation. Altogether, twenty-three nearly complete, and about three hundred partial skeletons have been uncovered in Utah quarries. These skeletons have ranged in length from six feet to eighty-four feet. Most of them were found in a good state of preservation. The bones have been petrified, or replaced by mineral matter. Not only dinosaurs are found in the formation but other reptiles, mollusks, primitive mammals, and a large variety of fossil plants. The Morrison Formation is well exposed near Jensen, where

Dinosaurs in their Utah environment during Morrison times. Painting by Ernest Untermann.

one of the world's best dinosaur quarries has been preserved as Dinosaur National Monument. The Morrison Formation is also exposed in Carbon and Emery counties where there are quarries. The Cleveland-Lloyd Dinosaur Quarry is located in Emery County, east of Cleveland. The prehistoric Museum at Price displays dinosaur fossils from that region.

4. HOW UTAH'S LANDSCAPE OF MOUNTAINS, VALLEYS, AND PLATEAUS WAS FORMED

The Rocky Mountains were gradually lifted. Near the end of the Age of Reptiles, extensive flooding of the land took place. Another sea moved from the south over the area of Utah and the American Midwest. The earth's surface slowly folded and broke because of forces deep in the earth, and the Rocky Mountains were gradually lifted in rugged fashion, high above the surrounding country. Sediments from the newly uplifted mountains were then washed down to the valleys and basins. The rock core of the mountains was left exposed. The Wasatch and Uinta ranges are the major divisions of the Rocky Mountains in Utah.

The Great Basin was left a lower region. To the west of the Rocky Mountain uplift was a broad, lower region which became known as the Great Basin. Within this basin was block faulting which resulted in mountains contrasting sharply with those of other regions. The mountains are usually isolated, short, north-south tending ranges that rise abruptly above the desert plains and have faults on each side of them. The Pacific Coast was an elevated area, and the Great Basin was about the same size as it is now.

Great faults produced great cliffs in southern Utah. After the disruption that produced the Rocky Mountains took place, widespread faulting (breaking in rock strata) took place from the northern to the southern end of Utah. Faulting occurred at weak places in the earth's crust when one portion of earth was raised and the earth immediately next to it slipped and was lowered, exposing great portions of the earth's inner layers. Along the west side of the Wasatch Mountains in northern Utah is the Wasatch fault. In the southern part of the state are great cliffs formed by the Hurricane fault. This fault system extends from Montana south into Arizona. West of the faults is the Great Basin.

The plateaus of southern Utah were lifted. In southeastern Utah, the whole area was lifted into high plateaus of different heights. Waters draining from these plateaus cut their way to the east. As time went on, waters washed through the thick sediments and volcanic lavas of the earlier periods to cut vast and impassable canyons. As the canyons deepened, brilliantly colored layers of rock were exposed. Further faulting gave an even more complex picture to the land. The great canyons of southern Utah were formed at this time.

5. DURING THE ICE AGE, LAKE BONNEVILLE COVERED MUCH OF WESTERN UTAH

The last major shaping of Utah's landscape took place in the Ice Age. During the

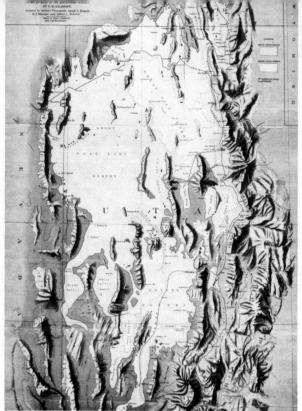

Map of ancient Lake Bonneville drawn by
G. K. Gilbert for the United States Geological Survey.
Gilbert wrote the first significant study
of Lake Bonneville.

Ice Age, an immense ice cap covered much of North America. It did *not* reach as far south as Utah, but the extremely cold climate formed glaciers in the Wasatch and Uinta mountains. The glaciers carved the land as they moved down the mountains into the valleys.

Lake Bonneville was Utah's Ice Age Lake. This lake covered much of western and central Utah and parts of Nevada and Idaho. It had an area of 19,750 square miles, was 145 miles wide and 346 miles long. The lake's irregular shore line measured 2,550 miles. At its greatest depth, the surface was about 1,000 feet above the present level of Great Salt Lake. The water inched out onto the level plains of the Great Basin and washed against the foothills. It extended deep through some Utah canyons and into such mountain valleys as Cache, Ogden, Morgan,

and Heber. The waves of Lake Bonneville washed the shores until a broad land terrace was formed, a bench that can easily be seen on the sides of the Utah mountains. As the lake's source of water slowly diminished and the climate warmed, the lake dropped to a lower level. Then the climate changed, and the lake filled again, this time to a level higher than the first level. Here it remained for some time. At the northern end of the lake the waters broke through and flowed over Red Rock Pass. The waters poured through the narrow outlet and from there flowed north into the Columbia Basin to drain into the Pacific Ocean. In a relatively short time the waters had cut through about 374 feet of rock until a base of harder rock was reached, halting erosion considerably. At this level (the Provo level) the lake remained for a long time and along its shoreline the lake's waves created the Provo Terrace—the largest of all terraces left by Lake Bonneville.

In time, climate changed again. Dry seasons followed, and the sun increased evaporation. The level of the lake dropped gradually, sometimes halting for a time, leaving other benches along the way. The Stansbury Terrace, midway between the Provo level and today's level of Great Salt Lake, is the most prominent of these benches.

When the level of the lake fell below its old benches, the mountain streams had to cut through the benches on their way to the lake. The streams picked up soils dropped earlier and carried them down to the lower lake level. At the mouths of the canyons where streams emptied into Lake Bonneville, *deltas* and *alluvial fans* were created. From a height one can clearly see where the rivers have cut through the benches and made the deltas and fans. Here some of the best soil in the state was deposited. Many of Utah's communities rest on these deltas and fans, be-

Along the southwest base of the Simpson Mountains on the Tooele-Juab county lines is a famous group of shore terraces, known as the Snowplow.

The outlet of Lake Bonneville was at Red Rock Pass, in southern Idaho. Waters flowing through this pass emptied into the Columbia River system and eventually into the ocean.

Numerous streams coming out of the Wasatch Mountains have formed alluvial fans such as this one. Many Utah communities are built on or near these alluvial fans.

cause of the good soil and water to work it.

Before the level of the lake fell below the Red Rock Pass outlet, the lake was fresh water. As the water level fell, the lake gradually became salty, for there was no outlet to carry off the salts dissolved out of the earth by the waters. Warm dry climate continued, the last glaciers receded, and the lake gradually lost its waters. The lake level dropped, rising and falling as the weather changed. The remnants of old Lake Bonneville in Utah today are Great Salt Lake, Utah Lake, Rush Lake, Sevier Lake, and Little Salt Lake.

During the Ice Age the glaciers of Utah were confined to the higher mountains and canyons. The Uinta Mountains contain thousands of glacial lakes, and in the Wasatch Range there are perhaps fifty glaciated canyons, two of the best examples being Little

Cottonwood Canyon and the higher reaches of Big Cottonwood Canyon. The glaciers helped create the great natural water storage basins in Utah's mountains which make irrigation agriculture possible. They also produced some of our most beautiful alpine lakes and summer resort areas.

6. THE FORCES OF NATURE ARE STILL SHAPING THE LAND OF UTAH

Since the times of ancient Lake Bonneville, earthquakes, wind, water, plants, and animals, as well as man, have all contributed to change the appearance of the land.

Earthquakes are a reminder that the earth is still shifting. Utah experiences many minor quakes, or tremors, which are hardly felt; but some are severe. Utah has about one major earthquake a year—usually along the Wasatch Mountains and High Plateau areas. In many places, through the ages, the benches of Lake Bonneville have actually shifted so that the once-level lines of a terrace are now irregular.

Wind and running water have continued to alter the landscape. Man has often speeded the process of change by contributing to erosion and destroying the natural scenery. In man's use of the land, it is important that he try to preserve its natural beauty and the plant and animal life so future generations might enjoy the land also.

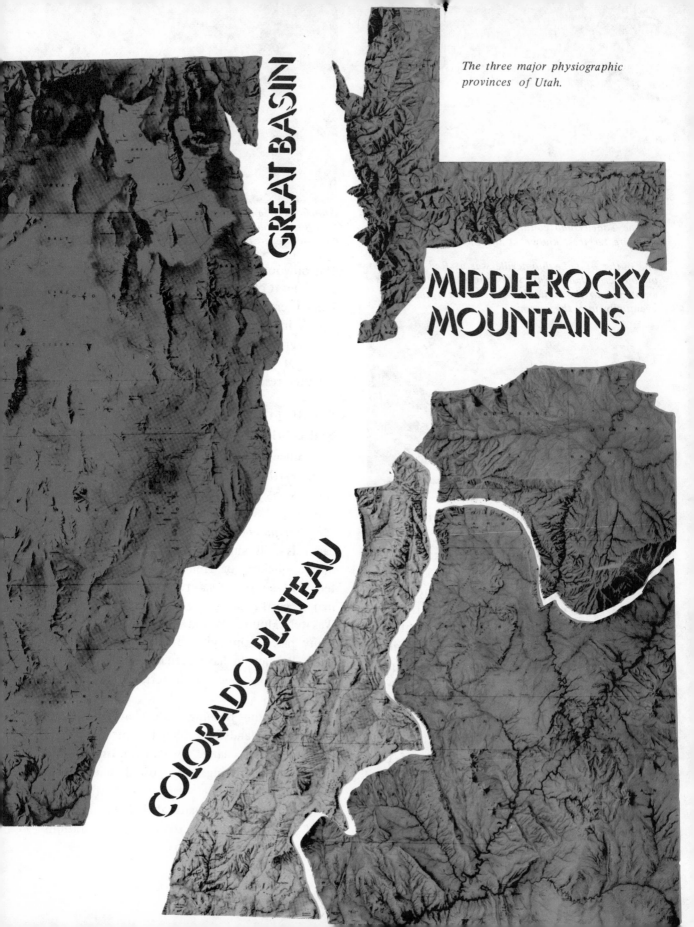

GREAT BASIN

MIDDLE ROCKY MOUNTAINS

COLORADO PLATEAU

The three major physiographic provinces of Utah.

THE FACE OF THE LAND

Utah's colorful landscapes have given the state the name of the "Rainbow Land." There are forested mountains, rough mountains with jagged cliffs, broad plateaus with deep canyons, vast deserts, sparkling clear mountain streams, slow-moving muddy rivers, beautiful green valleys, and mountain lakes. There are distinctly different natural regions, or physiographic provinces, in Utah characterized by these varied land forms.

IN THIS CHAPTER WE WILL LEARN

1. Three major physiographic provinces meet in Utah.

2. A rich variety of plant and animal life is found in Utah.

3. The mountains and high plateaus are important for Utah's water supply.

4. The face of Utah is marked by unique features.

2

Great Salt Lake is the most famous landmark of Utah.

The Wasatch Mountains as seen from Salt Lake Valley. They rise over a mile above the valley floor.

1. THREE MAJOR PHYSIOGRAPHIC PROVINCES MEET IN UTAH

Western North America is marked by mountains, basins, and plateaus. The Rocky Mountains extend from Canada into Mexico. East of these mountains lie the Great Plains. To the west is a series of plateaus and basins. Plateaus are high, fairly level areas frequently broken by deep canyons. Basins are broad low-lying regions that receive or drain waters from the surrounding mountains. West of the basins and plateaus and separating them from the Pacific Coast are high ranges of mountains, chiefly the Sierra Nevada.

In Utah three major physiographic provinces meet: the Middle Rocky Mountains Physiographic Province, the Basin and Range Physiographic Province, and the Colorado Plateau Physiographic Province.

The Middle Rocky Mountains Physiographic Province is a long spur of the Rocky Mountains that extends from Canada to New Mexico. In Utah that spur is made up of two mountain ranges: the Wasatch and the Uinta.

The Wasatch enters Utah from the north and extends to central Utah, ending near Nephi. The west face of the Wasatch Mountains presents a mile-high panorama of exposed rock which dates back to the earliest geologic ages. On the east side, the Wasatch Mountains slope less abruptly. They meet the Uinta Mountains along their northern portion and the plateaus of the southwest along their southern boundary. The crest of the Wasatch Mountains rises from 9,000 to over 11,000 feet in elevation. The highest peaks are Mount Nebo (11,877 feet above sea level), Mount Timpanogos (11,750), Twin Peaks

(11,319), Lone Peak (11,253), and Provo
Peak (11,068). In Salt Lake Valley the mountain peaks rise 7,000 feet above the valley
floor.

In the Wasatch Mountain range are several narrow fertile valleys: Cache, Ogden,
Morgan, and Heber. Lake Bonneville flooded
into these valleys and left rich soil. These are
also river valleys, for streams from the surrounding mountains flow through each of
them and empty into the basin to the west.
These valleys offer some of the lands best
suited to intensive cultivation in Utah.

The Uinta Range of mountains is the
highest in the state and affords magnificent
scenery. This range is about 130 miles long
and from 40 to 50 miles wide. It is the highest range in the United States with an east-
west axis. Kings Peak is the highest in the
state, rising 13,498 feet above sea level. Next
highest peaks are Mount Emmons (13,428),
Gilbert Peak (13,422), Mount Lovenia
(13,229) and Tokewanna Peak (13,175).
There are many other peaks above 12,000
feet.

The Basin and Range Physiographic Province, America's vast inland desert, is part of
western Utah. It is a region of great variety,
with many differing sections. The Great Basin
is the section that concerns us most in Utah
history.

The Great Basin has no outlet to the
sea. As its name implies, it is like a large flat
bowl. Rainfall is scanty. There is little or no
water surplus for any part of the region at
any season. Occasionally, torrents of rain fall,
and then shallow lakes appear which dry up
with a few days of hot weather. Streams running from the surrounding mountains creep
onto the basin floor and sink into the ground
or dry up on the way. The Humboldt River
in Nevada is an exception. It runs a 315-mile
course southwestward across the northern por-

*Hayden Peak is one of the highest peaks in the Uinta
Mountains. It is seen from Mirror Lake, one of
hundreds of glacial lakes in the mountains.*

*The Great Basin affords limited grazing where
grasslands are maintained by conservation practices.*

tion of the Great Basin. Even so, the river is
often narrow and shallow. Its banks are nearly barren and near the end of its course the
water is salty. The Sevier River in Utah runs
a long, winding course from the High Plateaus
to drain in the flats of the Great Basin.

The floor of the basin is a tableland
4,000 to 5,000 feet above sea level. Rugged
mountains rise sharply above the flat plain.
Shifts in the earth's surface have broken the
valley floor into many small basins. The short
and narrow north-south tending mountains
rise abruptly 1,000 feet to over 8,000 feet
above the floor of the basin, and from 5,000
to 12,000 feet above sea level.

The Great Basin is a desert with hot
days and cold nights. Plant life is scarce and
animal life limited. Good soils exist in the
desert basins which were once the bed of
Lake Bonneville. However, these soils frequently contain so much clay that they resist
the entrance of water and plant roots. They
are also salty. But salty soils which contain
adequate proportions of sand and silt can be
reclaimed through drainage and irrigation.

A desert monument of the Colorado Plateau.

This deep, narrow canyon has been formed by erosion.

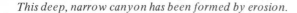

The Colorado Plateau Physiographic Province is the third of Utah's three major natural regions. This province covers southeastern Utah and includes the High Plateaus, the Uinta Basin, and the Canyonlands.

The Colorado Plateau Physiographic Province occupies two-thirds of the state. This large area is bounded on the west by the Great Basin, on the north and east by the Rocky Mountains, and on the south by the southern sections of the Basin and Range Physiographic Province. The waters of this area drain into the Colorado River which empties into the Gulf of California.

The Colorado Plateau Physiographic Province is a highland region made of nearly level layers of sedimentary rock. Many of these deposits have been deeply eroded and are exposed in cliffs that rise abruptly a thousand feet above the valley floors. These cliffs may extend as much as a hundred miles. In places the plateaus have been cut by streams and rivers into canyons hundreds of feet deep with nearly vertical walls. There are hundreds of magnificent canyons throughout the region. Here also are natural bridges, tall monuments, spires, and domal mountains.

The Colorado Plateau Physiographic Province includes many subdivisions or sections. Three major sections are in Utah: the High Plateaus, the Uinta Basin, and the Canyonlands.

The High Plateaus section occupies a central portion of the state, extending from

Nephi and Soldier Summit on the north to the Arizona border on the south. This belt of plateaus is from 25 to 80 miles wide, about 175 miles long and rises to elevations of 7,000 to 11,000 feet above sea level. On the south, the plateaus present dramatic cliffs named for their colors: the Pink Cliffs (the highest), White Cliffs, Vermillion Cliffs, and Chocolate Cliffs. The plateaus tilt slightly to the east. Their west face is steep and rugged. On the east, however, they are steep but often present a gentle and rolling appearance.

In the southern portion the High Plateaus section is made up of three north-south tending belts of plateaus with valleys between. These valleys are drained by the branches of the Sevier River and its tributaries into the Great Basin. Valleys along the Sevier and the San Pitch rivers are among the important valleys of Utah.

The greater part of the High Plateaus section is drained to the east by streams flowing into the Colorado River.

The Uinta Basin is the second of the sections of the Colorado Plateau Physiographic Province in Utah. This area received its name from its basinlike character and from the Uinta Mountains on the north. The Uinta Basin is about 170 miles long and 100 miles wide at its broadest point. It is well drained by a series of streams from the Uinta Mountains which empty into the Duchesne and Green rivers. These rivers cut across the basin to empty south into the Colorado River.

The Uinta Basin looks like a desolate, unproductive region, a land of scanty vegetation and little rainfall. But, there are promising farmlands along the stream courses, and south of the Uinta range are large areas with soils similar to those of the Wasatch valleys and the Great Basin plains. Under irrigation these lands produce abundant crops.

The Canyonlands section occupies the large remaining portion of the Colorado Plateau Physiographic Province in Utah. This region lies in southeastern Utah, east of the High Plateaus and south of the Uinta Basin. It is a rolling plateau country with narrow, deep canyons, and sudden-rising knoblike mountains. Much of it is "bad lands" with a barren, rocky surface, showing an array of fantastic shapes and colors—spires, cathedrals, towers, needles, and goblins. Natural bridges abound in the area. Rainbow Bridge has been called "the most famous and beautiful natural bridge in the world." It is so high (309 feet high) that the United States capitol building (278 feet high) could easily rest under it. One is impressed with the deep, narrow canyons caused by erosive floods. Here are broad valleys—Castle Valley and Grand River Valley. Here, too, are the Green River Desert and the Great Sage Plain. In the southeast corner of the state is a portion of the Navajo section of the Colorado Plateau, famous for its Monument Valley.

Rising above the plateaus are high domal mountains, reaching almost as high as mountains in the Wasatch and the Uinta ranges. The La Sal Mountains are the second highest range in the state. Mount Peale, the highest peak, rises to 13,089 feet above sea level. The Henry Mountains, a notable landmark, may be seen for miles. The highest peak, Mount Ellen (11,615 feet above sea level), contrasts its dark green covering against the color of the Canyonlands. The Abajo Mountains rise above the Sage Plain to eight independent summits.

Most of the area of the Canyonlands has little value for agriculture though it is used for winter grazing. Occasionally along the river bottoms there is opportunity for agriculture. Only in Castle Valley, Castle Creek Valley, Moab Valley, and Spanish Valley is there farming to any notable extent.

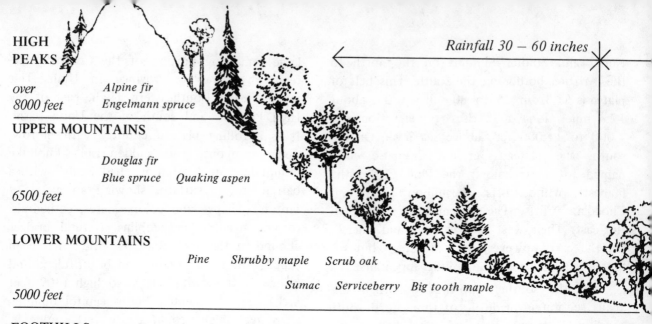

HIGH PEAKS

over 8000 feet

Alpine fir
Engelmann spruce

UPPER MOUNTAINS

Douglas fir
Blue spruce   *Quaking aspen*

6500 feet

LOWER MOUNTAINS

Pine   *Shrubby maple*   *Scrub oak*

Sumac   *Serviceberry*   *Big tooth maple*

5000 feet

FOOTHILLS

4000 feet

Chokech

GRASSLANDS

DESERTS
3000 feet

WATER COURSES

Rainfall 30 – 60 inches

Until very recently (the 1950s) the region was generally shunned and was perhaps one of the least known areas in the United States. In recent years explorers have gone into the region to hunt for uranium, oil, and gas.

2. A RICH VARIETY OF PLANT AND ANIMAL LIFE IS FOUND IN UTAH

Several reasons help explain why Utah has such a variety of plant and animal life. The wide range of plant life zones gives opportunity for many varieties of plants to grow. The plants furnish food for an equally large variety of animals. The Indians did not destroy what they found, and the varieties of plant and animal life were left relatively undisturbed until a little over a hundred years ago.

Plants and animals find certain regions more congenial for life than others. The Wasatch and Uinta mountains, and the High Plateaus are similar enough in elevation and rainfall that they have much the same life zones. The Great Basin and the Canyonlands sections also are much alike.

Some plants and animals are to be found generally throughout the state, while other areas have plants and animals unique to that region.

Plant and animal life in the mountains and plateaus of Utah. *Plant life.* The Wasatch and Uinta mountains are covered with a great variety of grasses, shrubs, and trees, varying according to the altitude. In lower elevations surrounding the mountains are areas of sagebrush, a little higher, piñon and juniper. In Utah the juniper is commonly called cedar. On higher elevations are the broadleaf trees and still higher the evergreens.

26

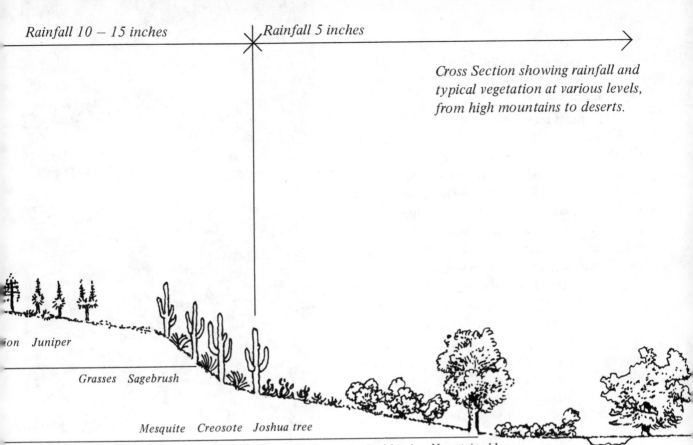

Rainfall 10 – 15 inches *Rainfall 5 inches*

Cross Section showing rainfall and typical vegetation at various levels, from high mountains to deserts.

ion Juniper

Grasses Sagebrush

Mesquite Creosote Joshua tree

Willows   Cottonwood   Red birch   Mountain alder

If we should go into one of the many canyons of these mountains and climb to the high peaks above, we would see the whole range of Utah mountain plant life. Along the water courses and in the canyons grow the cottonwood and the box elder. Bordering the canyon streams are a variety of shrubs—the red birch, the mountain alder, the hawthorn, and varieties of willows. Great thickets of bigtooth maple, scrub oak, chokecherry, sumac, serviceberry, and mountain mahogany grow up the canyon hillsides. The shrubby maple gives the autumn mountain landscape a carpet of bright color when its foliage turns into fantastic combinations of green, yellow, gold, brown, and red. At higher elevations in the mountains are forests of quaking aspen, Douglas fir, white fir, and blue spruce. Wild flowers cover the ground between the stands of timber. In the high mountains are deep

forests of Englemann spruce and alpine fir. These forested heights with their grassy parks of flowers reach to the timber line. In the alpine zone above grow the little sedges and herbs, and alpine shrubs and mosses.

To go from the desert floor to a mountain peak in these ranges gives one the same experience so far as climate and plant life are concerned as one would get in traveling from Mexico City to the Arctic Circle, for the plant life of the region west of the mountains is the same as that of the valley of Mexico City, and the plant life at the mountain tops is similar to that of the Arctic Circle.

The animal life varies from region to region. Although some animals are found throughout the state, others are found only in certain regions.

Throughout the state there are varieties of native rats and mice. Larger mammals

27

Coyote

found almost everywhere in the state include the porcupine, coyote, long-tailed weasel, badger, skunk, bobcat, mountain lion, and the mule deer.

Unique to the Wasatch and Uinta mountains and the High Plateaus are varieties of small mammals including tree squirrels, gophers, chipmunks, beaver, weasels, ferrets, minks, pikas, and rabbits. Larger mammals include the black bear found in the high mountains of the south and southeastern part of the state. The grizzly bear was once found in the Wasatch and Uinta mountains, the high regions of the High Plateaus, and the Raft River Mountains (in the northwest corner of the state). The ermine and the Canada lynx are also found in Utah's mountain areas. The moose is said to be accidental in Utah, being quite rare, and then only in the Wasatch and Uinta mountains. However, the North American elk (wapiti) is to be found throughout the Wasatch, the Uintas, the High Plateaus, the Raft River Mountains, and in the Pine Valley Mountains area (the southwest corner of the state). Otter are found in the Wasatch, Uinta, and Raft River mountains.

Collared lizard   *Cougar in snowy tree.*

Black Bear

Black-tailed prairie dog

Weasel in winter coat.

28

The High Plateaus have many of the same characteristics as the mountains. In these high regions one witnesses the same general patterns of plant life. Along the valleys is desert vegetation typical of similar elevations in the Great Basin, particularly the salt bush. Along the foothills are extensive areas of sagebrush. Above the sage and brush lands are the piñon and juniper. At higher elevations are forests of aspens, firs, and spruces typical of the mountains in northern Utah. To the east, as the High Plateaus drop off and away into the Canyonlands, the vegetation similarly changes, giving way to piñon and juniper with areas of desert shrubs. The valleys of the High Plateaus become important agricultural lands when placed under irrigation. The surrounding plateaus furnish excellent grazing for livestock.

The animal life of the High Plateaus is very similar to that of the Middle Rocky Mountain Physiographic Province. Here are the animals found throughout the state as well as those peculiar to the Wasatch and Uinta mountains. The southern borders of the High Plateaus are drained by the branches of the Virgin River. Along the courses of this stream and in the immediate surrounding areas are found an occasional ground squirrel and the pocket gopher. Beaver are found in the river courses, and the red and the gray fox are in this region, too.

In the Great Basin plant life is scarce, and animal life is limited. There are a few trees and desert shrubs adapted to live in the dry desert region. Toward the southern reaches of the Great Basin, the creosote bush dominates the landscape together with the mesquite and the Joshua tree. Farther north in cold desert areas and at the lower elevations, the shadscale marks the landscape of

This view of the southern end of the High Plateaus, Zion National Park, shows the spectacular effects of erosion.

nearly barren ground. In the broad high valleys and lower foothills, in an even colder region, is the sagebrush, occupying more area than any other vegetation in the Great Basin. Many nutritious grasses that provide good winter, spring, and autumn grazing for cattle and sheep are found in protected sagebrush areas. Utah pioneers learned that sagebrush indicated the presence of rich soil. Where sufficient water is available from streams and underground supplies, irrigation agriculture can produce alfalfa, grain, potatoes, sugar beets, and truck crops. Piñon, juniper, yellow pine, and oak, aspen, and fir at higher levels, grow on the Great Basin mountains.

Only a few animals live in the Great Basin area. Besides those animals found throughout the state, there are mice, rabbits, prairie dogs, and squirrels. Unique to the Great Basin are the pigmy rabbit and the kit fox. Larger mammals include only the pronghorn antelope, the mule deer, and the mountain lion. Gophersnakes, rattlesnakes and several species of lizards are found here.

In the Canyonlands desert region are the small mammals—mice and rats, the Say chipmunk, the ground squirrel, the cottontail and the black-tailed jack rabbit, the beaver, the pocket gopher, and the prairie dog. The gray fox lives in the Canyonlands as well as in the Uinta Basin.

3. THE MOUNTAINS AND HIGH PLATEAUS ARE IMPORTANT FOR UTAH'S WATER SUPPLY

Utah's major water supply is brought to her mountains by moist winds or clouds moving eastward from the Pacific Coast. The sun evaporates water from the ocean into clouds that move eastward. As these clouds meet mountain ranges, they drop some of their moisture, with the heaviest load of moisture falling on the western slopes. The remaining clouds move on at high elevations. Succeeding

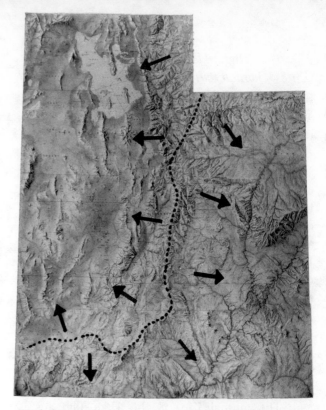

Utah has two major drainage systems. The Bonneville Drainage Basin drains waters from the Wasatch Mountains and the High Plateaus into the Great Basin area. The Colorado River Drainage Basin drains waters into the Colorado River system.

Aerial view of the Wasatch Mountains showing erosion and drainage into the valleys.

ranges of mountains bring down more moisture on their western slopes. The process is repeated time and time again as the clouds move eastward.

Across the Great Basin region from the Sierra Nevada into Utah, little moisture is dropped because the mountains are not high enough to reach the clouds moving high above. However, Utah's Wasatch and Uinta mountains as well as the High Plateaus are high enough to receive large quantities of moisture from the clouds before they move eastward. Throughout Utah, mountains which are high enough receive good supplies of moisture, but the low regions receive little rainfall and must depend almost entirely on irrigation.

The forested mountains and plateaus of Utah are watersheds or storage basins for water. Moisture which falls during the winter months is stored as snow. As the warmer spring months come, frozen moisture thaws and runs off in canyon streams that flow down into the valleys. The heaviest runoffs are in the spring and early summer. In the fall and winter, canyon streams are often nearly dry. The forested watershed regions of Utah must be protected if we are to have an adequate supply of life-giving water.

As runoff waters flow from the higher elevations into the valleys, they become part of a drainage system. There are two major drainage systems in Utah: the Colorado River Drainage System, and the Bonneville Drainage System. (Some waters falling in the extreme northwestern corner of the state drain into the Snake River and on to the Columbia River.)

The Colorado River Drainage System drains the eastern and southern portions of the state. The Colorado River drains the entire Colorado Plateau and empties its waters into the Gulf of California. One of the major

The entrance to Hidden Passage in Glen Canyon of the Colorado River is faced by a huge wall of Navajo sandstone.

Aerial view of drainage through the Colorado Plateau.

rivers to empty into the Colorado River is the Green River which originates in the Wind River Mountains of Wyoming. It receives water from the northern slopes of the Uintas, makes its way through Flaming Gorge and other canyons along the northern and eastern edges of the Uinta Mountains, and continues on south where it receives additional water from the Duchesne River which has drained much of the Uinta Basin.

The Colorado River receives water from the eastern slopes of the High Plateaus through a complex of streams and rivers. The Price and San Rafael rivers flow into the Green River and hence into the Colorado. The Fremont (Dirty Devil), Escalante, and Paria rivers flow through confined mountain valleys or narrow canyons into deep canyons of the Colorado River. The San Juan River drains the Four Corners region and empties into the Colorado River just above Rainbow Bridge National Monument. The Virgin River in southern Utah drains the southern slopes of the High Plateaus and flows southwest to join the Colorado River near the Arizona-Nevada border. The Colorado River then flows on into the Gulf of California.

The **Bonneville Drainage System** drains the large area including that once covered by ancient Lake Bonneville. This drainage system is perhaps the most important to the state because the majority of Utah's communities have been established along its stream courses. Unlike the streams which flow into the Colorado River, these Great Basin streams flow through fertile valleys. This water can be used.

Numerous rivers and streams drain into the Great Salt Lake from the surrounding mountains, chiefly those to the east. The Bear River is one of Utah's longest streams. It originates near Hayden Peak in the Uinta Mountains, flows northward into Wyoming, into Utah's Rich County, into Wyoming again, into Idaho (where it receives the overflow from Bear Lake), then south into Utah's Cache Valley. It continues westward through the mountains into Box Elder County's Bear River Valley, and finally empties into the northeastern bay of Great Salt Lake. In its five hundred mile course the Bear River receives water from many mountain streams and provides irrigation water to numerous communities. Also coming from the north into Great Salt Lake is the Malad River which waters part of Bear River Valley.

The Ogden River and the Weber River join near Ogden and flow as the Weber River directly into the Great Salt Lake.

The Canyon streams of the mountains east of Utah Valley—Dry Creek, American Fork, Provo River, Hobble Creek, Spanish Fork, and Spring Creek—empty into Utah Lake. Utah Lake drains north out of Utah Valley by the Jordan River which flows through Salt Lake Valley into Great Salt Lake. Along its way through Salt Lake Valley, the Jordan River picks up waters from the streams flowing out of mountain canyons east of Salt Lake Valley—Little Cottonwood Creek, Big Cottonwood Creek, Mill Creek, Parleys Creek, Emigration Creek, and City Creek.

The Sevier River system drains the interior valleys of the High Plateaus. The Sevier River originates on the slopes north of the Pink Cliffs. It flows northward through Panguitch Valley to Junction where it picks up water from the eastern valleys, drained by Otter Creek originating from the north, and the East Fork of the Sevier coming from the south. The Sevier continues flowing northward through Circle Valley, Marysvale Valley, and Central Sevier Valley until it reaches Gunnison where it is joined by the waters of the San Pitch River which has drained the Sanpete Valley to the northeast. The river meanders northwest, west, then southwest onto the desert floor to end in Sevier Lake.

Along the western front of the High Plateaus, at the edge of the Great Basin, little steams flow out of the highlands and onto the floor of the Great Basin, soon to evaporate and sink out of sight. However, these streams pass productive lands, and along some of them communities have been established. Some of the streams and the communities they support are Chalk Creek (Fillmore), Meadow Creek (Meadow), Corn Creek (Kanosh), Beaver River and North Creek (Beaver), Parowan Creek (Parowan), and Coal Creek (Cedar City).

The Wasatch and Uinta mountains and the High Plateaus constitute the most impor-

tant single geographic factor for life in Utah. These mountains and plateaus reach into the sky to bring down the moisture necessary to sustain life. The soils of Utah's best farming areas have come from these high lands. Here also are found rich mineral deposits that have made Utah a leading mining state. Extensive highland grazing areas are well used by Utah ranchers and farmers. Some of Utah's most beautiful scenery is found in these mountainous regions, along their fronts and in their canyons.

4. THE FACE OF UTAH IS MARKED BY UNIQUE FEATURES

Some of Utah's most noteworthy geographic landmarks are her lakes and deserts. *Utah Lake* in Utah Valley is a fresh water remnant of Lake Bonneville. It is about twenty-four miles long, from eight to twelve miles wide, and lies 4,488 feet above sea level. It receives its waters from the Wasatch Mountain canyons to the east, and empties north by way of the Jordan River into the Great Salt Lake.

Great Salt Lake is the most distinguished and famous landmark of Utah. A dead sea remnant of ancient Lake Bonneville, it is approximately seventy-five miles long and from eighteen to forty-four miles wide. It is the largest inland body of salt water in the Western Hemisphere. It is also the largest lake at its elevation (4,200 feet) in the world. The lake has a salt content of about 25 percent (that is, four buckets of salt water, after evaporation, yield one bucket of salt). The lake provides a moderating influence on the temperatures of the surrounding country throughout the year. Birds of western North America have always found the streams and marshes at the north edge of the lake a favorite stopping place on their seasonal migrations.

Great Salt Lake is not only rich in salt but many other minerals. The lands being exposed by the receding waters are now offering a new field for mining and processing minerals, such as magnesium, potassium, and lithium.

The Great Salt Lake Desert to the west and south of the Great Salt Lake is the dried-up bottom of Lake Bonneville. The old lake bottom is so nearly flat that a slight change in the depth of the water in Great Salt Lake greatly changes the shoreline. Most of the desert region around the lake is only twenty-five to thirty-five feet above the present lake level. Bonneville Salt Flats, near the Nevada border, are world famous for their hard flat surface which makes them ideal for speed-car racing.

Other deserts of the Great Basin in Utah include the Sevier Desert, the Escalante Desert, and the Black Rock Desert, which adds up to most of the Great Basin region in Utah.

Sevier Lake is another desert lake. A brackish, salty basin, it is almost dried up because the waters formerly going to it have been turned aside for irrigation. This region, too, was once the bed of Lake Bonneville.

We have seen that the Utah landscape is remarkable for the variety of its landforms and for the dramatic scenes presented along the lines where the three major natural regions meet. Before we understand how well man can live in the region, we must look at the climate, supply of water, nature of the soils, the sub-soil resources, and other natural resources. The face of the land is not only beautiful but it offers most of the natural resources that make possible a fruitful and varied living for man. These features of Utah we study next.

THE LAND AND MAN 3

We have seen how the land was formed through the long ages of earth's history. We have seen that creation left a great variety of natural regions in Utah—valleys, basins, plateaus, mountains, canyons, and deserts.

We now turn to the question: What opportunities does the land offer man to make a living? Man's life is largely if not wholly dependent upon the quantity and the quality of the natural resources available to him, his knowledge of these resources, and how to use them to his life purposes.

The basic natural resources are sunshine, air, water, soil, forests, minerals, and wildlife. Sunshine is essential to life and Utah rates well in this respect. In an average year there are 180 sunny days, 110 that are partly cloudy, and 75 cloudy days. Air is essential, too, especially pure, clean air. The purity of Utah's air must be safeguarded. Water is a natural resource which the people of Utah are much concerned about, both for the amount available and its purity. Soil is the home of almost all plant life. Its quality determines what will grow and what man can harvest from it. Utah has some excellent soils, and many more areas of good soils which need only water to make them productive. Forests provide lumber and a multitude of by-products, besides holding the soil and waters in the mountains, creating watersheds so important to the life of Utah. Forests are the home of wildlife, and furnish excellent pasture lands for grazing cattle. Favorite recrea-tion areas are in our national and state forests. A great variety of minerals provides Utah with raw materials from which many useful products are made. Coal, gas, and oil are other valuable mineral resources found in Utah. Wildlife abounds in all regions of Utah.

Much of the history of Utah is concerned with the attempts of man to make fullest use of natural resources. Because they are so important to life in the state, each generation must be charged with the responsibility of wise use, management, and conservation of natural resources.

IN THIS CHAPTER WE WILL LEARN

1. Utah is north, high, and inland.

2. Water, land, and climate combine to make human communities possible in Utah.

3. Forests are among Utah's most prized natural resources.

4. Wildlife and plant life are important natural resources.

5. Utah is rich in mineral resources.

6. Valleys offer the best places for man to live in Utah.

7. Human effort is necessary for man to benefit from nature's gifts.

Mount Timpanogos, a glaciated mountain
which serves as a watershed.

1. UTAH IS NORTH, HIGH, AND INLAND

Utah's climate is essentially determined by the fact that Utah is situated far north of the equator, is high in elevation, and far inland from the principal source for her moisture, the Pacific Ocean.

Utah is north. Utah is located on the globe between 37° and the 42° north latitude. This places her in the North Temperate Zone, the climate zone of the earth in which half of the people of the world make their homes.

Utah is high. Utah is one of the most elevated of the states in the Union. Most of the state is 3,000 to 7,000 feet above sea level. Only a small area in the southwest corner of the state lies below 3,000 feet. Most of Utah's communities are situated at elevations of 4,200 to 5,000 feet above sea level. Three-fourths of Utah has an altitude of a mile or more. The average elevation is estimated at 6,100 feet above sea level.

Utah is inland. Utah is 400 to 800 miles from the Pacific Ocean, the state's major source of moisture.

Because Utah is inland and has neither harbors nor outlets to the sea for shipping goods to other areas, she must depend upon overland means of transportation to carry goods in and out of the state.

2. WATER, LAND, AND CLIMATE COMBINE TO MAKE HUMAN COMMUNITIES POSSIBLE IN UTAH

Every human community is made up of a little land, a little water, and a little humanity. And so it is in Utah. Our water, combined with good soils and a suitable climate, have made possible the establishment of human communities in Utah.

Water resources. Compared to most areas of the world where mankind makes a living, *Utah is dry*. Utah is a desert land, with an arid and semi-arid climate. The mean annual precipitation at the levels occupied by most of Utah's population—at the valley and basin floors—is between 10 and 15, or about 12.75 inches. The mountain ranges, of course, receive more, 30-60 inches a year, whereas the desert areas receive 5 inches or less a year. Most of Utah's moisture falls during the winter and spring, from December to May. However, portions of eastern Utah receive large amounts of rain from thundershowers during the summer months, the moisture coming from the Gulf of Mexico. When the rain falls on barren rocky land, it quickly drains into the gullies and canyons, causing summer flash floods.

During the growing season—May to September—little rain falls in most agricultural areas. The spring runoffs, which are heaviest in April, May, and early June, give more moisture than can be used easily during the spring months. The waters are gone by the time crops of the late growing season need the water most for successful maturing. To solve this problem, man has built dams in Utah's canyons to store water from the early runoffs for use later in the season. Dams provide a dependable water supply if sufficient moisture falls during the storage season.

Utah's reliance on water from the mountains means that water users must cooperate in the use of the water and in protecting the watershed from any use that would destroy its ability to absorb water and later release it in a gradual runoff.

Each year about 53 million acre-feet of water falls in Utah. Additional water enters

A canyon stream.

the state by rivers. Of course some leaves by river streams such as the Colorado and Virgin rivers to the south. The great bulk of Utah's precipitation is consumed by seepage, evaporation from watersheds, and transpiration from vegetation. About 5 percent of the state's total water supply is consumed in producing crops on irrigated lands, and another 1 percent falls on dry farm land. City and town lots, and industrial sites use only about .2 percent of the total supply. About 4.3 percent of the state's total supply finds its way as runoff to the rivers that leave the state. It appears that only about 6 percent of the water supply is used intensively—for irrigated crops, dry farm crops, and for cities, towns, and industries.

The basic problem with regard to water in Utah is getting enough water in the right place at the right time. The *amount* of water is not the problem so much as is the lack of water *when* and *where* it is needed. The waters of the Green and Colorado river drainage systems are largely lost because of the nature of the country through which they pass. Plants use valuable ground-water supplies. Much of the ground-water of the Great Basin is too salty for use. In some areas where there is inadequate drainage, water-logging has resulted, making land unuseful and a health hazard.

More land could be cultivated in Utah with an additional dependable water supply. It is estimated that 1,429,000 acres of land suitable for agricultural production now dormant could be put into use with water. This would double Utah's agricultural crop land. Of Utah's presently irrigated lands (1,138,000 acres), only one-fourth has an adequate and dependable water supply.

New sources for water supply lie in the development of underground reserves, storage of flood waters, and harnessing Utah's principal rivers—the Green, the Colorado, the Bear, and the Virgin. Some Utah farmers are conserving water by using concrete-lined ditches and canals. Many inefficient canal systems exist which need improvement.

While Utah's development in the past has been possible because of wise management and use of water, in the future water may well be Utah's limiting resource. Increased agricultural requirements for water, and increased demands for water for new industries and new population centers, call for careful water management, and for large and comprehensive plans for the storage, conservation, and transportation of Utah's life-giving water. If the people of Utah want to use their water for industry, clean it up and reuse it for agriculture, Utah can support a greater population than at present.

The land. Mountains, high plateaus, and deep canyons give Utah a rugged surface that offers little opportunity for intensive crop farming. Even so, of Utah's 52,721,550 acres of land, about 90 percent is used for some form of agricultural production. Of this only about 4.1 percent is used for crops (2.6 percent in irrigated crops and 1.5 percent in dry farming), while about 86 percent is used for grazing.

Most areas in Utah are used for grazing during some part of the year. Through the winter months, when the weather is cool and moisture falls, winter grazing is possible at the lower elevations, in the desert regions of the Great Basin, plateaus, and canyon lands. During the hot and generally dry summer months, the best ranges are high in the mountains where precipitation is greatest and the temperatures are cooler. During the spring and fall good forage is available from the grasses of the intermediate regions characterized by the sagebrush, piñon-juniper, mountain brush, and related plant groups. By moving cattle and sheep from one range to the other, according to the season, it is possible to provide year-round range and thus make full use of the land.

Slightly more than 10 percent of the land surface of Utah could be used for producing good crops if adequately irrigated. In the valleys and basin plains are *three types of soils*: mountain, dry valley, and alkali. Mountain soil is loose, loamy, and comparatively rich in organic matter, but poor in lime. Dry valley soil is rich in minerals and poor in lime. Alkali soils contain large amounts of salts which have been dissolved from the earth and accumulated in ancient lake beds and at the termination points of streams. The heavy concentration of salts interferes with the growth of most plants. Mild alkali soils produce sweet clover, alfalfa, and sugar beets, but strong alkali regions remain poor range or wasteland.

Utah's climate. Utah enjoys four distinct seasons of the year—cold winters, short warm

UTAH CLIMATE STATISTICS

City	Elevation (Feet above sea level)	Mean Temperature Daily Maximum	Daily Minimum	Annual Mean Precipitation (inches)	Growing Season (days)
Beaver	5,860	64.0	30.9	11.25	106
Blanding	6,036	63.8	35.5	11.95	147
Brigham City	4,335	63.6	38.4	17.73	157
Bryce Canyon	8,000	56.9	25.2	15.83	60-80 (plateau)
					110-120 (bottomland)
Cedar City	5,980	64.7	36.1	10.27	142
Coalville	5,550	61.5	26.9	13.98	67
Duchesne	5,515	60.4	28.4	9.43	115
Emery	6,210	60.4	31.3	7.64	132
Farmington	4,267	64.6	38.2	19.52	168
Fillmore	5,250	66.3	38.4	14.10	155
Green River	4,058	70.1	35.2	5.78	158
Heber	5,593	60.5	27.5	15.84	77
Kanab	5,010	70.5	39.3	12.38	163
Levan	5,300	63.8	34.7	13.54	137
Logan	4,775	59.1	37.0	16.66	164
Manti	5,515	62.1	32.5	12.99	130
Milford	5,028	64.8	33.2	8.44	128
Moab	4,000	72.7	41.0	8.26	182
Morgan	5,070	62.6	29.1	14.68	92
Ogden	4,280	63.4	37.6	17.23	160
Panguitch	6,720	61.3	24.8	9.19	67
Price	5,560	64.2	34.7	9.77	153
Provo	4,470	64.9	34.1	13.50	126
Richfield	5,300	66.9	32.4	8.35	129
Saint George	2,880	77.6	44.7	7.81	213
Salt Lake City	4,220	63.9	38.7	14.74	202
Tooele	4,820	62.6	40.2	15.83	170
Vernal	5,280	61.4	27.0	8.52	119

springs, hot summers, and long warm autumns. In northern Utah, the winter season predominates, spring is short, and summer extends into a long autumn. In the southern part of the state, summer predominates, with the winter neither cold nor long.

Temperatures in Utah, as in other parts of the world, vary according to latitude (the distance from the equator) and altitude (the distance above sea level). The temperature becomes about 3° colder for each thousand feet rise in altitude and from 1.5° to 2° colder for each degree increase in latitude. This means that the lower valleys are warmer than the higher valleys, and that the communities in southern Utah have an average annual temperature from 6° to 8° warmer than those at similar altitudes in northern Utah.

Even so, Utah temperatures are neither excessively hot nor excessively cold. In the hottest months of the summer temperatures average in the 80s and 90s. Even on hottest days, the nights are usually cool. In the coldest months of winter the average warmest temperatures are in the high 20s and 30s while the average coldest temperatures range (in different localities) from 0° up to 24°. The state average of lowest temperatures on record is −28.57°. Temperatures below zero are uncommon in most parts of Utah, and long periods of extremely cold weather are also rare. The daily range of temperature at one place may be from 20° to 40° or more.

The Great Salt Lake has a moderating effect on temperatures in the neighboring region. In January (Salt Lake City's coldest month) the mean temperature is 26.5°, and in July (her warmest month) the mean temperature is 76.6°.

Utah has a short growing season. The growing season is the period of time an area is free from killing frost—the period between the last freeze in the spring and the first freeze in the fall. The length of the growing season determines to a large degree how successful man's life based on agriculture can be. If the growing season is too short, many crops cannot mature.

The growing season in Utah lasts generally from four and one-half to five months depending on the area. Farmers in Salt Lake Valley and in Saint George area have a growing season of six to six and one-half months. Farmers in Cache, Box Elder, Davis, Weber, and Tooele counties may expect from five to five and one-half months of freeze-free weather. Farmers in Utah County and other communities along the edge of the Great Basin and High Plateaus front may expect a four and one-half month growing season. Sanpete and Sevier counties and the Uinta Basin usually have a four month growing season. Communities of the Canyonlands region have a five month growing season.

What does this mean for Utah's agriculture? It means that Utah has a short growing season, and that the length of the growing season varies from valley to valley. Even in the same valley, a difference of two weeks in the growing season is often noted between the bottom lands and the foothills.

Farmers must know and depend on the usual climate patterns when planning their crops each year. Unusual climate conditions can be disastrous. Early frost in autumn can destroy a crop that is almost ready for harvest. Late frost in the spring can freeze the blossoms on early blooming trees, ruining their crop for the year.

One feature of weather patterns in Utah valleys makes possible fine orchards. On clear nights the colder air drains down to the valley bottoms while the foothills and bench lands remain relatively warm. For this reason farmers plant the hardier grains and vegetables in the bottom lands and the delicate fruits, berries, and vegetables on the bench lands.

3. FORESTS ARE AMONG UTAH'S MOST PRIZED NATURAL RESOURCES

Forests play a special role in Utah's mountain-valley way of life. Forests provide watersheds, shelter varieties of wildlife, yield timber, offer pastures for grazing livestock, and give man fine places for recreation—to hunt and fish, picnic and camp, and become close to nature.

Good forest lands provide excellent *watershed*. The natural growth of plants provides an excellent cover for the earth, holds the soil, and prevents rapid runoff. A well-forested watershed stores water, stabilizes stream flow, and assures us water for irrigation and city use. More than 20 million acres of land in Utah are classified as watershed land, and much of this is forested. About 80 percent of Utah's usable water comes from mountains with elevation above 7,000 feet, the region of her forests.

Utah is *lightly forested*, compared to other regions of the United States and the world. About one-third, or 16,219,000 acres, of the land of Utah is forest land (including piñon and juniper). Of this acreage 3,854,000 acres are classed as commercial forests, that is, having timber that is profitable for use in industry. Most of the commercial forests are in the Uinta and Wasatch mountains, and in the High Plateaus in the southern part of the state.

There are seven major national forests in Utah, with a combined area of over 8 million acres. National forests are managed by the United States Forest Service.

4. WILDLIFE AND PLANT LIFE ARE IMPORTANT NATURAL RESOURCES

Man has made use of many of the wide varieties of plant and animal life in Utah. Early explorers, visitors, and settlers hunted animals for food. The wildlife of Utah today is a natural resource of importance—for food, recreation, and an appreciation of nature.

The mammals of Utah. The large mammals of Utah—the buffalo, elk, moose, big

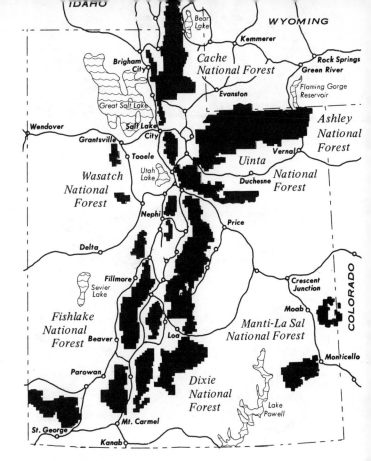

This map shows the national forests of Utah.

horn sheep, mule deer, antelope, and others—have been hunted for meat and fur. Buffalo lived only in the northwestern portion of the state, especially in Cache, Bear River, and Salt Lake valleys. There was a well-used buffalo wallow on the Jordan River where it empties into Great Salt Lake. Buffalo were killed in Salt Lake Valley as late as 1833, but by 1843 they were gone. Pioneers found only buffalo bones. Elk were hunted until they became scarce by 1895. The antelope, numerous in early times, ranged widely, through the west, south-central, and northeastern sections. The mule deer had the widest range; it was found almost everywhere. The big horn sheep was a favorite game animal of the Indians, particularly those living in the canyons and on the mesas of the Colorado and Green rivers. Today small herds are

41

Double-crested cormorants   Canada goose

Rainbow trout

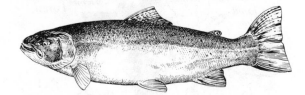

Snow geese

Mule Deer

Bison cows and calves

still in those areas, and in the La Sal and Uinta mountains. The bobcat, cougar (mountain lion), and some black bear are in the back country.

Utah's fur-bearing mammals are the beaver, badger, fox, marten, muskrat, ringtail cat, skunk, and weasel.

Native fish abounded in Utah's many streams and fresh water lakes in early times. From twenty to twenty-six native species of fish are known to have lived in Utah waters when the first settlers arrived. The most important of these fish were the Utah cutthroat trout, mountain whitefish, Utah chub, Utah sucker, and mountain sucker. In Bear Lake are native fish which are found no place else in the world. These are the Bonneville Cisco, Bonneville whitefish, and Bear Lake whitefish.

The introduction of new species of fish into Utah waters began in the 1870s for the purpose of supplementing the food needs of the settlers. Some introductions failed, but many were successful, such as the German carp, the rainbow trout, and the brown trout. Today it is estimated there are forty-nine different species of fresh-water fish in Utah waters, twenty-six of which are classed as native.

The birds of Utah. The waterways of Utah have always been favorite spots for the birds of North America to stop, rest, feed, and sometimes breed, on their annual migrations between Canada and Mexico, the Pacific Coast valleys and the Mississippi Valley. Utah's marshes and lakes attract great varieties of birds in large numbers. Utah's canyons have a variety of habitat and so are visited by a wide variety of birds.

About 350 kinds of birds (species and sub-species) have been observed and named in Utah. Of the birds named, 65 are counted as permanent residents, 160 as summer residents, and 25 as winter visitants. The others are transient or accidental visitors.

Ducks and geese in great variety and number are in Utah. In early times members of the grouse family were abundant—the dusky grouse, the ruffed grouse, the prairie chicken, the sharptailed grouse, and the sage hen. Sage hens, pine hens, and ruffed grouse are still found in Utah's uplands.

The golden eagle is the largest of the predatory birds. Hawks and owls are quite numerous.

A number of seagulls are here, the most famous is the California gull, the state bird.

The islands of the Great Salt Lake are favorite nesting places. Several species of birds have well-established breeding colonies there, among them the Treganza great blue heron, California gull, the double-crested cormorant, and white pelican. The islands are also headquarters for egrets, ibises, and avocets.

Somewhat unique to Utah are the Utah horned lark, the Utah red-winged blackbird, and the gray titmouse. In southern Utah crows and vultures are common. On the swift streams of the canyons may be seen the water ouzel, or dipper bird. Other common birds include the robin, the house finch, the cedar jay, the magpie, and the little marsh wren. The English sparrow was imported by early settlers. The starling is a recent arrival.

The Indians, Mountain Men, explorers, and early settlers took birds and their eggs for food. The greatest service of birds is their role in helping maintain the balance of nature.

The major plant forms, as they grow in the various physiographic provinces, were named in the last chapter. In the forested areas, man has hunted game and harvested nuts and berries for food, taken trees and other plants for shelter, and grazed cattle and sheep.

The valley floors were used for grazing livestock by the pioneers. From early times until shortly after permanent occupation, varieties of tall grasses covered the land. Contrary to popular notions, the valleys were not barren wastes, but covered with grasses, small clumps of dwarf oak and willows, and occasionally, trees along the water courses. The valley floors were the first pastures for pioneer livestock.

5. UTAH IS RICH IN MINERAL RESOURCES

Primitive man was quite unaware of the existence of the many rich deposits of metals, minerals, and other sub-soil treasures of Utah. His chief use of minerals was restricted to obsidian and flint for making arrow points. Early settlers knew only a little about mineral resources, though they made good use of coal and iron deposits. Only as man developed the need for more metals and minerals has exploration revealed their existence. Today Utah is known to be rich in these resources. It is possible that even greater stores of sub-soil wealth will be found.

Utah has the largest variety of minerals and metals of any state in the Union. Not only does she possess this variety, but her annual production of these minerals today ranks her high in the nation, both in quantity and in the value of the products. Utah ranked sixteenth in the nation (1969) in the value of her mineral products.

Utah's production is particularly high in the quantity and the value of the following *metals and minerals* (1969 rankings): asphalt (second), copper (second), gold (third), lead (third), molybdenum (second), potassium salts (second), silver (third), and vanadium (fourth). Utah is also a leading producer of cement, coal, fluorspar, gypsum, iron ore, lime, magnesium compounds, perlite, phosphate rock, pumice, salt, sand and gravel, stone, tungsten, uranium, and zinc. Utah ranks third among the states in the production of carbon dioxide, and ranks high in the production of natural gases.

Utah's *salt* reserves could supply the world for a thousand years. The shores of Great Salt Lake are beginning to supply many other minerals as well. Only recently have the mineral salts of the Great Salt Lake been extracted from the brine. Now large evaporation vats produce numerous minerals from the lake water.

The Colorado Plateau area stores a very rich supply of *petroleum* and *natural gas*. In Utah also are found these *unique minerals*: Gilsonite (found only in Utah), ozokorite (one of the most perfect insulators known, found only in Utah and Austria), and elaterite (an elastic mineral resin)—useful for making waterproofing compounds, varnishes, and insulating materials. Utah is a leading producer of potash, phosphates, and nitrates—useful mineral fertilizers. Other non-metallic minerals produced in Utah include soda ash, sulfur, gypsum, silica, sand, clay, cement, limestone, and lime. Helium and carbon dioxide are also important mining products.

Utah is poor in *precious stones*. However, she does produce agate, jet, chalcedony, jasper, garnet, opal, obsidian, olivimite, rock crystal, and topaz.

Utah has a supply of useful *building stones*, and these are used in various forms of construction. Marble exists in short supply only. Colorado marble, a pure marble, is found in the Fillmore area. Granite has been quarried from time to time, most notably for the construction of the Salt Lake Temple and the state capitol building. Oolite, a sandstone, is used extensively in the Sanpete County area, most notably and beautifully in the building of the Manti Temple. Picture stone is quarried east of Saint George and used in

that area. Extensive beds of sandstone, limestone, and some quartzites have been tapped for building materials. These materials are used chiefly in the pulverized state in mixtures that go to make up stone veneer and other building and construction materials. Sand and gravel, a rich supply left Utah by Lake Bonneville, is most important to Utah's building and construction business. It is used extensively in making concrete and building highways.

6. VALLEYS OFFER THE BEST PLACES FOR MAN TO LIVE IN UTAH

Land, to be useful to man for agricultural purposes, must have good soil, enjoy a suitable climate and sufficient water in order to promote vegetation growth. The union of these factors occurs only in a few places in Utah, chiefly in the valleys.

The mountain-valley relationship. The high mountains and plateaus receive the all-important moisture. Through time the valleys and basins have accumulated soils washed from higher areas. Streams of clear water move from the mountains through good lands and onto the valley floors. Timber is in the neighboring uplands. Native plant life and wildlife abound in the mountains and the valleys. This relationship of natural elements, called the mountain-valley relationship, makes the valleys the best places in Utah to live.

Utah valleys are often connected by low passes or canyons, making transportation and communication by land relatively easy. This ease of communication tends to promote a degree of unity within the state that could not exist if the valleys were more isolated.

Human activities in Utah center in the valleys. Here the Indians made their homes. Here the Mountain Men and explorers set their camps. Overland emigrants passed through the valleys and basins. Permanent set-

The mountains and valleys of Utah.

The valley-mountain system is illustrated where narrow valleys are watered by small streams. Farms can be maintained and livestock can be grazed in the surrounding range lands.

tlement took place in these valleys, and the early settlers wrote poems and hymns about the mountain valleys.

The valleys of the Great Basin. Along the line where the border of the Great Basin touches the Wasatch Mountains on the north and the High Plateaus on the south there are groups of valleys which make up the major population centers of Utah today. Most of these valleys are watered by streams from the east. Most have mountains or plateaus to their east and the Great Basin landscape to the west. All are in the Bonneville Drainage System.

Around the east and south of the Great Salt Lake is the Greater Salt Lake Valley—a group of valleys from Mona in Juab Valley on the south to Fielding in Bear River Valley on the north. The drainage of these valleys is closely related to the Great Salt Lake. This string of valleys is sometimes referred to as the Wasatch Front. There are several sub-valleys. Along the Wasatch Front are Bear River Valley on the north, Weber Valley around Ogden, and Salt Lake Valley proper (Greater Salt Lake City). Just west are valleys in the Great Basin: Skull Valley, Tooele Valley, Rush Valley, Cedar Valley, and Tintic Valley.

Salt Lake Valley proper, to the south and east of Great Salt Lake, is the area of Greater Salt Lake City or Salt Lake County today. It is a fertile and well-watered valley. The most desired lands, like those in other valleys, are those that are around and below the foothills and on the level plains near the mountains. Salt Lake Valley became the historic center of Utah and has since become the political, economic, social and religious center of Utah.

Utah Valley, south of Salt Lake Valley, is crescent shaped and curves around the eastern shore of Utah Lake. Fertile and well watered, Utah Valley is one of Utah's most important valleys.

South of Utah Valley is a string of small valleys which resemble their Great Basin environment and have the appearance of basin valleys. These valleys are higher and colder, and receive less water than their northern neighbors. These are Juab Valley, Pavant Valley, Beaver Valley, and Parowan Valley (sometimes called Little Salt Lake Valley for the small salt lake there).

The Great Basin valleys are only slightly separated from each other. The passes or saddles between them are low, and it is quite easy to move from one to the next. Indian trails became the wagon roads of the pioneers and the highways of today, north and south, east and west. Ease of transportation made for the development of commercial and industrial centers at crossroads.

The valleys of the Wasatch Mountains are surrounded by mountain ranges whose streams water the valleys and pass into the Bonneville Drainage Area. Cache Valley on the north was a bay of ancient Lake Bonneville. Its elevation is near that of communities in Salt Lake Valley and Utah Valley and has a growing season of five and one-half months. Other valleys in the Wasatch Range are higher, colder, and have a shorter growing season, usually about three months. These valleys are often named for the stream that passes through and drains the valley. They are: Ogden Valley (the valley of the Ogden River), Morgan Valley (the valley of the Weber River, west of Echo Canyon), and Provo Valley (valley of the upper Provo River). (The valley was named Provo Valley in early Utah history, but has been more recently called Heber Valley from its chief city.) Where the Bear River flows through Rich County there is the Bear River Valley. (Utah has another Bear River Valley in Box

A valley in the Bonneville drainage system.

Elder County.) About Bear Lake is Bear Lake Valley. In the mountains east of Great Salt Lake and Utah Lake are small mountain valleys: Rhodes Valley, Heber Valley, and Thistle Valley.

The valleys of the High Plateaus. The High Plateaus section is broken into two and sometimes three separate plateaus with valleys in between. Here along streams that drain the plateaus are the valleys of the High Plateaus. On the north is Sanpete valley, with an average elevation of 5,200 feet above sea level and a growing season of about four months. The valley is drained by the San Pitch River which empties south into the Sevier River west of Gunnison.

Along the Sevier River are several important valleys. (Let us proceed from south to north, following the river's course from its source.) South, in the high country of the source of the west fork of the Sevier River,

Ferron Reservoir stores water for valleys of the Colorado Plateau.

is Panguitch Valley, with an elevation of 6,720 feet and a growing season of just over two months—Utah's highest and coldest valley. Northward, along the stream course, is Circle Valley and then Marysvale Valley, somewhat similar to Panguitch Valley. The Sevier River then passes on northward and lower into the Central Sevier Valley, extending from Joseph on the south to Gunnison on the north. Here the elevation is about 5,300 feet above sea level, and the growing season is just over four months.

East of this line of valleys is Grass Valley, which is drained by the east fork of the Sevier River and Otter Creek.

The southern face of the High Plateaus looks out over the desert country toward the Utah-Arizona border. This area is drained by the Virgin River. Along the course of this stream are narrow, small valleys which afford some land and water and a long growing season because of their subtropical climate. South of Panguitch Valley, over the drainage divide, is Long Valley, tending south, about twenty miles long and averaging less than a mile wide. The Virgin River is fed by its East Fork (which begins above Glendale in Long Valley), receives additional waters from its North Fork, LaVerkin and Ash Creeks, and the Santa Clara River, which sources in the Pine Mountains. The Virgin River leaves Utah south of Saint George and flows south to empty into the Colorado River. The growing season in the Virgin Valley—Utah's Dixie—is from five to seven months, the longest in the state. Pine Valley is in the Pine Valley Mountains, north of Saint George. Water is the most precious resource in the Virgin Valley; it must be controlled most carefully to insure crop production.

Valleys of the Canyonlands. The eastern side of the High Plateaus slopes into the Canyonlands Section of the Colorado Plateau. Some important valleys lie in this region. Rabbit Valley is on the Fremont River. Castle Valley, a long, broad valley, is frequently crossed by streams such as the Muddy Creek (which later joins the Fremont River to form the Dirty Devil River), the San Rafael River, and the Price River. These streams furnish water for crops which have a growing season of from four to five months. (Rabbit Valley has a three-month growing season.) In the Green River country are Gunnison Valley and the San Rafael Valley. Spanish Valley (the area of Moab) is a small valley on lowlands neighboring the Colorado River. There are other valleys in the Canyonlands Section, some of which are suited for agriculture, but their areas of good soils are small, and there is little water.

The Uinta Basin and valleys. Streams drain south out of the Uinta Mountains and join with the Strawberry River (from the Wasatch Mountains) to form the Duchesne River. Along the Duchesne River are areas suitable for raising crops and for grazing. Though the area receives only from eight and one-half to nine and one-half inches of rainfall a year and has a growing season of four months, irrigation agriculture is able to produce basic crops and this with the surrounding grazing lands has made for good livestock raising country. Along the bottom lands and the moderately rolling terrain of Ashley Creek is Ashley Valley, the region of Vernal, center

of much of the life of the Uinta Basin. There are also other small areas of alluvial soils along the Green River.

7. HUMAN EFFORT IS NECESSARY FOR MAN TO BENEFIT FROM NATURE'S GIFTS

While Utah is rich in many resources, she is poor in others. She has areas of good soil and available water, but it takes know-how and effort to put the water on the land during the growing season. Utah has fine stands of timber, but it takes effort to get it out. Utah is rich in mineral wealth, but it requires knowledge and skill to locate, mine, and process those metals and minerals. However rich Utah might be in these resources, hard work is required to make use of them.

Utah's resources are not sufficient for all our purposes. The people of Utah are not self-sufficient. There are very few places on the earth where people are. It requires careful husbandry to care for Utah's water supply. We do not produce enough timber for all our present needs. We import much of our food supply and manufactured goods.

Utah makes her contributions to the world in certain goods and services and she receives essential goods and services in return. This requires communication and transportation. It has always required resourcefulness, ingenuity, hard work, and good relations with people far away to make a living in Utah. Man does not live to himself alone and survive. Living in Utah teaches that lesson.

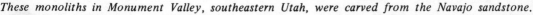
These monoliths in Monument Valley, southeastern Utah, were carved from the Navajo sandstone.

UNIT TWO
UTAH'S NATIVE PEOPLE

When does Utah history begin? If we think of history beginning with written records, then Utah history begins with the Spanish in Utah in the 1600s or 1700s. If we think of history as all that man has done, then Utah history begins with the Indians. The Indians have lived in this region for thousands of years and deserve our attention as the first people to know the land as home and to make a living on it. Too frequently the Indians are studied only when they are met by white men in the historical narrative, and told about only from the white man's point of view. Utah Indian cultures in their own right are worthy of our study.

Since the Indians did not have a written language to record their life activities, we must depend upon their material remains and what others wrote about them. The account of the earliest Indians told in chapter 4 is based on the work of anthropologists who make a special study of mankind from his material remains (in this case). The remains found at campsites, in caves, or in cliff dwellings have been carefully studied and compared with other findings. Since we do not have as much evidence as we would like to have, we are not sure about all the details of

their lives. The account of Utah's Indian tribes in chapter 5 is based upon the reports of earliest white men to meet these Indians and record their information. The descriptions in writing are very close to the descriptions of the Indian way of life made by the anthropologists from material remains alone.

For untold generations Indians made Utah their home. They knew where to harvest food and where to hunt. They knew how to make full use of nature's gifts. Their lives show us how man without the knowledge and skills learned in other parts of the world could survive in the Mountain West. We are impressed by the remarkable skills the Indians developed and how much they knew about nature. They lived with nature and were one with nature. It is doubtful that the Indian modified the natural environment very much. In contrast, when the white man came, he changed the natural environment, upsetting both the natural environment and the Indian way of life based upon it. It is important for us to study the Indian ways of life for their own values, to appreciate the remarkable accomplishments of the Indians, and how they were able to make this land their home.

This large panel of petroglyphs has been named Newspaper Rock.

The name Hovenweep, meaning deserted valley, is given to these ancient ruins located in Utah.

Petroglyphs in Nine Mile Canyon, Carbon County.

EARLY MAN IN THE MOUNTAIN WEST

The Indians were the first people to make a living on the land that is Utah today. They were Utah's first explorers, hunters, farmers, and village dwellers. They explored the valleys, basins, and mountain canyons. They knew where to find food and where to find protection from the cold. Utah's later explorers followed Indian trails. Utah's pioneers settled in areas that had once been occupied by Indians.

Primitive people have always depended upon nature for their living. In Utah, nature produced very little for man to live on. The desert country limited the development of the Indians. Even so, the Indians made a living

and met the challenge of a stingy nature.

A study of the lives of Utah's Indians teaches us about the ways man deals with nature. It teaches us how man first gathered and hunted for a living from raw nature. This will give us an appreciation for the achievements of those Indians who were able to build dwellings in the cliffs and master the art of agriculture in an unpromising region. It will also help us understand the obstacles the pioneers had to overcome when they came to make homes in this region.

We will study the Indians in two chapters. In the first we will learn about the earliest Indians of Utah. In the second we will learn about the Indian tribes living in Utah just before the first white men came.

IN THIS CHAPTER WE WILL LEARN

1. The American Indians had different ways of life.

2. The Desert Gatherers lived throughout the Southwest from early times.

3. The Anasazi achieved a high culture in the San Juan River region.

4. The Fremont were Desert Gatherers who acquired some of the Anasazi ways.

5. The Indians of the early Mountain West were peaceful.

6. The Fremont and Anasazi ways of life came to an end in Utah about 1300 A.D.

Pictographs in Barrier Canyon, Wayne County.

4

The people of Hovenweep built fine structures of stone including rectangular buildings, circular towers, pit houses, and underground kivas. Check dams and irrigation ditches point to their skill in agriculture.

1. THE AMERICAN INDIANS HAD DIFFERENT WAYS OF LIFE

The manner of life of a group of Indians depended upon the land, the climate, the native plant and animal life, as well as their knowledge of how to make a living from nature. The Indians learned from experience, from nature, and from other Indians. They exchanged ideas about weapons, tools, crafts, agriculture, and religion.

Although the Indians had much in common, they differed from region to region. They differed in language, in types and varieties of their food, in shelter, and crafts. When we speak of the *culture* of a people, we refer to their way of life—all the things they did. Culture traits are learned. They are taught by one generation to the next.

Most of the Indians of the Americas moved from place to place in search of their living. However, there were some Indians who had developed village life, even building great cities. These groups practiced the arts of agriculture and trade, developed the crafts necessary to build cities, and established customs and laws for a successful society.

There were three major groups of sedentary Indians in the Americas when Columbus came. These people had developed complex societies based on agriculture, and were living in great cities. In South America there was the Peruvian civilization as illustrated by the Inca. In the area of present-day Yucatan and Guatemala high civilizations had flourished for centuries, including the Maya. Later, in central Mexico the Aztec Empire had developed a high civilization.

There were other people, less advanced

but developing the arts of civilization. The Chibcha of northern South America and the Pueblo of southwestern United States are examples. The arts of civilization, based on agriculture, spread northward from Mexico into the American Southwest, and the Indians of Utah learned some of the arts and crafts of these groups.

The Indians who lived in what is now the United States are divided into five major culture groups. In eastern United States, east of the Mississippi River, lived (1) the *Indians of the Eastern Woodlands*. These were the Indians met by the colonists who founded our nation. West of the Woodlands Indians were (2) the *Hunters of the Plains* who lived on the Great Plains, from Canada to Mexico, and west to and including the Rocky Mountains. In the Pacific Northwest were (3) the *Fishers of the Northern Streams*. Utah Indians had little or no contact with these Indians. Throughout California and the Great Basin and part of the Colorado Plateau area were (4) the *Gatherers*, or *Desert Gatherers*. In New Mexico and Arizona, and extending into southeastern Utah lived (5) the *Pueblo Indians*, or *Village Dwellers*, one of the high culture or civilized groups of Indians.

2. THE DESERT GATHERERS LIVED THROUGHOUT THE SOUTHWEST

Long before any of the Indians of the Americas learned the arts of civilized life, there lived throughout much of the American Southwest Indians we call the Desert Gatherers. Their way of life is referred to as the Desert Culture. The Desert Gatherers lived west of the Rocky Mountains, through much of the Colorado Plateau and the Great Basin. Their culture dates from about 9000 B.C.

The Desert Gatherers moved in search of food. They moved from one place to another, from the basin floors to the uplands, always

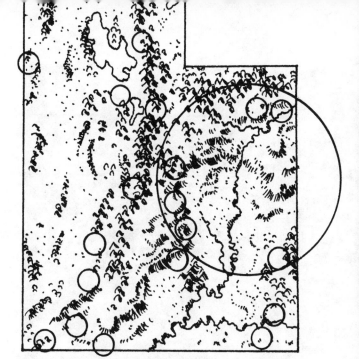

The Fremont Culture area included not only the Canyonlands and the Uinta Basin but spread into the High Plateaus and to the edge of the Great Basin.

in search of a living from what nature could provide. They lived in harmony with nature. They knew what nature provided in certain places at certain times of the year. They timed their movements to be in the right place at the right time to gather the plants and to hunt the animal life. Desert Gatherers did not plant or cultivate. They only harvested from nature's growth. Their entire life was dependent upon the resources of the land.

Only a few scattered groups of people could be supported by the plant and animal resources of the desert valleys and mountains. These people probably moved in *small family units* of fifteen to thirty individuals. The group possibly included a man, his wife or wives, their children and their families. Among the Desert Gatherers there was no strong tribal organization, or, if it existed at all, it was not effective. Small family units made up the basic Indian group. The constant search for food required most of the energy of the group. The continual round of gather-

The Fremont people built storage houses in crevices or in small rock shelters. Well concealed and often high on canyon walls, they were hard to get at. Sometimes these ruins are called Moki houses.

ing and moving filled the individual's entire lifetime.

The Desert Gatherers built no permanent dwellings. While on their seasonal rounds, they came to know the best stopping places. They preferred caves or overhang locations where high cliffs provided a protective recess in their walls or at their bases. In between stops at such locations, they made simple campsites in open country.

The Desert Gatherers used a wide variety of plant and animal life for food. They depended mostly on seeds and rootstock (rhizomes). They gathered acorns, piñon nuts, grass seeds, sunflower seeds, and the seeds of weeds. They especially liked the bulrush, sego lily bulbs, and other roots and bulbs. They gathered many kinds of berries. These people also hunted animals on a small scale. By use of the trap, snare, or other weapon, the Desert Gatherers hunted nearly every animal of the desert. The prized game was antelope

and mountain sheep. Bison were rare in the region. There were very few deer at that time. Food was scarce enough that no animal life was refused. The Desert Gatherers ate rats, mice, gophers, rabbits, and birds.

Cooking occupied much of their time. Seeds were sometimes parched with live coals in a flat basket. The seeds and rootstocks were usually ground into flour or paste on a stone slab. The flour was then prepared as mush or gruel and cooked by placing heated stones into the basket mixture. Meats were most often roasted. Small animals were simply thrown upon the fire and eaten when they were cooked.

The Desert Gatherers had few tools and little equipment. Especially important in their life were the basket and the flat milling stone. Baskets were made from plant fibers. Flat baskets were used for winnowing and for parching. Deep cone-shaped baskets were used for gathering and carrying. Tightly woven jug-like baskets were lined and covered with piñon gum and used as water carriers. From plant fibers the Desert Gatherers also made sandals and cordage (rope, string, thread). Some of their cordage was as fine as today's machine-twisted sewing thread. From cordage they made nets, bags, ropes, snares, and traps. They wove rabbit and mouse skins, and sometimes bird feathers, into light, warm robes or blankets.

Their chief weapon was the spear or dart and the dart thrower, called the atlatl. By about 1000 B.C. they acquired or developed the bow and arrow. They did expert work in flint for atlatl and arrow points. Other tools were made of bone and wood. Their entire crafts production was aimed at helping them gain food, whether on the desert floors or in the valleys and mountains. In the streams they caught fish, and for this purpose they made fine nets and fishhooks. Some of them even made decoys for hunting ducks in the marshes.

Desert Gatherers lived a simple life. Yet they learned how to live with nature and survive. They adapted their way of life to the region they called home. The way of life remained much the same down to historic times. They had no leisure time in which to develop an elaborate religion with complicated rituals. They took no time to decorate their baskets or darts. They were peaceful; they did not learn war.

3. THE ANASAZI ACHIEVED A HIGH CULTURE IN THE SAN JUAN RIVER REGION

In the American Southwest—in Arizona, New Mexico, Colorado, and Utah—more complex cultures developed among the Desert Gatherers. Desert Gatherers developed a higher culture by borrowing good ideas and new ways of doing things.

Good ideas spread among groups of wandering Indians. As Indians moved from place to place they met other Indians who had different ways of life. Sometimes they merely exchanged a few words, sometimes goods, and sometimes ideas of how to make life better. We know the Desert Gatherers traded goods at great distances because they possessed shells from the Pacific Ocean. They must have traded these shells with neighboring peoples who had contact with the Pacific Coast. So possessions of one group came to be in the hands of another group. In this way the Indians borrowed ideas for better tools, better ways of making baskets and pottery, or better ways of obtaining food.

On the mesas and in the canyons of the San Juan River, Indians originally lived much like the Desert Gatherers of western Utah. Eventually some features of the civilization of the people in central Mexico spread to north-

ern Mexico. Probably from these people or their neighbors, the San Juan River people obtained the ideas of agriculture and permanent dwelling places. The earliest Indians in the San Juan River region to adopt these new ideas are called Basketmakers. They are given this name because they made such fine and beautiful baskets which served important functions. When these same people came to live in large numbers in villages we call them Pueblo, from the Spanish word meaning villages. Later Indians referred to the Basketmaker-Pueblo people as Anasazi, or "the ancient ones." We call the culture of these ancient ones of the San Juan River region the Anasazi Culture.

The Anasazi Culture had its center along the San Juan River. It spread into the canyons and along the plateaus of the tributaries of the San Juan. Along the river bottoms and in the canyons were a few green stretches where gardens could be planted. On the mesa tops, too, were some good garden spaces. It was a dry land, but it had one advantage—summer rains, which came in the growing season. In the heart of the Anasazi country the boundaries of four states—Utah, Colorado, New Mexico, Arizona—meet today. This region is referred to today as the *Four Corners region*. This was the homeland of the Anasazi.

The Anasazi Culture began a little before the time of Christ and lasted to about 1300 A.D. in Utah. The history of the Anasazi is usually divided into four periods. The first two periods are named from their chief product, the basket; the second two periods are named from their dwellings, the pueblos. Names and dates of these periods are: Basketmaker Period (to about 500 A.D.), Modified Basketmaker Period (500-700 A.D.), Developmental Pueblo (700 to about 1050 A.D.),

*The dioramas shown here are in the Mesa Verde
National Park Museum and illustrate the four periods
through which Anasazi culture developed.*

---

*1. The Basketmaker Period (A.D. 1 to 400). These
first farmers in the Mesa Verde area lived in caves,
raised corn and squash on the mesa tops,
and gathered other food. Without the knowledge
of pottery they made beautifully
woven baskets, bags, sandals, and sashes.*

*2. The Modified Basketmaker Period
(A.D. 400 to 750). During this period the Anasazi
learned to make pottery and built roofed dwellings.
They also began to use the bow and arrow. The
population increased, and soon there were hundreds
of villages in the caves and on the mesa tops.*

and the Great Pueblo Period (from about
1050 to 1300 A.D.).

Basketmaker Period (to about 500 A.D.).
Agriculture was the most important new idea
borrowed by the Anasazi. By the time of
Christ the Anasazi had obtained from Mexico
maize or Indian corn, squash, and the knowledge of how to raise them. Before the time
of Christ, these people had moved from place
to place to gather or hunt for food. They
continued to gather and hunt, but their new
crops furnished the main parts of their diet.
As they improved their skill, planting more
gardens and harvesting more corn and squash,
they could remain in one place for a long
time and build permanent houses. Caves
which had long been used as brief stopping
places during the wanderings of the Indians
became permanent homes. Since the crops
harvested by any one farmer supplied him
with more than he and his family could eat
at once, there was a need for storage; so
storage pits were dug in the cave floors.
People could now depend on a supply of
food. They had enough stored for their use
until the next harvest. Since they did not
have to spend all their time in food gathering
and hunting, they had leisure time. Leisure is
one of the most important gifts to man, and
it comes mainly from agriculture that gives
man a dependable food supply.

*Modified Basketmaker Period (500-700
A.D.).* The Anasazi realized the advantages of
their farming culture. They borrowed other
ideas from their neighbors to the south. From
Mexico, again, there came new varieties of
corn, and then beans. *Beans* are an important
source of protein, and this meant that the
Anasazi now had a more balanced diet. They
would be healthier and live longer. It meant
they did not have to depend upon hunting
meat as much as they had before. The Ana-

sazi also borrowed the idea of *pottery* and how to make it.

Developmental Pueblo Period (700-1050 A.D.). As the population increased, the Basketmakers moved out of their caves and onto the mesas near their gardens. Here they built *villages*, now called pueblos. In time they joined their houses together into *compact clusters*. Sometimes they arranged their houses in one continuous square, sometimes in an L-shape, or a semi-circular unit. It was a time of experimentation in the development of pueblos. This is why the period is called Developmental Pueblo. These Indians experimented not only in the forms of their villages, but also in the types of walls they built for their homes. They used adobe and poles, adobe and stone, and finally they used cut stone laid evenly. In Utah the *jacal wall* (pronounced hacal) construction was popular. Jacal walls were made by setting posts upright, close together, and plastering mud between the posts to make a solid wall about six inches thick. Usually their houses were joined together leaving an open court in the center. In the open court pit houses were constructed. In time they were used not so much for storage as for ceremonial rooms, now called *kivas*. In the kivas the men of the village gathered for religious ceremonies. Public religious ceremonies were performed in the open courts. Dances were also held in the courts.

Religion grew more important and was centered around agriculture and the worship of nature. The priests or medicine men performed ceremonies to insure a good crop, to bring rain, and to ward off damage to crops.

The fine crafts developed by the Basketmakers were continued and improved. Elaborate weaving was done on looms. The art of making pottery was greatly developed. For designs on the pottery these people adapted the fine designs used in their basketry. They

3. *Developmental Pueblo Period (A.D. 750 to 1100). This period saw the beginning of true village living. In these villages, or pueblos, built on the mesa, the houses were joined in a long curving row. About the villages are the fields. A spring is nearby.*

decorated the pottery with black designs on a white base. The bow and arrow replaced the atlatl completely as the major weapon.

A new crop was introduced from the south during this period—*cotton*. Soon cotton blankets replaced the earlier fur robes. Breechcloths and blankets were woven for the men and blanket dresses for the women.

The Great Pueblo Period (1050-1300 A.D.) marked the greatest achievement in the Anasazi Culture. During this period *large buildings* were constructed. Some were *cliff dwellings* with hundreds of rooms and many kivas, others were terraced apartment houses

4. *The Great Pueblo Period (A.D. 1100 to 1300). Spruce Tree House, shown in this diorama, contains over a hundred rooms and eight kivas. Cliff dwellings such as this were built beginning about 1200 A.D. During this last century the Anasazi people reached their highest level of development.*

capable of housing a hundred families. Some pueblos were built of mud, stone, and wood, but the finest were built by horizontal masonry with well-shaped stones laid in adobe mortar. Walls were smoothly plastered and often decorated with designs in red, yellow, black, and white. Most pueblos were small with only a few rooms and a small kiva, but some were large and housed hundreds of people.

In Utah, the villages of the Anasazi of this period were on the mesa tops or along the smaller stream beds where there was good land for gardens. The Utah Anasazi found expert ways of conserving and using water. They made dams, dikes, and reservoirs, which enabled them to use all the available water with little loss.

The daily life of the people was spent in providing the necessities of life—food, clothing, and shelter. The men did most of the farming and hunting, and wove the cloth. They spent many hours in the kivas and taught their sons their skills and the rituals of the kiva. The women had the greater chores and created the finest crafts. They gathered food plants and plant materials for basket making. They made baskets and pottery and decorated them. They built and repaired the houses, made the clothing, and prepared the food. The women even gathered the wood. As they worked, the women taught their daughters how to do these chores as well.

The workmanship of the Anasazi of this Great Pueblo Period was the finest they ever produced. Their pottery was well shaped, carefully fired, and elaborately decorated with geometric patterns and animal figures. They also made cooking and storage pots, ladles, mugs, and bowls of clay. Their finely woven cotton cloth was decorated with colorful designs. From plant fiber and human hair they made string and cord. They continued to

The Anasazi made beautiful pottery which they used for storage.

make feather robes. They adorned themselves with jewelry in the form of wristlets, necklaces, and pendants made of turquoise, other brightly colored stones, coral, and Pacific shell. Flint knives, tools of bone, and household furnishings were also made.

4. THE FREMONT WERE DESERT GATHERERS WHO ACQUIRED SOME OF THE ANASAZI WAYS

While the Anasazi were developing their way of life, the Desert Gatherers to the north and west continued their nomadic ways in search of food. In their wanderings they met people who told them of the ways of their Anasazi neighbors—about their great villages, fine gardens, beautiful pottery and other crafts. *Desert Gatherers to the north borrowed some of the Anasazi ways of life*, as the Anasazi had earlier borrowed from their neighbors to the south. However, the Desert Gatherers did not acquire all of the Anasazi ways. They had their own way of life which they wanted to preserve as much as possible, for they respected the ways of their fathers. Yet they wanted to use some of the good ideas of the Anasazi. They borrowed what they wanted and could use, and adapted the new ideas to their old ways of life.

The art of gardening was the first and most important of the Anasazi ways borrowed by the Desert Gatherers. They began to plant gardens of corn, squash, and beans. They next borrowed the idea of *permanent dwellings and storage bins* which they constructed near their gardens. They also acquired the technique of making pottery. Gardening, dwellings, and pottery were the main features they added to their old way of life.

Fremont Culture is the name given to the Desert Gatherers who added these ideas to their old ways. The name Fremont was chosen because the remains of this way of life were first found in the Fremont River drainage area of the Colorado Plateau in southeastern Utah. The art of gardening was borrowed about 500 A.D. The Fremont people came to live in more or less permanent dwellings about 800 or 850 A.D. By 1200 A.D. most of the Indians of Utah were living in small villages and practicing gardening.

The Fremont way of life spread over much of Utah. It spread into the Canyonlands region, the Uinta Basin, the valleys of the High Plateaus, the Great Basin, and the area around the shores of the Great Salt Lake. However, the way of life of different groups of Indians varied somewhat throughout this region.

The Fremont way of life was based primarily upon gardening. Corn, squash, and beans were grown by most peoples of the Fremont Culture. Some built irrigation ditches to water their gardens. They continued to gather wild plants for food and to hunt and fish. They depended much more on gathering and hunting than the Anasazi to the south.

The settlements of the Fremont people were very small. Possibly the same small family groups now built dwellings which they

alone occupied. These small family settlements were located near their gardens. In the Canyonlands and Uinta Basin areas, Fremont people planted their gardens along river bottoms or by the banks of small streams. Dwellings were built nearby in cliff caves or along the river bottom under overhanging cliffs, or on high, isolated hills. In the Great Basin and the Sevier River drainage area, dwellings were located along the bases of the mountains at the mouths of canyons where there were water and soil for their gardens. The Fremont people continued their gathering and hunting and built storage bins in isolated stopping places along their routes.

A typical settlement included a pit house and granaries. A pit house was the lodge or dwelling room for people of the settlement. Granaries were storage places for the foods to be used during the year. Pit houses were usually of an irregular circular shape, constructed partly underground. Four center posts supported the roof. Side poles sloped

This cross-section drawing shows the construction of a typical pit house. Pit houses varied in depth from one to three feet and in width from ten to thirty feet. A round, adobe-rimmed fireplace, often paved with thin stone slabs, was near the center on the floor. Walls were sometimes plastered with adobe or masonry. Entrance was usually through the roof; a circular stone slab served as a door. Often the floors were covered with a layer of adobe.

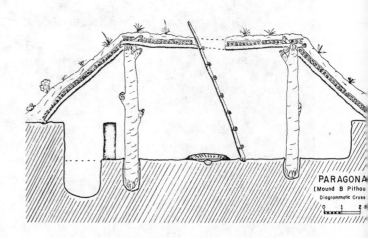

PARAGONA
(Mound B Pithou
Diagrammatic Cross

The Coombs Village is located at Boulder, Utah. This drawing represents the artist's conception of the village as it was about 1100 A.D.

A kiva at the Steer Palace site in Castle Wash. On the circular bench are stone supports for a ground-level roof. The excavation at the right shows the depth of Indian excavation; on this level a floor of prepared clay was laid.

from the roof to the edge of the pit. To make the roof, small poles, twigs and branches were laid over the opening, then covered with thick mud plaster. Near the center of the floor was a fireplace, paved with thin stone slabs and rimmed around with adobe. Granaries were built above ground with rectangular walls and roofs of timber, twigs, branches, and mud plaster. Granary walls were often built of adobe, but sometimes they were built of expertly cut stone, laid in straight walls with square corners. Frequently walls were made by setting posts in the ground close together on end, and laid up and plastered with adobe to make a solid wall about six inches thick. Entrances to pit houses and granaries were usually through an opening in the roof, covered by a thin stone slab. Granaries were also built in isolated places among rocks, in small cave openings or ledges. Walls of these granaries were usually of mud and rock with a small opening in the wall.

Pottery making was also borrowed by the Fremont people. Their pottery was usually gray, simply shaped into jars, pitchers, and bowls. Sometimes black designs were painted on the gray pots. Other types of pottery and stone work were also borrowed from the Anasazi.

The Fremont people made excellent coiled baskets. They had various kinds of grinding stones. They made bone awls, and from stone they made choppers, hammerstones, blades, scrapers, and drills.

Their clothing was made of leather, woven textiles, and fur. Men wore kilts, and women wore short skirts. Hide moccasins covered their feet.

The Fremont people also borrowed from the Hunters of the Plains. From their contacts with peoples of the Great Plains, the Fremont borrowed such ideas as the use of

buffalo and other animal hides and how to make leather, moccasins, and medicine pouches. Other features borrowed from the Plains Indians included horned headdresses and buffalo hide shields.

Not all Anasazi traits were borrowed by the Fremont people. We do not know why, but the Fremont people did not borrow the use of turkeys, cotton, grooved axes, sandals, the kiva, the multi-storied, apartmentlike house units, or the finest types of Anasazi pottery.

Even so, Indians of the Fremont Culture made some contributions of their own, such as moccasins, figurines, pictographs, isolated small granaries hidden among rocks and under ledges, the use of asbestos for waterproofing baskets, their own gray pottery types with different styles of decoration, lean-to houses in caves, and vaulted walls in masonry structures.

5. THE INDIANS OF THE EARLY MOUNTAIN WEST WERE PEACEFUL

The Indians we have studied in this chapter were people of peace. The Desert Gatherers, the Anasazi, and the Fremont were peaceful Indians. They respected each other and the other people they met. Evidence they left indicates that they exchanged ideas and goods, but not blows. They felt life was best when they were spending their time in gathering and hunting for their food, tending their gardens, building dwellings, making baskets, pottery, clothing, and other useful objects for this life. They passed these peaceful ways on to their children from one generation to the next.

6. THE FREMONT AND ANASAZI WAYS OF LIFE CAME TO AN END IN UTAH IN ABOUT 1300 A.D.

Great changes came upon the Fremont

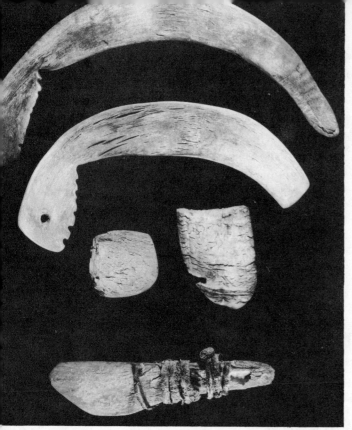

The Anasazi made these tools from mountain sheep horns. Pictured at the top are sickles used in seed gathering. The other tools were used for digging; wooden handles were attached to these tips.

and Anasazi people between the years 1250 and 1300 A.D. The events that occurred during that half century resulted in the end of the Fremont way of life among the Desert Gatherers and the removal of the Anasazi from the Four Corners region to northern New Mexico and Arizona. The Anasazi left their cliff dwellings and mesa pueblos and moved to the east and south leaving their former homes empty. Among the other people of Utah there was a great change, too. No longer did these people keep gardens. No longer did they build and live in permanent dwellings. They also lost some of the fine Anasazi ways they had borrowed. By 1300 A.D. the higher forms of Indian life had disappeared from Utah, and the culture of the ancient Desert Gatherers had been taken up again.

What happened to cause such a great change? Several explanations have been given, though it is not known exactly what happened or what caused it. (1) *Drought.* Tree rings indicate that the year 1276 was a very dry year, and that it was followed by a drought that lasted to the year 1299. Without moisture there could be no gardens. As garden foods became scarce or disappeared entirely, many of the young and the old people died. The Anasazi had to go somewhere else for food. They left their settlements and moved eastward into New Mexico and southward toward southern New Mexico and Arizona. (2) Another explanation is that *war* came among these people; that there was fighting among the villages, and that the pueblos were burned after their inhabitants were killed. (3) *Invasion* by northern Indians is given as a third explanation. It is possible that the warlike Navajo and Apache Indians came from their ancient home in Canada about this time and raided the settlements of the Fremont and Anasazi people, eventually driving out these peaceful Indians. The Navajo and Apache finally settled in New Mexico and Arizona, preserving their warlike ways but also adopting some of the ways of the Pueblo Indians.

No one of these explanations answers all our questions. Until we know more about those times, we will have to be content to know that during the last half of the thirteenth century a great change came upon the native people of the Southwest. The Anasazi moved. The Fremont people either left the region or simply gave up living in permanent dwellings and depending upon gardening. However, pottery making and gardening continued in some places. Other than this we can say that the people of Utah took up again the ways of the ancient Desert Gatherers. The great days of the Anasazi were soon to become only a memory.

The excavation of this burial site revealed the skeletal remains of an adult who died about 1150 A.D.

Chief Washakie and some of his band encamped in the Wind River Mountains, Wyoming, 1870.

UTAH'S INDIAN TRIBES

Our understanding of the Indians of Utah has been based, not on a written language of the Indians, for they did not write, but on physical remains in stone and clay, in pottery and baskets, tools of wood and bone, buildings very much in ruin, and pictographs. Often we have found only what was discarded or left behind. Even so, these remains tell us a great deal. But learning about the Indian way of life from what they threw away or left behind is a little like learning about our civilization from what is found in our garbage dumps or in ghost towns.

Another way of learning about the Indians is to read what the first white visitors said about them. Our first written account of the Indians of Utah comes from Father Escalante who visited Utah in 1776 and left his diary. (We will study about the Spanish coming to Utah in our next chapter.) Others followed and gave us additional information. From such writings we can tell the life habits of the Indians who were living in Utah at the time of the first white contacts. We refer to these Indians as historic Indians.

IN THIS CHAPTER WE WILL LEARN

1. The historic tribes of Utah were Desert Gatherers who spoke the Shoshonean language.

2. The Gosiute lived in northern and northwestern Utah.

3. The Paiute lived in southern and southwestern Utah.

4. The Ute of central and eastern Utah were Desert Gatherers until they obtained the horse.

5

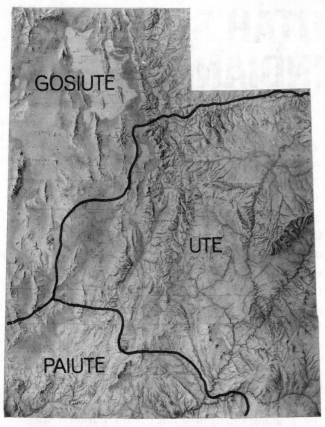

Three major groups of Indians occupied the Utah area from historic times: The Gosiute in the northwest, the Southern Paiute in the southwest, and the Ute in the central and eastern part of the state.

Chief Washakie's lodge and encampment, Wind River Mountains, Wyoming, 1870.

1. THE HISTORIC TRIBES OF UTAH WERE DESERT GATHERERS WHO SPOKE THE SHOSHONEAN LANGUAGE

In historic times (when we have written records) many Utah Indians lived in a manner similar to that of their Desert Gatherer ancestors. Some of these people had been little affected by the Anasazi and Fremont ways. For others, when the Anasazi and Fremont cultures ended, there was a return to most Desert Gatherer ways.

These Indians lived as three different culture groups, each speaking dialects of the Shoshonean language.

The three culture groups of Indians in Utah in historic times were the Gosiute, the Paiute, and the Ute. The Ute and Paiute, though speaking different dialects, could understand each other fairly well, but they could not understand the Gosiute. All these people lived in small family associations like their ancestors. Only the Ute developed a tribal system, and that was late in their history. Many of the differences in their way of life were determined by the nature of the country which they occupied.

2. THE GOSIUTE LIVED IN NORTHERN AND NORTHWESTERN UTAH

The Desert Gatherers who lived in the northern part of the Great Basin in Utah were a group of western Shoshoni Indians, but they are generally referred to as the Gosiute. Because of the necessity of digging for roots and burrowing animals and insects, early white visitors called the Gosiute "diggers" or "Digger Indians."

THE GOSIUTE INDIANS OF UTAH, MAY 1859

As described by Captain J. H. Simpson:

May 11, Camp No. 9, east slope of Antelope Valley.– ...

Found some Root-Diggers here, one a very old woman, bent over with infirmities, very short in stature, and the most lean, wretched-looking object it has ever been my lot to see. ...

These Indians appear worse in condition than the meanest of the animal creation. Their garment is only a rabbit-skin cape, like those already described, and the children go naked. It is refreshing, however, in all their degradation, to see the mother studiously careful of her little one, by causing it to nestle under her rabbit-skin mantle.

At first they were afraid to come near us, but bread having been given to the old woman, by signs and words she made the others in the distance understand that they had nothing to fear, and prompted them to accompany her to camp to get something to eat. Notwithstanding the old woman looked as if she was famished, it was very touching to see her deal out her bread, first to the little child at her side, and then, only after the others had come up and got their share, to take the small balance for herself. At camp, the feast we gave them made them fairly laugh for joy.

Near our camp I visited one of their dens or wick-e-ups. Like that already described, it was an inclosure, 3 feet high, of cedar-brush. ...

These Shoshoni, with many characteristics similar to the Plains Indians, lived on Utah's northern border and sometimes came into Utah. This is an encampment of Chief Washakie's band in the southern foothills of the Wind River Mountains, Wyoming, near South Pass.
Taken by William H. Jackson, 1870.

Several groups of Gosiute lived in the valleys west of Great Salt Lake and Utah Lake and north of the Great Salt Lake. Small family groups of Gosiute lived in Sink Valley, Skull Valley, Tooele Valley, Rush Valley, Cedar Valley, and Tintic Valley. Two small groups lived at the base of the Deep Creek Mountains near the Nevada border. A group of about two hundred lived at the foot of the Goose Creek Mountains near the northwest corner of Utah. Four villages of Gosiute lived along the northern shore of the Great Salt Lake between Promontory Point and the

A Gosiute dwelling drawn by artist with the James H. Simpson expedition of 1859.

last miles of the Bear River. On the Weber River there was a group mistakenly called "Snakes" and "Weber Utes."

The family was the basic unit among the Gosiute. Marriage was often between cousins. For his bride the male gave so many gifts that it amounted to bride purchase. Sometimes a man had more than one wife, and sometimes a wife had two husbands, but the usual pattern was for one man to have one wife. The small family group moved from place to place in search of food. Groups of families sometimes came together for communal hunts and dances, but usually only for a few days; then they dispersed. When families did gather in winter villages, they were led by a village headman whose main functions were to receive and pass on information about where to find food and to arrange for communal hunts.

Food gathering and preparation. The Gosiute lived in one of the most desolate regions of Utah and consequently their life was very difficult. Families spent almost their entire time in gathering for a living. They made use of every possible food—plant and animal. They especially relied upon insects, rats, lizards, rabbits, and a great variety of seeds.

Plant food was used throughout the year. They took seeds, berries, roots, and used some leaves for greens. Grass seeds were gathered in large flat tray-baskets. They gathered acorns in the Wasatch Mountains and piñon nuts throughout the area. In the fall the Indians came together and moved into the mountains to harvest the piñon nuts. Surplus nuts were stored. Seeds and berries were often pounded and made into small sun-dried cakes.

Small animals were dug from their holes, or taken by traps constructed to kill the animal by a falling stone. Insects, rodents

(especially ground squirrels), and rabbits were important to the Gosiute, who were also alert for larger game. Indians who lived near the forested mountains sometimes hunted deer, antelope, mountain sheep, and bison or buffalo. The bison, deer, and mountain sheep were usually hunted by individual Indians or small groups, but antelope and rabbits were hunted by the Indians in communal drives.

Rabbits furnished meat as well as fur for clothing. For rabbit drives, the Gosiute circled a large area and drove the rabbits into nets set to form a V-shape. The open ends were closed when the rabbits came into the V. In Cache Valley, when rabbits became numerous, a crowd of Indians simply surrounded them and killed them with clubs. Sometimes rabbits were hunted by making a large circle of fire and burning the grass and brush toward the center, driving the rabbits into the smaller area until the Indians could kill the rabbits easily. Because the burning method destroyed the range, Indians did not resort to it very often.

Antelope were hunted by driving them into a V-shaped trap. At the end of the narrowing V, there was a corral ready to hold the antelope. The Indians then killed the animals as needed or as fast as they could dry the meat and tan the hides.

Of the insect foods, crickets were very important to the Gosiute. The crickets were driven into a pit or caught in baskets as they floated down a stream. They were firebaked or sundried, then ground fine and made into cakes. Sometimes they were parched.

Fish were taken wherever they could be caught. Promontory Indians took fish from the Bear River.

The shelter most commonly used by the Gosiute was the wicki-up. This was made by arranging branches and brush in a cone or dome shape to form a crude shelter. This served as little more than a windbreak unless covered with skins. Often the Indians simply crouched behind a willow windbreak when the weather was stormy. Caves and rock shelters frequently served as winter homes.

Clothing was limited by the difficulty of obtaining skins. Early white visitors found the natives had little clothing. In summer, the men wore only a G-string or breechcloth, and women an apron or grass skirt. In winter they wore blankets made of strips of rabbit fur. Moccasins were worn only occasionally. Sometimes women wore a crown of twigs with leaves attached for a sunshade, but they had no basketry hats like Southern Paiute women.

Weapons and crafts. The chief weapon was the bow and arrow, used almost exclusively for hunting. Baskets of a poor quality were the chief craft of the Gosiute. In earlier times they made a little pottery, but this art had all but disappeared by the time white men first visited them. No pottery, poor basketry, bows and arrows, a few simple sewing tools with which to sew rabbit skins into blankets—these were the possessions and crafts of the Gosiute.

The Gosiute were peaceful Indians; war was almost unknown among them. Usually the only fighting was over the stealing of a wife. If the thief was from another group such as the Paiute, then there was more serious fighting.

The Gosiute played many *games* of skill and amusement in which both men and women participated. Games included such sports as shinny (in which a ball was propelled by a curved stick), hoop-and-pole games (such as throwing the pole at a rolling hoop), dice (using long sticks marked by colored designs), and archery. A kicking game and wrestling were also popular sports.

While the Gosiute had no chiefs, they did have their *medicine men*. The medicine man, or shaman as he is sometimes called, obtained his medical powers from dreams. The Indians believed that he had special powers with the unseen world of gods, demons, and spirits of ancestors. He treated all sorts of ailments.

3. THE PAIUTE LIVED IN SOUTHERN AND SOUTHWESTERN UTAH

Two main groups of Paiute Indians lived in western America. The *Southern Paiute* lived in southern and southwestern Utah and as far south as the Colorado and the Little Colorado rivers, and in the desert regions of southern California. The *Northern Paiute* lived

A Las Vegas Paiute dressed in the best of clothes.

The Kaibab Paiute of northern Arizona were photographed by John K. Hillers, photographer with the John Wesley Powell expedition which explored the Colorado River in 1873. The Indians put on their best clothing and even borrowed from the Powell party.

Two young women seed gatherers display the uses of basketry.

in the mountain regions of California, the desert regions of Nevada, in southeastern Oregon, and part of Idaho. In Utah history we deal mostly with the Southern Paiute.

Among the Southern Paiute with whom Utah settlers had contact there were four groups, named from their locale: the *Saint George Paiute* (living on the Virgin and Santa Clara rivers), the *Kaibab Paiute* (living on the Kaibab Plateau north of the Grand Canyon of the Colorado in Arizona), the *Moapa Paiute* (living in Moapa Valley along the Virgin River in southeastern Nevada), and their neighbors the *Las Vegas Paiute* (living at and near "The Meadows," Las Vegas).

The Southern Paiute lived in one of the most barren, isolated desert regions of America. While the Gosiute of the north also lived in a severe desert region with cold winters, hot summers and only about sixteen inches of moisture a year (Tooele Valley), the Paiute lived in a desert region of warm winters, even hotter summers, especially in the regions of lower elevation, and about eight inches of moisture a year as in Saint George.

The Southern Paiute way of life was very much the same as that of the Gosiute with one important exception. The Southern Paiute were semi-sedentary; that is, they spent much of their time in one place because they practiced some agriculture.

Agriculture, food gathering and preparation. The Paiute, like the Gosiute, relied mainly on seeds and roots for their food. However, along the Santa Clara and the upper Virgin rivers the Paiute cultivated crops of maize and calabashes (gourds), an art they had probably retained from the Anasazi and Fremont cultures. They borrowed other foods from the first white men to come into the region. By the time Mormon settlers came to live in the area the Paiute were raising wheat, melons, amaranth, and indigo. To water these crops they built crude irrigation ditches leading from the small streams to their fields. Trees and brush were cleared from the land to make plots for farming. Their total cultivated land may have amounted to as much as a hundred acres. The Paiute occupied most of the small places in the area where there was a little flat land and irrigation water nearby.

Apart from their agriculture, the Paiute were diggers and gatherers—taking small animals from their holes, digging roots, gathering seeds, berries, and nuts. Mesquite beans, seeds from the amaranth and yucca, and piñon nuts were favorites. Seeds were ground fine on *metates*, or flat stone grinding slabs, and then molded into cakes for cooking. Sometimes seeds were parched by coming in contact with hot coals shifted rapidly on flat tray baskets.

Autumn seems to have been the time for movement to other grounds, for they went into the Kaibab region to hunt and harvest. They relied only secondarily on hunting the larger game animals.

Shelter was little needed during the spring, summer, and autumn months, but winters were cold enough to require a shelter. The wicki-up, very similar to that of the

Two elderly Paiute, living in Moapa Valley, on the Muddy River in Nevada, are making the addition of "five and three are eight."

An old woman making a basket, seated outside her brush shelter (wicki-up).

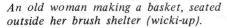

The Circle Dance in winter costume is watched by Major John W. Powell.

71

Ta-peats is shown outside his home, in the vicinity of Saint George, Utah, 1873.

These four Las Vegas Paiute were named by Hillers "The Old Gamblers."

Two young women carrying water.

Gosiute, was used extensively. Sometimes the Paiute simply stopped under a large tree for shelter.

The Paiute usually wore very little *clothing*, needing very little in the warm and hot seasons. The children wore none at all during the warm seasons. The men wore a simple breechcloth, and the women a simple skirt. Both wore rabbitskin blankets for a covering. Men and women had shirtlike coverings, and the men wore leggings at times. Moccasins were known among them but seldom worn. The women wore headdresses of basketry.

The Southern Paiute made fine *basketry*, using coiling and twining, techniques employed by the advanced basketmakers of the American Southwest. They made basketry hats, conical seed or burden baskets, seed beaters, winnowing and parching trays, flat trays, water jugs or ollas, and bowls. The basketry hats, worn only by the women, were used to protect them from the pitch when gathering piñon nuts and for protecting their heads from carrying straps attached to burdens.

The Paiute were peaceful like their relatives the Gosiute. Their *weapons* were used almost exclusively for hunting and food gathering. Besides the bow and arrow, they used a club and a flint knife. Their flint knife was made by placing a chipped flint blade into the end of a short wooden handle which was then wrapped just below the blade. Rodent hooks, to help in digging rodents from their holes, were long sticks with a hooked or slightly forked end. When inserted into the burrow and turned, the hook would catch in the fur of the rodent, and the animal could then be pulled out.

Fire was made by use of a stick drill twirled between the palms of the hands while an assistant held some bark tinder in which to catch the spark.

Pah-ri-ates in native summer dress.

4. THE UTE WERE DESERT GATHERERS UNTIL THEY OBTAINED THE HORSE

The Ute Indians, in historic times, lived in the region from the Uinta Basin on the north to the San Juan River on the south, and from central Utah on the west to the Great Plains east of the Rocky Mountains. Several bands lived in Utah. The *Timpanogots Ute* lived in Utah Valley and the region immediately east. The *Sampits Ute* lived south of the Timpanogots in Sanpete Valley and Juab Valley and as far south as Salina. The *Pahvant Ute* lived in the Sevier Desert region east of the Pavant Mountains. In the Uinta Basin were the *Uintah Ute*. The *Yampa Ute* lived to the south of the Uinta Basin. The *Pavagogwunsin* or *Fish Ute* lived in the high plateau region around Fish Lake. The *Sheberetch Ute* lived in Castle Valley and surrounding regions.

In prehistoric times the Fremont Culture had spread through much of the land occupied by the Ute. After about 1300 A.D., as was learned in the last chapter, the Indians discarded their Fremont ways and went back to the ways of their Desert Culture ancestors. Now Desert Gatherers again, their way of life was similar to that of their relatives the Paiute. Small family groups moved from place to place gathering a living from favorite gathering and hunting grounds. The struggle for a living was almost as hard here as in other parts of Utah. Some Ute improved their living by going into the Rocky Mountains to hunt deer and antelope. Some even went on to the Great Plains where they hunted buffalo. The Ute lived in this manner as Desert Gatherers for about three hundred years after the Fremont Culture ended. Then they began to pick up new ways from some of their neighbors.

Neighbors of the Ute. To the south and east of the Ute lived the *Navajo* and the

A camp scene showing babe in cradle.

A warrior and his bride.

Breaking up camp.

Encampment and tree lookout.

Apache. The Navajo had settled among the Pueblo or Village Dwellers of the Southwest and acquired many sedentary traits from these people. The Apache lived in the mountainous country of New Mexico, Arizona, and Mexico. They lived on game and wild plants, and sometimes moved onto the plains to hunt buffalo. They also raided peaceful Indians.

To the east lived the *Hunters of the Plains*. These Indians made their homes on the Great Plains and occasionally moved into the Rocky Mountains. The Ute Indians moved about and became acquainted with the Hunters of the Plains as well as the Apache and the Navajo.

The Ute had other very important neighbors after 1598. In that year *Spanish soldiers, missionaries*, and *settlers* came into New Mexico. The Spanish brought with them many things of importance to the Indians, but nothing quite so important as *the horse*. The Apache, Navajo, Ute, and Plains Indians in time acquired the horse—sometimes by stealing and sometimes by trading. The Ute came

to prize the horse so much that some of them traded their children to the Spanish for horses. The Spanish trained the Indian children to tend sheep and herd cows for them, and to do other tasks as servants or slaves.

The horse radically changed Indian ways of life. The Ute, Apache, Navajo, and Plains Indians now became horsemen, hunters, and warriors. They could now move about quickly and easily over great distances. They could follow the buffalo rather than waiting for the buffalo to come to them. From the buffalo they obtained their food and skins to provide their clothing and shelter. The whole life of these Indians became bound up with the buffalo. Plains Indians sometimes moved into the mountains where they could hunt deer, the Rocky Mountain goat, beaver (for furs), and porcupine (for needles). The Ute of the Colorado Plateau region rode their horses across the mountains to the Great Plains where they raided horses from the Plains Indians. Sometimes, however, there were peaceful encounters between the Ute and Plains Indians.

74

In all these contacts the Ute learned many things and borrowed new ways. They obtained not only the horse, but horse regalia, war equipment, the tepee, the travois, and the use of rawhide.

With the coming of the horse, it was possible for the Ute to obtain a living from a larger area. As they moved to lands held by other Indians there was war. *Tribal organization* was necessary in war as well as for hunts and raids. Bands of Indians grouped together under a strong leader and held a valley or several valleys as their own. The several bands of Ute formed a very loose confederation. In the 1700s the Ute were powerful and warlike, making raids onto the Great Plains. Raids continued into the 1800s when one Ute chief, Walkara, was known to have led his band from their Utah home in Sanpete Valley as far as the plains on the east and to California on the west. (See chapter 10, section 4.)

Where there were plenty of buffalo, Indians with horses made full use of the new ways of life. In less favored places and among less favored Indians, some of the Old Desert Gatherer ways remained. There were Ute Indians who knew the extremes of these different ways of life, and many mixed a few of the ways of each.

The *tepee* was an invention of the Plains Indians borrowed by the Ute. The tepee was made with long poles which were stood on end around a circle and at the top tied together where they crossed to make a frame for a tentlike dwelling. The hides of buffalo, expertly sewn together, covered the pole frame to provide a warm home. To move from one place to another the tepee was taken down and put onto the *travois*, a carrier made from two poles tied to a horse and braced apart to support a load. Many of the tepees of the Plains Indians were beautifully painted. The Ute tepees were usually quite plain. In summer the Ute used the wicki-up for shelter.

Meat was the staple food of these Indians. Meats were cooked over coals or preserved in two forms: *jerky* was made by cutting raw meat into long thin strips and drying it in the sun; *pemmican* was made by pounding dried meat, dry seeds, berries, and fat. This could be eaten dry or cooked by *stone boiling*. Fish were taken wherever found in streams or lakes. The Timpanogots Ute made their home in Utah Valley partly because of the excellent fishing in the lake. The Pahvant Ute fished the Sevier River and Fish Lake. When meat and fish were not abundant, the Ute turned to gathering wild plants. The yucca fruit, camas bulb, bitterroot, grass seeds, piñon nuts, wild potatoes, serviceberries, and chokecherries were popular. Occasionally, the Ute raised a little corn.

The women became very skillful in dressing and tanning the skins of the buffalo, deer, antelope, elk, and mountain sheep. From these they made *clothing*. The men wore shirts or robes, breechcloth, leggings, and moccasins. Women wore belted gowns that extended below the knees, leggings, and moccasins. The women also wore basket hats for everyday wear. At special dances or ceremonies the Ute men wore elaborate feathered headdresses. At such times the men painted their bodies and faces with black and yellow paints. The Ute did not cut their hair but wore it in long braids.

The women not only made the clothing, but also made the lodging and household utensils, prepared the meals, and reared the children. They did most of the work of moving camp. The men spent their time making weapons, hunting, and fighting. Favorite weapons included the bow and arrow, and the lance. Ceremonials were the affairs of men.

The Ute made a poor quality of pottery which they left undecorated. From willows they made basket water jugs, burden baskets, harvesting fans, and basket hats.

These, then, are the major groups of Indians living in the Utah region at the time the first white men came. In these homelands the Indians had lived out their lives from time beyond memory. Here they had developed their own patterns of life in harmony with nature. The coming of the white man was to bring permanent changes in old and honored ways of life.

MANY UTAH PLACE NAMES ARE INDIAN NAMES

The Indians named the mountains, streams, and valleys. Many of their place names were perpetuated by the Mountain Men, explorers, and settlers. Here are a few ex amples of the place names, with the Indian group that gave the name, and the Indian meaning.

Awapa Plateau, Wayne County	Paiute, a stream or water hole among the cedars.
Gosiute, Juab County	Shoshoni, dust people.
Hovenweep, San Juan County	Ute, deserted valley.
Ibapah, Tooele County	Gosiute, properly aibimpa, water tinged with clay silt.
Juab County	Ute, flat or level.
Kaiparowitz(s) Plateau	Paiute, a small elevation near the north end; or, the mountain home of these people.
Kanab, Kane County	Paiute, willow.
Kanosh, Millard County	Ute, man of white hair; name of a Pahvant headman.
Koosharem, Sevier County	Ute, for an edible tuber used by the Ute.
Markagunt Plateau	Paiute, highland of trees.
Mukuntuweap, North Fork of the Virgin River	Paiute, straight canyon.
Onaqui Mountains, Tooele County	Gosiute, salt.
Oquirrh Mountains	Gosiute, wooded mountain.
Ouray, Uintah County	Ute, for Chief Ouray.
Pahreah River, Pahreah, Paria	Paiute, dirty water.
Pah Vant, Pahvant, Pavant	Paiute, water people.
Paiute, Pah Ute	Paiute, true Ute, water Ute.
Panguitch, Garfield County	Paiute, the place where fish are.
Paragonah, Iron County	Paiute, a thin sheet of brackish water.
Parowan, Iron County	Paiute, marsh people.
Parunuweap, Washington County	Paiute, roaring water canyon.
Paunsaugunt Plateau (Garfield-Kane)	Paiute, home of the beaver.
Quitchupah Lake, Iron County	Paiute, bed ground, watering place.
Timpanogos, Utah County	Ute, Rock River (Provo River).
Toquerville, Washington County	Paiute, black mountain.
Uinta, Uintah County	Ute, pine land.
Yuta, Utes, Utahs, Ute	Ute, home or location on the mountain top.
Wah Wah Mountains	Paiute, salty or alkaline seeps.
Wasatch Mountains	Ute, a low pass over a high mountain range.

UNIT THREE
RIVALRIES FOR EMPIRES AND FURS

We have learned something of the nature of the land and the ways of the Indians in Utah. We now turn to a narrative history of Utah based upon written records. We will read the stories of the deeds of men who are known to us by name and by the records they left. History is the story of men in action.

It was not until 1847 that Utah was permanently settled by white men. During the seventy-one years from 1776 to 1847, Utah was entered, crossed, and recrossed by hundreds of explorers and travelers. These men found the Indian trails and followed them. They wanted to know the resources of the land. They wanted to claim the land for their own country—for farming and for mining precious metals such as silver and gold. They wanted to convert the Indians to Christianity. Some of those who crossed Utah were simply traders who hauled goods between New Mexico and California. Others came seeking beaver pelts which could be traded for a living. Some explorers sought a short and easy route across the plains, mountains, and deserts to help people move west and find new homes.

From 1776 until 1848 there was serious rivalry for the West between European countries and the United States. Great Britain, Russia, Spain, and later Mexico, and the United States rivaled each other for this land. The United States finally won it by war with Mexico in 1848. During this period of rivalry, this was the only major encounter in the form of war. Most of the time the rivalries took the form of explorations and establishing trails, trading routes, fur trapping expeditions, and forts in the region.

The Spanish were the first to come into Utah. Then British, French, Spanish, and American Mountain Men explored the region in search of beaver. When the United States wanted to help Americans move west to the Pacific Coast, government explorers were sent to map routes for emigrants to follow. In time hundreds of emigrants, headed for the coast, made their way across Utah. Utah was well explored before the Mormon pioneers made the first permanent settlement here in 1847.

Utah Lake

Duchesne River

Vernal

SEPTEMBER 11
ENTERED UTAH

SEPTEMBER 23-25
IN UTAH VALLEY

Delta

OCTOBER 1

SEPTEMBER 1

OCTOBER 8
DECIDED TO RETURN
TO SANTA FÉ

Cedar City

OCTOBER 11
LOTS DRAWN

NOVEMBER 7
CROSSING OF
THE FATHERS

Kanab

Navajo Mountain

OCTOBER 16
CROSSED UTAH—
ARIZONA LINE

Moenkopi Plateau

NOVEMBER 22

LEFT SANTA FÉ
JULY 29, 1776

RETURNED TO SANTA FÉ
JANUARY 2, 1777

Albuquerque

*The Escalante Trail led northward out of Santa Fé into
Colorado, into Utah near Jensen, westward to Utah Valley, southward past Cedar City, into northern Arizona,
crossed the Colorado River in Utah's Glen Canyon region,
and continued across northern Arizona to Santa Fé. This
modern map showing the route and camp sites of the Escalante Expedition is based on the map of the Escalante
Trail compiled by Herbert E. Bolton.*

THE SPANISH PENETRATION INTO UTAH

6

The Spanish were the first Europeans to penetrate the region that became Utah. Although they left no permanent settlements in Utah, they did leave an important heritage and gave us an interesting chapter in Utah's early history.

Spain was the first European country to establish colonies in the New World. The Spanish sought rich lands and civilized people whose wealth they could take. They also wanted to convert the natives to Christianity. America was theirs for the taking. In their conquests they established cities, missions, and forts to protect their holdings.

Spain had colonies in the New World a century before other European countries. Spanish settlements were made in New Mexico (1593) before Jamestown, Virginia was settled by the English (1607). The Spanish had explored most of the southwestern part of our country before the first English explorers came here. Though the Spanish came first, by the 1820s their position was seriously contested by other powers. The British and the Russians pressed down from the north, and the Americans from the east. The Utah region was in the middle of a great international contest. We should keep checking the map of the Utah region to see the changes that took place.

Spanish interest in the Utah region came out of a need to find a good route between their missions and forts in northern California and those in New Mexico. The Spanish also wanted to shorten their frontier along the north to protect it from other nations. Between the two widely separated northern frontiers of Upper California and New Mexico, there was no road nor were defense positions known to them. An expedition was sent to find a route for easy communication and better protection along this frontier. This expedition is known as the Escalante Expedition. It traveled through much of Utah without finding a route to Monterey in California. However, the expedition did result in several benefits for Utah.

From the Spanish penetration into Utah, we have our first written description of the land with its plant and animal life, and of the native Indians. We obtain also the first map of the region based on personal observation. Trails established by the Spanish became, in part, portions of important highways of Utah today.

The story of the Escalante Expedition and its results is the main subject of this chapter. We will study the background for that expedition and notice also what happened in Utah after the expedition returned to Sante Fé.

IN THIS CHAPTER WE WILL LEARN

1. Utah history is part of world history.

2. The Spanish made conquests in America for empire and the Christian faith.

3. The Spanish established missions and forts in New Mexico and California.

4. The Escalante Expedition sought a route between Santa Fé, New Mexico, and Monterey, California.

5. The Escalante Expedition gave us our first description and our first map of the Utah region.

6. After Escalante, a few Spanish traders came into the Utah region.

7. The Spanish explorations influenced later Utah History.

1. UTAH HISTORY IS PART OF WORLD HISTORY

No man lives to himself alone. We have learned that the history of one people at one time is influenced by events taking place in a neighboring region. We really cannot look at the history of one place or country without realizing that it is being influenced by its neighbors—near or far. We will, therefore, study events in other places when they come to influence affairs in Utah.

After the Indians, Utah was first explored and settled permanently by white men who came from Europe. From Spain by way of Mexico came Utah's first explorers. Later, from Great Britain and France came trappers searching the rivers and streams for beaver. From the United States came other explorers, trappers, and Utah's first permanent settlers.

2. THE SPANISH MADE CONQUESTS IN AMERICA FOR EMPIRE AND THE CHRISTIAN FAITH

The Americas were opened up to European conquest and colonization when Christopher Columbus discovered the New World in 1492. European countries at the time were seeking overseas empires for the purpose of founding colonies, trade, and converting people to the Christian faith. Spain and Portugal were leading in this race for empire. Spain took immediate interest in the New World. She sent soldiers, colonists, and priests to conquer, colonize, and convert the people of the New World. For over a century, the Spanish advanced throughout most of the Americas without any serious threat from another European country. During the century following Columbus, Spain took most of South America (Portugal took Brazil), Central America, and some of North America.

The West Indies served Spain as a base from which to conquer the New World. The Spanish conquest spread from the islands of the Caribbean to the shores of the mainland. Soon the Spanish were in Florida, Panama, and Mexico. From Panama the conquest spread southward toward the Chibcha peoples of northern South America and the Inca of Peru and Ecuador. From Panama the conquest also spread northward. With the conquest of the Aztec Empire, the conquest moved southward to the Maya and then northward toward the land of the Chichemecs and their neighbors to the north, the Pueblo.

The Spanish had several motives for their conquest of the New World. They sought land which would make up a great empire and supply Spain with wealth in the form of gold, silver, and raw materials.

Spanish priests wanted to convert the natives to Christianity. Explorers and priests traveled together, and sometimes priests were explorers as well. The Spaniards found little wealth in the form of silver and gold until they conquered the Aztec Empire and the Inca Empire. Then the rest of the hemisphere was explored in hopes of finding other civilized people and their wealth.

A Spanish map of America made in the 1700s.

3. THE SPANISH ESTABLISHED MISSIONS AND FORTS IN NEW MEXICO AND CALIFORNIA

Spanish expansion northward out of Mexico followed two lines. One went northward by land through the interior of Mexico and resulted in the establishment of missions and forts in New Mexico. The second went northward along the Pacific Coast through Baja (Lower) California into Alta (Upper) California and resulted in the establishment of missions and forts in California.

New Mexico. The hope of finding "other Mexicos" full of wealth led the Spanish to explore northward from Mexico into western North America. In 1527, Cabeza de Vaca and a few companions, after sailing from Cuba to Florida and there being left for lost, made their way along the coast to Texas, across Texas through some of the southwest and back to Mexico. Soon there were stories in Mexico of the rich Seven Cities of Cibola. An expedition in 1539, guided by one of Cabeza de Vaca's companions found the six villages of Zuñi pueblos near present Gallup. The next year a major expedition was formed un-

Indian villages such as this led Spanish explorers to return to Mexico with stories of the rich Seven Cities of Cibola.

The Palace of the Governors, Santa Fé, is the oldest public building in the United States, built in 1610. From here the Escalante Expedition set out on July 29, 1776, in search of a route to Monterey, Upper California.

der the command of Francisco Vasquez Coronado.

The Coronado Expedition (1540-42) set out from northern Mexico early in 1540 and made its way northward to the Zuñi pueblos near the Arizona-New Mexico border. The Spaniards easily conquered the villages but were disappointed in finding no riches to compare with those of Mexico and Peru. Nevertheless they asked the Indians for information about riches in neighboring areas. The Indians were glad to tell them of riches some place else, if only to get the Spaniards to move on.

Coronado sent *García Lopez de Cárdenas* with a small expedition to explore among the Moqui Indian villages and westward in northern Arizona. The Cárdenas expedition found only more poor Pueblo Indians, but did march as far north as the south rim of the Grand Canyon of the Colorado River, about fifty miles south of the Utah-Arizona border.

Coronado was led by the Zuñi Indians to believe in the existence of riches farther to the east in a land called Gran Quivira. He

and his men marched eastward through New Mexico, Texas, Oklahoma, and Kansas, to find only disappointment. The Coronado Expedition found no rich cities, but did discover and describe much of the southwestern part of the United States.

After Coronado's expedition there was little interest in the Pueblo Indians for forty years. Then missionaries went into the region, only to be killed. In 1598 Don Juan de Oñate was named governor of New Mexico, and was sent with an expedition to establish a permanent colony. Don Juan de Oñate made settlements and explored again most of the region first explored by Coronado. In 1609 a new governor moved the capital to a new settlement named Santa Fé.

Santa Fé became the most important city on the northern interior frontier of the Spanish possessions. Through the years that followed, Santa Fé was the main center for defending that portion of the Spanish frontier and for missionary work among the Pueblo Indians. Explorers were sent out in all directions from Santa Fé.

After the founding of Santa Fé there must have been some explorations north and west into the Colorado Plateau region and the Utah of today. In March of 1686 a report was made describing the land of *Quivira* (the land east of the mountains, the Great Plains area) and the land of *Teguayo* (the land west of the mountains, the Colorado Plateau area, and the Great Basin). Much was known about Quivira but very little about Teguayo: only that there were Indian tribes living in the region, that there was a lake there with people living about it, and that buffalo came into the region. Less than a century after this report, traders are known to have moved into the Colorado Plateau area of west central Colorado.

California. The second line of Spanish advance northward from Mexico was along the Pacific Coast to California. The coast was first explored by Juan Rodríguez Cabrillo in 1542. In 1602 Sebastián Vizcaíno with three ships and two hundred men explored and made maps of the coast from San Diego to Cape Mendocino. Vizcaíno recommended establishing a colony at Monterey. However, military posts were not set up until the threat of Russians moving down the Pacific Coast from Alaska and fear of the British interest in the area grew. Presidios and missions were established at San Diego in 1769 and at Monterey in 1770. The *presidio* was a military post presided over by a governor. Nearby was the *mission* where Catholic priests lived and did missionary work among the Indians.

4. THE ESCALANTE EXPEDITION SOUGHT A ROUTE BETWEEN SANTA FÉ, NEW MEXICO, AND MONTEREY, CALIFORNIA

To supply and help hold California, Spain had to open a new route from Mexico to California. To meet the Russian threat to California holdings, the Spanish needed a route between Santa Fé and Monterey over which messengers, soldiers, and traders could travel. The California holdings were not able to supply their own food needs. Food had to be obtained from the older agricultural settlements in Arizona and New Mexico. If possible, Spain would establish villages, missions, and presidios along the new route to help hold the territory and supply her empire.

Two persons were especially interested in seeking a route between New Mexico and Northern California—Father Francisco Garcés and Father Silvestre Vélez de Escalante. *Father Francisco Garcés* was stationed at the mission San Xavier del Bac (near Tucson, Ari-

San Xavier del Bac Mission, near modern Tucson, Arizona, was the base of operations of Fathers Escalante and Garcés, missionaries among the Zuñi of New Mexico, who recognized the importance of opening up the heart of the continent by exploration.

zona). From his post he explored the regions of the Gila and Colorado rivers. A route was established from Arizona to Monterey. It was believed, however, that New Mexico could supply Monterey better than Arizona, so Father Garcés explored even farther. A route needed to be found that could either go around the Colorado River or cross it easily.

Father Silvestre Vélez de Escalante, stationed among the Zuñi Indians of Arizona-New Mexico, knew of the explorations of Father Garcés. He also knew of the importance of a route to Monterey. He himself had explored in northern Arizona. He also knew that there had been several explorations out of Sante Fé into the country north of Santa Fé, among the Ute Indians of the Colorado Plateau. It was thought that a good route could be found through this country that would lead northward around the Colorado River and then west to Monterey.

The Escalante Expedition was formed during the month of July 1776, the same month and year that English colonies on the eastern American seaboard declared their independence from Great Britain. The expedition was made up of ten men, including the Catholic fathers, Spanish soldiers, and Indian servants. Indian guides were picked up from time to time. Each had a saddle horse. Pack animals carried baggage and provisions. Extra mounts, and a herd of cattle to provide fresh meat on the journey were also taken.

The expedition was led by *Father Francisco Atanasio Domínguez*, who was the official leader, and *Father Silvestre Vélez de Escalante*, who kept the diary of the expedition. Without his diary we would know little of the expedition. Because of Father Escalante's leading part in getting the expedition started and because he kept the diary that preserved the memory of the expedition, his name is most often given to the expedition.

Also in the group was *Don Bernardo Miera y Pacheco*, a Spanish-born soldier and civil leader of considerable experience. Miera joined the expedition as astronomer and map maker. He drew the famous map of the route of the expedition.

The expedition set out from Santa Fé on July 29, 1776, in search of a route to Monterey, California. Through August and early September the explorers made their way across the eastern edge of the Colorado Plateau area in Colorado. They met Indians of the Ute tribe from whom they obtained guides and interpreters.

The expedition entered what is today Utah on September 11. The explorers entered from the present site of Rangely, Colorado, traveled westward, passing near the site of present Jensen on the Green River, and about a mile south of the dinosaur quarry of Dinosaur National Monument. They followed

Typical country through which the Escalante Expedition traveled.

The Escalante Expedition emerged from Spanish Fork Canyon, September 23, 1776, to gain its first view of Utah Lake. From a painting by Paul Salisbury.

Father Escalante and later visitors to Utah mentioned the bearded Indians. This Paiute, one of John Wesley Powell's guides, was photographed in 1873 by J. K. Hillers.

the Duchesne River westward through the Uinta Basin, past the sites of present Myton and Duchesne. They then crossed over into Strawberry Valley and through the Wasatch Mountains by way of Spanish Fork Canyon into Utah Valley, arriving September 23.

Utah Valley was one of the most impressive sights to the Spanish on their entire journey. As they entered the valley they saw that the Yuta Indians were sending up smoke signals to spread the news of their coming. They went onto the plain and camped on one of the southern meadows of the Spanish Fork River, a short distance south and east of the present site of the town of Spanish Fork. That same day some of the party went northward to visit the Yuta Indian villages on

the Provo River. Through their Indian interpreter, the Spanish explained the peaceful intent of their mission and their desire to teach the Indians their religion. The Spanish did not baptize any Indians but promised to return and teach them and establish their religion among them. The Spanish stayed in Utah Valley three days—September 23, 24, and 25. They were impressed with the valley—the peaceful character of the Indians, their desire to have the Spanish missionaries come and live with them and teach them, the fertile land and the number of settlements it could support. Escalante described the valley and the Indians in his diary. The Spaniards did not go farther north than Utah Valley. They did not see Great Salt Lake. Before they left, the Spaniards bought large quantities of dried fish from the Indians, and obtained the services of a guide to lead them to the other Indians to the west and south.

A DESCRIPTION OF THE INDIANS IN UTAH VALLEY, 1776

From the diary of Father Escalante:

September 25. ... Round about it [the lake] are these Indians, who live on the abundant fish of the lake .... Besides this, they gather in the plain grass seeds from which they make atole, which they supplement by hunting hares, rabbits and fowl of which there is great abundance here. There are also buffalo not very far to the north-northwest, but fear of the Cumanches prevents them from hunting them. Their habitations are ... little huts of willow, of which they also make nice baskets and other necessary utensils. In the matter of dress they are very poor. The most decent clothing they wear is a buckskin jacket and long leggings made of the same material. For cold weather they have blankets made of the skins of hares and rabbits. They speak the Yuta language but with notable differences in the accent and in some of the words. They have good features and most of them have heavy beards. ... The plain ... is all clear land ... of good quality, and suitable for all kinds of crops. ... the valley would provide for as many pueblos of Indians as there are in New Mexico. ...

To reach Monterey, the Escalante Expedition had to press westward; they were already farther north than Monterey. To the west were desert lands, more barren than any they had seen before. Nowhere did they hear of a possible route to the ocean. To find a pass through the deserts they moved southward. Their journey took them from Utah Valley through Juab Valley to near the site of Levan, then westward to near present Mills and then southward to present Scipio. From this point they pressed directly westward to the region of the Pavant Butte, thence southward, but found no passage to the west.

Discouragements set in. It was early October, and autumn temperatures and colors were beginning to warn of the coming winter. On October 6 a heavy snow fell all day.

October 7, Escalante wrote in his diary: "Although we were greatly inconvenienced by the lack of firewood and the excessive cold, we were unable to leave San Atenógenes today either, because, with so much snow and water, the land, which here is very soft, was impassable." The next day "a very sharp north wind never stopped blowing." Mountains in all directions were covered with snow. The fathers feared mountain passes would be closed. Provisions were low, and they feared the men might be left in the desert without food. They knew they were still very far from Monterey. Considering these facts, the party decided to return to Santa Fé. They planned to continue southward to the Colorado River, then toward the Cosnina, the Moqui, and the Zuñi Indian villages so well known to Father Escalante, and from there on to Santa Fé. All members of the party were not satisfied with this decision; some wanted to reach Monterey at all costs. On October 11 they decided "to inquire anew the will of God by means of casting lots ... ." When lots were drawn, it was decided in favor of returning to Santa Fé by way of Cosnina. "Now, thank God," wrote Escalante, "we all agreeably and gladly accepted the result."

The decision to return to Santa Fé was reached when the expedition was near the present site of Milford. The lots were drawn when the party was east of present Lund. Moving southward from Escalante Valley, the expedition passed on into Cedar Valley, passing near present Cedar City, then southward past present Kanarraville, Pintura, Toquerville, La Verkin, and Hurricane. On October 15 the Escalante Expedition crossed what was to become the southern boundary of Utah into Arizona. The expedition had been in what is today Utah from September 11 to October 15.

The Escalante Expedition crossed the Colorado River here in November 1776. This spot is now known as the Crossing of the Fathers.

Across the plateaus of northern Arizona the expedition made its way with great hardship. The men crossed into Utah again east of present Kanab then southward around the border of Paria Plateau until they came to Marble Canyon of the Colorado River. The fathers spent days trying to find a passage across the canyons of the Colorado. They made their way northward along the edges of Glen Canyon into Utah and on November 6 they finally found a way to the river, by way of Padre Creek. Even here, as Escalante wrote, "it was necessary to cut steps in a rock with axes" to make it possible for men and animals to climb down to the canyon bottom. This point on the Colorado River is marked on our maps today as *the Crossing of the Fathers.* All were safely across the river

on November 7 and celebrated the safe crossing by "praising God our Lord and firing off a few muskets as a sign of the great joy which we felt at having overcome so great a difficulty ... ."

From the Crossing of the Fathers, the Spanish explorers made their way southward to the Indians known to Father Escalante and then eastward until they reached the Rio Grande where they turned north to reach Santa Fé on January 2, 1777.

5. THE ESCALANTE EXPEDITION GAVE US OUR FIRST DESCRIPTION AND OUR FIRST MAP OF THE UTAH REGION

Although the Escalante Expedition failed to find a route between Santa Fé in New Mexico and Monterey in northern California, the expedition accomplished a great deal. It learned about the nature of the country north of New Mexico and Arizona and gave the world its first idea of what the Utah country was like. Escalante recommended that settlements and missions be established in various places, especially at Utah Lake. The report discouraged any further explorations into parts of the region, but encouraged trading in the Utah region.

The Escalante Expedition cannot be considered a failure. It left us a record of what the fathers saw on their trip. The knowledge acquired on this journey in the wilderness was preserved in at least three ways. Members of the expedition *reported orally* to their superiors and companions. The *diary* kept by Escalante was turned over to the Spanish authorities at Santa Fé for immediate and future use. The *map* constructed by Miera was preserved and showed the Spanish many of the things written of in the diary.

The Escalante diary is the first written account made concerning western Colorado and Utah. Drawn from personal observation, the account is our first description of the nature of the land, the plant and animal life, and the Indians. The diary is a very important reference work.

The Miera map is the first map drawn from personal observation of the interior region of western America. On the map mountains, rivers, lakes, Indian tribes, Indian villages, and Spanish settlements are shown. Miera also marked the map with symbols showing the camping sites of the expedition on their long journey. The map is beautifully drawn, though not to our standards of accuracy in all details. Even so, we appreciate the map for the things it does tell us. It must have been studied a great deal by the Spanish after 1776. It probably served as a basis for other maps which were used as guides into the same territory later.

The map drawn for the Escalante Expedition by Don Bernardo Miera y Pacheco. In this first map of the Utah region, Miera noted geographical features, expedition camp sites, Spanish villages, and Indian villages and dwelling sites.

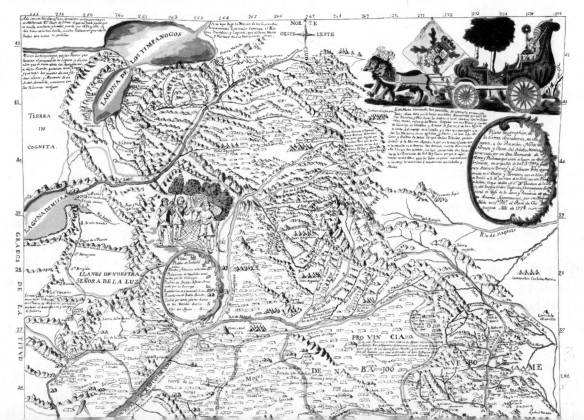

6. AFTER ESCALANTE, A FEW SPANISH TRADERS CAME INTO THE UTAH REGION

The Spanish did not follow up immediately on the explorations of the Escalante Expedition. They did not send other explorers to continue the search for a passage through the deserts and mountains to Monterey, nor did the fathers send missionaries among the Indians. There was still a need, though, for a route over which the Spanish could send goods from Santa Fé to the struggling California settlements.

In the years after the return of the Escalante Expedition, Spanish traders followed the Escalante Trail into Utah Valley. Shortly after the turn of the century the trade from Santa Fé to Utah was fairly regular, and it lasted for many years. The traders did not take the Escalante Trail exactly or the entire distance. Shortcuts in the trail were explored and followed which took the traders west from the Dolores River, south of the Book Cliffs, through Price Basin and into Utah Valley.

An early hunting and trading expedition into Utah Valley was led by *Mauricio Arze* and *Lagos García.* This party of seven left Abiquiú, New Mexico, March 16 and returned July 12, 1813. The party made its way to the lake of the Timpanogos (Utah Lake), where they remained three days. The records of this trading expedition seem to indicate that the routes were well known, that the Spaniards were familiar with most of the Indians, and that language was not a serious problem.

How many trips like this were taken by the Spanish, both before and after 1813, is difficult to say, for these traders seldom kept records of their travels. Nevertheless it is known that trading increased between Santa Fé and the Indians of north central Utah.

Out of this trade came expeditions that finally established a useful route—the *Old Spanish Trail.* In time, as we shall see in the next chapter, the Old Spanish Trail was added to on the west end and connected to Los Angeles. These additions were made by Mountain Men, fur trappers, and traders chiefly from the United States.

7. THE SPANISH EXPLORATIONS INFLUENCED LATER UTAH HISTORY

The Spanish made no settlements in Utah; they only traveled across the area. They left little influence on Utah's history, but the influences the Spanish did leave are worth mentioning.

THE ESCALANTE EXPEDITION

Herbert E. Bolton comments:

... They made one of the most notable explorations in North American history, and their fame is as secure as that of De Soto, Cabrillo, Zebulon Pike, or Lewis and Clark. They explored more unknown territory than Daniel Boone, George Rogers Clark or even Lewis and Clark. For the opening of new vistas they belong with Coronado and the splendid wayfarers of Mexico and South America. For their relations with the strange peoples encountered they stand in a class almost by themselves.

The Spanish were the first white men to have contacts with the Indians. They helped break down the resistance of the Indians to the coming of other white men. The Spanish furnished the Indians with horses and guns which greatly changed the Indian way of life.

The Spanish gave us our first maps. They also put on the map many names we use today.

We cannot say that the only influences on the Indians were due to the Spanish. During the same time, Mountain Men in this region were also influencing the Indians. We will study the Mountain Men in the next chapter.

SPANISH NAMES ON OUR MAP

Abajo Mountains, San Juan County

From *Abajo*, meaning low; the Low Mountains.

Arido Creek, San Juan County

From *aridio*, meaning dry; Dry Creek.

Boneta, Duchesne County, Bonita Bend of the Green River

From *Bonita*, meaning graceful, beautiful.

Castilla Springs, Aguas Calientes, Utah County

Aguas Calientes, hot waters. Named by Escalante and the later Spanish traders.

Dolores River, Grand County

Named *Río Nuestra Senora de los Dolores*, River of our Lady of Sorrows, and contracted by Americans to *Río Dolores* or Dolores River,

The Crossing of the Fathers, on Colorado River a few miles north of Utah-Arizona line

El Vado de los Padres, so named for the experiences of the Escalante Expedition.

Escalante Desert, Iron County, Escalante River, Escalante, Garfield County

Named by Utah settlers in memory of Father Escalante.

Green River

Named by Escalante the *Río Buenaventura*, Good Fortune. Later *Río Verde*, Green River. Known to the Mountain Men as Spanish River.

La Sal Mountains

Sierra de Sal, a mountain range of salt. An important landmark on the Old Spanish Trail.

Meadows of Santa Clara or Mountain Meadows, Washington County

Las Vegas de Santa Clara, important resting place on the Old Spanish Trail.

La Verkin Creek, Washington County

The name is likely a corruption by Americans of the Spanish name *Río de la Virgen*.

Little Dolores River, Grand County

Río Dolores Chiquito, named by the Spanish from the larger Rio Dolores to the south.

Virgin River, Washington and Kane counties

Río de la Virgen, named River of the Virgin; anglicized by Americans to Virgin River.

Santa Clara River, Washington County

Río Santa Clara, River of Saint Clara, in honor of Saint Clara of Assisi, foundress of the order of Franciscan nuns.

San Rafael River, San Rafael Valley

Río San Rafael. Franciscan friars dedicated the river to San Rafael Archangel, the angel of the spirits of men.

Salina, Salina Creek, Salina Canyon, Sevier County

Named by the Spanish for the rock salt and the adjacent salt seeps. *Salina*, a salt marsh or pond.

San Juan River, San Juan County

Río San Juan Bautista, Saint John the Baptist River. There are various explanations of origin: for Don Juan Oñate; perhaps by Escalante for Don Juan María de Rivera who went northwest from Santa Fé in 1765.

Sevier River, Sevier County

Corrupted by the American Mountain Men from Río Severo (*Severo*, rigorous, grave, serious) to Sevier River.

Spanish Fork, a stream, a city, a canyon, a mountain peak in Utah County

Derived from the fact of the Escalante expedition in 1776 passing these points.

Spanish Valley, Grand County

Known for the Spanish encampments there.

White River, Uintah County

Río Blanco, named by Escalante; anglicized to White River.

THE MOUNTAIN MEN 1807-1840

Long after Fathers Domínguez and Escalante made their historic trek into Utah, and while the Spanish traders pressed their way into Utah, other men seeking the riches of the land came into the Utah region. These were the Mountain Men – fur trappers. They came to trap the beaver whose pelt they sold to be made into fine hats. British and French-Canadian trappers came from the north, and American Mountain Men came from the north and the east. Northward out of Santa Fé and Taos came French, Spanish, and American fur hunters.

The fur trade flourished in the American West from 1807 until about 1840. The fur trade opened here shortly after the Lewis and Clark Expedition when it was first learned that the streams of the Great Plains and the Rocky Mountains were rich in beaver. Fur trapping lasted as long as the beaver were plentiful. By about 1840 most of the beaver had been killed. At the same time, however, the demand for beaver fur ended.

Through the period of the Mountain Men, the Utah region was claimed by Spain and after 1822 was owned by Mexico. British and American trappers as well as Spanish fur men hunted Utah streams for beaver. There was not only rivalry for beaver pelts but rivalry for the land itself.

The Mountain Men were among the most important of Utah's early frontiersmen. They were among the first great explorers of the continent. They explored the streams, rivers, valleys, mountains, plateaus, and deserts. They found the passes in the mountains. They found the Indian trails and made them into more permanent trails that would in many cases become our modern highways. They had long and intimate contacts with the Indians. The Mountain Men ended the isolation of the Indian, broke down his resistance to the white man, and made it much easier for the white man to make permanent settlement in the land that the Indians had formerly held to themselves.

The knowledge of the West gained by the Mountain Men was sometimes shared in letters to people in the East. Many of these letters were published in newspapers. Trappers' notes were sometimes included on new maps of the West. The Mountain Men spread their knowledge of the West and made it available to settlers who came after them. Even after the beaver were gone, many of the Mountain Men stayed in the mountains, set up forts to supply emigrants or served as guides to emigrant parties going across the continent in search of new homes. Utah and Utah's settlers owe much to the Mountain Men.

IN THIS CHAPTER WE WILL LEARN

1. There were rivalries between nations for possession of the American West.

2. How the fur trade operated and helped open the West.

3. After Lewis and Clark, American fur trappers swarmed the Missouri River and its tributaries.

4. The Mountain Men thoroughly explored and trapped the Utah region during the 1820s.

5. During the 1830s, the Utah region was visited less frequently by Mountain Men.

6. The Mountain Men were important as explorers and trail makers.

1. THERE WERE RIVALRIES BETWEEN NATIONS FOR POSSESSION OF THE AMERICAN WEST

We learned in the last chapter that *Spain* did all she could to establish missions, presidios, and trade routes in the American Southwest in order to hold her lands against the intrusion of other powers. *Great Britain* wanted a hold in the Northern Hemisphere and sent ships of discovery along the northern Pacific Coast. *Russia* continued her expansion eastward across Siberia, into Alaska, and down the west coast of North America. The *United States* was interested in the American West, too. She had nearly doubled her territory in 1803 when she purchased the Louisiana Territory from France. This vast region bordered the holdings of Spain and Great Britain. The Louisiana Purchase gave the United States an interest in the West. In order to hold her land, the United States must know all about it and occupy it.

The United States sent the Lewis and Clark Expedition westward to learn about the Louisiana Purchase and the Pacific Northwest. The expedition, organized by President Thomas Jefferson and led by Captains *Meriwether Lewis* and *William Clark*, was instructed to explore the Missouri River and beyond even to the western ocean and report on all matters relating to the country—its plant and animal life, and the native Indians—as well as possibilities for trade and settlements. The expedition was in the West from 1804 to 1806, but especially important for the story of this chapter was the fact that Lewis and Clark reported the western streams were full of beaver. This work touched off a

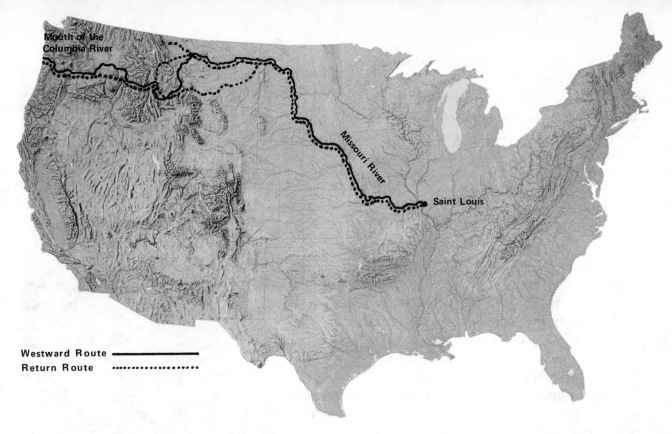

The route of the Lewis and Clark Expedition, 1804-6.

Westward Route ——————
Return Route ••••••••••••••••

rush by Americans into the West to trap beaver.

2. HOW THE FUR TRADE OPERATED AND HELPED OPEN UP THE WEST

From earliest times man has used the furs of animals to clothe himself. For hundreds of years there was a demand for beaver fur. From the dark brown, soft underfur came the hairs from which the finest felt was made. Beaver felt was made into the best of men's hats. In England and Europe, tall-crowned *beaver hats* were popular. In order to supply the demand for these furs, explorers and trappers went in search of the beaver.

Early European explorers soon learned **America was rich in beaver.** Companies formed to engage in the trade. The first was the Hudson's Bay Company organized in

Beaver hats

The D'orsay (1820)

The Continental cocked hat (1776)

A clerical hat (Eighteenth century)

The Paris beau (1815)

95

1670 to trap and trade in British North America. There followed the North West Company, also British, formed in 1783. In the 1780s, John Jacob Astor, an American businessman, got into the fur trade. Following the return of Lewis and Clark, many American companies were formed to trade for pelts and trap beaver in the West.

The beaver lives in wooded areas along the banks of streams and lakes. He lives off the bark and leaves of trees, especially the aspen, cottonwood, and willow. His home or lodge is either in the bank of a stream or in the stream itself, built of limbs, twigs, and mud. The beaver builds dams to stop fast flowing streams and form ponds or lakes of sufficient depth for his lodge and to give himself and family a place to swim.

Throughout the wooded and watered regions of the West, beaver lived in large numbers. They were found in green forested regions and in the streams of semi-arid regions.

The beaver is a large animal, becoming two feet in length, not counting his ten-inch tail, and weighing thirty to forty pounds, though often much more. The pelt of a full-grown beaver usually weighs from a pound and a half to two pounds. The pelt of a pup weighs about half that amount. At Saint Louis, where most of the pelts were eventually sold, beaver pelts sold for $4 to $6 a pound. Later, when trappers sold their furs in the mountains, they received $3 a pound, or from $5 to $6 a pelt.

After a beaver was trapped, his skin was removed and cured, then folded with the fur inside and packed in bundles by means of a crude press. Bundles were then tied with green buckskin thongs, which contracted while drying and tightened around the bundle like an iron band.

The Mountain Man was daring, carefree, and independent. He loved adventure. He

The beaver pelt was sought for its usefulness in making felt for men's hats.

Beavers built dams creating ponds in which they built their lodges.

liked to travel and see new places, leaving a home of comforts and security to live in the wilderness. He stayed alive in the wilderness by adopting Indian ways and learning Indian skills. Some Mountain Men took Indian girls for wives. The Mountain Man always had to be careful in dealing with the Indians. He had to keep his wits about him to stay alive—in friendly or in hostile Indian country. He was well trained and educated in the knowledge of frontier life.

The trusted weapon of the Mountain Man was his small-bore, long-barreled rifle. He carried his own flints, hickory ramrod, powder horn, bullet pouch, and made his own bullets. He was never without his short-handled axe or tomahawk, and a keen-edged skinning knife. An outfit for his horse, a few blankets, and cooking gear made up his equipment. His costume was unique. It was an adaptation of Indian materials to the white man's way of dress, fitted to living in the mountains.

Like the Indian, the Mountain Man lived off the country as much as possible, except that he usually had with him a scant supply of salt, flour, tea, and coffee. His favorite meat was the buffalo, from which he took humps, ribs, steaks, and bone marrow. He also enjoyed deer, elk, antelope, and bear.

For transportation, the American Mountain Man relied for the most part on his horse and pack mules. Occasionally he went by water. For water travel he usually made his own bullboat, a sort of leather tub, with a frame made of curved limbs, covered with tightly sewn and water-proofed buffalo skins. It was light enough to carry on his back, small enough to hide easily, and just big enough to float a trapper and his packs.

The life of a trapper was dangerous. Indians were the most constant threat. Grizzly bears often attacked Mountain Men. Jedediah Smith and Hugh Glass suffered terribly from bear maulings and lived to tell about it.

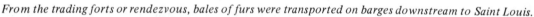

From the trading forts or rendezvous, bales of furs were transported on barges downstream to Saint Louis.

Mountain Men setting traps for beaver.
Watercolor by Alfred Jacob Miller.

Mountain Man Joseph Walker and his Indian wife.
Painting by Alfred Jacob Miller.

JEDEDIAH SMITH IS MAULED
BY A GRIZZLY BEAR

From the journal of James Clyman:

[In the Black Hills country the party was coming down a valley, Jedediah Smith in lead, when he met a bear, face to face.] Grissly did not hesitate a moment but sprung on the capt taking him by the head pitc[h]ing sprawling on the earth [the bear was eventually killed] ... none of us having any sugical Knowledge ... I asked the Capt what was best he said one or 2 [go] for water and if you have a needle and thread git it out and sew up my wounds ... I ... began my first Job of d[r]essing wounds ... one of his ears was torn from his head out to the outer rim after stitching all the other wounds in the best way I was capabl and according to the captains directions the ear being the last I told him I could do nothing for his Eare O you must try to stich up some way or other said he then I put in my needle stiching it through ... over laying the ... parts togather as nice as I could with my hands water was found in about ame mille when we all moved down and encamped the captain being able to mount his horse and ride to camp whare we pitched a tent the onley one we had and made him as comfortable as circumstances would permit this gave us a lisson on the character of the grissly Baare which we did not forget

There were often quarrels among the Mountain Men themselves, and there was always danger of hunger, thirst, storm, accidents, and disease to contend with. The Mountain Men had to be their own doctors.

The Mountain Men were almost constantly in contact with the Indians. In the early days of the fur trade, the Mountain Men persuaded the Indians to trap the beaver and sell the pelts to them in exchange for goods. Later, Mountain Men did the trapping themselves, learning from the Indians the trails and rivers and neighboring tribes, and trading with the Indians for horses or goods they wanted. By the time the fur frontier reached the Rocky Mountain West, white men did most of the trapping.

Most of the Mountain Men had little education, yet some were well educated, intelligent, and gentlemanly. Some of these men

The Mountain Men, in search of beaver, explored much of the Mountain West.
"Mountain Men," a painting by William Henry Jackson.

left us fine diaries, letters, and memoirs telling of their experiences. Mountain Men were not religious as a rule, though a few were. Jedediah Smith was a devout Christian, faithful in his daily prayers and reading the Bible. Peter Skene Ogden was another religious man. While on the march he gathered his men together daily for public prayers. Some of the Mountain Men read a good deal—the Bible, Shakespeare, and the famous works of English fiction.

The fur trading company was a well-organized partnership of fur trappers. Many free trappers outfitted themselves and disposed of their furs on an individual basis. More men, however, trapped as employees of a company. The company hired the trappers, furnished the equipment, and bought all that its trappers caught.

Most of the fur trading companies had their headquarters in Saint Louis, and from this center company men and free trappers set out for the hunting grounds. Company trapping expeditions included from fifty to a hundred trappers, sometimes even more. When such an expedition arrived in the mountains, it would separate into small groups that went into the surrounding country to explore and trap. Before separating, they agreed to meet again at a certain spot at a certain time, sometimes a year later.

For winter camp, trappers usually found a secluded, well-watered, timbered valley or canyon where a small cabin shelter could be built away from the eyes of wandering Indians. There the trapper, with sufficient wood for fuel, forage for his animals, and the possibilities of hunting his own food supply, lived through the winter.

A trapper could not always carry with him his entire catch of furs. He had to deposit his furs, from time to time, in some safe hiding place and in such a way as to protect them from being seen by Indians. Such a hiding place was called a *cache*, a word borrowed from the French trappers meaning to hide, to conceal, to disguise. The cache was usually a hole or pit dug in a dry place, well constructed and covered to keep its contents dry and safe from wild animals, and the detection of Indians. In it he stored supplies, food, and furs.

A trapper could not well afford the time to carry his furs each year to Saint Louis. To save this time and hazard to life and furs, two practices developed: the trading post and the rendezvous.

The *trading post* was developed earliest and was used almost entirely in the Missouri River Valley. Posts were built at strategic locations in the beaver country. The post was a fortified center that served as defense against the Indians of the region. It also served as a depot, where the trapper could deposit or exchange his furs for supplies and equipment. From the trading post, the collected furs were floated down the river on a keelboat to Saint Louis.

The *rendezvous* was a substitute for the trading post. The trading post was fixed at one place, but the rendezvous was simply a meeting place in the wilderness. The rendezvous moved with the trappers, wherever the trapping grounds were best. Once a year between 1825 and 1840 the trappers of the Ashley and Henry men or the men of the Rocky Mountain Fur Company met at a predetermined spot in the mountains. To the rendezvous the company men from Saint Louis would bring a large supply of goods for the trapper. For the trapper himself they brought blankets, powder, lead, rifles, traps, tea, coffee, sugar, and salt. For the trapper to trade to the Indians, they brought bright-colored shawls and calicoes, little bells and mirrors, and beads. These items the Mountain Man would trade to the Indians for beaver pelts or horses or anything else needed from the Indians. For these supplies, the Mountain Man sold to the company his furs, gathered at such risk and cost through the year, for three dollars a pound. For the goods he received, he was charged high prices, but he had to have them, and there was no place else to buy them. The rendezvous was not only a time for trading. It was also a time of fellowship, renewing acquaintances, exchanging

discoveries and knowledge about the country, and of enjoying human society after isolation in the wilderness. Drinking, gambling, fighting, racing, shooting, telling tall tales—that was the rendezvous.

CHRISTMAS DINNER, 1840, SITE OF PRESENT OGDEN *From the journal of Osborne Russell:*

... The first dish that came on was a large tin pan 18 inches in diameter rounding full of Stewed Elk meat The next dish was similar to the first heaped up with boiled Deer meat (or as the whites would call it Venison a term not used in the Mountains) The 3d and 4th dishes were equal in size to the first containing a boiled flour pudding prepared with dried fruit accompanied by 4 quarts of sauce made of the juice of sour berries and sugar Then came the cakes followed by about six gallons of strong Coffee already sweetened with tin cups and pans to drink out of large chips or pieces of Bark Supplying the places of plates. on being ready the butcher knives were drawn and the eating commenced at the word given by the landlady....

Between 1825 and 1840 sixteen rendezvous were held. The first rendezvous were held in northern Utah or on its present borders: 1825, Henrys Fork of the Green River on the Utah-Wyoming line; 1826, in southern Cache Valley (near Hyrum); 1827, at the south end of Bear Lake; and in 1828 near Laketown on Bear Lake. As the beaver of this region "played out," and the Indian menace to the north lessened, the rendezvous were shifted a little northward into the Wyoming region, usually on the Green River or Little Popo Agie River.

3. AFTER LEWIS AND CLARK, AMERICAN FUR TRAPPERS SWARMED THE MISSOURI RIVER AND ITS TRIBUTARIES

Just as soon as Lewis and Clark returned from the West in 1806 with the news of rich beaver lands in the West, eager young men gathered at Saint Louis through the winter of 1806-7 and made preparations for setting out the next spring to hunt beaver.

Manuel Lisa was one of the first fur

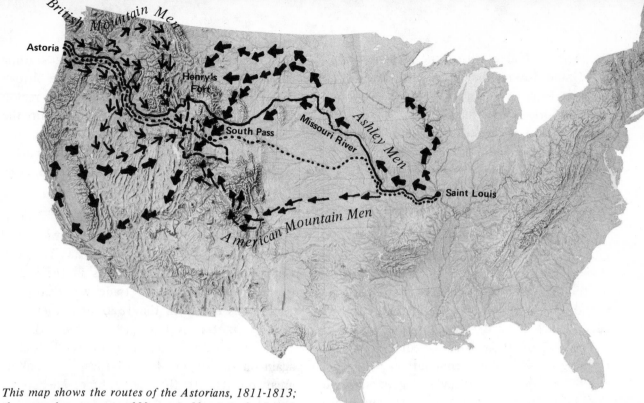

This map shows the routes of the Astorians, 1811-1813; the general movements of Mountain Men into the American West; and the Oregon Territory under joint occupation by the U.S. and Great Britain from 1818-46.

traders to send men into the West. April 19, 1807 his expedition of forty-two men left Saint Louis for the upper Missouri River country, returning the next year. Lisa not only sent out men to trap but to explore. He sent his agents in all directions to visit the surrounding Indians and make arrangements to trade with them for furs. One of his agents was John Colter who reached the Yellowstone National Park area in the autumn and winter of 1807-8. He discovered its geysers and canyons, and reported the rich beaver lands of the Rocky Mountain region in which it lay. Manuel Lisa formed the *Saint Louis Missouri Fur Company* with William Clark, Andrew Henry, Pierre Chouteau, and others as partners. This company sent out expeditions yearly, some with 350 men. The company was reorganized in 1812 with William Clark as president and Lisa as director and was dissolved in 1814 when Lisa formed the *Missouri Fur Company*.

Andrew Henry made regular hunting trips far up the Missouri River. In 1810 he and his men went southwestward from the Three Forks of the Missouri into the region west of the Tetons, and set up a few cabins (Henry's Fort) on a fork of the Snake River now called Henrys Fork, and there wintered. It was from Henry's Fort that one of the earliest expeditions came toward or into Utah.

John Jacob Astor's trappers, known as *Astorians*, were the first Americans to trap in the Far West. To challenge the British companies, Astor planned a two-front attack: one by sea and one by land. He sent the ship *Tonquin* around South America to the mouth of the Columbia River where his men established Astoria, a fort and fur-trading post, in March 1811. The Overland Astorians left Saint Louis in October 1811, led by Wilson Price Hunt, and proceeded up the Missouri to the Arikara Indian villages near the mouth of the Grand River. They then cut westward to Jackson Hole south of the Tetons and on to Henrys Fork of the Snake River. Five Astorians chose to remain in the region to explore and trap. The main group proceeded up the Snake to the Columbia, arriving at Astoria in January 1812, the second American group to complete an overland trip to the Pacific.

As this group made the return trip to pick up their fellow trappers, on the Snake River in western Idaho they came upon four of the five men who remained. One had deserted. These men were in a bad way, having been attacked twice by Indians and having lost most of their horses, equipment, and clothing. Before the second attack, they had covered a wide area. They had gone south to the Bear River and followed it southward, possibly into Utah but not far enough to learn about the Great Salt Lake. They went into Wyoming and then back into Idaho.

The two groups of Astorians now joined and proceeded eastward through southern Idaho. Their route took them over South Pass, which they discovered. However, they did not publicize the discovery, and it was not until 1824 that the pass was rediscovered and used.

4. THE MOUNTAIN MEN THOROUGHLY EXPLORED AND TRAPPED THE UTAH REGION DURING THE 1820s

During the 1820s the Utah region was thoroughly explored and trapped by the Mountain Men. They explored the rivers and streams, the valleys, and even the desert lands. The first four rendezvous were held in Utah or on her northern border. By 1830 most of the nooks and corners of the area of Utah today were well known to these explorer-trappers.

The Mountain Men of the 1820s came into Utah from three directions. The British trappers kept coming into the Utah region from the northwest. Americans came into the region from the east out of Saint Louis, and from the southeast out of Santa Fé, having come to Santa Fé from Independence, Missouri.

Between 1812 and 1815 the United States and Great Britain were at war. The British took over Astoria and the American Fur Company's men and posts in the northwest. The American fur trade was disrupted, and it was not until the 1820s that there was an important revival in the fur trade. But by 1821 Americans were trapping and trading again on the upper Missouri River and making great profits. At that same time, Mexico revolted against Spain for her independence and opened Santa Fé to American trade. Thus, during the 1820s Americans went west—to the northwest and to the southwest.

From the South, out of Santa Fé, along part of the Escalante Trail and parts of what was shortly to become the Old Spanish Trail, Mountain Men came into the Utah region. Many made their journey across the southern Great Plains following the southern rivers, especially the Arkansas, to the mountains. The first trappers to get into this region, under Spanish and Mexican control, were put into jail for illegal entry into the country. When Spain lost control of Mexico, the Mexicans became more lenient with the Americans, and by 1823 Santa Fé was open to American trappers. During the 1820s, American trappers used the cities of Santa Fé and Taos as bases of operations to trap northward into the southern Rockies and into the Utah regions.

One of the early trappers to work out of Santa Fé was *Etienne Provost.* A French-Canadian by birth, Provost came to Saint

Louis by 1815 and that year trapped on the upper Arkansas River. During the winter of 1823-24, Provost and his partner, a French-Canadian named LeClerc, left Taos and went northwest into the southern Rockies of Colorado trapping beaver.

During the winter of 1824-25 there were several groups of Mountain Men in the Utah region from New Mexico. *Joseph* and *Antoine Robidoux, William Becknell, Ewing Young, Sylvestre Pratte*, and later the *Bent brothers* and *Ceran St. Verain*—all were in on the fur trade that took them to the Green, the Grand, and San Juan rivers. That fall Joseph Robidoux' party suffered an attack by Plains Indians, and several men were killed and others robbed. In 1825 the Robidoux brothers trapped the Gunnison and the Uncompaghre rivers.

In the fall of 1824, Provost and LeClerc went farther north and west into the Uinta Basin of Utah. That fall, Provost pushed west up the Strawberry River and over the Wasatch Mountains to the river that bears his name. He followed the Provo River into Utah Valley. He then pressed northward into the valley of the Great Salt Lake. Here he had a serious encounter with Snake Indians.

Provost met a Snake chief probably on the Jordan River. The chief, anxious to revenge injuries to his people by other whites, invited Provost and his men to smoke with him, but insisted that it was bad medicine to have any metallic object near while they smoked the peace pipe. Provost and his men put aside their weapons and entered in on the ceremony. At a signal the Indians attacked the trappers with knives they had hidden in their robes. Provost and three or four of his men escaped. The rest were slaughtered. Provost fled east over the mountains and rejoined LeClerc in the Uinta Basin.

During the spring of 1825, Provost was again in the Wasatch Mountains with about thirty men. In May he was on the Weber River where he met British and American trappers.

From the Northwest, British trappers came into the Utah region. After the British took over Astoria during the War of 1812, Americans did very little trapping in the Northwest. After the boundary settlement of 1818, which provided for joint occupation of the Oregon country by British and Americans, the trappers of the North West Company and the Hudson's Bay Company trapped all the furs they could out of the country south of the Columbia, for they guessed that those lands would go to the Americans when joint occupation ended.

British penetration into the Utah region resulted from several expeditions called the Snake River Expeditions. The Northwesters conducted Snake River Expeditions in 1818, 1819, and 1820, and the Hudson's Bay Company (which took over the North West Company in 1821) conducted them in 1823, 1824, and 1824-25. During the 1819 expedition, the British trappers reached Bear River (named by Michel Bourdeau "from the great number of those animals on its borders"). They followed the Bear River almost certainly to Bear Lake and also into Willow Valley (Cache Valley) where Bourdeau gave his own name to a stream (which name was later changed to Blacksmith Fork). In 1823 the British were again on the Bear River. None of these expeditions reached Great Salt Lake.

The Snake River Expedition of 1824-25 was led by *Peter Skene Ogden*. It left Flathead Post December 20, 1824, and was to reach Weber Canyon in Utah before turning back. With Ogden and his large party was a group of American trappers led by Jedediah

Smith. The Americans were to give Ogden's party good-natured competition and some difficulties.

From the East, out of Saint Louis, came Americans under the Fur Company headed by William H. Ashley and Andrew Henry. In 1822 at Saint Louis a partnership was formed between William H. Ashley and Andrew Henry, two important fur traders. The trappers assembled in 1822 by these men included the most notable Mountain Men: Jedediah S. Smith, James Clyman, Thomas Fitzpatrick, James Bridger, John H. Weber, Daniel T. Potts, David E. Jackson, William L. and Milton G. Sublette, Moses (Black) Harris, Hugh Glass, and Jim Beckwourth. Later others joined up, including Joseph R. Walker, Joe Meek, Kit Carson, and Old Bill Williams.

The Ashley-Henry men opened up the wealthiest fur sections of the West. They were the first trappers to do the major part of the trapping themselves rather than trading with the Indians for furs. Furthermore, Ashley and Henry dealt with their men as independent trappers, paying them for beaver pelts delivered in the mountains. This way, the trapper could spend all his time in the mountains and save himself yearly trips to Saint Louis. The *rendezvous* was an essential feature of this system, founded by Ashley and continued by his men. *The Ashley-Henry men are especially important in our Utah heritage because they did more than any other group to explore the Utah region and help prepare the way for eventual settlement.*

In the fall of 1823 *Jedediah S. Smith* was put in command of this important beaver hunting party. The group went west from Fort Kiowa, on the Missouri River, breaking a new trail toward the mountains. They tried to cross the snow covered mountains north of the Wind River Mountains, but turned south and struck upon the Sweetwater River. They

James (Jim) Bridger played an important role in the fur trade. His fort was a trading post important to overland emigrants including the Mormons. From a painting by Waldo Love.

Jedediah Strong Smith was a leader of the American fur trappers who explored Utah so thoroughly during the 1820s. From a sketch made by a friend, from memory, after Smith's death.

went west and discovered South Pass in March 1824.

South Pass is a level area on the continental divide that separates the waters that flow eastward and drain through the Mississippi River Valley into the Gulf of Mexico, and those that flow west and empty into the Pacific Ocean or drain into the Great Basin. The Smith party was not the first group to cross South Pass, but it was the first to make this pass well known to fellow Americans. Smith sent Fitzpatrick back to Saint Louis to tell Ashley about the discovery. Soon it was announced widely in the newspapers.

The rediscovery of South Pass meant a great deal to Americans. It meant that emigrants might get to the West by wagon more easily than by river transportation through the difficult mountainous country to the north first explored by Lewis and Clark. Americans could perhaps now get into the Oregon country before the British could settle it in large numbers. In the years that followed, South Pass became the highway for trappers and missionaries. It made possible the rapid settlement and American acquisition of Oregon, and the early immigration to California and Utah.

Jedediah Smith and his men trapped west of South Pass on the Green River, then separated into two groups to explore and trap the surrounding country. Smith led a small party, and John H. Weber led the larger group.

Smith's smaller group went on west to the Snake River Country and met Indian trappers of the Hudson's Bay Company Snake River Expedition of 1824. The Indian trappers they met had been robbed of their equipment and were lost. Jedediah Smith bargained to guide them back to their post in exchange for all their furs. He spent the fall of 1824 at Flathead Post learning all he could of British fur operations and the geography of the land the British trapped.

The larger group of Smith's American trappers headed by John H. Weber may have numbered up to fifty trappers. Jim Bridger and Daniel Potts were in the group. The Weber group went west from Green River by

way of Blacks Fork and struck the Bear River, went down that stream into Willow Valley (Cache Valley), Utah-Idaho, where they wintered on the Cub River. During the autumn of 1824, a bet was made among the men as to the course of the Bear River beyond Cache Valley. Jim Bridger was selected to follow the course of the river and determine the bet. With others, on horseback, he followed the river to the Bear River narrows, and discovered Great Salt Lake on the other side. He tasted the water and concluded that it was an arm of the Pacific Ocean. (That same fall of 1824 Etienne Provost was also in Salt Lake Valley on the Jordan where he lost men in an encounter with the Snake Indians. Records are so inadequate for these men that it is impossible to tell for certain which was the first discoverer of the Great Salt Lake, though Bridger is usually given the honor.)

The Weber men trapped Willow Valley (Cache Valley) during the fall of 1824 and the spring of 1825. They then moved southward, trapping along the way, to the valley of the Great Salt Lake. They began trapping along some of the streams emptying from the Wasatch Mountains into the lake. They were based near present-day Ogden when other trappers came into the area: Jedediah Smith and men, and Peter Skene Ogden and men, in turn, from the north, and Etienne Provost and his men from the east.

The British did not appreciate the entrance of Americans into trapping grounds they wanted all to themselves. Believing the Snake country worth holding, the British had given command of the Snake River Expedition of 1824-25 to a tough fighter, *Peter Skene Ogden.* Among all the Mountain Men of the 1820s, Peter Skene Ogden stands second only to Jedediah Smith among the great explorers and leaders in the fur trade.

Peter Skene Ogden's Snake River Expedi-

Peter Skene Ogden was the leader of several Snake River Expeditions of the Hudson's Bay Company.

tion left Flathead Post December 20, 1824, "the most formidable party that has ever set out for the Snakes." It was made up of Ogden, William Kittson, and fifty-seven trappers. Jedediah Smith and his party followed after. The two parties proceeded south together in this manner until March 19 when Smith and his men went out ahead of Ogden's large party. Thereafter, Smith and his men trapped a day or two ahead of Ogden's men, taking most of the beaver, much to Ogden's disgust. During the last of April they arrived at the Bear River. Ogden and his men trapped along Bear River which led them into Cache Valley, where they also trapped. Jedediah Smith and his men followed the Bear River out of Cache Valley and into Salt Lake Valley and there met the men of his party led by John H. Weber.

On May 16 Ogden crossed south from Cache Valley into the next valley, naming the "hole" and river New Hole and New River, but afterwards they were called Ogdens Hole

and Ogden River. Here the British trapped with great success for a few days until they were interrupted by the news that there were two parties of Americans in the neighborhood. On May 22, Ogden crossed over from Ogden Valley south to Morgan Valley and the canyon of the Weber River. The next morning Ogden met Etienne Provost and his men who had come from the Uinta Basin. That afternoon Ogden and his men met face to face twenty-five Americans and fourteen British deserters. The meeting between British and American fur trappers came near to bloodshed and an "international incident."

Threat of war in Weber Canyon, May 23-25, 1825. One of the problems facing the Hudson's Bay Company was desertion of its trappers to American companies who paid more money for pelts and charged less for supplies than the British. There was also rivalry over the trapping grounds. When Ogden and his remaining trappers were camped in Weber Canyon, Gardner Johnson of the American company challenged the British to a fight. He claimed that they were on American soil and that the British had no right to be there. Ogden contended that the Oregon country was still under joint occupation, and he had equal rights there. Actually both parties were in Mexican territory. Ogden kept a cool head during three days of dispute, refusing to open fire on the Americans. Finally the British withdrew and retraced their steps to Oregon. However, Ogden was to return later to the Utah region on trapping expeditions.

William H. Ashley came to the mountains in 1825, explored the Green River and Uinta Basin, and established the first rendezvous. When Jedediah Smith and his men rediscovered South Pass in March of 1824, Fitzpatrick was sent back to Saint Louis to tell Ashley the news. Ashley acted at once, leaving Saint Louis with a party of trappers and arriving on the Green River in April 1825. After arranging for his men to meet in rendezvous on July 10, he then set out with a few men to explore the Green River, making the first trip by boat down that river. He passed through the deep canyons from Flaming Gorge to Split Mountain, then on until he reached the treacherous rapids of Desolation Canyon about fifty miles south of present Roosevelt, Utah. He bought horses from friendly "Eutau" Indians, learned from them the nature of the country to the south, and then retraced his course upstream to the Duchesne River. Ashley met Etienne Provost and twelve men who were returning from the Weber Canyon encounter with the British. Provost helped Ashley retrieve a cache buried on the Green River, and then guided him over the mountains to the rendezvous site.

Their route took them into Strawberry Valley, over the mountains and down Center Creek to Heber Valley, north to Kamas Prairie and on to the Weber River, then to Echo Canyon, across the Bear River Divide and east to Henrys Fork.

The first rendezvous was held on Henrys Fork of the Green River, July 1825. For the rendezvous Ashley's 120 trappers came from throughout the Middle Rockies. Ashley could be proud of the accomplishments of these men. They had rediscovered South Pass, explored and trapped the Green, Snake, and Bear river valleys, searched out the Great Salt Lake and neighboring valleys, and now explored the Green River and crossed the Uinta Basin. The discoveries of these men, coupled with their successful encounter with the British, gave the Americans control of the Rocky Mountain beaver trade.

The rendevous was an annual meeting of the Mountain Men of a company. Here they sold or traded their year's catch for supplies, exchanged information about the West, and prepared for the next year's trapping. "Rendevous on the Green River," a painting by William Henry Jackson.

At rendezvous, Ashley bought 8,829 pounds of beaver pelts, worth $45,000 to $50,000 in Saint Louis. To the trappers he sold sugar, coffee, tobacco, lead, powder, knives, bar iron, and Indian trinkets. Once the bargains had been concluded and trapping fields assigned, the trappers went back into the wilderness.

During the 1825-26 season, Ashley's men explored even farther in the Utah region. Jedediah Smith accompanied Ashley to Saint Louis, where he became a partner with Ashley (Henry had withdrawn in 1824). He was soon back in the mountains trapping in parts of Wyoming, Utah, and Idaho. Throughout the Great Salt Lake area there were scores of trappers. In the spring of 1826, Jim Bridger and others worked from Cache Valley up the Bear River and around to Bear Lake. It was likely at this time that the name Willow Valley was changed to Cache Valley for there were a number of caches dug in the valley. During the spring of 1826, Jim Clyman and three others went around the Great Salt Lake in "skin boats" to learn whether any other streams with beaver emptied into the lake. The men learned that the lake was dangerous, the land around it was desolate, and that there was no outlet to the sea. That same spring, Jedediah Smith explored west and northwest of the Great Salt Lake.

The second rendezvous was held in Utah in 1826. The records are not clear as to the site, but it is believed by most that it was held in *Cache Valley* (near Hyrum or in the south end of the valley). At this rendezvous Ashley brought the usual supplies and bought pelts from his trappers. However, he soon sold out his interests in the company to David E. Jackson and William Sublette. Smith retained his interests and the three now formed the firm of Smith, Jackson and Sublette.

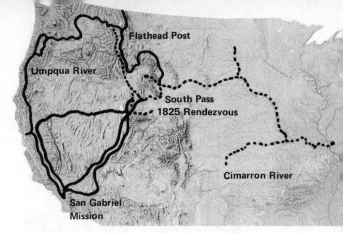

This map shows the travels of Jedediah S. Smith who conducted five expeditions into the West between 1822 and 1831: 1) 1822-23, up the Missouri River; 2) 1823-24, South Pass, Green River, Bear River, Flathead Post; 3) 1826-27, first southwest expedition; 4) 1827-29, second southwest expedition; 5) 1831, Smith massacred en route to Santa Fé.

The new partnership of Smith, Jackson and Sublette was the sole inheritor of the wilderness empire. Jackson was assigned to be resident partner, working in the trapping end of the business in the Middle Rockies. Sublette was to supply the men with equipment and transport the supplies and the furs. Jedediah Smith was given the special task of purposeful discovery and exploration.

Jedediah Smith explored central and southern Utah on his first southwest expedition, August 1826 to July 1827. From the rendezvous about August 15, Smith took fifteen men and proceeded to Great Salt Lake Valley, on south into Utah Valley, down Juab Valley to the Sevier River. He followed the Sevier River south, past the future sites of Gunnison, Salina, Richfield, and Marysvale. When the country began to close in about him, he followed Clear Creek west to the site of Cove Fort, then turned south again, following the future route of U.S. 91 or Interstate 15. He reached the Virgin River and followed it down to the Colorado, and followed the Colorado to the Mojave Indian villages (present Needles, California). Through all these desert lands, Smith sought a river that would take them west to the Pacific Coast. He found none. He also searched for beaver trapping country. He found so little it was not worth stopping to trap. His men had difficulty finding food. There were no buffalo south of Utah Valley, only an occasional antelope, a mountain sheep, or the black-tailed jack rabbits. Two weeks were spent crossing the Mojave Desert until they reached Cajon Pass and went into San Bernardino Valley and to the San Gabriel Mission. After some difficulty with Mexican authorities, Smith went north up the San Joaquin Valley still searching for a river to the sea. Always there was the high, impassable Sierra Nevada range. Finally, at the Stanislaus River in northern California he left most of his men to cache the furs they had trapped chiefly in California and camp for the winter, while he and two men crossed the Sierra Nevada and made their way across the central Nevada desert of the Great Basin (May 20, 1827). They passed Walker Lake, then crossed central Nevada and in desperate condition finally reached the south end of Great Salt Lake. Smith was overjoyed to be "home" at last.

JEDEDIAH SMITH REACHES GREAT SALT LAKE

From the journal of Jedediah Smith:

... The Salt Lake a joyful sight was spread before us.

Is it possible said the companions of my sufferings that we are so near the end of our troubles. For myself I durst scarcely believe that it was really the Big Salt Lake that I saw. It was indeed a most cheering view for although we were some distance from the depo, yet we knew we would soon be in a country where we would find game and water which were to us objects of the greatest importance and those which would contribute more than any others to our comfort and happiness.

Those who may chance to read this at a distance from the scene may perhaps be surprised that the sight of this lake surrounded by a wilderness of More than 2000 Miles diameter excited in me those feelings known to the traveler who, after long and perilous journying, comes again in view of his home. But so it was with me for I had traveled so much in the vicinity of the Salt Lake that it had become my home in the wilderness.

Smith and his two companions crossed the Jordan by raft, and made their way north, most likely through Cache Valley and Logan Canyon, to Bear Lake where they arrived at the site of the rendezvous, July 3, near present Laketown. Of his reception, Smith wrote: "my arrival caused a considerable bustle in camp, for myself and party had been given up as lost. A small Cannon brought up from St. Louis was loaded and fired for a salute."

At the third rendezvous (July 1827), at the south end of Bear Lake, Utah, Smith learned that while he was away in the Southwest, his partners had been trapping the surrounding country, doing well, and putting the partnership on a successful financial footing. Because Smith had left men and furs in California, he was assigned to take another trip to the Southwest.

On his second southwest expedition (July 1827 to August 1829), Jedediah Smith took the same general route through Utah to the Mohave Indians where he lost several men in an Indian attack. Then he went on into California, where he again had trouble with the Mexican authorities who detained him. Finally freed, he proceeded north, found his men, sold the furs to the skipper of a Yankee sailing ship, and bought horses to drive into the mountains to sell. He did not want to go across the desert again, so explored northward to Fort Vancouver. At the Umpqua River he lost all but two of his men in a massacre. Smith finally made his way into the Snake River country and by August 1829 joined Jackson and Sublette in Montana. During 1829-30 he trapped with his partners and men in the upper Missouri and the Yellowstone country. Leaving the mountains forever, he arrived in Saint Louis, October 7, 1830. He began the work of preparing his journals and maps for publication, but then yielded to the temptation to join a trading expedition to Santa Fé. On the Cimarron River in western Kansas, his party was attacked by a Comanche war party. Smith was killed May 27, 1831.

The contributions of Jedediah S. Smith are many. He rediscovered South Pass. In his two southwest expeditions, he found a way to southern California. He was the first man to go all the way from Saint Louis to the California coast. He was the first man to travel the length and breadth of Utah. He was the first to travel the length of California and Oregon, from San Diego to Fort Vancouver on the Columbia. He was the first to cross the breadth as well as the length of the Great Basin. He clearly demonstrated that there was no river draining from the Great Salt Lake region to the Pacific Coast.

Peter Skene Ogden came into the Utah region again during the fall and winter of 1828-29. His fourth Snake River Expedition took him from southeastern Oregon south to what was later named the Humboldt River by Frémont. He followed it east and beyond until he reached the deserts bordering the north side of the Great Salt Lake. He then went north into the Snake River country, but returned to explore the Humboldt west to the Humboldt Sinks in present western Nevada. The discovery of this long inland river in the middle of the northern Great Basin was a most important discovery to future overland travel.

During the four years following the discovery of Great Salt Lake (1824-28), the Utah region was well explored and very nearly trapped out. During these four years of trapping, the Mountain Men trapped the streams of the Wasatch and the Uinta mountains, the valley of the Sevier River and into the upper Virgin River country. The desert regions had been avoided, but wherever there were beaver in the streams of the mountains,

the trappers had found them. By 1830 the northern and central areas of Utah were well known to the Mountain Men.

5. DURING THE 1830s THE UTAH REGION WAS VISITED LESS FREQUENTLY BY MOUNTAIN MEN

Most of the first wealth of beaver had been stripped from the country, and trappers now had to range over a larger area than ever before to make trapping profitable. In 1830 the partnership of Smith, Jackson and Sublette sold out its fur trapping interests to the *Rocky Mountain Fur Company* with Jim Bridger, Thomas Fitzpatrick, Milton G. Sublette, Henry G. Fraeb, and Baptiste Gervais as partners. That same year the American Fur Company expanded its operations into the Mountain West. More competition was coming to the fur trade in the mountains.

The name of *Benjamin L. E. Bonneville* is prominent in the later years of the fur trade, mainly because he had a good biographer, Washington Irving. He himself did not get into the Utah region. However, Joseph R. Walker, one of his men, led an important exploring and trapping party into Utah.

Bonneville was a captain in the United States Army. He obtained leave to work up support for his interest in the fur trade and to explore the western country to provide the army with information about the country and the Indians beyond the Rockies. He came to the mountains in 1832 with 110 men, hauling equipment by wagon over South Pass. (He proved that wheeled vehicles could be taken over South Pass.) He went up the Green River to the 1833 rendezvous at Horse Creek. Bonneville sent men out in all directions to trap and learn about the country. He met with little success, for there were too many who had come earlier and who knew the country better. After the rendezvous Bonneville sent out the Walker expedition which proved very important in establishing western trails.

The Walker expedition (1833-34) set out from the Green River rendezvous July 24, 1833 with more than forty well-equipped men. It reached the Great Salt Lake about the middle of August. Walker took his men around the northern shore of the lake, then westward into the Great Salt Lake Desert. After great suffering from thirst and lack of food, the company came upon the Humboldt which they followed west to the Humboldt Sink, the Carson Sink, and Walker Lake. Later this route to California was to form part of one of the important highways of America.

The Walker expedition crossed the Sierra Nevada, discovered Yosemite Valley, and stopped for awhile in the San Joaquin Valley. Mid-February 1834 the party began its return journey. Walker led his party southward, around the southern portion of the Sierra Nevada (Walker Pass) and then northward along the east base of the Sierra Nevada to his former route along the Humboldt. He cut north to the Snake River and east to meet Bonneville. His march like that of Jedediah Smith clearly proved there was no river that emptied from near the Great Salt Lake or the Great Basin into the Pacific Ocean.

Osborne Russell, a trapper of the 1830s, visited the Utah region and left a good description of the Salt Lake area. Russell came to the mountains in 1834, helped build Fort Hall on the Snake River, and trapped surrounding regions. The next spring Russell went south into Utah Valley and traded with the Indians. "I passed the time as pleasantly at this place as ever I did among Indians," he wrote, "in the daytime I rode about the val-

Joseph Reddeford Walker made important explorations around Great Salt Lake, across northern Nevada, in California, and through Utah.
Portrait by Alfred Jacob Miller.

Fort Hall, a painting by William Henry Jackson.

ley hunting waterfowl who rend the air at this season of the year with their cries."

Thomas L. "Pegleg" Smith led a party of American Fur Company men into Utah and Arizona in 1841. Besides Smith and James Baker (who wrote about the trip), there were forty other trappers and seven

111

Shoshoni Indians. The party came down from the north following Bear River, then to the Weber, and on to the Provo in Utah Valley. On their return trip from trapping in southern Utah and Arizona, the party again camped on the Provo River.

As the fur trade declined in the 1830s, fewer trappers visited the Utah region. Some *Mountain Men built forts* as supply stations and rendezvous points for trappers. Such forts were built in Utah by Antoine Robidoux, Philip Thompson and David Craig, Jim Bridger, and Miles Goodyear.

Antoine Robidoux, we learned earlier, was one of the early trappers to work out of Santa Fé into the Utah region. During the winter of 1837-38 he built the first trading post in Utah, on the Green River near the mouth of the White River. He soon moved it to the Whiterocks Fork of the Uinta River. During these years *Fort Uintah* was a famous gathering place for trappers. While on a visit to Missouri in 1841, Robidoux advised the first emigrant wagon train to the Pacific on the best route to take. Later, the hostility of the Ute Indians caused Robidoux to abandon Fort Uintah, and it was destroyed in 1844 by rival traders.

Fort Davy Crockett was built by Philip Thompson and David Craig in 1837 in Browns Hole, on the Green River near the Utah-Colorado boundary line.

Fort Laramie was built during the summer of 1834 by William L. Sublette and Robert Campbell at the junction of the Laramie and North Platte rivers in Wyoming. Fort Hall was built the same year by Nathaniel J. Wyeth at the junction of the Snake and Portneuf rivers in Idaho. Both forts played important roles in later Utah history.

We will learn of the forts established by Jim Bridger and Miles Goodyear in the next chapter.

6. THE MOUNTAIN MEN WERE IMPORTANT AS EXPLORERS AND TRAIL MAKERS

Spanish traders and Mountain Men combined their efforts to make the Old Spanish Trail. The Escalante Expedition had sought a trail from Santa Fé to northern California. In the following years the hope remained that a northern route to California could be found. In the 1830s a trail was established, not to northern California, but through Utah to Los Angeles in southern California—the *Old Spanish Trail*. This famous trail was put together, so to speak, by combining parts of the Escalante Trail, parts of the trails used by the Spanish traders among the Utah Valley Indians, and other trails made by the Mountain Men.

Antonio Armijo took an early step toward such a trail in 1829-30 when he took goods from Santa Fé to Los Angeles, going by way of the Four Corners region, northwestern Arizona, and Cajon Pass. The first party to make the trip on the Old Spanish Trail started during the winter of 1830-31 and was headed by *William Wolfskill* and *George C. Yount*. The next year *Antonio Santi-Estevan* led the second trading trip from Santa Fé to Los Angeles. As years passed, shortcuts were made until it was a well-defined route. From Central Utah to California the trail made use of traces left by Jedediah Smith and other Mountain Men.

Antoine Robidoux inscribed this message in French on a canyon wall on his way to the Uinta Basin. Translated, it reads: Antoine Robidoux passed here the 13 November 1837 to establish a trading house at the Green or Uinta river.

THE MOUNTAIN MEN LEFT NAMES ON OUR MAP

Ashley Creek, Ashley Valley, Ashley National Forest	Named for William H. Ashley, explorations in 1825.
Bear River, Bear Lake	Named by the British fur trapper Michel Bourdeau 1819.
Beaver River, Beaver, Beaver County	Beaver River so named because of the abundance of beaver.
Browns Hole, on Green River, Daggett County	Site of 1837 Fort Davy Crockett built by Mountain Men.
Cache Valley, Cache County	Named by Jim Beckwourth, probably 1825-26, from Willow Valley; favorite place to cache furs.
Duchesne River, Fort Duchesne, Duchesne, and Duchesne County	Named for a French fur trapper Du Chesne who was in Uinta Basin, about 1840. Perhaps named by Father DeSmet after Rose Du Chesne.
Great Salt Lake	Named by 1824-25; first Big Salt Lake.
Henrys Fork, Green River	Named for Andrew Henry, associate of William H. Ashley.
Logan, Cache County	Possibly named for Mountain Man Ephraim Logan or Logan Fontanelle, a friendly Indian chief who had been so named by French-Canadian trappers in region, 1820-1839.
Malad River, Box Elder County	From French, *malade*, sick. Trappers got sick from eating beaver on this creek; the beaver had eaten poisonous roots.
Ogden, Ogden River, Ogden Valley, Ogdens Hole, Ogden Peak	Named for Peter Skene Ogden, of the Hudson's Bay Company, in the region from 1825.
Portage, Box Elder County	From the French, *porter*, to carry. Where one must carry his boat.
Provo, Provo River, Provo Canyon	Named for Etienne Provost.
Weber River, Weber Canyon, Weber County	Named for John H. Weber.

From about 1830 to about 1850, the Old Spanish Trail was the route over which yearly caravans of travelers and traders made their way between Santa Fé and Los Angeles. The people of New Mexico had great sheep herds. From the wool they made fine *sarapes* and *fresadas* (shawls and blankets). The people of California raised herds of fine horses and mules. Furthermore, the Californians received silks and other luxuries from trade with China. Traders using the Old Spanish Trail packed on their mules the woolen goods of New Mexico and transported them to California to trade for horses, mules, silks, and other goods, which were in demand in New Mexico.

By 1840 the era of the Mountain Man was coming to an end. The beaver were being trapped out and the demand for beaver fur fell as silk hats became popular. Many of the Mountain Men returned to the states to live out their lives. Some went to Oregon and California to settle and farm. Others remained in the mountains and lived with the Indians, or alone. During the years before, the Mountain Men had explored most of the Mountain West and laid trails for others to follow. Their contributions to the settlement of the West were many. Some of those who remained in the mountains established trading posts or became guides to government explorers and overland emigrants. They continued to serve as guides to the West long after beaver trapping was given up.

OVERLAND MIGRATIONS AND EXPLORERS

Most of what the Mountain Men knew about the West they kept in their heads. Only a few wrote letters, and even fewer kept journals. Some letters were published in the newspapers of the time, and others were sent to government officials who made them a matter of record. The explorations of Jedediah Smith were known and were shown on a map of the period. Gradually the American people were learning about the American West.

During the 1840s two types of people came into the Utah region: (1) government explorers and (2) home seekers bound for California and Oregon. The explorations of the 1840s were different from those of the Mountain Men. The Mountain Men wanted to trap the beaver streams. The explorers of the 1840s wanted to describe its plant and animal life, to map the region scientifically, and especially to show possible routes of travel to the Pacific Coast. The government was anxious to have Americans occupy the Oregon country and other parts of the American West.

Emigrants, bound for the Pacific Coast to make homes, passed through the Utah region. These emigrants often wrote letters back East, and some even wrote books of their journeys across the continent. The explorers and emigrants of this period helped open the way for permanent settlement in Utah. The Utah pioneers of 1847 owe a great debt to those who went before, especially those who passed through Utah in 1846.

Permanent occupation of homes in the Utah region was not to come until the year 1847. Even so, in the years from 1840 to 1846 there were forts or trading posts built by Mountain Men. These dwellings may rightfully claim to be Utah's first dwellings occupied by white people.

The explorers and emigrants who crossed Utah in this period were not intent on settling in Utah; they had other goals in mind. However, their roads and their reports and maps helped those who followed.

The important things to look for in this chapter are the making of wagon trails, the reporting and mapping of the Utah region, and the solving of the boundary disputes between the United States and her neighbors.

IN THIS CHAPTER WE WILL LEARN

1. The United States was growing rapidly and expanding westward.

2. Indian and trapper trails became wagon roads in the 1840s.

3. John C. Frémont made several explorations of the Utah region.

4. In 1846 several overland companies followed the Hastings Cutoff through Utah.

5. Miles Goodyear established a trading post on the Weber River in 1846.

6. The boundaries of the United States were expanded in the 1840s.

Government explorers made surveys necessary to draw accurate maps of the region described in their reports.

This painting by William H. Jackson suggests the heavy westward migration, such as that of 1843, moving over South Pass.

8

1. THE UNITED STATES WAS GROWING RAPIDLY AND EXPANDING WESTWARD

In the years following the beginning of her national life in 1789, the territory of the United States expanded rapidly. There was a feeling that it was the "manifest destiny" of the United States to own and to occupy the continent west to the Pacific Coast. The government felt a need to follow upon the work of the Mountain Men, to put settlers on the land, in order to help claim those western lands for the United States.

During the early 1840s, Americans took gigantic steps west. They crossed the Great Plains and the Rocky Mountains and settled in the Oregon country or in California. The Oregon and California trails were being well defined by annual migrations. Utah was at the crossroads of the West even in those

days, and emigration to California and Oregon gave Utah some of her most interesting history.

2. INDIAN AND TRAPPER TRAILS BECAME WAGON ROADS IN THE 1840s

Through the centuries, Utah's Indians had made many trails. The Mountain Men had followed these trails, creating only a few new ones. Man walking along a trail, with his horse and pack animals, leaves a trace of his passing by. When a wagon is drawn over the ground, a greater trace is made. Soon wagon trails are made which become roads in time. The first wagon trails were made in northern Utah in the 1840s.

The first wheeled vehicle to cross over South Pass was the cannon carriage Ashley sent to the 1827 rendezvous at the south end of Bear Lake in Utah. In 1830, wagons were brought to the Wind River, and in 1832 Bonneville used wagons over South Pass, taking his supplies by wagon to the Green River. By 1840 a wagon trail had been made to Oregon. Soon people were to drive wagons across northern Utah on their way to California.

The first wagon train to cross Utah was the Bidwell-Bartleson party of 1841. In the spring of 1841 there gathered at Independence, Missouri, a group of people who wanted to get to California by wagon. John Bidwell and John Bartleson were leading figures. It seems they were partly influenced by the glowing descriptions of Joseph Robidoux who was in Independence at the time. The group left Missouri May 19, 1841, and proceeded west along the Platte, the North Platte, over South Pass to the Green, and then along the Bear River to Soda Springs, Idaho. Here the party split into two groups; one continued on north to Oregon, the other turned south to California by crossing the

Utah and Nevada regions. This latter group followed the Bear River south and then turned north around Great Salt Lake. In this company were the first white women to enter Utah, Mrs. Kelsey and her nineteen-year-old daughter Nancy. Crossing the Great Salt Lake Desert they encountered many difficulties. They finally reached Pilot Peak, abandoned one wagon and a few days later abandoned the other wagons in eastern Nevada. Pushing on with their animals, they reached the Humboldt River which they followed to the Humboldt Sinks, then crossed to the Carson River and to the Walker River, up the west branch of the Walker River to the mountains. They reached the summit of the Sierra Nevada October 18 and found it covered with snow. Yet they got through, worn to skin and bones. On November 4 they reached the San Joaquin Valley of California. No one was to travel this same route again, but it did become known that emigrants could reach California by such routes.

More significant than this early wagon train, and more important to the future settlement of Utah than the explorations of the Mountain Men, were the scientific explorations and published reports of explorations by Captain John Charles Frémont of the United States Army Topographical Corps.

The Bidwell-Bartleson party of 1841 undertook a new route from Soda Springs to the Humboldt River by going around the northern edge of the Great Salt Lake Desert.

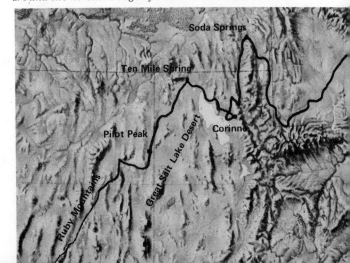

John C. Frémont, significant government explorer of the West in the 1840s, prepared reports and maps which were of considerable help to overland emigrants, including the Mormons.

3. JOHN C. FRÉMONT MADE SEVERAL EXPLORATIONS OF THE UTAH REGION

John C. Frémont was one of America's greatest explorers of the West. Frémont was a handsome, daring person. He was filled with enthusiasm for his work, and he was also steady, patient, and industrious. He could endure hard work and personal sacrifices. He was well educated for a life of explorations. He was trained in mathematics, the natural sciences, and in all that related to the out-of-doors. In his youth he had practical experience surveying railroad routes in wilderness country. Frémont was interested in exploring the West. His marriage to Jessie Benton, daughter of Senator Thomas H. Benton of Missouri, gave him the support he needed. Senator Benton was a close friend of William

Clark of the Lewis and Clark Expedition. The senator was influential in getting Frémont named as the leader of exploring expeditions. Frémont was a good choice. He had a keen intellectual interest in the plant and animal life, the geography, and trails in the West. Frémont was one of the first scientific explorers of the region west of the Mississippi.

Frémont led five expeditions to explore, report, and map the American West. The first was conducted May to October 1842 and took him to the Wind River Mountains and back to Independence, Missouri. He charted the route along the Platte, the North Platte, to and around South Pass. *His second and third expeditions took him into the Utah region*, and we will study them in detail. His other expeditions were later and do not relate to Utah at this time.

Frémont was a scientist. Each day he took readings to determine the longitude, latitude, and altitude. He took the temperature at different times each day. He observed the character of the landscape, the soil, the plants (naming many of them by their scientific names), and animal life, the tribes and habits of the Indians. He wrote each day in his journal all things worthy of mention for later use in publishing a report of his march.

Frémont did not blaze new trails, but rather followed the paths others had made. His most important contributions are that he charted or mapped these paths and trails, and described the land, plant and animal life in the surrounding country. Furthermore, he gave Americans his findings by promptly publishing his reports. With his reports were excellent maps.

Each day's march followed a routine. The camp was up at daybreak. The animals were set to grazing while the men ate breakfast. They marched all day, and camped an hour before sunset to give time to pasture

An artist's conception of John C. Frémont raising the American flag in the Wind River Mountains, 1842. The sketch was drawn for use in Frémont's campaign for president of the United States, 1856.

the animals and build whatever security was needed for the camp during the night. Guards were set to watch the camp at night. Frémont himself was often up during the night to make observations and record his instrument readings.

John C. Frémont's second exploring expedition (1843-44) took him into the Utah region. The purpose of this expedition was to explore to the Columbia River and on to Oregon, and hopefully to help emigrants get to Oregon. Whichever country placed the most people into Oregon country would claim it. The United States was anxious to get settlers there quickly. Frémont was to report on the country and explore routes of travel with the view to helping more people get to the West Coast.

Frémont set out in May 1843 with forty well-equipped men. Thomas Fitzpatrick, a fur trapping companion of Jedediah Smith and other Ashley men, served as guide. Later Kit Carson joined the expedition. Many of Frémont's men were Mountain Men. Frémont's route took him west by a new route to the Rockies then north to the Oregon Trail. He continued across South Pass and southwest till he reached the Bear River, August 21. He followed the Bear River northward (passing into Rich County, Utah) to Soda Springs and then south to the Great Salt Lake where they arrived September 6. Frémont and his men stayed about one week on the shores of Great Salt Lake, camped on Weber River. A small party took a rubber boat to a small nearby island (Fremont Island) and returned the next day. Frémont contented himself with this exploration of the lake and promised himself a more thorough look at a future time. September 12 they began their northward journey retracing their steps up the Bear River. Frémont reported many interesting things about the Salt Lake region and especially about Bear River Valley.

JOHN C. FRÉMONT DESCRIBES BEAR RIVER VALLEY

From the Report of his Second Exploring Expedition:

[Having visited Great Salt Lake, Frémont returned northward up the Bear River Valley, in present Box Elder County.]

September 14.— ... the bottoms of this river, and of some of the creeks which I saw, form a natural resting and recruiting station for travelers, now, and in all time to come. The bottoms are extensive; water excellent; timber sufficient; the soil good, and well adapted to grains and grasses suited to such an elevated region. A military post, and a civilized settlement, would be of great value here; and cattle and horses would do well where grass and salt abound. The lake will furnish exhaustless supplies of salt. All the mountains here are covered with a valuable nutritious grass, called bunch grass, from the form in which it grows, which has a second growth in the fall. The beasts of the Indians were fat upon it; our own found it a good subsistence; and its quantity will sustain any amount of cattle, and make this truly a bucolic region.

119

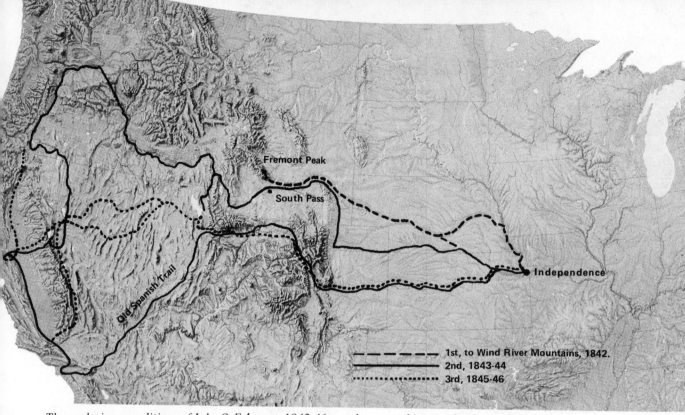

The exploring expeditions of John C. Frémont, 1842-46, are shown on this map. On the second expedition Frémont entered Utah from the north and later from the south. On his third expedition he crossed Uinta Basin and the Great Salt Lake Desert.

Map labels: Fremont Peak, South Pass, Old Spanish Trail, Independence

1st, to Wind River Mountains, 1842.
2nd, 1843-44
3rd, 1845-46

Frémont went on to the Snake and Columbia rivers, then south through Washington, into Nevada and California. Working his way south through the San Joaquin Valley, he then cut east through Walker Pass and west to reach the Old Spanish Trail on April 18, 1844.

Frémont made a second major entry into the Utah region on this return trip. His party followed the Old Spanish Trail to Las Vegas and the Virgin River Valley. By May 10 he had reached "a halting-place of very good grass on the clear waters of the Santa Clara fork of the Rio Virgen." They were in Utah. Here the mountains "began to be wooded with cedar and pine, and clusters of trees gave shelter to birds—a new and welcome sight—which could not have lived in the desert we had passed." The changed appearance of the country gave everyone "a more lively spirit."

At or near Mountain Meadows the party was joined by Joseph Walker, the Mountain Man who took an expedition west of Great Salt Lake for Captain Bonneville. He had guided a company of emigrants to California and now met Frémont's party.

The trip up through central Utah from the south passed by the Little Salt Lake (where the Old Spanish Trail turned east into the plateaus), northward to the Sevier River country (which impressed Frémont very much), through Juab Valley and into Utah Valley on May 25. After a day's rest the party turned east by way of Spanish Fork River, Diamond Fork Creek, and Strawberry River to reach the Duchesne River and Fort Uintah June 3. Robidoux was not there at the time, but Frémont refreshed himself and went on to Ashleys Fork, Browns Hole, then east through Colorado, to the Arkansas River, and back to Missouri.

JOHN C. FREMONT DESCRIBES CENTRAL UTAH

From the Report of his Second Exploring Expedition:

May 17.– ... [Sevier River country] We had now entered a region of great pastoral promise, abounding with fine streams, the rich bunch grass, soil that would produce wheat, and indigenous flax growing as if it had been sown. Consistent with the general character of its bordering mountains, this fertility of soil and vegetation does not extend far into the Great Basin. ...

May 25-26.– ... in general and comparative terms ... [this region] would be inferior to the Atlantic States, though many parts are superior for wheat; while in the rearing of flocks and herds it would claim a high place. Its grazing capabilities are great; and even in the indigenous grass now here, an element of individual and national wealth may be found. ...

By August 1844 Frémont was back in Saint Louis, writing his report for publication. His *Report* was published immediately and enjoyed a wide circulation. It stimulated great interest in California and Oregon. One of the most significant declarations of the report was the description of the true nature of the *"Great Interior Basin."* Jedediah Smith had traveled around the basin and crossed parts of it. Joseph Walker talked to Frémont about the idea of a basin, for Walker fully believed the interior country to be a basin. It was Frémont, however, who scientifically explored and observed the region surrounding the basin in sufficient detail to establish that it was a land with no outlets to the sea. On his map he wrote: "The Great Basin: diameter 11° of latitude, 10° of longitude: elevation above the sea between 4 and 5000 feet: surrounded by lofty mountains: contents almost unknown, but believed to be filled with rivers and lakes which have no communication with the sea, deserts and oases which have never been explored, and savage tribes, which no traveler has seen or described."

On his third exploring expedition (1845-47), John C. Frémont again visited the Great Salt Lake region and crossed the Great Basin to California. By the time Frémont's *Report* of his second expedition was published, the United States government was ready to send him on a third expedition. Americans were anxious to gain possession of the Oregon country and California. It was important to get emigrants there by the best routes. Frémont was instructed to explore more thoroughly the Great Salt Lake region, the Great Basin, the Sierra Nevada, and the Cascade Range. Part of the explorations planned would be in Mexican territory. There were several disagreements between the United States and Mexico, and a definite prospect of war between them. Furthermore, Frémont's presence might add to the difficulties. Frémont wrote that "the eventualities of war were taken into consideration."

The expedition assembled at Bent's Fort on the Arkansas River in August 1845. Joseph Walker and Kit Carson were guides. Frémont's large, well-equipped party crossed the Rockies and into the Utah region by way of the White River. Crossing the Green River, and pushing up the Duchesne River to the Provo River and down that stream the party arrived in Utah Valley the second week in October.

Frémont and his party spent a couple of days in Utah Valley, then proceeded north to the southern shore of the Great Salt Lake. On the future site of Salt Lake City they spent two weeks (October 13 to 27, 1845). From base camps here, explorations were conducted around the lake and up the streams emptying into it. Frémont noted the temperatures, rains and snow on the mountains, and the plant life. Toward the end of the month he prepared for his most important exploration–a route west from Great Salt Lake to California.

When Frémont's party reached the southwest corner of the Great Salt Lake (near Cedar Mountains), he sent a scouting party

Pilot Peak served as a guide landmark for Frémont in 1845 and overland emigrants in 1846 who made their way across the Great Salt Lake Desert. Springs were found near the base of the mountains.

The springs near Pilot Peak.

Christopher (Kit) Carson led an exciting and varied life as Mountain Man, guide to Frémont, Indian agent, and soldier in the Mexican and Civil wars.

headed by Kit Carson across the salt flats to find water and grass. Far to the west and about sixty miles north, could be seen a high peak—they would steer for that peak in hope of finding water at its base. Carson was to signal with smoke if he found water. Carson and his scouts, with a pack-mule loaded with water and provisions, started out at night to make the crossing. The next afternoon, without the assurance of water, Frémont led the rest of his company out onto the desert and traveled into the night. Before morning, Frémont made his own fire signals to tell Carson where he was. Soon one of Carson's men came into Frémont's camp with the word that at the peak they had found water, grass, and wood. The party pressed on, and that afternoon all were at the base of the peak Frémont named *Pilot Peak*, for it had guided them across the salt flats of the Great Salt Lake Desert. Frémont was at Pilot Peak October 30 and 31. He had made a track across the desert that was to be important to the emigrants of the next year 1846.

Shortly after this, Frémont divided his party into two groups in order to survive better the ordeals of the desert and also to learn more about the Great Basin they were now crossing. He appointed Lieutenant Theodore H. Talbot to command one group, guided by Joseph Walker. Frémont led the other part of his company, exploring a region of central Nevada previously unexplored by white man. Frémont arrived at Sutter's Fort in northern California December 9, 1845.

4. IN 1846 SEVERAL OVERLAND COMPANIES FOLLOWED THE HASTINGS CUTOFF THROUGH UTAH

During the years John C. Frémont was on his explorations, emigration continued along the Oregon Trail to the Pacific Northwest. The *Report* of Frémont stimulated American interest also in California, and many Americans were anxious to settle there.

The big problem to California-bound emigrants was the great distance. Emigrants followed the Oregon Trail to near Fort Bridger. From there the Oregon Trail led northwest along the Bear to Soda Springs, then on to Fort Hall. The California Trail left the Oregon Trail west of Fort Hall and went southwest to the Humboldt River, then fol-

lowed that stream to western Nevada, and continued over the Sierra Nevada into California.

Mountain Men knew ways through the mountains. **The important thing was to get a wagon route through the mountains.**

By 1845-46 people were ready to consider the idea of a shortcut to California if someone could chart the route for them. Someone did. And people took the cutoff. That cutoff went through Utah. Some emigrants made it with success. Others made it, but not without tragedy. Some did not make it at all. That is the story of the emigration of 1846. That year wagon trails were made into Salt Lake Valley, one of which was followed by the Mormon pioneers the next year.

The idea of a cutoff by way of the Great Salt Lake began with Lansford W. Hastings.

Lansford W. Hastings had gone to Oregon in 1842, then to California the next year. He fell in love with the country. He wanted to do big things in California; and for his plans, he needed American people there. He wrote a book encouraging people to go to California. In this book, *Emigrants' Guide to Oregon and California* (1845), he spoke of a time and distance-saving cutoff west from Fort Bridger. Hastings met John C. Frémont at Sutter's Fort, Christmastime 1845, and they talked for four days on the possibility of a shortcut by way of the Great Salt Lake. Hastings had not been over any such route when he wrote his book. Frémont believed such a shortcut was possible, and Hastings agreed.

The next spring, Hastings went east to meet the migration on the Oregon Trail to persuade them to go to California by his proposed *Hastings Cutoff*. He left Sutter's Fort April 11, 1846. With him was J. M. Hudspeth. Soon he picked up James Clyman,

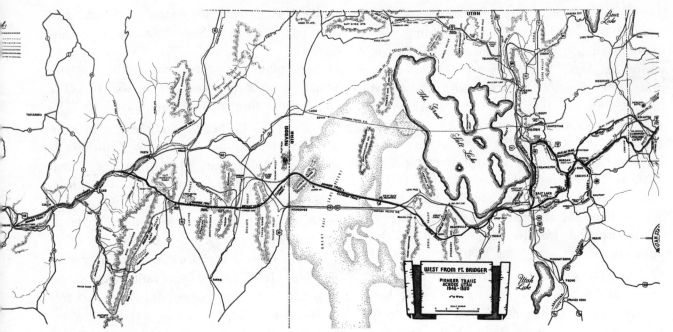

Hastings Cutoff led from Fort Bridger to the Humboldt River by way of Great Salt Lake, eliminating the necessity of following the longer distance of the California Trail by way of Soda Springs.

Mountain Man. Their route took them eastward along the trails already established to the Humboldt River. With difficulty they then picked up traces left by the Frémont men the year before until they reached Pilot Peak. They crossed the salt flats to the south edge of Great Salt Lake, traveled eastward across Salt Lake Valley (June 2), pressed into Parleys Canyon, turned north, crossed Big Mountain, followed East Canyon Creek to the Weber and went on east to Fort Bridger arriving June 7. Early in June, Hastings went east to meet the emigration on the Oregon Trail. Just east of South Pass on July 7 he penned a letter to the emigrants which he sent by an east-bound traveler. Then he went back to Fort Bridger to wait for people to come his way.

Westbound on the overland trail were several emigrant groups who would cross Utah by way of the Hastings Cutoff. In the large emigration of 1846 there were at least *five separate groups* that took the Hastings Cutoff from Fort Bridger through the Great Salt Lake area to the Humboldt River, eliminating the long route to the north. These groups were, in the order they came through Utah, (1) the Edwin Bryant party, (2) the Harlan-Young party, (3) the James Mathers party, (4) the Heinrich Lienhard party, including the Hoppe group and T. H. Jefferson, and (5) the Donner-Reed party. Let us follow each of these groups through.

The Edwin Bryant party was made up of Edwin Bryant, a Kentucky newspaper editor, and several friends bound for California. They left the Missouri frontier early in May and reached Fort Bridger the evening of July 16. Here they remained a couple of days talking to Hastings and Hudspeth. Bryant and his friends decided to sell their wagons, trade for mules and horses and ride over the Hastings Cutoff for California. The party of nine, accompanied by "Hudspeth and three young men from the emigrant parties," set out on the new route, on horseback, July 20. They went south and west from Fort Bridger crossing the Big Muddy Creek and the Bear River, to Yellow Creek and along that stream, over the divide into Echo Canyon, down Echo Canyon to the Weber River, then down the Weber, past Devil's Gate, to Salt Lake Valley. Along the last five miles of its course through the Wasatch Mountains, the Weber River cuts a deep and narrow defile. The river bottom was filled with boulders over which the great stream tumbled and splashed. On July 26 the Bryant party went through this canyon. Bryant wrote: "Entering between the walls of the mountains forming the canon, after laborious exertions for several hours, we passed through it without any serious accident. The canon is four or five miles through, and we were compelled, as heretofore, to climb along the side of the precipitous mountains, frequently passing under, and sometimes scaling, immense overhanging masses and projections of rock."

From the mouth of Weber Canyon the Bryant party turned south along the base of the mountains. They enjoyed very much the "dozen salmon-trout, from eight to eighteen inches in length; and the longest weighing four or five pounds." They crossed the Jordan River and made their way west around the south end of Great Salt Lake, crossed the Stansbury Mountains and Skull Valley, proceeded west across the salt flats to Pilot Peak, and southwest eventually reaching the Humboldt. They got through to California in fairly good order. Their contribution was that *they had established a route from Fort Bridger into Salt Lake Valley*. On other parts of their journey they followed the trails others had made before them.

The Harlan-Young group was second through the Utah mountains westbound for California. George Harlan was from Michigan. When Hastings' *Guide* came to him, he read

Devils Gate, Weber Canyon. It was the experience of taking wagons down the Weber River through such narrows as these that led Hastings to recommend that the Donner Party take another route through the Wasatch Mountains.

it and decided to go to California. He arrived at Westport (Kansas City), Missouri, in October 1845 and remained there through the winter preparing a company for the spring trek. At Westport he met others who joined him. There were Samuel C. Young, his wife and their children with families. There was the Peter L. Wimmer family who were said to be Mormons. The Harlan-Young group joined in the big migration of 1846, arriving at Fort Bridger July 16, the same day Edwin Bryant and his friends arrived. The Harlan-Young men talked with Hastings and Hudspeth and decided to follow the Hastings Cutoff. Hastings agreed to guide their forty wagons through the mountains to California.

The Harlan-Young group left Fort Bridger July 20. They made good time through the first part of their journey, passing quickly into Echo Canyon, and down the Weber. They made the rough passage through Weber Canyon. Their wagons must have suffered considerably, but they made it, to go on into Salt Lake Valley, following the general route taken a few days before them by the Bryant party on horseback.

The Harlan-Young party had such difficulties in the canyon of the Weber River that Hastings felt an obligation to warn members of the wagon trains that were following.

James Mathers arrived at Fort Bridger July 21, and was soon joined by the rest of his company. Mathers decided to take the Hastings Cutoff and left on that route July 25, following the trail of the Harlan-Young party just five days ahead at outset. His party reached the Weber River July 29, but did not emerge from the canyon of the Weber River until August 5. Two days later the Mathers company was at the south edge of Great Salt Lake, having caught up with the Harlan-Young party with whom they traveled on to California.

The Heinrich Lienhard party consisted of several small groups. There were the "five German boys"—Lienhard and four Swiss and German companions who had recently come to America and were caught up in the "fever" for California. Heinrich Lienhard's journal tells much about the groups between the Bryant and the Donner parties. The German boys had a wagon, three span of young oxen, and two young cows. Traveling close by were the three wagons of Samuel Kyburz and family. Then there were Jacob D. Hoppe and his family in two wagons. At Fort Bridger several other wagons joined the party. We will refer to all these groups as the Lienhard party. In the group was T. H. Jefferson who drew a remarkable map of the region and the routes taken by the Hastings Cutoff emigrants.

On July 26 the Lienhard party set out on the Hastings Cutoff, following the line of march of those just days ahead. Hastings himself came back from guiding the Harlan-

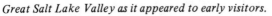

Great Salt Lake Valley as it appeared to early visitors.

Young party to help these later wagons through by telling the leaders the best routes to take. They shortened the trail in one place only, otherwise following the route of others before them. In Morgan Valley, August 3, Hastings met the Lienhard company and warned them of the canyon of the Weber. Hastings had advised the first companies to turn south here for an easier route into Salt Lake Valley, but they had gone on in spite of his advice. By good luck they had gotten through. The Lienhard group decided to keep with the Weber. On August 5 and 6 the groups got through the narrows of Weber Canyon and the next day reached the shores of the Great Salt Lake. The group went south along the base of the mountains, crossed the Jordan River, in which they bathed "and relished it," and went on to the south edge of the lake where they had the unique experience of bathing in salt water. The Lienhard group followed the trail of others across the salt flats to Pilot Peak and beyond to the Humboldt. This was the only group of the year to lose neither wagon nor animal in the crossing.

AN 1846 IMPRESSION OF SALT LAKE VALLEY

From Heinrich Lienhard's journal:

On the 7th [August] we reached the flat shore of the magnificent Salt Lake, the waters of which were clear as crystal, but as salty as the strongest salt brine. ...The land extends from the mountains down to the lake in a splendid inclined plane broken only by the fresh water running down from ever-flowing springs above. The soil is rich, deep black sand composition doubtless capable of producing good crops. The clear, sky-blue surface of the lake, the warm sunny air, the nearby high mountains, with the beautiful country at their foot, through which we on a fine road were passing, made on my spirits an extraordinarily charming impression. The whole day long I felt like singing and whistling; had there been a single family of white men to be found living here, I believe that I would have remained. Oh, how unfortunate that this beautiful country was uninhabited! ...

The Donner-Reed party followed the Lienhard party and was the last of the 1846 emigration to use the Hastings Cutoff. The Donner-Reed party is one of the best known of all overland emigrant parties, mainly because of the tragedy that came to them in the Sierra Nevada. They arrived at the heights of those mountains just a few days after a heavy storm sealed off the passes and forced them to remain in the mountains through a long and cold, starving winter. A few days would have made the difference between life and death to many of them. Had they started earlier, had they not lost a few days here or there along the way, had they not stopped to build a road in the Wasatch Mountains, had they been better organized and unified, had they cooperated more—they would have escaped their tragic fate. Their most significant delay was in the Wasatch Mountains—a delay that cost many of them their lives, but which gave considerable advantage to the Mormon pioneers who followed their exact route just eleven months later.

The Donner-Reed party was made up at first of the families of James F. Reed, and George and Jacob Donner, all of Springfield, Illinois. Many others joined them, until they were nearly two hundred strong. They left Independence, Missouri, late in the season of 1846 and followed the usual route to South Pass and on toward Fort Bridger. On the Little Sandy, July 19, before reaching Fort Bridger the large party divided into two groups. The larger decided for "the longest way round" by way of Fort Hall. The remaining group decided for the Hastings Cutoff. In this latter group were eighty-seven men, women, and children, with twenty-three wagons. After the separation the smaller group elected George Donner captain, so they were called the Donner company.

They reached Fort Bridger July 27. Here

the party rested several days to strengthen their cattle for the trek ahead. On July 31 the Donner company left Fort Bridger on the cutoff, eleven days after Hastings had led the Harlan-Young company out, and five days after the Lienhard company had left. They followed the route of the previous wagons (except the Lienhard shortcut in Wyoming) to Echo Canyon, down Echo Canyon to the head of Weber Canyon. Here (August 6) they found a letter from Hastings sticking in the top of a sage brush. He stated that if they would send a messenger after him he would return and pilot them through a route much shorter and better than Weber Canyon. The company sent messengers after Hastings, and camped August 7, 8, 9, and 10 near present Henefer waiting for the pilot. The messengers were Reed, McCutcheon, and Stanton. Reed and companions caught up with Hastings at Black Rock on the south end of Great Salt Lake. Hastings took Reed up Emigration Canyon to Big Mountain "where we could overlook a portion of the country that lay be-

tween us and the head of the canyon, where the Donner Party were camped." Hastings then showed Reed the route by which he could pilot his company south from the Weber to this point. They parted, and Reed went north by the route his party must come. Reed arrived back in camp the night of August 10. The company voted to follow Reed and build a road to Salt Lake Valley rather than follow the Weber River through the canyon.

The Donner-Reed party cut timber and thicket to make a road from the Weber south to Big Mountain. Twelve days were taken up (August 11-22) in cutting and opening a road along Dixie Hollow, up part of East Canyon Creek to Big Mountain. At the west foot of Big Mountain they crossed "Small Mountain" (now Little Mountain) into Emigration Canyon and cut a road on into the valley.

August 23 the Donner Company camped at the Jordan River. The next day they reached the Oquirrh Mountains. They had taken eighteen days from first reaching the

Emigrants often lost wagons and goods in the salt flats of the Great Salt Lake Desert.

Weber River. They estimated they had made only thirty miles, but it was more like forty. Even so, they had lost a week or more cutting a road through thicket, pine, and aspen, at great labor and exertion. Building this road was one of the most notable achievements of any emigrant train that year. But it cost them time—most precious at this moment. That road was to save the Mormons some work the following year and give them that equally precious time for crops.

The trek of the Donner party from the shores of the Great Salt Lake was marked by quarrels, deaths, and delays. In crossing the salt flats, oxen were lost so wagons had to be abandoned, and goods cached never to be seen again. After reaching Pilot Peak the company lost valuable time by taking the long way around the Ruby Mountains instead of going around their northern end, the shortest route to the Humboldt. There were quarrels. Fears of never getting to California alive haunted them; fears of starvation and thirst drove them to distraction. A man savagely attacked Mrs. Reed, and was killed by Mr. Reed. For this murder Mr. Reed was expelled from the company and his family forced to continue without his help. Reed went ahead to send back relief. The party also sent men ahead to solicit help, and in time some help came, but it was too little to last long enough.

Finally the divided and worn party reached the Sierra Nevada, arriving at Truckee (now Donner) Lake the end of October. The snows had begun a couple of days before, and a long season of stormy weather was upon the mountains. Attempts were made to cross the mountains by wagon without success, then by foot without success. The Donner party dug in for a winter in the tops of the Sierra Nevada. Storms continued, and starvation set in. Death followed. Some resorted to cannibalism. Relief attempts were made from California through the winter. Finally, after heavy loss of life, the last were brought out. Of the eighty-seven persons who started from Fort Bridger on the Hastings Cutoff only forty-eight lived to get through to California. Their story is one of indescribable hardships. It is a story of great heroism and courage on the part of some, and of the worst human characteristics on the part of others.

Many lessons were taught by the Donner party to future emigrants. Among the lessons taught were: (1) start early, there is a "too late" date; (2) do not delay, keep moving—long rest stops can cost you your lives; (3) be united, quarreling and bickering can be just as destructive to good progress on the route as savage Indians, starvation, or storms; (4) do not be afraid to travel light, to save goods at the expense of one's life will never get you through (some in the Donner party were jealous of their expensive outfits and furnishings); (5) know the route or have someone along who does know it well; (6) know how to live in the wilderness or have someone along who does.

5. MILES GOODYEAR
ESTABLISHED A TRADING POST
ON THE WEBER RIVER IN 1846

At Fort Bridger the same time as the Donner party was Mountain Man *Miles Goodyear* and his English partner Mr. Wills or Welles. These two men planned to leave the fort within a few days "to settle at some favorable point on the Salt Lake, which in a short time will be a fine place for emigrants to recruit their teams, by exchanging broken down oxen for good teams."

Miles Goodyear had come to the mountains to engage in the fur trade in 1836. He traded at Fort Hall, Fort Uintah, and Fort

Miles Goodyear built this cabin on the Weber River west of Ogden in the fall of 1846. There he hoped to establish Fort Buenaventura, but the Mormons bought him out in 1847.

Bridger. He had married "a beautiful Indian woman," a Ute, and had two children by her. Watching the heavy emigration on the cutoff the summer of 1846, Goodyear decided it was time to set out for himself and establish a trading post to help that emigration and make himself a living.

In early August, Goodyear and his partner went to Salt Lake Valley and set up a trading post on the Weber River at the present site of Ogden. This site had been used by the Mountain Men since 1825. Goodyear called his post *Fort Buenaventura*. (The name Buenaventura had been given by some mapmakers to a mythical river that supposedly drained or connected Great Salt Lake to the Pacific Ocean.) Here Goodyear built a cabin, fenced a piece of land and began a garden. He had sheep and cattle, too. He did not remain in the cabin during the winter of 1846-47, but his English partner did. Goodyear went to California with a pack of furs, to return the next spring with horses to sell to the overland emigrants.

6. THE BOUNDARIES OF THE UNITED STATES WERE EXPANDED IN THE 1840s

Besides the migrations into California,

settlers continued to push into the Oregon country. As a result the United States tried to end joint occupation and settle the boundary question in the Oregon country in favor of American citizens now living there. In 1846 the Webster-Ashburton Treaty established the present boundary between the United States and Canada in the Oregon country.

Americans moved into Texas in the 1820s and 1830s. By 1835 Americans in Texas revolted against Mexican rule, declared their independence, and set up the Republic of Texas. In time these Americans wished to have Texas become part of the Union. In 1845, by a joint resolution of Congress, the Republic of Texas was annexed to the United States as the state of Texas. Mexico was not pleased with these actions by Americans in her northern provinces. The annexation of Texas, together with boundary disputes and other issues, led to war between the two nations (May 13, 1846 to February 2, 1848). The Mexican War was ended by the Treaty of Guadalupe Hidalgo. By that treaty the United States received most of the American Southwest. In 1835 the United States purchased lands south of the Gila River from Mexico to establish the mainland boundaries of the United States as we have them today.

UNIT FOUR
MORMON PIONEERS PLANT CIVILIZATION IN UTAH

Before 1847 Utah had been crossed and recrossed by Indians, explorers, trappers, traders, and overland emigrants. But there had been no attempt at permanent settlement. The westward movement was taking people across the plains and the mountains to the West Coast. If Utah had followed the usual patterns of American occupation of the West, she would have waited many years before permanent settlement took place. As it was, the region was settled early by a large group of people of one religious faith who sought a place they thought no one else wanted, a place where they could establish their own society as they thought best. These were the Mormons, members of the Church of Jesus Christ of Latter-day Saints.

The transplanting of civilization in the heart of the Mountain West was a notable achievement by the Mormon pioneers. It required great courage, excellent leadership and planning, and devoted followers. The Mormons came to their task well prepared by

their experiences in the East. Not only was the initial migration of 1847 a success, but each year thereafter until 1869 Mormon emigrant trains made their way across the plains to Utah. During the first years there may have been doubts as to the possibility of surviving in these valleys, but soon the dangers were past and settlement spread throughout the area. By the 1860s the Mormons had extended settlements through much of Utah and formed their society on a firm base.

The Mormons were not the only people, however, to help build Utah. Other people came to Utah from the beginning. However, since the Mormons made up the major portion of the population in those first decades, the credit should go to them for the initial planting of life and civilization in Utah. In Unit Five we will study the contributions of other people who came a little later and in fewer numbers, but whose contributions were important, nonetheless.

C. C. A. Christensen came to Utah with the handcarts of 1857, sketching en route. In 1869 he began to paint significant scenes in the history of the Mormon church, including his own experiences. He sewed his canvases together, rolled them on a long pole, placed them in his wagon, and went from village to village giving illustrated lectures on Mormon church history.

Mormons arriving at Commerce, Illinois, where they established the city of Nauvoo.

THE MORMONS COME TO UTAH

While other people were passing over Utah for the more attractive lands of California and Oregon, the Mormons settled the Utah region because they believed no one else wanted it, thus allowing them to establish their own society and their own religious life as they thought best.

The Mormon settlers gave Utah much of her unique history, set the patterns for her villages and cities, and determined much of the way of life of her people, even to the present time.

The Mormons were well prepared for their role as settlers of the West. They had experience in moving large numbers of people. They had built cities and governed themselves. They had a strong leadership and were united in their purposes.

Theirs is a story of personal sacrifice, of great physical effort against severe odds, of collective group effort in building successful communities, and of following their ideals with a dedication and a practical common sense. It took much daring to move thousands of people into the distant American West and risk survival in a relatively unknown land. It took vision and practical know-how to establish cities and provide for the necessities of life from the surroundings. The qualities necessary to do all this were developed among the Mormons as a group in their experiences before 1846.

IN THIS CHAPTER WE WILL LEARN

1. Utah was settled by the Mormon people for religious purposes.

2. Mormon experiences in the East helped prepare them for pioneering in the West.

3. The Mormon migration to Utah was by land and by sea.

Joseph Smith, Jr., as founder and prophet of the Church of Jesus Christ of Latter-day Saints, had great influence on the history of Utah. Many of his ideas and practices found expression in the thought and institutions of the people of Utah.

1. UTAH WAS SETTLED BY THE MORMON PEOPLE FOR RELIGIOUS PURPOSES

Settlement for religious purposes was in the American tradition. The Pilgrims and the Puritans came to America to practice their religion as they saw fit. Protestants and Catholics alike founded colonies on religious principles. Religious freedom and tolerance are part of the American ideal, although many Americans then and now are not as tolerant as they should be.

The Mormons were not the only people to come to Utah for religious purposes. Jews, Catholics, and Protestants also came, some for distinctly religious purposes. We will study these groups in a later chapter. We will try to understand the ideas and purposes of each group. In historical studies such as this, we are not concerned with whether the religious ideas of any group are true or false. Our interest is to try to understand the influence of those ideas on the lives of men and on history.

The Mormon religion. On April 6, 1830, under the direction of Joseph Smith, Jr., the Mormon church was organized. First it was called the Church of Christ, then the Church of the Latter-day Saints, then the Church of Jesus Christ of Latter-day Saints. The Mormons were so called for their belief in the *Book of Mormon*. The Mormons held most of their religious beliefs in common with other Christian faiths, but differed in some points important to our study. They claimed their leader was a prophet of God who received the word of God by direct revelation, that they were to restore the true Christian faith and build a real Kingdom of God on earth. Believers were expected to break off ties, abandon old associations and move to "Zion," or a gathering place with all other Mormons where they could establish their religion fully. The villages of Zion would form the basis for the Kingdom of God. The establishment of the Kingdom of God, in preparation for the Second Coming of Christ, was a dominant purpose of the Mormons in the nineteenth century. All the affairs of life would conform to the church's ideal. Mormonism concerned itself with religious, social, economic, and political matters. Mormons believed they had received the authority and power of God, the priesthood, for the benefit of mankind. They must preach their religion to the world. Missionaries went from friend to friend, and relative to relative, spreading the Mormon faith in the United States.

2. MORMON EXPERIENCES IN THE EAST HELPED PREPARE THEM FOR PIONEERING IN THE WEST

The urge to a western Zion was to lead the Mormons to settle time after time on the westward frontier. At each gathering place they built for permanence. As the first converts were made, a gathering place was designated at Kirtland, Ohio, the center of one of the first scenes of missionary success.

Kirtland, Ohio, was the center of Mormon activities from 1831 to 1838. The village grew with Mormon immigration and became a thriving, prosperous town. In March 1836 the first Mormon temple was dedicated there. Here the foundations of Mormon religious beliefs and church organization were given to the people. At the head of the church was the First Presidency with Joseph Smith and two counselors. A Quorum of Twelve Apos-

At Kirtland, Ohio, their first gathering place, the Mormons built a city and erected their first temple.

tles was chosen from proven missionaries and defenders of the prophet. Seventy elders, named the Seventies, were chosen to preach. In large communities, such as Kirtland, there was a stake president with two counselors and a High Council of twelve members to rule the church there. There was a presiding bishop over the church who had special concern with the economic affairs of the church and the economic welfare of the members.

Independence, Jackson County, Missouri, was a gathering place of the Mormons from 1831 until 1833 when the original settlers, jealous and fearful of the increasing number of Mormons, drove about twelve hundred Mormons from their lands and burned their homes, store, destroyed their press and other property. The Mormons fled north across the Missouri River into *Clay County* where they were well received and settled in peace until 1836 when they decided to avoid further conflicts with the older settlers and moved north into what became Caldwell County. The Mormons laid out their farms on the Missouri prairie and built a new village, *Far West*, where they enjoyed peace for a couple of years. Plans were made for a temple. In

1838 a new settlement farther north was laid out in Daviess County called *Adam-ondi-Ahman*. But increasing conflicts mounted between the Mormons and their neighbors, and in October 1838 Governor Boggs ordered the Mormons to leave the state or be killed. On Crooked River, two Mormons were killed on October 25. On October 30, a mob came upon the Mormon settlement of *Haun's Mill* and killed seventeen men and boys. Through the fall and winter of 1838-39 the Mormons prepared to leave Missouri. By the summer of 1839 most were out of the state. About twelve to fifteen thousand Mormons were expelled from Missouri and settled on the Illinois side of the Mississippi River, above Keokuk.

Some of the difficulty in Missouri was based on the fact that Mormons bought up good lands for their fellow Mormons which frustrated Missourians who had planned to buy those lands. In elections the Mormons voted as one, and the large Mormon vote threatened political control by the Missourians. Most Mormons were Northerners and were opposed to slavery and said so, and this challenged the Missourians who were slave

Nauvoo, Illinois, "the city beautiful" of the Mormons was built on a big bend of the Mississippi River. On the hill overlooking the city rose their temple. A contemporary sketch.

holders. Many Mormons sounded self-righteous, and this irritated the Missourians. Joseph Smith was jailed the winter of 1838-39, and it fell to Brigham Young, one of the twelve apostles, to direct the evacuation of all the Mormons from Missouri, a good experience for him for the future.

Nauvoo, Illinois, was the largest and the last of the cities built by the Mormons in the East. From Missouri they had fled to Keokuk, and then they found a site north on the swampy shores of a big bend in the Mississippi River. On the broad flat area near the river, a town was laid out with straight streets running at right angles, according to the plan of Joseph Smith for the City of Zion. The population soon swelled with the Missouri exiles, Mormons gathering from the East, and new converts from Britain. The city was soon marked by hundreds of cabins, some frame houses, and a few homes of brick and stone. Rising on the hill overlooking the city were the white walls of the temple, not completed until 1845-46. But Mormon settlements spread beyond Nauvoo, into the surrounding countryside in Illinois and across the Mississippi River into Lee County, Iowa. By 1845-46 there were possibly forty to forty-five thousand Mormons in the general area. Nauvoo was the largest city in Illinois at the time.

In Illinois the Mormons were able to obtain from the legislature a liberal charter for their city, Nauvoo. The charter gave the Mormons great political power and enabled them to govern themselves for the most part, with their own militia, city council, courts, and police.

From Nauvoo missionaries were sent to all parts of the world. From eastern United States and from England, converts gathered to Nauvoo. Joseph Smith led his people in religious affairs, expanding church organization, elaborating church doctrine.

In time, troubles developed between the Mormons and their Illinois neighbors. The Illinois people came to fear the political and military power of the Mormons besides objecting to some of their religious practices. When the Mormons came to Illinois from Missouri, they found the Whig party and the Democratic party about evenly divided. The votes of the Mormons for Whig candidates gave Whigs a victory, and they rewarded the Mormons with the Nauvoo Charter. This angered the Democrats. In time the Mormons decided to vote for the Democrats which led the Democrats to win. This angered the Whigs. In 1844 Joseph Smith declared himself a candidate for president of the United States on his own party ticket. This angered both the Whigs and the Democrats. Newspapers, owned and operated by political parties in those days, stirred the people against the Mormons. Antagonisms reached a pitch in 1844 when Joseph Smith was running for president of the United States, and the Nauvoo Legion, his militia, was active.

Troubles came to Joseph Smith, not only from without, but more dangerously from within the church. On June 7 a few members of the church who now considered Joseph Smith a fallen prophet because of some new doctrines and practices he had started, printed an opposition newspaper called *Nauvoo Expositor*. Three days later the press of the paper was destroyed by order of the Nauvoo City Council (Joseph Smith was mayor). This attack on the freedom of the press was the last straw to the non-Mormons. Mob violence threatened the Mormons. Joseph Smith was imprisoned at Carthage, the county seat, awaiting trial. On June 27, the jail was attacked by a mob, and Joseph Smith and his brother Hyrum were killed.

To Brigham Young fell the responsibility of leading his exiled people from Nauvoo to a new home in the West.

Leadership of the Mormon church fell to the twelve apostles with *Brigham Young* as their head. (While others believed that Brigham Young was not the rightful leader, no other strong leaders emerged at this time, and it was he who led the majority of the Mormons to safety and built for them their place in history.)

These experiences helped prepare the Mormons for their trek West. By 1846 the Mormons had built cities, governed themselves, established an emigration system to bring converts from Europe to America, developed a strong group of efficient leaders, given those leaders experience in moving masses of people long distances, and developed a strong spirit of unity among themselves.

A migration is forced upon the Mormons. After the death of Joseph Smith, there was comparative peace between the Mormons and their neighbors until September 1845 when violence again broke out. To begin with, there were burnings of farms and houses in the outlying Mormon settlements. Serious disturbances followed. The state militia was called out. The Mormons were forced to promise that they would leave Nauvoo the next spring. The winter of 1845-46 was spent preparing wagons and belongings for the trek to find a new home.

The first problem the exiled Mormons faced was to find a place for their settlement. They had to find a place where there would be land, water, and timber in sufficient quantity for a large population—at that time and in years to come. Because of their past experiences they wanted to be the first settlers in a region, and they wanted a place that no one else would want so they could have it to themselves. Yet they would have to be able to establish communications with the "outside world" to get their missionaries out and their convert-immigrants in, to say nothing of the exchange of essential goods.

The Mormon leaders studied about the West in preparation for the migration. How much did the Mormons know about the West in 1845? They had lived on the frontier of American settlement for fifteen years. At Independence, Missouri, they were at the outfitting point for the Santa Fé Trail, so they knew or could have known about that trade into the Southwest. Their church newspapers at Independence and Nauvoo carried news items and reports from Mountain Men and explorers. They knew more about the West, in a general way, than most Americans knew at the time. But they made special studies, too. They read Frémont's *Report* and inserted excerpts in the columns of the *Nauvoo Neighbor*. Notices also appeared announcing Hastings' *Emigrants' Guide* which told of the suggested shortcut by way of the Great Salt Lake. In 1842 Joseph Smith had prophesied that the Mormons would go to the Rocky Mountains. The leaders thereafter were interested in the West. They planned exploring expeditions to the Rocky Mountain region, but these did not go. In 1845 the twelve apostles read in their council meetings Frémont's *Report* (telling of his visit to the Great Salt Lake, Bear River Valley, the Sevier River country, Utah Valley, and the valley of the Great Salt Lake). They read about irrigation methods. Various possible places of future settlement are mentioned in their records: "Rocky Mountains," "Vancouver," "California," "the Great Salt Lake." They studied before they moved. But they would not decide upon a place until they had seen it.

3. THE MORMON MIGRATION TO UTAH WAS BY LAND AND BY SEA

In 1846 the Mormon population was concentrated in Nauvoo and the surrounding countryside of Hancock County, Illinois, and across the Mississippi River in Lee County, Iowa. As the migration began, there was a general dispersal of the Mormons. Many followed their leaders into Iowa and remained in the migration. Many, however, moved into neighboring states to work and earn enough money before they could move west. Others went to Saint Louis to live. But there were also many Latter-day Saints living in congregations in the East who had not yet gathered. Most of these people adopted a policy of "wait and see." There were some, however, who wanted to join the migration at once.

They were the first to get into the American West, and they did so by leaving from New York City and going by ship to the Pacific Coast.

The ship *Brooklyn* carried Mormons from New York City to San Francisco Bay in 1846. In September 1845 Brigham Young wrote Orson Pratt and *Samuel Brannan* in New York City suggesting that they arrange to take the church's newspaper press and a large company of emigrants to the bay of San Francisco in California. He suggested that since the Mormon church would be moving to the Pacific Coast, the Mormons on the east coast could get there more easily by water than by the overland route. Passengers were solicited. Samuel Brannan was placed in charge of the company, and the ship *Brooklyn* was chartered. On February 4, 1846, the *Brooklyn* sailed from New York harbor with 70 men, 68 women, and 100 children. The ship sailed into the Atlantic, south around the Horn and up the west coast of South America. The first stop was at the Juan Fernandez Islands (where Daniel Defoe placed his imaginary character Robinson Crusoe). Here the ship's passengers refreshed themselves with bathing and washing their clothes, while the ship was restocked with water, food, and wood. The *Brooklyn* then sailed to the Sandwich (Hawaiian) Islands where the passengers were again refreshed before proceeding on their voyage. They arrived at San Francisco Bay and landed at the little Mexican village of Yerba Buena (the future site of San Francisco) the last of July 1846.

When the *Brooklyn* landed, it was learned that the United States and Mexico were at war and that California had been taken by American forces. The *Brooklyn* passengers, strangely enough, outnumbered the inhabitants of Yerba Buena, and that village became a Mormon settlement. The men found various occupations. Some cut timber to pay for their passage. Others began farming. In time a Mormon farming community named Port Hope was established on the Stanislaus and the San Joaquin rivers. Samuel Brannan remained with the Mormons in California until the spring of 1847 when he proceeded east over the California Trail to meet the Pioneer Company moving overland.

Across Iowa. The exodus of the Mormons from Nauvoo began February 4, 1846, the same day the ship *Brooklyn* sailed from New York harbor. Brigham Young and others of the apostles took the lead. Others followed soon after. It took until September for all the Mormons to evacuate Nauvoo, leaving it for local citizens to step in and occupy. It was winter when the migration began. The first wagons crossed the Mississippi River on ice. Later, others would be ferried across. Traveling across Iowa was most difficult. The Mormons had to blaze a new road. The only significant road building done by the Mormons on their entire trek was across Iowa. Winter rains turned the rich soil into mud. Swollen streams caused delays. Through timbered country, trees had to be cut to make roadways. It all added up to a great deal of difficulty and slow travel.

The Mormon Battalion, on its march to California, is pictured here as it reached the Gila River after a fifty-two-hour, ninety-mile forced dry march.

On their way across Iowa, Mormons went to work for the few settlers in the region. Mormons built roads, fences and bridges, dug wells, and helped build houses. In exchange for these services they received goods they badly needed.

At Garden Grove and Mount Pisgah the Mormons built houses, fences and bridges, cleared land, plowed and planted. The pioneers then went on, knowing that there would be many to follow who would appreciate the crops that could be harvested.

The migration across Iowa swelled as the Mormons left Nauvoo. During these winter and spring months there were 15,000 Mormons, 3,000 wagons, 30,000 head of cattle, a great number of mules and horses, and immense flocks of sheep on their way across Iowa.

By June 14, the Pioneer Company led by Brigham Young had reached the Missouri River.

Before leaving Nauvoo, Brigham Young asked many people for assistance for their overland trek. He wrote to Queen Victoria of England asking in behalf of her subjects now in America if they could settle on Vancouver Island. He wrote governors of the states asking for refuge. He sought financial aid from the federal government as well, proposing that the government hire Mormons to build forts on the overland trail. Thus the Mormons could work their way west and be paid for it. All but one of Young's attempts failed. He appointed Jesse C. Little to go to Washington and solicit aid for the Mormon migration. Little's efforts resulted in the call of the Mormon Battalion.

The Mormon Battalion marched from Iowa to California during the War with Mexico. The call of the Mormon Battalion came as a result of Brigham Young's request for government aid in the overland trek of the Mormons. In January 1846 he sent Jesse C. Little to Washington to seek aid for the Mormon migration. When Little arrived in Washington, war had been declared on Mexico, and President Polk saw the possibility of the government and the Mormons being served in one movement. He offered to give them aid in the form of a special battalion of soldiers to serve in the Mexican War. The soldiers would be given arms and equipment (to be retained upon discharge) and pay for military duty. Little accepted, and the orders were issued. Captain James Allen was sent to the Iowa camps of the Mormons to accept the services of those who would volunteer. He appeared at Mount Pisgah June 26. By July 16 the companies of the Mormon Battalion were recruited and organized. In the battalion were 549 persons, including officers, privates, and servants. Families of several of the officers and their men accompanied the battalion on the march.

The route of the march of the Mormon Battalion took the soldiers from the Mormon camps in western Iowa to Fort Leavenworth for two weeks where they received arms and equipment. On August 13 and 14 the companies started west along the Santa Fé Trail, arriving in Santa Fé in October. Three groups of sick left the battalion and wintered at Pueblo, in present Colorado. The next year they joined the Mormon migration on the overland trail. The battalion left Santa Fé (October 19) and marched south to the Gila River and followed that stream west. The

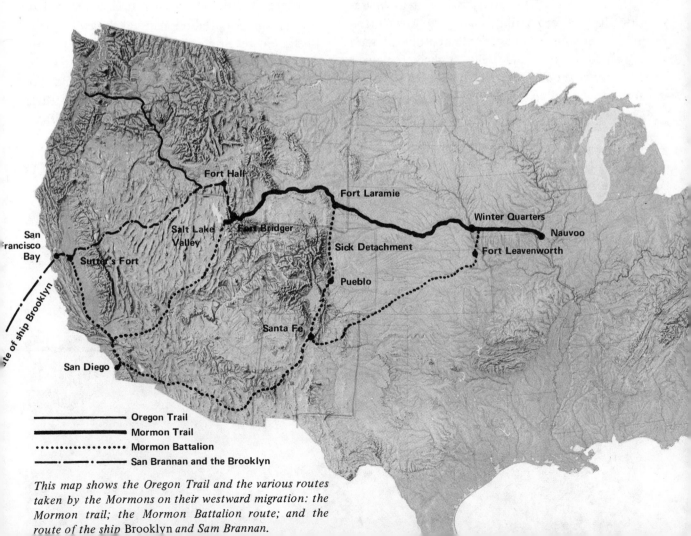

This map shows the Oregon Trail and the various routes taken by the Mormons on their westward migration: the Mormon trail; the Mormon Battalion route; and the route of the ship Brooklyn *and Sam Brannan.*

troops crossed the Colorado River, and southern California to arrive at the Mission San Luis Rey (January 27). In Southern California the battalion served at San Diego and built a fort near Los Angeles.

After the battalion disbanded, July 16, 1847, its members were to be found throughout much of the West. Some reenlisted and served near San Diego. Some went to northern California where they joined the *Brooklyn* people. Some battalion men went east in 1847 to join their families. Others remained in California for a time. Some worked for James W. Marshall near Sutter's Fort, building a mill race. Here some were working on January 24, 1848 when Marshall discovered gold. This discovery set off a race from the United States and many parts of the world for the California gold fields. It caused a great migration to California immediately following the 1848 announcement. Some battalion men remained in the gold fields. Others remained in southern California. It took many months for the battalion men to get back to their families.

The march of the Mormon Battalion helped the Mormon migration westward. Mormon soldiers got west and were paid for going. Although some died on the way, none lost their lives as a result of encounters with the enemy. They did not even see the enemy. The pay they received went to help their families and the church. Members of the Mormon Battalion watched for good places to colonize. Some of them later settled on the Gila River in Arizona. Battalion members also helped explore trails to Utah, giving the church leaders more information about the West.

At Winter Quarters. When the first pioneer company reached the Missouri River, it was decided to go no farther west that season but to spend the winter of 1846-47 in winter quarters. The season was late, and the call of the Mormon Battalion had taken away many of the men. Brigham Young obtained permission from the Omaha Indians to camp on their lands west of the Missouri, and most of the Mormons crossed over the Missouri River and established themselves in *Winter Quarters*.

On the banks of the Missouri River the Mormons made their Winter Quarters, 1846-47.

Here on the Missouri bottom land (soon called "Misery bottoms") the gathering Mormons built a temporary settlement. By December there were 548 log houses and 83 sod houses, inhabited by 3,483 people. By spring there were a thousand dwellings. The winter of 1846-47 was very hard on the destitute Mormons. Lacking in food, clothing, shelter, and proper sanitary conditions, many died.

During the winter, plans were laid for the trek to begin in the spring. An advance party, called the *Pioneer Company*, would go west, explore, and determine a site for future settlement. Then the migration could follow rapidly. During the fall of 1846 Father Pierre-Jean De Smet, Catholic missionary among the Indians of the Oregon country and Great Plains, visited the Mormon leaders. "They asked a thousand questions about the regions I had explored," he wrote. They spoke of the basin of the Great Salt Lake, which "pleased them greatly from the account I gave of it." The Mormon leaders had read John C. Frémont's *Report*, and they had his map of his 1843-44 trip. They seemed to favor the region of the Great Salt Lake though other places were still being considered. The Mormon leaders kept studying and asking questions about the Mountain West.

The Pioneer Company established a route and found a permanent settling place for the Mormons. Early in April 1847, the Pioneer Company was organized, and by April 16 it was on its way. It consisted of 143 men and boys, 3 women, and 2 children. Among the men were 3 Negroes. The women were wives of Brigham Young, Lorenzo Young, and Heber C. Kimball. The company traveled in 72 wagons, with 93 horses, 52 mules, 66 oxen, 19 cows, 17 dogs, and some chickens. Scientific instruments were taken along to enable Orson Pratt to make all the necessary

observations of elevation, temperatures, and latitude of camp sites. Maps of the route to Oregon were carried as well as Frémont's 1843 map.

The company was organized into groups of "tens," five tens making a "fifty," and two fifties a "hundred." Captains were set over the two "hundreds," the five "fifties" and the fourteen "tens." Later a military-type government was set up with Brigham Young as lieutenant general and Stephen Markham as colonel, with majors and captains. A couple of days out, April 18, a daily camp routine was established. This organization and daily routine was followed by tens of thousands of emigrating Mormons in the years to come.

The Pioneer Company created the Mormon Trail over the first half of the journey, from Winter Quarters to Fort Laramie. Their route went west until they reached the north bank of the Platte River. They followed that

The Pioneer Company set the pattern for Mormon emigrant companies in crossing the plains. Each night the wagons were drawn in a circle. Samuel Jepperson Utah artist, painted this scene, "Our Coming to Zion," as part of his Remembrances of My Boyhood.

river westward past Grand Island (where the Oregon Trail began to follow the south bank of the Platte River) and along the Platte and then the North Platte to Fort Laramie, which they reached the first of June. On the first of the journey they had a few encounters with Indians, lost two horses by stealing and two by killing. Although some of the prairie on the north side of the Platte had been burned, the Mormons chose to remain on that side. On the other side of the river were emigrants on the Oregon Trail. To avoid quarrels over wood, grass, and water, the Mormons chose to make their own road across the level prairies.

At Fort Laramie the Pioneer Company was joined by a group of Mormons from Mississippi who had traveled directly from their homes to Pueblo where they wintered with the sick detachment of the Mormon Battalion. The Mississippi group had arrived at Fort Laramie two weeks before and now joined the Pioneer Company going west. On June 16, the sick detachment of the Mormon Battalion under Captain James Brown arrived at Fort Laramie and followed the Pioneer Company.

At Fort Bridger the Pioneer Company rested, repaired their wagons, and prepared for the last third of their trek. Here they took the Hastings Cutoff, following the traces of the overland emigrants of 1846.

West from Fort Laramie the Mormons followed the Oregon Trail to Fort Bridger. At Fort Laramie the Pioneer Company crossed over to the south side of the North Platte. Thereafter to Fort Bridger they were on the Oregon Trail. They established a ferry on the North Platte to aid the Mormon migration to follow. From the North Platte they followed the Sweetwater to South Pass then traveled southwest to Fort Bridger, arriving July 7.

THE DAILY ROUTINE OF THE PIONEER COMPANY, 1847

From the journal of William Clayton:

Sunday, [April] 18th.– ... At 5:00 p.m., the officers of the camp met with President Young, and he told the order for traveling and camping hereafter, which was communicated to the companies by the Captains of 10's as follows:

At 5:00 in the morning the bugle is to be sounded as a signal for every man to arise and attend prayers before he leaves his wagon. Then cooking, eating, feeding teams, etc., till seven o'clock, at which time the camp is to move at the sound of the bugle. Each teamster to keep beside his team, with his loaded gun in his hands or in his wagon where he can get it in a moment. The extra men, each to walk opposite his wagon with his loaded gun on his shoulder, and no man to be permitted to leave his wagon unless he obtains permission from his officer. In case of an attack from Indians or hostile appearances, the wagons to travel in double file. The order of encampment to be in a circle with the mouth of the wagon to the outside, and the horses and stock tied inside the circle. At 8:30 p.m. the bugle to be sounded again at which time all to have prayers in their wagons and to retire to rest by nine o'clock. ...

Along the route, the pioneers met people who told them much about the country, the route ahead, and the region around the Great Salt Lake. While they were at South Pass (June 26-28) they had conversations with Mountain Man *Moses (Black) Harris.* Orson Pratt wrote, "We obtained much information from him in relation to the great interior basin of the Salt Lake, the country of our destination. His report, like that of Captain Frémont's, is rather unfavorable to the formation of a colony in this basin, principally on

Joseph Smith, commanding officer, is shown here reviewing the Nauvoo Legion. Painting by C. C. A. Christensen.

Leaving Nauvoo. Painting by C. C. A. Christensen.
The Mormons had agreed to leave in the spring, but they were forced to leave in mid-winter.

account of the scarcity of timber. He said that he had traveled the whole circumference of the lake, and that there was no outlet to it." The afternoon of June 28, the pioneers met *Jim Bridger*, a man they had looked forward to seeing for they knew of his reputation for knowing the Mountain West. Bridger was on his way to Fort Laramie, but he remained overnight in camp with the Mormons and gave them a full description of the route ahead and of the regions around the Great Salt Lake and Utah Lake. Two days later, June 30, the pioneers met *Samuel Brannan*, the man in charge of the *Brooklyn*. He had come east to meet the Pioneer Company and tell them about California. Brannan had followed the California Trail eastward, past the site of the Donner tragedy in the Sierra Nevada, along the Humboldt, then to Fort Hall, and on to Fort Bridger. A couple of days after the pioneers left Fort Bridger, on July 10, they met *Miles Goodyear* who was on his way to meet the overland migration to trade with them. Goodyear gave the pioneers "much information in regard to the country," including information about himself and the fort he had established on the Weber River.

The Pioneer Company followed the Hastings Cutoff from Fort Bridger to the valley of the Great Salt Lake. The pioneers halted at Fort Bridger July 7-8, setting wagon tires, shoeing horses, and preparing for the mountainous road ahead on the Hastings Cutoff. The Mormons followed generally the route taken by the wagons of 1846, though "this route is but dimly seen, as only a few wagons passed over it last season." They crossed the Bear River July 12, were in Echo Canyon the next day, and on the fourteenth were at the junction of the Echo and Weber rivers. Here the Pioneer Company divided into two groups. Mountain fever had struck many in the company, including Brigham Young.

Young's group followed behind while the advance scouting group of forty-two men and twenty-three wagons were to explore ahead "and endeavor to find Mr. Reed's route across the mountains." The Mormons had been told they could not get through Weber Canyon because of the depth and swiftness of the stream.

The advance scouting group was led by Orson Pratt. He explored to the canyon of the Weber and then searched for and found Reed's route south along East Canyon Creek and over Big Mountain. Pratt's men took axes and spades and cleared the Donner Road, a task that "required considerable labor," despite the great exertions of the Donner party eleven months before. July 19 Orson Pratt and John Brown went up Big Mountain, down the other side, across Little Mountain and down Emigration Canyon, following the Reed trail. They were the first of the Pioneer Company to see the Salt Lake Valley. On

ORSON PRATT AND ERASTUS SNOW ENTER GREAT SALT LAKE VALLEY

From the Journal of Orson Pratt:

July 21.– ... [In Emigration Canyon] To avoid the kanyon the wagons last season had passed over an exceedingly steep and dangerous hill. Mr. Snow and myself ascended this hill, from the top of which a broad open valley, about 20 miles wide and 30 long, lay stretched out before us, at the north end of which the broad waters of the Great Salt Lake glistened in the sunbeams, containing high mountainous islands from 25 to 30 miles in extent. After issuing from the mountains among which we had been shut up for many days, and beholding in a moment such an extensive scenery open before us, we could not refrain from a shout of joy which almost involuntarily escaped from our lips the moment this grand and lovely scenery was within our view. We immediately descended very gradually into the lower parts of the valley, and although we had but one horse between us, yet we traversed a circuit of about 12 miles before we left the valley to return to our camp, which we found encamped 1½ miles up the ravine from the valley, and 3 miles in advance of their noon halt. It was about 9 o'clock in the evening when we got into camp. ...

July 21 Orson Pratt and Erastus Snow traced the same route and then made a circuit of about twelve miles in the valley before returning to camp in the canyon. On July 22, several of the advance party went into the valley and explored as far as the hot springs north of present Salt Lake City. The advance

A DESCRIPTION OF THE VALLEY

From the Journal of Orson Pratt:

July 22nd. – ... After going down into the valley about 5 miles, we turned our course to the north, down towards the Salt Lake. For 3 or 4 miles north we found the soil of a most excellent quality. Streams from the mountains and springs were very abundant, the water excellent, and generally with gravel bottoms. A great variety of green grass, and very luxuriant, covered the bottoms for miles where the soil was sufficiently damp, but in other places, although the soil was good, yet the grass had nearly dried up for want of moisture. We found the drier places swarming with very large crickets, about the size of a man's thumb. This valley is surrounded with mountains, except on the north: the tops of some of the highest being covered with snow. Every 1 or 2 miles streams were emptying into it from the mountains on the east, many of which were sufficiently large to carry mills and other machinery. As we proceeded towards the Salt Lake the soil began to assume a more sterile appearance, being probably at some seasons of the year overflowed with water. We found as we proceeded on, great numbers of hot springs issuing from near the base of the mountains.
... We travelled for about 15 miles down after coming into the valley, the latter parts of the distance the soil being unfit for agricultural purposes. ...

camp was now in the valley. The next day, Orson Pratt moved his camp onto City Creek, called the camp together, and offering prayer, gave thanks for their safety in traveling, and dedicated the camp and the land to the Lord. Plowing was begun. A dam was built across City Creek in order to carry water onto the plowed land. On July 24 the last of the Pioneer Company including Brigham Young came into the valley. Many years later, Mormon memories recalled that when Wilford Woodruff's carriage wagon carrying the fever-sick Mormon leader came to the high point from

which the valley of the Great Salt Lake could be seen, Brigham Young raised himself from his bed to study the scene. After gazing upon the broad valley, he is remembered as saying, "This is the right place. Drive on."

From the records of 1847 it appears that the Mormons had thought seriously all along of selecting the valley of the Great Salt Lake as a future settling place for the Latter-day Saints. But first an exploration must be made, and the exploring party had now reached the valley. The leaders would explore thoroughly before making a final decision. The region must meet many demands.

Sentinel of the Plains. Painting by J. T. Harwood.

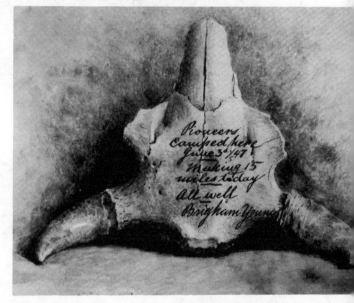

The Pioneer Company made a new trail along the north bank of the Platte River. Painting by C. C. A. Christensen.

The pioneers enter Salt Lake Valley. Painting by William Henry Jackson.

10 THE FIRST YEARS

The beginning of a city, early summer 1850. At the left is the Old Tabernacle. At the right is the Council House with the scaffolding still up. In the center are the Mint and the predecessor of Brigham Young's Beehive House.

Once the Mormons found a place for settlement they faced many problems. There was the problem of securing enough timber and building materials for their homes and buildings. There was the problem of raising food. Was the growing season long enough? Was there sufficient rainfall or water? Was the soil fertile? Were there other natural resources in sufficient quantity to supply their needs? To these people of much faith, the prospects looked good. They went to work with zeal.

How did they solve these problems? What happened during those first years? These were exciting years during which the experiment was sometimes in doubt.

The experience of the Mormon pioneers was comparable to that of early man anywhere on the earth—taking the land the way nature had left it and planting life and civilization there. It is important to see how resourceful these pioneers were in making good use of the tools and equipment they had.

IN THIS CHAPTER WE WILL LEARN

1. The first years were a struggle for survival.

2. During the first years the pioneers made important decisions and began lasting practices.

3. The pioneers governed themselves.

4. New settlements were founded north and south of Salt Lake City.

5. Overland emigrants to the California gold fields traded goods and services in Utah.

6. By 1850 the Utah settlers had established the beginnings of civilized life.

1. THE FIRST YEARS WERE
A STRUGGLE FOR SURVIVAL

The first week in Salt Lake Valley. Orson Pratt and Erastus Snow were the first of the Mormon pioneers to enter the valley of the Great Salt Lake. They entered on Wednesday, July 21, 1847. They went north as far as City Creek and then returned to their camp. The next day, Orson Pratt and eight others went into the valley on horses "to seek out a suitable place to plant some potatoes, turnips, etc., so as to preserve the seed at least." They went as far north as the hot springs, then returned to their camp. They found the advance company and the main company encamped in the valley, about five and a quarter miles from the mouth of the canyon, on Parleys Canyon Creek.

On Friday, July 23, the advance camp moved a couple of miles up onto City Creek where the grass appeared even "richer and

One of the first acts of the Pioneer Company was to turn water onto the land for crops, thus beginning irrigation agriculture in Salt Lake Valley.

thicker" than at their last camp, and the soil "rich, black and a little sandy." A meeting was called. Prayers of thanksgiving were offered and a plea made for rain. "Orson Pratt dedicated the land and themselves unto the Lord." After prayers were said, the men went to work. Committees were appointed to different tasks. "A patch 20 by 40 rods was staked off, in which to plant potatoes, and another piece for beans, corn, and buckwheat." Three plows and a harrow were put to work and continued working the ground the rest of the day. Midafternoon, a dam was built across the creek, and trenches were cut to convey the water to irrigate the soil. Later in the afternoon men began mowing grass and preparing space for a turnip patch.

On Saturday, July 24, plowing continued. Potatoes and early corn were now planted. The water of City Creek was turned upon the soil until it was well soaked. *This was the beginning of Mormon irrigation agriculture in the Great Salt Lake Valley.* In the afternoon, Brigham Young and the last of the Pioneer Company arrived at City Creek Camp.

Reports of the Mountain Men and the observations made by the pioneers made them wonder about two important features of this land: summer rains and sufficient timber. They would have to explore to determine if there were sufficient timber resources to support a large population. The most important tasks immediately ahead of them were those of plowing, planting, and irrigating their crops, and the exploration of the valley.

According to custom, Sunday was devoted to religious services, no work being performed that day. Monday, July 26, the men continued their plowing, planting, and irrigating. A group began building a road in City Creek Canyon to get timber out. Two men were sent to the mountains to the east to explore for timber. They were gone two days

and returned to report "an abundance of good timber, principally pine and balsam fir, with a little cottonwood, but access to the same was very difficult." Two other men were sent to explore the west mountains; they returned that night reporting the less favorable nature of the land west of the Jordan River.

With the planting and explorations for timber going on, Brigham Young and other leading men climbed to the top of Ensign Peak to survey the valley and surrounding country. When they came down, they explored the west base of the peak, visited the warm springs, and came upon the lands sloping toward the north course of the Jordan River. Here they "could but remark all along, the richness of the soil and the abundance of high, good looking grass." They returned to camp on City Creek that evening to find that the men had planted about three acres of potatoes, some peas and beans, and were then planting four or five acres of corn. Some men had gone two miles southeast (Sugar House area) and started a garden. ". . . their operations and industry are truly pleasing and noble. The more I view the country," wrote William Clayton, "the better I am satisfied that the Saints can live here and raise abundant crops."

Tuesday, July 27, plowing, planting, and irrigating continued. Burr Frost set up his forge and began blacksmithing. Carpenters rigged up more plows. Indians came into the valley and traded with the Mormons.

Brigham Young led a group of sixteen men west along the Jordan River, crossed it, and explored westward to the Great Salt Lake. Near Black Rock they bathed in the lake. Some explored westward to the entrance to Tooele Valley. They camped for the night and the next morning explored southward along the east base of the Oquirrh Mountains.

Orson Pratt went three miles farther south and from Sandy Ridge (near Point of the Mountain) saw Utah Lake and Utah Valley. That afternoon (Wednesday, July 28) the party was back at the City Creek encampment.

"Some of the party," the record shows, "wished to explore the country further, for a site for settlement." Brigham Young observed that he was "willing that the country should be explored until all were satisfied, but he believed firmly, every time a party went out, and returned, that they would agree that the place already chosen was the place for them to locate."

By Wednesday evening, July 28, one week after the first entrance into the valley, the Mormon pioneers had explored the valley of the Great Salt Lake rather well. They had visited the canyons and crossed the valley from one end to the other. They had seen the streams, sampled the soil and observed the vegetation. They had found the Indians "very peaceable and gentle."

About five p.m. Brigham Young took some others to a spot between the two forks of the City Creek and said that would be the site of the Temple Block. Here they would build a temple. The plat for the city was also approved. At eight p.m. a public meeting was held. Brigham Young called on the men "to express their feelings on the subject" of locating here. Many of the men were in favor of settling in the valley. "It was moved and seconded," wrote Howard Egan, "that we should locate in this valley for the present, and lay out a city at this place; which was carried without a dissenting voice."

During the first month in the valley there was a continuation of activities which marked the first days. There was continued exploration, plowing, planting, and irrigating. *In early August explorations were made*

into Tooele Valley, Utah Valley, Bear River Valley, and Cache Valley. Early in August two men explored Tooele Valley. Lewis B. Meyers explored Utah Valley and returned August 3, reporting plenty of timber. He was soon on his way to Cache Valley too. Jesse C. Little led parties into Utah Valley and into Cache Valley. On August 4 and 5, Little, Samuel Brannan, and others went into Utah Valley. They reported "a handsome valley about six by eight miles wide." They proved for themselves that the Jordan River was the outlet from Utah Lake. Little and others went along to explore up the Bear River and into Cache Valley. On their way north they stopped at Miles Goodyear's Fort Buenaventura, "which consisted of some log buildings and corrals stockaded in with pickets." Mr. Wells, Goodyear's man in charge, had a herd of cattle, horses, goats, and "some sheep that needed shearing." In his small garden "there was corn in tassel, planted June 9, beans ripe, carrots a foot long, cabbage, radishes, etc., looking well." ". . . although it had been neglected, it looked well, which proved to us that with proper cultivation it would do well." The report on Cache Valley was favorable—it "looked beautiful from the summit of the mountain"—but the explorers regretted that there was no more timber there than in Salt Lake Valley, except up the ravines in the mountains.

The beginnings of irrigation agriculture were proving quite successful, despite the lateness of the season. By July 31, as a result of eight days' labor with thirteen plows and three harrows, three lots of land totaling fifty-three acres had been broken, of which thirty-four were planted. About twenty-three acres were planted with buckwheat, corn, and oats. One lot of eight acres was planted with corn, potatoes, and beans. A garden of ten acres had been broken, of which four acres had been sown with garden seed. Howard Egan wrote, "We have put in a few of almost all kinds of seeds." Three acres of corn were already up two inches above the ground, and some beans and potatoes were up too. Soon all the crops were up and doing well. The experiment had proven the land fertile. By August 10 another thirty acres had been plowed and mostly planted, making a total of about eighty acres under cultivation. Men now turned to building grist mills for making flour, digging pits for their pit saws, and blacksmithing.

Basic industries developed rapidly in Salt Lake Valley. While many men worked at plowing, planting, and irrigating, others worked at their special trades or crafts. Some made buckskin clothes and others repaired shoes. A pit was dug and a pit saw was installed for making rough lumber. Burr Frost and Thomas Tanner built a blacksmith shop. Some men went to the shores of Great Salt Lake to obtain salt and harvested 130 bushels with twenty-four hours of labor. Good stands of timber were located in the mountains and roads built to them. Crews of woodsmen went into the canyons, took out logs, and brought them to camp to be cut into lumber or prepared for use in cabins. A few hunted successfully for wild game.

Laying out the city and constructing *the first buildings* were special tasks. The first building was a temporary *bowery*, twenty-eight by forty feet, erected July 31 on Temple Block. It was built by placing posts upright in the ground. Timbers were then laid across the tops of the posts and covered with brush. *It was a shaded place for holding religious services and business meetings of the community.*

The task of surveying the city and laying out its streets was entrusted to Orson Pratt and H. G. Sherwood. On August 3 a base

The pit saw served until true sawmills could be erected, making use of water power.

line was run, and the surveying of the Temple Block began. By August 20 the laying out of the city was completed. The survey ran 15 blocks north and south and 9 blocks east and west. It was composed of 135 blocks, each containing ten acres, subdivided into eight lots, each lot containing one and one-fourth acres. The streets were eight rods wide. Three public squares were provided in different parts of the city. Temple Block, at first planned to be forty acres, was made like the rest and contained ten acres. The streets were named on August 16. On August 2 the three camps of pioneers moved into one camp on the Temple Block.

Once the decision was made to establish themselves in the valley, preparations had to be made for the coming winter. The pioneers decided not to live in their wagon boxes but to build cabins inside *a stockade or fort.* The

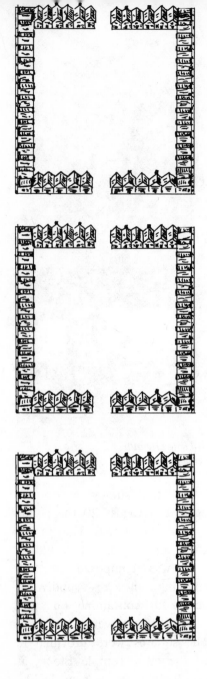

This drawing suggests how the Old Fort may have looked.

use of Spanish *adobe* was adopted. Wet clay or mud mixed with straw or plant fiber, then molded into bricks and dried in the sun, made excellent building bricks. Adobe were 18 inches long, 9 inches broad, and 4 1/2 inches thick. The walls of the fort were 27 inches thick and 8 or 9 feet high. Work began on August 10. Many men set to making adobe, while many others got timbers from the canyons. By August 23, twenty-nine log houses had been built inside the fort. Each house was 8 or 9 feet high, 16 or 17 feet long, and 14 feet wide. Eleven of them were roofed with poles and soil. The cabins faced a common green used for pasturing some animals. This arrangement was known as the Old Fort. Its pattern was to be duplicated, with some variety, in many of the Mormon settlements.

Immigration and emigration. All this work was not done by members of the Pioneer Company alone. Others soon came into the valley. On July 29 the sick detachment of the Mormon Battalion arrived in military formation, many of them mounted, followed by their wagons. Headed by the fifes and side drum, the detachment of 150 men marched to the site of the City Creek camp. They were followed by about 50 Mississippi Mormons who had also wintered at Pueblo and accompanied the detachment into the valley. Altogether, there were about 350 people in the valley to perform the labors of laying the foundations of the city.

But there was also an out-migration. On August 2, Ezra T. Benson and others were sent back on the trail to help the coming emigrants. On August 9, Samuel Brannan, Captain James Brown of the battalion, and others left for San Francisco. Some of the battalion men now in the valley were so anxious to get to their families in Winter Quarters that they secretly left camp to return there. Those who would return to Winter Quarters were divided into two groups: those with ox teams and those with horse teams. On August 16 and 17, the ox teams left the valley for Winter Quarters. In this company were 24 of the pioneers and 46 battalion men. On August 26, Brigham Young and his company of 107 pioneers and battalion men left the valley to return to Winter Quarters, arriving October 31, 1847. On December 5, Brigham Young was sustained by his people as president of their church. He spent the winter of 1847-48 preparing the Mormons for the 1848 migration to the valley.

The first winter in the valley. While Brigham Young and his company were on their way east to Winter Quarters, the 130 Mormon settlers in Salt Lake Valley prepared for the winter ahead. However, in September the first real immigration arrived in Salt Lake Valley. Companies of Mormon emigrants had followed the Pioneer Company, feeling confident that a place would be found for them. In all, these companies numbered 1,540 people, with 580 wagons, 124 horses, 9 mules, 2,213 oxen, 887 cows, 358 sheep, 35 hogs, and 716 chickens. These people had come to stay. They were under the general supervision of Parley P. Pratt, one of the twelve apostles. With them was John Taylor, also one of the twelve apostles, and John Smith, uncle of the Prophet Joseph Smith.

For government the Mormons simply used their church organization. John Smith was named to preside over the community. He was given two associates called counselors. A High Council of twelve men was named. These fifteen men and a clerk performed the usual functions of city government from October 1847 to January 6, 1849. (We will study more of how the early settlers governed themselves later in this chapter.)

Most families in early Utah lived for a time in log cabins such as this of the Osmyn Deuel family.

The September 1847 immigration so swelled the population that the original ten-acre fort was inadequate to care for all the people. Two additional ten-acre squares were added on the south, enclosed with an adobe brick wall. Cabins were built along the inside walls, but independent of the walls. Later, a fourth square was added. Even so, some of the people that winter lived outside the fort in cabins near the fort or on other locations in the valley. The population that first winter numbered about 1,670 people living in about 423 cabins.

Food was the big problem not only during the first months but also during the first years in the valley. The crops that grew from the July plantings were lost. Late in September, after the large immigration came in, "cattle and horses entirely destroyed the crops sown, except the potatoes, the tops of which they ate smooth with the ground." There would be seed potatoes for the next spring, but little more. The people would have to live off the goods they brought with them. Seed for spring planting also would have to be brought in. They had hoped the July planting would yield seed.

The winter was hard for many people. There were no vegetables and little flour. Some were fortunate enough to have milk cows. Sometimes a beef was killed, but since the cattle had been worked so hard, the beef often had to be boiled all day to make it tender enough to eat. The Indians taught the Mormons to dig roots and thus helped them survive. The bulbs of the sego lily were particularly appreciated. The sego lily has since become Utah's state flower in recognition of the life-saving role it played the first winters.

The weather during the first winter was "remarkably mild and pleasant." There were severe frosts and several light snows, but the days were warm and the snows soon melted away. Much of the work of pioneering continued through the winter months. The settlers spent time gathering fuel, taking care of their cattle, and improving their cabins by adding doors, flooring, tables, bedsteads, and chairs. In January the project of fencing the community and its farm lands was begun again. The fence enclosed the area designed for the city and the area set aside for farming called the "Big Field." Farm lands were located south of the Old Fort. By March, 872 acres of land had been sown into winter wheat, and plans were made to plant the rest of the city site with spring and summer crops.

By the end of the first year in the valley there were three saw mills in operation by water power and another nearly completed. Two grist mills were nearly ready to use. There was in operation a water-powered threshing machine, which threshed between one and two hundred bushels in twelve hours.

Spring planting began early in March 1848. Corn, beets, onions, peas, beans, cu-cumbers, melons, squash, lettuce, and radishes were now planted. Lettuce was ready to harvest by May 4 and radishes by the middle of May.

Despite the promise of an abundant first harvest from the virgin land, frost and crickets came to destroy many of the vines, peas, beans, and some nursery trees and grain. The pioneers had planted too early for some crops, and late frosts did their damage. The mild winter had spared many insects and pests. Black crickets were especially destructive. When the cricket attack worsened some pioneers began to quit work and talked of going to California to live. Some wanted to send messengers to Brigham Young telling him not to bring any more people here, for there would not be food for them. The men of the Mormon Battalion said, "God has sent us here, and here we are going to stay, come weal come woe." John Smith kept the people working at their tasks and caring for their crops as well as they could. In time gulls from the lake came in large flocks and devoured multitudes of crickets, saving many crops. In grateful remembrance to the gulls for helping save the 1848 spring crops, the California gull has been named the Utah state bird.

Despite losses due to frost and crickets, the pioneers regarded their first harvest with satisfaction and thanksgiving. Some wheat was harvested during the first week in July. The pioneers now thought they could live here. Corn was ready the first week in August. Some ten thousand bushels of winter and spring wheat were harvested by August, and it was expected that the grain harvest would total twenty thousand bushels. Other crops did well, too. "The people had eaten green peas until they were tired of them."

On August 10 several hundred people met under a large awning and celebrated *a first thanksgiving* feast in the valley. The feast included "almost every variety of food, all produced in the valley." Prayer and thanksgiving, music and dancing, and firing a cannon, marked the festival.

Exploration of the region continued. In April of 1848 a group of six men explored the islands of the Great Salt Lake. In May A. A. Lathrop and E. K. Fuller, with a company of nineteen men and five hired Indians, came into the valley from California by way of the southern route (the Old Spanish Trail). The men brought with them about 150 head of cattle and "fruit cuttings of various kinds."

In June and July 1848 Parley P. Pratt and others explored to find a shorter route from the valley to the Weber and Bear rivers. Pratt found a new route through the mountains, but it was not used until 1850. In 1862 the Mormon immigration used this route, and thereafter the route over Big and Little mountains was neglected. The route of highway U.S. 40 to Kimball's Junction and U.S. 189 north to Echo Canyon very nearly follows Parley P. Pratt's road explored in 1848.

Brigham Young returned to the valley September 20, 1848. For the second year he had led Mormon emigration westward. Following his company were other companies that kept arriving in the valley until the last of November. In all some 2,417 settlers, including 24 Negroes, came into the valley that fall. There may have been 4,500 people in the valley for the second winter.

The Old Fort served as home for the new settlers during the second winter as it had the first. Additions were made. Some 450 buildings were inside the fort. Some people lived outside the fort as they had the year before.

During the fall, *land was further divided*

Cottages were soon built on city lots. A Salt Lake City street scene, looking eastward, 1852.

out to the people. By October 1848 the city plot had already been allotted to families. The size of the city was extended both north and south. The Big Field was divided into lots for farming—5, 10, 20, 40, 80 acre lots. Families then applied for farming lots which they held in addition to their city lots. Some 863 applications were made in October, and 11,005 acres of land were thus taken up.

The winter of 1848-49 was a harsh, cold season. Near the end of November a severe cold spell surprised everyone and caught many unprepared. During the winter heavy snows came regularly, and while there were thaws, snow covered the ground for three months. Cattle could not find grass as they had the winter before. The heavy snows made it difficult to get firewood. The immigrants of 1848 had not brought enough foodstuffs to last till the next harvest. By mid-February many families were destitute. Many were reduced to eating "rawhides, and to digging sego and thistle roots for months to subsist on." But there was sharing, whenever there was anything to share. "Those persons who had provisions, imparted measurably to those who had not, so that all extremity of suffering from hunger was avoided."

During the worst of the winter, wolves and other predatory animals came out of the mountains to menace the settlers. A hunting contest was arranged. Two groups of men hunted the animals and killed 2 bears, 2 wolverines, 2 wild cats, 783 wolves, 409 foxes, 37 mink, 9 eagles, 530 magpies, hawks and owls, and 1,026 ravens.

The heavy snows and the alternating thaws convinced the people in the Old Fort that they needed timber roofs instead of dirt roofs. A quick February thaw ruined many dirt roofs and some adobe walls so that cabins had to be abandoned. People had already begun to move out of the fort and onto their city lots. During spring the Old Fort was abandoned. As new cabins were built on the city lots, Salt Lake City began to take on the appearance of a city.

Early in the spring of 1849 the crops were planted. March and April were mild months. The crops soon looked good. But again, small crickets made their appearance. This year, not the gulls, but "large flocks of plover" came and made "heavy inroads" on the crickets. The plover did the same service for the settlers as the gulls had the year before. Cricket plagues were to be a common terror to the settlers for many years, and most of the time there were no birds to save the crops. But the crops of 1849 turned out well. There would not be an overabundance, but there would be food for all.

2. DURING THE FIRST YEARS THE PIONEERS MADE IMPORTANT DECISIONS AND BEGAN LASTING PRACTICES

During the first years decisions were made that started practices which were to give Utah much of its distinctive character.

Mormon families did not live to themselves alone. The Mormon pioneers believed that they should *take care of each other* and *make provision for those who came after them*. Each family was expected to take care of itself and help others besides. When projects of community benefit were undertaken, individuals willingly responded to the call to do the job. It was customary for all to work for the common good. They often placed community requests before family considerations. This *unity of purpose* made it possible for them to achieve much more than the usual frontiersmen achieved.

Natural resources. The leaders made important decisions very early with regard to the use of *land, water, timber,* and other natural resources. It was determined that so far as possible all Mormons in the valley now and in time to come should have equal opportunity to possess land. Land was not bought; it was not to be sold. Here was the frontiersman's dream of *free land*. Land would be measured out to every man, both a city lot and land for farming purposes. He could till his land as he saw fit, but he must be industrious and take care of it. A man should not hold more land than he would cultivate. The amount of land, in addition to a city lot, a man might receive depended upon his occupation. A farmer might obtain forty or eighty acres, whereas mechanics and artisans would need only five acres, for they would earn their living by their trade as well as by some farming. Pieces of land were divided among the people by "lot," by drawing numbers.

Water, timber, and other natural resources were considered to belong to the community. No one person was to own water, timber, or other natural resources like coal and iron deposits. These belonged to the community to be used by all for the benefit of all. *Water* from the canyon streams would be divided among the land holders whose lands would be watered by those streams. Each farmer would receive water as determined by the amount of land he had. A system of irrigation canals was constructed, owned, and managed by the men of the community. The water was controlled by the users. And in the early days the whole system was under the direction of church leaders. Church meetings attracted most of the men of the community. It was here that matters relating to the water and other resources were often discussed. In time, irrigation companies were formed to construct larger canals. In 1853 the Provo Canal and Irrigation Company (the first in the territory) was incorporated by the territorial legislature. The next year the legislature authorized the construction of a canal from Utah Lake to Salt Lake City. Each of these projects was to be paid for by taxes on the land under irrigation.

Timber was managed on a similar basis. Timber resources were carefully guarded. Other natural resources were also controlled by the community for the benefit of all.

3. THE PIONEERS GOVERNED THEMSELVES

Many factors led to the success of the early Mormon pioneers. They were united in their purposes and actions. They accepted the call of their leaders to do the work necessary to build the communities. One of the most important factors was the *effective Mormon church organization*. It served as the means by which most of the pioneer accomplishments were made.

The Mormons used their church organization for the first government in Salt Lake Valley. Church organization had directed the Mormon migration from Nauvoo. It was both easy and natural for the Mormons to continue to use that organization for their governmental needs. When they arrived in Salt Lake Valley they were in Mexican territory, but they simply followed an American tradition of providing their own form of government. However, they violated the prevailing American tradition when they united church and state.

The High Council was the first governing body in Salt Lake Valley. When Brigham Young left the valley in August 1847, he proposed that John Smith should preside with two counselors over the High Council. These officers were accepted by the people October 3, 1847. The High Council was the ruling authority over the Mormons in the West from that date until the return of Brigham Young on September 2, 1848. It retained control of municipal affairs until January 6, 1849. The High Council continued to have influence in city affairs for years afterward.

The High Council performed all the functions of government. It passed laws, administered the laws, and tried cases involving violation of the laws. About 130 ordinances were passed by the High Council. It passed the first tax on October 24, 1847: "every man in the Old Fort should be taxed sufficient to pay for gates for the same." The High Council named committees to handle some functions such as drafting laws, hearing and adjusting claims between citizens, assessing and collecting taxes, regulating trade with the Indians, locating a cemetery, and establishing prices on goods and on the grinding of meal. The High Council granted the first divorce in the city. It directed the purchase of Miles Goodyear's claim to land on the Weber and his improvements there.

Law enforcement was in the hands of a marshal. Stealing seems to have been the most serious crime. In the absence of a jail, the whipping post was used for the punishment of violators of the law.

On November 7, 1847, the first *wards* were organized in the valley. These wards were *ecclesiastical divisions* of the Mormon church. The Mormon ward is similar to a congregation and is presided over by a bishop. The Mormon bishops' duties included performing some functions of government such as trying cases involving conflicts between members of their congregations. Thus the Mormons had their own court system within their church.

The Mormon pioneers had settled in Mexican territory, but this was soon changed by the outcome of the war between the United States and Mexico, in which the Mormon Battalion had served. **The war with Mexico was ended by the Treaty of Guadalupe Hidalgo (February 2, 1848).** By this treaty the United States received undisputed title to Texas, California, and the region between lying north of the Gila River and south of the 42° north latitude. The Utah region was now United States territory.

When news of the treaty reached Salt Lake City, the people set to work to form a political government. After forming this government they applied to the Congress of the United States for admission into the Union as a state. Early in March 1849 a convention was held in Salt Lake City. On March 10 the convention adopted a constitution creating the *State of Deseret.* Two days later an election was held to select officers. Only one slate of officers was presented to the people. There were no political parties. There was no opposition vote. There were 624 votes cast for the following who were elected: governor, Brigham Young; secretary, Willard Richards; chief justice, Heber C. Kimball; associate justices, Newel K. Whitney and John Taylor; marshal, Horace S. Eldredge; attorney general,

Daniel H. Wells; assessor and collector, Albert Carrington; treasurer, Newel K. Whitney; supervisor of roads, Joseph L. Heywood. For magistrates the election named the bishops of each of the wards in the valley. The Mormons simply named their top church officials to the top government positions. A memorial was sent to Congress asking admission of the State of Deseret into the Union. An elected delegate and others were sent to petition Congress. In the meantime, the government of the State of Deseret functioned as though it were a legal government recognized by the federal government.

The State of Deseret functioned as the political government in this region from 1849 to 1851. The General Assembly held several sessions between July 1849 and March 1851. Executive and judicial officers were sworn in. The Senate and the House organized for business. The state was divided into counties and precincts. During these years, as settlements expanded, counties were created and cities incorporated. Counties created were Great Salt Lake, Weber, Utah, Sanpete, Juab, Tooele, and Davis. Cities incorporated were Salt Lake City, Provo, Manti, Ogden, and Parowan.

The State of Deseret expected to include the Great Basin, the Colorado River drainage area, and access to the sea.

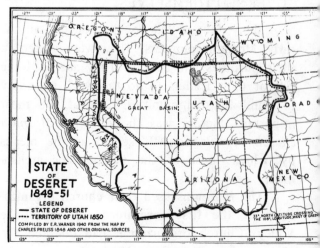

160

County courts were established with judges, clerks, sheriffs, justices, and constables. A supreme court was created to hold annual sessions in Salt Lake City. Ordinances were passed creating a state militia. The University of the State of Deseret (later the University of Utah) was incorporated.

The Mormons were disappointed in their desire to have the State of Deseret admitted into the Union. Their representatives in Washington, Almon W. Babbitt and John M. Bernhisel, worked with the Congress in vain. The United States was facing serious problems over the extension of slavery in territories recently acquired by the United States. Finally a series of compromises was worked out in an effort to give both the North and the South as many concessions as possible. By the Compromise of 1850, California was admitted as a state without slavery. New Mexico was organized as a territory, "with or without slavery" when it should come into the Union as a state. The Territory of Utah was created by the act of September 9, 1850, "with or without slavery" when it should come into the Union as a state. Instead of statehood, the Mormon people obtained a territorial government. (We will study more of this government in chapter 13.)

4. NEW SETTLEMENTS ARE FOUNDED NORTH AND SOUTH OF SALT LAKE CITY

The establishment of numerous settlements was important to the Mormons. Settlements would allow them to control and lay claim to land and to provide gathering places for future immigration. As soon as places could be explored and it was determined they could be settled safely, settlements were begun.

Bountiful. Just three days after Perregrine Sessions arrived in the valley, September 26, 1847, he took his wagons and accompanied by Samuel Brown went about ten miles north of the Temple Block to a spot near the mouth of North Canyon. They encamped on the future site of Bountiful. The next summer several other families joined in the Sessions Settlement. About twenty-five families spent the winter of 1848-49 there.

Farmington. At the same time Sessions went to his camp site, another companion of the overland trek, Hector C. Haight, took a herd of cattle northward and located about five miles north of Sessions' cabin. Haight was joined by other familes who settled at different points on the streams in the vicinity of what is now Farmington. Daniel C. Davis of the Mormon Battalion settled on a creek that was named for him, and in 1850 a county was named for him. During the winter of 1848-49 about twenty-five families lived in the region.

Ogden. Captain James Brown returned to the valley from California November 15, 1847, with pay for the services of the Mormon Battalion. With this money, on direction

A scene, north end of Salt Lake City, about 1860. Ensign Peak is in the background.

from the High Council, he bought Miles Goodyear's claim to land and holdings on the Weber River. Cattle were soon put to graze there, and soon afterwards Brown moved there with the Chilton, Myers, and Thurlkill families. In 1848 Brown moved most of the old Goodyear cabins away from the Weber bottoms a short distance southeast where he built Brown's Fort. During 1848, cereal grains, potatoes, vegetables, and watermelons were grown. The stock did well too. The little settlement took care of itself during the next year. In September 1849, Brigham Young and others visited Brown's Fort. It was decided that a city should be laid out on the south side of the Ogden River, "at the point of bench land between the forks of the Ogden and the Weber rivers, so that water from both streams might be taken out for irrigation and other purposes." In August of the next year the plan of the city was decided. Brigham Young advised the settlers "not to scatter in the country, but to move to the city lots, build good houses, with schoolhouses, meeting house, and other public buildings, fence their gardens, and plant out fruit trees, so that Ogden might be a permanent city and a suitable headquarters for the northern country."

Tooele. At the south end of the Great Salt Lake, just beyond the Oquirrh Mountains and about twenty-five miles west of Salt Lake City, is Tooele Valley. It was explored by Brigham Young three days after he entered the valley. In 1849 it was used by Captain Stansbury as a grazing ground for cattle. During the fall of 1849, three men, Cyrus and Judson Tolman and Phineas R. Wright, went to work there building a mill for Ezra T. Benson, and in December the first settlers located in what is now Tooele. About a dozen families spent the winter there. In 1850 the community of Tooele was organ-ized. John Rowberry was named president of the church branch, April 24, 1850.

Mormon Indian policy was put to the test when settlement expanded southward from Salt Lake Valley. Brigham Young held to a policy of peaceful coexistence with the Indians, and Indian and Mormon relations were good. But both Indians and Mormons knew of the very real problem created by the whites coming in and taking Indian lands and upsetting Indian sources for a livelihood.

Brigham Young wanted to avoid conflict with the Indians. When Indians began trading with the settlers in Salt Lake Valley, he required the trading to be done by Alexander Williams and Dimick B. Huntington. He believed his people should not expect the Indians to behave as the Mormons did. The settlers should tolerate the Indians, educate them and teach them the arts of civilization. When difficulties arose in May 1850, he advised the people to "feed the Indians more or less until they could raise grain or provide for themselves, and to set them an example worthy of civilized men." Use biscuits, not bullets, was his advice. "It is cheaper to feed the Indians than to fight them," he is quoted as saying.

The Mormons did not know it, but Salt Lake Valley was considered by the Ute, Shoshoni, and Gosiute to be neutral ground between them. Here Indians came for salt which they all needed. All western tribes knew that in this valley they did not fight. While the Indians of Utah were naturally peaceful, they must have realized a little late the magnitude of the Mormon migration into their lands. One possible source of trouble was Walkara (sometimes Walker), a Timpanogos Ute chief.

Walkara led a band of Ute Indians that roamed on their horses from the Utah region on the north to Mexico on the south, and from southern California on the west to the

Great Plains on the east. His band made raids for horses on the Spanish settlements and the great ranches of southern California. The horses were taken to other regions and traded, sometimes to white people. By 1847 Walkara was doing an excellent business in this horse traffic.

Walkara was disturbed at the coming of the Mormons. The Mormons did not ask him if they could settle on these lands, and for this he was offended. On the other hand, he hesitated to make war on the Mormons, for he had heard that they were like the Spanish Fathers Escalante and Domínguez, who had come among them seeking only to teach them their religion. Besides, the Mormons themselves might buy or trade with him for his horses.

Walkara changed his position from time to time. He wanted war with the Mormons at one time and peace at other times. He seems to have been anxious for war at first, but soon changed his mind.

Indians came to visit the Mormon settlement a few days after the first soil was turned in 1847. Trading took place from time to time. During the summer of 1848 Chief Walkara and his brother Sowiette, accompanied by hundreds of Indian men, women, and children, visited the Mormon settlement in Salt Lake Valley. They had with them several hundred head of horses for sale. Parley P. Pratt describes them and their conversations:

"They were good looking, brave, and intelligent beyond any we have seen on this side of the mountains. They were much pleased and excited with every thing they saw, and finally expressed a wish to become one people with us, and to live among us and we among them, and to learn to cultivate the earth and live as we do. They would like for some of us to go and commence farming with them in their valleys, which are situated about three hundred miles south."

Both the Mormons and the Ute spoke of peace. The Ute even sent a peace party to an encampment of Shoshoni Indians then in the valley, seeking a peace treaty with them.

With the main tribes of Indians, the Mormons were able to maintain peaceful relations through the early years. Difficulties arose with little bands which had either broken off or which lived separately from the main tribes. These small bands took whatever opportunities they could to take cattle and horses from the Mormon settlers. The Indians did not share the white man's attitudes toward private property.

Early in 1849 a small band of Indians took cattle and horses from settlers in the Tooele and southern Salt Lake valleys and then went into Utah Valley. At the end of February Captain John Scott and thirty or

"Wakar, Later Chief of Utah Indians."
A contemporary portrait by Solomon N. Carvalho, 1854.

forty men tracked the Indian party into Utah Valley and with the help of Timpanogos Ute followed them to their encampment on a creek since known as Battle Creek (Pleasant Grove). There a skirmish took place. The Timpanogos Ute did not fight but stood back watching the battle. Four Indians were killed. This was the first fight between settlers and Indians.

Whatever conflicts Walkara had in his mind between peace and war with the settlers, he came to the position of his brother Sowiette and the older men that the only policy for them to follow was that of peace with the Mormons. In May 1849 Chief Walkara told a Mormon interpreter that "he looked upon the 'Mormons' as his fathers, mothers, brothers, and sisters, and that none of his people should meddle with their cattle." Walkara was anxious for the Mormons to settle in his area, southward in Sanpete Valley, also in Little Salt Lake Valley.

Provo. The settlement of Utah Valley came from the desire to find grazing lands, establish a fishery, and teach the Indians. In January 1849 a group of men was sent to Utah Valley to look into the possibilities for livestock grazing. Shortly after the Indian fight on Battle Creek, preparations were made for a settlement. Early in March 1849, John S. Higbee and thirty settlers went to Utah Valley and made a settlement on the Provo River. They immediately began plowing and planting and building a fort which they named Fort Utah. A cannon was placed in the center on a raised platform, as a protection against possible attack by the Indians. When Brigham Young and his company of visitors came to Fort Utah in mid-September, they went two miles southeast of the fort and began to lay out a city. They explored the valley for sites for other settlements and inquired into the nature of the country south.

HIS WINTER HOME, PROVO, WINTER OF 1849-50

Described by Captain Howard Stansbury, U.S. Army:

... Our quarters consisted of a small unfurnished house of unburnt brick or adobe, unplastered, and roofed with boards loosely nailed on, which, every time it stormed, admitted so much water as called into requisition all the pans and buckets in the establishment to receive the numerous little streams which came trickling down from every crack and knot-hole. During this season of comparative inaction, we received from the authorities and citizens of the community every kindness that the most warm-hearted hospitality could dictate; and no effort was spared to render us as comfortable as their own limited means would admit. Indeed, we were much better lodged than many of our neighbors; for, as has been previously observed, very many families were obliged still to lodge wholly or in part in their wagons, which, being covered, served, when taken off from the wheels and set upon the ground, to make bedrooms, of limited dimensions it is true, but yet exceedingly comfortable. Many of these were comparatively large and commodious, and, when carpeted and furnished with a little stove, formed an additional apartment or back building to the small cabin, with which they frequently communicated by a door. It certainly argued a high tone of morals and an habitual observance of good order and decorum, to find women and children thus securely slumbering in the midst of a large city, with no protection from midnight molestation other than a

Fort Utah, Provo.
From a lithograph in Stansbury's 1852 publication.

wagon-cover of linen and the aegis of the law. In the very next enclosure to that occupied by our party, a whole family of children had no other shelter than one of these wagons, where they slept all the winter, literally out of doors, there being no communication whatever with the inside of their parents' house.

The founding, within the space of three years, of a large and flourishing community, upon a spot so remote from the abodes of man, so completely shut out by natural barriers from the rest of the world, so entirely unconnected by watercourses with either of the oceans that wash the shores of this continent—a country offering no advantages of inland navigation or of foreign commerce, but, on the contrary, isolated by vast uninhabitable deserts, and only to be reached by long, painful, and often hazardous journeys by land—presents an anomaly so very peculiar, that it deserves more than a passing notice. In this young and progressive country of ours, where cities grow up in a day, and states spring into existence in a year, the successful planting of a colony, where the natural advantages have been such as to hold out the promise of adequate reward to the projectors, would have excited no surprise; but the success of an enterprise under circumstances so at variance with all our preconceived ideas of its probability, may well be considered as one of the most remarkable incidents of the present age.

During the winter of 1849-50 the Indians were very troublesome to the Fort Utah settlers. Cattle and horses were stolen from the herds and grain from the fields. Occasionally an Indian arrow would hit near a settler as he was gathering wood in the river bottoms. The fort itself was fired upon. The Indians began to threaten war, calling the settlers cowards for not fighting. They threatened to get other Indians to help them wipe out the settlement. By January the settlers asked Brigham Young for permission to protect themselves. The local militia went into Utah Valley with a show of force against the Indians.

A battle between the Indians and the militiamen took place on the Provo River February 8 and 9, 1850. The Indians occupied a double log house, abandoned by a settler and his family who had fled to the fort. It took the militia two days to take the

house. In this fight one settler was killed and several others wounded. The Indians fled at the end of the second day. The next day the militiamen followed the Indians and fought and defeated them at the south end of Utah Valley. They then attacked other Indians in Rock Canyon. The total Indian loss was about forty, more than half the number of Indians in the fight. When peace came to the valley, the Indians were pushed away from the area, and the settlers moved onto city lots and farms.

Manti. The settlement of Sanpete Valley came in response to an invitation from Chief Walkara to Brigham Young for the Mormons to come to their valley and teach them how to farm and build. Explorations were made in the fall of 1849. In November Isaac Morley led a company of 224 settlers, 124 males and 100 females, to the distant valley. They arrived November 22, 1849. No sooner had they arrived than snow fell; a bitterly cold winter closed in on them before they had time to erect cabins or build a fort. The Indians who had been so friendly now appeared with demands for food. They were fed and saved from starvation. Measles spread among the people. Children died of the disease. At last, Indians helped the settlers. Men were able to get to Salt Lake and back on snowshoes, bringing much-needed supplies. In May, ten teams with grain arrived from Salt Lake Valley to help the Sanpete settlement. As soon as winter ended, the settlers went to work building shelters, plowing the land, and fencing their farms.

Chief Walkara showed his feelings for the settlers when on March 13 he was baptized a Mormon. On July 7, 1850, when Isaac Morley asked Walkara if some of his people wanted to be baptized, 120 of the 250 in the region became members of the church.

When Brigham Young visited the settle-

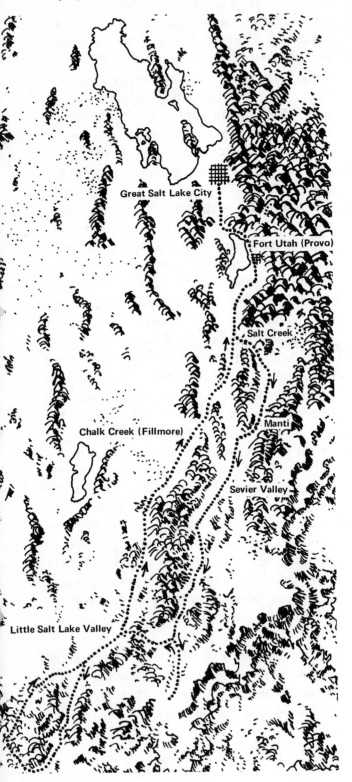

This map shows the route of the Southern Exploring Company, 1849-50, led by Parley P. Pratt.

Great Salt Lake City

Fort Utah (Provo)

Salt Creek

Chalk Creek (Fillmore)

Manti

Sevier Valley

Little Salt Lake Valley

ment in August 1850, he selected a site for the permanent city to be named Manti. The survey was made, marking out a city with 110 blocks, "each 26 rods square, with eight lots in a block, streets six rods wide." By the end of 1850 the settlement numbered 365 people.

The exploration of central Utah. By 1849 the pioneers knew the valleys of northern Utah well. They needed reports on the possibilities of settlement in the valleys to the south. In November 1849, Parley P. Pratt was appointed head of a group of about fifty men known as the *Southern Exploring Company*. They were to explore southward to observe the natural resources and to choose sites for settlements in the valleys of central and southern Utah.

The Southern Exploring Company set out from Salt Lake Valley November 25 and proceeded to Fort Utah. The streams and settlement sites in Utah Valley were carefully noted. The explorers then crossed into Juab Valley, proceeded south to Salt Creek (Nephi), and followed Salt Creek into Sanpete Valley. The explorers went on to the Sevier River and followed it southward toward its source. When the country began to narrow they turned back and then west, and with great difficulty made their way across the plateaus and down into Little Salt Lake Valley. This region impressed the explorers very much. They decided to leave some wagons and oxen with men (under David Fullmer) to rest while another party led by Parley P. Pratt explored southward.

The Pratt group went south to Muddy Creek (present Cedar City), then crossed the rim of the Great Basin into an "almost indescribable country, thrown together in dreadful confusion . . . ." They followed Ash Creek to the Virgin River, and down the Virgin (past the site of Saint George) to its junction with the Santa Clara. On the Virgin they met Indians who were raising crops of corn, pumpkins, and squash by irrigation. Deciding to go no farther south, they followed the Santa Clara northward, passed through Mountain Meadows, then north and eastward to the Little Salt Lake Valley, arriving on January 8. Here the two groups were reunited.

Fullmer's camp had become well acquainted with Little Salt Lake Valley and recommended it most highly for a settlement. They had discovered excellent timber stands and deposits of iron ore.

Through January the Southern Exploring Company made its way northward through Beaver and Pavant valleys. At Chalk Creek (present Fillmore) winter bore so heavily on the explorers that they decided the entire group could not go on with their limited supplies. Wagons and sufficient supplies were left with part of the company to winter on Chalk Creek. The others (led by Pratt) went on to Provo. They made their way slowly through almost constant snow storms. They finally reached Fort Utah January 31 and Salt Lake City February 2, 1850. The members left at Chalk Creek survived the winter and made it to Salt Lake City in March.

The Southern Exploring Company traveled seven hundred miles during the worst time of the year, through cold and storm. They had learned the nature of winters in the southern regions of Utah. They had explored the chief valleys and determined many of the best settlement sites throughout central and southern Utah. The Mormons now had their own first hand observation and description of the important central valleys. This was a most significant exploration.

Little Salt Lake Valley: Parowan. When Parley P. Pratt returned from his southern exploring expedition, one place he especially recommended for settlement was the valley of the Little Salt Lake. Iron ore in the mountains especially attracted the explorers. Plans were soon made to send a colony to this valley, 265 miles south of Salt Lake City.

The expedition journeyed southward through the unsettled country in zero degree weather. They had to make their way over five ranges of hills and mountains before arriving on Center Creek, January 13, 1851. As soon as a site for the town of Parowan was selected, the men began to build a six-mile road into the canyon to obtain timber for dwellings and public buildings. One of the first poles cut was a ninety foot pole which they erected on their town site, and on it raised the Stars and Stripes. The land was dedicated, and their religious and civil liberties were celebrated by the raising of the flag and the firing of their cannon.

During the winter they built a fort of hewn logs, in the shape of a Greek cross. In the fort were located dwellings, a meeting house, a school, and a watch tower. This fort served Parowan for fifteen years.

George A. Smith was the leader of this community. His ability, energy and great enthusiasm did much to civilize southern Utah. He was the civil leader of the community as well as the religious leader. He taught English grammar around the campfires that first winter. He apparently conducted town meetings in a democratic manner, for he wrote: "our deliberations were conducted in a general assembly, which we called 'the quorum,' by the light and warmth of immense fires of dry scrub cedar and pinion pine. These debates of our farmers and mechanics were among the most animated scenes of my life."

5. OVERLAND EMIGRANTS TO THE CALIFORNIA GOLD FIELDS TRADED GOODS AND SERVICES IN UTAH

Gold was discovered in California Janu-

Here at Sutter's Mill, on the American River, California, on January 24, 1848, Mormon Battalion members were digging a millrace when gold was discovered, setting off the famous gold rush of 1849.

ary 24, 1848, while Mormon Battalion men were working for James W. Marshall on a sawmill on the stream at Sutter's Fort. As news of this discovery spread, thousands of people throughout the world rushed to California to stake a claim in the gold fields, and "strike it rich." News did not reach the East in time for people to get across the continent in 1848, but many were ready in 1849. It is estimated that nearly fifty thousand forty-niners made it across the continent that year. Of these, ten to fifteen thousand went by way of the Great Salt Lake. From June until October forty-niners flooded through the Salt Lake Valley. The presence of so many emigrants in Utah made important changes in the life of the people.

The forty-niners and the Mormons helped each other. Many of the forty-niners had brought too much of some things with them. They needed to lighten their wagons of surplus goods—food items, tools, equipment, clothing, and household goods. They needed fresh supplies of certain foods, oxen, and other animals. Some needed to have grain ground for them. They needed to have their wagons repaired. Some needed new wagons and harnesses. The Mormons could provide these services and foods. They had fresh oxen and other animals to spare. And the Mormons badly needed some food items, and clothing, for their clothing was wearing out. There were no stores, and they had little or no money. Tools and equipment had become worn out, damaged, or destroyed. Thus, the forty-niners traded their surplus goods for foods and services the Mormons could provide. The rate of exchange greatly favored the Mormons who were able to trade at one-fifth to one-half of eastern market value.

Mormon blacksmiths, wagonsmiths, teamsters, laundresses, and millers were kept busy. Mormons stationed at ferries on the major streams of the overland trail earned money for ferrying the California-bound wagons.

Some forty-niners, realizing it was better to get to California with less rather than not get there at all, abandoned goods on the side of the trail. Metal goods were among those most frequently dropped. The Mormons needed these badly, and men working the trail picked up such goods and brought them into the valley.

Before the gold rush, the Mormon settlers had little money in circulation. They knew the difficulty of living by barter. They appreciated the money that came to Utah with the forty-niners.

When several hundred forty-niners arrived too late to make it to California, many decided to winter in the valley. But such a large increase in the population, with stores of food already decreased through trade, threatened famine. To help the emigrants through, Captain *Jefferson Hunt* of the Mormon Battalion, who had gone over the southern route to California on two different occasions, offered to pilot them south and over the Old Spanish Trail to southern California. The large group left early in October 1849. Near Beaver Creek some advocated taking a shortcut to Walkers Pass, about which they had heard. But no one knew the country in between. There were no maps. Jefferson Hunt refused to guide them over any route but the one originally agreed upon. Many took the "shortcut" and suffered terribly on the desert, later known as Death Valley.

The scenes of 1849 were repeated in 1850 as the number of forty-niners in Salt Lake Valley doubled. About one thousand gold-seekers wintered in Salt Lake Valley before going on to California the next spring. In exchange for food and lodging, these emigrants worked on farms and helped the community in other ways. By 1851 the gold fever was dying, and perhaps only five thousand gold-seekers came through the valley.

The Mormons lived at the crossroads of the West. They could not live in complete isolation because their settlements were on the routes to California. In this case, as in instances to follow, the Mormons benefited by being on this crossroads of the West.

6. BY 1850 THE UTAH SETTLERS HAD ESTABLISHED THE BEGINNINGS OF CIVILIZED LIFE

By 1850, within four summers after the pioneers entered the Salt Lake Valley, the Mormon settlers had successfully transplanted the basic elements of civilization. They had established a large population. They were successfully engaged in agriculture and supplying their basic food needs. The essential trades were also established. Salt Lake Valley was the chief center of population and of agricultural and mechanical production. Several settlements had been established beyond the borders of Salt Lake Valley, and they showed promise of success.

The population. By 1850 there were 11,380 people in the settlements. They were located chiefly in the Great Salt Lake Valley, but also in the new settlements to the north and to the south. These people were *young*

By 1851, when this sketch was made, Salt Lake City showed evidences of rapid growth and was an important stopping place for emigrants on their way to California.

people. Three-fourths of the people were under age thirty and more than half of them were under age twenty. Most of the Mormon leaders were in their late thirties and forties. About 82 percent of the people had been born in the United States and 10 percent of those had been born in the territory of Utah. About 18 percent were foreign born, and most of them were from the British Isles and Canada. The population was about evenly divided between males and females.

SALT LAKE VALLEY, 1849

As described by Captain Howard Stansbury, U.S. Army:

A city had been laid out upon a magnificent scale, being nearly four miles in length and three in breadth; the streets at right angles with each other, eight rods or one hundred and thirty-two feet wide, with sidewalks of twenty feet; the blocks forty rods square, divided into eight lots, each of which contains an acre and a-quarter of ground. By an ordinance of the city, each house is to be placed twenty feet back from the front line of the lot, the intervening space being designed for shrubbery and trees. The site for the city is most beautiful: it lies at the western base of the Wahsatch Mountains, in a curve formed by the projection westward from the main range, of a lofty spur which forms its southern boundary. On the west it is washed by the waters of the Jordan, while to the southward for twenty-five miles extends a broad level plain, watered by several little streams, which, flowing down from the eastern hills, form the great element of fertility and wealth to the community. Through the city itself flows an unfailing stream of pure, sweet water, which, by an ingenious mode of irrigation, is made to traverse each side of every street, whence it is led into every garden-spot, spreading life, verdure, and beauty over what was heretofore a barren waste. On the east and north the mountain descends to the plain by steps, which form broad and elevated terraces, commanding an extended view of the whole valley of the Jordan, which is bounded on the west by a range of rugged mountains, stretching far to the southward, and enclosing within their embrace the lovely little Lake of Utah.

On the northern confines of the city, a warm spring issues from the base of the mountain, the water of which has been conducted by pipes into a commodious bathing-house; while, at the western point of the same spur, about three miles distant, another spring flows in a bold stream from beneath a perpendicular rock, with a temperature too high to admit the insertion of the hand, (128 Fahr.) At the base of the hill it forms a little lake, which in the autumn and winter is covered with large flocks of waterfowl, attracted by the genial temperature of the water.

... The facilities for beautifying this admirable site are manifold. The irrigating canals, which flow before every door, furnish abundance of water for the nourishment of shade-trees, and the open space between each building, and the pavement before it, when planted with shrubbery and adorned with flowers, will make this one of the most lovely spots between the Mississippi and the Pacific. One of the most unpleasant characteristics of the whole country, after leaving the Blue River [of Missouri], is the entire absence of trees from the landscape. ... The studding, therefore, of this beautiful city with noble trees, will render it, by contrast with the surrounding regions, a second "Diamond of the Desert" ... .

The land. There were 926 farms. A total of 46,849 acres had been taken up, of which 16,333 acres were under cultivation and 30,516 were in pasture.

The *fertility of the soil* is well shown by the *production of basic crops* in 1850. Enough food was produced for the whole community as well as some for the overland migration en route to California.

The value of *livestock* was totaled at $546,968. The population of 11,380 owned 5,266 working oxen, 4,861 milk cows, 2,489 "other cattle," 2,429 horses, 325 mules, 3,262 sheep, and 914 swine.

Fruit tree cuttings had been brought into the valley from California in May 1848. We are not informed by the records exactly what fruits were represented or how well these cuttings did. But in 1850 it was recorded that "Peaches were raised this year, the first raised in the Great Basin, though they were destroyed by the children before they were ripe." Even so the 1850 harvest was abundant.

The Utah family in 1850. The typical family in Utah in 1850 was made up of five members, two parents in their twenties or early thirties, with three children probably under fifteen, and possibly one of them born in Utah. In each household the father was engaged in some occupation, and every third family had an additional member over fourteen employed in some occupation. Fully half of the work force was engaged in farming. The other half was engaged in trades.

The typical farming family lived on a farm of fifty-one acres, one-third of which was cultivated and two-thirds in pasture. The family had two working oxen, two milk cows, one horse, a sheep or two, and every other family had a pig. In 1850 the family farm produced 116 bushels of wheat, 10 bushels of Indian corn, 11 bushels of oats, 46 bushels of Irish potatoes, 2 bushels of barley, 5 tons of hay, and garden vegetables worth (or sold at) $24.56. The household also made eighty-nine pounds of butter and thirty-two pounds of cheese. Some farming families grew rye, buckwheat, clover seed, flax, tobacco, and hops. Some made molasses, and one or two families had bees. The farm implements and machinery were worth about $90, and the cash value of the farm, including personal and real property was about $337.

The families engaged in the trades lived on their city lots and some of them may have farmed on small five-acre lots outside the city, though most of them might have confined their farming to the back part of their city lot. Half of the men in the trades were engaged in building and construction, blacksmithing, tanning and shoemaking, lumbering and making furniture, and brick making. There were only a few people in Utah in 1850 who lived by trading and by professions like law, teaching, and medicine.

11

The near-annual visits of Brigham Young to the settlements were welcomed by the people
and used by the Mormon leader as a means of promoting unity among the scattered settlements.

EARLY MORMON SETTLEMENT OF THE MOUNTAIN WEST

One of the most important contributions of the Mormons to the development of the American West was the establishment of settlements throughout Utah and the Mountain West. If it had not been for Mormon settlement, it is likely that Utah would have been only sparsely settled by mining and ranching communities. The Mormon village gave Utah a special character and served other areas of the Mountain West in many ways. The Mormons established an agricultural oasis in the Mountain West. Surplus agricultural products were freighted to rail centers and mining camps. Utah communities were on the route to California and had many opportunities to help emigrants.

Mormons gathered in Utah from many parts of the world. Here they settled in an orderly fashion and built communities. They brought with them many of their national habits and ways of life. Utah became a "melting pot" for peoples from many lands. Many of their ways were kept alive. Others were changed and became part of the Mormon pioneer way of life that developed in Utah.

IN THIS CHAPTER WE WILL LEARN

1. Why the Mormons planted settlements throughout Utah and the Mountain West.

2. The Mormon settlers came to Utah from many parts of the world.

3. How new settlements were founded.

4. From 1847 to 1857 settlements spread into the major valleys of Utah and to the borders of Deseret.

5. Settlements were built up by continued immigration.

6. How unity was kept in the far-flung Mormon empire.

173

north

1. WHY THE MORMONS PLANTED SETTLEMENTS THROUGHOUT UTAH AND THE MOUNTAIN WEST

Between 1847 and 1900, the Mormons founded about five hundred settlements. Most of these were in Utah, but many were in the neighboring states of California, Nevada, Arizona, New Mexico, Colorado, Wyoming, and Idaho. Mormon settlements were also made in Canada and Mexico. Over three hundred settlements were founded during Brigham Young's lifetime. Under his successors in the presidency of the Mormon church, John Taylor and Wilford Woodruff, the expansion of Mormon settlement continued without pause.

There were several reasons why the Mormons established settlements in Western America. Most of these reasons were religious, but some were political and economic.

The Mormons had a genuine desire to gather their fellow believers from throughout the world to their Utah Zion. They believed they had been led to the valley of the Great Salt Lake and that the surrounding regions were part of the gathering place. Belief in a gathering demanded that the Mormon leaders find a place for church members to settle. Land opportunities must be provided not only for those now of the Mormon faith, but for those who would yet become converted to the church. The gathered Latter-day Saints, as they believed, would make up a temporal and spiritual Kingdom of God on earth.

Many settlements were founded to help achieve the Mormon ideal of self-sufficiency. In many ways it was a practical necessity to be self-sufficient. Salt Lake Valley was hun-

The Mormon missionary system brought converts to Utah from many lands.

dreds of miles from eastern cities or the Pacific ports. The settlers must try to produce for themselves most of what they needed. It was also important for them to produce some goods in excess so thay could sell them for money with which to buy necessities. Money was scarce in early Utah.

The ideal of complete self-sufficiency was impossible to realize. Utah did not have sufficient natural resources to make it possible for the settlers to supply all their needs.

In order to supply their needs as well as they could, the Mormons founded settlements for the special purpose of producing goods like iron, coal, and cotton.

Some settlements were founded to convert Indians to Christianity and to Mormonism. It was Brigham Young's desire to teach the Indians the art of farming and building homes. He also wanted to teach them his religion. Mormons were sent on missions to live among the Indians, teach them their religion, agriculture, and the industries. Settlements were founded in connection with this Indian missionary effort. Often such missionary efforts were necessary to make peace with the Indians before settlements could be founded in these areas.

Outposts, way stations, or supply stations were set up along routes leading into the Mormon settlement area. Around the borders of Deseret, on the major routes, outposts were established that served as supply points for Mormon emigrants on their way to the central settlements.

2. THE MORMON SETTLERS CAME TO UTAH FROM MANY PARTS OF THE WORLD

The Mormon missionary system brought converts from many lands. The Mormons acted on the idea that their religion was for all people in all lands. So missionaries were sent to all the world, first the United States, then Canada, England, and Europe. Missionaries also went to the Pacific Islands, Australia, and the Orient.

Mormonism spread from western New York into eastern New York and on into the New England states. From gathering centers in Ohio, Missouri, and Illinois, the early Mormon missionaries went eastward into the more populous states. Gradually the new religion spread into most of the United States. Converts came from cities and villages of the most populous region of the country. A comparative few came from the sparsely settled frontier areas.

From New York, Mormonism spread northward into Canada. In turn Canadians and Americans in 1837 took Mormonism to England where they achieved remarkable success. Mormonism spread into various cities in the British Isles. From the British Isles the faith was taken by British subjects to outposts of the British Empire: Malta, Gibraltar, India, Australia, South Africa, and China. Australia became a significant center of Mormonism.

Between 1849 and 1853 Mormonism spread from Great Britain onto the continent of Europe where converts were made in small numbers in France, Switzerland, Italy, and Germany. Much more success, however, was enjoyed in the Scandinavian countries where large numbers of converts were made in Denmark, Sweden, and Norway.

Wherever the missionaries went, they praised their home in the mountains and taught their converts to gather in the Utah Zion.

Mormon converts brought to Utah their own ethnic characteristics and talents which contributed greatly to the development of the culture of Utah. From the cultures of Europe and other parts of the world, Mormon converts brought fine traditions and practices to Utah. Traditional ways survived in Utah, and her communities have been richer because of the contributions of people from so many lands.

The missionaries who thus spread their religion were the same people who pioneered the settlement of the Mountain West. A man might be founding a settlement one month, and the next month be called upon to leave his family and new home and go on a mission.

Great Britain and Scandinavia contributed the largest number of foreign-born converts to the Mormon migration. From 1840 to 1869, 28,063 British converts emigrated to America. From 1850 to 1869, 11,441 Scandinavian converts joined the Mormon migration to Utah. On an average each year about 800 British converts and about 580 Scandinavian converts emigrated to the United States. Switzerland, Germany, France, Italy, and other European countries contributed fewer, but nevertheless important, people to settling Utah.

Mormons gathered not only from Europe and Great Britain, but from other parts of the world. Immigrants came from Australia, India, South Africa, and the Near East. Most of the immigrants were British subjects.

Ways and Means of Immigration to Utah. From European countries converts went to Liverpool, England, where they were organized for their journey to America. Ships were chartered to carry them. Between 1840 and 1854, ships carrying converts from Liverpool docked at New Orleans, Louisiana. Immigrants then were transported up the Mississippi River on steamboats to Saint Louis. After 1855 ships docked at New York, Philadelphia, or Boston. From these ports immigrants took trains as far west as the rails ran, and then wagons to outfitting places in Iowa or Missouri. At outfitting places the immigrants were equipped and prepared for the overland trek. Immigrant companies were organized in much the same fashion as the 1847 Pioneer Company was organized. They traveled through the summer to arrive in Salt Lake Valley in September and October.

Some converts were able to pay the entire cost of their passage to America and their journey to Utah. Others were able to pay only a portion. To help poor emigrants

At Liverpool, England, Mormon converts from European countries boarded ship for America.

Mormon emigrant ship leaving Liverpool in 1853.

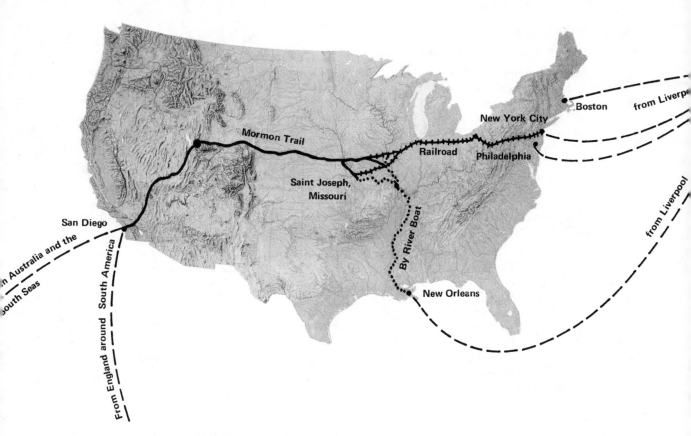

This map shows the ways immigrants were transported to Utah.

the *Perpetual Emigrating Fund Company* was organized in 1849. The fund was built by donations of money, oxen, wagons, and food stuffs. Donations were converted into cash or credit, which was then used to pay the expenses of transporting converts from Liverpool to Utah. When the immigrant was able to repay his indebtedness to the PEF, as it was called, he did so. In order to improve their finances, some immigrating Mormons stopped off in New Orleans, Saint Louis, or New York and worked for a season before making the overland trek to Utah.

A successful, unique, and distinctly Mormon method of travel employed the use of *handcarts*. The handcart was a two-wheeled cart supporting a box that held the traveler's essential belongings. The people walked and pulled or pushed the cart. Ox-drawn wagons carrying camp equipment and supplies accompanied the handcarts. By this method ten handcart companies, totaling nearly 3,000 people, crossed the plains between 1856 and 1860.

Upon arrival in Salt Lake Valley, the immigrants usually camped on a city square for a few days. Here they were visited by church leaders and instructed in the ways of Mormon community life. Places to settle were recommended. Sometimes "calls" were made for certain immigrants to go to certain valleys and help build settlements there. The newly arrived were often greeted by friends they had not seen since leaving their old homes.

THE HANDCART SONG

A favorite Mormon folk song commemorates the handcart:

Ye Saints who dwell on Europe's shore
Prepare yourselves, for many more,
To leave behind your native land,
For sure God's judgments are at hand.
For you must cross the raging main
Before the promised land you gain,
And with the faithful make a start,
To cross the plains with your handcart.

CHORUS

For some must push and some must pull,
As we go marching up the hill;
So merrily on the way we go
Until we reach the Valley.

The lands that boast of modern light
We know are all as dark as night,
Where poor men toil and want for bread,
Where peasant hosts are blindly led.
These lands that boast of liberty
You ne'er again would wish to see
When you from Europe make a start
To cross the plains with your handcart.

As on the road the carts are pulled
'Twould very much surprise the world
To see the old and feeble dame
Thus lend a hand to pull the same.
And maidens fair will dance and sing—
Young men more happy than a king,
And children, too, will laugh and play,
Their strength increasing day by day.

But some will say: It is too bad
The Saints upon the foot to "pad"
And more than that, to pull a load,
As they go marching o'er the road.
But then we say, It is the plan
To gather up the best of men
And women too—for none but they
Will ever travel in this way.

And long before the Valley's gained
We will be met upon the plains
With music sweet and friends so dear,
And fresh supplies our hearts to cheer.
And then with music and with song,
How cheerfully we'll march along,
And thank the day we made a start,
To cross the plains with our handcart.

When you get there, among the rest
Obedient be and you'll be blest;
And in God's chambers be shut in
While judgments cleanse the earth from sin.
For we do know, it will be so,
God's servants spoke it long ago;
We say it is high time to start,
To cross the plains with our handcart.

Mormon emigrants on their way to Utah halt on the road at a watering place.

Handcart travel was used by Mormon immigrants from 1856 to 1860. During that time ten companies totalling 2,945 persons started out. Tragedy struck the Willie and Martin companies (1856) when repeated winter storms came upon them after they reached South Pass. Before rescue teams could arrive from Salt Lake Valley, 122 had died of cold or starvation.

The Salt Lake Valley Mormons provided food, shelter, and comforts to the immigrants to make them welcome and help them get acquainted until they settled themselves more permanently.

A most important question to the newly arrived immigrant family was where to make their home. Many immigrants settled in Salt Lake Valley and remained there. Their skill and services were needed, and they found opportunity to make a good living. Some went into the neighboring valleys and made homes.

A MORMON OVERLAND EMIGRANT TRAIN, 1850

As described by Captain Howard Stansbury:

Monday, September 2.— ... Ninety-five wagons were met to-day, containing the advance of the Mormon emigration to the valley of the Salt Lake. Two large flocks of sheep were driven before the train, and geese and turkeys had been conveyed in coops, the whole distance, without apparent damage. One old gander poked his head out of his box and hissed most energetically at every passer-by, as if to show that his spirit was still unbroken, notwithstanding his long and uncomfortable confinement. The appearance of this train was good, most of the wagons having from three to five yoke of cattle, and all in fine condition. The wagons swarmed with women and children, and I estimated the train at one thousand head of cattle, one hundred head of sheep, and five hundred human souls.

In Salt Lake City the newly arrived emigrants were welcomed.

Others were called to found new settlements, to be truly pioneers in their own rights. Some went through the experience of helping found and build up new settlements several times in their lives.

3. HOW NEW SETTLEMENTS WERE FOUNDED

Most of Utah's communities were founded as a direct result of the planning and the direction of Mormon church leadership. The establishment of settlements and village life was an important phase of the church's work. Brigham Young and his associates planned and worked out the details of immigration and establishing settlements. Only a few communities were founded by individuals or groups of families acting on their own and these were soon brought under church organization.

The founding of distant settlements was a unique experience. It was not enough for some Mormon converts to have crossed the ocean and the continent to Utah. Some were asked to go many miles farther and settle virgin land just as the pioneers of 1847 had done in Salt Lake Valley.

Half of the settlements founded between 1847 and 1857 were located along the Wasatch Front. Families founding these settlements did not have to travel very far. The region was well explored. Indians were not a menace. There was security in numbers in the region. Between 1847 and 1858 more than fifty communities were founded in Weber, Davis, Salt Lake, and Utah counties.

The establishment of settlements farther away from Salt Lake Valley was much more difficult. Yet nearly fifty distant villages were founded between 1847 and 1858. These communities stretched from southern California to central Idaho, from Carson Valley in western Nevada to Moab on the Colorado River in eastern Utah.

Most of the settlers who founded new communities went through the same general experience. From the beginning of the settlement of Utah, Mormon pioneer leaders developed a pattern by which each new distant settlement was founded.

(1) The first task was to search out by exploration a place to settle. The pioneers of 1847 set the pattern. Before they chose Salt Lake Valley they learned all they could about it from the reports of Frémont and Mountain Men. They personally explored the valley, followed the streams into the canyons, searched the canyons for timber. Brigham Young wanted to know as much as could be learned about a place before he chose it as a site for permanent settlement. An appropriate site must have good land, ample water, ample timber, all near each other.

(2) A leader of the new settlement must be chosen. It was most important that the leader of the new settlement be experienced in guiding a migration and founding a settlement. He must be qualified to serve in the new settlement as religious, political, and economic leader. Many of the early leaders of settlements had experience in the Middle West, having helped found Mormon communities in Missouri and Illinois; most had taken a leading part in the overland migration and the settlement of Salt Lake Valley.

(3) Choosing the settlers was the next task. Each settlement must have persons who were skilled in the essential occupations and trades, like farmers, blacksmiths, carpenters, masons, tanners, millers, and sawyers. If the settlement had a special mission, persons with the necessary skills must be included in the number chosen to found the settlement. They must have the necessary equipment, not only in wagons, teams, tools, and firearms, but also any special equipment to help fulfill the mission assigned the settlement. Livestock,

poultry, seeds, and sufficient food to last a year must also be taken.

It was the practice in many instances for Mormon leaders to call settlers to go to certain valleys to make settlements. The call to found a new settlement was accepted just the same as a call to preach.

(4) Once the leader was chosen and the settlers called, a rendezvous point was announced at which the entire group would gather and organize for *the journey to the new settlement site.* Most groups going south met and were organized in Utah Valley. The organization used on the overland journey was used on these journeys. The leader was given authority and expected obedience. Careful instructions were given by Brigham Young or an associate. The settlement leader was expected to follow these instructions. He was to exercise his best judgment. Supplies were checked to make sure all necessary tools and equipment were present.

Covered wagons drawn by ox teams were the common mode of transportation. The trek was begun. Camps were made on creeks or at water holes. Settlers going into southern Utah, Arizona, and Nevada had serious troubles from the lack of roads and water, and hostile Indians.

(5) Arriving at the site of their future home, the settlers set to work to lay the foundations of their settlement. Sometimes a temporary camp was made and the site for the village determined after thorough exploration of the locale. Sometimes the settlers chose the site at once and began laying out the village. The leader directed all phases of life and activities in the new settlement.

The site for the settlement had to be close to timber, water, and good land. A site near the mouth of a canyon offered several advantages. Timber was in the mountains. The canyon stream supplied the water needs of the settlement. Also the richest lands were to be found near the mouths of canyons or by the beds of streams.

If settlers came at the right time of the year, *planting* began immediately. The *construction of a road into the canyon* was begun at once, too, to obtain timber with which to build a fort and cabins. While cabins were being built, people lived in their wagon boxes that had been removed from the wagon bed. *Timber* was cut and hauled down the canyon on the wagon beds. Communities with large enough canyon streams floated timber down the stream. Another first task was the building of *irrigation canals* to carry the water from the canyon stream to the village site. Gristmills and sawmills were begun as soon as possible.

The next task was to *build a shelter* against the weather and protection against the Indians. Very often the settlers spent the first year living in *dugouts*. These were half-caves dug in the side of a hill, fronted up with logs and roofed over with logs, branches, and sod. Sometimes *log cabins* were built at once, and a *stockade* of poles reinforced with rocks and adobe bricks was erected around the cabins. The pattern for cabin arrangement in a *fort* had been set in Salt Lake Valley, though improved upon by later settlements. While it was policy to be at peace with the Indians at almost any cost, it was also policy to be cautious. The stockade, meant to protect the settlers from an Indian attack, was used as a corral for the cattle. The cattle were brought into the stockade nightly and during any threat of Indians stealing or killing them. It was important to have a water supply in the fort, either from streams or wells.

When the Indian menace proved unreal or disappeared (usually within a year or two), the fort was abandoned, and *the settlers moved out onto their city lots* and their farms.

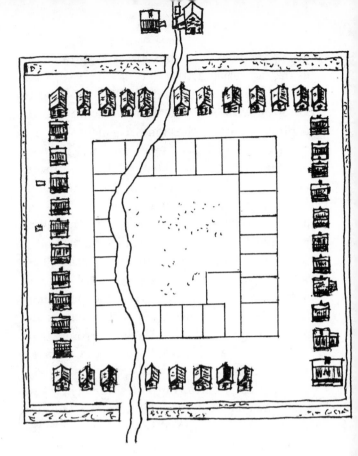

Many Mormon villages were first forts, with cabins arranged in a protective square.

Surveying the city lots and farms was usually begun at once, but always within the first year or two. In settlements near Salt Lake City, Brigham Young visited within months after their beginning and helped choose the site for the town and lay it out.

4. FROM 1847 TO 1857 SETTLEMENTS SPREAD INTO THE MAJOR VALLEYS OF UTAH AND TO THE BORDERS OF DESERET

In the last chapter we studied the beginnings of settlement in Salt Lake Valley, Utah Valley, Sanpete Valley, and Little Salt Lake Valley. We saw how settlements expanded into neighboring regions. The Mormons wanted to settle all the areas they could as soon as possible, to be the first settlers there, and establish their society in these valleys.

It will not be possible to narrate the history of each settlement or the expansion of settlement in each valley. We will concern ourselves with the general movements and directions taken by Mormon settlement.

During the first ten years of Mormon settlement of the Mountain West, four movements can be seen. First, initial settlements were established as soon as possible in the major valleys of the Utah region spreading from the Ogden region on the north to the Little Salt Lake Valley on the south. These valleys had been settled by 1851 as we learned in the last chapter. Second, many new settlements were made in the valleys immediately west of the Wasatch Front, from Utah Valley on the south to the Ogden region on the north. Third, more distant valleys were settled. Fourth, outpost settlements were established along the routes into the Mormon country. These outposts served as supply stations to help the Mormon migration and other Mormon business coming into the central valleys.

The Wasatch Front was rapidly settled. Along the western front of the Wasatch Mountains from Provo on the south to Brigham City on the north, settlements were made in rapid succession. There was little Indian threat in Salt Lake Valley and northward.

In *Salt Lake Valley* many settlements were established the first years. During the summer of 1848 people moved from the Old Fort out onto excellent sites for settlements and laid the foundations of Big Cottonwood, East Mill Creek, Sugar House, South Cottonwood, North Jordan and West Jordan. In 1849 Little Cottonwood, Brighton, Granger, and Draper were settled. Herriman and Midvale were settled in 1851 and Crescent in 1854.

Davis County settlements had an early beginning. In 1848 settlement expanded from Bountiful and Farmington to Centerville and Kaysville, and in 1850 Layton was founded.

Ogden's beginnings date from James Brown's purchase of Miles Goodyear's holdings on Weber River. The settlement grew, and from Ogden as a center, other settlements soon were made in the surrounding region: Mound Fort (1848), Lynn (1849), Harrisville, Marriott, Slaterville, Uintah, and West Weber (1850), North Ogden, Farr West, and South Weber (1851), and South Hooper (1852).

Ogden, looking north on today's Washington Boulevard, about 1860.

THE MORMONS PUT PLACE NAMES ON THE MAP OF UTAH

In naming their settlements, the Mormons chose names from many sources: names of their leaders, names from the Bible or their *Book of Mormon*, or names of their homes in the British Isles and Europe. Here are a few examples of each.

Places named for church leaders:

Abraham, Millard County	Abraham H. Cannon
Benson, Cache County	Ezra Taft Benson
Brigham City, Box Elder County	Brigham Young
Cannonville, Garfield County	George Q. Cannon
Clawson, Emery County	Rudger Clawson
Fielding, Box Elder County	Joseph F. Smith
Heber, Wasatch County	Heber C. Kimball
Hyrum, Cache County	Hyrum Smith
Iosepa, Tooele County (*Iosepa*, Hawaiian for Joseph)	Joseph F. Smith
Taylor, Weber County	John Taylor
Thatcher, Box Elder County	Moses Thatcher
Widtsoe, Garfield County	John A. Widtsoe
Woodruff, Rich County	Wilford Woodruff
Ivins, Washington County	Anthony W. Ivins
Joseph, Sevier County	Joseph A. Young
Lyman, Wayne County	Frances M. Lyman
Maeser, Uintah County	Karl G. Maeser
Marion, Summit County	Francis Marion Lyman
Parleys Park, Summit County	Parley P. Pratt
Parleys Canyon	Parley P. Pratt
Penrose, Box Elder County	Charles W. Penrose
Saint George, Washington County	George A. Smith
Snowville, Box Elder County	Lorenzo Snow
Talmage, Duchesne County	James E. Talmage

Place names drawn from the Bible and the Book of Mormon:

Bountiful, Davis County

Deseret, Millard County

Enoch, Iron County

Ephraim, Sanpete County

Jordan River

Lehi, Utah County

Manti, Sanpete County

Mount Carmel, Kane County

Mount Nebo, Utah County

Nephi, Juab County

Salem, Utah County

Moab, Grand County

Moroni, Sanpete County

Place names drawn from homes in Europe and the British Isles:

Avon, Cache County	Avon, England
Glendale, Kane County	Glendale, Scotland
Leeds, Washington County	Leeds, England
Lynne, Box Elder county	Lynne, Scotland
Wales, Sanpete County	Wales, England
Elsinore, Sevier County	Elsinore, Denmark
Venice, Sevier County	Venice, Italy

Settlements expanded not only along the base of the mountains on the streams of the Ogden and Weber rivers, but *up the Weber River into Morgan Valley.* The rich lands of Morgan Valley attracted settlers and soon settlements were made there: Morgan and Peterson (1855), and Milton (1856). Wanship (1854) and Peoa (1857) were founded on the upper Weber.

From the Ogden area settlers moved northward too. Settlers of Harrisville went northward to the site of Willard where they laid foundations for that settlement in 1851. Pleasant View and Brigham City were settled in 1851. Perry was founded in 1854, and north of Brigham City, Call's Fort (Harper) was established in 1853.

From Salt Lake Valley settlement expanded westward into *Tooele Valley* in 1849 when Tooele and Grantsville were founded.

The beginnings of Batesville date from 1852. In 1854 Clover was settled.

As soon as the Indian menace had passed, *Utah Valley* rapidly filled up with settlements. Provo beginnings date from 1849. The next spring Lehi was settled, and in the summer Pleasant Grove was established on Battle Creek. That fall (1850) these settlements were begun: Springville, Payson, Alpine, Spanish Fork, American Fork, and Lindon. In 1851 Santaquin and Salem were settled. Mapleton was founded in 1856, and Goshen in 1857.

West of Utah Valley is *Cedar Valley*, a dry valley in the desert regions of the Great Basin. Two settlements were founded there: Cedar Valley (1852) and Fairfield (1855).

As settlement in Utah Valley swelled, it overflowed southward into *Juab Valley*. In 1851 Nephi and Mona were founded in that valley.

Distant valleys were settled. Nearly half of the settlements founded between 1847 and 1857 lay beyond the Wasatch Front. About thirty-eight settlements were founded north of Brigham City, and south of Utah Valley. People were more frequently called to establish these distant settlements, and the typical procedures of founding a settlement (section 3) were more closely followed.

Cache Valley had its initial settlement in 1856 when droughts in Tooele Valley sent Peter Maughan looking for a better place to settle. Brigham Young encouraged him to try Cache Valley. Cattle had been grazed there the year before. Maughan's Fort (Wellsville) was established in 1856. The next year additional population came into the valley, and Mendon was founded just north of Wellsville.

Sanpete Valley was initially settled in 1849 and 1850 with the founding of Manti, as related in the last chapter. In 1852-53 Ephraim was settled, and Spring City in 1852. The beginnings of Mount Pleasant date from this same time, though the settlement was abandoned because of Indian troubles until 1859.

The Mormon pioneer leaders fully expected settlement to expand throughout the Utah region. They thought the future capital of the territory should be in the geographical center. For this purpose Fillmore was established in *Pavant Valley* in 1851. Two other settlements came a little later when Holden was founded in 1855 and Meadow in 1857.

Parowan, settled in 1851, served as a supply station on the route between Salt Lake City and California and as a significant center from which many other settlements were founded. Late in 1851 Cedar City was founded. These two settlements were the center of the *Iron Mission*, an attempt to produce iron from iron ore discovered west of Cedar City. For seven years great effort and money were put into the project with only moderate success. Paragonah was settled in 1852. *Beaver* was settled in 1856 by a group of people from Parowan.

From Parowan settlers pressed farther south into Utah's *Dixie* country. Here along the Santa Clara and Virgin rivers the Indians practiced a little agriculture. Settlements spread into this region very early: Harmony on Ash Creek (1852), Pine Valley (1855), Pinto (1856), Washington on the Virgin River (1856), Gunlock on the Santa Clara (1857), and Price on the Virgin (1858).

Outposts of the Mormon empire were established along the emigrant routes leading to the central valleys of Utah. These outposts were settlements serving especially as forts or supply stations. Some had a special mission of making peace with the Indians by converting them to Mormonism and teaching them the arts of civilization.

On the Overland Trail *Fort Supply*,

about twelve miles south of Fort Bridger, was established in 1853. In 1855 the Mormons bought *Fort Bridger*. These forts were important to the Mormons for supplying immigrants with flour made from the grain raised there.

Genoa in Carson Valley (now western Nevada) was laid out as a Mormon settlement in 1854 although Mormons had established Mormon Station there as a trading post as early as 1849.

San Bernardino, California, was established in 1851 as a typical Mormon settlement. Early in 1851 Amasa M. Lyman and

San Bernardino, California, was an important outpost of Mormon settlement, founded in 1851, near Cajon Pass on the Old Spanish Trail.

Fort Supply, built by the Mormons on the overland trail in 1853, served as a supply point and resting place for emigrants before the last part of the journey to Salt Lake Valley.

The Mormon outpost of Genoa, at the east foot of the Sierra Nevada, as drawn by H. V. A. von Breckh, artist with the Simpson expedition of 1859.

Charles C. Rich led a company of some five hundred Mormons and 150 wagons by way of the Old Spanish Trail to California. At the foot of the mountains, near Cajon Pass, the city of San Bernardino was laid out on the lands of the old San Bernardino Ranch, bought by the Mormons for their settlement. Soon the community was among the most prosperous of Mormon settlements. It served as a stopping place for missionaries and immigrants from the Pacific Ocean area and from England. It supplied food and other essentials to emigrants making their way to the central valleys of Utah.

Las Vegas, or "The Meadows," was established in 1855 as a Mormon outpost on the Old Spanish Trail. The primary purpose of the Las Vegas Mission was to induce the Indians to ways of peace, teach them Mormonism and the arts of civilization. Also food stuffs were grown in the small meadows and supplied to companies of travelers going to and from California. Las Vegas was over 200 miles from Cajon Pass—desert all the way—and about 120 miles from the settlements on the Santa Clara. Thus, Las Vegas was an important supply point, furnishing water and food to weary travelers.

Two outposts were established for the primary purpose of converting the Indians. The *Elk Mountain Mission* (May-September 1855) took a company of forty-one men, fifteen wagons, and the usual supplies from Manti eastward to the site of present *Moab*. When they arrived at their destination the Indians at first welcomed them; however, shortly the Indians' mood changed and they laid seige to the little fort. The Mormons then abandoned the mission and returned to Manti. This mission has been called "the most disastrous and futile of its kind."

The *Salmon River Mission* (1855) established *Fort Limhi* (now spelled Lemhi) on the Lemhi Branch of the Salmon River in Idaho about four hundred miles north of Salt Lake City. The mission, which was among the Bannock and Shoshoni Indians, gave signs of success. It made progress among the Indians. Grain and vegetables were raised. But a sudden Indian uprising in February 1858 led to the abandonment of Fort Limhi late that year. No attempt was made to re-establish the mission.

By 1857 the central valleys of Utah were well filled with small communities. More distant valleys had received initial settlement and showed signs of successful beginnings. The region of Deseret had been rimmed with outposts in strategic places.

5. SETTLEMENTS WERE BUILT UP BY CONTINUED IMMIGRATION

Once settlements had been established, it was important for them to be built up with additional citizens who would help them become centers for religious, social, economic, and political life.

As a result of Mormon missionary work, there was a continual flow of emigration to Utah. An average of about three thousand immigrants arrived in Salt Lake Valley each year between 1847 and 1869. The population of Utah Territory had increased from 11,380 in 1850 to 40,273 by 1860. About two-thirds of the total population lived in the five counties along the Wasatch Front: Salt Lake County, 11,295; Davis County, 2,904; Weber County, 3,675; Box Elder County, 1,608; and Utah County, 8,248. In neighboring Tooele County there were 1,008 people. In 1860, Cache County population numbered 2,605; Juab, 672; Millard, 715; Sanpete, 3,815; and Washington, 691.

6. HOW UNITY WAS KEPT IN THE FAR-FLUNG MORMON EMPIRE

Without the advantages of modern means of communications, the Mormons developed a truly remarkable system by which they maintained a fundamental unity among their far-flung settlements. There was a sameness to all villages, not only in their physical layout, but in their internal life.

This unity was achieved by various means. A *strong leader* was chosen to establish the major settlements, and he had influence with leaders of neighboring settlements. From the pulpit the village leader gave instruction in all fields, not only for religion but for the everyday operations of the village. Village leaders went twice each year to Salt Lake City to attend the *general conferences* of the church. Here they received instructions and answers to their problems. During the October conference of the church the *annual fair* was held; examples of what communities had done were displayed. *Brigham Young made frequent visits* to the settlements, inspecting, inquiring, giving instructions and encouragement, and reporting on general church developments to encourage the settlers in their work. Through the columns of the church newspapers, such as the *Deseret News* (founded 1850) and the *Latter-day Saints' Millennial Star* (printed in England since 1840), the same instruction went to all Mormons. Through all these means the church leadership kept their people united.

Brigham Young visited distant settlements. Here he is in Arizona, 1870. These long trips offered ample opportunity to discuss goals and methods, and to become acquainted with local leaders and the people.

Salt Lake City looking eastward on South Temple Street about 1859. The Deseret Museum and the Mint are at the left, the Lion House and Beehive House are in the center, and the home of Daniel H. Wells is at the right.

LIFE AND LABOR IN THE EARLY SETTLEMENTS

How did the first settlers live once they were in their villages? An understanding of how they lived and worked will help us appreciate what they did to secure a hold in this region.

Most communities in America, and especially on the western American frontier, grew up in an irregular manner without planning, streets developing from cowpaths or Indian trails. Not so in Utah. Here villages were planned. The life lived in those villages conformed largely to patterns set by church leaders. Cooperation was required to effect these patterns. Community goals were achieved by individual sacrifice. Work, industry, thrift, and sobriety were virtues required of all.

IN THIS CHAPTER WE WILL LEARN

1. The Mormon village followed a city plan that was repeated in all settlements.

2. Utah village life was based on agriculture and related trades.

3. Home life in the early Utah village was primitive.

4. The economic life of Utah was advanced by the efforts of many people.

5. Pioneer social life emphasized religious activities, recreation, and education.

12

Salt Lake City, Utah's first permanent settlement, soon became the political, commercial, social, and religious center of the territory. An 1853 view.

This 1860 plat of Salt Lake City shows the pattern by which the capital city as well as most other Mormon villages were laid out.

1. THE MORMON VILLAGE FOLLOWED A CITY PLAN THAT WAS REPEATED IN ALL SETTLEMENTS

The Mormon village in the Mountain West was patterned after Joseph Smith's "City of Zion." The City of Zion planned for a community of farmers and associated trades. There was to be a central residential area; barns, corrals, and farms and farm buildings were to be located outside the residential limits. A central square was to be reserved for the village tabernacle. This plan, it was hoped, would bring people together into a closely knit society where they could work together more easily for common goals. Most Utah settlements were laid out according to the plan, but the ideal was difficult to realize.

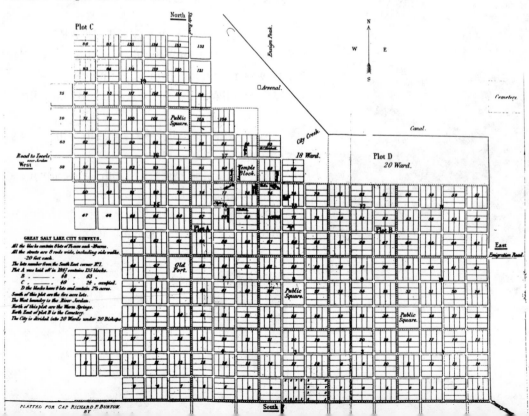

The Utah village blocks were square, the streets wide and running at right angles, always in north-south and east-west directions. Blocks were usually about ten acres each, and eight house lots were planned for each block. This gave each household about one and one-fourth acres for house and garden.

Salt Lake City was laid out according to this plan. The immigrant to Utah saw his first City of Zion when he entered Great Salt Lake Valley. Here he became acquainted with the village pattern of life to be followed in settlements he would help establish.

Most families lived in the Old Fort one or two years, then moved onto their city lots, built small cottages, and planted their gardens and fruit trees. Gradually Salt Lake City began to look like a city.

Salt Lake City held a special place in the minds and hearts of the people of Utah. It had been the first settlement, and it became the leading city. It was the headquarters of the Mormon church, the home of Brigham Young and other leaders. It was the religious, social, and commercial center.

Important first buildings, after the Old Fort and cottages, included *boweries* and

The Council House, one of the most important public buildings in early Utah, stood on the southwest corner of Main and South Temple streets.

The Social Hall, entertainment center, stood a half block south of Eagle Gate, on the east side of the street.

The block east of the Temple Block (Hotel Utah corner today) was an important commercial center in early Utah. The Deseret Store and General Tithing Office and Bishop's Storehouse are shown on the corner (1 and 2). Also shown are Brigham Young's stables (3), the Mint (4), Deseret News Building (5), Brigham Young's first home (6), the Lion House (7), the Beehive House (8), and the city wall (9).

191

The Temple Block, from the beginning, was the religious center of Salt Lake City. This early view shows the Old Tabernacle (3) and the brush-covered bowery to the right.

Eagle Gate, entrance to Brigham Young's property, has undergone several changes and remains today a landmark in the city. The original wooden eagle was carved by Ralph Ramsey.

tabernacles, in which meetings were held. On the Temple Block, now known as Temple Square, the first bowery was erected. The Old Tabernacle was completed in 1851 and served until the present tabernacle was completed in 1867. The site for the temple was marked by Brigham Young on July 28, 1847. On February 14, 1853 the ground was dedicated, and on the following April 6 the cornerstone of the Salt Lake Temple was laid.

The *Council House*, completed in 1850, was an important center for church, government, education, and printing activities. The *Social Hall* was the early entertainment center. It housed the first theater west of the Missouri River and was used for stage plays, dances, and other entertainments.

The residences of Brigham Young were important buildings in early Salt Lake City. The *Beehive House*, built in 1852, was his personal residence and sometimes his office. Immediately west of the Beehive House, Brigham Young constructed in 1852 a one-storied adobe building, the *Governor's Office* or *President's Office*. Church records were kept at the *Historian's Office*, built in 1854. The *Lion House* was built in 1855 as another residence for Brigham Young and his family.

The Beehive House, the President's Office, and the Lion House, all built for Brigham Young, were the most impressive buildings in Salt Lake City in the early years. An 1858 photo by D. A. Burr, taken from near the Social Hall.

Brigham Young's property extended east and north up City Creek. Just east of the Beehive House, he built a *private school* for the education of his children. In 1859 he constructed the *Eagle Gate*, which spanned the road giving entrance into his properties to the north.

Directly east of the Temple Block the buildings and yards of the church's *General Tithing Office and Bishop's Storehouse* were erected between 1850 and 1852. On the corner fronting south was the Deseret Store, a general store serving people doing business in the tithing system. This store was the home of the *Deseret News* for many years. Just east of these offices was the *Mint* (1849).

When a business district emerged in Salt Lake City, it grew out of residential areas along Main and State streets. In Mormon villages "Main Street" usually developed close to the central square or along the main road through town. Salt Lake City was first to develop a business district. Other settlements took years to develop a small business district or main street. Many tradesmen took care of their business in their cottages until a business district emerged.

Important to every settler was "water in the ditch" for irrigating crops. Fences were important, also, to keep livestock where it belonged.

Utah villages were established near the mouths of canyons or high on streams where fresh water could be obtained for household uses and irrigation. The compact villages helped conserve limited water resources. Easy access was also had to timber in the nearby canyons. Location near the mountains may have helped give protection against Indians.

Setting up an **irrigation system** was a primary task. The men went to work digging ditches from the streams to the village blocks in such a way as to provide an even flow of water to all sections of the village. The life-giving water, used for drinking, kitchen use, and irrigation, flowed along the sides of the streets in neat ditches.

Fences were an absolute necessity, to keep one's own livestock at home and keep another's livestock out of one's yards and pastures. "Good fences make good neighbors" was a wise and important proverb.

2. UTAH VILLAGE LIFE WAS BASED ON AGRICULTURE AND RELATED TRADES

Agriculture was the economic base of Mormon settlement in the Mountain West. Farming was the first occupation of the people. Food was produced in each village. There could be no reliance on bringing in food supplies from distant supply centers, so each village had to produce as much of its own food as possible.

Major crops were wheat, maize (Indian corn), oats, Irish potatoes, peas, and beans. Some rye, buckwheat, and barley were also grown. Sorghum molasses served as a sugar substitute. The important grain-raising valleys were Salt Lake, Utah, Sanpete and the lands in Davis and Weber counties. By 1860 Box Elder and Cache valleys were beginning to produce a variety of crops, and Iron County produced quantities of wheat and corn.

Not all grist mills were as extensive as this one owned by Brigham Young. At the grist mill wheat and other grains were ground into flour or other forms for use.

James Henry Ellsworth, blacksmith, worked at his trade in Payson, Leeds, and Kanab in Utah before settling in Arizona in the 1880s.

During the 1850s, when the population increased two and one-half times, the number of farms increased almost four fold, and the area of improved land increased almost five times. Wheat production increased three fold, corn ten fold, Irish potatoes three fold, peas, beans, wool, and flax eight fold. Fruit trees were imported in large numbers in the 1850s, and Utah's orchards were begun. Orchard products for the year 1859-60 were valued at $9,281. The counties produced fruit valued as follows: Salt Lake, $7,296; Sanpete, $1,335; Tooele, $300; Utah, $160; Davis, $140; and Weber, $50.

By the end of the 1850s the people passed beyond fear of starvation. Yet there were bad years. Crickets and grasshoppers were a constant threat, and they continued to be a threat for years. Crickets destroyed many of the crops of 1848 and 1849, and in these years gulls or plover came to help halt the ravages of the crickets. The crops of 1850 were good, but 1851 was known as a famine year. Bounteous crops were raised the next years, but in 1855 and 1856 the crickets were at their worst. The territory was laid waste, and famine was upon the people. These two years were the most critical years for the settlers. The crops of 1857 were good, and thereafter enough was raised that the fear of famine began to pass. Yet in each new settlement there was always the threat of famine during the first years.

But not all people lived by farming. From the beginning nearly half of the working men were engaged in other **essential trades** and businesses. In each village there was need for saw mills, grist mills, tanneries, and blacksmith shops. People often had to travel short distances to the *grist mill* to have wheat ground and made into flour. *Saw mills* were set up on good streams to cut logs into convenient sizes for construction. Not every village or even valley had a *tanner*; there was

a great demand for leather and leather goods, especially harnesses, boots, and shoes. The *blacksmith* worked in metals to provide shoes for horses and oxen, iron tires for wagon wheels. He not only made wagons and carts, but tools, guns, and nails. His was the most basic industry after food production, for without his services few other activities could go on.

In most communities one would find a blacksmith, sawyer, miller, and carpenter. In the larger communities one would find cabinetmakers, tanners, makers of pottery, tin wares, copper and sheet-iron, and cordage, yarns, and hats. There were also gunsmiths, watchmakers, carpenters, and masons.

3. HOME LIFE IN THE EARLY UTAH VILLAGE WAS PRIMITIVE

As the village was the center of life in Utah, so the home was the center of life in the village.

In moving out onto the American frontier, families were often reduced to primitive living. They could stow away only essential belongings in their wagons, and they sometimes had to live out of wagons for months. Everyone had to work at the essential occupations of life, supplying food, clothing, and shelter. Gradually these primitive conditions changed to something a little more comfortable.

The pioneer home evolved from the wagon box and crude dugout to a small cottage. When a new settlement was started, whole families lived from the wagon box for days, weeks, and sometimes months. Sometimes a tent covered the wagon box, or was used alone. The next home might be a *dugout*, a dwelling dug in the side of an earth embankment, a front wall with door, some partial sides, and a short roof, thickly covered with sod. The interior of the dugout provided a dark, damp, and smoky apartment at best— a dirt floor, back walls of dirt, no windows, a crude door, and some kind of fireplace. In southern Utah where stone was more plentiful than timber, this same type of dwelling was made with stones laid up instead of timbers for the front walls.

A third type of home might be a *cabin* of logs but more frequently of adobe. Timber was needed for door and window lintels and for roofing. Where there was sufficient timber, the cabin might be made of logs, laid up and chinked with adobe. Roofs were made of board slabs or a few timbers and branches covered with dirt sod. Shingles came later.

The cabin had only one door and small windows in order to help keep out dirt and cold. Besides, there was no glass for windows and only poor substitutes such as greased paper or factory cloth. For light one depended on tallow candles. Beds were built by setting an upright post in the floor and join-

*After years of work a settler might have
a comfortable log cabin for his family.*

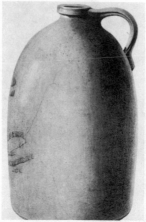

Stone jug

Sleigh chair

Winding reel

Wooden chair

Friendship quilt

ing it to the cabin walls by horizontal poles secured to the post. Ropes or strips of rawhide were stretched from poles to walls, and on this framework the bedding was placed. Straw mattresses were common until enough feathers were collected for a feather mattress.

The fireplace was the center of activity. Here was warmth as well as the cooking center. One might also see the tools of the man's trade, a spinning wheel, a cupboard covered by a cloth curtain, log benches, rough tables, and a rocker. For the baby there was a cradle on rockers. The water pail had to be filled from the ditch or well and brought in. Water was drawn in this manner for drinking, cooking, and bathing. Baths were usually taken in a large tub set on the floor, but in summertime young people bathed in a nearby creek.

Cottages were placed at the front of the lot to give regularity to the streets. Space was provided for ornamental trees, shrubs, and flowers. Behind the cottage was the family's vegetable garden and small orchard. Trees were planted on the street ditch bank. Water from the street ditch was taken by a smaller

196

Iron   *Lantern*

ditch onto the lot, watering the shrubs and irrigating the garden. A family could produce much of its own food needs on an acre of garden, with enough of some crops to last through the winter.

The straight streets were soon accented by the lines of young trees growing along the sides. Some trees were transplanted from the mountains—locust, maple, and cottonwood—while others were imported—the lombardy poplar, the carolina poplar, the black locust, and the honey locust. Peach, apricot, plum, cherry, and apple trees were brought in for home orchards, and did well once they made a start.

Food. From the beginning of settlement, food was a problem for each community. Settlers took a supply of dry food staples with them, and they had to eat from these stores for months, perhaps a year, until their crops matured. Even when yields were good, the farmer could not think of himself alone. There were heavy demands for his produce from the newly arrived immigrants, overland emigrants, the Indians, and his fellow settlers who were following trades.

The *basic foods* were meat (chiefly beef), wheat (made into bread and cereals), corn, potatoes, and seasonal foods from the garden and orchard. In the spring and sum-

mer months there were peas, beans, squashes, cabbages, beets, cauliflower, and lettuce. And when nut and fruit trees were producing, the settler had walnuts, apricots, quinces, cherries, plums, currants, raspberries, and gooseberries.

Wild plants and wild game were also eaten. Deer, elk, and antelope were hunted. Fish were taken from the streams. In early summer, children might gather eggs of geese, ducks, curlews, and plovers found in the thick grass of the marshy flats about the lakes and valley streams.

Wild berries were eaten raw or cooked, and made into syrups and jellies. Among the native berries used were the golden currant, the serviceberry (or sarviceberry), blue huckleberry (or blueberry), grouse whortleberry, wild raspberry, western thimbleberry, chokecherry, and blueberry elder. Greens such as miner's lettuce, dandelion plants, and water cress were important for food. Roots and bulbs of different kinds were also used, such as the Indian parsnip, wild onion, the brandegee onion, and the arrowleaved balsamroot, sometimes called "Mormon biscuit." Wild rhubarb was found and used. The blue camas lily was much desired by Indians and whites alike. The bulb of the sego lily was used by

Rag carpet

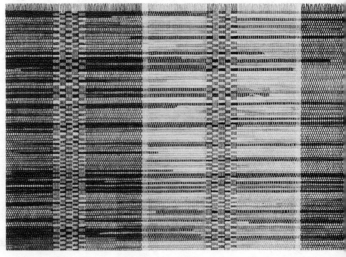

the Indians who taught its use to the early settlers and thus helped them survive.

Some plants were imported by the settlers: mustard plants, the sunflower, catnip (a medication for colic), horehound (used in making the popular horehound candy), and mint.

The pioneers were resourceful in supplying their food needs as shown by this list of the total variety of foods available. However, few people had access to all these foods. Most families in a new settlement were deprived of all but a few foods, and the hardest trial was the monotony of their diet, the necessity of getting along on the same food items, week after week.

Clothing. As soon as clothing brought to Utah was worn out, the settlers had to make their own. One could not buy clothes from stores in the early days of any settlement. It took years to develop trade with the States and to obtain enough money to buy goods. Shoes were especially hard to replace. It took years for tanners to establish themselves. Children often went barefoot. A pair of moccasins might be made for wear on special occasions such as Sundays. Wool was taken from sheep and carded into fleecy rolls which the girls spun into woolen yarn, using the spinning wheel. Cloth was woven from the yarn, then cut and made into clothes for the family. The cover from the covered wagon might be borrowed. Well-worn and bleached, it was cut and made into men's shirts and pants. A pair of pants might be made from an elk skin, and a hat from straw.

Other home manufactures included soap, candles, molasses, beverages, brooms, wooden bottles, pottery, combs, and dyes. *Soap* was an essential item. Animal grease from cooking and butchering was saved through the year. Lye was made from wood ashes in leach barrels. The grease and the lye were boiled to-

Churn   *Copper kettle*

gether in large pots out-of-doors. It was a full day's work. It took many bushels of ashes and many pounds of grease to make a barrel of soap, but that much soap lasted a long time. Soapmaking was a spring activity.

Making tallow *candles* was an autumn activity, in preparation for the time when light would be needed during the long winter nights and short days. Tallow was melted and poured into molds in which the wick had been placed. Sometimes wicks were dipped slowly and cooled and the process repeated until the tallow built up around the wick and a candle was produced.

"Necessity is the mother of invention," it was often said, and members of the family developed resourcefulness in meeting their needs. It was a habit of life to "make-do"—to use what was available for many purposes. "Eat it all, wear it out, make it do, or do without," was the motto of many families.

4. THE ECONOMIC LIFE OF UTAH WAS ADVANCED BY THE EFFORTS OF MANY PEOPLE

Men working together can do many things that individuals alone cannot do. The people of Utah expected each man to use his energies and skills for the community good as well as his own. Work projects were planned and sponsored by Mormon church leaders. The legislatures of the State of Deseret and of the Territory of Utah made grants of money to church enterprises and private enterprises to help develop the resources of the territory for the benefit of the people.

BRIGHAM YOUNG

As described by Captain Howard Stansbury:

... President Young appeared to be a man of clear, sound sense, fully alive to the responsibilities of the station he occupies, sincerely devoted to the good name and interests of the people over which he presides, sensitively jealous of the least attempt to undervalue or misrepresent them, and indefatigable in devising ways and means for their moral, mental, and physical elevation. He appeared to possess the unlimited personal and official confidence of the people; while both he and his two counsellors, forming the presidency of the church, seemed to have but one object in view, the prosperity and peace of the society over which they presided.

The Mormon church took the role of leadership in developing many aspects of the economy. It planned, directed, sponsored, encouraged, and called upon laborers to work on many projects.

Working for the common good and the use of church income and resources led to some unusual economic practices in Utah. *Tithing* among the Mormons was a voluntary income tax, paid in money or "in kind" (goods). Goods paid as tithing "in kind" were placed in a bishop's storehouse, which received all types of produce and products. There was a bishop's storehouse in nearly every community or valley. Storehouses might exchange goods to keep a balance of supplies on hand. People could buy from the storehouse. They could turn in more than their tithing and receive credit which they could use as they needed to buy goods in the storehouse. Tithing credit was issued sometimes as tithing scrip, which served as a money substitute. The bishop's storehouse, then, served as a tithing receiving store, a bank, and a grocery store.

There was little *money* in early Utah. Cash was very scarce. Most people relied on tithing scrip or barter. When gold was discovered in California, Brigham Young sent men to mine gold and bring it back to Utah to be minted into coins. Gold coins were minted in Salt Lake City from 1849 until about 1861. These coins were few in number, and few people benefited. In order to keep money in Utah, rather than have it paid to people outside Utah for goods, Brigham Young encouraged the people to be self-sufficient and trade at home.

Public works program. The church took advantage of the large number of laborers available to construct public buildings and structures. When an immigrant arrived, he needed work, and Brigham Young saw that he was put to work on a public works project. For his labor he received pay in goods from the General Tithing Office or in tithing scrip.

Under the public works program, directed by Daniel H. Wells, shops were set up for carpenters, painters, stonecutters, and blacksmiths. At the adobe yard bricks were made for the public buildings; extra bricks were sold to private persons. A machine shop operated between 1852 and 1864, making tools, wheels, locks, knives and swords, saws, and other tools and parts. A foundry shop (1854-64) made castings in iron, brass, copper, and lead, for machine parts and tools. A nail factory (1859-65) supplied the all-important nails.

From two to five hundred men were kept busy during the 1850s on a number of public buildings. The Council House, the Old Tabernacle, Social Hall, Endowment House, Bath House, General Tithing Office and Bishop's Storehouse, and ward schoolhouses (meeting houses) were built under this program. A wall was built around the Temple Block, and a wall was begun around the entire city (1853-54). Brigham Young's Beehive

Pioneer sugar factory, Sugar House, south of Salt Lake City, was built in 1853 as part of the unsuccessful attempt to produce sugar from the sugar beet.

House and his President's Office, as well as residences of other church officials, were built by men working in this program.

Industries. To provide for some basic needs, projects were undertaken to use the natural resources of the region, promote industries and establish businesses that would help the people with goods they could not supply themselves. Their aim was self-sufficiency.

The Deseret Pottery factory was established in 1851. Paper mills were set up to produce *paper* for printing the *Deseret News*, but most of these were not altogether successful until 1860 when a good mill was brought in. To satisfy the demand for *sugar*, a sugar factory was designed in France, built in England, shipped to the territory, and set up five miles southeast of Salt Lake City in an area later called Sugar House. Sugar beets were to be converted into sugar. After much labor and money were spent, however, this proved a failure, and it was not until the 1890s that sugar was manufactured in Utah.

In an attempt to produce *iron*, Mormons were called to settle near Parowan and produce iron from the ore discovered west of Cedar City. Skilled workers were sent, but the difficulties were too great, and only a little iron was produced.

Woolen and cotton mills were set up, and by the 1860s they were supplying some wool and cotton cloth to the people.

Coal was needed for heating homes and by blacksmiths for making coke for their forges. During the 1850s and 1860s Utah was for the most part without coal. In 1851 coal veins were discovered east of Cedar City, and in 1855 other coal reserves were discovered near Wales in Sanpete Valley. Near Chalk Creek (close to present Coalville) coal was discovered in 1859. During the 1860s coal was supplied in small quantities from these beds. Later, with the coming of the railroad, the coal problem was largely solved.

Transportation. Although the Mormon settlers wanted to be self-sufficient, they knew it was not entirely possible. They were not able to produce some essential goods. They wanted also to sell their surplus products for money with which to buy the goods they could not produce.

To help in this trade, they asked Congress for improved roads to Utah, for a railroad to Utah, and for a telegraph system. Serious efforts were made to establish boat transportation along the Yellowstone, the Snake, and the Colorado rivers. All these efforts met with little success. They did have success, though, freighting across the plains.

Ox-team wagon trains annually made their way back and forth across the plains between Salt Lake City and the trade centers along the Missouri River. Twelve oxen usually pulled a canvas-covered wagon, which carried three or four tons. Twenty-five or twenty-six wagons made up a train. The trip from the

Coke ovens, such as shown here, were used in pioneer mining operations to melt the metal from the rest of the ore.

Missouri River to Salt Lake Valley usually took from twelve to fifteen weeks. In 1856 Brigham Young organized the *Brigham Young Express and Carrying Company* to help solve the transportation problem. This company succeeded and for a short time gave Brigham Young a monopoly of the mail, passenger, and freight business of the Mountain West.

Merchants. Resident and non-resident merchants gave Utah her first stores and provided the settlers with fresh supplies of eastern store goods. The people of Utah received their first store goods from emigrants en route to California in exchange for food and services. Merchants saw the possibility of making a living supplying store goods to the people of Utah and went into the business. They brought their goods from the east to arrive in the fall so that those attending October conference could make purchases at that time. Often the merchants accepted produce and cattle in exchange for the goods. The merchants then sold the produce and cattle in California where they made another profit.

Among the early merchants were Living-

Henry Dinwoodey's cabinet and chair shop, one of the early private businesses, began a long tradition of service in the furniture business.

ston and Kinkead, who brought $20,000 worth of goods from the States in 1849; J. M. Horner & Co., who brought $200,000 worth of goods in 1854; John B. Kimball, the Walker brothers, Henry W. Lawrence, Levi Stewart & Co., H. S. Eldredge & Co., William Hooper, and William Jennings. The most successful merchants were non-residents of Utah, and those who were residents were usually non-Mormons.

The store of Livingston and Kinkead, early merchants, is shown in this 1858 scene of Main Street, south of the Council House.

There was a great variety of stores on Main Street in 1860.

5. PIONEER SOCIAL LIFE EMPHASIZED RELIGIOUS ACTIVITIES, RECREATION, AND EDUCATION

Social life among the Mormons centered around church activities. To the Mormon the Sunday church service was a time of rejoicing, where he met with family, friends, and church leaders, where songs were sung and sermons given not only on religious themes but also on the practical affairs of life. The first Thursday of each month Fast Meeting was held. Members went to this service after fasting through the day and had the opportunity to stand and speak as they wished. (In 1896 the day was changed to the first Sunday of the month.)

Twice a year, April and October, leaders and members met in General Conference. Sermons were heard at meetings held for several days. It was also a time for business, meeting with friends and relatives, and evening socials.

Music played a prominent role in Mormon life. Choirs were formed in many wards. When the Old Tabernacle was finished, the choir that had sung in the Bowery was named the Tabernacle Choir, the predecessor of the present world-famous choir.

Bands were popular. The Nauvoo Brass Band continued in Utah. In the 1850s Captain Ballo's Band was justly famous. Ballo, a Sicilian by birth, had been a musician in the West Point band. He came to Utah and organized a band which played for religious services, public celebrations, and dances, until his death in 1861.

A strong tradition of singing developed in Mormon homes. Religious music was sung, and folk songs were passed down from generation to generation. Violins and guitars were easily brought to Utah, and by 1855 there were five pianos in the territory.

Dancing was perhaps the most popular recreation. In Salt Lake City, dancing parties were held often and late into the night. A Legislative Ball might start with a dinner, followed by dancing. The dancers ate the last of the dinner for their breakfast before ending the party near dawn. Orchestras usually consisted of two violins, a flute, and bass violin. Sometimes a band furnished the music. The most popular dances were square dances. Dancing parties of Salt Lake City were imitated in the smaller settlements. Dancing was a vigorous recreational exercise for a hard-working people.

The *Deseret Dramatic Association* was organized in Salt Lake City in 1853 to present stage plays. The popular plays of the time, and sometimes Shakespearean dramas, were presented by local talent who performed only for the applause they received. Dramatic societies were formed in Provo, Lehi, Parowan, and Brigham City during the 1850s.

The most popular of holiday *celebrations* was the Twenty-fourth of July, commemorating the arrival of the pioneers in Salt Lake Valley. The Fourth of July was celebrated, too, but the Twenty-fourth of July became the official annual holiday. Picnics in the canyons, parades, programs with speeches, and evening dancing marked the day.

Schools. The Mormons have always shown a keen interest in education. They had schools in Ohio and Missouri and a university in Nauvoo. School books were printed for the future before leaving Nauvoo. Around the evening campfires en route to Salt Lake Valley, classes were conducted for the young people. Although Mormon educational ideals were high, educational development in Utah was comparatively slow. However, Mormon communities were likely to be more advanced in education than other communities on the frontier. In the early years several types of schools were conducted.

(1) Voluntary schools were conducted by a teacher using his own tent or cabin and asking no salary. Contributions may have been given as partial payment. The first school held in the valley, by Mary Jane Dilworth, was a voluntary school, held in her own tent the winter of 1847-48. In most settlements there were able teachers who held this type of school.

(2) Private schools were held by persons interested in making some of their living by teaching. These teachers opened their schools to all and charged a tuition fee.

(3) Ward schools were established in each ward or settlement in Utah. The meeting house at first was the schoolhouse. Teachers were appointed by the bishops. Though the schools mainly taught religious subjects, schooling was free to all. By 1854 there was a schoolhouse in every ward in the territory.

(4) The common school or the territorial public school was created by law and was the officially recognized public school of the time. Sometimes this was the same as the ward school.

(5) Special schools (perhaps they were more like clubs) were begun by individuals and groups for educational, professional, and social purposes.

The University of Deseret was created February 28, 1850. It was to be a school for teachers and to supervise education in the territory. The Parent School, the school for teachers, began in November 1850 with great promise but soon passed out of existence for the lack of means to obtain books and equipment. The university was little more than a name until after 1868.

Brigham Young built this schoolhouse for the use of his own family.

Willard Richards was a Thompsonian doctor who took the lead in early Utah in health matters. An apostle and counselor to Brigham Young, he also served as church historian, secretary to the State of Deseret, did much of the secretarial work of the Territory of Utah, presided over the council of the legislative assembly, and was postmaster of Salt Lake City. He died in 1854.

The midwife was the practical nurse of the day, assisting women in childbirth and illnesses.

Books were scarce. A few McGuffy Readers and spellers were available. Students provided their own slates and slate pencils.

By 1860 there were 173 schools in Utah, taught by 220 teachers, with 5,585 students. That year it cost $27,838 to support the schools.

Health and medicine. The early Mormon view on health was that sickness was of man's own making, caused by bad habits. They believed that under certain conditions illness could be cured by faith in God's healing power. There was a general attitude that doctors were not needed. At that time, medical science was in its infancy, and most practicing doctors were poorly trained. Their usual practice was to bleed a person to get rid of impure blood they believed was causing the illness. They gave calomel, a powdered form of mercury and chlorine, for most sicknesses. Both these practices could be fatal and doctors were sometimes more feared than the disease. The Utah pioneers liked the Thompsonian doctors who used simple herbs, cold and hot packs and steam baths as stimulants to cause the body to rid itself of the disease. Willard Richards was a Thompsonian doctor.

Midwives were used in every settlement to deliver babies. They performed great services for the women. Often a midwife was called by church leaders to this responsible service. As a group they were highly successful. Only a few did not practice sanitary methods and thus spread disease.

One of the most dreaded diseases was cholera, spread by infected water, milk, raw foods, flies, and soiled hands. There was a world-wide epidemic of cholera in the 1850s, but the people of Utah were not severely affected by it. Measles broke out among the Indians during the winter of 1847-48 and left many dead. There were epidemics of diphtheria, typhoid fever, and enteritis during the first years.

The greatest number of deaths occurred among the young. One-third of the deaths were among babies under one year of age, and two-thirds of all deaths were among children under five years of age.

UNIT FIVE
UTAH'S TERRITORIAL PERIOD

During the period 1851 to 1896, Utah lived under a territorial form of government and was ruled by officers appointed by the federal government in Washington. It was thought that these officers would properly represent the interests of the federal government and train the people of Utah in self-government in preparation for statehood when they would rule themselves. For the Mormons it was a long and difficult experience. They believed they were already capable of governing themselves under statehood.

Several major movements mark this period. For the Mormons it was a period of expansion of settlement and the establishment of the Mormon way of life. Other people came to Utah to live who contributed, in their way, to the political, economic, social, and religious life of the territory. During this period the telegraph and the railroad came to Utah. Mining and other industries and businesses were now made possible because of easy transportation.

The coming of new people led to conflicts between different ways of life. There were serious conflicts between the Mormons, emigrants, government officials, churchmen, and businessmen. The Mormons insisted on freedom to set up their society according to their religious beliefs. Others insisted that some of those ways were not in harmony with current American practices. It was a matter of freedom in a democracy, of minority rights as contrasted with majority rights, of tolerance for diversity. Misunderstandings, hard feelings, prejudice, and ignorance played a large role in these affairs. It will be our task to study these different ways of life and attempt to understand the points of view, beliefs, and goals of each group. It is not our task to attempt to determine, even if we could, who was right or wrong, though we may draw lessons from these experiences. It is important to realize that periods of conflict were limited in time, and usually between certain persons. The desires of the people to live in peace finally prevailed, adjustments were made and Utah achieved statehood.

The territorial militia was called the Nauvoo Legion, a continuation of the Mormon militia in Nauvoo, Illinois. These troops were ready to defend their homes against what they considered an invasion of Utah.

CONFLICTS AND WARS MARKED UTAH'S EARLY TERRITORIAL DAYS

During the 1850s Utah began to have political conflicts which were to mark her history for decades. The separation of church and state, the problem of minority and majority rights, and the contrast between strong local political leadership and weak federal appointees were some of the major problems. Most of the time it was a matter of honest men having honest differences of opinion.

Several governments existed side by side in Utah. The Mormon ecclesiastical government could and often did serve all the needs of church members. In addition, Mormon leaders had founded a state government under the name of the State of Deseret, which lasted from 1849 to 1851. On the other hand, the United States government gave the people of Utah a territorial form of government.

IN THIS CHAPTER WE WILL LEARN

1. The Territory of Utah served as the political government of Utah from 1850 to 1896.

2. Brigham Young faced many problems as governor of Utah Territory, 1851-57.

3. The Utah War was a blunder based on misunderstandings.

4. Governor Alfred Cumming helped establish patterns of territorial government in Utah.

5. In the Civil War, Utah stood on the Union side.

6. Territorial government was a source of conflict between Utah and the federal government.

An officer of the Nauvoo Legion.

1. THE TERRITORY OF UTAH SERVED AS THE POLITICAL GOVERNMENT OF UTAH FROM 1850 TO 1896.

In the American system of government, **territorial government** was meant to serve as a preparation for statehood. Utahns lived under territorial government for forty-five years before attaining statehood. Under territorial government, United States officials appointed the governor, other executive officers, and judges. The people of the territory elected members of the legislature. Appointed officers were usually political friends of those in power in Washington; sometimes they were well qualified, sometimes they were not. If the people of Utah had been given statehood, they would have elected their own governor and executive officers, judges, and legislature. In addition they would have elected two senators to the United States Senate and at least one representative to the House of Representatives. Under territorial government they sent a delegate to Congress who could listen but not vote, and speak only when invited. The people of Utah felt that they already had the necessary experience for statehood and could govern themselves. They did not like territorial government for they considered that it placed them under the rule of foreigners.

Although statehood was denied in 1850, Utahns were appointed to territorial offices. On January 27, 1851, news reached Utah of the creation of the Territory of Utah. The following were appointed territorial officers: Brigham Young, governor; Lemuel G. Brandebury, chief justice; Perry C. Brocchus, associate justice; Zerubbabel Snow, associate justice; Broughton D. Harris, secretary; Seth M.

Blair, attorney general; and Joseph L. Haywood, United States marshal. Young, Snow, Blair, and Haywood were Utahns. On February 3, 1851 Brigham Young took the oath of office as governor of the Territory of Utah.

The *governor* was the chief executive officer in territorial government. The responsibility for the territory was his. He was to report directly to the secretary of state (after 1873 to the secretary of the interior) of the president's cabinet. When the governor was absent from the territory, the secretary of the territory became acting governor. The *secretary* served as correspondent and record keeper for the territory.

The *three justices* sat as district judges over three separate judicial districts. When a case was to be appealed from a district court to the territorial supreme court, the three justices sat as one court with the chief justice presiding.

The *territorial legislature* was elected by the people and was empowered to write the laws for the territory. Their laws must be in harmony with those of the United States. The Council of thirteen members was presided over by a president, and the House of Representatives with twenty-six members was presided over by a speaker.

The *delegate* to Congress, members of the territorial legislature, and city and county officers were elected by the people.

2. BRIGHAM YOUNG FACED MANY PROBLEMS AS GOVERNOR OF UTAH TERRITORY, 1851-57

Brigham Young had very close and cordial relations with the territorial legislature. The legislature met in annual forty-day sessions, beginning the second Monday of December. Heber C. Kimball, Brigham Young's close friend and counselor, was frequently elected president of the Council, while other close friends and churchmen at various times were elected speaker of the House. The legislature met in Salt Lake City, usually at the Social Hall, except for the fifth session (1855-56) which met at Fillmore. As early as 1851, Fillmore had been designated the capital of Utah Territory. The sixth session also met at Fillmore but adjourned at once to Salt Lake City. It returned to Fillmore only once thereafter. Salt Lake City has since remained the capital.

The legislature was concerned with many features of government. In addition to legalizing the laws passed earlier by the State of Deseret, the territorial legislature located the seat of government at Fillmore, created counties, chartered companies for the development of iron and other resources, paid bills, looked into forming a mail service, established probate courts and appointed probate judges. The legislature also provided for the construction and maintenance of roads, bridges, and ferries, for the management of the penitentiary, and for the collection of territorial taxes.

Governor Young addressed the sessions of the legislature. The unity existing among

Utah's first statehouse was in Fillmore. Built in 1855, the legislature of 1855-56 met there.

the legislators is shown by the comment that the seventh session passed "without the occurrence of a negative vote on any question or action during the session."

In contrast to his cordial relations with the legislature, **Brigham Young sometimes had marked differences of opinion with federal appointees.** The first appointees arrived in Salt Lake Valley by the end of August 1851. Difficulties began at once. On September 7, at a conference meeting of the church, Brigham Young invited the officials to the stand and asked Judge Perry E. Brocchus to speak. The judge spoke in terms uncomplimentary to the women in the congregation, and Young at once defended them and Mormon practices, saying harsh things about some federal officers. On September 22, the legislature was called into session. In the first week there was a dispute over the funds given the secretary for the expenses of the legislature. The non-Mormon appointees (Secretary Harris, Judges Brandebury and Brocchus) left the territory for Washington, D.C., taking the $24,000 meant for the legislature. Thereafter these officials were called "run-away officials." In Washington they complained about Brigham Young as governor. New appointees were named, and they arrived in the autumn of 1852.

Without federal judges, Utah was without a court system. So the legislature transferred powers of the federal courts to the probate courts which were manned by residents of the counties. This was all according to law. Most judges coming to Utah found no fault with the system.

Indian affairs. One of Brigham Young's chief responsibilities was handling Indian relations. As governor he was also superintendent of Indian affairs. Brigham Young wanted peaceful coexistence with the Indians, but, he also wanted to safeguard the lives and property of the settlers. The Indians objected to the white man taking over their lands. Indian slavery was another issue.

Slave traders from New Mexico came into Utah Territory trading horses and ammunition for Indian children whom they sold into slavery. When Brigham Young learned of this, he did all he could to stop it. One trader, arrested and forced to free some Indian slaves, took revenge by supplying firearms and ammunition to the Indians and stirring them up against the Mormons. By proclamation and by law (1852) the slave traffic was forbidden. Many persons were saved from slavery, and Mormon families took Indian children into their homes. But this deprived traders of their profitable business, and it deprived Indians of a source for horses and ammunition. Older Indians were angered at Young's interference.

Between July 1853 and May 1854 the *Walker War* was fought. Indians regularly threatened the settlements in Salt Lake, Utah, Juab, and Sanpete valleys. The militia was ordered to stay ready for attack. Protective walls were ordered built around each settlement including Salt Lake City. The order was to "fort up." In armed encounters nineteen settlers and many Indians were killed. Several smaller settlements were abandoned, and the people moved into the larger towns. Late in May 1854 Brigham Young met with Chief Walkara, his braves, and Kanosh, chief of the Pahvant Indians, in Walkara's tent at Chicken Creek, Juab County, and made a formal treaty of peace. Walkara died the next January and was succeeded by Arrapeen, a brother.

In 1855 peace treaties were signed with Ute and Shoshoni Indians. Yet there were troubles. The Elk Mountain Mission (near Moab) was broken up because of troubles between the settlers and Indians. Governor

Kanosh, chief of the Pahvant Indians, sought peaceful relations with the white settlers.

Chief Walkara and his brother Arrapeen, sketched from a painting by W. W. Major. Walkara was succeeded as chief of the Ute in central Utah by Arrapeen, who continued a general policy of cooperation and peaceful coexistence with the Mormons.

John W. Gunnison was leading a United States survey through Utah when his party was attacked by Indians. He and seven of his men were killed.

Young ordered out part of the militia to protect settlements in the eastern part of the territory. Early in 1856 the *Tintic Indian War* broke out, involving Indians and settlers in Utah, Cedar, and Tintic valleys.

Gunnison Massacre. Midway in the Walker War a massacre took place. Emigrants en route to California had given Indians trouble, and the Indians sought revenge on the next white people to come through. The next group to come through was a United States government exploring party led by Lieutenant John W. Gunnison of the U.S. Topographical Survey, surveying for possible routes for the proposed Central Pacific railroad. The Indians, renegades from Chief Kanosh's Pahvant Indians, attacked Gunnison's party early on the morning of October 28 and killed Gunnison and seven others. Since the Pahvant Indians were at peace with the Mormons, some people mistakenly thought the Mormons were responsible. Much criticism came to the people of Utah and to Indian Superintendent

Garland Hurt, Indian agent, fled the territory when he believed a Mormon alliance with the Indians put his life in danger. He is shown here leaving the Spanish Fork Indian farm, late September 1857, for the East. His reports supported the Buchanan administration in its decision to send troops to Utah.

Brigham Young over the Gunnison massacre.

To help solve the white man's problems with the Indians, Brigham Young in November 1855 recommended the establishment of *Indian farms*. Farms were established at the mouth of the Spanish Fork River in Utah Valley, on Twelve Mile Creek near Gunnison in Sanpete County, at Corn Creek near Fillmore in Millard County, and at Deep Creek in western Juab County near the Nevada line. These farm lands were fertile and capable of supporting agriculture, and lay adjacent to hills where the Indians could hunt. Mormon farmers were sent to teach the Indians how to farm, with the intent of making the Indians self-sufficient farmers. By June 1856 the farms were successfully producing wheat and other crops. At Corn Creek in 1858, eighty acres were in wheat production. But the Indian agent, Garland Hurt, while publicly supporting the Indian farms, was suspicious of a Mormon-Indian alliance, and his reports to Washington cast negative reflections on the

Mormons and Young's Indian policy. His reports led the government to take little or no action to help Utah's Indians. The government sent promises but neglected to send money.

Colonel Edward J. Steptoe in Utah. Brigham Young's term of office ended in 1854, and President Franklin Pierce did not reappoint him. It was known that Colonel Edward J. Steptoe was the president's choice for governor, yet Pierce delayed making an appointment. In the meantime, Governor Young was, by law, to serve as governor until his successor was appointed and took office. On August 31, 1854, Colonel Steptoe arrived in Salt Lake City at the head of two companies of artillery and one company of infantry, altogether 175 soldiers and about 150 employees of the quartermaster. Steptoe's instructions were simply to examine the possibility of constructing a road from Salt Lake City to California, and to investigate the Gunnison Massacre. Colonel Steptoe assisted in the prosecution of Indians charged with murder in that massacre. Late in April 1855 Steptoe received a commission as governor of Utah Territory. The colonel declined the appointment because, he said, if he had accepted it, he would have had to give up his military commission. Earlier, he and his officers and other federal appointees had joined in signing a petition sent to the president December 30, 1854, asking that Brigham Young be appointed for another term. Brigham Young was appointed to a second four-year term.

Disagreements developed between Utah and federal officials over land and Indian policies, mail contracts, and the probate court system. After the run-away officials left Utah Territory in 1851, there was peace until 1855 when new appointees came to Utah. By this time Governor Young's policies were more fully developed. New appointees were outspoken and were fearful of the power exercised by Young as both governor and church president. While some early officials had kept their criticisms from the Mormons, by 1855 and 1856 the disagreements were open.

David H. Burr, surveyor general of the territory, made *land surveys* and helped legalize the settlers' occupation of the land in harmony with federal practices. Some thought his efforts were aimed at the eviction of the settlers from their lands. He objected to the practice of entrusting timber rights to certain individuals for management for the entire community. He feared that the church was becoming an agent for control of the land, contrary to federal practice. In the spring of 1857 Burr left Utah for Washington, D.C., where he complained about the situation in Utah.

Jacob Holeman and *Garland Hurt*, Indian agents, clashed with Brigham Young over his *Indian policy*. Brigham Young was superintendent of Indian affairs, and the agents had to follow his lead. Hurt, an educated and respected citizen, at first got along with Brigham Young and helped establish Indian farms on which to teach the Indians agriculture. But when Mormons believed that Hurt was turning the Indians against the settlers, he left the territory in September 1857 for Washington where he made reports to the government adverse to the Utahns.

Mail service was very important to people on the frontier, and they wanted the best service possible. Trouble came to the Mormons when W. M. F. Magraw, a frontier businessman and friend of President Buchanan, lost the mail contract he had to take mail to Utah. The contract was won by Hiram Kimball of Utah and taken over by the Brigham Young Express and Carrying Company. This loss so angered Magraw that he wrote a letter to the president, October 3, 1856, denouncing the Mormons and complaining of affairs in Utah.

The probate courts. After the run-away officials left Utah in 1851, the territorial legislature transferred powers of the federal courts to the probate courts. Probate courts were county courts usually headed by a leading person in the county. The transfer was quite legal, but it offended some judicial appointees, especially Associate Justice *W. W. Drummond* who came to Utah in September 1855. Judge Drummond opposed the probate courts in Utah and by words angered the Mormon people. He went to Carson Valley to hold court, and from there he went on to California and to Washington, D.C., where on March 30, 1856, he resigned as judge and wrote a letter to the United States Attorney General detailing many accusations against Brigham Young and the Mormons, concluding with this suggestion: "I do believe that, if there was a man put in office as governor of that Territory, who is not a member of the church (Mormon), and he supported with a *sufficient* military aid, much good would result from such a course . . . ."

The election of 1856. In the presidential election campaign of 1856 the new Republican party advocated the abolition in the territories of those "twin relics of barbarism—slavery and polygamy." Thus the "Mormon Question" had entered national politics. While the Republicans did not win that election, they attracted a great deal of support for their views and the Democrats, who did win, had to pay attention to their demands.

By early 1857 most of the important non-Mormon federal officers of Utah Territory were in the East, often in Washington, circulating their complaints against the people of Utah. Newspaper editors printed their stories, which stirred public opinion against

James Buchanan, president of the United States, is remembered in Utah history for sending an expeditionary force to Utah to suppress an alleged rebellion against the government.

The federal army sent against Utah made its way across the plains during the summer of 1857.

the Mormons. On March 4 a Democratic administration, with James Buchanan as president, was inaugurated, and action was soon taken on these complaints.

3. THE UTAH WAR WAS A BLUNDER BASED ON MISUNDERSTANDINGS

The reports about affairs in Utah that reached the new administration demanded that the government take stern measures against the people of Utah for their alleged defiance of the government of the United States. Public opinion, as expressed in the press, supported and encouraged this view. President Buchanan asked cabinet members for reports in their files on conditions in Utah. There were the letters of Burr, Holeman, Hurt, Magraw, Drummond, and others. The letters of Magraw and Drummond were most influential. By May 20, 1857, the president had decided to take Drummond's suggestion to replace Brigham Young as governor and to send a military expedition to Utah to install the new governor and to insure obedience to federal law in Utah.

An army marches against Utah. On May 28, 1857, units making up the forces of the Utah Expedition were ordered to assemble at Fort Leavenworth, under the command of Brigadier General W. S. Harney. The units were the Fifth Infantry, eight companies of the Tenth Infantry, the Second Dragoons of cavalry, and two batteries of the Fourth Artillery Regiment. These troops assembled slowly at Fort Leavenworth. On July 18, troops began to move out from Fort Leavenworth for Utah. General Harney never joined his command; he was called to other duties. Colonel Edmund Alexander was the senior officer in an army without a commander. He was unfit for top command; he lacked the ability to make correct decisions quickly. Through the remainder of July and through

August, the troops moved westward along the overland trail, experiencing many desertions.

In the meantime the government had difficulty in obtaining a new set of appointees for the political offices in Utah. However, the list was complete by late July. The following persons were named: Alfred Cumming, governor; D. R. Eckles, chief justice, and Charles E. Sinclair and John Cradlebaugh, associate justices; John Hartnett, secretary; Alexander Wilson, attorney; Peter K. Dotson, marshal; and Jacob Forney, superintendent of Indian affairs. These officers caught up with the troops later. General Harney's successor, Colonel Albert Sidney Johnston, assumed command September 11 and brought with him six companies of the Second Dragoons, guided westward by Mountain Man Jim Bridger. Lieutenant Colonel Philip St. George Cooke and companies of the Dragoons came even later, not starting until September 16.

Utahns learned of the coming of the army on July 24, 1857. President Buchanan did not notify Governor Young that he was no longer governor. Nor did the president inform him of the coming of the army and its purpose to support a new governor in office. The Mormons learned of the expedition on July 24, 1857, while many were at the head of Big Cottonwood Canyon at a grand picnic celebrating the holiday. Mormon mail carriers had seen the expedition shortly after it formed, learned of its mission, and raced to Utah with the message. To Brigham Young and the Mormons it was a challenge of war. Without word from the president, and without further investigation or negotiation on the part of Brigham Young, the Mormon leader considered the action to be another persecution upon the Mormons.

Brigham Young acted at once for the defense of Utah. Missionaries were called home from posts around the world. Settlers in out-

Albert Sidney Johnston commanded the expeditionary forces against Utah for alleged rebellion against federal authority. After the Utah War, General Johnston distinguished himself as a Confederate general in the Civil War.

lying settlements and outposts were asked to leave or sell their homes and move into the central valleys of Utah. San Bernardino and Carson Valley were to be given up. Scouts were sent out onto the Great Plains to spy on the movements of the army. Armed defense of the valleys was planned. Firearms were manufactured or repaired. Daniel H. Wells, commanding officer of the Nauvoo Legion, the Utah militia, organized his forces and then organized the territory into military districts to meet the emergency.

Almost from the start the federal government had second thoughts about sending the expedition. General Winfield Scott warned against sending the forces so late in the season. Shortly after the troops left Fort Leavenworth, upon direction from Washington, *Captain Stewart Van Vliet was ordered to Utah* to make inquiries regarding the reception of the army and provisions for the troops.

Captain Van Vliet arrived in Salt Lake Valley September 8. That evening and the days following he had discussions with Young and other leaders. The captain learned of the falsehood of some of Drummond's charges. He heard the Mormon side of the argument. He learned that the Mormons considered the army no more than a mob sent to exterminate them or take their leaders, and that the Mormons were determined to fight for their lives. He heard Brigham Young preach to the people on Sunday. The church leader asked the congregation for a show of hands of all those who would burn their homes rather than see the army come in. All hands went up. On Monday, September 14, Captain Van Vliet and Delegate John M. Bernhisel left Salt Lake City for Washington, where a report favorable to the Mormons was given.

The day following Van Vliet's departure *Governor Brigham Young issued a proclamation declaring martial law in Utah Territory.* "Citizens of Utah—We are invaded by a hostile force, who are evidently assailing us to accomplish our overthrow and destruction." He recounted persecutions suffered by the Mormons and blamed their present situation on "letter writers," "corrupt officials," and "howling editors." His proclamation (1) forbade all armed forces from entering the territory, (2) ordered all forces in the territory to be ready "at a moment's notice to repel any and all such invasion," (3) forbade any person to pass or repass into or through, or from the territory without a permit from the

proper officer. A state of war existed.

The most terrible event of the Utah War took place in southern Utah at *Mountain Meadows*, about thirty-five miles southwest of Cedar City. To alert the settlers to the invasion of Johnston's army, George A. Smith, founder of Cedar City and apostle to the southern settlements, spent August preaching fiery sermons and reminding the settlers of past persecutions, stirring them to resist the coming enemy. About the same time a group of emigrants came through Utah en route to California, consisting of the Fancher train and a group of horsemen who called themselves "Missouri Wildcats." Smith had instructed the settlers to save all food stuffs and not to sell any to emigrants. This Missouri group missed this expected food supply and resented the Mormon action.

The "Wildcats" stirred up trouble: one claimed to have helped kill Joseph Smith; another wanted to go back and kill Brigham Young and Heber C. Kimball. Settlers believed these men poisoned a spring resulting in the death of cattle and people, and that they fed poisoned beef to Indians, causing deaths. The Indians were enraged. Governor Young wondered whether or not the Indians could be controlled. He feared for the settlers. He had hoped for an alliance between Mormons and Indians against the army if necessary.

The settlers of southern Utah were already tense. Added to the threat of an army from the north was the possibility of an Indian war at home. In this atmosphere southern Utah leaders met at Cedar City, Sunday afternoon, September 6. Some argued for vengeance, others for peace. A rider was sent to Salt Lake City to get Brigham Young's direction. The rider left on Monday and reached Governor Young at noon on Thursday. Within the hour Governor Young wrote instructions to let all emigrants pass through in peace and sent the rider back at top speed. But the rider arrived too late. On the same day the rider left Cedar City, Indians attacked the emigrants at Mountain Meadows. When word of the Indian attack reached Cedar City, Mormon volunteers were sent to bury the dead. At night three emigrants slipped away to seek help from the people of Cedar City, but one was killed by Indian ambush, so the other two fled to California. This event compounded the fears of Mormon military leaders that an Indian war would break out. With an army invading Utah, an Indian war had to be avoided at all costs. We do not know who decided what should follow, but orders were given and on Friday, September 11, Indians and men of the Utah militia went to the emigrant camp. The emigrants (about 120) were lured from their defenses, disarmed, and slain. Seventeen children were spared and taken to the settlements. The affair is the darkest event in Utah history. It can be accounted for only in relation to the hysteria of war: the threat to life from an invasion from without and Indians at home who demanded vengeance on the emigrants or on the settlers.

Military action between the federal troops and the Utah militia began near South Pass. Leaders of the Mormon militia in this action were Colonel Robert T. Burton, Major Lot Smith, Major John McAllister, and Adjutant General James Ferguson. Burton left Salt Lake City August 15 with seventy-five men to scout the army. Near South Pass, September 24, he raided the troops and stampeded their cattle. This was the first military action of the war. Other militiamen were sent to scout various routes by which the army might enter.

Utah militiamen were sent to Echo Canyon to prepare defenses and to defend that canyon. Other troops were in readiness should they be called up. In Echo Canyon stone walls were built on the upper slopes, and trenches were excavated along the canyon walls from which soldiers could fire upon the enemy. Boulders were placed so they could be pushed easily onto troops below. Deep ditches were dug to make it possible to flood the army's path.

On October 3, General Daniel H. Wells and his staff resolved to destroy Fort Bridger and Fort Supply lest they serve the enemy. The Mormons planned a scorched-earth policy. Instructions were given to commanders to harass the army, annoy them, delay them, burn grass before them, drive off their animals, destroy their supplies, but not take any human life. These tactics were designed to keep the military action on the Great Plains and so delay the troops that they would not be able to take the campaign into the mountain valleys, but be forced to winter in the mountains.

Daniel H. Wells, apostle and counselor to Brigham Young, was general of the Nauvoo Legion during the Utah War.

Major Lot Smith went right to work. The next day, October 4, he found two supply trains, burned them, and the following day found and burned a third. In all, seventy-two wagons carrying 300,000 pounds of food, mostly flour and bacon, were destroyed.

Colonel Alexander of the U.S. Army at this time decided to avoid Echo Canyon and take a route northward along the Bear River and enter Utah from the north. October 7 his command moved on these orders, but they found the road impassable. Bad weather had set in. Alexander turned back to his former camp, arriving there November 2. During this time Major Joseph Taylor of the Utah militia was captured by the army. Colonel Alexander learned his orders and Mormon strategy and tactics.

The new commanding officer, Albert Sidney Johnston, made contact with his command and ordered all troops back to Hams Fork. He arrived there November 2. But this was a poor place to winter, so Colonel Johnston directed his troops toward Fort Bridger. The winter grew severe. The troops lost many animals in the snow and cold. At Fort Bridger they found that all had been burned but the stone walls. The troops rebuilt the fort to provide a winter habitation. On November 20, Lieutenant Colonel Philip St. George Cooke arrived at Fort Bridger with his troops. They had suffered a hard march, lost many soldiers by desertions, and had lost 130 of their original 144 horses. His troops could go no farther. Colonel Johnston decided the army would have to winter near Fort Bridger. The new federal appointees caught up with the troops as they went into winter quarters. Governor Alfred Cumming, his wife, the judges, and others suffered through the winter with the troops.

Throughout the fall the Mormons manned their defenses in Echo Canyon. In time they learned that the federal troops were going to winter quarters at Fort Scott (near Fort Bridger). Delaying tactics had won for the Mormons. By the end of November most of the Nauvoo Legion had left the mountains and gone home for the winter. A few militiamen stayed in the mountains through the winter on patrol duty.

When news reached Washington that the expedition was forced to winter in the mountains and had failed to capture the Mormon community, there was a flood of criticism upon President Buchanan. He was now blamed for sending the troops out so late, and for not sending an investigating committee first. For a successful military campaign against the Mormons, there would have to be more troops and money. Congress, although anti-Mormon, was reluctant to put more troops and money into "Buchanan's Blunder."

President Buchanan felt the weight of this criticism, and now had Captain Van Vliet's report, favorable to the Mormons and denying the state of rebellion. Early in Janu-

Philip St. George Cooke, who had led the Mormon Battalion, was a lieutenant colonel in Johnston's army. His respect for the men of the Battalion led him to march bare-headed through the city.

Thomas L. Kane, "friend of the Mormons," by his personal diplomacy contributed significantly to the peaceful settlement of misunderstandings between the federal government and the people of Utah.

ary 1858 the president was visited by *Colonel Thomas L. Kane* of Pennsylvania, a distinguished American and friend of the Mormons. Colonel Kane offered to go to Utah at his own expense to learn the truth of the situation and report to the president. Without giving Kane any official capacity, the president encouraged him to do so.

Colonel Kane left at once, assuming the name of "Dr. Osborne." He took passage for California on a steamer and hastened from San Bernardino to Utah. He arrived in Salt Lake City February 24. In his talks with Brigham Young and others, he was assured of the intention of the Mormons to welcome Governor Cumming, if he would come without the troops. On March 8 Kane left for Fort Scott. There he met Governor Cumming and explained his mission and his findings in Salt Lake Valley. Over the protests of the military leaders, Governor Cumming, Colonel Kane, two servants, and a Mormon escort left Camp Scott for Salt Lake City where they arrived April 12. They were well received by the Utah leaders. Governor Cumming was given residence in the fine home of William C. Staines. He had talks with Brigham Young and other leaders. He had the opportunity to speak to about four thousand people in the Old Tabernacle where he explained his plans as governor and heard the complaints of the people. He visited the Utah library and saw the records and seal of the U.S. District Court, the supposed destruction of which had been one of the charges Drummond made that helped bring about the war. Governor Cumming could now report to the president that he had been received by the people of Utah, his authority was acknowledged, and that peace could come.

But the people of Utah prepared for the worst. Should the army come against them in the valleys, it would find only scorched earth.

To meet the threat of an invading army, Brigham Young called people from distant settlements to the central valleys of Utah. At Provo, shanties were constructed to house the people during the emergency.

On March 21 the citizens agreed to abandon all homes north of Utah Valley and move to Provo. In May the "move south" began. People left their homes filled with straw so that they could be quickly burned if necessary.

In the meantime there were **peace developments** from another source. President Buchanan, under criticism from the national press and Congress, with the report of Captain Van Vliet and the assurances of Colonel Kane before him, sent a peace commission to Utah Territory. He named two distinguished public servants: ex-Governor L. W. Powell of Kentucky and Major Ben McCulloch of Texas. These men were given the president's terms of peace and authority to negotiate. They arrived in Salt Lake City June 7, 1858.

The peace commissioners met at the Council House with Utah leaders on June 11. Commissioner Powell reported the president's proclamation, in which the Utahns were accused of treason, charged with crimes, but offered pardon if they would be subject to the Constitution and laws of the United States, and let the troops be quartered in the territory. Brigham Young objected strongly to the charges, but said he would accept the president's pardon for Major Lot Smith's burning government supply trains. The people of Utah had always been loyal and always would be, Brigham Young said, but they wanted *"hands off!"* The troops could reside in the territory if stationed more than forty miles away from Salt Lake City. Young wanted peace, but not subjection; his people would fight for their freedom. The commissioners wished peace, so peace came.

The next day the commissioners wrote Johnston the terms of the agreement. Johnston at Camp Scott agreed. The troops moved out on June 17 and entered Salt Lake Valley June 26. That day they marched through the city. Strict order and discipline prevailed. The valley was in absolute stillness save for the sound of marching troops. The city was to be burned if the troops should so much as stop. Lieutenant Colonel Philip St. George Cooke marched beside his troops, with head uncovered, as a token of his respect for the men of the Mormon Battalion he had com-

The federal troops were permitted through the vacant city only on the condition that they not stop within the city; otherwise guards would set fire to the city and leave only scorched earth for the army.

The headquarters of the expeditionary forces under General Johnston was located at Camp Floyd, west of Provo, in Cedar Valley.

manded in the Mexican War. The army passed over the Jordan River and camped in the church pasture. Soon they marched south into Cedar Valley where they established Camp Floyd near the new settlement of Fairfield. Johnston's army was to remain from two to three years.

The peace commissioners and Governor Cumming visited the uprooted people in Provo and encouraged them to return to their homes. Brigham Young and other leaders left Provo on July 1 for their homes, and soon others followed the example. Slowly the people resumed their normal routine of life. The peace commissioners left on July 3 for Washington with their report. The Utah war was ended.

4. GOVERNOR ALFRED CUMMING HELPED ESTABLISH PATTERNS OF TERRITORIAL GOVERNMENT IN UTAH

During the **administration of Alfred Cumming**, the governor did all in his power to enforce the laws of the United States and at the same time be just to both Mormons and non-Mormons. Governor Cumming faced a difficult situation. For the most part he was successful, winning more friends than enemies. He often had more trouble with federal appointees and the army than with the Utahns.

The army at Camp Floyd settled down to the life of a typical frontier military post. Barracks were erected, stores established, and other buildings put up. The troops had little more to do than maintain their garrison life. When soldiers obtained leaves to visit the settlements, sometimes there was trouble with the local citizens.

The three justices were assigned to the three judicial districts. One of the judges, John Cradlebaugh, wanted to bring Brigham Young to trial as the man responsible for the

Mountain Meadows Massacre. He asked Johnston, who had been promoted to general, for troops to protect his court in Provo. This alarmed the people. Governor Cumming objected, too, and ordered the troops withdrawn. Johnston contended that his orders were superior to those of Cumming. For weeks there was trouble between the two. Finally a decision from Washington supported Governor Cumming—the civil authority is supreme and over the military in our government.

At Camp Floyd the troops were encamped in tents and log shelters from June 1857 until the end of the occupation of Utah in July 1861.

Alfred Cumming was governor of the Territory of Utah from 1857 to 1861.

Largely because of his just performance of duties, Governor Cumming got along well with the legislature and the people of Utah. He helped them become accustomed to having a non-Mormon governor. He was able to write: "A community is seldom seen more marked by quiet and peaceable diligence, than that of the Mormons."

The **outbreak of the Civil War** ended the military occupation of Utah and the administration of Alfred Cumming. Even before war broke out, General Johnston had left Utah (March 1, 1860), leaving Philip St. George Cooke in command. When war broke out, some troops were ordered to duty in Arizona and New Mexico. The last of the troops left Camp Floyd in July 1861. Governor Cumming left in May 1861 for his home in Atlanta, Georgia. He cast his lot with his native state and the Confederate cause.

What was the cost of the Utah War? We may never know or be able to tell. It cost the United States government a great deal in money and in military services. Although no blood was shed in military action, tragedies were experienced by the army and people of Utah because of the conditions of this war. The American people continued to suspect the people of Utah and have ill feelings toward them. One can hardly count the cost of these values. When Camp Floyd was abandoned, the Utahns gained by the sale of surplus goods. About $4,000,000 worth of goods went into the hands of Utah businessmen for about $100,000.

5. IN THE CIVIL WAR, UTAH STOOD ON THE UNION SIDE

With the outbreak of the Civil War, the people of Utah declared their support for the Union. Very few Utah citizens sympathized with the Southern cause. Most citizens were from northern states or from the working classes of Europe, and they did not sympathize with the southern slaveholders. Some Utahns went east to fight on the Union side. While Confederate troops came into the American Southwest, none invaded Utah.

During the Civil War, however, Utah underwent a second military occupation by American troops. Colonel Patrick Edward Connor, at the head of companies of California volunteers, occupied Utah Territory in October 1862. While these troops were sent to Utah to protect the overland mail route and the telegraph lines from the Indians, it was believed by Connor and others that the real purpose of the California volunteers in Utah was to keep a watchful eye on the Mormons. (We will discuss Colonel Connor and his men in the next chapter.)

From the outset of the war until the California volunteers arrived in Utah, **the Nauvoo Legion performed short-term volunteer service** at the request of the War Department. In April and May of 1862 Colonel Robert T. Burton led twenty mounted men eastward over the emigrant road to guard the coaches and wagons carrying passengers and a large quantity of mail. In response to an authorization from the adjutant general in Washington (at the direction of President Abraham Lincoln) Brigham Young called up a full cavalry company of one hundred men and ten supply wagons for ninety days' service to protect the stage and telegraph lines and overland mail routes in Green River County, Utah Territory (now Wyoming). These troops served until August when they were mustered out of service.

6. TERRITORIAL GOVERNMENT WAS A SOURCE OF CONFLICT BETWEEN UTAH AND THE FEDERAL GOVERNMENT

While Governor Cumming tried to rule with justice for both Mormons and non-

Mormons, his successors often gave up that ideal and tried to enforce federal law against the Mormons, sometimes at the sacrifice of justice. The long history of Utah territorial government is one of conflict between federal appointees and the people of Utah.

With the arrival of Governor Cumming, Brigham Young seemed to retire from civic affairs and put his full attention to church affairs. Yet the Mormon people looked to him for direction in all their affairs, and he did not disappoint them. He gave leadership. The story is told that one territorial governor, upon coming to Utah, went to Brigham Young and told him, "I'll have you know that I am governor of this territory." To this the church president replied, "You may be governor of the territory, but I am governor of the people." True or false, the story illustrates the truth that Brigham Young governed the Mormon people, and that territorial governors were not altogether important or effective.

The Mormons really wanted to be left alone and to govern themselves. To a large degree they did govern themselves. Their church government answered most of their needs. Under territorial law they governed themselves in their communities. They elected their representatives in the territorial legislature. Although Utah was occupied by federal troops after 1862, the Nauvoo Legion functioned until 1870. Much local government was taken care of by the county or probate courts until 1874.

Mormon leadership had such a variety of programs for the development of the territory and the people that other agencies seemed to do little in comparison. It would seem that many of the programs that developed and advanced the territory originated with the Mormon leadership and were accomplished through church agencies.

Utah was under territorial government from 1850 to 1896. Through all these years governors and judges were named in Washington. After the Utah War, rarely was a Utahn or Mormon given a federal appointment in Utah territorial government. Federal officers came and went, in many instances almost without effect on the people and the development of the territory. Some governors were very capable men; others were without necessary qualifications. All were political appointees of the party in power, appointed as a reward for service to the party.

The governors performed the essential service of maintaining federal relations with the territory. Territorial government was managed by them. Rarely did the governors get along well with the Utah legislature. It is doubtful that the legislature was a very important agency for the development of the territory.

Some distinguished judges were appointed to the Utah courts, and, of course, some were much less than able.

Conflict arose because of honest differences of opinion on important matters. Usually the conflict was between the federal appointees and Mormon leaders. The majority of the people were unaffected by this controversy, except that the spirit of conflict and harsh feelings spread among the people.

(The struggle of Utah to gain statehood is told in chapter 18.)

Various bands of Indians in conference with the U.S. Commission near the Virgin River. Major John Wesley Powell, leader of two expeditions down the Colorado River, 1869-71, appears at left of picture.

The Reverend Daniel S. Tuttle, Episcopal bishop of Utah, 1869-86, made significant contributions to early Utah.

MANY PEOPLE MAKE THEIR CONTRIBUTIONS TO UTAH

The Mormon contribution to the development of Utah was great and cannot be minimized. The Mormons made the first permanent homes, established irrigation agriculture, established cities, roads, government, some of the first businesses, and developed the natural resources. But the Mormons were not the only people to pioneer Utah. During the 1850s and 1860s other people came and made their contributions. These people brought with them their way of life. They came as merchants and businessmen, soldiers, teachers, churchmen, explorers, railroaders, and miners.

IN THIS CHAPTER WE WILL LEARN

1. The American westward movement caught up with Utah.

2. American soldiers made significant contributions to early Utah.

3. Jews came to Utah as resident merchants.

4. Catholic priests came to Utah to serve their members living in the area.

5. Protestant ministers and teachers came to serve their members and as missionaries to the Mormons.

6. Government explorers made contributions in mapping and describing the Utah landscape.

14

225

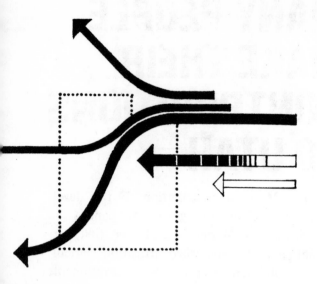

1. THE AMERICAN WESTWARD MOVEMENT CAUGHT UP WITH UTAH

When the first settlers landed on America's shores they turned their backs on Europe and faced to the west. From that time on, Americans moved west to seek new lands and establish new homes. The Mormons had participated in the westward movement in moving onto the frontier of western settlement in Ohio, Missouri, Illinois, and finally in Utah. During the 1840s and 1850s the westward movement bypassed the region between the Mississippi Valley and the Pacific Coast. The region, regarded as the "Great American Desert," was forbidding as a place to settle. It took years for Americans to realize the value of these lands for homes and ranches. The Mormons were the first white men to settle in the central mountain regions of this great American West.

The Hayden survey of 1871 camped in Cache Valley. Here they determined the location of the Utah-Idaho boundary, a fact which led to political problems in Idaho over the Mormon question.

The movement of people onto the western frontier often followed this order: the hunter, the trapper, the fur trader who went into the distant West, cattlemen, miners, farmers, and town dwellers. The pattern was different in the case of Utah. The fur traders had come and gone, and the farmers and the town dwellers came as Mormon settlers. The cattlemen and the miners came later. The fact that the Mormons had already established an agricultural oasis in the Mountain West was a great help to the miners, cattlemen, and others who came into the neighboring regions, for the surplus agricultural products of Utah helped to feed these non-farming frontiersmen.

The Utah region was attractive not only to the Mormons but to other Americans. From the beginning of exploration, travelers had seen the beauty of the land, and after Mormon settlements were made, they saw the fine opportunities of making a living here.

Emigration to California went through Utah before and after 1847. Some California-bound emigrants ended their trail and settled in Utah. During the 1850s to a small extent and during the 1860s to a larger extent, Americans on the western frontier came into the Utah region to do business and to make a living. Gradually the American frontier was catching up with Utah.

The total number of non-Mormons who came to Utah was not great. Even in the later years of the century non-Mormons numbered only about 10 percent of the total population. But their influence was much stronger than their numbers would indicate, and their contributions were far reaching.

2. AMERICAN SOLDIERS MADE SIGNIFICANT CONTRIBUTIONS TO EARLY UTAH

Soldiers of the United States Army arrived in the territory for various duties. The first of these groups was led by Lieutenant Colonel *Edward J. Steptoe*. He was in Utah from August 1854 until the end of the next April. Steptoe was sent to Utah to investigate the Gunnison Massacre and apprehend the murderers, and to look into the possibility of a military road from Utah to California. Steptoe established a military reservation in Rush Valley where livestock was wintered. The officers and men rented quarters in Salt Lake City. The colonel won the praises of the Mormon leaders as an officer and a gentleman. Inevitably some conflicts arose between troops and citizens. There were some affairs approaching brawls, but there were also many pleasant social events, especially dances, to which the soldiers were invited.

The second body of soldiers to come into the territory was under the command of **Albert Sidney Johnston** in connection with the Utah War in 1857. About four thousand troops and about three thousand suppliers and camp followers eventually located in Cedar Valley at *Camp Floyd*. Like Steptoe's troops, the soldiers spent money in Utah.

The presence of so many troops and camp personnel in the territory had important economic effects. The Mormons sold their surpluses to the army. They traded dried fish, vegetables, butter, eggs, buttermilk, pies, and "Valley Tan" whiskey to the troops in exchange for money, clothing, tea, coffee, iron, and stoves. The church contracted to supply large quantities of grain, hay, and lumber to Camp Floyd. This trade was profitable to the citizens. In addition, many citizens found employment at the camp, chiefly as carpenters, masons, and blacksmiths. The army did not live entirely upon the products of the settlers, thus threatening a famine among the people. Rather, much of its need was supplied by hundreds of wagons freighting supplies in from the East each year. At one time the freighting firm of Russell, Majors and Waddell sold 3,500 large freight wagons (which cost from $150 to $175 apiece in the east) for $10 each. Surplus oxen, mules, and horses were also sold to the citizens. When Camp Floyd was abandoned, there was an auction of army equipment and goods. Goods sold included iron, tools, equipment, livestock, feed, and food in the form of beans, flour, and meat. The loss in value to the government proved to be of great value to the settlers. In the end, the invading forces had benefited the settlers economically, making some Mormons comparatively rich.

The Civil War brought the third body of soldiers to Utah. To protect the overland mail and telegraph lines against Indian attack, volunteer soldiers were recruited in California and Nevada and sent to Utah under the command of Colonel *Patrick Edward Connor.* The troops, about 750 in number, arrived in October 1862 and on October 22 founded *Camp Douglas* on the east bench overlooking Salt

Patrick Edward Connor commanded the California Volunteers in Utah. He was one of the most influential non-Mormons in Utah's territorial history. He founded Fort Douglas in 1862, led military campaigns against the Indians, was the father of Utah mining, and was a leader in the anti-Mormon crusade.

Camp Douglas (later Fort Douglas), located on the east bench overlooking Salt Lake City, was an important military post in the Mountain West.

Lake City. Camp Douglas became one of the United States Army's most important installations in the West. The contributions of the camp and the soldiers stationed there through the years have been many.

However, the Mormons felt they were under military occupation for the second time. At first and for many years, citizens and soldiers feared each other. At Camp Douglas the soldiers published the *Union Vedette* (a weekly and then a daily newspaper, November 20, 1863 to November 27, 1867) and circulated it not only in Salt Lake City but sent copies back east to newspapers and government officials in Washington. The paper was anti-Mormon and asked the government to protect Americans from the Mormon people.

Camp Douglas served as an outlet for some goods produced by the settlers. But Connor felt that Mormon prices were too high, so most camp supplies came from the East.

Indian campaigns. One of the activities of the soldiers was their primary objective of suppressing Indians in their attacks against the overland mail and telegraph.

When the *California volunteers* arrived in Utah, Indian troubles awaited their attention. Shoshoni and Bannock were encamped in Cache Valley and held captive an emigrant boy whose parents had been killed by Indians. Major Edward McGarry was placed in command of sixty cavalrymen who rode at once to the Indian camp where, near Providence, November 23, 1862, there was a skirmish in which three Indians were killed and one wounded. No soldiers were hurt. The chief surrendered the boy, and the troops returned to Camp Douglas. A few days later Major McGarry was again in command of a unit which was sent north to Bear River to recover stolen livestock. Four Indians were taken hostage, but when the other Indians refused to return the cattle, the hostages were killed and the soldiers returned to camp.

The Battle of Bear River (January 29, 1863) was the major engagement of the California volunteers, and one of the most significant battles in the Mountain West. Indians had been attacking wagon trains on the overland route in southern Idaho. They had also made life miserable for the Cache Valley settlers by thieving and demanding supplies. Early in January the Indians attacked a company of miners en route from Montana to Salt Lake. The leader of the company lodged a complaint with government authorities in Salt Lake City whereupon Chief Justice Kinney issued a warrant for the arrest of the chiefs of the offending tribes of Shoshoni. Judge Kinney requested that Colonel Connor take soldiers to support the arresting officer and to chastise the Indians.

Connor took his force of about three hundred cavalry and infantry on a forced march under cover of darkness, reaching Franklin (now Idaho) during the night of January 28. Two Franklin men guided the military forces to the Indian village located at the juncture of Beaver Creek and Bear River. Here about six hundred Shoshoni were entrenched in a ravine. About one-third or one-half of the band were women and children.

At dawn, a surprise attack was launched, and bitter hand-to-hand fighting followed in which Indian men, women, and children fought to defend their lives. After more than three hours of fighting some of the Indians broke and ran; a few escaped by swimming the Bear River.

About 300 Indian men and 50 women and children were massacred. The Indian survivors were fed and allowed to go. The soldiers found a great deal of plunder the Indians had taken from settlers and wagon trains. They recovered valuables and burned the village.

The Battle of the Bear River took place where Beaver Creek (now Battle Creek) flows into the Bear River in this valley, about ten miles north of Franklin, Idaho (on the Utah-Idaho border). After crossing the Bear River, Connor's troops made a two-front attack on the Shoshoni encampment, massacring about half the inhabitants.

229

In the battle soldier casualties included 22 killed, 45 wounded, and 79 incapacitated by frozen limbs. The army moved back to Franklin where it spent the night—the settlers doing all they could to care for the soldiers and the wounded. The troops were back in Camp Douglas on February 4.

One military historian has said that the Battle of Bear River was "the largest engagement ever fought between Indians and white men west of the Rocky Mountains." It was perhaps "the only instance in the history of Indian warfare in which red men deliberately assumed the defensive and fought from trenches." Surely there are elements in this massacre which compare with those in the Sand Creek Massacre (Colorado, November 29, 1864) and the Battle of Wounded Knee (South Dakota, December 29, 1890).

The Battle of Bear River is significant for Utah settlement, for Indian strength was broken. Indian resistance to settlement came to a virtual end in southeastern Idaho and northern Utah. Settlers now moved out of their forts onto lots. The white victory helped make the overland route safer for emigrants, mail, and wagon trains of supplies.

The California volunteers made several other contributions to the security of the Utah settlers and to the overland routes. They escorted mail and passenger coaches, emigrant and supply trains, patrolled the telegraph lines, and built military roads. During the spring and summer of 1863 troops were called to suppress Indians west of Salt Lake City, in Skull, Cedar, and Utah valleys. Soldiers stationed at Fort Bridger brought about a peace treaty with the Shoshoni in that area. Similar peace treaties were signed by Indians in Utah and Nevada. For many months after October 1863, the routes of travel through and around Utah territory were used without fear of Indians.

Mining. General Connor and the California volunteers made a significant contribution to Utah's development when they opened up mining for precious metals. The Mormons had mined salt, coal, iron, and lead. The development of mining precious metals, however, was begun by the volunteers. The troops from California were really miners in uniform, for they had gone to California to mine, and they looked upon Utah's mountains with searching eyes. But little could be done until the Indians had been checked. (The mining activities of the California volunteers will be discussed in chapter 15.)

Military forts were established in Utah. *Camp Douglas* remained a permanent post in Utah, garrisoned periodically by from two to four hundred regular troops. The name was changed to Fort Douglas, December 30, 1878. Fort Douglas became the principal army post in the Mountain West.

Fort Cameron was established at Beaver in 1872, for political reasons, to keep a check on the Mormons. Barracks and officers' quarters were built, as well as a hospital, a commissary store, and headquarters building.

Barracks at Fort Cameron, Beaver, about 1918, after the buildings had been put to use by the Murdock Academy.

About 125 officers and men were stationed there during its ten-year history. In 1883 it was abandoned, and its buildings were used for a school, a branch of the Brigham Young Academy, later called the Murdock Academy. Other forts were established when need arose in the 1870s and 1880s (see chapter 16, section 5).

The construction, maintenance, and sale of the forts built by United States soldiers were a source of cash income to settlers. The soldiers' contribution in mining was significant, leading to the introduction of more people into the territory, enlarging the business community, and putting more power into the hands of non-Mormons.

3. JEWS CAME TO UTAH AS RESIDENT MERCHANTS

During the 1860s and especially after the coming of the railroad in 1869, people of different ethnic backgrounds and religious faiths came to Utah, to make a living and establish homes. In establishing their own churches, varieties of religious faiths came to be represented in Utah. Though few in number, they nevertheless made important contributions to the early development of Utah.

Jews were among the first non-Mormons to come to Utah. They came as merchants who wanted to make permanent homes here. They made significant contributions to the economic life of early Utah.

It is believed that Julius Gerson Brooks and his wife Fanny, who came in the summer of 1854, were the first Jews to remain in Utah. Many Jews who were in the California gold rush looking for places to settle after the mining booms were over, came to Utah from California and Nevada. Because of the Mormon emphasis on agriculture and manufacturing, there was ample room for merchants and businessmen.

In the mid-1860s there were about fifty adult Jews in Salt Lake City and a few others scattered throughout the territory. Numerous businesses were represented, including merchants, salesmen, and shopkeepers.

The first Jewish religious services were held October 11, 1864. The formal organization of the Jewish congregation was effected in 1881 under the title "B'nai Israel of Salt Lake City." The first synagogue was completed in 1883 at a cost of $14,000. This was outgrown, and a larger synagogue was built in 1891, costing $37,500.

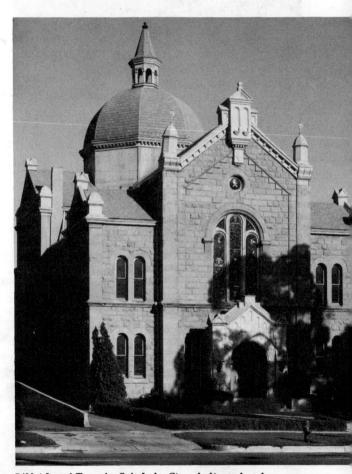

B'Nai Israel Temple, Salt Lake City, dedicated and consecrated in 1891, was patterned after the famous Jewish temple in Berlin. The Auerbach family, members of the congregation, brought Philip Meyer, a nephew and architect, from Germany to draw the plans for the synagogue.

*Jewish merchants were among Utah's first businessmen.
This view southward on Main Street in Salt Lake City
shows the stores of the Kahn brothers
N. S. Ransohoff, the Siegel brothers, and others.
The Masonic Hall is in the center.*

*The Saint Mary Magdalene Catholic Church, consecrated
in 1871, is shown in the center of this picture
of Salt Lake City looking northward. Also shown
are the John W. Young home, lower left, the
Daniel McIntosh home, the Feramorz Little lumber
yard, and the Wells Fargo stables, across
the street from the church.*

Brigham Young counted the Jews his friends, and he showed this friendship when he donated land for the Jewish cemetery and more than once made Mormon church buildings available for Jewish religious services. As the years passed strong friendships grew between many Jews and Mormons. When Protestants began to establish congregations in Utah, the Jews responded to calls from Protestants in raising funds to build churches. One Jew served as a trustee to a Protestant church while remaining a Jew. Some Jews were converted to the Mormon church, and a few Mormon women married Jews and became members of that faith.

Despite individual friendships, when the bitter days of conflict between Mormon and non-Mormon came in the late 1870s and the 1880s, the Jews as a group were committed like other non-Mormons to fight against Mormon control.

The Right Reverend Lawrence Scanlan, Catholic bishop of Salt Lake City, was a significant religious leader in Utah from 1873 until his death in 1915.

4. CATHOLIC PRIESTS CAME TO UTAH TO SERVE THEIR MEMBERS LIVING IN THE AREA

The earliest Catholics in Utah came as visitors, remaining but a short time. They include Fathers Dominguez and Escalante, and some of the Mountain Men (Etienne Provost and Thomas Fitzpatrick). The earliest known resident Catholics were among the volunteers from California and Nevada who came in 1862, Patrick Edward Connor among them. Among the troops at Camp Douglas there were always some Catholics. To answer their religious needs the Reverend *Edward Kelly* came on assignment to Salt Lake City during the summer of 1866. He celebrated mass in the Old Tabernacle on Temple Square, and purchased land on Second East Street for a church. (Brigham Young helped clear the title for him.) Because of poor health, however, Father Kelly left in a couple of months and returned to San Francisco.

The first resident pastor was the Reverend *James P. Foley* (in Salt Lake City from summer 1868 to autumn 1870), who was followed by the Reverend *Patrick Walsh* (in Salt Lake City from early 1871 to July 1873). For the three or more Catholic families in the city and the soldiers at the camp, Father Foley held services in the dilapidated adobe structure on the property Father Kelly had bought two years before. Father Walsh put his energies into the building of the first Catholic church in Utah. The old adobe structure was replaced by a brick church in honor of Saint Mary Magdalene, at a cost of $12,000. The church was consecrated by Archbishop Alemany from San Francisco on November 26, 1871. Father Walsh also held the first services in Ogden. During this time the Reverend Patrick J. Dowling from San Francisco was appointed the resident pastor to Corinne, where he served during the boom days of that town, 1872-73.

The most important name in the history of the growth of Catholicism in Utah is that of the Reverend *Lawrence Scanlan,* who arrived August 14, 1873, as pastor of Salt Lake City. He had the largest geographical parish in the United States at the time, with eight hundred Catholics in his parish, only ninety of whom were in Salt Lake City and Ogden. He was to spend the rest of his life in Utah, serving in turn as pastor, vicar-forane, vicar-apostolic, and bishop, until his death in 1915, forty-two years later. Within two years he repaid the $6,000 debt on the original church building, then built churches, schools, and hospitals not only in Salt Lake and Ogden, but in the mining towns of Utah then in their hey-day. In 1875 a school was opened and a hospital begun by sisters in Salt Lake City. In Ogden a church was built in 1876 and a sisters' school opened in 1878. In 1879 a church and a hospital were built at Silver Reef. In 1881 a church and school were built in Park City, and the same in Eureka in 1885 and 1886. All Hallows College, a school for boys, was built in Salt Lake City in 1885.

Father Scanlan made his visits much of the time on horseback or on foot, to Ogden and Provo, and the mining camps at Ophir, Stockton, Alta, Castle Gate, Park City, and Bingham; and wherever there was prospect of establishing a parish, he erected a church.

While Father Scanlan was at Silver Reef in 1879, he received an invitation from the Mormon leaders in Saint George to use the tabernacle there for Catholic services. Father Scanlan accepted the invitation. Inasmuch as the services for Sunday—missa cantata and sermon—called for a choir singing Latin, he thought that part of the service would have to be omitted. However, the Saint George tabernacle choir leader asked for the Catholic music, the Peter's mass, and in two weeks the choir knew the mass and could sing it in Latin. On May 18, high mass was sung in the Saint George Tabernacle. Since most of his congregation was Mormon, he explained before the services the meaning of the vestments used at mass. Father Scanlan won the esteem and good will of the Mormons, and the Mormons won the gratitude of the Catholics for their willing cooperation.

5. PROTESTANT MINISTERS AND TEACHERS CAME TO SERVE THEIR MEMBERS AND AS MISSIONARIES TO THE MORMONS

Some religious groups came to Utah with the major purpose of spreading education and the Christian religion. In order to do this, missions were established in Utah.

The first group to come to Utah to make converts among the Mormons were members of the **Reorganized Church of Jesus Christ of Latter Day Saints**. They held Joseph Smith III and not Brigham Young to be the rightful successor to the presidency of the church. In 1863 representatives came to Utah where they converted a few families and built a chapel in Salt Lake City. In time there were annual out-migrations of these people to California or back east.

The Congregational church. Believing that Protestant services in Salt Lake City would help the community, General Connor exerted influence to have the Reverend Norman McLeod sent to Utah by the American (Congregational) Home Missionary Society. Connor offered Reverend McLeod the position of chaplain at Camp Douglas until he might be appointed pastor of a church. Reverend McLeod held his first services January 22, 1865 and a few weeks later organized the First Congregational Church. Non-Mormons in Salt Lake City gave encouragement and helped build *Independence Hall* which was the home of the Congregational Church in Salt Lake City for many years. In 1866 Reverend McLeod went east to raise money for the church and did not return. It was not until 1874 that the Reverend Walter M. Barrows came and reorganized the church. Since that time there has been a steady growth of the Congregational Church in Utah.

Schools were founded by the Congregationalists in Salt Lake City and other Utah settlements. *Gordon Academy* began its first term in September 1878 with classes held in Independence Hall, then in Hammond Hall. The academy later became known as the Salt Lake College. Three schools were built in Salt Lake City between 1882 and 1886. Ogden had a school in 1884 and Provo an academy in 1883. Twenty-three schools were also operated in rural Utah. Their success helped to show the need for a better school system.

The Episcopalians built churches, schools, and hospitals in Utah. The third Protestant group to come to Utah before the coming of the railroad was the Episcopal church. In May and July of 1867 the Reverend Daniel S.

The Reverend Daniel S. Tuttle, Episcopal bishop in Utah, was a founder of schools, churches, and hospitals.

In the nineteenth century, the Episcopalians only gradually extended their church services to other centers in Utah. In 1888 Bishop Abiel Leonard, Bishop Tuttle's successor, established congregations in Park City and Eureka.

The Presbyterians came to Utah with the dual purpose of serving their own members and establishing schools for the education of Mormon children. Making use of the newly completed transcontinental railroad, Presbyterians came to Utah and set up a church in Corinne in July 1870. The Reverend Josiah Welch began working with the Presbyterians in Salt Lake City in October 1871, preaching his first sermon in Faust's Hall, over Mulloy and Paul's Livery Stable. Three years later a

Saint Mark's Day School, Salt Lake City.

Saint Mark's Episcopal Cathedral, Salt Lake City.

Tuttle, Episcopal bishop of "Montana, with Jurisdiction in Idaho and Utah," with four other ministers and their families moved to Utah. Services were held in Independence Hall. Under Bishop Tuttle's able direction, schools, churches, and hospitals were built. Saint Mark's Day School in Salt Lake City was set up in July 1867, the School of the Good Shepherd in Ogden (1870), Saint John's School in Logan (1873), Saint Paul's in Plain City (1873), Saint John's in Layton (1886), and Rowland Hall-Saint Mark's, a college preparatory school for girls in Salt Lake City 1881. These schools operated into the new century, and Rowland Hall-Saint Mark's is still one of Salt Lake City's fine schools.

Saint Mark's Cathedral was completed in 1871 in Salt Lake City, one of the most distinctive landmarks in the city. In Ogden the Church of the Good Shepherd was consecrated in February 1875.

Saint Mark's Hospital was started in 1872 in a small adobe building. It moved to its present site after 1879.

235

church was built costing $29,500 and seating 515. It was the first home of the Salt Lake Collegiate Institute. In December 1874 the Presbytery of Utah was organized.

Between 1875 and 1883 the Presbyterians established thirty-six mission schools and four academies with sixty-five teachers. Mission schools were begun by ministers and often taken over by well-trained, competent women teachers. Though Presbyterian children attended the schools, the greatest number of pupils were Mormon children. In some communities there was serious opposition to the schools; however, from the number of students taught during the years the schools were in operation, it would seem that some Mormons willingly sent their children. About fifty thousand children were taught in these schools. Many of the smaller towns in Utah had Presbyterian mission schools.

The Synod of Utah was organized in August 1883. One of the most influential leaders was the Reverend Dr. Robert G. McNiece who came to Salt Lake City in 1877 and remained for twenty years. The Reverend George W. Martin and wife were in Manti for forty years.

During the 1870s various Protestant denominations established churches in Utah communities. This Methodist church was built in Richfield.

The other Protestant church groups that came to Utah in the 1870s and 1880s were the Methodists, the Baptists, and the Lutherans. They came to bring the services of their churches to their members. The Reverend G. M. Peirce was the leading Methodist from 1870 to 1876, during which time he organized churches and church schools in Salt Lake City, Corinne, Tooele, Provo, and Beaver. The Baptists first held services in 1871 when the Reverend George W. Dodge, Indian agent for the Territory of Utah, conducted services during his tenure here until 1874. The Reverend Dwight Spencer was the next to come to Utah to hold Baptist services. He came to Ogden in January 1881 and soon organized the First Baptist Church of Ogden. Dr. G. B. Morse led the church in Salt Lake City. The Lutherans came to Utah in 1882 and organized the Zion Evangelical Lutheran Church in Salt Lake City, July 18, 1882. They built their church at Second South and Fourth East streets in 1885 at a cost of $7,000. The pastor in Salt Lake City served other preaching stations including Sandy, Bingham Canyon, Park City, Eureka, and Provo. The Disciples of Christ (Christian) church came to Utah in 1890 and established churches in Salt Lake City and Ogden that year.

The Swedish Evangelical Lutheran Church, Salt Lake City, was built in 1885.

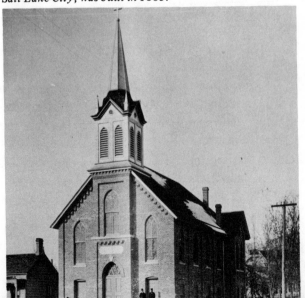

6. GOVERNMENT EXPLORERS MADE CONTRIBUTIONS IN MAPPING AND DESCRIBING THE UTAH LANDSCAPE

While Mountain Men, overland emigrants, and settlers had explored much of the American West, government explorers scientifically described and mapped the area. To aid emigration westward, Congress authorized agencies of the War Department and the Department of the Interior to undertake scientific explorations. Surveys of major existing routes and explorations of routes proposed for a transcontinental railroad and wagon roads were made. Special exploration and mapping was done on the Colorado River and the Colorado Plateau.

Within two years after the Mormon settlement of Salt Lake Valley, Captain *Howard Stansbury* of the Corps of Topographical Engineers was in Utah exploring and surveying the valley of the Great Salt Lake. His maps of the route to the valley and of the Great Salt Lake area were drawn by Lieutenant John W. Gunnison and Charles Preuss (who had served with John C. Frémont). Stansbury and his party were in Utah from August 28, 1849 to August 28, 1850. He visited Fort Hall, explored around Great Salt Lake and Utah Lake, and on his return eastward explored from Fort Bridger to Fort Laramie. His description of possible railroad routes along his line of exploration influenced the route later followed by the overland stage and the railroad. His published report gives one of the first accurate descriptions and appraisals of the region around Great Salt Lake, including plant and animal life. While in Utah, Lieutenant Gunnison gathered information for a book which he published in 1852 entitled: *The Mormons, or Latter-day Saints, in the Valley of the Great Salt Lake: A History of Their Rise and Progress, Peculiar Doctrines, Present Condition, and Prospects, De-rived from Personal Observation during a Residence among Them.* It is one of the finest accounts of the Mormons and the early settlement of Utah.

The course of the Colorado River was not known in the early 1850s. Other rivers carried their share of commerce, why not the Colorado? Settlers and the government were equally anxious to use the river for moving goods and people. Lieutenant *Joseph C. Ives* of the Topographical Bureau was ordered by the secretary of war "to ascertain the navigability of the Colorado, with especial reference to the availability for the transportation of supplies to the various military posts in New Mexico and Utah." During 1857-58 Lieutenant Ives made a detailed study of the Colorado River, upstream to Black Canyon, the site of Boulder Dam. Ives used for part of the exploration a steamboat of special design named the *Explorer*. Ives did not go as far as the Virgin River, but concluded that the practical head of navigation was Black Canyon, not far from Las Vegas (the Meadows), a resting place on the road from California to Salt Lake City. A road could be built from the river to the emigrant road. In addition to a well-illustrated, scientific report of the expedition, Ives compiled a map of the area covered by the reconnaissance. Ives recommended the use of the Colorado River for commerce. The Mormons gave serious attention to the recommendation, with the idea of shortening the voyage for immigrants coming to Utah by water. Mormon explorations resulted in establishing in 1864 Call's Landing, about fifteen miles upstream from Black Canyon. Though promoters said prospects for bringing immigrants by water to this point were good, the scheme was abandoned because of practical problems with this route and the coming of the transcontinental railroad.

Call's Landing, on the Colorado River about forty-five miles south of present Overton, Nevada, was established in 1864 by Anson Call as part of an attempt to bring immigrants from Europe to Utah by water.

The government's first attempt at a systematic and comprehensive survey of the trans-Mississippi West came when Congress in 1853 authorized the secretary of war to undertake the survey of four possible east-west routes for a railroad from the Mississippi River to the Pacific Ocean. These surveys made possible the first accurate topographical map of the West. In their reports the explorers included descriptions of the country passed through, maps, sketches of the scenery, Indians, plant and animal life.

The survey for a central railroad route was commanded by Captain *John W. Gunnison*, who had been in Utah with Stansbury in 1849-50. His party was to explore westward from Saint Louis toward San Francisco, and locate a route through the Rocky Mountains by way of the Huerfano River and Cochetopa Pass, or another accessible pass. His explorations led him to the Gunnison and Green rivers, and then to the Sevier River in Utah. By this time he had traced a new military road to Taos, another southern emigration wagon road to California, and proved it

would be very difficult to build a railroad route along the thirty-eighth parallel. When the party was on the Sevier River, about fifteen miles southwest of present Delta, the morning of October 26, 1853, a party of renegade Pahvant Indians attacked the camp and killed Captain Gunnison and seven of his men. (See chapter 13, section 2.) Lieutenant *E. G. Beckwith* assumed command of the expedition and completed the survey. Beckwith made his way to Salt Lake City, then surveyed a route westward along a line near the forty-first parallel to the Pacific Ocean by way of the Humboldt Mountains and Mud Lakes.

Government surveys were also made for wagon roads useful for emigrants and settlers. One of the most frequently traveled areas was between Fort Laramie and Salt Lake Valley. In 1858 the Corps of Topographical Engineers compiled a map of this route, based on the explorations of Frémont, Stansbury, Beckwith, and others. Routes practical for wagons were shown. Lieutenant *Joseph Dixon* compiled a map from a variety of sources of a wagon road from Salt Lake Valley to Fort Hall, to the Columbia River, and the Willamette Valley in Oregon. Captain *James Hervey Simpson* made productive surveys of Utah territory in 1858 and 1859. He charted a road between Fort Bridger and Camp Floyd. He also searched out a direct wagon route from Camp Floyd, across the Great Basin, to Genoa in Carson Valley, saving about two hundred miles over the old emigrant road. The Pony Express and the telegraph line followed these routes. He also found a pass through the Uinta Mountains to the Green River, Fort Bridger, and to Fort Leavenworth.

Between 1867 and 1879 four great surveys were made mapping the geology and natural resources of the West. The Hayden survey, 1867-79, led by Dr. *Ferdinand V.*

The Hayden survey party in camp. Photos of this expedition are by William H. Jackson, survey photographer.

Ferdinand V. Hayden led a major government survey of the West, 1867-79. He was largely responsible for the creation of Yellowstone National Park and helped organize the United States Geological Survey.

In 1871 Hayden led a survey party to the Yellowstone country. At Ogden they left the train and made their first camp.

Hayden, covered a vast area of the Rocky Mountains and the Colorado Plateau regions. Yellowstone National Park was created (1872) largely through his efforts. *Clarence King* directed an exploration in an area fifty miles on each side of the fortieth parallel, extending across the ranges of mountains from eastern Colorado to the California boundary. This survey passed through Utah along the line of the Uinta Basin. King was perhaps the first geologist to give a clear reconstruction of the geologic history of the Rocky Mountain region. In 1871 Lieutenant *George M. Wheeler* was given the responsibility of systematically mapping the entire region west of the hundredth meridian. While these three surveys added to knowledge of the geology and geography of the West (and all related to Utah), the fourth survey was of particular interest to Utah.

Major *John Wesley Powell* was the most colorful of the government explorers who came to Utah between 1850 and 1880. Largely self-taught in the natural sciences he nevertheless obtained a teaching position at an Illinois college after his service in the Civil

The Powell party is ready to start a second exploration of the Colorado River, 1871.

John Wesley Powell, explorer of the Colorado River, is also called the father of reclamation, an interest he gained on his visits to Utah in 1869, 1871, and 1889.

War (he lost his right arm to the elbow at the Battle of Shiloh). In 1867 and again in 1868 he organized and conducted parties of students and amateur naturalists across the plains to the mountains of Colorado, where in 1868 he saw the gorges of the Green and Colorado rivers. He conceived the daring scheme of exploring those river canyons by boat. Reports of his dramatic achievements captured the interest of scientists and made him a public hero.

Exploring the canyons of the Green and Colorado rivers was exploring the last frontier of the United States. By hard work Powell obtained necessary financial and government backing for his exploration. On May 24, 1869 all was ready, and Major Powell and nine companions entered the Green River (in Wyoming where the transcontinental railroad crosses the river). Four boats had been built specially for the trip. Powell and his men floated down the Green and the Colorado rivers, passing through the deep gorges, sometimes through placid waters, but frequently running wild rapids. Mishaps were frequent, food became wet and spoiled, and one boat

was wrecked. At one point the voyage became so uncertain that three of Powell's men withdrew, climbing out of the canyon to seek safety, only to be killed by Indians. Reduced now to two boats and with food for only five days, Powell and the six remaining men proceeded through the Grand Canyon reaching the Colorado's confluence with the Virgin River August 30. They had been more than three months on the river, and covered nine hundred miles. In spite of hardships, they had made scientific readings which made it possible to map the river. Powell became aware of the need for a study of the arid regions of the West to learn how best to make use of this great drainage system.

Before Powell's second expedition down the Colorado in 1871, he spent time in Utah making friends with the Indians. Jacob Hamblin and Brigham Young both encouraged the Indians to listen to Powell and treat him as a friend. As a result of Powell's studies he learned much about the Indians and their way of life in the arid plateau regions. Powell was impressed by the ability of the Indians to adapt their way of life to a dry and

Powell's boat, with his chair fastened, is moored in the canyon of the Colorado River.

Major Powell (the white man nearest the camera) and Jacob Hamblin, on Powell's right, meet with Paiute Indians in a tribal council.

sparsely vegetated area. He noticed how the Mormons used the available water to support a large population and believed it was through community use of water that success had come to the Utah pioneers.

Major Powell's interest in the West brought him to Utah again in connection with the Powell Survey of Arid Lands, 1889. On this visit he studied the drainage systems of Utah streams and located lands which could be brought under irrigation. Reservoir sites were studied, along with stream flow, and the amount of evaporation from the lakes and streams. Ten sites were selected where reservoirs could be built. These sites were Bear Lake, Utah Lake, Cottonwood Creek in Big Cottonwood Canyon, and seven sites on the Sevier River and its tributaries. This survey changed water use in Utah by bringing federally financed reservoirs and dams to Utah in place of the cooperative use of water the early settlers had maintained. It resulted in greater quantities of water stored, hence opening up more land for cultivation.

Major Powell sought to avoid duplication in the surveys of the West. His work resulted in the creation of the United States Geological Survey in 1879. In this agency he was named the first director of the Bureau of American Ethnology, and succeeded (1880) Clarence King as director of the Geological Survey. Powell had considerable influence on the promotion of studies of the Indians of the Colorado Plateau region. Many of his proposals were put into effect; such as the withdrawal of public lands for the public good, the harnessing of the waters of the Colorado River, setting up a bureau of forestry, and a federal agency for the encouragement of science. He spent thirty years of his life working in the United States Geological Survey, the Bureau of American Ethnology, and the Bureau of Reclamation.

Major Powell's most significant writings include *Report on the Lands of the Arid Region of the United States* (1879), *Explorations of the Colorado River of the West and Its Tributaries* (1875, issued in 1895 in revised and enlarged form as *Canyons of the Colorado*). John K. Hillers, a photographer, was with Powell on his expeditions. He has left many excellent photographs of the Ute

Clarence Edward Dutton made the most extensive geological survey of Utah's mountains and plateaus.

and Paiute Indians he met along the course of the Colorado River.

  Clarence Edward Dutton is another explorer who made a notable contribution to our understanding of Utah geology. Dutton began his geological career with Powell in 1875 and devoted the next ten years to the study of the plateaus of Utah and Arizona. In 1879-80 he published his *Report on the Geology of the High Plateau of Utah*. His geological knowledge and literary skill give a most readable and graphic description of the plateaus and canyons. He pointed out that the Wasatch Range ends at Mount Nebo, that the plateaus are no relation to the Wasatch Range, being of a different age and structure. He published his *Tertiary History of the Grand Canyon District* in 1882 and his *Mount Taylor and the Zuñi Plateau* in 1886. His works are illustrated with magnificent drawings.

  These government explorers gave us

Major Powell speaks with Tau-gu, a Paiute, near Cedar City.

John K. Hillers, photographer with Powell, 1871-72, recorded the scenic beauty of the Canyonlands as well as the Indians of Utah.

scientific descriptions and accurate maps of major portions of the Mountain West. We have them to thank for much of our knowledge concerning the geology of the Utah region. They gave us basic information concerning the historic Indians of Utah and their way of life. Their work led to federally financed reclamation projects which have conserved our water, provided power plants, and extended our irrigation systems.

Paiute Indians are playing the game Kill the Bone, Kaibab Plateau, 1873.

At Promontory Summit, Utah, May 10, 1869,
the tracks of the two railroads met, completing the transcontinental railroad. This unusual view shows the troops
and crewmen present. At the right is the telegraph pole from which was flashed the message "Done!"

AND MINING FRONTIERS COME TO UTAH

The way of life of the people of Utah in the 1850s and the early 1860s was changed slightly by the non-Mormons who came during those decades. However, during the late 1860s their way of life changed significantly. Utah became tied more closely to the nation, and some of her geographical isolation ended. Non-Mormons continued to make important contributions to the development of Utah.

The American westward movement caught up with Utah during the 1850s, and during the 1860s and 1870s Utah participated even more in national movements in the West. With the westward movement of people came overland freighting and faster means of carrying passengers, goods, and mail, climaxing in the Pony Express, the overland telegraph, and the transcontinental railroad.

These advances came as a result of the normal expansion of American business interests in the West to provide better service and to make larger profits. But these advances were speeded up by the concern of the federal government to bind the nation more closely and quickly in a firm Union. It was feared by some that California and other western states and territories might join the Confederacy in the Civil War. Close contact by news and mail, through the Pony Express, telegraph, and rails, could help keep these western people in full support of the Union.

These improved means of communication and transportation were most welcome in Utah. Years ago Utahns had asked Congress for an overland telegraph and a transcontinental railroad, to pass through Salt Lake City. The people of Utah wanted to keep in touch with people in the East, speed up immigration, and receive eastern goods that could be brought in more cheaply by trains. More people would come in: Mormon immigrants, people servicing the telegraph and the railroad, as well as people who wanted to make their homes in the West. A mining frontier accompanied the railroad to Utah because the railroad made it possible to profitably mine the precious ores.

Some people felt that the coming of the railroad would break up the Mormon experiment. That the Mormon pioneer way of life was preserved as much as it was is due to the planning of the Mormon leaders to take full advantage of the benefits of the railroad and to establish institutions which helped guard against the disadvantages (to them) of the coming of the railroad. Even so, life was changed significantly for everyone in Utah.

The study of the coming of these changes is a continuation of the theme established in the last chapter—the contributions of many people to Utah's development.

IN THIS CHAPTER WE WILL LEARN

1. Overland freighting, the stagecoach, and the Pony Express brought goods and mail.

2. The Overland telegraph and Utah's Deseret Telegraph Company helped bind Utah to the nation.

3. The rails of the first transcontinental railroad met at Promontory, Utah, May 10, 1869; thereafter, railroads were built into the valleys of Utah.

4. The railroad brought many changes to Utah.

5. The mining frontier came to Utah once the railroads were built.

1. OVERLAND FREIGHTING, THE STAGECOACH, AND THE PONY EXPRESS BROUGHT GOODS AND MAIL

Freighting goods into Salt Lake Valley began with the first pioneer immigration. With the establishment of more villages, the demand for eastern goods increased; and with the opening of mines and the establishment of mining camps and towns in California and the Mountain West, there was even greater demand for goods from the East. Miners were so busy mining that almost everything they used, ate, or wore, had to be freighted in to them. And their demand for mail was great.

Overland freighting was one of the most

Main Street, Salt Lake City, 1865. Freighting brought in goods not locally produced which merchants sold to their customers.

important enterprises in the West between 1850 and 1870. Companies were formed, large and small, to carry goods and mail to the miners and settlers of the West. The federal government offered mail contracts and sometimes large subsidies to these companies, grants which made it possible for them to survive and make a profit. After the completion of the transcontinental railroad in 1869, *freighting* continued as an important business, carrying goods from the railroad to distant settlements and mining camps. The people of Utah were involved in both the overland freighting and the freighting within the Mountain West region. Increasingly, freighted goods came into Utah during the 1860s. Freighting was a way of life for some people and the people of Utah benefited from goods brought in.

The hazards of overland freighting were great. Storms, floods, poor roads, few if any bridges, Indian attacks, all made the risks great. Heavy expenses made the cost of goods quite high. Lucrative profits were made. It was big business. During the 1860s along the overland trail, hundreds of wagons could be seen passing one point in a single day. Thousands were on the trail during the summer.

One of the most important overland freighting companies was the partnership firm of *Russell, Majors and Waddell*, formed in 1855 and for several years the major freighting firm operating through Utah. This firm freighted the goods in for Johnston's army during the Utah War. Their wagons carried food stuffs and industrial goods to the army and mining camps, and brought back such goods as hides, and especially ores from the mines. Each wagon train consisted of twenty-five or twenty-six covered wagons, each wagon carrying about six thousand pounds of goods, and pulled by six yoke of oxen. The wagon train was directed by a wagon boss.

There was brisk trade between northern Utah communities and the mining towns of Idaho and Montana.

There was also an assistant wagon boss, a night herder, and a man to drive the extra animals, and a few spare drivers. Walking beside each wagon was a "bullwhacker." In driving the oxen he used a twelve-foot bullwhip which he cracked over their heads. The train averaged from twelve to fifteen miles a day. At night the wagons were formed into a circular corral according to overland travel custom. It was a long haul. It took a summer for a wagon train to make the journey and return.

The Stagecoach. The freighting wagon was too slow for passengers and mail, and to meet this demand the *stagecoach* came west. Companies were formed in order to obtain government contracts to carry the mails. Passenger trade helped pay the expenses. Stations were established along the way for the exchange of horses and for a food and rest stop for the passengers. The central route passing through Salt Lake City was used by private firms taking the overland trail.

A stagecoach stops in Salt Lake City. Wells, Fargo & Co., one of the most important stagecoach lines in the West, specialized in carrying passengers, mail, and money.

The Bear River Hotel, near present Collinston, was an important stagecoach stop on the route from Ogden to Montana.

The Pony Express. Russell, Majors and Waddell, the great wagon freighters, devised a faster means of carrying the mails, the *Pony Express*. By a system of relays of horsemen, the mails could be carried between Missouri and California in ten days. By such a plan they hoped to obtain the government contract for carrying the mails.

The Pony Express was a remarkable success in performance, though it proved a financial failure. It operated from April 3, 1860 to October 24, 1861, less than nineteen months. However, this was an important time during the early years of the Civil War for the East and West to be tied together by mail services. It helped bring the Far West closer to the East and helped to hold the Far West and its treasures closer to the Union. It hastened the coming of the telegraph and the railroad.

The Pony Express route ran 1,966 miles between Saint Joseph, Missouri, and Sacramento, California. From Saint Joseph to Fort Bridger the route followed much of the Oregon Trail. From Fort Bridger the route led into Salt Lake City. Out of Salt Lake City, the route led south out of the valley and then west across the Great Salt Lake desert country through the Nevada deserts across the Sierra Nevada and on to Sacramento.

Along this route, 190 relay stations were set up with four hundred keepers and stock tenders. The stations were set, ideally, ten miles apart. Over four hundred horses were in use by eighty riders. Riders had to be slender, wiry fellows in their late teens or early twenties, expert horsemen, courageous, daring, dependable, devoted to duty, and willing to risk death daily. Their horses were the fastest that could be obtained. The rider's daily run was from seventy-five to one hundred miles. He made two round trips a week between the stations on his section of the route. The riders rode day and night in all kinds of weather. Riders started out with their fast ponies, with the *mochila* (a square leather pad with mail pouches fitted at each corner) slung over the saddle, trying to make nine miles an hour. Two minutes were allowed at the next station for a gulp of water, a chunk of bread, and throwing the *mochila* on a fresh mount. The most dangerous part of the ride was in Utah and Nevada. The Paiute Indians of western Utah and Nevada looked upon the riders and stations as threats to their hunting. Stations were burned, keepers killed. Fighting Paiute Indians in the Great Basin disrupted the Pony Express for two months. Yet otherwise the mails went through, and few riders were killed by Indians.

Mail was carried west from Saint Joseph and east from Sacramento. Altogether three hundred runs each way were made, delivering nearly 35,000 pieces of mail, with the loss of only one pouch. The fastest time made was seven days and seventeen hours, when the

At a Pony Express station a rider quickly changes his mount. Painting by W. H. Jackson.

mails carried the news of Lincoln's inauguration and address. At first, letters were carried for $5 a half ounce. Later the price was reduced to $2 and then to $1 a half ounce. The company received an average of $3 a letter, but it cost $16 to deliver a letter.

The Pony Express first came to Salt Lake City, April 7, 1860, 11:45 p.m., four days out of Sacramento. The *Deseret News* exclaimed that this speed now brought "us within six days communication with the frontier, and seven days from Washington—a result that we Utonians, accustomed to receive news three months after date, can well appreciate." In time, as news of great moment came from the East, the *Deseret News* put out "extras" known as the *Pony Dispatch*. Thanks to the Pony Express the newspaper was able to print Lincoln's inaugural address eight days after it was delivered in Washington. It was the Pony Express that brought to Utah the news of the outbreak of the Civil War.

But the Pony Express was not doing it all alone. Throughout the East were networks of railroads and telegraph lines, carrying mail

249

The Deseret News *quickly noticed the arrival of the Pony Express and sometimes printed a special edition, the* Pony Dispatch, *carrying the latest news brought by pony.*

The Deseret News

TRUTH AND LIBERTY

ELIAS SMITH.....EDITOR AND PUBLISHER.

Wednesday..............April 11, 1860.

The Pony Express.

The first Pony Express from the West left Sacramento city, Cal., at 12 p.m., on the night of the 3d inst., and arrived in this city at 11: 45 p.m. of the 7th, inside of prospectus time. The roads were heavy and the weather stormy. The last 75 miles was made in 5 hours, 15 minutes, in a heavy rain.

The Express from the East left St. Joseph, Missouri, at 6: 30 p.m. on the evening of the 3d and arrived in this city at 6: 25 p.m. on the evening of the 9th. The difference in time between St. Joseph and this city is something near 1 hour and 15 minutes, bringing us within six days communication with the frontier, and seven days from Washington—a result which we Utonians, accustomed to receive news three months after date, can well appreciate.

Much credit is due the enterprising and persevering originators of this enterprise and, although a telegraph is very desirable, we feel well satisfied with this achievement for the present.

The weather has been disagreeable and stormy for the past week and in every way calculated to retard the operations of the company, and we are informed the express eastward from this place was five hours in going to Snyder's mill, a distance of twenty-five miles.

We are indebted to Mr. W. H. Russell for a copy of the St. Joseph *Daily Gazette*, printed expressly for Utah and California, with dates from Washington and New York to the evening of the 2d, and from St. Joseph to 6 p.m. of the 3d instant.

The probability is, the express will be a little behind time in reaching Sacramento this trip, but when the weather becomes settled, and the roads good, we have no doubt they will be able to make the trip in less than ten days.

Court Proceedings.

The Probate Court for Great Salt Lake County has been in session since Monday. J. B. Atkins alias Atkinson, indicted for larceny, was arraigned yesterday and plead guilty; also William Brattan alias Hiram Mecham, on an indictment for horse stealing, on being arraigned confessed to his guilt. Each case was inquired into as required by law, and they will receive their sentence to-day.

John Mowry alias George Harrison alias George Wyers, accused of horse stealing, was tried and acquitted.

Charles Manhard was arrested by Sheriff Burton, yesterday evening, on a warrant issued some weeks since, two bills of ind ctment having been found against him for larceny during the first week of the court, on one of wh ch he was tried and acquitted. The other was not presented by the grand jury till after he was discharged, since which time he has kept out of sight till within a short time of his arrest. He made a vigorous attempt to escape and two associates drew pistols but did not deter the Sheriff from doing his duty. On seeing that Manhard was secured, the other two put spurs to their animals and fled.

The Union Academy

Was opened, pursuant to previous notice, on Monday morning, 9th inst., at 9 o'clock, in the large and commodious building on the east side of Union Square, formerly known as the Union Hotel.

Up to Tuesday morning the number of students who had presented themselves, was only twenty-six.

Two departments have been formed, thus far, including the whole number of students. The first department comprises the class in mathematics, thirteen in number, which is under the supervision of Mr. Orson Pratt. This class has entered upon the study of algebra, Day's algebra being chiefly used as text books.

The second department is under the supervision of Mr. James T. Cobb, comprises the classes in the lower branches; namely, arithmetic, geography, history, &c. Reading, writing and other rudimental branches will not be taught in the Academy, for the present, at least.

Although the Academy is under the general supervision of Professor Orson Pratt, his immediate services, probably, will not be required till the classes in the higher branches shall have become farther advanced, or until applicants present themselves, prepared to enter into the study of the more abstruse sciences.

The auspices under which this Academy has been opened and the interest manifested by many in its success, together with the zeal already exhibited by the students in the prosecution of their studies, are strong guarantees of the permanency of the institution.

The opportunity here offered by President Brigham Young, to our young men, of acquiring a thorough, practical, scientific education cannot but be gratefully acknowledged and, we trust, will be duly improved by all whose circumstances will permit them to avail themselves of it. The benefits to be derived therefrom will doubtless be more fully understood and appreciated in years to come. Our most ardent wishes are for its complete success.

In this connection we may also state that a school has been opened in the building commonly known as the "Holladay & Warner" store, nearly opposite the Tabernacle, by Mr. Henry I. Doremus, who is favorably known to most of our citizens as an experienced and qualified teacher. His school already numbers about fifty scholars, mostly under fifteen. He will be able to accommodate a much larger number and, as he informed us, should a sufficient number of older scholars present themselves, he will place the younger classes under the care of suitable assistants, in another apartment, and devote himself to the instruction of those more advanced.

The school taught by Mrs. Hulda Kimball, one of our most experienced female teachers, in the 17th Ward, is in a flourish ng condition —the average attendance being about fifty, with a pleasing degree of regularity, promptness and interest on the part of the scholars. Truly, we have seldom been more highly gratified than during a recent passing call at this school.

What other schools are now in operation in this city, we are not prepared to state; but it is to be hoped that, wherever the winter terms have expired, the schools will be re-opened, in every ward throughout the city and throughout the Territory, as soon as practicable, that our children may be instructed in every branch of knowledge whereby they may be better prepared for the duties soon to devolve upon them.

Release of Prisoners.—The *Mountaineer* of Saturday announced to the public that Judge Eckles had discharged the five prisoners taken from the penetentiary on writs of Hebeas Cor-

LATEST NEWS FROM THE EAST ! !

BY THE PONY EXPRESS.

From the Washington correspondence of the St. Louis *Republican*, dated March 26, we learn that the Senate Committee on Territories have authorized three bills to be reported, namely:

1. A bill to organize the Territory of *Arizonia*, instead of *Arizona*.

2. A bill to organize the Territory of Jefferson, (Pike's Peak).

Then follows an elucidation of the Senate Committee's proposition for finally disposing of the "knotty question" of "Mormon Utah", only a single paragraph of which we are able to insert, on account of our limited space, which we quote from the letter, as follows:

3. A bill *amendatory* of the act organizing the Territory of Utah — by which the seat of government is to be removed from Salt Lake City to Carson Valley, and the name of the Territory changed from Utah to Nevada. The bill also makes the *male* population the sole basis of apportionment, and confines the elective franchise to citizens of the United States, thus excluding the previous large vote of unnaturalized foreigners. The Committee hope by this policy to pass the political power of the Territory from Salt Lake to Carson Valley —from the hands of the Mormons to those of the Gentiles. The removal of the seat of government to Carson Valley, in connection with the rich mines lately discovered there, it is believed will soon attract a large population, while the change in the basis of apportionment will reduce the representation from the Salt Lake region in the legislature.

These proposed amendments, it is understood, are not to interfere with our present delegate, the Hon. W. H. Hooper, or the present political status of the Territory.

The change of the name of the Territory, writes this correspondent, is designed to break the charm which "Utah seems to have acquired over a certain portion of Europe and arrest, if possible, at least in some degree, the immigrat on of foreign Mormons."

Another proposition for the *relief* of Utah, concerning which some members appear to have great concern, is to so change the organic act as to give the President of the United States the power to appoint the members of the territorial legislature.

Capt. Hooper, we are informed, was before the committees several times, giving information, and, "by his ready and clear responses and his gentlemanly and ingenuous manner, made a most favorable impression upon every member of the committee."

The Senate Committee have had and will have no conferences with the House Committee, but act altogether upon their own judgment.

The admission of Kansas into the Un'on is yet uncertain.

It is confidently asserted that the Territorial policy of the Senate will not be endorsed by the House.

With many democrats the motto is, "No more new Territories."

In the House, on March 30, an amendment to the post office laws was passed, providing that if any person endorses on a letter that it is to be returned to him in thirty days, if not called for, it shall be so done, instead of being sent to the Dead Letter office.

On April 2, the bill for the suppression of polygamy was considered in the House, which elic ted a leng hy debate, but no action was taken thereon.

On the 29th of March, the House bill, authorizing publishers to print on their papers the date when subscriptions expire and reducing the postage on town and city drop letters to one cent, passed both Houses of Congress.

On the 31st of March, the Post Office Committee of the House had Mr. Gwin's Pacific Telegraph bill under favorable consideration.

Private letters from Arizona state that all communication with New Mexico is severed

the morning of which day a great manifestation in favor of the Pope had taken place at the Vatican. Letters from Rome state that the agitation is so great that it is doubtful whether the French army will be able to restrain it much longer.

A foreign letter says: "Meanwhile Rome is quiet. Folks stick knives into each other on the Corso in broad daylight, but quiet, peaceably and without noise."

The verdict in the second trial of the great breach of promise case, Garstang vs. Shaw, which has been going on in St. Louis for some weeks, was in favor of the defendant. A motion for a new trial was filed immediately upon the rendition of the verdict.

Latest News by Mail.

By the Eastern Mail which arrived Sunday afternoon dates from New York to the 15th, and from the frontier to the 20th of March were received.

The news was not very important. Congress was doing little or nothing but quarrelling over the sectional and political differences.

The House elected Mr. Stockton chaplain, March 6, on the second ballot. He received 111 votes. On the first ballot there were between twenty and thirty candidates voted for.

On the 9th on motion of Mr. Grimes, it was ordered that the letter of the Delegate of the Territory of Utah, in Congress, inclosing the memorial of delegates of the convention which assembled at Great Salt Lake City, and adopted a constitution with a view to the admission of Utah into the Union as a State, together with a copy of that constitution, on the files of the Senate, be referred to the Committee on Territories.

Western Utah.

The news from the mining districts in the Western part of the Territory by last mail was not very interesting to those who prefer peace and good order to such scenes of rowdyism and bloodshed as are of frequent occurrence in that ill-fated region.

The shooting business continued brisk, and there was no probability of there being any decline during the season, as the floating population of California was pouring over the Sierra Nevada, and filling up the country by thousands wherever gold or silver had been found.

The Farmington Mill.

The new grist mill at Farmington, Davis county, was put in motion on the 5th instant, and is now in successful operation. The people in that vicinity who have wheat, can have it ground hereafter if they wish, on short notice near at home, without being subjected to the inconveniences they have suffered heretofore, in consequence of having to go abroad to get their grinding done.

The expense incurred in the erection of the mill has been far greater than was anticipated at the time the building was commenced, owing to circumstances that were then unseen; and if an example of perseverance and going ahead against "wind and tide" is or can be of any benefit to those who are naturally inclined to quail and shrink on the appearance of a dark cloud and yield to every reverse of fortune they may have to encounter while passing through the world, the one that has been set in this instance should not be lost upon those who are thus disposed, if any there are among the number who have watched the progress of events and been familiar with the circumstances.

If the mill does not do good work as now arranged, it can be fitted up so that it will; and no effort will be spared to have all things pertaining thereto done in a manner satisfac-

and messages. The Pony Express ended with the completion of the transcontinental telegraph. It had been a remarkable success in carrying the mails, though it led to the bankruptcy of its founders.

The Butterfield Overland Mail, a stagecoach line, carried most of the passengers and mail in and out of Salt Lake City, between Missouri and California, for a few years after 1861. Ben Holladay then came into the field, bought the interests of Russell, Majors and Waddell, and operated stagecoaches across country and between mining camps. In 1866 Ben Holladay sold out to Wells, Fargo & Company. This company spread throughout the Mountain West, serving the mining camps, carrying mail and gold or silver bullion.

2. THE OVERLAND TELEGRAPH AND UTAH'S DESERET TELEGRAPH COMPANY HELPED BIND UTAH TO THE WEST AND THE NATION

At the time the Pony Express was in operation, the overland telegraph was being built. To build the overland telegraph it was necessary to erect poles and string wires from Omaha, Nebraska, to San Francisco. The central route across the continent was chosen and the first pole was set in July 1861. Financed by the federal government, two companies raced to complete the task, the *Pacific Telegraph Company* building from the east and the *Overland Telegraph Company* building from the west. Utah citizens participated in the contracts and the labor. Brigham Young supplied poles for 750 of the 1100 miles of the eastern section, while Little & Decker of Salt Lake City furnished poles for the line from Salt Lake City to Ruby Valley, Nevada. On October 18 the eastern line reached Salt Lake City and one week later, October 24, 1861, at Salt Lake City, the lines were connected completing the overland

telegraph. Now instead of a message from the East taking ten days to get to Sacramento, the same message was electrically flashed across the continent in seconds.

Unlike the Pony Express, the telegraph was here to stay. The telegraph performed a genuine service in helping to break down the geographical isolation of Utah. While the costs were high at first and the wires sometimes cut or broken, the lines served Utah and the West well. The editor of the *Deseret News* remarked on January 8, 1862: "The Overland Telegraph line, by which our city is in daily communication with the Atlantic and Pacific States and the British North American Provinces, is one of the greatest and grandest institutions of recent construction."

The Mormons built their own Deseret Telegraph line. Brigham Young planned immediately to have a telegraph line unite Salt Lake City with the Mormon settlements of the Mountain West. Plans were put into motion at once, but it was not until after the Civil War that the necessary wire and other equipment could be obtained. On October 15, 1866, the church wagon train arrived—sixty-

Telegraph lines were erected from the east and from the west; the lines connected at Salt Lake City, October 24, 1861, ending the Pony Express and bringing almost instantaneous communications with the rest of the country. In time, Utah communities were connected by the wires of the Deseret Telegraph Company.

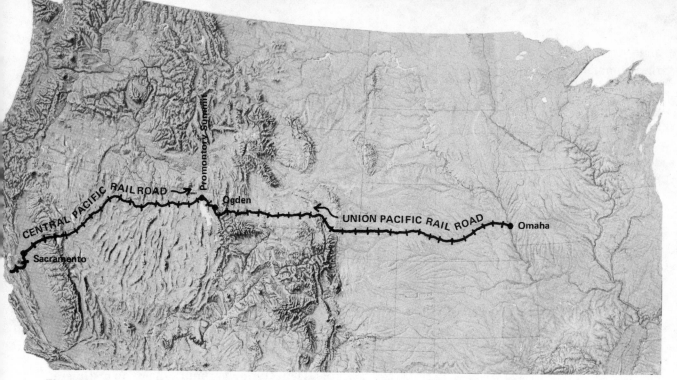

The transcontinental railroad was completed May 10, 1869 when the tracks of the Union Pacific, building from the East, and the tracks of the Central Pacific, building from the West, met at Promontory Summit, Utah.

five wagons with eighty-four tons of wire, insulators, batteries, and other equipment. The building of the Deseret Telegraph line was a cooperative enterprise. Donations were sought from each settlement to pay for the equipment. Each community was to recruit and support its local operators. The people of each valley assumed the responsibility of constructing, equipping, and staffing that part of the line running through their valley and half way to the next. Some work was done during the summer of 1866, and when the wire and equipment came, the five-hundred-mile line was soon finished. One line connected Salt Lake City with Logan on the north and Saint George on the south (completed on January 15, 1867), with a side line running into Sanpete Valley. The Deseret Telegraph Company was organized March 21, 1867. As the years passed, the line was extended to nearly all Mormon settlements from southern Idaho on the north to northern Arizona on the south, and into many of the Utah and southern Nevada mining towns. By 1880 over a thousand miles of line served sixty-eight offices or stations.

3. THE COMING OF THE TRANSCONTINENTAL RAILROAD OPENED THE RAILROAD ERA IN UTAH

The people of Utah looked forward to the coming of a railroad for years. Many of them had seen railroads and ridden trains in the East, and knew the speed, comfort, and inexpensiveness of that form of travel as compared to horse and ox team. They not only wanted a transcontinental railroad to come through Salt Lake City, but they wanted railroads in Utah between the settlements. Memorials were sent to Congress in 1852, 1854, and 1860 urging the construction of a railroad to and through Utah. In 1856, at Ogden, Brigham Young advised the settlers there to stop competing with each other in their various forts for growth but to move into the central city of Ogden, for, he said,

The Union Pacific Railroad, organized in 1862, built westward from Omaha across the Great Plains. In the Wasatch Mountains of Utah the construction crews met great difficulties building bridges to span the canyons and streams.

In Weber Canyon the Union Pacific cut a tunnel through the mountains.

"Here a large city will be built up, and railroads will make it a city of importance." When the ground breaking ceremonies took place for the Union Pacific at Omaha, Brigham Young sent a congratulatory telegram promising Mormon help in building the road.

Railroad building in the United States had expanded rapidly in the 1830s, 1840s, and 1850s. After the Civil War, railroad lines were extended into the Far West. On July 1, 1862 Congress authorized the construction of a continuous railroad and telegraph line starting west from Council Bluffs, Iowa. Land grants and bond issues were offered to help finance construction. The Central Pacific Railroad Company was organized in 1861 and authorized to build eastward from Sacramento, California. The Union Pacific Company was organized in 1862 in Chicago to build west from Omaha, Nebraska. From Omaha west the route was surveyed. Between June 1 and October 28, 1864, Samuel B. Reed was in Utah surveying the road from the Green River to Salt Lake City. Brigham Young helped him with men, transportation, and subsistence. In May 1868 Brigham Young obtained a contract from the Union Pacific to help build the road from the head of Echo Canyon. Beginning July 10, 1865, when the first rail was laid at Omaha, the rails moved west. Hundreds of workmen, many of them Irishmen fresh from the Union Army, performed the heavy and sometimes dangerous work.

The people of Utah played a part in building the transcontinental railroad. In May 1868 Brigham Young obtained a contract for $2,125,000 from the Union Pacific for the grading and masonry work on the railroad line from near the head of Echo Canyon, through Weber Canyon, to the shore of the Great Salt Lake or to Salt Lake City, "de-

ECHO CANYON

A railroad song of 1868

At the end of great Echo, there's a railroad begun,
And the Mormons are cutting and grading like fun;
The say they'll stick to it until it's complete,
For friends and relations are longing to meet.

CHORUS

Hurrah! hurrah! the railroad's begun,
Three cheers for our contractor, his name's Brigham Young;
Hurrah! hurrah! We're honest and true;
And if we stick to it, it's bound to go through.

Now there's Mister Reed, he's a gentleman too,
He knows very well what the Mormons can do;
He knows in their work they are lively and gay,
And just the right boys to build a railway.

Our camp is united, we all labor hard,
And if we work faithfully, we'll get our reward;
Our leader is wise and industrious too,
And all things he tells us we're willing to do.

The boys in our camp are light-hearted and gay,
We work on the railroad ten hours a day;
We're thinking of the good times we'll have in the fall,
When we'll take our ladies, and off to the ball.

We surely must live in a very fast age,
We've travelled by ox teams and then took the stage,
But when such conveyance is all done away,
We'll travel in steam cars upon the railway.

The great locomotive next season will come,
To gather the saints from their far distant home,
And bring them to Utah in peace here to stay,
While the judgments of God sweep the wicked away.

pending upon which end of the lake the road passes." This covered a distance of about sixty miles, through some of the most difficult of the Union Pacific road. Work was begun on the contract June 9, 1868. With plenty of labor and little or no cash in Utah, this was a welcome opportunity, one sought by the Mormon leader for his people. By this means they could turn their labor into money to pay their debts and buy machinery and goods to establish mercantile stores in their settlements. Subcontracts were let out to the bishops of wards, who then recruited laborers from among their ward members. The Mor-

mon laborers began at the head of Echo Canyon and were soon building the grade in Echo Canyon, Weber Canyon, and into Salt Lake Valley. By January 15 the Union Pacific reached Echo.

On March 8, the Union Pacific reached Ogden where it was received with a great celebration. Thousands and thousands of citizens "feasted their eyes and ears with the sight and sound of the long expected and anxiously looked for fiery steed." By late afternoon the tracks were laid into the city. Great crowds thronged the scene. Bands played amid cheers of the crowds and speeches. Banners waved the message: "Hail to the Highway of Nations! Utah bids you Welcome!"

The Central Pacific Railroad built eastward from Sacramento, California. Most of the building was done after 1866. Many Chinese laborers were brought in for the hard heavy work of crossing the Sierra Nevada. A contract was signed by Mormons to construct the line from Humboldt Wells, Nevada, to Ogden, some two hundred miles. Brigham Young saw that the contracts were managed as church cooperative projects. By June 1868 the Central Pacific had crossed the mountains and reached the California-Nevada boundary line. With the most difficult road behind them, a race was on. In April 1869 the workmen were laying track in western Utah, and on the twenty-ninth of that month Central Pacific crewmen laid a record breaking ten miles of track in one day. The usual was from four to seven miles of track a day.

As the two lines raced—the Union Pacific west from Ogden, and the Central Pacific east toward Ogden—they actually passed each other in laying parallel beds for track, each hoping their distance would be accepted so their road would receive the land grants and other benefits. Congress finally established

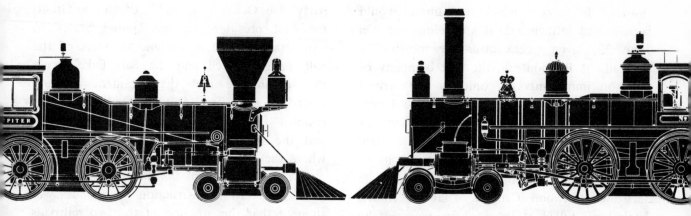

Union Pacific's No. 119 and Central Pacific's "Jupiter," which met at Promontory Summit May 10, 1869.

Promontory Summit as the place where the rails would meet.

On May 10, 1869, the two lines met at Promontory Summit, Utah, about fifty miles west of Ogden. The first transcontinental railroad was completed. The Union was tied east and west by iron rails. The east coast and the west coast were now only eight days apart. From Omaha to Salt Lake City was now only thirty-eight hours by rail (at about twenty-eight miles an hour, average time), a distance which took the Mormon overland emigrants and others months to cover. The West would never again be the same. The Old West was passing away rapidly. A new epoch in the history of the nation, the West, and of Utah had come.

HOW LONG DID IT TAKE

To travel from the Missouri River
to Salt Lake Valley?

The 1847 Pioneer Company	100 days
A handcart company	90 days
A wagon company	80 days
A stagecoach	14 days
The Pony Express	6 days
The railroad	1 ½ days

In western Utah the Central Pacific construction crews laid ten and a half miles of track in one day, a record which stood until recent years.

The Central Pacific Railroad, organized in 1861, built eastward over the Sierra Nevada. Chinese workers, with picks and shovels, chisels and hammers, carts, and black powder, carved their way over the granite range.

Many firsts for Utah soon followed the completion of the transcontinental railroad, showing the ways in which the railroad would benefit and influence Utah's development. On June 25, seven weeks after the meeting of the rails at Promontory, the first company of Mormon immigrants to come by rail arrived at Taylor's Switch near Ogden on the Union Pacific. On July 25, the first shipment of Utah ore by rail left Ogden for San Francisco. The shipment consisted of ten tons of ore from the Monitor and Magnet mine in Little Cottonwood Canyon. That December, Utah beef, killed at Promontory, was sent by refrigerator car to San Francisco where it sold at twelve cents a pound. During the last week in December 1870, 60,000 pounds of dried peaches were shipped east from Utah by rail. Utah was to continue thereafter to send its agricultural products and its minerals and metals to distant points. Distinguished visitors, as well as thousands of tourists were also to come through Utah on their way east and west. On May 28, 1870, the first through train from the Atlantic to the Pacific, from

At the end of the tracks, near Promontory Summit, rose the town of Corinne, Utah's first railroad town of significance. Corinne became the non-Mormon center of Utah for a few years and threatened to become a railroad center.

Boston to San Francisco, came to Utah, carrying the Boston Board of Trade excursion party. On October 3, 1875, Ulysses S. Grant, the first president of the United States to visit Utah, arrived in Ogden. Members of the Salt Lake Council and the Salt Lake reception committee met the president's private railroad car. The Salt Lakers' train was coupled to the rear of the president's car, and the party proceeded to Salt Lake City where the president was entertained.

The little city of *Corinne* grew up at the last railroad construction camp. It was thought that the junction of the two railroads would be at Corinne, which would make Corinne a major city in Utah. Corinne had been one of the "hell on wheels" camps— with all the rough life characteristic of such camps. Corinne became the non-Mormon capital of Utah. Brigham Young wanted Salt Lake City to be the junction, but that city had been missed by the railroad when the decision was made to pass west through Ogden. This decision gave the Mormon leaders two problems: (1) the possibility of Corinne becoming a major city of commercial importance giving travelers an unfavorable view of Utah, and (2) the necessity of bringing a rail-

road connection from Ogden to Salt Lake City.

Preferring Ogden as the junction for the two railroads, Brigham Young used church money to buy land for a railroad depot and shops and offered the land to the Union Pacific Railroad as a gift for their depot and shops. The offer was accepted, and Ogden became the center of railroading in Utah.

The Utah Central Railroad. To keep Salt Lake City equally on the railroad map of Utah and to bring the benefits of the railroad to Salt Lake City, the Mormon church built a railroad from Ogden to Salt Lake City (thirty-six miles) under the name of the Utah Central Railroad. The company was organized March 8, 1869. Construction was begun in September and finished to Salt Lake City by January 10, 1870. The railroad was built as a church cooperative project by volunteer Mormon laborers. The workmen were paid in stocks or bonds in the company, railroad tickets, or in the form of credit on their indebtedness to the Perpetual Emigrating Fund. Except for the Union Pacific and Central Pacific roads, no other railroad built in Utah was of so much value to the people as the Utah Central. Its connection with Ogden was vital. It served the area where most of Utah's mining, manufacturing, and trade were concentrated. It was used to speed up immigration and reduce immigration costs. It ran conference specials and summer excursions. It gave an outlet for the farm produce of Utah's richest valleys, hauled coal to Salt Lake City, hauled ores bound for Ogden and the transcontinental railroad, and gave impetus not only to the mining but to every branch of

The Mormons built the Utah Central Railroad from Ogden to Salt Lake City, connecting the capital to the transcontinental railroad January 10, 1870.

The Utah Central Railroad was operated for a few years as a Mormon railroad, carrying passengers and freight.

Ogden became the railroad center of Utah, chiefly through the efforts of Brigham Young. Transcontinental lines and lines running north and south centered here. This photograph shows the Union Depot and yards in 1890.

industry. By March 1870 two passenger trains were running daily between Salt Lake and Ogden.

Other railroads were built south from Salt Lake City. The *Utah Southern Railroad* was a southern extension of the Utah Central, built from Salt Lake City south through the following settlements: to Sandy (September 23, 1871), to the Point of the Mountain south of Draper (August 9, 1872), to Lehi (September 23, 1872), to American Fork (September 23, 1873), to Provo (November 25, 1873) where there was a grand celebration, and to York, Juab County (February 16, 1875).

Early Utah railroads. Between 1869 and 1890 railroads connected many settlements and mining towns.

(1) Central Pacific, (2) Utah Northern, (3) Union Pacific, (4) Utah Central, (5) Wasatch and Jordan Valley, (6) American Fork, (7) Utah Southern, (8) Utah Southern Extension, (9) Utah Western, (10) Salt Lake, Sevier Valley and Pioche, (11) Salt Lake and Eastern, (12) Echo and Park City, Utah Eastern, (13) Denver & Rio Grande Western, (14) Salt Lake and Western, (15) Bingham Canyon and Camp Floyd, (16) California Short Line, (17) Summit County, (18) Utah and Pleasant Valley.

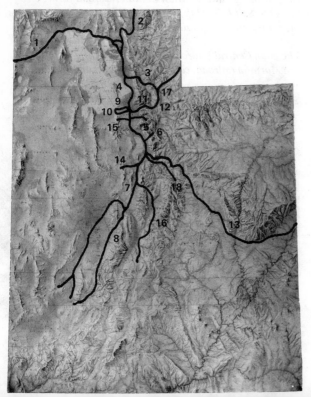

Spurs and branch lines ran from the Utah Southern Railroad to nearby communities and mining districts. A junction was made with the main road at the Sandy Station and run to the granite stone quarry. This line was used in hauling granite from Little Cottonwood Canyon for the building of the Salt Lake Temple. Another line ran from the Salt Lake station to the Temple Block. The first stone was delivered by rails to the Temple Block April 4, 1873. A spur was also constructed to Bingham Canyon in 1873, and in 1875 a spur line was extended on up Little Cottonwood Canyon to the Alta mining district.

The Union Pacific bought into the Utah Southern Railroad company as early as 1872. In January 1879 a new company was formed to extend the rails farther south to serve especially the mines of Frisco in Beaver County. This was the *Utah Southern Railroad Extension Company.* Soon the rails were being laid again to Juab (June 13, 1879), to Milford, Beaver County (May 15, 1880), and to Frisco (June 23, 1880). In 1881 the Utah Central, the Utah Southern, and the Utah Southern Extension were consolidated under the Union Pacific, into one company under the name *Utah Central Railway System.* After this transaction Mormon influence in railroad building and policy declined.

The railroad line from Frisco on the south to Ogden on the north, together with branches and spurs, opened up many mining districts, and gave the settlements transportation for their people and their products.

Railroads were also built north from Ogden. The *Utah Northern Railroad* was another Mormon railroad in its beginning. There had been a brisk freighting business between Utah communities and northern mining towns since the opening of the Idaho and Montana mines. The Utah settlements supplied agricultural products and other goods to the mines. Now that goods for the mines came to Utah by rail, the freighting business was better than ever, and a railroad could serve the purpose very well. Corinne served as the major depot for this freighting trade. To provide transportation for the settlers in northern Utah and to improve trade with the Montana mines the Utah Northern Railroad was organized August 23, 1871. It too was a church cooperative railroad in its construction, using local labor and materials, but bringing in the iron rails and rolling stock. The beginning point was Brigham City. The first rail was laid in March 1872. By July 1, freight and passenger trains were running twice daily to Hampton's Station at the edge of Cache Valley. Mendon was reached December 19, 1872. The rails were completed to Logan on January 31, 1873, and to Franklin, Idaho, May 2, 1874. In the meantime connections were made from the Brigham City junction to Corinne (June 9, 1873) and to Ogden (February 5, 1874). A passenger could leave Ogden at 9:40 a.m., arrive in Logan at 12:50 noon, and in Franklin at 2:24 p.m. That was averaging twenty miles per hour including stops. The road north to Franklin was built by Mormons. Thereafter the lines were built by the Union Pacific under the name of the *Utah and Northern Railroad Company* (formed October 4, 1877). Between 1878 and 1881 the lines were extended northward through Pocatello, Blackfoot, and Camas, Idaho, and to Dillon, Silver Bow Junction, and Butte, Montana. In 1884 the line went on to Garrison, Montana, where it met the Northern Pacific transcontinental railroad.

The construction of the Utah Northern was a great help to the northern settlements. The railroad helped settlers move to northern Utah and southern Idaho. Cache Valley laborers were employed on the construction of the road from 1877 to 1881, bringing cash into the valley.

In addition to these major north-south running Utah railroads, there were several shorter **intra-Utah railroads** built during the 1870s that carried services to the various communities and mining districts. Roads were built west into the mining districts in the Oquirrh and Tintic mountains. A railroad was built from Provo into Pleasant Valley, Carbon County, to bring out coal (1879). Lines were built also into Sanpete and Sevier valleys.

One of the most important railroad lines to come to Utah was the **Denver and Rio Grande Western Railroad**, a subsidiary of the Denver and Rio Grande Railway of Colorado. The D & RGW was incorporated in Utah in 1881 and that year it acquired the short roads into Bingham Canyon and into Little Cottonwood Canyon, and in 1882 the Utah and Pleasant Valley Railroad. It soon had a through line from Pleasant Valley to Salt Lake Valley. Between 1882 and 1883 the road was extended so that by the spring of 1883 there was a line from Ogden to Denver, Colorado. Benefits to Utah were felt immediately in the delivery of coal to the populous valleys. The near-monopoly held by the Union Pacific on the interstate traffic was also broken and the people of Utah were given better prices for transportation and better service. (The Union Pacific had bought into Utah railroads until it owned most of them by the 1880s.) The D & RGW built or took over branch lines, not only into the mining districts but also into Sanpete and Sevier valleys. This railroad opened new sections of the territory, at first the Carbon County coal fields, and later the agricultural lands east of the Wasatch Mountains.

In Salt Lake City, rails were laid for streetcar and street railroad systems. In 1872 the *Salt Lake City Railroad Company* was

Main Street of Salt Lake City shows the coming of horse-drawn streetcars in the early 1870s.

Salt Lake City, looking eastward on First South Street, at the time of the construction of the streetcar line in the 1870s. At the left is the Salt Lake Theatre. Other civic and religious buildings are in the background.

formed. On June 20 the first streetcar was put into service. It was a heavy car drawn by four horses. That summer the tracks extended a mile and a half down the center of Salt Lake's wide streets. In time the tracks were extended into various parts of the city, including northward to the Warm Springs Bath House, a popular resort. A line from the Utah Southern-Utah Central depot was built

to the Temple Block to carry stones and equipment for the construction of the Salt Lake Temple. By 1883 the company had fourteen cars in operation, nine miles of track, eighty-four mules, and thirty regular employees.

The *Salt Lake and Fort Douglas Railroad*, a street railway system, was opened for operation June 1, 1888. It ran along Eighth South Street up onto the east bench where it branched north and south, running north to Fort Douglas, and south through Sugar House (where it connected with the railroad to Park City) and on to Mill Creek.

4. THE RAILROAD BROUGHT MANY CHANGES TO UTAH

With the coming of the transcontinental railroad to Utah in 1869 and the various railroads in Utah in the 1870s, many changes came to the economic, political, social, and religious life of the people. The coming of the railroad signaled the end of the long trek across the plains by wagon or handcart, and the end of the annual church teams freighting in goods from the East. It meant easy transportation for immigrants and tourists, better and cheaper goods, cheaper mail rates, and faster mail service. It meant the opening of the mines, the establishment of banks and large stores with a great variety of goods. It meant an increased opportunity for Utah to export surplus agricultural products and the ores from her mines.

The economic life of the territory was affected at once. While some teamsters were put out of work, no doubt, it took years for railroads to reach some communities. In the meantime many Utah men and boys earned their income *freighting* goods from the ends of the railroad lines to distant communities and mining camps.

Utah manufacturers had been able to

produce some items more cheaply than they would cost if hauled across the continent on wagons. With the lower rates of the railroad, eastern goods came in much cheaper than they could be produced in Utah. As a result, many local manufacturers went out of business or adjusted to the new conditions. Prices fell so sharply on some goods that merchants had to sell at a loss. Home manufacturers had a difficult time. They were forced to improve methods of production and reduce wages.

THE CROSSROADS OF THE WEST

From the Deseret News, *March 6, 1867:*

... Geographically Utah is their center, and must remain so unless the topographical aspect of this western region can be changed. And this city must be the commercial capital of these States; the emporium from which they will draw supplies, the depot where the east and west will consign their stores for distribution through them; the centre from which lines of travel will radiate in many directions. Our position, the country we inhabit, and the nature of our resources emphatically point to our becoming manufacturers as well as agriculturalists. Our farms, our orchards and our gardens, are admitted by all honest travelers, who pass through our Territory, to be marvels of industry, care and taste. We can produce cotton to supply the outside markets to an immense extent. Our vineyards flourish; the silk worm has been successfully kept here, though in a small way, and a beautiful quality of silk has been obtained; and we have facilities for sheep raising and obtaining wool that are difficult to excel.

Ogden and Salt Lake City emerged as important transportation centers, not only for the east-west traffic, but for the north-south traffic as well. Salt Lake City increasingly became the capital of the Mountain West. Here was the banking center, the business center, the mining center, and the transportation center of the Mountain West.

Mining now began to boom with the railroads running to the mines. During the 1860s mining seemed to be sleeping, waiting for an easy, inexpensive way of hauling the ores to smelters and refineries. Immediately with the coming of the railroad and extension lines into Salt Lake Valley and west into Rush Valley, there were rich mines opened in Bingham Canyon, Little Cottonwood Canyon, in the Oquirrh Mountains, and in the Tintic Mountains. Many smelting and stamp mills were built in the early 1870s. An 1872 report counts twenty-one smelting works in operation, processing 686 tons of ore a day, and four stamp mills and two steam batteries with a combined crushing capacity of 100 tons a day. The railroad made profitable the processing of Utah's rich mineral products. (We will read more of the mining boom in Utah in the next section.) Railroads and mining developed side by side.

With the coming of the railroad and the development of mining, which brought more non-Mormon merchants and businessmen, miners and railroad workers into Utah, **Utah became tied more closely to the nation**; and the Mormon way of life was challenged. The large number of newcomers to Utah had an influence, not only on the economic life of Utah, but on the social, religious, and political life. These people demanded a voice in the direction of the economic and political life of the territory.

Utah became better known to the American people as tourists and distinguished visitors came in larger numbers, often stopping to take a good look at the Mormons. Actors and actresses came to appear on the stage at the Salt Lake Theatre, adding significantly to the cultural life of the people.

5. THE MINING FRONTIER CAME TO UTAH ONCE THE RAILROADS WERE BUILT

The history of mining in Utah in the nineteenth century may be divided into three periods: (1) Mormon mining from 1847 on, (2) individual prospecting, the recording of claims, and organization of mining districts

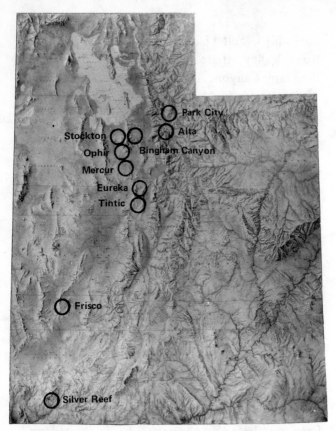

The major mining areas of Utah were opened up with the coming of the railroad.

Mission was in operation in the Coalville area and the first coal was hauled from those mines by wagon in 1863. Some oil was produced from oil shale near Levan in the late 1850s, no doubt used for lamps, harness oil, and other lubrication needs. In time the settlers found good clay for making bricks, and the making of adobe was abandoned in favor of burnt brick. In 1884 there were twenty-eight brick plants in operation in Utah, and by 1900 there were forty brick plants.

A new era in mining history in Utah opened in 1863 with the discovery of precious metals in Bingham Canyon. This period is marked by the search for gold and silver and other precious metals, though the prospectors found Utah richest in silver and lead, copper and zinc, and less rich in gold. This phase of mining history is also marked by the location of mining claims by individuals, and the organization of mining districts which initiated mining on the basis of individual ownership, investment, and profit. From 1863 to 1866 there was a great rush of prospecting on the east side and then on the west side of the Oquirrh Mountains, and then in the Wasatch Mountains in Little Cottonwood Canyon, Big Cottonwood Canyon, and in American Fork Canyon. Claims were staked out and recorded. Mining districts were organized. Only a little smelting was done. By 1866 activity on these new discoveries had come to a stop. Much money had been spent, but more would have to be spent. Costs were too high until the transportation problem could be solved.

With the coming of the railroad, mining became profitable, and Utah experienced a mining boom, with rushes into the various mining districts. Mining towns grew up overnight.

The major mining rushes and districts in early Utah.

from 1863 to 1866, and (3) the great increase in mining production with the coming of the railroad.

Mormon settlers sought the mineral wealth of the territory to help in their goals of building a self-sufficient economy. Every community needed building stone, clay for making adobe bricks and lime for mortar. They needed coal for heating their homes and public buildings, and for making coke for the blacksmith's forge. They needed lead for bullets. They needed iron for making implements and tools. At the outset they harvested salt from the shores of the Great Salt Lake. To obtain vital minerals, an Iron Mission was begun in the Cedar City area in 1850-51, and a Lead Mission was sent to work near Las Vegas in 1856. In the early 1860s a Coal

The mining of precious ores in Utah began when rich ores were discovered in Bingham Canyon in 1863. Profitable mining on a large scale began with the coming of the Bingham and Camp Floyd Railroad. The full-scale operation, cutting away the mountain side, was to wait until after the turn of the century.

Bingham Canyon mining operations took out silver and lead, copper and zinc, and gold.

Bingham Canyon. The history of mining in Bingham Canyon is in many ways the history of mining in Utah. It was Utah's first mining district and it has continued to produce through the years, sharing the ups and downs of mining fortunes, and is today Utah's chief mining attraction.

The Bingham brothers, Sanford and Thomas, were the first to discover the rich ores of the Canyon. Sent by Brigham Young in 1848 to the area, they farmed, grazed their herds, and turned to prospecting. But Brigham Young advised against it: "Instead of hunting gold, let every man go to work at raising wheat, oats, barley, corn and vegetables and fruit in abundance that there may be plenty in the land." The ore-finds were covered and soon forgotten as the Binghams went on church missions and settlement assignments.

Nevertheless, the canyon continued to be used as a grazing ground and for its timber. In 1863 it was being used by George B. Ogilvie, Archibald Gardner (bishop of West Jordan Ward), and soldiers from Camp Douglas. One afternoon in mid-September, George Ogilvie and others were dragging out logs when they uncovered silver-bearing ore. Ogilvie recognized the ore and sent a sample to General Connor who had it assayed. Further explorations were made and claims staked out. The Jordan Silver Mining Company was formed at once, with twenty-five members, including the discoverers, General Connor, Utah citizens, and officers and men from Camp Douglas. The West Mountain Quartz Mining District was organized September 17, 1863, to include the Oquirrh Mountains and west to the 114° line. This was the first recorded mining claim and the first mining district to be formally organized and recorded in the territory of Utah. Soldiers soon swarmed into Bingham Canyon and

263

neighboring areas. New claims were staked out as discoveries were made. The Wasatch Mining District was next organized to include the Wasatch Mountains from Weber Canyon south to Provo. Soldiers were sent into the mountains of southern Idaho, of southeastern Nevada, and the Uinta Basin to make new discoveries. The *Union Vedette* carried news of the discoveries with the intent of bringing on a mining boom in Utah. Connor felt one way to solve "the Mormon question" was to introduce a large non-Mormon population into the territory. The next spring the western slopes of the Oquirrh Mountains were being prospected and claimed. The Rush Valley Mining District was organized June 11, 1864, taking in the western slopes of that range. By the fall of 1865 over five hundred mining claims had been located in the Rush Valley Mining District. The city of Stockton had been founded and had a population of four hundred. General Connor put about $80,000 of his own fortune into operations at Stockton.

After Ogilvie and others established the first mining claim, a town grew up, but because of lack of transportation and high expenses it was nearly abandoned. Placer mining saved the community when men turned to washing ores to recover gold. The Clay Bar was the richest placer mine at the time, yielding more than $2,000,000 in gold by 1868.

When the Bingham and Camp Floyd Railroad came to the canyon, lode mining was revived and soon rich strikes were paying off. Mills, smelters, and concentrating plants were built in the early 1870s. For the most part it was lead and silver mining; no one at that time thought much of mining for copper. It was not until the turn of the century that Bingham Canyon was to become a copper producer.

Stockton, Ophir, Mercur. From Bingham

Ophir experienced a mining boom during the late 1860s and 1870s. Ores were hauled from here to the Great Salt Lake where they were boated to Corinne and the railroad. This 1910 photograph shows the mining town after the early rushes were over and before the mines produced again when new mining methods were applied.

Canyon prospectors went over the ridge of the Oquirrh Mountains to the west side where in 1864 other rich discoveries were made and mining districts organized. General Connor founded *Stockton*, naming it for his home in California. By 1865-66 there were fifty buildings there. In 1864 he built Utah's first smelter. Eight others were built in the same area that year.

When, in the late 1860s, the soldiers learned that in a canyon south of Stockton the Indians mined silver and gold for trinkets and lead for bullets, they looked for themselves and staked a claim. Soon the mining town of *Ophir* was growing up with shacks, saloons, and gambling halls. The news of Ophir's wealth spread rapidly and the rush was on. The mines produced well, but the ore beds were shallow and were soon exhausted. Later when it was learned how to sink deeper shafts and when more efficient

Ore carts, such as these being used at Ophir, were employed in many mines.

smelting techniques were developed, the mines came back into production.

Soldiers also discovered silver ore in a canyon farther south. When one man made an $80,000 haul from his mine, the news attracted miners from all around. But one company put in $700,000 developing a mine and received only $175,000 in return. By 1880 the boom was over and the town of Lewiston was a ghost town. In 1882, however, Arie Pinedo, a Bavarian prospector, came into the same area and located the *Mercur* lode, a quicksilver deposit, after which the town was named. But it was too difficult to get the gold separated out from the ore and the miners left. It was not until 1893 when the cyanide separation process was discovered that the Mercur mines flourished. Millions of dollars worth of gold, silver, and lead came out of these mines.

Alta. In the Wasatch Mountains, south of Camp Douglas, up Little Cottonwood Canyon three famous mines were founded: the Emma, the Prince of Wales, and the South Hecla. These mines attracted thousands into the canyon between 1865 and 1873. At first the going was hard and the ores were carried in cowhides down the canyon to ox-drawn wagons which took the ore to the railroad at Ogden, then on to San Francisco. Ores from these mines were then shipped by sailing vessels around Cape Horn to Wales, British Isles. After all transportation and smelting charges were paid, the owners still received $180 a ton for the ore. The Emma mine was bought out, in time, by British investors for $5,000,000. Shortly after that purchase the mine gave out. British investors suggested fraud and deception, creating a crisis between Great Britain and the United States. Finally it was determined by visiting British geologists that the ore body had been cut off by a fault and the mining had come to its natural end. Later the continuation of the vein was discovered and mined. The mining of silver in the area has continued, off and on, from that time until recent years.

Park City. In the mountains south from Kimballs Junction on the emigrant road into Salt Lake Valley (up Parleys Canyon from Salt Lake City), three soldiers from Camp Douglas are said to have stumbled onto a

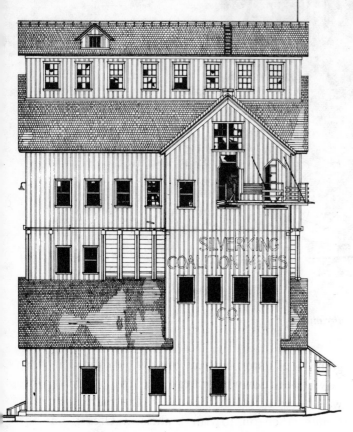

Silver King Ore Loading Station, Park City.

Little Cottonwood Canyon was the site of the mining town of Alta, famous for rich strikes and booming days between 1865 and 1873. This photo, taken about thirty years later, shows the town in decline.

Park City mines have produced for over a century. Some are still in operation.

bold outcrop of quartz. They marked the spot with a red handkerchief, broke off a chunk, and took it to Camp Douglas for assay. The ore was rich in silver, lead, and gold. A mining rush followed and the mining town of Park City grew up. After the Flagstaff mine was opened in 1870, others soon followed: Walker Gulch, Webster Gulch, McHenry Gulch, the Jones Bonanza, and in 1872 the Ontario (located by Rector Steen), a mine that produced ore running four hundred ounces of silver to the ton. Soon the mountains were dotted with claims, but the ore ran deep and was difficult to get out, and when miners tunneled for it they struck water and were flooded out. Only by merging interests, consolidating claims, and applying advanced engineering skills were the miners able to overcome these problems. Park City has been one of Utah's most successful min-

ing areas, for it has continued to produce to the present time.

Tintic. Named for Indian Chief Tintic, who gave the early settlers so much trouble during the 1850s, the Tintic mining district was one of Utah's richest in gold, silver, copper, lead, and zinc. The first claims were staked in December and January of 1870-71, and soon several important mines were producing ore worth $86 to $6,000 a ton. Millions of dollars worth of ore was taken out in the 1870s. Mills and furnaces were set in

Workmen at the action front inside the Ontario Mine, Park City, about 1900.

operation. In 1883 the Salt Lake & Western Railroad reached the Tintic mines.

Frisco. West of Milford in the San Francisco Mountains was discovered the Horn Silver Mine, said to be the richest silver producer in Utah. The story is told that it was accidentally found in 1875 by two prospectors from Pioche, Nevada. They had found a good water hole, Squaw Springs, and did not want to leave it, so they looked around for ores. "This ledge looks kind of good," said one as he struck his pick into the ledge. Glistening galena ore was exposed—they had struck a bonanza. They sank a twenty-five foot shaft in solid ore said by some to be so rich it could be whittled, and the slivers curved like the horn of a mountain sheep, thus giving the mine its name. The two prospectors sold their claim for $25,000 to three men who sank a shaft 280 feet and took out 25,000 tons averaging $100 a ton. In 1879 the property was sold to the New York financier Jay Cooke for $5,000,000. The town of Frisco boomed. Cooke came to Salt Lake City and induced the Mormon leaders to extend the railroad to Frisco. This was done with the additional help of New York financier Jay Gould and Union Pacific Railroad President Sidney Dillon. By 1880 the Utah Southern Extension reached Frisco and Milford.

After 1880 the mine produced heavily as the owners pushed the miners feverishly to greater production. But the owners disregarded mining safety rules and one morning in 1885 as the night shift came off work and the men of the day shift were ready to be hoisted into the shaft, they were stopped by officials saying there had been a trembling in the shaft. While they were standing around, the mine caved in with a crash that broke windows in Milford, fifteen miles away. A new shaft was sunk, but most of the miners

267

Coal mining was an important industry in Utah. Coal was made into coke which was used in the smelting process, and coal was used for heating homes and other buildings.

moved out, leaving the town nearly deserted. The mine was not worked for years, but in 1928 a new company was organized that brought the mine into producing 10,000 tons a year.

Silver Reef. In the mountains northwest of Leeds, Washington County, another rich silver mining district was established in the 1870s. Stories differ as to how it was discovered, but John Kemple is credited with assaying the ore in 1868 and organizing a district in 1871. Little was done however until 1874 and 1875. By this time the Walker brothers of Salt Lake City took interest and sent William Tecumseh Barbee and others to investigate and begin operations. By 1876 the Silver Reef was being mined with great success. The mines in neighboring Pioche, Nevada, were playing out and the miners there rushed into the Silver Reef area, creating a boom that built a town of 1,500 people. In-

dividual claims were being consolidated by 1880 and companies were operating efficiently. There was a leaching plant and a stamp mill. In 1877 one mill was turning out a thousand-ounce brick of silver every day. Ore was valued from $30 to $400 a ton. After 1881 the mines went into decline and then out of operation, to be opened at later dates. Between 1876 and 1903 the mines at Silver Reef yielded silver valued at over $10,500,000.

These are some of the major mining districts opened in Utah in the 1870s. Eventually mining extended into each of Utah's counties, each producing mineral wealth at one time or another. There have been 135 mining districts in all. Many of the mines lasted only a short time and were soon deserted, leaving ghost towns, while others have continued to produce to the present time.

From 1863 to the turn of the century,

268

gold, silver, and lead were the most important metals mined. Mines, smelters, and mills were set up to produce and process these metals. In 1872 Utah produced 11,785 tons of lead which was 45 percent of the United States total that year. But Utah's uniqueness in mining is in the diversity of its mineral wealth. In the first decades of mining, other minerals and metals were also mined with profit. We have seen that coal was mined at Coalville and in Pleasant Valley. By 1878, 102,600 tons of coal were mined in Utah. In 1884 Gilsonite was discovered and by 1888 some 700 tons were mined and hauled out. This mineral is mined only in Utah to the present day. Sulphur was produced also (but the demands then were few—chiefly for sheep dip, gun powder, and medicine). Gypsum was first produced near Nephi in 1882. Today there has been a greater development of all of Utah's mineral wealth; the value of its annual production has multiplied a hundred times since the 1870s.

Mrs. Gramb's boarding house, Silver Reef, 1880s. The people in the picture are from left: W. O. Carbis, Mrs. Gramb, G. M. Ottinger, Mr. Crockwell, Mr. Case.

Life in the mining towns. While each of Utah's mining towns had its own character, all mining towns had much in common. The first miners hurriedly put up shanties or tents, then came more substantial but still flimsy buildings for the most part, spreading up along the gulch or over the flat. Often there was only one street that wound its way up the narrow canyon toward the mines. Every mining town had a boarding house, hotel, general store, blacksmith shop, livery stable, meat market, saloons, dance halls, and a cemetery. At its height Alta had a hundred buildings (including twenty-six saloons and six breweries) spread out over the flat, housing five thousand people. There was usually a telegraph line into town, and a Wells, Fargo & Co. express office. In the rush days at Mercur, six stagecoaches arrived daily. And of course, if the mines operated long enough, the railroad eventually came to town. Catholic churches were built in Park City and in Silver Reef; elsewhere there were halls where the Protestant ministers held services when they came to town. A few of the towns had newspapers. Silver Reef had a race track, for which race horses were brought from as far away as Sevier Valley and the Kanab region. At Silver Reef the Catholics had a church school and a hospital administered by the sisters, and the Protestants had their Citizen's Hall, an educational, social, and religious center.

Water was often miles away and had to be hauled in to be sold at from four to ten cents a gallon. The scarcity of water hurt miners and mining. Wells were sunk, but often without success. At Tintic a wooden pipeline was constructed in the 1880s from the Jenny Lind Spring, and from this pipe the householders obtained their water in pails. Frisco never had running water, a factor in its decline.

Life in the mining towns included a wide variety of activities, once miners had become family men. Here is the Mercur Junior Band about 1900.

The miners expected to get rich, and some did. But those that made it rich usually "mined the miners"—that is, they worked to take the money from the miner by selling him goods and services. Businessmen in the town usually made out rather well. As for the miners, they were usually poor, and next year they would possibly be poorer. Yet there was always the exception of striking it rich in those imaginary rich lodes just over the hill.

The effect of mining on the development of early Utah. The number of people in mining towns in Utah in 1870 might have reached two thousand or more. In 1880 the number may have reached eight or ten thousand, and in 1890 may have amounted to ten thousand or more. At the most the population of the mining towns made up from 2 to 5 percent of the population of the territory.

While the number of miners was small,

A group ready to go into town for supplies.

A boarding house at the Buckhorn mine, Ophir, about 1903.

their influence on Utah's development was great. The mines and miners had to be supplied with equipment and goods. Hauling loads of materials from the terminals of the railroad to the mining towns fell to men and boys in the neighboring settlements. Food stuffs from the villages were also freighted or peddled to the mining towns. This freighting and peddling brought cash into the hands of the settlers, making it possible for them to buy goods they otherwise could not obtain. Saint George churchmen expressed the belief that the discovery of silver at Silver Reef was a godsend. Certainly the trading with the mines and mining population helped save some communities from abject poverty.

The establishment of mines also stimulated railroad construction which in itself brought money to Utah communities. The railroads in turn brought in goods and people.

The routes of the railroads helped to develop Ogden into one of the most important transportation centers in the Mountain West, and helped develop Salt Lake City as a transportation, financial, and mining center for the Mountain West.

The businessmen and financiers connected with railroading and mining became persons of influence in Utah communities. They also were very influential in establishing in Utah the two-party political system, the secret ballot, economic competition, and progressive reforms in some of the cities. They sought to establish the practices of American political and social life to which they were accustomed in Utah, where only Mormon institutions had prevailed to that time. We will see in a later chapter how conflicts between these people and the Mormon way of life were solved.

Salt Lake City, urban center of Utah, was a city of over twenty thousand people when this photograph was taken in 1882. The Salt Lake Temple is under construction.

UTAH CITIES AND THE EXPANSION OF SETTLEMENT

The coming of the railroad and mining had an impact on labor and life in Utah, especially in Salt Lake City and Ogden and in the villages near the mining camps. But while Salt Lake City, Ogden, and a few other communities were taking on the characteristics of cities, the Mormon villages at great distances from the urban centers along the Wasatch Front retained their original Mormon flavor.

Agriculture supported not only the Mormon settlers, but other people who came to Utah. In time when Utah produced agricultural crops in surplus of needs, the surpluses were freighted to neighboring communities and territories and sold. The Mormons created an agricultural oasis in the Mountain West that benefited not only themselves but their neighbors and those who passed through Utah.

During the later decades of the nineteenth century, the expansion of settlement continued at about the same rate as earlier. Settlements expanded into distant valleys in Utah and into neighboring territories. This continued expansion convinced the Indians that they could not live in peace with the white settlers and keep their old way of life. Furthermore, as Mormon settlement expanded, it met the expanding cattle frontier of Americans coming from the east and the southeast. Sometimes this meeting of conflicting cultures led to difficulties.

IN THIS CHAPTER WE WILL LEARN

1. Urban centers developed in Salt Lake City and Ogden.

2. The economic development of Utah reflected the influence of the railroad and mining.

3. Mormon settlements expanded throughout Utah and into neighboring regions.

4. The expansion of settlements led to the Black Hawk War.

5. After the Black Hawk War, settlement expanded into eastern Utah.

16

1. URBAN CENTERS DEVELOPED IN SALT LAKE CITY AND OGDEN

In the first years of settlement, life was much the same in all Utah villages. As years went on, however, some cities grew until their size gave them a different way of life from the smaller villages. Large city centers are called *urban centers*, and the process of growing into such centers is called *urbanization*. In small farming villages people depended more on their own resources for food and other necessities of life. Each man performed many tasks in supplying his needs. He built his house, made his furniture, farmed his land, herded his cattle, made his own

One of Utah's most famous corners—the homes and offices of Brigham Young. The Lion House, the President's Office, and the Beehive House, Salt Lake City.

harnesses and some other farm equipment. As agricultural surpluses were produced, it was possible for some people to perform tasks other than farming. As more people came to live closer together, individuals could confine their efforts to one trade or occupation, being paid for those services, and in turn paying others for those things they did not produce.

Salt Lake City developed as Utah's urban center. Salt Lake City almost doubled its population each ten years from 1850 to 1890. In 1850 there were 3,150 people residing in the city, and in 1890, 44,843. Salt Lake City was always Utah's largest city, and Salt Lake County had one-fourth of Utah's total population from 1860 to 1890.

Several factors contributed to Salt Lake City's growth as an urban center. It was Utah's first city and became the headquarters of the church to which 90 percent of the people belonged during the territorial period. It became the political capital of the territory, located in the center of the most productive valleys of Utah. The richest mines were in the canyons of the surrounding mountains. Salt Lake Valley was fertile and could support a large population. It was connected to other fertile valleys on the north and south.

Both Salt Lake City and Ogden were on the crossroads of western travel. In 1846, the year before settlement, Salt Lake Valley was on the route of emigrants to California, and it remained an important stopping place for travelers bound for California. The junction of the two main railroad lines at Ogden gave Ogden an important element for future growth. The construction of the Utah Central Railroad from Ogden to Salt Lake City helped keep the capital city on the transportation map as well.

The growth of Ogden into an urban center was assured by the establishing of a railroad junction, depots, and yards there. Many employees of the railroad resided in Ogden. Their wages supported many other people. Ogden became the distributing point for the freight coming from all directions. In 1860 there were 1,463 settlers in Ogden, and in 1870, the year after the railroad came, there were 3,127 residents. During the next ten years the population doubled, and it doubled again in the next decade to 14,889 in 1890. With the development of the livestock industry, Ogden became the livestock shipping center of the Mountain West.

A street scene in Ogden at about the time of the coming of the railroad.

The growth of Ogden as an urban center was furthered by the junction of railroads at Ogden in 1869.

Farmington about 1896. The scene is typical of many Utah towns along the Wasatch Front.

2. THE ECONOMIC DEVELOPMENT OF UTAH REFLECTED THE INFLUENCES OF THE RAILROAD AND MINING

The population. During the decades after 1860, the population of Utah continued to grow. From 1860 to 1870 the territory more than doubled its population (from 40,273 to 86,786), and in the next decade it almost doubled again (143,963 in 1880). By 1890, Utah had a population of 207,905, a five-fold increase in thirty years.

Through these decades about one-half the population of the territory lived in the counties of Salt Lake, Weber, Davis, and Utah. This shows the trend of the Wasatch Front counties toward urbanization. Brigham Young and other church presidents were also able to extend and increase the population of the outlying settlements of Utah. The number of people in the smaller villages trebled from 1860 to 1870, and nearly doubled from 1870 to 1880.

Fully half the people of Utah territory in 1880 lived in communities with populations from 250 to 500. There were 150 communities with an average population of 350, and 25 communities with a population of from 1,000 to 2,000. The four leading cities in 1880 were Salt Lake City (20,768), Ogden (6,069), Provo (3,432), and Logan (3,396). In each settled valley a major city grew, with a few communities of lesser size, and a larger number of small villages. For example, in Utah Valley there were Provo, with a population of 3,432, six communities with populations averaging 1,915, and eight villages with an average population of 365. This pattern was typical of Salt Lake Valley, the Weber County region, Cache Valley, Sanpete Valley, and others.

Occupations and the labor force. *Agriculture* was from the beginning the most important occupation because if the people were to survive, they had to supply themselves with food. Similarly they had to supply themselves with other necessities.

In the 1850s, 1860s, and 1870s about half of Utah's labor force was engaged in agriculture. As more land came under cultivation and production increased, and as more goods were brought in by the railroad, it was possible for proportionally fewer farmers to supply the people with their food needs. So while the actual number of farmers kept increasing, the percentage of farmers in the total labor force began to drop after 1870 so that in 1860 just over a third, and in 1890 just under a third of the workers were engaged in farming.

When enough food was being produced, the settlers could turn to *other trades and occupations.* Most of the Utah immigrants came from industrial areas, from cities in the United States, England, and Europe. They were skillful artisans, trained mechanics, schooled in manufacturing and other trades. These people had become farmers upon coming to Utah, but in the decade after the coming of the railroad, many returned to their native trades. After 1870, the number of persons employed in manufacturing increased from 2,259 (1870), to 4,931 (1880), to 7,704 (1890).

This painting by Lorus Pratt shows a typical harvest scene in Utah.

Agriculture. By 1890 about 30 percent of the laboring force was engaged in agriculture. Agriculture became more diversified as farmers began growing a larger variety of products.

The *introduction of alfalfa* helped solve the problem of winter feeding of livestock. As native grasses on the open grazing lands were eaten or taken over by the expansion of city and village lots, a greater need arose for a forage that could be harvested and stored. Alfalfa was brought into Utah in 1848, spread slowly, and became established as a basic crop. By 1890 there was more land in alfalfa than wheat, the next largest crop in acreage.

Another important development in agriculture was the development of *artesian wells*, made by drilling into the earth to reach water. Internal pressure causes the water to flow to the surface. Usually Utah farmers had to drill about 146 feet at a cost of about $78, and they ordinarily obtained a flow of about thirty gallons of water a minute. The water was used for household as well as irrigation purposes. By 1890 5,802 acres of land were being irrigated from artesian wells.

Irrigation continued to be the backbone of Utah agriculture. Utah pioneered in irrigation and retained a strong leadership in irrigation science. In 1890, only California had more farmers using irrigation than Utah. Utah ranked fourth in the number of acres irrigated. However, Utah's farms, averaging 27 acres each, were the smallest farms in the

Mountain West. In 1890, one-half of 1 percent of Utah's total land surface was under irrigation. On Utah farms, alfalfa, wheat, oats, barley, corn, and rye continued as basic crops, besides the truck garden crops.

Livestock raising grew into an important aspect of agriculture in the 1870s, 1880s, and 1890s. Increasingly the lands of the territory were used by ranchers for grazing cattle and sheep.

Very little *farm machinery* was brought to Utah by the pioneers other than a few plows. Thus, blacksmiths were in demand in all communities, as one of their most important tasks was to make tools and machinery. Resourceful farmers did much of their own repair work. After the railroad came, there was a large increase in farm machinery purchased. The dollar valuation of farm machinery in 1880 was more than double what it was in 1870.

The railroads employed hundreds of workers: 520 (1870), 1,001 (1880), and 2,094 (1890), averaging about 2.5 percent of the total labor force in Utah. At the same time, almost as many people were engaged in wagon transportation. The freighting business was still important—goods had to be moved from the railroad lines to the people.

Mining employed hundreds of people. The census records show only those actually in the mining towns at the season of the year the census taker visited the towns. In 1870, he counted 575; in 1880, 2,648; and in 1890 he counted 3,819. These figures suggest that about 5 percent of the labor force was actually engaged in mining. Undoubtedly more should be counted here because of all the people who came to the mining towns to supply the miners with goods and services.

The building trades and construction laborers were still very important, making up

over 5 percent of the total labor force through these years.

Manufacturing. From 1860 to 1900 there was a steady growth in manufacturing as the materials produced at home were gradually replaced by store goods. While home industries had been developed, the people had never been wholly satisfied with their own production. However, many manufacturing establishments grew up that made it possible for the people of Utah to use Utah industries and Utah products.

Mormon cooperative stores. One of the most significant events in the economic history of the territory was the establishment of *Zion's Co-operative Mercantile Institution*, October 1868, in Salt Lake City. ZCMI was formed by Brigham Young for the control and regulation of trade for the benefit of the Mormon people. There were three fundamental reasons for the establishment of this cooperative merchandising program: (1) to take full advantage of the services of the railroad in bringing in eastern goods at cheaper prices, (2) to keep non-Mormon merchants from entering Mormon trade and profiting at the expense of the Mormons, and (3) to encourage home industries by putting the profit from a cooperative store system into buying machinery and other essentials for the establishment of industries to produce goods for the people.

Brigham Young felt that non-Mormon merchants charged excessively high prices for goods and that they would continue to do so in the future. If non-Mormon merchants monopolized trade at the expense of the Mormons, Brigham Young felt they could "destroy the Saints." Brigham Young wanted to take advantage of the railroad but guard against disadvantages he saw accompanying its services.

A central institution was established in

An early home of the Zion's Cooperative Mercantile Institution, Main Street, Salt Lake City.
From this center the cooperative movement among the Mormons in Utah was directed.

Salt Lake City to buy goods in the East and import them to Utah for sale. From the central warehouse goods were distributed to branch or local retail stores which sold the goods at uniform prices. Local retail stores were established in every ward or community and were expected to control the trade in that locality. The Mormons were expected to trade only with the ZCMI, and not with "outsiders." The profits from the system were to be spent in establishing home industries, shops and factories, and in producing essential goods.

Many merchants already in business put their supply of goods into the cooperative enterprise in exchange for stock in the ZCMI. On March 1, 1869, the parent ZCMI opened for business in the Eagle Emporium of William Jennings. On April 21, 1869, the first retail store opened in the building formerly occupied by N. S. Ransohoff and Company. Soon retail stores were in operation in each ward in the city, and by 1870 every ward and community had a retail ZCMI store.

Between 1869 and 1884 this cooperative system for the production and distribution of goods extended throughout Utah. The parent store was an immediate success, doing $1,750,000 worth of business the first year, and about $4,000,000 worth of business each year thereafter. It was estimated that in its first four years of operation the institution saved the Mormon people $3,000,000 because of its lower prices.

The ZCMI operated a tannery, boot and shoe factory, and a clothing factory. Local cooperative stores spent their earnings in establishing cooperative butcher shops, blacksmith shops, dairies, carding machines, grist-mills, sawmills, tanneries, boot and shoe shops, molasses mills, furniture shops, and in buying threshers and mowing machines for the farmers of the community. Cooperative livestock herds were also established.

The essential cooperative nature of the system was based on the fact that anyone could purchase stock in the institution. Dividends were declared and paid to the stockholders as the institution made money. From the beginning, however, a relatively few people held most of the stock, and as the years passed the merchants in a community tended to increase their holdings in the store until only a few owned stock in the store. As this happened, the cooperative aspect began to disappear. In the early 1880s this form of cooperation almost disappeared, though the local stores kept in business, patronizing the central parent ZCMI.

3. MORMON SETTLEMENTS EXPANDED THROUGHOUT UTAH AND INTO NEIGHBORING REGIONS

During the 1860s and 1870s the familiar

After the Utah War, there was a rapid expansion of settlement in many valleys. Primitive conditions prevailed at the founding of these new settlements. The upper is an artist's sketch of the settlement of Hyrum, summer 1860. The lower sketch illustrates a fort-style arrangement of cabins at Hyrum.

As in the 1850s, Mormon settlers called to found distant settlements usually met near Salt Lake City, were organized, and then departed for the site of their new homes. These people are bound for the settlement of Saint George.

patterns of settlement followed those set in the 1850s. (See chapter 11, and chapter 13, section 3.) New settlements were founded at about the same rate as during the first decade. Many settlements were founded by persons who were called, while others were founded by people who moved from one settlement to another, searching for a better place to live.

During the 1850s the valleys along the Wasatch Front had been settled. The big move during the Utah War led many people to settle other valleys instead of returning to their old homes. After the war, settlement expanded into the mountain valleys of the Wasatch Mountains, from Cache Valley on the north to Heber Valley on the south.

Cache Valley had two settlements—Wellsville and Mendon—in 1857. These settlements were reoccupied after the Utah War, and in 1859 settlements were founded at *Logan, Providence, Richmond, Millville, Franklin,* and *Smithfield*, and in 1860 at *Hyde Park, Paradise, Hyrum*, and *Avon*. Indian troubles kept the people close to their forts. However, after the Battle of Bear River (January 29, 1863), settlers moved out onto farms; other settlements were founded and widespread cultivation of farm lands began in Cache Valley.

From Cache Valley settlers moved eastward through the mountains into **Bear Lake** country. In the fall of 1863, Apostle Charles C. Rich and others were called to settle the country. They went into the valley on horseback, picked a site for a settlement and returned. The settlers in their wagons made the forty-six-mile trip through the mountains in eight days and arrived at the site of future *Paris*, Idaho, September 26, 1863. Other settlers followed. The townsite was surveyed and cabins built. From thirty to forty families spent the first winter there. Others arrived

the next spring, and when Brigham Young and his party visited the settlement in May, there were thirty-four cabins. In 1864 neighboring settlements were founded: *Bloomington, Saint Charles, Ovid, Montpelier, Fish Haven, Liberty,* and *Bennington*; and *Wardboro* in 1865, and in 1870, *Georgetown*, followed shortly by others. (All these communities are in Idaho today.) Soon settlements extended southward (into present Utah): *Laketown* (1867), *Meadowville* (1869), *Randolph* (1870), *Woodruff* (1870-71), and *Garden City* (1877). The northern Bear Lake settlements were considered part of Utah in those years, and even after the survey of 1872 divided the settlements into Idaho and Utah, the Idaho settlements sent representatives to the Utah legislature. These communities have always been closely tied to Utah.

Settlement also extended at the same time eastward into other **valleys of the Wasatch Mountains.** Settlers had gone eastward from Brigham City, into Little Valley in the 1850s, but it was not until 1863 that Danish settlers began permanent settlement of *Mantua*. From Ogden, settlements were extended eastward up the Ogden River into Ogden Valley, where *Eden* was founded in 1859 and *Huntsville* in 1860. Settlers had moved up the canyon of the Weber River in the 1850s, but in 1860 settlers founded *Morgan, Richville*, and *Porterville*, and *Croyden* in 1862. In 1859 and 1860 many families moved eastward from Utah Valley into Heber Valley to establish *Heber, Midway, Charleston*, and *Center Creek*. Other families settled in Rhodes Valley (Kamas Prairie) at *Kamas* and *Peoa* in 1860, and up along the Weber River. In 1859 settlements were begun at *Coalville, Hoytsville*, and *Wanship*.

Sanpete Valley. Shortly after the Utah War, in 1859, new settlements were founded in Sanpete Valley: *Fountain Green, Moroni,*

A major purpose in settling southern Utah was the production of cotton. This cotton mill, built in Washington in 1866-67, operated for almost half a century, producing at times up to 550 yards of cloth a day.

Mount Pleasant, Fairview, and *Gunnison.* Upper Thistle Valley was used as a herd ground by the people to the south, and in 1861 settlers surveyed the meadow lands, divided the land, and settlement began at *Indianola.* West of Moroni on Currant Creek the people of Moroni planted orchards, and settlers moved there to found *Freedom* in 1870. Manti people used lands to the south as herd grounds and this led to the settlement in 1872 of *Sterling.* From Gunnison, people moved onto Twelve Mile Creek to the site of an ancient Indian camping ground and there in 1871 founded *Arrapeen* (later named *Mayfield*). In 1864 an Indian showed Brigham Young a piece of black rock, saying that it was rock that burned. Coal was thus discovered west of Moroni. In 1869 Welsh settlers moved there to mine coal and named the community *Wales.* From Spring City, *Chester* was settled in 1870. A few miles northwest

of Gunnison, *Fayette* was founded in 1861. In 1870 there were 6,786 people in Sanpete Valley, and in the next ten years the population increased to 11,557.

Southern Utah and the Cotton Mission. After the Utah War, Brigham Young turned his attention more and more to southern Utah and the valleys along the Virgin River and its tributaries. With the coming of the Civil War in the East, the supply of cotton from the southern states was cut off. Besides, Brigham Young wanted his people to be self-sufficient. Utah could have her own *Dixie*—a semi-tropical land that would grow cotton and other semi-tropical products. Brigham Young knew the possibilities of the region, and by 1860 there were small farming villages at *Harmony* and *Toquerville* on Ash Creek, *Santa Clara* and *Gunlock* on the Santa Clara River, *Washington, Harrisburg,* and *Tonaquint* along the Virgin River, and *Virgin City* and *Grafton* on the Virgin east of Ash Creek. In the mountains there were *Pine Valley* and *Pinto.*

At the 1861 October conference Brigham Young called over three hundred men and their families to settle in southern Utah on the Virgin River. The objective was to grow enough cotton for Zion. The settlement was to become a central point for all southern Utah settlements, to be an important point on the road to California, and a center from which Arizona might be settled by Mormons. The importance of this *Cotton Mission* is indicated by the fact that two apostles, Orson Pratt and Erastus Snow, were placed in charge. Settlers were called from Salt Lake, Utah, and Sanpete valleys. Among the trades represented in the group were farmers, mechanics, coopers, blacksmiths, carpenters, masons, cabinet makers, plasterers, clerks, teachers, and musicians.

The large caravan of settlers reached

their destination in December 1861 and named the site of their community *Saint George* in honor of Apostle George A. Smith, who was in charge of all southern Utah settlements. The Paiute Indians were not a threat; it would not be necessary to build a fort. The townsite was surveyed. One block was set aside for a public square. Agricultural lands were divided and the major problem of water for their lands was solved. Houses were built of adobe, though later homes were built of fine stone. A schoolhouse was built early in 1862, and by April a sawmill was operating. There were about as many people in the Cotton Mission as in all other settlements in the Virgin Valley combined. Saint George became at once the center of Utah's Dixie.

Settlement moved on up the Virgin River and its forks; *Duncan's Retreat, Rockville,* and *Shonesburg* were founded in 1861. Settlers went in 1862 up the North Fork to found *Springdale* and *Zion Park.* For a livestock-raising area, Dixie people found the region of Shoal Creek suitable and founded *Hebron* in 1862. Settlements expanded up the East Fork into Long Valley where *Mount Carmel* and *Glendale* were founded in 1864, and *Alton,* in 1865. A few miles to the south, where Kanab Creek flows out of the Vermillion Cliffs, the village of *Kanab* was founded in 1864. Some forty miles to the east, ranchers founded a small community *Pahrea* (Paria), in 1865. During the 1860s, Utah's Dixie increased from 691 to over 4,500 people.

The Muddy Mission. One of the most difficult of all Mormon settlement missions was to the Muddy Valley (now Moapa Valley, Nevada), midway between Saint George and Las Vegas. The purpose of the mission was to establish settlements in a semi-tropical valley where cotton and other products could be grown, and at the same time establish a way

ONCE I LIVED IN COTTONWOOD

George A. Hicks was called to settle Dixie

Oh, once I lived in "Cottonwood," And owned a little farm,
But I was called to "Dixie," which gave me much alarm;
To raise the cane and cotton, I right away must go,
But the reason why they sent me, I'm sure I do not know.

I yoked old Jim and Bally up, all for to make a start;
To leave my house and garden, it almost broke my heart.
We moved along quite slowly, and often looked behind,
For the sands and rocks of "Dixie," Kept running through my mind.

At length we reached the "Black Ridge," where I broke my wagon dow
I could not find a carpenter, We were twenty miles from town,
So with a clumsy cedar pole, I fixed an awkward slide,
My wagon pulled so heavy then, That Betsy could not ride.

While Betsy was a walking, I told her to take care,
When all upon a sudden, She struck a prickly pear,
Then she began to blubber out as loud as she could bawl;
If I was back in "Cottonwood," I wouldn't come at all.

And when we reached the Sandy, we could not move at all.
For poor old Jim and Bally, began to puff and lawl.
I whipped and swore a little, but could not make the rout
For myself, the team and Betsy, were all of us give out.

And next we got to Washington, where we stayed a little while:
To see if April showers would make the verdure smile:
But Oh, I was mistaken, and so I went away,
For the red hills of November, looked just the same in May.

I feel so sad and lonely now, there's nothing here to cheer,
Except prophetic sermons, which we very often hear.
They will hand them out by dozens, and prove them by the Book;
I'd rather have some roasting ears, to stay at home and cook.

I feel so weak and hungry now, I think I'm nearly dead,
'Tis seven weeks next Sunday, since I have tasted bread:
Of carrot tops and lucerne greens we have enough to eat,
but I'd like to change my diet off for buckwheat cakes and meat.

I brought this old coat with me, about two years ago,
And how I'll get another one, I'm sure I do not know.
May Providence protect me against the wind and wet,
I think myself and Betsy, these times will ne'er forget.

My shirt is dyed with wild dockroot, with greasewood for a set;
I fear the colors all will fade when once it does get wet.
They said we could raise madder, and indigo so blue
But that turned out a humbug, the story was not true.

The hot winds whirl around me and take away my breath;
I've had the chills and fever, till I'm nearly shook to death,
"All earthly tribulations, are but a moment here."
And Oh, if I proved faithful a righteous crown shall wear.

My wagon's sold for sorghum seed, to make a little bread,
And poor old Jim and Bally, long, long ago are dead.
There's only me and Betsy left to hoe the cotton tree,
May heaven help the Dixieite wherever he may be.

This view of Richfield was taken in 1876, twelve years after initial settlement. Most pioneer settlements in Utah had an appearance like this in their first years.

station on the route between southern California and Utah settlements. Plans included establishing a warehouse at a landing on the Colorado River near the Muddy River (*Call's Landing*, 1865) for emigrants from Europe who would be brought by water, by way of Panama and the Gulf of California, then up the Colorado River to that point, thus doing away with the transcontinental trip.

Early in 1865 the settlers arrived in the narrow Muddy Valley and made their chief settlements: *Saint Thomas, Saint Joseph*, and *Overton*. In February 1865 a warehouse was erected at Call's Landing. It was a difficult mission because of the lonely situation, the desert country all around, the Indians who sought to gain all they could from the settlers, and the difficulty of reclaiming land with insufficient water. Yet the settlers were beginning to succeed when the region was made part of the newly created and enlarged state of Nevada. Nevada taxes had to be paid in cash, and the settlers had no money. In

1871 the improvements were left, and the people moved back to Utah, most of them settling in Long Valley, Kane County. (In the 1880s, several Mormon families settled again on the old sites of Saint Thomas, Saint Joseph, and Overton.)

The settlement of the Sevier Valley. The occupation of Sevier Valley came somewhat after the settlement of neighboring regions. The long valley with its tributary valleys remained in the possession of the Indians who kept pretty much to their old ways during these years. In the fall of 1863 groups of men moved into central Sevier Valley. A couple of families lived in a dugout during the winter of 1863-64 at the site of *Monroe*. Early in January 1864, about twenty families formed a settlement at the site of *Richfield*. That same year families settled *Salina, Glenwood*, and *Joseph*.

Farther to the south, up the Sevier River, three important settlements were made in 1864: *Marysvale, Circleville*, and *Panguitch*. A few families were at the site of Marysvale in the fall of 1864, and the next spring sixteen other families joined the settlement. Circleville was settled by people from Sanpete who had come in December 1863, followed by about fifty families who were called there in the spring of 1864. Panguitch was settled by fifty families called from Parowan.

4. THE EXPANSION OF SETTLEMENTS LED TO THE BLACK HAWK WAR

Settlements expanded at the expense of the Indians whose best hunting and gathering grounds were disturbed and taken up by townsites, grazing lands, lumbering, and mining activities. As settlements increased, the Indians were reduced to preying on the settlements for food, attacking wagon trains, or begging for handouts.

The *Indian farms* established in the late

1850s by Brigham Young had shown real promise, but the Utah War, the Civil War, and a succession of difficulties with Indian agents and the government encouraged many Indians to leave the farms. Some Indians moved from the farms and settled on lands adjacent to white settlements. Most Utah Indians had kept to their old ways of making a living by hunting and gathering. By the early 1860s many Indians were reduced to stealing or starving.

In 1863 the United States negotiated *a series of treaties* with the Indians of Utah, Nevada, and Colorado. It is likely the Indians did not fully understand what they surrendered, but in general, the Indians agreed to cease their hostilities; to permit the whites to build roads, military posts and stations, telegraph, and stage lines, and railways on their lands; and to permit the establishment of mines, mills, and ranches, and the taking of timber. The Indians further agreed to remove to officially established reservations whenever the president of the United States deemed it appropriate. In return, the Indians were to receive sums of money for specified periods of time, in compensation for the loss of game on their hunting grounds.

In 1861 President Abraham Lincoln designated the *Uinta Basin* as an Indian reservation. In 1864 Congress passed the Indian Removal Act which required Utah Indians to vacate and sell lands they then held and remove to the Uinta Basin, which was set aside for their "permanent settlement and exclusive occupation." To effect these removals, the superintendent of Indian affairs for the territory, in the presence of Brigham Young and other leading Mormons, made a treaty with the principal Indian chiefs of Utah at the Spanish Fork Indian farm on June 8, 1865. While this treaty was never ratified by the United States Congress, Congress did approve

and supply money for the establishment of the *Uintah Indian Reservation*.

By the mid-1860s, however, many Indians were disappointed over the failure of the government to help them. They realized that peaceful coexistence, however benevolent Brigham Young's policy, was not working for them, and that they were losing their lands and their means of making a living. Indian resentment at the occupation of their lands and their resistance to removal led to war.

The Black Hawk War, 1865-68 was the most serious and devastating of Utah's Indian wars. It started at Manti in April 1865 and lasted for three years, extending throughout central and southern Utah. The Ute Indians were under Black Hawk. The fundamental causes of the war have been mentioned. Actual hostilities opened with the following events.

Black Hawk led Ute Indians against white settlers in central and southern Utah, 1865-68, in response to the expansion of white settlement.

Sanpete Indians had been taking stray cows, and the settlers objected. On the other hand the Indians had suffered a smallpox epidemic brought to them by the whites. At a meeting between the whites and Indians at Manti, April 9, 1865, the talks were heated and reached a climax when John Lowry dragged an Indian from his horse, thrashed him, then went home for a gun. When he returned, the Indians were gone and war threatened. The Indians began raiding and stealing livestock and occasionally killing whites. The whites retaliated by pursuing the Indians. The Indians were highly successful in guerrilla warfare—surprise attacks, ambush, swift retreats, concealments, and unexpected attacks on distant settlements.

Most of the attacks were in the Sanpete and Sevier valleys. But settlements farther south also came under attack. These Indian disturbances led other Indians, usually peaceful, to steal and kill. The Navajo, and to a lesser extent the Paiute, caused trouble for white men in southern Utah, northern Arizona, and in the Muddy settlements. Settlers fortified their villages. Special forts were constructed, such as Fort Deseret (1866) and Cove Fort (1867). Men worked in their fields

Cove Fort, built midway between Fillmore and Beaver in 1867, served as a refuge for families during the Black Hawk War.

with their guns at their sides. Troubles became so bad that newer and smaller settlements had to be abandoned as the inhabitants moved to older and larger settlements for protection. The people of Salina left in April 1866 for Gunnison. In May the settlers in Piute County moved into Circleville. In June the settlements on the Sevier River south of Richfield were broken up. In April 1867 Richfield was abandoned. In all, more than twenty-five settlements were abandoned in central and southern counties.

On August 19, 1868, Colonel F. H. Head, territorial superintendent of Indian affairs, and Dimick B. Huntington, Indian interpreter, had a council with the Indians at Strawberry Valley. Here a treaty of peace was made. The war was over. Black Hawk died September 26, 1870, near Spring Lake in Utah County. Yet there were other raids until June and July 1873 when other treaties were signed ending the difficulties.

Before the war ended from fifty to seventy settlers lost their lives; an equally large number of Indians lost their lives; and a vast number of horses and cattle were lost, killed, or stolen. The expenses of the local militia amounted to about $1.5 million. The federal troops had refused to help, so the local militia under Daniel H. Wells shouldered the responsibility.

With the war over, the program of *removal of the Indians* remained. The Ute, under Chief Tabby, who favored peace, agreed to move to the Uinta Basin. While about 1,500 Ute were removed to the Uintah Indian Reservation during the next year or two, most Indians chose to remain on or near their ancestral lands.

The Gosiute refused to move but settled down to farming in Deep Creek and Skull Valley. William Lee, a Mormon, lived with the Gosiute in Skull Valley and taught them how to farm. During the next forty to fifty years, however, the Gosiute became a forgotten people.

The Paiute in southern Utah continued to live in small groups on the fringe of white settlements. Some of these groups were formally established on private lands or on Mormon church property. The Paiute were neglected by the federal government, but the Mormons continued to give assistance. In 1891 the Southern Paiute were removed to the newly created Shivwits Indian Reservation outside Santa Clara. In 1907 other Paiutes were moved to the Kaibab Reservation in Arizona.

5. AFTER THE BLACK HAWK WAR, SETTLEMENT EXPANDED INTO EASTERN UTAH

When the Black Hawk War was over, many people returned to their abandoned homes, while others moved to other valleys. By this time, non-Mormon ranchers and miners had come into central Utah. A few ranches had been set up and a few mines begun. Some miners made use of abandoned settlements.

Sanpete and Sevier valleys. From 1871 to 1875 there was a filling in of settlements in central Sevier Valley with the establishment of *Annabella* and *Vermillion* (1871), *Central* (1872), *Venice* (1873) and *Prattville* (1873), *Elsinore* (1874), and *Redmond* and *Aurora* (1875).

Settlement extended up Otter Creek to *Burrville* (1873) and *Koosharem* and *Greenwich* (1874).

South of Panguitch, *Hillsdale* was founded in 1871. Excellent grazing lands were found south of Panguitch for the community's cooperative herd. The Hatch family began a settlement there in 1872, named *Hatch*.

Canyonlands. East across the plateaus from Panguitch, in the Canyonlands, settlers found water and land suitable for settlements. *Cannonville* was settled in 1874. *Escalante*, which had been explored early in 1875, was settled that June by upper Sevier people who wanted a warmer climate. From Cannonville settlers moved to *Henrieville* in 1883. *Tropic* was settled seven years later.

In the Canyonlands, to the north of Escalante country, other settlements were made. The Fremont River originates in the Fish Lake Mountains and flows eastward to join the Dirty Devil River (thence to the Colorado River). This area is now Wayne County. Along the course of the Fremont River are small valleys offering farm and range lands. Between 1876 and 1892 eleven villages were founded: *Fremont* (1876), *Thurber* (1879, renamed *Bicknell* in 1914), *Teasdale* (1879), *Carcass Creek* (1880, named *Grover* in 1888), *Loa* (1885) and nearby East Loa or *Lyman*, *Torrey* (1886) and *Fruita* (1892). Settlers also went farther downstream into the south desert country to *Pleasant Creek* (1881-82, later known as Floral, Hank's Place, or *Notom*), and *Caineville* (1883), and beyond the Upper Hills to Graves Valley and *Hanksville* (1883). By 1900 there were 1,907 people in these small settlements in the isolated valleys of the canyonlands of Wayne County.

Castle Valley. During the Black Hawk War, Sanpete Valley men had chased Indians eastward across the Wasatch Plateau into Castle Valley, and recognizing the possibilities for settlement, they explored the headwaters of the San Rafael River, Ferron, Cottonwood, and Huntington creeks. They made favorable reports of the area. At a meeting at Mount Pleasant in Sanpete Valley, September 22, 1877, encouragement was given to the settlement of Castle Valley, and Mormon leaders began the selection of men to be called to settle there. That fall men made their way, sometimes cutting new roads, into Castle Valley, arriving November 2. Farms were laid out and a small log cabin built. Early in 1878 others came, planted crops, and founded *Castle Dale, Ferron, Orangeville, Huntington,* and *Price.* Other settlers came in 1879 and *Wellington* was settled. In 1880 the territorial legislature created Emery County. In 1881 the site of *Emery* on Muddy Creek was settled. From Huntington, settlement extended to *Cleveland* (1885), and thence to *Elmo* (1902).

The coming of coal mining and the Denver & Rio Grande Railroad into the Price basin gave rise to coal mining and railroad towns. *Green River, Helper, Colton,* and *Soldier Summit* were founded during the early 1880s in connection with railroad and mining activities. Coal mining towns paralleled this growth: *Scofield* and *Clear Creek* (1880), *Coal City* (1885), *Castle Gate* (1888), *Sunnyside* (1899), and *Hiawatha* (1909).

West of the La Sal Mountains, Pack Creek flows through Spanish Valley and Moab Valley to the Colorado. Here is the site of the Elk Mountain Mission that failed in 1855. In the 1870s ranchmen from the east moved into the area, raising sheep and cattle. Mormons returned to the region, some of them buying out some of the non-Mormon ranchers. *Moab* was named and a post office established in 1879.

The *San Juan Mission* was one of the most difficult of colonization efforts. The mission was to locate a settlement on the San Juan River in southeastern Utah. Late in 1879 a number of families were called from Parowan and Cedar City. The expedition was under the charge of Silas S. Smith. The company made its way eastward over the mountains to Escalante, then made a road over the difficult desert plateau country southeastward

to the Colorado River. To get down to the river, they had to cut away rock cliffs to make a slide-road from the high cliffs down to the river bank. This Hole-in-the-Rock trek was one of sheer courage and extreme hardship. After crossing the river, the settlers had even more difficult country to pass through until they reached the San Juan River where they established the community of *Bluff.* Eight years later, *Monticello* was founded, and when the Bluff settlers decided to pull out in 1904, they settled *Blanding.* Crop agriculture was the main occupation until cattle grazing proved profitable.

Uinta Basin. While explorations had been made into the Uinta Basin earlier, Mormon settlement did not begin until the fall of 1877, a few years after several hundred Ute Indians had been settled on the Uintah reservation. Non-Mormon ranchers were in the region when Mormon settlers arrived. When Mormons learned that there were good lands to the east suitable for farming and ranching, and not included in the boundaries of the reservation, they settled on them. Ashley Fork Center (present *Vernal*) was established in 1878 on Ashley Creek. Lars Jensen (a non-Mormon) had located on the Green River and

When the San Juan Mission pioneers reached the rim of the canyon of the Colorado River they were able to reach the river only by making their way down through this narrow pass called the Hole-in-the-Rock.

put a ferry in operation in September 1877. In December a Mormon settled nearby. Others soon followed and established the community of *Jensen*. Up Ashley Creek some fifteen miles, others established a small settlement on Dry Creek known as *Mountain Dell* (1878). That same year Mormon settlers went a few miles west of Ashley Fork Center to establish *Maeser*. A sawmill and a flour mill were erected, giving the name *Mill District* to the settlement. South and east of Ashley Fork Center others established *Naples* (fall 1878). And in 1880 land was taken up two and a half miles southwest of Ashley Fork Center at *Glines*. These small farming and ranching communities were the only Mormon settlements in the Uinta Basin until 1905.

As the population of the Uintah Indian Reservation grew, forts and trading posts were established. The Bureau of Indian Affairs established an agency at Ouray in 1881. *Fort Thornburgh* was built about six miles north of Vernal at the mouth of Ashley Creek Canyon and served from 1881 to 1884. In 1886 *Fort Duchesne* took over the task of aiding the Uinta Basin Indians. This fort was situated about three miles above the junction of the Duchesne and Uinta rivers, midway between the headquarters of agencies at Whiterocks and Ouray. The special mission of Fort Duchesne was to guard the Indian frontier in eastern Utah, western Colorado, and southwestern Wyoming. The number of troops stationed there varied during the first years from 275 to 126. Roads were built from the reservation to Fort Bridger, Park City, and Price. A telegraph line connected the fort with Price. The fort spent thousands of dollars for labor, hay, wood, and other goods, besides paying for the services of freighters.

Mormon settlement of the Mountain West continued under Brigham Young's successors with the same force and direction he had given it. Under Presidents John Taylor, Wilford Woodruff, and Lorenzo Snow, settlements were founded in Utah, neighboring states and territories, Canada, and Mexico. Settlement expanded southward into Arizona (1873, 1876), New Mexico (1875), Colorado (1877), and on into Mexico (1887). Northward settlement expanded into Idaho (1860s and 1870s), Wyoming (1876), and into Canada (1887). Mormon leaders realized that population was increasing and that available land was rapidly being taken up. There was a need to find new land to satisfy the younger generation and the immigrants who were coming into the territory in a constant flow. The Mormon settlement movement lasted into the early twentieth century, when it came to a close after about fifty years.

The expansion of settlements in these later years, however, faced problems not known in earlier times. The frontier of Mormon settlement now met the frontier of American settlers—cattlemen and miners moving into Mormon Country. When these two frontiers met, there were some open conflicts, though for the most part the people lived peaceably.

San Juan Mission settlers crossed the Colorado River at this site.

Stone houses, built of native stone and fitting beautifully into the landscape, marked the coming of an age of stability. Most stone houses were built in the 1870s and 1880s.

17

THE OLD WAY OF LIFE

Through the nineteenth century and well into the twentieth, Utah and the area of the Mountain West settled by the Mormons was considered Mormon Country. As many as 90 percent of the people of Utah were Mormons, and Mormon ways characterized life in the villages as well as the cities. The Mormons had come to Utah to build a kingdom of God and to establish a society influenced in all details by their religion.

The Latter-day Saint Temple at Manti, built in the 1880s, is one of the most beautiful of Mormon temples. Others in Utah are of a similar design.

As a study of colonial America requires consideration of the way of life of the Puritans and Pilgrims, so a study of early Utah requires a consideration of the way of life the Mormons established. The religion of the Latter-day Saints dominated all aspects of life in early Utah. Mormon teachings and practices showed in the pattern of the villages, in political ideas and practices, in economic life, and in social affairs, including architecture, music and the theater. Church influences were felt in daily work, recreation, home life, reading, and conversation. Many of the old ways survived well into the twentieth century and remain in the memory of many people as an ideal for the future.

The old way of life was an outgrowth of the first pioneer days and was also the foundation upon which modern Utah was built. The pioneer generations worked hard for the comforts of life, and at the same time worked to establish organizations and practices which would make life richer for them and their children, in family and community life, in education, in religion, and in the cultural aspects of life.

IN THIS CHAPTER WE WILL LEARN

1. Mormon church leaders aimed to establish a kingdom of God on earth.

2. Church organizations and institutions helped further Mormon goals.

3. The United Orders were unique communitarian experiments in equality and cooperation.

4. Life in the Mormon villages was hard.

5. Architecture and the fine arts showed church influence.

6. Educational institutions reflected the religious life of the people.

7. Mormon practices were opposed by some people.

Brigham Young, more than any other one person, was the founder of Utah.

1. MORMON CHURCH LEADERS AIMED TO ESTABLISH A KINGDOM OF GOD ON EARTH

The Mormon goal of establishing a kingdom of God on earth dominated much of what happened in nineteenth century Utah. The Mormons believed they were building an earthly kingdom to which Christ would come and from which He would rule the earth. Thus it was important to occupy as much land as quickly as possible to the exclusion of others, lay out communities, and people them. The Mormons must be united in all things. Loyalty to church leaders and fellow Mormons, and obedience to Mormon teachings became primary virtues. Unity was a foremost ideal; the Mormons must be one; there must be no divisions among them. All programs established had a religious orientation. Supporting church candidates for political office showed loyalty to leaders. Economic policies were formed to help the Mormons become independent from the outside world; Mormons were to avoid indebtedness to the non-Mormon world. Mormons were asked to cooperate with each other in all things, to think of the other fellow, to sacrifice personal wishes for the good of the kingdom. Instruction to help meet these goals was given in sermons, often repeated, in the pulpits in Salt Lake City and in all the settlements, and usually printed in the church's newspaper, the *Deseret News*. Obviously, the important figures in early Utah were church leaders.

Church leaders occupied a place of influence unlike any body of leaders in other territories or states. Presiding over all the church's activities were the *general authori-*

ties: the three members of the First Presidency, members of the Quorum of Twelve Apostles, the Presiding Bishopric, and the Presiding Patriarch. A stake president and two counselors presided over church affairs in stakes, units equivalent in area to a valley or county. Because of the faith and confidence of Mormons in their officers, these men had considerable influence in the lives of the people.

No name is so important to Utah's early development as that of *Brigham Young*. As Mormon church president for thirty years, he served his people as religious, political, economic, and social leader. He led one of the great mass migrations in American history. He directed programs for the conversion and immigration of thousands of converts and the establishment of over three hundred settlements throughout the mountain West. He designed and laid out cities and villages. He built tabernacles. He saw the Saint George Temple to completion and dedication. He planned the Salt Lake, Logan, and Manti temples, and supervised construction of the Salt Lake Temple during his life. He founded newspapers and schools. He was a contractor for the construction of railroads and telegraph lines. He was businessman, economic and political statesman, and religious leader to his people. He was supported directly in his goals by many people of considerable talent who accepted his leadership and put his plans into operation. He frequently made spring and summer visits to the settlements, both north and south, giving encouragement, instructions, and leadership; some thirty such trips were made in his lifetime. He loved his people. To the time of his death, August 29, 1877, he was fiercely loyal to his religion and his followers. He met great opposition only from those who did not believe as he did. "He had much courage, and superb equipment."

Closely associated with Brigham Young, serving as members of the First Presidency, at various times, were Heber C. Kimball, George A. Smith, Willard Richards, Jedediah M. Grant, and Daniel H. Wells. The chief responsibility for much of Utah's development rested with these men. The Quorum of Twelve Apostles was an important body, and exerted leadership and influence. Most of the apostles lived in Salt Lake City, but a few took leadership roles in distant settlements. It was practice to send an apostle to head the settlement of a major distant valley. These men were regarded as spiritual and temporal leaders. Bishops, who presided over congregations (or villages), took instructions from these valley leaders. In 1877 Brigham Young brought most of the apostles to Salt Lake City and put stake presidents (with counselors and a High Council of twelve men) over bishops of wards in what was called a stake organization.

Peter Maughan,
Cache Valley

Ezra T. Benson,
Cache Valley

Lorenzo Snow,
Brigham City

Isaac Morley,
Sanpete Valley

Among the founders of Utah were the leaders of stakes and settlements in the distant valleys.

Jacob Hamblin,
Southern Utah

George A. Smith,
Southern Utah

Erastus Snow,
Southern Utah

Franklin D. Richards,
Weber County

Abraham O. Smoot,
Utah Valley

Lorin Farr,
Weber County

Charles C. Rich,
Bear Lake

John D. Lee,
Southern Utah

After the death of Brigham Young the First Presidency was not reorganized until October 10, 1880, when John Taylor was sustained as president, with George Q. Cannon and Joseph F. Smith as counselors. Presidents Wilford Woodruff and Lorenzo Snow, who succeeded President Taylor, retained his counselors.

2. CHURCH ORGANIZATIONS AND INSTITUTIONS HELPED FURTHER MORMON GOALS

To meet the needs of the church in attaining its goals, various organizations were established. Basic to the entire church structure were the quorums of priesthood. In the Mormon church the priesthood was held by the male members. There was no separate class of priests or pastors. On the basis of his worthiness, a man was chosen to serve in one of several offices in the priesthood.

The Mormon bishop was an important figure in early Utah. Usually each community was organized as a ward, presided over by a bishop. The bishop conducted religious services and was responsible for church buildings and properties. Through him the church religious, economic, political, and social programs were effected. He presided over the bishop's court which settled disputes between members of his ward. He worked closely with the women's Relief Society in matters of charity and relief, funerals, and burials. Because members paid their tithing to him "in kind," that is, in the form of goods produced, he became a merchant of sorts who received and stored the produce, gave of it to the needy, kept records of any surplus and traded this for goods his people needed. The bishop took care of fruit, vegetables, hay, livestock, chickens, fresh eggs, butter, and cheese, until these goods were needed. He was indeed the "father of the ward." Some bishops served for as long as twenty-five years in one community. Such men were community founders and leaders.

As a member of the Mormon priesthood, a man could expect at least once in his lifetime to be called on a mission for from two to three years. Most missionaries went to the British Isles, the Scandinavian countries, northern Europe, or to the eastern states of the United States. During his mission, increased responsibility and work were placed on his wife, sons, or brothers. For as much as he gave, he received many benefits, and brought to Utah cultural influences from foreign lands which made Utah richer and far less narrow and isolated than it would have been otherwise.

Various organizations were established to help meet the needs of church members. As needs arose, individuals and church leaders began organizations which spread to all wards. These organizations were the means by which the church spread its teaching, and most of the population of Utah grew up under the influence of organizations which continue to the present time.

Sunday Schools among the Mormons began with Richard Ballantyne, who held the first school on Sunday, December 9, 1849, in the Fourteenth Ward of Salt Lake City. The movement grew and on November 4, 1867, the church brought all Sunday Schools under one board with George Q. Cannon as president. For the guidance of the schools the *Juvenile Instructor* magazine was begun January 1, 1866.

Primary associations were begun in 1878 by Mrs. Aurelia Spencer Rogers of Farmington, Davis County. With no kindergartens and few elementary schools, Mrs. Rogers felt children needed weekday religious education. Eliza R. Snow was appointed to head the or-

ganization and Mrs. Rogers began the first Primary Association, in Farmington.

With the coming of the railroad, new movements were begun in the church to help meet the threats the railroad brought to Mormon customs and goals. On November 28, 1869, Brigham Young called his daughters together in the Lion House and organized the *Retrenchment Society*, "for the promotion of habits of order, thrift, industry, and charity ... ." He asked his daughters to avoid "extravagance in dress, in eating, and even in speech." They were to dress modestly in clothes of their own make, preferably of cloth from Utah's mills. At their meetings they were to receive gospel instruction. The movement spread throughout the settlements. In 1878 the name was changed to the *Young Ladies' Mutual Improvement Association*.

During the 1860s a number of literary societies were formed by individuals in Salt Lake City and Odgen. In June 1875, when there were seven such societies in Salt Lake City, Brigham Young asked Junius F. Wells to organize these groups into the *Young Men's Mutual Improvement Association*. The first association was organized in the Thirteenth Ward, Salt Lake City, June 10, 1875. The association was formed to further the moral, intellectual, and spiritual growth of young men, and to provide needed recreation under church supervision.

The women's *Relief Society* was originally organized by Joseph Smith in Nauvoo in 1842 but was not revitalized and put into full operation until 1866 when Eliza R. Snow was named president. Units were organized in the wards and settlements. Women were encouraged to be self-sufficient, develop home industries, live frugally, administer to the poor, and to help the poor provide for themselves.

To provide fine clothing inexpensively,

Among the leaders of Mormon women were (left to right) Elizabeth Ann Whitney, Emmeline B. Wells, and Eliza R. Snow.

they engaged in raising silk. The Deseret Silk Association spread information on silk culture. Mulberry trees were planted, silk worms imported, and silk projects set up in about 150 local organizations. It was estimated that in 1877 there were five million silk worms in the territory. Some women were successful in producing enough silk cloth to make a complete outfit of clothing from the silk of their own silk worms. During the 1870s the women undertook a wheat project, in which they gathered and saved surplus wheat.

In 1872 Lula Greene started a newspaper called the *Woman's Exponent* which became the magazine of the Relief Society. Emmeline B. Wells, an early contributor, became associate editor in 1874 and editor in 1877. She and Eliza R. Snow were among the leaders of Utah women and worked for women's rights. While attending a Women's International Council and Congress in London, Mrs. Wells was received by Queen Victoria. She became president of the Relief Society in 1910 and continued to edit the *Exponent* until 1914. The magazine's name was then changed to the *Relief Society Magazine*.

3. THE UNITED ORDERS WERE UNIQUE COMMUNITARIAN EXPERIMENTS IN EQUALITY AND COOPERATION

One of the basic ideals of the Mormon religion was that the Mormons should be equal in all things, temporal and spiritual, and that they should live in unity, cooperation, peace, and brotherly love. This utopian ideal was shared by many groups in the United States during the early decades of the nineteenth century. These groups tried new forms of community economic organization with the view to eliminating the extremes of poverty and wealth. Communities attempted to live as families. Each member was required to work according to his ability and each member received goods according to his need.

In trying to reach this goal, the Mormons experimented with a variety of economic organizations at different times. In Missouri, the Mormons practiced these principles under the "Law of Consecration and Stewardship." Under this arrangement a person deeded (or consecrated) his properties to the church and received back (as a stewardship) only those he absolutely needed. The surplus was put into the bishop's storehouse to help the poor. In Utah in the 1850s there was a short-lived revival of the principle called the Consecration Movement. In 1864 Apostle Lorenzo Snow established a mercantile cooperative in Brigham City in an attempt to live some of these cooperative principles. Within ten years this community cooperative operated a general store, tannery, woolen mill, cooperative herds, farms devoted to special crops, and other branches relating to industry and agriculture in Bear River Valley.

The most serious attempt to live these principles by the Mormons was during the 1870s. The coming of the railroad had tied Utah to the economy of the nation and when the nation suffered economic depression in

1873 Utah was hurt also. Brigham Young took this opportunity to organize his people in what he called united orders to combat the nationwide depression and the influence of non-Mormon ways in Utah.

The United Order movement was launched by Brigham Young in Saint George January 11, 1874, when he delivered the "Great Sermon." A month later over three hundred persons volunteered to enter the United Order. The movement began when Saint George and Santa Clara farmers established a cooperative farm. United Orders were soon established in other Dixie communities. Brigham Young and his company next made their way northward, organizing one community after another into the United Order, arriving in Salt Lake City April 20. In two months over thirty settlements had been or-ganized into the United Order. The annual conference (May 7-10) was devoted entirely to the subject. After conference the movement spread throughout the territory.

The movement, however, was only a short experience. In most instances the organizations lasted only a few weeks, or at most a year or two. Villages founded for the express purpose of living the United Order appear to have had greater success, such as *Bunkerville* (Nevada), *Kingston* (Piute County), and *Orderville* (Kane County).

The *Kingston United Order* was centered around the family of Thomas R. King who wanted his family to live the order. Some thirty families were in that order from 1877 to 1883. Their homes were built in a fort style, with the dining hall in the central building. Farming and ranching were the chief

The United Order at Orderville was the most successful attempt by the Mormons to live their ideal of economic unity. Here is shown the Relief Society building (1); the Dining Hall (2), the center of community life; the Big House (3); the Blacksmith Shop (4); Carpenter Shop (5); Commissary Department (6); and the United Order Office and Shoe Shop (7). The dwellings (8) were arranged in a partial fort-style. The stables (9) were against the hills, and the fields (10) were to the south. Painting by Elbert Porter.

occupations, though they also built a grist mill, a woolen factory, and a tannery.

The longest and most successful experience was in the little village of *Orderville* on the Virgin River in Long Valley, Kane County. Begun at Mount Carmel in March 1874, the people in the order moved a few miles north a year later and founded Orderville. The village was laid out in a square with dwellings around the west, north, and east sides, all attached to each other in fort style. Central in the square was the dining hall, at the north of which was the kitchen and the bakery. Across the streets about the dwellings were shops, school, and the order office. North of the village next to the hills were the stables. The fields were outside the village, up and down Long Valley.

All things were done by common consent under the leadership of a presidency and a board of directors who were elected by majority vote. All meals were taken in the community dining hall, freeing many women for other tasks. Each person worked according to his abilities and the assignments given. Under community management, the Orderville people raised their own livestock, grew their own grains and vegetables, milled their own flour, made their own molasses, had their own dairy herd, and manufactured "almost all the necessaries of life": cloth, leather, shoes, tinware, cooperware, brooms, and furniture. As their wealth increased they bought neighboring ranches.

Social life centered around the dining hall with its Big Table. Here the people ate their three meals each day. The dining hall served also for church services, daily community prayers, and socials after the evening meal. Singing, spelling bees, and dances were especially popular with the young people.

Orderville began with about twenty-four families of 150 persons. It grew until it reached about 700 persons in 1884. These remarkable people were highly successful in keeping the order going for ten years. The order broke up when external pressures, such as federal prosecution of polygamists, forced its abandonment in 1884.

These examples of United Orders are of the communal type, and are not typical of all those established. Other communities were organized by Brigham Young along other lines, depending upon the situation, resources, and experiences of the community.

4. LIFE IN THE MORMON VILLAGES WAS HARD

Even as the goals of personal life were set by religion, so **life in the Mormon village centered around the church,** or the meeting house, as it was called. In Salt Lake City the regular services which attracted the most attention were the regular Sunday afternoon tabernacle services, at which the general authorities spoke to large crowds of Saints and visitors. In the wards in the communities, religious services were held weekly. There were also the meetings of the Sunday School, Relief Society, Primary, and in most communities the Young Men's and Young Ladies' Mutual Improvement Associations. The major Sunday service was the sacrament meeting. The first Thursday of each month was "fast day," when the faithful fasted for two meals, attended the fast meeting, and bore testimony concerning their belief in the church and its teachings. "Block teachers," usually two high priests, made monthly visits to the homes of the Mormons residing on the block to which they were assigned, learning about the welfare of the members of the families and leaving a message.

In Mormon villages, during the 1870s the first adobe homes were replaced by houses of brick, stone, and well-milled lumber.

In each village the **basic occupations** were farming and livestock raising. However, a few citizens provided essential services to the community. Each village had a blacksmith. Carpenters and cabinet makers were also in demand, as were brick and stone masons. Usually each village had a school teacher, though he would have other means of making a living too. Few villages had any services comparable to those of the doctor or lawyer, though each village had midwives.

Most valleys had gristmills, and sawmills were located in some valleys where there was good cutting timber in the mountains. Co-operative stores were established in many Utah villages in their early days. The ZCMI movement took over some of these cooperative stores and put its own cooperative stores in other villages. The later co-op stores were well designed and usually built of brick or stone. The lower story was the sales room where goods were displayed for sale. The upper story was used variously. It might store additional goods or be used for offices. In some communities the room was used as the village dance hall.

Cooperative stores, like the Cedar City Co-op Store, branches of the ZCMI in Salt Lake City, were established in most communities in Utah during the 1870s.

Entertainment. The settlers of Utah were men and women of many talents who provided entertainment for themselves through dramatic associations, choirs, debating societies, and their own abilities to have good times. The old forms of entertainment and recreation continued to meet their needs— dancing parties, outings, plays, and excursions, as in the earlier years. The Fourth of July and the Twenty-Fourth of July were times for excursions to nearby canyons for picnics, or for meetings where patriotic speeches were given. School children recited or sang, and if the local apostle or some other church leader was present, he gave the speech of the day.

The visits of Brigham Young and other church leaders to a community afforded special occasions for festivities. The people looked forward to such visits and did their best to make them enjoyable. Visitors were entertained with parades, parties, dinners, and dances. While the men talked over matters relating to the community, the townswomen met with the visiting wives and heard news of friends and discussed the latest fashions.

Local dramatic groups staged plays and pageants to relieve the monotony of life. Debaters took issues of the day to speak on, providing both entertainment and information. Some communities were able to imitate to a lesser degree the performances at the Salt Lake Theatre. Those plays appealed to many people. In the early days, play-goers could take produce, such as grain, chickens, or other merchandise, to the nearby tithing office and receive theater tickets in exchange.

Folk songs. The Mormons were known as the "singingest" people in the West. Besides hymns sung in religious services, they sang at home, in the fields, at socials. Many of these songs were folk songs—songs originating among the people who had little or no training in music. The songs were sung to tunes familiar to everyone, but the words were a special creation. Folk songs reflect the common experiences of the people. Folk songs were seldom written down, but were passed on from one singer to another and so were changed and added to in the singing. They were the most popular songs and were greatly enjoyed by everyone. They show a remarkable capacity on the part of the Mormons to portray their most personal feelings and their ability to laugh at themselves.

Life in Utah during the early years of community building was hard. By the later decades of the nineteenth century, however, many people were beginning to enjoy some comforts, and they were expecting better times.

Even though people worked hard, *they played* vigorously. The men and boys pitched horseshoes, played baseball, tested their strength in rope-pulling contests and in wrestling matches. The women had a good time preparing for special picnics, outings, and celebrations. They could have parties or socials in their homes by inviting friends and neighbors in for a quilting bee or a wool picking bee. They often invited friends over to eat something special from the garden or out of the oven.

Dancing was a favorite recreation for both young and old. The social hall was used, or a dance could be held in a large home by moving furniture out of large rooms. Each village had its town musicians who played for most occasions.

Play helped keep people happy as they worked hard and did without the comforts and conveniences some of them had known before coming to Utah.

The home. Managing the pioneer household was a full-time job. Just keeping a house warm in winter took work. The men had to haul wood from nearby hills, then chop it

into stove-size pieces and take it into the house where it was stacked for use in the kitchen stove, fireplace, or stoves in other rooms of the house. In cold weather the kitchen stove became the center of the home. It gave warmth and was at the center of the most important activity, food preparation. A woman might have a kettle of stew or soup cooking on top of the stove, while bread, meat, or a butter cake was baking in the oven. Kettles were rotated on the stove to take advantage of the different temperatures available on different parts of the stove top. Water was also heated on the stove for washing the dishes after meals, or for doing laundry or taking a bath.

Water from a well or nearby stream was carried to the house and used for everything from drinking to keeping the family clean. Water, like everything else, was used sparingly. Often a mother bathed more than one child in the same tub of water, or poured a rinse over those bathing second or third. She might then scrub the floor with the soapy water remaining.

Providing light for a home was a problem. Candles were useful, but when kerosene became available for use in lamps and lanterns, this gave greater light in the room for work, lessons, and reading during the evening hours.

A woman provided clothes for her family, sometimes by working directly from the wool sheared from the sheep. She would wash the wool, card it, spin it into thread and dye it before weaving it on her home loom or sending it to the woolen mills to be woven into cloth. Then she would cut, sew, and fit the clothing to the family member, doing all of the sewing by hand. She could buy or trade for linen and cotton cloth. Every article of clothing was valuable. It could be made over for someone smaller—

taken apart, turned inside out, and remade into a new style. Eventually it could become part of a quilt or a rug, or finally a mop rag.

During summer months, women grew vegetables and fruit in their gardens and orchards. Fruit could be dried or made into preserves or jam. Some vegetables were dried. The root vegetables were kept fresh in underground pits. Unusable produce was fed to pigs and chickens. Women took care of fresh milk by straining it and keeping it stored in a cool place. Cream skimmed from the large milk pans was used in cooking or set to sour for making butter. Extra milk was made into cottage or cheddar cheese. All dairy products were useful in trading for necessities the family could not produce. Chickens and ducks were useful as food and also for their feathers. Their feathers were saved and used to make pillows and feather beds. Beds could be made with a mattress stuffed with corn shucks or cattails, but a feather mattress was a prized possession.

Women always saved used fat for making soap, a chore usually reserved for the spring of the year. Houses were cleaned in the spring. The rugs were taken up, hung outside, and beaten until free of dust. Walls received a fresh coat of whitewash or calcimine. Furniture was washed and polished. With the clean rug again tacked down, the house was ready for another year of living.

Men also worked hard all the year round. The farmer planted in the spring after his field was prepared by plowing and leveling. In the summer he irrigated, weeded, and harvested cuttings of hay which he stored in his barn or in the open in properly made stacks. Fall was a very busy time finishing the harvest and preparing for winter. The farmer also had daily chores such as milking the cows, feeding and watering the animals, and keeping his stables and barnyard clean.

His farm equipment had to be kept in good repair, and harnesses mended. He had to maintain fences and irrigation ditches. Each spring he and other men cleaned the ditches and canals that carried irrigation water. During the winter he improved his home, grounds, and farm, as the weather permitted. His family usually saved shoe repairing and other such household chores for the days when storms or cold weather dictated indoor work. Winter was a time when women did most of their spinning, knitting, and sewing. They also had more time for making social calls and attending church meetings. Winter was a time for killing cattle and hogs, because the cold weather helped preserve the fresh meat. Hind quarters of beef could be wrapped in a sheet and hung on the north side of the house. Pork was turned into smoked hams, sausage, and headcheese. Parts of the meat could be exchanged with neighbors or traded for something else. Perhaps a freight wagon would take it to another town to sell or trade.

Freighters and peddlers were of great importance to the people of Utah. Through them such items as needles, thread, pins, lace, dye, cloth, tea, sugar, soda, and spices, as well as nails, wire, bolts, and tools were brought to the villages. Some peddlers walked through Utah with these in packs on their backs. They would exchange goods for food and lodging. Peddlers were eagerly awaited by the townspeople.

With the coming of the railroad and the formation of the ZCMI, these articles became more widely available. The ZCMI was able to order supplies from the East which were eventually delivered to the local co-op and sold to the individual for either cash or exchange goods. In this way a woman could order a bonnet from Saint Louis and pay for it with butter or cheese in her hometown.

The Mormon social institution which received the most publicity was **polygamy**. It is necessary and important to understand Mormon polygamy because (1) it was a unique feature of life in Utah that had importance to many Utah families; (2) it was a widely known aspect of Mormon life, becoming so prominent that Mormonism, Utah, and polygamy came to mean one and the same thing to most people who professed to know anything about the Mormons; and (3) most important for our study here, it became a national issue that led reformers and politicians to take up a crusade against it and other features of Mormon life.

The practice was publicly acknowledged and defended by the Mormons from 1852 to 1890. The Mormons practiced polygamy, they said, because it was God's command to them. Actually only a few men practiced polygamy. It is estimated that from 10 to 15 percent of the Mormon married men had more than one wife. A much smaller number had more than two wives, though some of the leaders had more.

The typical polygamous family was that of a man having two wives. Sometimes the two wives lived under the same roof, working together in the tasks of the household. Often the husband provided separate homes on separate lots, or even in different settlements. However housing was worked out, there still existed the problem of living in harmony together. Some families were more successful than others. Plural marriage was difficult for the husband and the wives. Most men and women resisted it with every argument at their command, and then when it was not a trial of religious faith, it was a "great trial of feelings."

Health conditions and medical services remained much the same through most of the territorial period. Only slight advances were made in medical knowledge, and those were as slow in coming to Utah as to other western territories. People came to realize that diseases could flourish in the valleys, and that it required care to enjoy health here. As cities grew in size, the dangers from diseases increased. Specific sources of diseases remained unknown, though the germ theory was just beginning to be discussed in the world and in Utah. Isolation and quarantines came to be used to reduce the spread of diseases. A yellow flag on the door or gate warned of a disease within. Disinfection was just being tried. Yet these means were inefficiently used and limited to very few people, and they largely failed. No one saw the danger, for example, in the unsafe, disease-breeding, out-door toilets.

After 1869 there were severe epidemics in Utah. In 1872 diphtheria, scarlet fever, and an epidemic bowel complaint caused great alarm. In 1880 a diphtheria epidemic took 749 lives. Whole families were wiped out. The funeral processions carrying the victims were vividly remembered for years. The high death rate among mothers and infants called for better knowledge of mother and infant care. This care rested on midwives, most of them without any formal training. Some midwives practicing good hygiene delivered hundreds of babies without a loss of mother or child, while others carried infection from one home to another, leaving tragedy wherever they went.

During the 1870s and 1880s Salt Lake City had small hospitals, a few doctors, and some schools to train midwives. The settlements were not so fortunate, though in time they had trained midwives.

Saint Mark's Hospital. With the coming of the railroad and the opening and enlarging of mines in the Salt Lake area, frequent industrial accidents required surgical care. A

Saint Mark's Hospital in Salt Lake City was Utah's first hospital.

Dr. Romania B. Pratt, Utah doctor.

Dr. Ellis R. Shipp, Utah doctor.

hospital was urgently needed. On April 30, 1872, Major Wilkes, a manager of one of the mines; Dr. John F. Hamilton, a practicing physician in Salt Lake City; and the Reverend R. M. Kirby—all identified with the Episcopal church—together with Warren Hussey, a prominent businessman in the city, began Saint Mark's Hospital in a small adobe dwelling on the northwest corner of Fourth South and Fifth East streets, with a capacity of six beds. In 1876, the hospital was moved one block north into a building with twelve beds. The hospital served as a county hospital until 1912 when the Salt Lake County Hospital was opened.

Holy Cross Hospital. The second hospital in Utah was founded by the Catholic church. When two nuns came to establish a school, they learned of the need for a hospital. They were in the mining camps collecting funds to open a school when they saw how many miners were ill or injured and needed care. With the aid of two more nuns, a hospital was opened in a rented fourteen-room house in Salt Lake City. There were beds for twelve or thirteen patients. The first doctors at the Holy Cross Hospital were Dr. Allen Fowler and two brothers, Drs. Dee and J. M. Benedict. In 1881 a new building was begun with a 125-bed capacity. It was completed in 1883. This building was enlarged in 1891 and again in 1903; the chapel was added in 1904.

Ten years after Saint Mark's and seven years after Holy Cross hospital was founded, the Mormons built the *Deseret Hospital*, sponsored by the Deseret Hospital Association, closely identified with the Relief Society. The forty-bed hospital opened on July 17, 1882. Before the hospital started, men and women were sent east to study medicine. Seymour B. Young, a nephew of Brigham Young, went to the University Medical College of New York, graduating in March 1874. Romania B. Pratt left her five children with her mother and went to Philadelphia to study at the Women's Medical College, graduating in 1877. Mrs. Ellis R. Shipp received her degree the following year from the same institution. These doctors worked in the hospital, carried on private practices, and taught classes that spread their knowledge throughout the territory. With more students going east to study, health conditions improved as the people lost their prejudices against doctors and adopted latest scientific practices. The Deseret Hospital continued to function until 1905 when the *Dr. Groves L. D. S. Hospital* was opened.

5. ARCHITECTURE AND THE FINE ARTS SHOWED CHURCH INFLUENCE

Throughout the ages, man has expressed his highest aspirations in architecture, sculpture, painting, music, and other arts. We are able to judge the greatness of a people largely through their artistic creations and their regard for the beautiful.

During the first years in Utah, the set-

The Pine Valley Ward Chapel, built in 1868 in central Washington County, is one of the most beautiful and unique Mormon meeting houses.

tlers were reduced to primitive living conditions. But they did not remain in such conditions for long. There was a constant effort to improve the physical comforts of the house, and to build beautiful churches and other civic buildings. What the settlers had known before they came to Utah, they brought with them. Skilled craftsmen came in large numbers from Europe. Their skills and the memories of fine architecture and other artistic efforts were brought to Utah and put to work.

Utah attained an artistic maturity earlier than some other territories because of the talents brought to Utah by these converts.

Architecture. During the 1860s, 1870s, and 1880s many new buildings were erected throughout the territory. The first rush to build protective homes of adobe and logs had

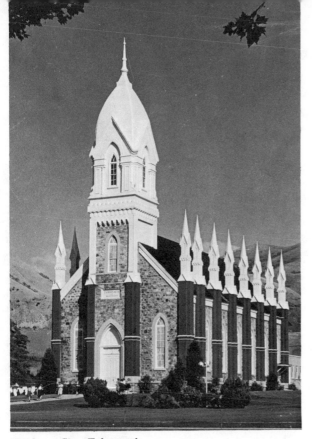

Brigham City Tabernacle.

Coalville Tabernacle.

Stake tabernacles, some of the most beautiful buildings, were religious and cultural centers in their regions.

Saint George Tabernacle, interior.

The Gardo House, Brigham Young's family home on east South Temple.

These drawings were made for the Historic American Buildings Survey, which attempts to identify and preserve buildings of historical importance.

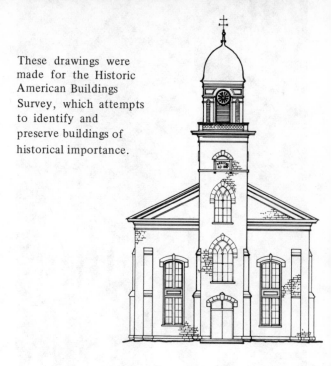

The east elevation of the Wasatch Stake Tabernacle, Heber City.

South elevation of the Staines-Jennings Mansion, Salt Lake City, known today as the Devereaux House. Constructed in 1857, the mansion was the first in Salt Lake City and was used to entertain such notables as territorial governor Alfred Cumming and U.S. president Ulysses S. Grant.

This drawing shows the cast iron front of the ZCMI Building, Salt Lake City.

long passed, and there was now time to build more enduring buildings. Most of the Salt Lake ward meeting or ward schoolhouses were rebuilt. The old adobe structures were torn down and brick and stone meetinghouses erected in their place. Latter-day Saint temples were built in Saint George, Logan, Manti, and Salt Lake City. The need for larger meetinghouses resulted in the building of many of the large tabernacles still in existence today. Craftsmen throughout the church were called to help create these beautiful structures. Some buildings were noted for their beautiful spires, stained glass windows, or paintings on the walls. Today they stand as a reminder of the skill, love, and aspirations of these workmen.

The Tabernacle. Perhaps Utah's most famous building is the Mormon Tabernacle on Temple Block, built between 1863 and 1867. The Old Tabernacle (1852) and the Bowery (1854) were not providing the seating space necessary for large conference gatherings, so a new tabernacle was built. William H. Folsom

and Henry Grow planned and superintended the construction of the building. Truman O. Angell designed the interior.

The large auditorium is elliptical in shape, 250 feet long, 150 feet wide, and 68 feet from floor to ceiling. It has a seating capacity of eight thousand. The self-supporting wooden roof rests on forty-four buttresses of red sandstone which stand ten to twelve feet apart around the circumference of the building. The wooden arches are ten feet in thickness and span 150 feet. The arches are of lattice stress construction, put together with wooden pins and strips of rawhide. Before the railroad came, nails and bolts and iron were in very short supply, so no nails or iron were used in the arches. The gallery was added in 1870. Construction cost is estimated at $300,000. When the Tabernacle was completed, the Bowery was torn down. The Old Tabernacle was left in service until 1877 when it was replaced by the present Assembly Hall, dedicated January 8, 1882.

The Mormon Tabernacle, Salt Lake City, under construction. Notice the arches of lattice stress construction resting on stone buttresses.

This 1869 photograph shows the Tabernacle shortly after completion.

The general conferences of the Mormon church have been held in the Tabernacle since October 1867. The auditorium is frequently used for public concerts and meetings of civic importance. Distinguished visitors including presidents of the United States have spoken there, and tourists to the City of the Saints often include a visit to the Tabernacle.

The renowned architect Frank Lloyd Wright described the Tabernacle as "one of the architectural masterpieces of the country and perhaps the world." The accoustical qualities of the building are remarkable.

Equally famous with the Tabernacle building itself is the *Tabernacle Organ*. Joseph H. Ridges, a carpenter who had worked in an organ factory in his native Australia, and who had brought a small pipe organ to Utah with him, drew the plans for and supervised the construction of the great organ. The best lumber for the large pipes, free from knots, and with little pitch or gum, was found in the white pine timber stands near Parowan and in Pine Valley, near Saint George. Ox

teams hauled the great timbers three hundred miles to Salt Lake. Glue was made by boiling hundreds of cattle and buffalo hides. A hundred men are said to have been employed constantly in the organ construction between January 1866 and the time it was dedicated in October 1867. When first put in operation it had 700 pipes. The organ was enlarged in 1885, 1900, and 1915, and rebuilt in 1945. Today there are 188 sets of pipes, totally 10,746 individual pipes.

The Salt Lake Theatre was an important institution in Salt Lake City. Opening in March 1862 it served as the entertainment center of Salt Lake City for sixty-six years. It staged great plays of the past and the best contemporary drama, most frequently produced and put on by amateurs, under the training of London theatrical professionals who had migrated to Utah. Occasionally the great actors and actresses of the day played seasons or short runs at the theater. After the coming of the railroad, many great artists came to Salt Lake City to play in the famous

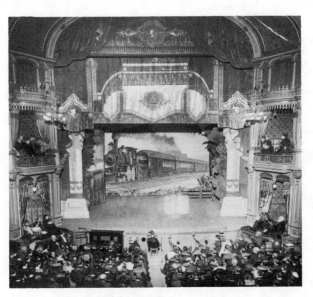

The Salt Lake Theatre, interior.

The Salt Lake Theatre was the center of theatrical and popular musical activities from 1862 to 1928.

theater. The theater orchestra of twenty members was first directed by Professor Charles J. Thomas from England. He was succeeded by George Careless, one of Utah's most notable musicians and composers. The first scenery was painted by George M. Ottinger, a gifted artist.

Music. Brass bands, choirs, individual singing, and playing musical instruments made up the major forms of musical expression in early Utah. It was not until the 1860s that persons trained in professional music came to Utah to influence musical developments. Much of this development centered around the Tabernacle organ and choir and the demands of the Salt Lake Theatre. The Tabernacle Choir, parent of so much musical development in Utah, began in the Bowery (built in 1849), continued in the Old Tabernacle, and carried on in the new Tabernacle, under the direction of Robert Sands (1867-69), George Careless (1869-80), Ebenezer Beesley (1880-90), and Evan Stephens (1890-1916).

In 1861 David O. Calder, Brigham

Young's chief clerk, interested the president in having classes for the study of choral music. As a result the *Deseret Musical Association* was organized and presented programs of "anthems, quartets, trios, duets, songs, readings, pianoforte, harmonion and concertina solos, with choice pieces of music by theatrical orchestra." In 1862 *Charles J. Thomas* came to Utah from the theaters of London and at once became the conductor of the Salt Lake Theatre orchestra. As conductor of the Tabernacle Choir, he raised the status of the choir from that of an ordinary country church choir to that of a metropolitan group, singing good anthem music. In 1864 he was called to Saint George where he continued to perform musical services.

One of the great Utah musicians was *John Tullidge* who came to Utah in 1863 from England where he had received an excellent music education and achieved a high place in English music circles. In Salt Lake City he taught voice and composition, and when his pupils were ready for recitals he

The Salt Lake Theatre Orchestra included some of Utah's leading musicians. This 1868 picture includes Josh Midgley, left, Ebenezer Beesley, David M. Evans, George Careless (leader), Mark Croxall, H. K. Whitney, and Orson Pratt, Jr.

toured the settlements giving concerts.

George Careless, also from England, became the most influential musician in early Utah. He had studied music at the Royal Academy of London and had played in orchestras at Exeter Hall, Drury Lane, and the Crystal Palace. He was appointed to conduct the orchestra of the Salt Lake Theatre. He began his demands for quality music by reducing the orchestra from twenty to seven players and induced Brigham Young to pay the players $3 a night for their services. He not only directed the orchestra but composed the dramatic music and the curtain music. He was conductor of the Tabernacle Choir from 1869 to 1880. He organized his own orchestra in 1879 and gave frequent concerts. The orchestra was a financial success, a tribute to

Salt Lake audiences in those days. A major event in music history in Utah was his June 1875 presentation of the oratorio the *Messiah* by G. F. Handel. Soloists and choral members were brought from all walks of life and from all denominations—it was truly a community production.

While Calder, Thomas, Tullidge, and Careless were the great leaders in the movement for better music in church and community, they were helped very much by three others. *Ebenezer Beesley* became conductor of the Tabernacle Choir (1880-90) and captain of the martial band of the Nauvoo Legion. He composed hymns, compiled books of hymns, conducted singing classes and glee clubs, and after 1890 did choir work in Tooele and Lehi. *Evan Stephens* was a con-

David O. Calder

John Tullidge

George Careless

Charles J. Thomas

Ebenezer Beesley

Evan Stephens

ductor and a composer who did professional study in Boston. Upon his return to Salt Lake City he organized an opera company, putting on favorite light operas. He was appointed conductor of the Tabernacle Choir and built the choir to three hundred voices and established it as a world famous choir.

He led the choir on tours, including the 1893 appearance at the World's Fair in Chicago, where the choir won second prize. *Joseph J. Daynes* was Utah's leading organist through these years. He was the first to play the new Tabernacle Organ in 1867 and served as organist from that time to 1900. He also composed hymns and instrumental music.

These early musicians set a standard and a tradition for excellence in choice of music and its professional performance. They greatly influenced music in the Mormon church which was carried into every settlement.

The visual arts. There was little encouragement to the artist in early Utah for several reasons. First, there were the all-consuming tasks of building homes, farms, and cities that took most of the people's energies. Second, there were not enough people of any wealth, during the first generation in Utah, to patronize the artists to make it possible for them to live by their art. The artists of early Utah found commissions to paint scenery in theaters and the decoration for some buildings. Later artists found employment in painting scenes in the temples. William Majors and William Ward, who came in the 1850s, stayed a very short time. In the 1860s artists came to Utah who were talented and produced some fine paintings. Among them were George M. Ottinger from Pennsylvania, Daniel Anthony Weggeland from Norway, and John Tullidge from England. Alfred Lambourne was the first artist of any note which the territory produced. John Hafen from Switzerland emerged in the 1880s as a significant artist. For the most part these artists painted portraits of local persons or landscapes of local scenes. Ottinger broke away from these themes and created scenes around ancient American subjects.

C. C. A. Christensen came to Utah with the handcarts of 1857, sketching en route. In

1869 he began to paint significant scenes in the history of the Mormon church, including his own experiences. He sewed his canvases together, rolled them on a long pole, placed them in his wagon, and went from village to village giving illustrated lectures on church history.

Charles R. Savage was Utah's major pioneer photographer. He and George M. Ottinger were partners from 1862 to 1872. Charles W. Carter was another early photographer of note. These men made a significant contribution to history by recording in photographs the images of persons and scenes in early Utah.

6. EDUCATIONAL INSTITUTIONS REFLECTED THE RELIGIOUS LIFE OF THE PEOPLE

Churches, schools, libraries, books, and newspapers are important to a society. Social and intellectual activities of life are among our richest experiences. The people of Utah sought a wide range of such experiences to improve their way of life.

Schools and libraries. Education was important to the settlers of Utah. Mormon schools in the wards and communities continued to operate through these later years of the century as they had before. Other private schools also continued to operate and to increase in enrollments. (These schools were mentioned in chapter 14, section 5.)

The *University of Deseret*, founded in 1850, existed almost in name only until 1868 when David O. Calder, one of the regents, opened a commercial college in the Council House. In 1869, however, Dr. John R. Park was appointed to reopen the university and establish courses for scientific and classical instruction as well as courses designed for the preparation of school teachers ("normal" courses they were called). With this appointment and the beginning of these classes the university began a remarkable growth. In 1869, 250 students were enrolled. The next

Main Building (University Hall), University of Deseret, 1884.

Brigham Young Academy, Provo, about 1890.

year there were 550 students, with fourteen faculty members. Advanced courses in mathematics, science, the arts, and a normal department were added. In the early 1870s a mining department was added. All this was done while meeting in the Council House. In 1881 a larger building was provided and the scope of the university enlarged. Dr. Park guided the university until 1892.

Two other institutions of importance were founded by the Latter-day Saints during these years: the Brigham Young Academy (now Brigham Young University) at Provo in 1875, and the Brigham Young College at Logan in 1877.

A report of 1888 shows there were 99 denominational schools in Utah, 6 of which were Mormon. In 1894, a similar report counts 113 denominational schools, of which 26 were Mormon, 33 Congregational, 33 Presbyterian, and 21 Methodist.

Libraries. Books were prized possessions in pioneer Utah. Only a few people had books in any number. Besides the collections of individuals and of the Mormon church, Utah's first library was the *Territorial Library*, authorized and paid for by Congress when the territorial government was established in 1850. Books were purchased in the East, and in February 1852 the library of three thousand volumes, located in the Council House, was opened to the public, with William C. Staines as librarian. Many subjects were represented: reference, literature, travel, philosophy, religion, and novels. Used by the territorial officials as a law library, it served also as a public library when the legislature was not in session. It lasted until 1890 when the books were turned over to the library at the University of Deseret.

The Mormons attempted several library programs. In 1864 the Seventies' Library or reading room was opened to the public in the Seventies' Council Hall in Salt Lake City. Many communities, following the seventies' example, started libraries as church libraries. Salt Lake Stake had an actively supported library from 1887 to 1897. It was supported by donations and benefit performances by the Salt Lake Theatre players. The University of Deseret, too, began a library program in the 1870s. Most of these failed due to lack of

313

financial support on a continuing basis. The non-Mormon Ladies' Library Association established a library, but when the ladies asked the city to finance the library and were refused, they boxed the books and that library closed. The Masonic Grand Lodge of Salt Lake City, however, established an important library. Its collections dealt mainly with the Mormons, Utah, and mining and chemistry. This library was used to the end of the century.

Newspapers and magazines were the chief reading materials and the means by which people could express themselves in writing. The *Deseret News* continued to be the newspaper of the territory, widely read in all the settlements. The *Salt Lake Tribune*, begun in 1871, grew out of the *Utah Magazine* and the *Mormon Tribune* as an opposition paper to the *Deseret News*. It was the strong minority voice. During the 1870s and 1880s most Utah communities had their own newspapers. Some communities had manuscript newspapers, written by members of the YMMIA and YLMIA, and circulated in single copies.

7. MORMON PRACTICES WERE OPPOSED BY SOME PEOPLE

Mormon ways dominated throughout most of the Utah territory. Mormon practices were particularly strong and unopposed in the rural villages. In the urban centers of Salt Lake City and Ogden, particularly, there was opposition to Mormon ways, chiefly from non-Mormons. Non-Mormon influences in the mining towns and at some railroad centers were as strong as Mormon influences were elsewhere.

No society stays the same forever. There were changes in the Mormon way of life as well as in the ways of the non-Mormons in Utah.

A *reform movement* begins with the

Long Sounds.			Letter.	Name.	Sound.
Letter.	Name.	Sound.	ꓶ		p
ϑ	e	as in eat.	Ꞝ		b
Ɛ	a	" ate.	ꓯ		t
ϑ	ah	" art.	Ꞓ		d
Ꝋ	aw	" aught.	C		che as in *cheese*.
O	o	" oat.	Ꝿ		g
Ꝍ	oo	" ooze.	Ꝋ		k
Short Sounds of the above.			Ꝍ		ga...as in...*gate*.
ꓲ		as in it.	P		f
ꓩ		" et.	Ꞓ		v
Ꝫ		" at.	L		eth..as in .*th*igh.
ꙍ		" ot.	Y		the " *th*y
Ꞁ		" ut.	Ꝫ		s
ꝗ		" book.	6		z
Double Sounds.			Ꝺ		esh..as in..fle*sh*.
Ꝭ	i	as in ice.	S		zhe " vi*si*on.
ϑ	ow	" owl.	Ꝓ		ur " b*ur*n.
Ꝩ	ye		Ꝇ		l
Ꞷ	woo		ꝏ		m
Ꝥ	h		Ꞃ		n
			Ꞑ		eng.as in.le*ng*th.

Ꞷꙍ ꝩꙍꝫ ϑ ꝩꝯꙫ ꙑꝩꙍ ꝩꞷꞃꙑ ꝏϑ.   Ꝺϑ ꝯꝯ ϑ ꝋꞷꝫꝯꙑ ꝏϑ, ꙑꝩꙍ ꙍꞃꝯ ꞃꙑꙑ ꙍꝯꙫ ꝩꞷꙑꙑ ꝏꙍ ꙫꝯꝯꙫ ꝩꝯꝯ.   Ꝺϑ ꝩꙫꝯ ϑ ꙍꝯꙍꙑ ꙫꙍꙍꝏ. Ꙓꝯꝩ ϑ ꝩꞷꙑꙑ ꝓꙍꙈ.   ꝺꞁ ꝩꙍꝯꙍꝯ ꙫϑꙍ Y ꙫϑꙍ ꙫꙫ ꙍꙈ.   Y ꙫϑ ꙫꙍꝯꙍ ꞁꙈ ꙫꝯꝯꙍ.   Ꞷꙍ ꝯꝯꝯꙑꞜ ꙫꙍꝯ ꙫϑꙍ ꙫꙫϑ ꙍꝩꞁꙑꙈ.

The Deseret Alphabet, created by Orson Pratt, Parley P. Pratt, George Watt, and others, was an attempt by early Mormons "to simplify the reading of English by children and foreigners" by using a new alphabet of phonetic symbols. Using the alphabet (above), you can read a page from a textbook printed in Deseret in 1868.

desire of some people to change ways of the society in which they live. Religion and religious denominations are almost always founded as reform movements. Much of Utah history tells of attempts on the part of religious leaders to change the ways of life of

William S. Godbe was associated with other Mormons in a movement to cooperate with the non-Mormon world.

their people. Sometimes reform movements come from within an organization, and sometimes they come from outside.

During the 1860s the Mormon church encouraged retrenchment and self-sufficiency through the formation of the Mutual Improvement Associations and the activities of the Relief Society. The United Order movement sought a fundamental reform of Mormon society. The cooperative movement (ZCMIs) began as a means of protecting Mormon society from threats which came with the railroad. However desirable the leaders thought these measures were, there were many Mormons who did not accept these policies and practices, and there were some who opposed them outright. One such group was called the Godbeites.

The Godbeite Movement was begun in 1868 by a group of prominent Mormons including William S. Godbe, E. L. T. Harrison, Eli B. Kelsey, Edward W. Tullidge, Henry W. Lawrence, T. B. H. Stenhouse, and W. H. Shearman. These men believed Utah should keep up with the developments of the rest of the world and have modern improvements. They wanted cooperation between Mormons and non-Mormons. They opposed Brigham Young's anti-mining policy, the system of cooperative stores, and the boycott against non-Mormon merchants. Godbe, although a polygamist himself, believed that polygamy would disappear from Mormon society if opposition to it ceased. He believed in education and equal rights for women. He believed in maintaining his plural family responsibilities and supported his wives and families throughout his life.

The Godbeites expressed their views in their publication the *Utah Magazine* (beginning January 1868), which was succeeded by a newspaper the *Mormon Tribune* (beginning January 1, 1870). Its name was soon changed to the *Salt Lake Tribune*. The newspaper was soon bought by anti-Mormons and for decades carried on the crusade against the Mormons and their way of life. The Godbeite movement was short lived, but the ideas expressed by its leaders took hold and some of them won out at last.

While unity was the Mormon ideal, and was generally achieved, there were those both in the church and out who disagreed with some policies and practices. There was room for initiative, and many programs begun by individuals were adopted later by the church. There was some room for differences of opinion, but Mormons did not question church authority without fear of being challenged. The church, as a voluntary body of like-minded believers, sometimes excommunicated those who differed excessively with generally accepted teachings and practices. (Most of the Godbeite leaders were excommunicated.) Opposition from within the church combined with opposition from without to change some of the old ways of life and lay the basis for twentieth-century Utah.

Delegates to the constitutional convention, Salt Lake City, 1895. These men wrote Utah's present constitution. From all parts of the territory, all walks of life, Mormon and non-Mormon, these men took important steps to end the conflict between Mormons and non-Mormons and lay the foundations for peace in Utah.

316

UTAH'S STRUGGLE FOR STATEHOOD

In this chapter is told the story of the long struggle for Utah statehood. From the very beginning of Utah's history there were conflicts between the Mormon community and the other people who came here. The Mormon way of life was different. The differences led to conflict with other Americans who came here to live. It must be kept in mind that this story of conflict is about only a few people, chiefly the leaders in the Mormon community and the leading figures in the non-Mormon community. The vast majority of people in Utah lived quite peacefully, side by side, showing many signs of cooperation, mutual assistance, respect, and tolerance. We should also keep in mind that there are many ways of looking at the things people do. The Mormon people had very good reasons for their way of life, and the non-Mormons the same. These people had honest differences of opinion. We should attempt to understand the various issues they disagreed about and the way each group thought about them.

This was an age when reform movements were common in the United States. National reform movements picked up the "Mormon question" as a major issue. The "Utah situation" became a national issue, and was finally solved on the terms of the people of the United States, not those of the Mormons.

This is the story of how the majority group in Utah, the Mormons, were prohibited from keeping the society they had set up. It shows how a small group in Utah, combined with the majority of the people of the United States, were able to make these remarkable changes. In the end, the Mormons were forced to make the major features of their way of life conform to the general way of life of the American people.

During this period there was much misunderstanding, prejudice and intolerance on both sides. There was a great need then as there is today for tolerance and understanding of different ways of life and the reasons for them.

In many ways, Utah's struggle for statehood is the culmination of Utah's history in the nineteenth century. The achievement of statehood was the most important event in Utah's history after permanent settlement in 1847. Statehood meant that the people of Utah could choose their own leaders, so it was worth fighting for, and worth the sacrifices made for it.

IN THIS CHAPTER WE WILL LEARN

1. The people of Utah wanted statehood for the advantages of self-government.

2. Many issues were contested which kept Utah from becoming a state.

3. A crusade was waged against the Mormons and their peculiar institutions.

4. When the Mormon church gave up its peculiar institutions, Utah gained statehood.

18

317

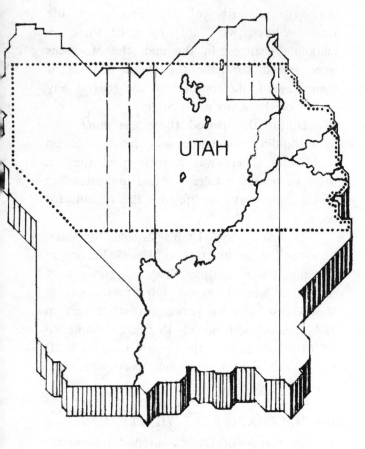

STATE OF DESERET

.... **TERRITORY OF UTAH**

— — **REDUCTIONS**

1. THE PEOPLE OF UTAH WANTED STATEHOOD FOR THE ADVANTAGES OF SELF-GOVERNMENT

Two forms of government were provided by the United States for its newly occupied lands. *Territorial government* was designed for newly occupied lands, where the people were few in number, and the major executive and judicial officials were appointed by the president of the United States. Under *state government*, the people in a region devised their own constitution (in harmony with the Constitution of the United States) and elected their own executive, judicial, and legislative officers. Territorial government might be thought of as "foreign rule" while state government was "home rule." Territorial government was designed to help a people become self-governing under the direction of leaders appointed in Washington.

Did the Mormon people need instruction in self-government? They had built cities in the East. They had governed themselves in Nauvoo. They had organized one of the most successful mass migrations in history, through self-government. In Utah, they had formed the government of the State of Deseret and ruled themselves under its constitution. They believed they were capable of ruling themselves. Besides, they believed the federal officials sent to Utah were not good leaders, and that they were perhaps the poorest examples that could be sent from Washington.

Repeatedly the people of Utah petitioned Congress for admission into the Union as a state equal with the other states of the Union. Constitutional conventions met on six different occasions: in 1849, 1856, 1862,

1872, 1882, and 1887. Each time Congress ignored the petition.

The people of Utah could not understand why they should not be admitted. They had population enough, experience, leaders, and they were loyal to the United States. Congress may have been willing to grant statehood in the early 1850s, but stories coming out of Utah about the Mormons tended to make Congress hesitant and suspicious. Federal officers in Utah, travelers, visitors, and residents of Utah kept the public informed about the "Mormon problem" in Utah. Much that was said was true; much was false. But misunderstandings and intolerance also played a role.

2. MANY ISSUES WERE CONTESTED WHICH KEPT UTAH FROM BECOMING A STATE

Conflict centered chiefly around the desire of the Mormons for unity in all they did. This ideal of unity was expressed in all aspects of pioneer life at one time or another—in government and economic activities especially. Mormons suppressed individual desires and conveniences for the common goal. On the other hand, non-Mormons stood for individualism, competition, and diversity as the best expression of American life—political diversity, economic competition, and individualism in all aspects of life.

Politics. The Mormons believed in majority rule, that the will of the majority should prevail. In the first years after settlement elective offices were filled with local people, Mormons; no one else was around. This was self-government. But when others came, there was no political party through which they could get into political office.

There were no political parties in Utah in the modern sense until 1870. Church leaders selected possible officers whose names

Among the leading territorial officials, about 1885, were these men, left to right: Orlando W. Powers, associate justice; Elwin A. Ireland, United States marshal; Eli H. Murray, governor; Charles S. Zane, chief justice; W. H. Dickson, United States attorney; and Jacob S. Boreman, associate justice.
These men took leading roles in the anti-Mormon crusade of the 1880s.

were put on a ballot and the people voted for them; no opposition candidates were listed. Elections were simply votes for the officers selected. When the railroad came, however, one of the first things the new arrivals did was to organize a political party. The *Liberal party* was formed at Corinne and Salt Lake City in February 1870. The non-Mormons of Utah and Mormons who differed from their leaders in political affairs, such as the Godbeites, joined it. Federal officers, railroad workers, miners, cattlemen, merchants, bankers, and businessmen were among those represented. They opposed what they considered to be church domination of the political life of the community. In response, the Mormons formed their own *People's party* the same month in Salt Lake City. Church leaders continued to name candidates.

The Council of the territorial legislature, 1888. These men represented the Mormon element in the territorial government, often in opposition to the members of the executive and judicial branches who were appointed and usually non-Mormon.

The *county courts* were a source of conflict. In each county there was a probate judge, who with three selectmen made up the county court or officers for county government. In 1852 the territorial legislature gave the probate judges "power to exercise original jurisdiction" in civil and criminal cases. The legislature had power to do this, and it was done because the federal judges had skipped out, leaving the territory without judges. When federal judges returned, however, they found they had little to do, handling only, or mainly, cases in which the United States was a party. Civil and criminal cases went first before probate judges. The Mormons took their cases before their bishops, though some cases between Mormons were heard in probate courts. Non-Mormons believed that they did not get justice in a "Mormon" court.

The territorial *militia*, made up of Mormon settlers, commanded by Mormons, was feared by some to be a "military arm" of the church. Actually the Nauvoo Legion, or territorial militia, fought against the Indians in the Black Hawk War, without help from federal troops. *The militia was needed here as in any other territory or state.*

Economics and business. The Mormon settlers insisted on the right to manage their own economic affairs. They built homes, schools, churches, tabernacles, temples, farms, and businesses of all types. This was done through central planning and direction, by many dedicated persons working together. Natural resources were reserved for the use of all the people. No person was to have the chance to build a monopoly. The cooperative movement and the United Orders were extensions of the spirit of cooperation.

Non-Mormons believed this central management of the economy benefited only the Mormons, that the church tried to obtain a monopoly of land and other natural resources. They believed that the natural resources were freely open to all people, and that there should be open competition for them. They believed the American way of life depended on individualism, not cooperative communitarian practices. The Mormons tried to be self-sufficient and economically independent; the non-Mormons believed in economic interdependence.

Education. Mormon schools were designed to meet the needs of the Mormon goal of the Kingdom of God, hence the schools, while teaching the three Rs, concentrated on religious education for the Mormon faith. The Protestants who came to Utah believed that one way to solve the "Mormon problem" was to give a broad education to the children, and they set up many excellent schools which probably gave the best education available in Utah. Mormon leaders, reared in the United States in the early decades of the century before there were free public schools, believed that education was like other commodities.

Those who received the goods should pay for them, hence the idea of free public schools was slow coming to Utah. The non-Mormons, coming to Utah when these ideas were taking hold in the nation, wanted free, public, tax-supported schools in Utah.

Immigration. The Mormons, in the American tradition, believed America to be a land of promise, that her strength lay in the immigrants, that America was a land of freedom to all people, that immigration should be encouraged. The non-Mormon felt that immigration of Mormons should stop. He found the continuing arrival of Mormon Europeans a threat to his chance for jobs and land.

Polygamy. The fundamental areas of conflict were in political and economic practices, but the sensational issue was the Mormon practice of plural marriage. The Mormons believed it to be a religious duty and obligation which they defended from the Bible. The non-Mormon view was that American life and morality was based on the family of a husband having but one wife, that polygamy was destructive of the family. The Mormons defended their practice on the grounds that it was a religious practice and the Constitution of the United States guaranteed religious freedom.

3. A CRUSADE WAS WAGED AGAINST THE MORMONS AND THEIR PECULIAR INSTITUTIONS

The Mormons may have been the majority in Utah, but they were a minority group in the United States. The non-Mormons in Utah wanted equal opportunity to make a living here and they sought a voice in government. They felt restricted and so set their task to change features of the Mormon way of life so as to guarantee privileges for themselves. The Mormon system, they contended, was a "menace," a threat to the American

way of life. So long as this group was loud in denouncing the Mormon society in Utah, statehood would not be considered. In time, it became evident that *statehood would be withheld from Utah until the people of Utah had a society—especially a political, economic, and family life—that conformed to the general pattern of American life.*

Congress held supreme power in the territories, so it was to the advantage of the crusaders to keep Utah a territory. At the same time appeal was made to Congress to enact legislation aimed at the destruction of the peculiar institutions of the Mormons. Once laws were enacted, violators of the law would be prosecuted through the courts.

Congress passed a law against the Mormon practice of polygamy (*Anti-bigamy Act,* 1862) when the Republican party filled its campaign promise to abolish slavery and polygamy. However, there was little attempt to put this law into effect. It was not until the anti-Mormon crusade of the 1870s stirred up national feelings that more concern was given to Utah.

Through the influence of Judge James B. McKean, who came to Utah in 1871, Con-

James B. McKean, chief justice of the Utah territorial court, helped launch the anti-Mormon crusade by prosecuting polygamists in court for violation of the federal law.

George Reynolds, a polygamist, was tried in the courts as a test of the constitutionality of the Poland Act and found guilty, the law being upheld.

The Utah Commission, set up by the Edmunds Act of 1882, supervised elections in Utah until statehood.

Rudger Clawson, who had narrowly escaped death at the hands of a mob in the Southern States while on a mission there, was tried for violation of the polygamy provisions of the Edmunds Act and found guilty. His case strengthened the anti-Mormon crusade in Utah.

gress passed the *Poland Act* of 1874 which changed the court system so that polygamists were no longer tried by Mormon judges and juries. George Reynolds, a polygamist, appealed to the Supreme Court to see if the law was constitutional. The law was upheld, and Reynolds was imprisoned. Other legal battles followed. George Q. Cannon, a member of the presidency of the church, was denied his seat in Congress as a delegate from Utah because he was a polygamist.

In 1882 Congress passed the *Edmunds Act*, setting up the Utah Commission to supervise elections in Utah. The commission required voters to swear that they were not polygamists, refusing to allow polygamists to vote. Because the Mormons doubted that the Edmunds Act was constitutional, another test case was sent to the Supreme Court. This time Rudger Clawson stood trial to test the law. His conviction was upheld, and he went to prison followed by many other Utahns. Fines of from $500 to $800 were paid, and prison sentences up to five years were served.

Between 1862 and 1882, only ten arrests

Utah territorial penitentiary, Salt Lake City. Here convicted polygamists served their sentences.

were made for polygamy. After 1883 arrests became common. In 1885 President John Taylor delivered his last public address, spending the rest of his life in hiding, or "on the underground," as it was called. He died in exile, July 25, 1887, at Kaysville. Other church leaders went on foreign missions or to the homes of trusted friends. Church colonizing in Canada and Mexico began, and many polygamists went to these countries. Those at home lived away from their families much of the time. Even so, by 1880 over a thousand men had been arrested and sent to prison. If polygamists were caught by U.S. marshals, they went to court, and if convicted, paid the fine and went to prison.

Only one Mormon polygamist was killed by a marshal. Edward M. Dalton of Parowan was indicted on the charge of polygamy but did not attend his trial. Instead, he went to Arizona for a visit. On his return he was shot by Deputy Marshal William Thompson, Jr., who let Dalton ride past him, then called "Halt!" and at the same time fired, shooting Dalton in the back. Deputy Thompson was tried for murder but acquitted.

While these raids and prosecutions were

taking place, still another law was passed. This was the *Edmunds-Tucker Act* of 1887, a law which had the power to destroy the Mormon church as an effective institution. It dissolved the corporation of the Church of Jesus Christ of Latter-day Saints, taking over all of its property. The Perpetual Emigrating Fund Company was dissolved. The right of Utah women to vote was abolished. All polygamists were refused the right to vote. Schools were placed under the rule of a new commissioner. The territorial militia law was annulled. Judges of probate courts were to be appointed by the president of the United States.

Financially the church was in trouble. Its buildings had to be rented from the government for several hundred dollars per month. Its herds of sheep and cattle, coal mines, shares of stock in the Deseret News Company, Deseret Telegraph Company, Salt Lake Dramatic Association, Salt Lake Gas Company, Salt Lake Street Railroad Company, Salt Lake Theatre, and Provo Woolen Mills were taken. With the church leaders in jail, before the courts, or under bond, large sums of money were going for legal fees and fines.

George Q. Cannon is shown with other Mormons convicted of polygamy serving their terms in the penitentiary. Cannon, a leading Mormon during the years of the crusade, was a delegate to Congress during the 1870s. After becoming a member of the Mormon First Presidency, he won the election of 1880 but was denied his seat after Congress passed the Edmunds Act of 1882.

In time the Mormon church was forced to borrow money from Salt Lake banks to pay the rent for use of its own properties.

At the same time Utah Mormons were struggling with the heavy burdens the Edmunds-Tucker Act placed on them, Idaho enacted a law taking the right to vote away from all Mormons in that state. The Utah Commission, in 1890, recommended this same law for Utah. That same year the Supreme Court ruled that the Edmunds-Tucker Act was constitutional.

4. WHEN THE MORMON CHURCH GAVE UP ITS PECULIAR INSTITUTIONS, UTAH GAINED STATEHOOD

By the summer of 1890 the world seemed to be falling in on the Mormon people. They no longer had any role in the administration of justice in the territorial courts. They no longer had any supervision of the territorial militia. The church had lost many of its properties and was relinquishing the role it had in developing the economy of Utah. And now, not only the polygamists but *all Mormons* were going to be deprived of civil rights. When the Supreme Court upheld the Edmunds-Tucker Act and the Idaho Test-Oath Law, the church was threatened with extinction or being reduced to a small, insignificant sect, rather than fulfilling its desire to become a world church with a universal

Wilford Woodruff, president of the Mormon church, 1889-98.

message. It was either survival or extinction.

On September 24, 1890, President Wilford Woodruff held a special meeting of the apostles, and received their approval to issue the *Manifesto*. This official declaration stated that the church was no longer teaching polygamy, or plural marriage, or permitting persons to enter into the practice, and that the president's "advice to the Latter-day Saints is to refrain from contracting any marriage forbidden by the law of the land." The next day the *Deseret News* carried the Manifesto, and at the October conference, President Woodruff read it, and nearly every hand went up to sustain the president in his decision.

Most anti-polygamy crusaders were not sure the Mormons were sincere; they would "wait and see." But the chief justice of the Utah Supreme Court, the man who had been most energetic in prosecuting polygamy cases in his court, accepted the Manifesto in good faith; to him the Mormons were "honest and sincere." Most Mormons took the president at his word, and accepted the Manifesto as a revelation; however, there were a few Mormons who secretly continued the practice of contracting additional marriages and this gave great trouble to the church and Utah.

Polygamy had been a sensational surface issue. The fundamental issues were economic practices and political control. The church's economic role was being destroyed by the confiscations of its property. Adjustments next came in the area of politics. Statehood would wait until there were national political parties in Utah instead of the lopsided local parties that divided Mormon against non-Mormon.

The coming of national political parties to Utah. One of the most important steps Utah had to take before attaining statehood was to form a two-party system which would ensure fairly close elections. It was to be similar to that of the nation—Republican and Democratic parties. Up until this time Utah had had some experience with more than one party. However, as a rule the Mormons voted for the candidates their leaders selected to run on the People's party slate. The non-Mormon party candidates could not win elections because they represented only about 10 percent of the population.

During the struggle for statehood the Liberal party won more and more power because Mormons were being disfranchised. The party was getting a stranglehold on Utah's economy and government. The Liberal party did not wish to give up these advantages in exchange for statehood, when Liberals would again become a minority political power and would no longer receive benefits from the

Utah economy. As a result some of these people fought statehood. But others with a more tolerant outlook wanted statehood so the bitter struggle would end. They used their influence to help convince the president and the territorial officials that Utah was preparing to become a state.

Although Utah had some Democratic and Republican organizations prior to the 1890s, they were used only to elect delegates to the national conventions of each party. In the spring of 1891, action was taken to establish the two major national political parties in Utah. The People's party was dissolved and Republican and Democratic clubs were organized in the communities.

Left to themselves, the Mormon people, for the most part, would have voted Democratic. To bring a near balance of strength between the two major political parties, the Latter-day Saints were instructed to participate actively in both parties. In order to make this balance, however, many Mormons were called by the church leaders to be Republicans, until there was a balance.

Between 1891 and 1895 the steps were taken for Utah to become a state. Most Mormons and most non-Mormons were in favor of taking these steps, but there were some on both sides who were fearful of the future, and they opposed the steps.

The first election to take place after Democratic and Republican clubs had been formed was in August 1891 to elect representatives to the territorial legislature. The Democrats polled 14,369 votes, the Republicans 6,397, and the Liberals 7,411. Clearly a more equal political system was emerging.

On December 19, 1891, the First Presidency of the church petitioned the government for amnesty for the polygamists. The petition was endorsed by Governor Arthur L. Thomas and Chief Justice Charles S. Zane.

Arthur L. Thomas was governor of the territory at the time of greatest adjustment toward statehood.

On September 15, 1892, the Utah Commission added its endorsement to the petition, and on January 4, 1893, President Harrison issued a proclamation of amnesty to the polygamists for past offenses. On July 18, the Utah Commission issued a resolution advising that polygamists be allowed to vote.

In the meantime, the 1892 election for delegate to Congress clearly showed that a two-party system existed in Utah, despite the continued power of the rebellious, backward-looking Liberal party. The Democratic candidate, Joseph L. Rawlins, won over Frank J. Cannon, the Republican candidate. It appeared to many that Cannon was a "church candidate," for he was the son of George Q. Cannon, a member of the First Presidency, and his opponent was considered an agnostic. If true, this would show that the church candidate did not win, even if church influence had been used in his behalf. The Liberals polled well in 1892, and took control of most of the political offices in Salt Lake County.

The following year, however, in an election for the legislature, the Liberals polled poorly and lost control of Salt Lake offices. The *Salt Lake Tribune* counseled the party to disband, and on December 18, 1893, the Liberal party officially disbanded.

Following the presidential pardon and the Utah Commission's recommendation that polygamists be allowed to vote, Delegate Joseph L. Rawlins presented to the Congress, September 6, 1893, a bill recommending statehood for Utah. The bill passed the House, December 13, without opposition, and then passed the Senate. The following July 18, 1894, President Grover Cleveland signed the Enabling Act, which authorized the people of Utah to elect delegates to a Constitutional Convention, write a constitution, elect officers, and apply for admission into the Union. For the first time in Utah's history, Utah was *invited* to join the Union. On September 27, President Cleveland issued a proclamation granting pardon and restoring the civil rights to all who had been deprived of them by the anti-polygamy laws.

Through these years there was still difficulty over church properties in the hands of the government. The Supreme Court had decided (January 18, 1892) the properties were to be used for the benefit of the public schools just coming into existence. The church objected on the grounds that this would be church support of the state, and recommended that the properties, if not returned to the church, go to the poor or to build churches. Congress then passed a law in conformity with the wishes of the church. On January 10, 1894, the First Presidency received back the personal properties it had surrendered. The losses were great; the church was bankrupt. It was not until 1896, after statehood came, that real estate properties were returned.

The November 1894 election was the

John Henry Smith, Mormon apostle, helped bridge the gulf between Mormons and non-Mormons. He was president of the constitutional convention.

first Utah election at which only national parties were in the field with candidates. The citizens elected Republican Frank J. Cannon delegate to Congress, and elected delegates to a Constitutional Convention. The Republicans showed strength by winning a majority of the delegates.

The Constitutional Convention was held in Salt Lake City between March 4 and May 18, 1895. During those sixty-six days, the delegates wrote Utah's constitution. According to the requirements of Congress, they wrote into the constitution provisions which clearly forbade the practice of polygamy and called for the separation of church and state.

That November 5, the people voted for or against ratification of the proposed constitution, and for a choice of officers of state government called for in the constitution. It was a Republican victory. The people elected as governor Heber M. Wells, son of pioneer leader Daniel H. Wells. As chief justice of the Utah Supreme Court, they elected Charles S. Zane. Zane had formerly been a leader in the judicial crusade against polygamists, but he had put full faith and confidence in the integrity of the Mormon leaders when the

Manifesto was issued. The people were grateful for his confidence.

The Utah Commission examined the election returns, as was its duty, and then presented the results to Congress and the president, whereupon President Grover Cleveland, on Saturday, January 4, 1896, issued the proclamation that Utah was admitted to the Union as the forty-fifth state. Two days later, January 6, 1896, the newly elected officers of the State of Utah were inaugurated, and Utah was a full-fledged part of the Union.

Significances. Utah's struggle for statehood and the coming of statehood meant many things to the people of Utah. *Peace came.* Former enemies turned to the ways of peace for the sake of progress and the future.

For the Mormons it meant giving up polygamy, economic cooperation on the scale earlier practiced, political unity, and church influence in politics. It meant survival as a church, and with that survival an opportunity to tie its relations to the world in order to fulfill its original and more fundamental purpose of carrying its message to the world. It meant greatly reducing Mormon economic and social experimentation, avoiding the "peculiarities" typical of the pioneer period. The church came to hold a conservative position in politics and economics. The Mormon people gained the privilege of being tolerated and heard, as they had never been before.

For the non-Mormons, the coming of statehood meant giving up rule by the minority (themselves) for majority rule (the Mormons had the most votes), but with the gentleman's assurance and understanding that there would be friendly agreements, that Mormon and non-Mormon would participate side by side in political affairs, without regard to religion.

Although for the people of Utah it meant increased taxes, this was far out-weighed by the advantages of statehood and the new services that would be received. The federal government now gave over seven million acres of land to the state for the benefit of its new school system. With a new school system possible, the people could develop as fine a system as existed in the nation.

Utah became one with the nation, with firm economic, political and social ties. Hereafter the future of Utah would be more closely tied with that of the nation. The people would share in the benefits and responsibilities of American citizenship as never before.

The people of Utah gained self-government. They would now have state officers of their own choosing, courts with judges of their own choosing. They would now have a voice in choosing the president of the United States and the privilege of sending two United States senators and one representative to the national capital to represent the people and interests of Utah with voting power and political influence.

Business confidence would come. Capital and population would be drawn to Utah. Businessmen elsewhere would now want to invest money and talent to develop Utah's many natural resources, all on a scale never possible under territorial rule or the trying conditions of the crusade.

That generation taught us there is no future in extinction, but in survival there are all sorts of possibilities of dealing with the problems of a changing world, that in a changing world, one must change too in order to live, and move, and have influence. They taught us courage to face the future optimistically and to take steps to ensure a greater future for us and our posterity. They were giants who were big enough to change some of their ways so that greater good might come to all.

328

UNIT SIX
UTAH IN THE PROGRESSIVE ERA
1896-1918

The coming of statehood to Utah was one of the most decisive events in Utah's history. It marked the end of one era and the beginning of another. The old ways of life were passing and new ways of life were taking their place.

History makes no leaps, and all ages are transitional. There was a gradual preparation for the coming of the new and a slow passing of the old. The new ways of life did not come without a struggle. Everyone did not accept the new ways at once. It took time.

The peculiar institution of plural marriage was officially ended in 1890, but it died slowly. The one-party system was replaced by the two-party system, but the charges against Mormon church influence in politics lasted for years. Free, tax-supported public schools came to Utah, but the Mormon and non-Mormon church schools continued in operation. And so it was in other fields. In some ways Utah and her new ways of life were not fully developed and accepted by the people of the nation until the time of World War I, 1917-18.

The change in government was sudden and most important. Home rule came to Utah. The changes in economic life were also sudden. The old forms of cooperation were replaced by a typical American individualistic and competitive way of doing business. Utah began to fit into the patterns of American political and economic life.

In the process of joining the Union as a state, Utah found that she received much from her new position, and in turn she was able to give much to the nation.

The history of Utah and the history of the United States have always run side by side. Utah history cannot properly be considered separately from that of the United States. During the territorial period, Utah tried to be different, and she was different in many ways. However, in those days Utah was greatly influenced by developments in the nation at large. During her life as a state, Utah became less unique and more like the other states. Increasingly the Utah experience in the twentieth century becomes more and more closely identified with that of the nation and the world.

GOVERNMENT UNDER STATEHOOD

The Great Seal of the State of Utah was adopted by the first state legislature, April 3, 1896.

Extravagant use of red, white, and blue bunting marked some store front decorations.

19

When Utah became a state, full political authority rested with the people. The people of the state had power to create the government they chose, on all levels, so long as it was representative in form; that is, it must be democratic, with departments and agencies representing the will of the people. State government was put into operation early in 1896, and Utah's people have lived under that constitution since then.

It is important to know the form of government the constitution of the state of Utah set up and how that government functions in serving Utah citizens. It is important also to know the relationships between the state of Utah and the federal government.

IN THIS CHAPTER WE WILL LEARN

1. Utah state government was established in 1896.

2. Utah's constitution furthered the ideals of American democracy in Utah.

3. The state legislature is the lawmaking body in Utah's government.

4. The governor is charged with enforcing state law and administering state government.

5. A system of courts operates in Utah bringing justice to the people.

6. City and county government is created by the state to serve local needs.

7. A close relationship exists between state and federal government.

Heber M. Wells was inaugurated Utah's first
state governor on January 6, 1896.
He served until January 1905.

1. UTAH STATE GOVERNMENT WAS ESTABLISHED IN 1896

On January 4, 1896, in his White House office, President Grover Cleveland signed the proclamation admitting Utah to the Union. Immediately after the signing, Utah officials in Washington—Delegate Frank J. Cannon, newly elected Representative C. E. Allen, Governor Caleb W. West, and Junius F. Wells, were shown the proclamation amid rounds of congratulations. In the proclamation President Cleveland declared that "the terms and conditions prescribed by the Congress in the United States to entitle the STATE OF UTAH to admission into the Union have been duly complied with, and that the creation of said State and its admission into the Union on an equal footing with the original States is now accomplished." The president's secretary telegraphed the news of the proclamation to Salt Lake City.

Utah's national guard battery marched to Capitol Hill and fired a twenty-one gun salute.

The feeling in Washington was one of "gratification that Utah is now at last a member on equal terms with other sister States and that the struggle and contest of long years past is over."

In Salt Lake City, receipt of the president's telegram at the Western Union office at 9:15 a.m. Utah time was the signal for widespread celebration. The excitement began when the Western Union manager, with the permission of the police, fired two shots into the air. Hundreds of people gathered to hear the oft-repeated cry, "Statehood has been proclaimed." Business was suspended. Crowds swarmed the streets, shouting, laughing, and shaking hands all around, to the accompaniment of bells ringing and whistles blowing. Several companies tied down the whistle strings to their steam-powered whistles. Near bedlam was reached when others fired giant firecrackers. The battery of the Utah National Guard marched to Capitol Hill and fired a twenty-one-gun salute. The news soon spread throughout the city and state, setting off statewide celebrations.

Monday, January 6, was *inauguration day*. The ceremonies took place in the Tabernacle, which was decorated for the occasion with draped American flags. The entire space at the west end, between the galleries, was decorated with a flag, 158 feet by 75 feet. The forty-fifth star was illuminated. "High up between the organ pipes, above the dates 1847 and 1896, hovered with outspread wings an effigy of the American eagle ...." Below was *UTAH* in electric lights. The building was filled to capacity; many stood outside. On the stand were leading citizens, officers of the territorial government, military officers from Fort Douglas, and the newly elected state officers. Territorial Secretary C. C. Richards conducted the exercises which began at 12:30 noon. The United States Sixteenth Infantry

Band, the "equally excellent" Denhalter Band, and the Tabernacle Choir furnished music. President Wilford Woodruff was present. George Q. Cannon offered the invocation. A chorus of a thousand children, "all waving flags and keeping time to the conductor's baton," sang "the Star-Spangled Banner." Joseph L. Rawlins read the proclamation. Governor Heber M. Wells gave his inaugural address. He congratulated the citizens, the state, and the Union on Utah's admission as the forty-fifth state. He pointed to the healing of old wounds and the great prospects for the state in the future. The choir sang "America," and the Reverend Thomas C. Iliff of the Methodist Church offered prayer. The band played "Hail Columbia" as the throng poured out of the Tabernacle into the winter sunshine.

At 3 p.m., by request of the governor, the legislature convened at the City and County Building to determine the time of the first regular session. Accordingly, the first session of the legislature convened Wednesday, January 8, when Governor Wells gave a com-

Inaugural ceremonies were held in the Tabernacle which was decorated specially for the occasion.

Throngs crowded the streets of Salt Lake City in celebration of the coming of statehood.

The Sego Lily is Utah's state flower. A small delicate flower, the Sego Lily grew profusely in Utah in early times. The Indians considered the bulbs a delicacy and taught the pioneers to use them in times of food scarcity.

prehensive message to the legislators on every aspect of state government and the various agencies and departments then in existence. Utah had begun her statehood experience.

Before narrating the history of Utah's political experiences, it is important to know something about the state's constitution. Much of this chapter will be devoted to a study of the Utah state constitution and the principles of government expressed in it.

2. UTAH'S CONSTITUTION FURTHERED THE IDEALS OF AMERICAN DEMOCRACY IN UTAH

When Utah was admitted as the forty-fifth state in the Union, she came into the mainstream of American political life and enjoyed more fully the ideals of American democracy.

The American system of government is the creation of the people. The *people* are the ultimate authority in the state. They created the government, and they elect the officers of their government. It is a representative democracy, a government by the elected representatives of the people who answer to the

"Utah, We Love Thee" was adopted by the legislature as the state song, February 10, 1917.

Utah, We Love Thee.

(State Song of Utah, Adopted by the Legislature, February 10, 1917.)
Words and Music by EVAN STEPHENS.

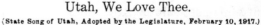

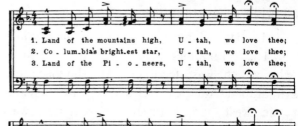

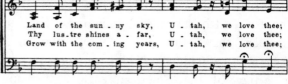

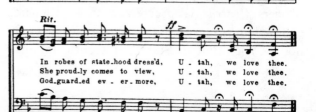

334

people. It is a government of the majority with protection of the minority.

The *dignity and worth of every human being* is a most fundamental concept of our democracy. Every person counts for something, everyone can contribute something of worth to the community. A democracy provides opportunities for every person to fulfill himself to the utmost of his capabilities and, in turn, accept his responsibility as a citizen of both the state and the nation.

Government exists for the benefit of the people. Its major purposes are to protect the country from foreign and domestic enemies, to provide for the general welfare, to provide justice for all, to protect the individual in his basic rights to hold property and to share in the economic life of the country. Each individual is guaranteed religious freedom and the freedom to learn, to know, and to speak and write freely within the bounds of decency and respect for the rights of others.

Everyone has an opportunity to play a role in government—to choose candidates for office, to vote for those officers, to make his voice heard by those officers, and if he chooses, to be a candidate and to serve in public office. The individual has the right to speak out in favor of government policy and to practice the equally important *right of dissent*—to speak in opposition to the policies and practices of those in office. He has the right to agree, to disagree, to be right, and to be wrong.

Since the success of a democracy depends on the judgment of the citizens and elected officials, *education* of all the people has been an important part of democracy.

Like the federal government, **Utah has a written constitution** which sets the rules for state government. The state constitution sets the limits on government and guarantees liberties and rights to the citizens. It does not conflict with the federal constitution or federal laws and treaties. As a state Utah is on equal footing with other states in the Union.

Utah's constitution established a government of *three distinct branches*: (1) the legislative, (2) the executive, and (3) the judicial. A system of *checks and balances* expressed in the federal constitution is also found in our state constitution. Power was given to the state to create counties, cities, and towns. The state was given the power to establish and maintain public schools, control the formation of business corporations, tax and set fees, borrow money, organize a militia, protect the interests of labor, preserve forests, establish public institutions, and manage state-owned lands. The constitution also spelled out the rights of citizens to vote and hold office and set the patterns for election laws.

Special provisions were written into the Utah state constitution. Some of these provisions reflect the problems involved in Utah's struggle for statehood and the requirements made by Congress before Utah could be admitted into the Union. Others reflect the progressive thinking of the men of the day.

"There shall be *no union of Church and State*, nor shall any church dominate the State or interfere with its functions. No public money or property shall be appropriated for or applied to any religious worship, exercise or instruction, or for the support of any ecclesiastical establishment." (Article 1, Section 4)

And again: "*Perfect toleration of religious sentiment* is guaranteed. No inhabitant of this State shall ever be molested in person or property on account of his or her mode of religious worship; *but polygamous or plural marriages are forever prohibited.*" (Article 3)

Any right to the *public domain lands* was disclaimed and the debts of the territory were assumed by the state. (Article 3)

The early state legislatures met in the Salt Lake City and County Building.

And: "The Legislature shall make laws for the establishment and maintenance of a system of *public schools*, which shall be open to all the children of the State and be free from sectarian control." (Article 3)

With regard to *labor*, the constitution was forward looking in requiring the legislature to prohibit the "employment of women, or of children under the age of fourteen years, in underground mines," in setting eight hours as a day's work "on all works or undertakings carried on or aided by the State, County or Municipal governments," and requiring the legislature to "pass laws to provide for the health and safety of employees in factories, smelters and mines." (Article 16)

Women citizens were given equal "civil, political and religious rights and privileges." (Article 4)

A "**Declaration of Rights**" makes up the first article in Utah's constitution. The framers of our constitution believed this declaration so important that they set it first.

The rights named here are the same as those in the Bill of Rights in the first ten amendments to the federal constitution, other amendments, and in the fundamental law of the land. These fundamental rights are *not bestowed* by government, *they are inherent in man's existence*, and the framers of these constitutions and amendments insisted that government recognize them and *guarantee* these rights to the individual. These rights include freedom of religion, freedom of the press, freedom of speech, freedom of assembly, freedom of petition, and the right to "enjoy and defend their lives and liberties," "to acquire, possess and protect property," and "to communicate freely their thoughts and opinions, being responsible for the abuse of that right." The Utah Declaration of Rights also listed the right to bear arms (militia), to trial by jury, to free elections, and other basic rights enjoyed under common law by Englishmen and Americans for hundreds of years.

The state constitution may be amended by the two-thirds vote of the legislature and by majority vote of the voting citizens. The constitution may also be revised or rewritten by a constitutional convention when the legislature and the majority of the voters at the next election approve such a convention. Amendments adopted by such a convention are not valid until a majority of the electorate of the state votes in favor of them. The constitution written in 1895 is still in effect and has been amended over fifty-five times.

The vote. In our democracy the will of the people is expressed in free elections, by casting one's ballot at the election poll. The right to vote is fundamental and should be considered a privilege and a duty. The Constitution of the United States leaves to the states the determination of the qualifications of the voter. In America women received the franchise to vote almost a century after establishment of the federal constitution. Wyoming and Utah were the first territories to grant this right, Wyoming in 1869, and Utah in 1870. However, that right was taken away from Utah women by the Edmunds-Tucker Act of 1887. The right was returned by the authors of the state constitution in 1896. An amendment to the federal constitution gives the right to vote to all citizens over eighteen.

The Utah State Capitol Building was designed by Richard K. A. Kletting and was completed July 3, 1915, at a cost of $2,739,528. It is considered by many as one of the most beautiful state capitol buildings in the nation.

Political parties. A political party is a group of citizens with similar political ideas and goals. The group organizes for the purpose of gaining political office to promote their ideas. Political parties serve many useful purposes. They help *select the candidates* for office. Once every four years, the national political parties (and the state political parties) *write a platform* representing their views and proposals on the issues of the day. This helps the voter decide how he wants to vote. Political parties also *help government work more smoothly*. When a majority of those elected to office are of the same political party, there is greater harmony, and the chances of good government improve.

But while it is important to have unity, it is just as essential that there be a healthy, strong opposition voice in government. The *loyal opposition* is a watchdog, a vocal critic of what the party in power is doing. The opposition helps keep the government officials honest, fair, and efficient.

America is said to have a two-party system. The federal constitution said nothing about political parties, but parties soon grew up and have since become an essential part of our political life. While in the past there have been other major parties, the Republican party and the Democratic party have come to represent the two major ways of looking at the role government should take in solving state and national problems.

But America also has a "third party" tradition. Third parties arise when people who cannot agree with either of the major parties, or who believe that the major parties are ignoring important issues and programs, organize to call problems to the attention of the public. Third parties have had great influence in American history. Many important reforms have come from third parties. Third parties "win" when they attract enough voters away from the major parties to make the major parties fear losing an election. In an effort to get back third party voters, the major party may adopt into its party platform some of the views (planks) of the third party. When a major party wins an election with a third party plank in its platform, it is under obligation to do something about the reform.

3. THE STATE LEGISLATURE IS THE LAWMAKING BODY IN UTAH'S GOVERNMENT

The constitution gives the legislative power (the lawmaking power) to a *Senate* and *House of Representatives*, together referred to as the *Legislature*. Senators and representatives are elected to express the will of the people in law. A senator or representative must be twenty-five years of age, a citizen, a resident of the state for three years, and a resident for one year and a voter in the district from which he is elected.

By the state constitution, the House of Representatives has been made up of representatives from each county. Each county has

The House of Representatives is shown meeting for the first time in the new State Capitol Building.

had one or more representatives in the House. There were forty-five representatives in all during the early years of statehood. For representation in the Senate, counties were grouped into twelve districts, and eighteen senators were elected from those districts. These figures have increased from time to time.

While there is still an attempt to have representatives from every county in the state, the fundamental principle is that senators and representatives *represent people*, not geographical areas. To achieve this, the constitution required that both houses of the legislature should be reapportioned every five years in accordance with changes in population. That is, every five years a census is called for, and the legislature should change the representation in the two houses according to the increase or decrease in population. (Article 9) While the legislature has been reapportioned from time to time, the reapportionment has been far behind the change in population.

Representatives are elected to two-year terms, and senators to four-year terms. Half the senators are elected every two years.

The state constitution allowed the first legislature to meet for ninety days, but limited each legislature thereafter to only sixty days. The legislature met every two years beginning the second Monday in January of the odd-numbered years. In 1968 the constitution was amended to provide for holding a general session of the legislature during odd-numbered years and a budget session during even-numbered years. The length of each session was limited, a general session to sixty days, a budget session to twenty days. The first budget session was held in 1970.

Powers of the legislature. Lawmaking is the primary function of the legislature. In addition, however, the legislature may propose amendments to the state constitution, confirm appointments recommended by the governor, and investigate matters relating to the function of lawmaking. The legislature may sit as a court in cases of impeachment (removal from office) of certain state officers for high crimes, misdeeds, or wrongful conduct while in office.

Initiative and referendum. The people of Utah may also make or repeal laws by the processes known as the *initiative* and the *referendum*. This participation by the people in the lawmaking process was authorized by a constitutional amendment approved November 6, 1900, though it was not until 1917 that the legislature passed measures to put the amendment in operation. Initiative is the process by which the people propose legislation. Referendum is the process by which the people bring before them for their approval or rejection some law already enacted. Either may be used on the state or local level. These processes have been used only once each; the referendum was used in November 1942 on a law passed by the legislature in 1941, and the initiative was used in 1952.

Lobbying. The people have a right to present their views to the legislators. When individuals representing a special group try to persuade the legislators to support a bill favoring that special group, it is called lobbying. Legislators must be receptive to the wishes of the people, but they must guard against being influenced by special-interest groups at the expense of the best interests of all the people.

A typical legislature, during its sixty days in session, goes through the following business: (1) elects officers, (2) hears the governor's message, (3) organizes into committees, (4) hears proposals for legislation and writes bills to be acted upon, and (5) votes on bills. (Until the Seventeenth Amendment to the Constitution of the United States, the state legislature also elected United States senators from Utah. The last legislature to exercise this function met in 1911; the first popular election of a United States senator from Utah was in 1914.)

All laws begin as bills. A bill is a proposal, written as a law, to be considered by the legislature. The bill may be written by a legislator or a group of legislators, by the attorney general (at the suggestion of the governor, perhaps), or by citizens.

4. THE GOVERNOR IS CHARGED WITH ENFORCING STATE LAW AND ADMINISTERING STATE GOVERNMENT

The *executive branch* of Utah's government is headed by five elective officers: the governor, secretary of state, state auditor, state treasurer, attorney general. The superintendent of public instruction was elective until 1951 when it was made appointive.

The *governor* heads the executive branch. He is charged with the faithful execution of state laws and with the administration of state government. He is commander in chief of the militia. He gives messages to the legislature setting forth the condition of the state, and recommends bills for the legislature to consider. He may call special sessions of the legislature. Bills passed by the legislature become law with his signature. If he does not like a bill, he may veto it. However, if the legislature wishes to pass the bill over his veto, it can do so by obtaining a two-thirds vote for the bill; then it becomes a law without the governor's signature. He has power to appoint and to remove certain officers. He can grant reprieves or pardons to persons convicted of crimes.

The *secretary of state* keeps a record of the official acts of the legislature and of the executive branch, and serves as acting governor when the governor is out of the state.

The *state auditor* examines or inspects the financial records of the state and sees that the funds are accounted for and records kept accurately.

The *state treasurer* is responsible for the public moneys. He authorizes the spending of state moneys according to the law.

The *attorney general* gives legal advice to the governor and other state officers. He is the attorney for all state offices.

The state *superintendent of public instruction* was given his duties by the legislature and was charged with the administration of the public school system. This office was named in the constitution and was elective from 1896 until 1951 when a constitutional amendment gave the State Board of Education the power to appoint the superintendent. This took the office out of politics.

The executive officers are elected for terms of four years. To be eligible for office, each must be a qualified elector and a resident citizen of Utah for at least five years. The governor and the secretary of state must be at least thirty years of age at the time of their election. The attorney general must be at least twenty-five years of age, must have been admitted to practice law before the Supreme Court of Utah, and must be in good standing in the legal profession. The state auditor and the state treasurer cannot succeed themselves in office.

In the absence of the governor from the state, or in case of the disability of the governor to carry out his duties, the secretary of state acts as governor during that time. If both the governor and the secretary of state are out of the state or disabled, the president of the Senate is acting governor.

The governor and other elective officers may be removed from office for high crimes, misdeeds, and wrongful conduct in office. The legislature tries such cases. The House of Representatives, by a two-thirds vote of all members, may accuse an official. The case is then tried before the Senate, which may convict only on a two-thirds vote of all members. In case of impeachment proceedings against a governor, the chief justice of the Utah Supreme Court presides.

To assist the governor and other executive officers in conducting the business of government, *departments, boards, and commissions* have been set up from time to time. Some of the main functions of these boards have been to look after mining safety, agriculture, land, water, taxes and taxation, banks and banking, health, fish and game conservation, examiners for practicing doctors and dentists and other professional services, the state fair, labor relations, roads, aeronautics, and such organizations as the Art Institute and the Utah State Historical Society. As Utah society has become more complex, these boards have increased with the increased role of government in the lives of the people. Today, there are over one hundred such agencies.

5. A SYSTEM OF COURTS OPERATES IN UTAH BRINGING JUSTICE TO THE PEOPLE

There are two separate systems of law operating in the State of Utah: federal and state, and two systems of courts: federal and state. The courts interpret the law and make judgments in cases of violations of the law. Federal courts hear cases involving federal laws and the federal constitution. State courts hear cases involving state laws and the state constitution. There are no contacts between these two systems on the state level. However, a case in the state courts may be appealed from the state supreme court to the federal courts and thence to the Supreme Court of the United States.

There are three levels of state courts. At the lower level are courts of limited jurisdiction, at the second level are the district courts or trial courts, and at the third is the supreme court of the state.

Courts of limited jurisdiction, by law, handle only certain cases. The nature of the offense, age of the person, and the sum involved largely determine in which court the case is heard.

Justice of the peace courts are established in precincts within counties where the justices are elected. Justice courts have jurisdiction in civil cases involving less than $300 and in criminal cases involving minor breaches of peace punishable by less than six months sentence or $300 fine.

Small claims courts were authorized by law in 1933 to operate in each justice's court to deal with cases involving less than $50.

City Courts were authorized by law in 1901 in county seat cities with a population of 5,000 or more and in cities of the first and second class (over 15,000 population). The number of judges in the city court depends on the population of the city. Salt Lake City has five city judges and Ogden two. All other city courts have one judge. The city courts have jurisdiction in civil cases involving actions under $1,000, in cases for alleged violations of city ordinances, and have the same jurisdiction in criminal cases as the justice courts. City courts take the place of justice courts in cities where they have been established.

Juvenile courts were established by the laws of 1905 and 1907. Six juvenile court districts were set up in Utah. These courts have jurisdiction in cases relating to the "neglect, dependency and delinquency of children" under eighteen years of age. In felony

The First District Court, Provo, is here pictured in session in the Utah County Court House.

cases, however, the juvenile courts and the district courts have concurrent jurisdiction.

District Courts. The district courts are between the courts of limited jurisdiction and the highest court in the state. These courts are trial courts which have general original jurisdiction in most civil and criminal cases. This means that certain civil and criminal cases must come before these courts first. Formal records of all proceedings are kept. District courts are established in seven judicial districts in Utah. They supervise the courts of limited jurisdiction. Cases from lower courts may be appealed to the district court. District court judges now serve six-year terms.

Supreme Court of Utah. The Utah State Supreme Court is the highest court in Utah. It has original jurisdiction in that it may issue certain writs (such as mandamus, certiorari, prohibition, quo warranto, and habeas corpus) and may direct state officers or others to perform lawful duties or refrain from unlawful acts. In all other cases, the supreme court is an appellate court; that is, it is a court to which cases from the district court may be appealed for review. Cases may be appealed

from lower courts to the higher courts; that is, from such courts as city courts to the district court and on to the supreme court.

At the beginning of state government the supreme court consisted of three justices elected on a partisan ballot for six-year terms. In 1917 a law increased the number of justices to five and the term to ten years. Thereafter, one justice was elected every two years for a term of ten years. After 1951 the office was considered nonpartisan. The justice whose term is nearest to expiration serves as chief justice for at least two years.

The state constitution outlined the general system of courts, and the legislature has provided for the detailed operation of the courts. The legislature may change the judicial system from time to time, within the provisions of the state constitution.

6. CITY AND COUNTY GOVERNMENT IS CREATED BY THE STATE TO SERVE LOCAL NEEDS

County and municipal government is established by the state and is controlled by the political authority of the state. The state constitution recognized the twenty-seven counties in existence in 1896 and instructed the legislature to establish a system of uniform county government. Cities and towns were to be classified according to population and a uniform system of government provided.

County government is established to serve the local needs of the people or rural areas outside incorporated cites. Counties may levy and collect taxes, conduct elections, enforce laws, purchase and control property and erect buildings necessary for the use of the county, provide for public health and welfare, provide fire protection, license businesses and trades, establish and maintain schools and libraries, and record property mortgages,

County Court House, Beaver. County government is centered in the county court house.

deeds, and other legal documents. As new conditions have arisen, county government has adjusted to provide essential services for the people.

County government is headed by a *board of county commissioners*, consisting of three commissioners. At each November election in even-numbered years, two commissioners are elected, one for a two-year term, the other for a four-year term. One of the three commissioners is chosen chairman. The board is responsible for all county affairs and the supervision of county officers and departments.

Other county officers include: (1) county treasurer, who collects taxes and other moneys due the county, (2) sheriff, who is the state law enforcement officer in the county, (3) county clerk, who serves as secretary to the board of commissioners, is responsible for maintaining court and election records, and generally is to the county what the secre-

tary of state is to the state, (4) county auditor, who investigates all claims against the county and pays the bills, and examines the financial books kept by other county officers to see that accurate and complete records are maintained, (5) county recorder who keeps the official records of the county, recording mortgages, deeds, and other documents involving property, (6) county attorney, who is the county legal officer, (7) county surveyor, who surveys and keeps an accurate record of all land surveys in the county, and (8) county assessor, who determines the value of properties for the purpose of taxation. These county officers hold office for four years, except the county attorney whose term of office is two years.

The county superintendent of public schools was elected to office in most Utah counties until 1905, when a law was passed requiring the county board of education to appoint him.

Precincts are created subdivisions of the county. Precinct officers are the justice of the peace and the constable.

City government provides us with many immediate and important services. Among the concerns of city government are water, lighting, plumbing and sewage disposal, public health, streets, parks and playgrounds, fire protection, police protection, cemeteries, animals, and zoning for residential and business districts. Regardless of how efficient federal and state governments might be, life would be difficult indeed without the services of the city government.

Since statehood, Utah cities and towns have had an increasing role to play in the improvement of life. As life has become more complex, city governments have had more and more to do to keep pace with the demands of modern living.

For purposes of prescribing the forms of

Salt Lake City and County Building, built in 1894, housed state government until the completion of the State Capitol Building in 1915.

The Ogden City Hall, about 1896. City government is centered in a city hall, but few communities have had such fine buildings as this.

government, the cities and towns of Utah since the 1880s have been grouped according to population into four classes: cities of the first, second, and third class, and towns. Sometimes the terms city and town are interchangeable. A special form of government is prescribed by law for cities in each class. For cities there is prescribed a *mayor*, for towns a *president*. Serving with the mayor in a city is a commission of four (cities of the first class), or a commission of two (cities of the second class), or a council of five (cities of the third class). The president of a town and four trustees make up a town board. All serve terms of four years, and the law prescribes that half those on a council or board are to be elected every two years.

The mayor-commission, the mayor-council, and the president-town board forms of government have much the same duties, though the law is specific as to their powers and responsibilities. These councils are administrative bodies charged with supervising city

affairs. They are also legislative bodies in that they enact ordinances to be observed as law in the city.

Most of Utah's cities have kept much the same form of government through the years. However, some changes have been made from time to time, and in recent years additional forms of government for cities have been permitted by law. Increasingly city councils have turned to choosing city managers under a city-manager form of government. The following are some Utah cities with city managers: American Fork, Bountiful, Blanding, Clearfield, Cedar City, Farmington, Monticello, Morgan, Nephi, North Salt Lake, Ogden, Orem, Parowan, Richfield, Roy, Vernal, and West Jordan.

7. A CLOSE RELATIONSHIP EXISTS BETWEEN STATE AND FEDERAL GOVERNMENT

Ours is a government of limited powers. Constitutions are written to limit government.

Certain powers were conferred on the federal government by the federal constitution. The federal government is concerned with the general welfare of the country, foreign relations, relations between states, the monetary system, and similar matters. The federal constitution prohibits the states from acting in these and other areas. At the same time, the federal constitution reserves all other powers not specified in the constitution to the states and to the people.

State government is concerned with the needs of the people within the state and performs services which are authorized by the state constitution or laws.

It is important for each level of government to operate and to be respected in its own domain. Sometimes there is overlapping of services by different levels of government. Governments try to avoid this situation. It can be avoided for the most part by each level of government taking full responsibility for its own domain and fully providing the services needed by the people at that level. When local government fails to do this, state and federal governments may step in.

Under the federal constitution, each state is represented in the federal government by two senators in the United States Senate and representatives (proportionate to the population of the state) in the United States House of Representatives. Utah had one representative until 1913, and since then has had two representatives. Senators and representatives are to express the will of the people of Utah in federal legislation and programs.

Agencies of the federal government have performed services for Utah from the beginning of her territorial existence. Postal service came early. Marshals helped protect lives and property, and judges presided in the courts. Land offices came in 1869 to enable the people to secure title to the lands they al-

Fire fighting in early Salt Lake City.
Local government provides many services,
including police and fire protection.

ready held or would obtain. Care for Indians was administered by agents of the federal Bureau of Indian Affairs. After statehood these services continued and many more were added.

One of the most important and immediate benefits to Utah from the federal government was the gift of 7,414,276 acres of land. These lands or the proceeds from the sale of these lands were given to support Utah's school system and for other projects.

In 1888 the provisions of the federal Morrill Act of 1862 were applied to Utah by the legislature for the creation of a land-grant college. The Morrill Act provided for the donation of public lands to the states for the establishment of agricultural and mechanical colleges. The Agricultural College of Utah, established by the legislature at Logan, opened its doors September 1890 and graduated its first class in 1894. A major function of the college centered in the Agricultural Experiment Station, a federally supported agency which conducted scientific experiments in agriculture relating directly to conditions in Utah. Some of the major benefits to Utah's agriculture have come through the research of this experiment station in Logan.

Caroline Bridge, a painting by Utah artist H. L. A. Culmer.

UTAH ADJUSTS TO ITS POSITION IN THE NATION

When Utah joined the Union, new life came into the people—a spirit of optimism, freedom, daring, and doing. That spirit paralleled the spirit of the Progressive Period in the United States. The Progressive Period in American history is so called because of faith in progress, and the forward-looking democratic reforms effected in our national life. Utah participated in some of these reforms.

Utah was in a transitional period from 1896 to 1920, during which time she emerged from her pioneer character to become a state in the modern world. In 1896 she still showed her pioneer character. By 1920, Utah ways, especially in the urban centers, were becoming more like those of other states.

At the beginning of the period there were people who believed the Mormons were not keeping their part of the bargain in getting statehood—that some Mormons were continuing polygamy, that the church was influencing the political and economic life of the state. By the end of the period the separation of church and state had been made, and there was little doubt in anyone's mind about the loyalty of the Mormons to American ways.

As America participated in world affairs, so did the people of Utah. Utah men joined the armed forces of the United States to fight for their country on foreign soil.

Utah participated in national affairs too, and national movements came to Utah. Reclamation and conservation were new but powerful movements of the time, and Utah was influenced greatly by the construction of dams and reservoirs, and the setting aside of forest reserves, and national parks and monuments.

IN THIS CHAPTER WE WILL LEARN

1. Conflicts between the old and the new died slowly.

2. Utah adjusted its political life to that of the nation.

3. Utah soldiers fought in America's foreign wars.

4. Federal reclamation projects brought more Utah lands under irrigation.

5. Federal conservation programs helped improve Utah's economic life.

6. National parks and monuments preserved some of Utah's natural beauty and natural wonders.

20

347

Joseph F. Smith, president of the Mormon church from 1901-18, effected his church's transition from the pioneer era to the modern world.

1. CONFLICTS BETWEEN THE OLD AND THE NEW DIED SLOWLY

The achievement of statehood did not end the bitter contest over the role of the Mormon church in Utah political and economic life. Peace over these issues did not come until the end of World War I. From 1896 to 1918 was a period of transition from the territorial days to a time when Mormons and non-Mormons worked closely together.

The achievement of statehood was one thing; it was quite another to create new patterns of life for the Mormon church. The task of moving the church from the old ways to the new ways fell principally to *Joseph F.*

C. C. Goodwin, editor of the Salt Lake Tribune, *1880-1901 carried on a running feud with the Mormon church and its* Deseret News. *He promoted many progressive causes in Utah and came to modify his views of the Mormons.*

Charles W. Penrose, editor of the Deseret News, *1880-92, 1899-1907. The contest between the* Deseret News *and the* Salt Lake Tribune *was carried on by succeeding editors until about 1917 when the old feud was ended.*

Smith, president of the church from October 17, 1901, until his death November 19, 1918. He saw the course the church must take and piloted it through troublesome times to days of peace. He was the object of much ridicule by his opposition, but he established new patterns for relations between Mormons and non-Mormons in political and economic affairs. No church president since has been so significant in Utah history.

Throughout most of this period the *Salt Lake Tribune* and the *Deseret News* maintained their long-time feud. C. C. Goodwin, *Tribune* editor, and Charles W. Penrose, *Deseret News* editor, waged battles on old issues. The *Tribune* had only bad words for the Mormons, President Smith, other leaders, and their intentions. Sometimes the *Deseret News* answered in kind; sometimes it ignored the opposition.

The national press echoed the Utah newspaper battles and added some warfare of its own. Magazines attacked the Mormon church—charging betrayal of agreements made for statehood, of church involvement in politics and economics. One magazine article went to the extreme by charging that the Mormon church controlled Wall Street and the economy of the nation through its tithing system.

In Utah, people were looking to their past and to their future. In July 1897, Utah celebrated the fiftieth anniversary of the coming of the Mormon pioneers into Salt Lake Valley. The celebration included parades and the dedication of the monument at the intersection of Main and South Temple streets in Salt Lake City to Brigham Young and the pioneers. The monument was designed by one of Utah's most distinguished native sons, the great sculptor, Cyrus Edwin Dallin. The Utah State Historical Society was founded on December 28, 1897, and on March 8, 1917, was made a state institution. In January 1928 it began the publication of a historical magazine, the *Utah Historical Quarterly*. Pioneer

The pioneer monument to Brigham Young was dedicated July 20, 1897, as part of the semi-centennial celebration.

Square (the block on which the first Old Fort was erected in Salt Lake Valley the fall of 1847) was dedicated as a public park by President Wilford Woodruff, July 24, 1898, just six weeks before his death. The Daughters of the Utah Pioneers was founded April 11, 1901, by Mrs. Annie Taylor Hyde, a daughter of John Taylor and the wife of a son of Orson Hyde. This organization was to perpetuate the names and achievements of the men, women, and children who pioneered Utah. Records were to be kept and historical material published by this organization.

There were other signs of change. The Deseret Telegraph Company's lines were bought by Western Union in February 1900. Utah's first state fair was held in October 1899; in March 1907 the name of the Deseret Agricultural and Manufacturing Society was changed to the Utah State Fair. The old Deseret Museum was moved in 1890 from its pioneer adobe building across the street to the newly erected Templeton Building, and soon thereafter it was succeeded by the Bureau of Information and Church Literature, opened on Temple Block in August 1902.

2. UTAH ADJUSTED ITS POLITICAL LIFE TO THAT OF THE NATION

Two-party system. One of the requirements for statehood in Utah was a functioning two-party system. The People's party (Mormon) disappeared in 1891 and the Liberal party in 1893. Members of the Liberal party moved into the Republican party while Mormons were divided between the Republican and Democratic parties. Church leaders recommended that Mormons join the party of their choice and remain loyal to it. However, if the Mormons had been left on their own, most would have joined the Democratic party because of past loyalties. To encourage a balance between the two parties church lead-

ers called some local church leaders to affiliate with the Republican party. This was done during the 1890s until there appeared to be a balance of strength between the two parties. It took until about 1900 for the two parties to achieve this balance. By that time, also, party leadership was developing.

The problem of Mormon church leaders holding political office. One of the major political questions in the generation after statehood was the influence church members and leaders might exert in political affairs. The continuation of church domination as in the territorial period was out of the question. But Mormons made up about 70 percent of the population and to deny them free exercise of political rights was equally out of the question. If a leading churchman wished to serve in a political office, should he be denied the privilege of serving both church and state? Would it not be a denial of freedom to prohibit a churchman from running for political office? If there were such a prohibition, would it not deprive the state of much excellent leadership? But how to maintain a separation of church and state? These problems were not solved for many years.

The election of 1895. In 1895 Mormon apostle Moses Thatcher and President B. H. Roberts of the First Council of Seventy announced candidacy for the United States Senate and for representative in Congress, respectively. For this action they were censured by President Joseph F. Smith, who wanted to protect the efficiency of the church. He believed any leader should consult with his superiors for permission before undertaking such a course. In the election of 1895, Roberts lost. In March 1896, Roberts agreed to abide by church rules as he now understood them and was continued in his church office. Moses Thatcher, however, refused to abide by this rule and his name was

Brigham H. Roberts was elected to the 56th Congress as a Democrat; he was denied his seat because he was a polygamist. He was a leading churchman and historian.

dropped from the Quorum of the Twelve Apostles.

The new *political rule of the church* was read to the April 1896 conference as a binding policy. It stated that before accepting any position which would interfere with the performance of ecclesiastical duties, a church officer should apply to the proper authorities and learn whether he could take upon himself the added duties and responsibilities of the new position. The document was signed by all the general authorities.

The Roberts case in Congress. Having secured permission, B. H. Roberts was candidate for Congress in 1898 and won that election over considerable opposition from the *Salt Lake Tribune* and the Salt Lake Ministerial Association (non-Mormon religious leaders). In Washington, Roberts was refused the privilege of being sworn in as a member. His case was referred to the House Committee on Privileges and Elections which recommended that he not be sworn in as a member. On January 25, 1900, by a vote of 268 to 50, the House of Representatives refused to seat Roberts. William H. King was elected to fill the vacancy in a special election held April 2, 1900.

United States senators from Utah. By constitutional provisions, the Utah legislature was to elect during its first session (1896) two senators, one for a long term and one for a short term. This was to make Utah's election patterns fit those of the nation. At the first legislature the Republicans won by electing Frank J. Cannon and Arthur Brown over the Democratic candidates, Moses Thatcher and Joseph L. Rawlins. Cannon drew the long term and Brown the short term. There seems to have been a gentlemen's agreement during these first years, that one United States senator would be a Mormon and the other senator a non-Mormon. This was observed for the first twenty years of statehood.

In the second legislature (1897) the legislators elected a successor to Arthur Brown. Joseph L. Rawlins became Utah's first senator to fill a six-year term. When the third legislature met, Frank J. Cannon sought reelection as a Silver Republican, a third party, hoping to gain votes from Democrats and Republicans. Alfred W. McCune was the chief Democratic contender, but the Democrats were divided. While McCune gained the largest number of votes, he could not poll enough to win and the legislature adjourned without electing a United States senator. Two years later the fourth legislature (1901) tried again; Thomas Kerns (R) won the four-year term seat. In 1903 Joseph L. Rawlins' term was up. The Republicans won the election of 1902; the fifth legislature named and elected Reed Smoot United States senator. But Smoot was a Mormon apostle and there was opposition to him as there had been to B. H. Roberts.

The Smoot case. Reed Smoot went to Washington, was sworn in as a senator, and took his seat. Ten months later the Senate Committee on Privileges and Elections took

Reed Smoot, Mormon apostle and United States senator from Utah from 1903-33, was a leader in the Republican party in Utah and the nation. Standing with the conservatives of his party, he helped create the image that Utahns were conservative, loyal Americans.

under consideration protests mounting against Smoot. The committee investigations lasted from January 1904 to February 1907. One protest charged Smoot with "having a legal and a plural wife." A second protest charged the Mormon church leadership, including Smoot, with control of the political affairs of Utah, thus creating a union of church and state contrary to the constitution of the state of Utah and the Constitution of the United States. The second protest also charged church leadership with encouraging the practice of polygamy. During the hearings, the committee examined Mormon church President Joseph F. Smith, Apostles Francis M. Lyman and Hyrum M. Smith, assistant church historian Andrew Jenson, and many other

Mormons from Utah. A large number of "conservative and influential citizens," mostly non-Mormons of Utah and Idaho were also called to testify. Special attention was given to matters surrounding the actions of two apostles, John W. Taylor and Matthias F. Cowley. These men had a difference of opinion with the other authorities in regard to plural marriages and had encouraged Mormons to perpetuate the practice. On June 11, 1906, the committee reported its findings, but the report was not unanimous. The Burrows Resolution, the majority report, found "the facts stated in the protest are true" and Smoot therefore not entitled to his seat. The minority report declared that Smoot met the qualifications of office, that the charges were false, and that he should retain his seat. The two reports went to the Senate for vote. The Senate rejected the Burrows Resolution and adopted the minority report in favor of Smoot by a vote of 42 to 28.

Several immediate effects came from the Smoot hearings. Apostle John W. Taylor was released from the apostleship, October 6, 1905, and was excommunicated March 26, 1911. Matthias F. Cowley "resigned" from the apostleship October 28, 1905. Cowley was not excommunicated. The church showed its determination to abide by the spirit of the Manifesto to end plural marriages among the Mormons. President Joseph F. Smith issued to the 1904 April conference an "Official Statement" declaring: "I hereby announce that all such [plural] marriages are prohibited, and if any officer or member of the Church shall assume to solemize or enter into any such marriage he will be deemed in transgression against the Church ...." This statement is sometimes referred to as the Second Manifesto.

The American party. Testimony given at the Smoot hearings led to the formation of an anti-Mormon political party known as the American Party of Utah. On September 7, 1904, about forty anti-Mormon politicians met in Auerbach Hall, Salt Lake City, and discussed prospects for an anti-Mormon political party in Utah. The featured speaker was Senator Fred T. Dubois, the old Mormon fighter from Idaho. He urged organization of the party to help protect the political rights of the citizens from what he called destruction at the hands of the leaders of the Mormon church. On September 30 the party met in the Grand Theatre and endorsed a slate of persons for state offices, and on October 11 held another convention during which they nominated county, legislative, and judicial candidates. The party showing in the November election was slight, but it won three successive Salt Lake City municipal elections and controlled the city government from 1905 to 1911. The party not only ran Salt Lake City for six years but it interested itself in progressive reforms. During Mayor John S. Bransford's administration, the commission form of city government was adopted for Salt Lake City. Party loyalties are less significant in the commission form of government and the American party began to lose support. After a defeat at the polls in 1911 the American party left the field, and the two major parties, now well organized, took over political affairs for the state.

Voting patterns. In national elections Utah has voted, with few exceptions, for the winning presidential candidate. In 1896 Utah cast 82 percent of its vote for William Jennings Bryan (D) instead of voting for the winner, William McKinley (R). In 1912 Utah voted for William Howard Taft (R) rather than Woodrow Wilson (D), the winner.

During the period 1896 to 1916 the Republicans dominated the elective offices. They held the governorship until 1916. The

1. *Heber M. Wells (R) 1896-1905*

- b. August 11, 1859, Salt Lake City
- d. March 12, 1938
- Son of Daniel H. Wells
- Salt Lake City recorder, 1882-90
- Clerk, territorial legislature
- Member, Constitutional Convention
- Banker, businessman
- Member, Board of Public Works

Major events or accomplishments during the administration:

- launched Utah state government
- began codification of Utah law
- eight-hour day law
- pioneered conservation of Utah's natural resources; conservation of forests
- founded branch of State Normal School, Beaver
- established national forests in Sevier and Wayne counties
- 50th anniversary, Pioneer Day (July 24), 1897
- creation of State Institute of Arts
- development of the state's resources
- improvement of roads
- office of state dairy and food commissioner
- state chemist
- Called out National Guard to maintain law and order at Scofield, Castle Gate, and Sunnyside, Carbon County. Discontent of miners.
- promoted display of Utah products, Trans-Mississippi Exposition, Omaha, Nebraska, 1898

2. *John C. Cutler (R) 1905-1909*

- b. February 5, 1846, Sheffield, England
  To Utah in 1864
- d. July 30, 1928
- Agent, Provo Woolen Mills, 1877–
- President, Cutler Brothers and Company
- Associated with banks and insurance companies, Utah Light & Power Co., Utah-Idaho Sugar Co., and Utah Hotel Co.
- Trustee and treasurer, LDS University
- Clerk, Salt Lake County; clerk of probate court, 1884-90

Major events or accomplishments during the administration:

- advocated construction of state capitol building
- adjusted finances of the state
- urged capital investment in Utah industry—railroads, mines, mills, industry
- created state board of park commissioners
- founded state juvenile court system
- state law compiled and coded: *Compiled Laws of Utah*, 1908
- established board of horticulture
- turned jurisdiction of Fort Douglas and Fort Duchesne to federal government
- approved establishment of an experiment station in central Utah
- act providing for registration of births and deaths in Utah
- name of Deseret Agricultural and Manufacturing Society changed to Utah State Fair
- lands in Uintah Indian Reservation opened up to white settlement, 1905

3. *William Spry (R) 1909-1917*

- b. January 11, 1864, Windsor, Berkshire, England
  To Utah 1875
- d. April 21, 1929
- Worked in railroading, blacksmithing
- State representative, Tooele County, 1903-5
- U.S. marshal, 1906-8
- U.S. commissioner of Public Lands, 1921-29

Major events or accomplishments during the administration:

- creation of Duchesne County, January 1915
- child labor law
- workshop for blind
- orphans home
- neighborhood house
- state capitol building completed
- Utah legislature held first meeting in new capitol building, February 10, 1915
- refused to intervene in the Joe Hill case
- established state banking commission
- established commission to investigate industrial accidents
- established irrigation and water rights commission
- state board of sheep commissioners
- state dairy and food bureau
- conservation commission
- registration and licensing of motor vehicles
- State Normal School at Cedar City made branch of Utah Agricultural College
- XVII Amendment to U.S. Constitution, popular election of senators, effective May 13, 1913

4.   *Simon Bamberger (D) 1917-1921*

- b. February 27, 1845, Darmstadt, Germany
  To America, 1859; to Utah, 1869
- d. October 6, 1926
- Interested in coal mining
- Built railroad spur from Nephi to Wales
- President, Bamberger Coal Company
- Member, Salt Lake City School Board; urged higher salaries and financial support for schools
- State Senator, 1902-6
- President, Salt Lake and Denver Railroad Company
- Utah's first war governor, first non-Mormon governor, and first Democratic governor

Major events or accomplishments during the administration:

- led Utah during war years to a high contribution to war effort
- statewide prohibition law
- budget system established
- utilities commission established
- Colorado River Project begun
- equalization of taxes in relation to mines

state legislatures were dominated by Republican majorities. They also dominated the congressional delegations except for the one term of Joseph L. Rawlins in the Senate and the terms of William H. King in the House. In 1916, however, the Democrats won the gov-ernorship, two seats in Congress, a seat in the Senate, and Utahns voted for the presidential winner, Woodrow Wilson, for a second term.

By 1920 Utah had so adjusted her political life to that of the nation that national opinion no longer associated Mormonism with radicalism or disloyalty. Rather the suggested association with the conservative Republican party gave the people of Utah an image of conservatism, which was emphasized by the career of Utah's senior senator, Reed Smoot, who was soon in the inner circles of the conservative wing of the Republican party.

3. UTAH SOLDIERS FOUGHT IN AMERICA'S FOREIGN WARS

One of the duties imposed upon Utah's men as citizens in the new state was service in the army. Other than the Utah National Guard, which had been organized in 1894, there was no standing army, nor an on-going selective service at the time of statehood. The United States had not engaged in a major foreign war since the Mexican War of 1846-48. Mormons served in that war, some Utahns performed service in the West during the Civil War, and others went east to fight.

The Spanish-American War. Early in 1898 relations between the United States and Spain deteriorated over affairs in Cuba to the extent that the United States demanded independence for Cuba and the withdrawal of Spanish armed forces from the island. Spain reacted by a declaration of war against the United States on April 24, and the next day the United States declared war on Spain. President McKinley issued a call for troops from each state, proportionate to the state's population. Governor Wells was asked for five hundred men from Utah. The governor issued a proclamation calling for volunteers. Within a week Utah's quota had been reached, and by May 4 nearly seven hundred had volunteered.

Utah volunteers for service in the Spanish-American War received basic military training at Camp Kent on the Fort Douglas military reservation.

These volunteers from Bountiful served with the Utah Light Artillery unit in the Spanish-American War. Charles R. Mabey, future governor of Utah, is second from the left.

Utah troops engage the enemy in action in the Philippine Islands, 1899.

Many business firms offered half pay to their employees who volunteered for service, and promised them their jobs back when they returned.

Volunteers reported to Fort Douglas for basic training. The men were formed into units made up solely of Utah men. The 663 Utah volunteers were organized into three batteries of light artillery and two troops of cavalry. Forty men were assigned to the Second Engineers of the United States Volunteer Engineers.

Battery A and Battery B, Utah Light Artillery, left Fort Douglas May 20 for San Francisco en route to the Philippine Islands (part of the Spanish empire) where they landed July 17. They engaged in various battles including that which resulted in the fall of Manila, August 13. After peace negotiations began, these batteries continued service in helping suppress the Filipino outbreak (1899). These batteries lost nine men killed and thirteen wounded, the only Utah casualties of the war.

Utah had been asked for one troop of cavalry, but the volunteers were so numerous Utah officials pleaded for an additional unit which was granted. Troop I, Second United States Volunteer Cavalry was mustered into service at Fort D. A. Russell, Cheyenne, Wyoming, May 18, where Colonel Jay L. Torrey had gathered the men for an exceptional unit of "frontiersmen who are marksmen and horsemen." Torrey's Rocky Mountain Cavalry left Fort Russell June 22 for Jacksonville, Florida, where they prepared for battle in Cuba. The Utah Troop I, however, was not called to Cuba but remained at Camp Cuba Libre until mustered out October 24.

The second troop of cavalry organized of Utah men was known as First Troop of Cavalry, Utah United States Volunteer Cavalry. These men left Fort Douglas May 24 for San Francisco where they were assigned to the Presidio in that city and then duty in Yosemite and Sequoia parks rather than going to the Philippines. They were mustered out December 23.

The Second Regiment of United States Volunteer Engineers served in Hawaii and Battery C of the Utah Light Artillery served at the Presidio and Angel Island, San Francisco.

Each of the units was given a special homecoming, but the men of Batteries A and B, because of their battle experience and lengthened service, were given special treatment, including a train chartered for their trip from San Francisco to Salt Lake City where they arrived August 19, 1899. The day

had been proclaimed by Governor Wells a state holiday of thanksgiving for the return of the soldiers.

Mexican border campaign. In 1916 the United States was having difficulty along the United States-Mexican border. Americans hired to operate Mexican mines had been killed by Mexicans; Pancho Villa, a revolutionary commander had led raids into Texas and New Mexico. General John J. Pershing was ordered to head an expedition of fifteen thousand men to pursue Villa into Mexico. President Woodrow Wilson, June 18, 1916, made a call on the Utah National Guard for service with Pershing. Mobilization of the units took place at Fort Douglas. Additional recruits brought the units to war strength. Ultimately eight cavalry troops and a battery of field artillery, a field hospital, and sanitary detachments were brought together for service. They served on the Mexican border until December 1916.

World War I. On April 6, 1917, less than

The Utah veterans of Batteries A and B were given an enthusiastic homecoming in Salt Lake City, August 19, 1899. The arch was at Second South and Main Streets.

357

President Woodrow Wilson on a visit to Utah in the interest of Liberty loans. A group of Boy Scouts greets the president on the steps of the State Capitol.

four months after the Utah guard units had returned from the Mexican border, the United States declared war on Germany. World War I had opened in July 1914 and spread until nations in Europe, the Americas, and Asia were involved. The world had never seen anything so extensive in the number of countries involved, nor so destructive of life and property.

Utah was immediately involved in the war. Caught up in the optimistic war spirit of the times, Utahns responded quickly to the demands of the federal government to contribute men, money, services, and material. Even before war was declared they expressed their feelings at a large mass meeting held in the Tabernacle on March 26. Addresses were given by Governor Bamberger, Senators Smoot and King, Mayor W. M. Ferry, and others. At the close of the program, the following resolution was adopted: "we solemnly pledge ourselves here and now to loyally support the President of this Republic in whatever course may become necessary to enforce our rights as a people, to preserve our honor as a Nation and to protect the lives of our fellow citizens at home or abroad, on land or sea."

During this war, the government found it necessary to add a selective service draft to the older practice of enlisting volunteers. Eventually, men between the ages of 18 and 45 were required to register for military service. About 21,000 men entered units of the land forces, and about 3,500 served in different branches of the navy. Slightly more than half of the Utah inductees volunteered. About 665 lost their lives in connection with war service: 219 were killed in action, 32 died of accidental deaths, and 414 died of disease.

While Utah men were assigned according to the needs of various outfits, some effort was made to keep them in units. The 91st Division, known as the "Wild West Division," was composed of men from Utah and other western states. The 362d Infantry was a Utah unit. Their chaplain was Calvin S. Smith, son of Mormon church President Joseph F. Smith. The division landed in France, July 22, 1918, and saw action in the Argonne-Meuse offensive, the Cheppy Woods area, the Chateau-Thierry offensive, and were pursuing the enemy at the time of the Armistice, November 11, 1918.

Utah's national guard units were organized as the 145th Field Artillery Battalion, commanded by Colonel Richard W. Young, a West Point graduate and veteran of the Spanish-American War. B. H. Roberts was chaplain. The unit landed in France September 2 and was poised for action when the armistice came.

Other Utahns performed valued services in the Red Cross and medical units overseas. Dr. Hugh B. Sprague recruited a motor ambulance company of a hundred men, known as the American Red Cross Ambulance Company No. 27 of Salt Lake City. The First Utah Field Hospital Company saw considerable action in France, also. As many as a hundred physicians and surgeons and seventy-three trained nurses from Utah also served overseas.

The home front in World War I. At home there was loyal support for the war. A patriotic spirit was cultivated. Citizens cooperated in building an efficient home defense system and an effective military establishment for service overseas. Agricultural, industrial, and financial resources were mobilized. At federal request the *State Council of Defense for Utah* was organized April 26, 1917. This council put Utah on a war footing. Local councils were established in the counties.

To help finance the war effort, Liberty Loan drives were conducted. Clarence Bamberger and Heber J. Grant were chairmen of the drives in Utah. In five drives—through the efforts of bankers, social clubs, businesses and the boy scouts—Utah citizens subscribed $72,509,000, a sum well over Utah's quota. Other contributions were made for a total of $79,855,440 to war finances.

Farmers expanded their holdings in an effort to produce more food for our soldiers and allies. Housewives economized to conserve food and fuel. Business and industry expanded to meet demands. Due to the heavy rail traffic through Ogden, that city was advanced as a distribution center.

Fort Douglas played an important part in the war. At the outbreak of the war only a quartermaster detachment with one officer and six men was stationed there. However, troops returning from the Mexican border and units mustering into service soon made it a post of importance. Units received equipment and training there. During the war the fort served also as a prisoner-of-war camp.

With the participation of Utah men in the battles of World War I and the full support of the citizens in home efforts, there was no doubt in the minds of the American people of the loyalty of the people of Utah to the United States government. The old charges of disloyalty could not be leveled

The Liberty garden of D. R. Allen in Salt Lake City, June 1918. Everyone was encouraged to grow his own food so more food would be available for the soldiers and our allies.

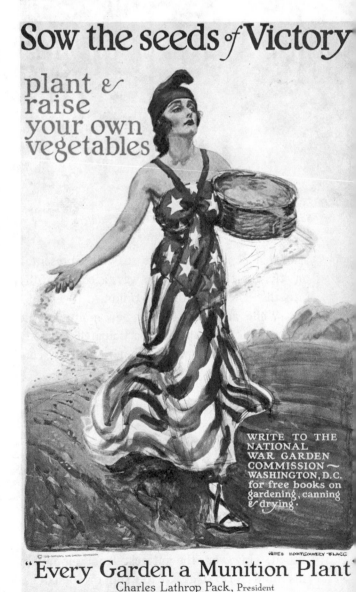

359

Salt Lake City welcomed home Utah's soldiers, June 1918.

against a people who were so well represented on the battlefield. Utah was accepted fully into the sisterhood of the Union.

While adjusting to her new political role in the Union, Utah also participated in many federal programs which benefited her economic life.

4. FEDERAL RECLAMATION PROJECTS BROUGHT MORE UTAH LANDS UNDER IRRIGATION

Utah public lands. One of the special benefits to Utah upon entering the union was the gift of 7,414,276 acres of public land. Money from the sale of these lands was to go into a special fund which was not to be disturbed. However, the interest from money in this fund was to go to the support of education.

Utah continued to benefit from the availability of public lands for settlement, agriculture, and other purposes. Utahns continued to take up land under the *Homestead Act* of 1862. By 1962, 16,798 Utah farmers had proved up on their entries, having settled 3,607,683 acres of land. The *Desert Land Act* of 1877 permitted individuals to acquire 640 acres at twenty-five cents an acre provided the land was irrigated within three years. Under this act 1,500 Utahns had taken up 259,335 acres by 1904. By 1914 several hundred thousand acres of desert land in Utah was still available for sale. In 1894 the *Carey Act* was approved which authorized the president to grant to each public-land state a maximum of one million acres within its boundaries for irrigation, reclamation, settlement, and cultivation. Surplus funds from this program were to go to reclaim other lands in the state. Under this act a person could take up to 160 acres of land at a cost of fifty cents an acre; the applicant had to construct this own irrigation system. In 1909 the *Enlarged Homestead Act* was applied to Utah. Applicants for land, under this act, could enter upon 320 acres or less of non-mineral, non-irrigable, unreserved, and unappropriated surveyed public land that did not contain merchantable timber. A special provision for Utah read that an applicant did not have to maintain continuous residence upon the land he entered. In the first five years under this act, 3,208 entries were made of about 300 acres each.

The conservation and reclamation movements. By the turn of the century many people had become aware of the value of the natural resources. Preservationists wanted to prevent the exploitation of timber, minerals, and water power, and to retain the scenic works of nature in public ownership for future generations. Conservationists wanted to

A party of photographers, Ogden, about 1899.

develop principles and programs for the wise use and management of the forests, minerals, and water power. Early national leaders in this movement included John Wesley Powell, Carl Schurz (secretary of the interior, 1877-1881), President Theodore Roosevelt, and Gifford Pinchot (chief of the U.S. Forest Service). It was under Roosevelt and Pinchot that many conservation ideals came to realization and many programs were successfully established. Roosevelt greatly increased the acreages in national forests and transferred them to the Department of Agriculture for better protection. He withdrew from sale great areas of mineral lands, retained water power sites in federal hands, required stockmen to pay fees for the use of ranges, and provided that the fees and other funds should go for the protection and improvement of the public ranges. Mature trees in the forests might be cut and sold, but the income would go to forest management.

President Roosevelt believed the federal government should help with projects in forest and water conservation. He believed that great acreages would be made available with additional water and that the sale of such lands would largely pay for the government's expenditure in building dams and canals. To help this process along he established the *Bureau of Reclamation* in 1902.

To promote reclamation ideas, a series of *irrigation congresses* were held in the West. William E. Smythe, the father of the congresses, chose Salt Lake City for the first National Irrigation Congress, held September 15-17, 1891. There were 450 delegates in attendance from sixteen states and territories. The delegates visited Lehi, Provo, and other places throughout Utah to see irrigation in action. Other irrigation congresses followed; each recommended reclamation of arid lands in the West by irrigation.

Out of these recommendations and President Roosevelt's recommendations, Congress responded with a most important law for Utah and the western states. In 1902 Congress passed a bill sponsored by Representative Francis G. Newlands of Nevada. By the *National Reclamation Act* (*Newlands Act*) the government agreed to use the proceeds from the sale of public lands for reclamation projects—dams and irrigation systems—to reclaim arid lands for agriculture. Settlers using water from the dams were to agree to repay the cost of construction, thus creating a revolving reclamation fund for the construction of other works. Under the provisions of this act, Utah has profited greatly by the construction of dams and reservoirs and the increased acreages of land reclaimed for agriculture.

The *Strawberry Valley Reservoir and Canal* was the first reclamation project in Utah constructed by the government under the Newlands Act. In Utah Valley there was more good farm land than could be watered by the Spanish Fork River. The problem was how to increase the water in the Spanish Fork River. The plan adopted took water from the Strawberry River, which flows eastward off the Wasatch Mountains into the

The Strawberry Valley Project takes water from the Strawberry River through the Wasatch Mountains to drain into the Spanish Fork River. The three pictures below show the dam site and camp, a grader taking dirt from a barrow pit, and the inside of the finished Strawberry Tunnel.

Duchesne River, and put it into the Spanish Fork River. This was done by building a dam across the Strawberry River in Strawberry Valley. Then the impounded water was diverted from the reservoir into a three-and-a-half mile cement-lined tunnel drilled through the Wasatch Mountains and onto the other side of the mountain into Sixth Water Creek that drains into Diamond Fork, thence into the Spanish Fork River and on into Utah Valley.

The Strawberry project was begun in 1905 and completed in 1922 though the first irrigation water was turned into the tunnel in 1915. Between 50,000 and 60,000 acres of land in southern Utah County came under irrigation at once. The communities of Mapleton, Spanish Fork, Salem, and Payson profited most. Some old canals were used; a new cement Highline Canal carried water to Payson. After the reservoir was completed, an electric power plant was built to provide power to drill the tunnel. By 1914 Payson, Salem, and Spanish Fork had electricity from this source.

5. FEDERAL CONSERVATION PROGRAMS HELPED IMPROVE UTAH'S ECONOMIC LIFE

The use of Utah's natural resources by the pioneers was essential to maintaining a living. Yet the very presence of white men changed the character of the land and left nature out of balance. Valley lands, covered with grasses, were taken up in farms and villages, or grazed by livestock. Irrigation waters flooded the patches of farm lands, sometimes washing away top soil, sometimes dissolving salts to the surface. It took a few years to develop proper irrigation practices. Timber and shrubs were taken for buildings, fuel, railroad construction, and mining. Wildlife was taken to supplement the food supply. Within a generation the ecological balance was sufficiently disturbed to alarm some pioneer leaders.

In October 1865 apostle Orson Hyde, who was in charge of Sanpete Valley settlements, reported his observations on what had happened to the land since 1847. He warned against those who took too much land and cared for it improperly. He then said: "I find the longer we live in these valleys that the range is becoming more and more destitute of grass; the grass is not only eaten up by the great amount of stock that feed upon it, but they tramp it out by the very roots; and where grass once grew luxuriantly, there is now nothing but the desert weed, and hardly a spear of grass is to be seen. Between here and the mouth of Emigration kanyon, when our brethren, the Pioneers, first landed here in '47, there was an abundance of grass over all those benches; they were covered with it like a meadow. There is now nothing but the desert weed, the sage, the rabbit-bush, and such like plants, that make very poor feed for stock. Being cut short of our range in the way we have been, and accumulating stock as we are, we have nothing to feed them with in the winter and they perish. There is no profit in this, neither is it pleasing in the sight of God our Heavenly Father that we should continue a course of life like unto this."

Utah was in a particularly dangerous situation because of the large number of small farms along the base of the mountains. Each farmer had a few head of cattle to graze and the forested areas in the mountains offered a nearby grazing ground. Soon not only the valley grasses but the meadows in the canyons and mountains were being destroyed through overuse.

By the turn of the century a general realization of the problems of overgrazing

Albert F. Potter, chief grazing officer, United States Forest Service, 1892.

awakened the people to the need for wise management of natural resources. In Utah the conservation movement was first expressed in forest and water conservation.

The national forest movement. In July 1902 Albert F. Potter, chief grazing officer, forestry division, the Department of the Interior (later the Forest Service, Department of Agriculture), conducted a five-month survey of natural resources of the Wasatch Mountains and the High Plateaus. Potter's job was to determine how the immediate needs of both the people and the land could best be met. In his tour of 145 days, he traveled 3,077 miles by train, wagon, and foot, but mostly on horseback. He visited communities and talked with people, but spent much of his time in the mountains observing the condition of the timber lands and grazing lands. He noticed the mining areas and newly established power plants. Potter got a good picture of the needs for control of the forest lands. He believed in conservation through wise use. He was interested in the livestock industry, but he also saw that the forest lands were very important as watersheds providing clean water for villages and for mining and lumbering.

Potter observed that most of the cattle

operations were small, but one group of stockmen had pooled their holdings until they had nearly 77,000 acres under lease. While cattle were tied to farm property and winter feeding, sheep ran winter and summer on the public domain. Sheep grazing reached unusual proportions in the years at the turn of the century. In some areas there were open conflicts between cattlemen and sheepmen. For the most part sheepmen and associated industries were opposed to Potter and the expected results from his study, while cattlemen, farmers, and townspeople generally favored placing the forests under reserve. Cache Valley residents welcomed Potter's survey and appear to have petitioned that a forest reserve be established quickly. Cache Valley people had observed the decline of the forests and wanted something done about it.

Even before the Potter survey, two national forest reserves had been established in Utah through the efforts of Utahns. However, the Potter survey of 1902 marked the beginning of wide-scale forest management.

Between 1897 and 1908 several national forests were created in Utah, putting under protective management several million acres of forest land. The Uinta National Forest was established February 22, 1897. Fishlake National Forest was established in 1899, receiving its present name in 1907. Cache National Forest dates from a proclamation of May 5, 1903, with additions in 1907 and its present name in 1908. In central Utah the Manti National Forest, was established May 29, 1903, to which was soon added the La Sal National Forest, established January 24, 1906. The southern portion of the High Plateaus was established as the Dixie National Forest, September 25, 1905. The Wasatch National Forest, which included the Salt Lake National Forest, was established August 16, 1906. In the Uinta Mountains area the Ashley National Forest was established July 1, 1908. These reserves have been consolidated, added to, and names changed from time to time. Today there are seven national forests in Utah totaling more than eight million acres. Several other national forests extend into Utah from neighboring states.

From the beginning of the national forest movement, the policy was that all land "be devoted to its most productive use for the permanent good of the whole people, and not for the temporary benefit of individuals or companies." This major policy found expression in three related policies: (1) "Use of the resources for the benefit of people, but in a manner that will assure perpetuity." (2) The policy of "multiple use." Lands usually support several resources at the same time, and each must be protected and used according to its importance. (3) Where conflicting interests occur, as they will under multiple use, "the question will always be decided from the standpoint of the greatest good to the greatest number in the long run." Through the years the Forest Service has tried to serve the people while maintaining the forests under these policies.

The conservation of water implies the maintenance of clean rivers and streams. This in turn assures a pure and adequate water supply to homes. In early pioneer days Utah was known for its clean ditches of fresh running water, so pure it could be used for household purposes. Penalties were attached to disturbing the ditches and streams. Unfortunately, such regard for the purity of water soon eased. However, enough people were concerned that the territorial legislatures of the 1890s enacted comprehensive health laws. The text of one law read: "Whatever is dangerous to human life or health, and whatever renders soil, air, water, or food impure or unwholesome, are declared to be nuisances and to be illegal ...." Penalties were prescribed for the violation of specific offenses.

6. NATIONAL PARKS AND MONUMENTS PRESERVE SOME OF UTAH'S NATURAL BEAUTY AND NATURAL WONDERS

One important way the federal government has acted on the ideals of conservation has been through the creation of national parks and monuments. The movement began in 1872 with the establishment of Yellowstone National Park.

National Parks are areas distinctly national in importance and interest, created by Congress out of federally owned lands. *National monuments* are public land areas set aside by presidential proclamation because of their biological significance, archaeological nature, historical value, or geological features. Most national monuments have been created under authority of the Antiquities Act of June 8, 1906. National monuments can be named as national parks.

Natural Bridges National Monument was the first national monument created in Utah. Though the region had been visited and the bridges seen by Cass Hite, a prospector, in 1883, and by Emery Knowles, John Albert Scorup, and other cowboys in 1895, it was not until 1904 that national publicity was given to the site by articles in the *Century Magazine* (August 1904) and the *National Geographic Magazine* (September 1904). The next summer, members of the Salt Lake Commercial Club undertook an expedition into the region. From these expeditions and reports came a movement to set aside the area for all the people. President Roosevelt created the monument April 16, 1908.

The monument is about fifty miles west of Blanding, in White Canyon, on the western edge of Grand Gulch Plateau. Here, in 2,649 acres set aside to preserve these wonders, are

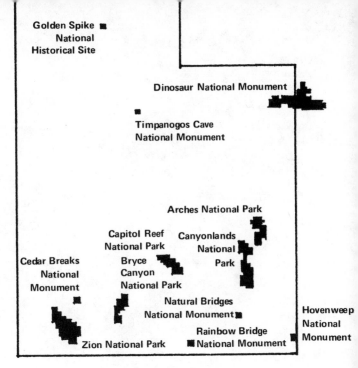

National parks and monuments in Utah today.

three of the world's largest natural bridges. Only Rainbow Bridge is larger. Recently the monument has been increased to 7,600 acres by including other areas on Grand Gulch Plateau, particularly areas containing Indian ruins.

Zion National Park. The beauties of Zion Canyon on the North Fork of the Virgin River were known to Mormon settlers from 1858 when the canyon was discovered by Nephi Johnson. Major Powell saw the canyon too. To the Mormons the canyon was Little Zion, for it is said to have reminded them of "towering temples of stone," of "houses built without hands," their "heavenly city of God." In the summer of 1908 Leo A. Snow of Saint George made a survey of the canyons of the Kolob Terrace, including Zion Canyon. As a result of his report, recommendation was made by the Department of the Interior to the president of the United States that the area be created as the Makuntuweap National Monument, using the Indian name for the North Fork of the Virgin River. The

This air view of Zion Canyon shows the deep canyons cut in the southern end of the High Plateaus, the area of Zion National Park.

Temple of Sinawava, Zion National Park.

Augusta Bridge, Natural Bridges National Monument. An oil painting by H. L. A. Culmer. The Bridge, named Sipapu by the Indians, is 220 feet high, spans 268 feet, and is 31 feet wide and 53 feet thick. It is one of the largest natural bridges in the monument.

monument was created in 1909. On March 15, 1918, the name was changed to Zion National Monument and the area enlarged to 76,800 acres. Senator Reed Smoot introduced the bill to establish it as a national park; the bill passed and was approved November 19, 1919, creating Zion National Park. A second Zion National Monument adjoining the park was established in 1937; in July 1956 it was added to the park and is known as the Kolob Canyon section.

Rainbow Bridge National Monument. At their recently established Indian trading post in Monument Valley, the John Wetherills heard of a rainbow-turned-to stone. They relayed the news to Professor Byron Cummings of the University of Utah. The summer of 1909 he was joined by two Indian guides, a government survey party led by W. B. Douglas, and several friends and students on a trek in search of a natural bridge. Cummings credited two Paiute Indians, Noscha Begay and his father, as the discoverers of the bridge.

Of seeing Rainbow Bridge, Professor Cummings wrote: "We were all overwhelmed at the sight of this mighty towering arch ... Even then [it] is dwarfed by the bare sandstone cliffs that rise far above it on every side. The wealth of color reflected from the cliffs and the deep shadows of the gorges make you feel you are in some giant paradise of long ago, that any minute huge forms of

This exploring party, west of Navajo Mountain, is in search of Rainbow Bridge, August 1909.

Rainbow Bridge, found by white men under the guidance of Indians, is one of Utah's most famous natural wonders. The area was soon made a national monument.

man and beast might come stalking out of the shadows and ask why such puny creatures as we disturb their solitude."

Rainbow Bridge was proclaimed a national monument on May 30, 1910.

The Dinosaur National Monument story centers around the life of Earl Douglass, a geologist and fossil collector for the Carnegie Museum, Pittsburgh, Pennsylvania. Prior to his coming to Utah, he collected fossils in Colorado, Idaho, Montana, and the Dakotas. During the summers of 1907, 1908, and 1909 he explored the Uinta Basin. On August 19, 1909, Douglass made the discovery which led to the development of the dinosaur quarry and the establishment of Dinosaur National Monument. He had been prospecting the Morrison formation for weeks when near the crest of a hard sandstone ridge he spotted a long section of dinosaur tail vertebrae exposed by erosion. Further digging disclosed more of the skeleton.

From 1909 to 1923, under Douglass' direction, the Carnegie Museum removed 700,000 pounds of dinosaur bones from the quarry, hauled them by wagon to Watson, Utah, and shipped them by rail to Pittsburgh. This wealth of fossils contained twenty-three nearly complete skeletons. Parts of three hundred dinosaur specimens were found. The longest skeleton was of Diplodocus, 84 feet. Altogether this was the richest known single source for dinosaur remains. Many of the bones have been assembled as complete skeletons and may be seen in museums in Pittsburgh, Washington D.C., New York City, Lincoln, Denver, Salt Lake City, and Toronto, Canada.

Dinosaur National Monument was established October 4, 1915, consisting of the quarry and eighty acres of surrounding land. The boundaries were extended in 1938 to include the scenic canyon country. The monu-

Earl Douglass discovered dinosaur fossil remains in Utah and was chiefly responsible for the development of the dinosaur quarry and the establishment of Dinosaur National Monument.

Monument (March 2, 1923), consisting of over five hundred acres in Utah and Colorado, protects a group of nineteen separate building ruins. Dating from the time of the Anasazi, these ruins are noted for their square, oval, circular, and D-shaped towers. *Bryce Canyon National Park* (June 8, 1923) is a natural amphitheater of fantastic rock sculpture eroded from an exposed face of the Pink Cliffs. Rain, snow, sun, and ice have worn away the cliffs leaving brilliantly colored sculpture suggestive of miniature cities, cathedrals, temples, organs, and people. *Arches National Monument* (April 12, 1929) near Moab contains more natural stone arches, windows, spires, and pinnacles, carved by the forces of nature than any other known section of the nation. It was enlarged in 1938 and 1969 and designated a national park in 1971. *Cedar Breaks National Monument* (August 22, 1933) offers superlative scenic values in its multicolored and fantastically eroded shapes. It covers a ten-mile amphitheaterlike area near Cedar City. *Capitol Reef National Monument* (August 2, 1937), east of Torrey, originally contained 33,168 acres of highly colored sandstone cliffs and fantastic forms created through erosion. It was subsequently enlarged to 254,241 acres and was designated a national park in 1971.

ment now covers over 206,233 acres in Utah and Colorado.

In later years other national parks and monuments were established within Utah. *Timpanogos Cave National Monument* (October 14, 1922) preserves a series of small but beautifully decorated underground chambers within limestone beds on the north slope of Mount Timpanogos. *Hovenweep National*

Wagons loaded with dinosaur bones enter the "U" circle at the University of Utah, about 1924, after the Carnegie Museum ceased work in the quarry.

Picnic excursion to Provo Canyon via the D & R G Railway.

The big problem, in the early days of the automobile, was roads. Some motorists just went too far, even with chains.

THE NEW WAY OF LIFE

During the period 1896 to 1920 changes came to Utah which were more revolutionary in their effect on economic and social life than the coming of the railroad. Utah emerged from the days of the candle and the oil lamp into the light of electricity. The horse and buggy began to disappear as automobiles and concrete highways appeared. Interurban railroads provided quick passenger and freight transportation between the cities of the Wasatch Front. The use of steel and concrete in building construction brought high-rising buildings to downtown Salt Lake City. Despite these radical changes, pioneer ways lasted well into the twentieth century for most Utahns.

Utah's economic life became more closely tied to nationwide patterns. Business improved, investment money came to Utah, and goods from Utah went far and wide.

Social and cultural changes were as significant as material changes. The Mormons adjusted their ways of life to a closer conformity to common American ways. Mormons and non-Mormons cooperated in business, politics and community development projects. Mormon businesses became more like "any other business" as distinctions gradually broke down. The immigration of Mormons declined, and there was a new immigration to Utah, part of the new immigration to the United States from southern Europe. These immigrants added much to Utah's economic and cultural life. Utah's society became more diversified.

Indians, moved onto the Uintah Indian Reservation in the last century, were deprived of many of those lands by governmental action which made some of the lands available to white homesteaders. Ute Indians made their last uprising against the advance of the whites, and failed.

Richfield baseball team, 1912-13.

21

IN THIS CHAPTER WE WILL LEARN

1. Utah's economic life prospered as it conformed to national economic patterns.

2. Electricity brought about a revolution in communication, lighting, and power.

3. Streetcars, interurban railroads, and automobiles effected a transportation revolution.

4. The new immigration added a new dimension to Utah.

5. A modern educational system emerged.

6. What happened to Utah Indians after they were moved to reservations.

Railroads played an increased role in life in the twentieth century. Salt Lake was connected with Los Angeles in 1905.

Saltair, built in 1893 on the shores of Great Salt Lake, offered swimming, dancing, a roller coaster, and other amusements. The famous resort was made possible by improved railroad services.

1. UTAH'S ECONOMIC LIFE PROSPERED AS IT CONFORMED TO NATIONAL ECONOMIC PATTERNS

In the spirit of statehood requirements the Mormon church withdrew increasingly from the area of economic development, sold many of its properties, disposed of stock in its businesses, and generally retreated from its former role in the economic life of Utah. Business relations grew friendlier, prejudices were broken down, and a spirit of business confidence rose. Outside investments helped develop Utah's industry and agriculture. There was general prosperity in all fields. Mining, manufacturing, and agriculture witnessed new developments.

Salt Lake City and Ogden continued to develop as financial, commercial, transportation, and distribution centers. Transcontinental railroads, north-south lines, and local railroads served to move goods in and out of Utah.

Railroad services increased. The Oregon Short Line Railroad Company, organized in Salt Lake City in 1897, acquired possession of the Utah Central, Utah Northern, Utah Southern, Utah Southern Extension, and Salt Lake and Western lines. Through these consolidations Utah was connected to the extensive farming and mining areas of Idaho, western Wyoming, Montana, and eastern Oregon. The Western Pacific Railway, built in the 1890s, connected Salt Lake City with the San Francisco area. The Lucin Cutoff, completed in 1903, shortened the Southern Pacific route between Ogden and Lucin by forty miles. A great engineering feat, the cutoff was 103 miles long. One-third of its length was built upon trestle work and fill-ins over the waters of the Great Salt Lake. In 1905 the Los Angeles and Salt Lake Railroad was completed, connecting Utah communities with the major cities of southern California. These were important developments for Utah trade relations with coastal cities. Spur lines led to Saltair, the popular resort at the south edge of Great Salt Lake, and to mining areas.

Population characteristics. In the thirty years between 1890 and 1920 the population of Utah more than doubled. The increase was from 210,779 (1890) to 449,396 (1920). Salt Lake City and Ogden doubled their population between 1900 and 1920. Provo and Logan doubled their population between 1890 and 1920. These four cities account for more than half of the state's population increase from 1900 to 1920. Though all the counties, except Juab and Rich, shared in this population increase, the growth was mostly urban.

Laying sewer lines, Salt Lake City, May 1915.
Many improvements came to Utah's urban
centers such as sewage disposal systems, natural gas,
sidewalks, and roads.

In 1890 36 percent of Utah's people lived in urban areas while in 1920 48 percent lived in cities. Half of the people of Utah lived in Weber, Davis, Salt Lake and Utah counties.

The number of families increased from 56,196 (1900) to 98,346 (1920). The rate of growth in numbers of families was double that of the entire pioneer period. The average size of the Utah family during the territorial period was slightly less than that of the average American family, but from 1890 on the size of the Utah family was slightly larger than that of the average American family. With improved health and sanitation conditions there were more older people than before.

In 1900 about 80 percent of Utah's population was born in the United States (chiefly New York, Illinois, Ohio, and Pennsylvania); 19.4 percent were foreign-born (chiefly England, Denmark, and Sweden). The census counted 2,623 Indians, 672 Negroes, 572 Chinese, and 417 Japanese.

With regard to church membership in 1900, of the total population of the state, Latter-day Saints or Mormons made up 68 percent, Catholics 3.4, Greek Orthodox 1.5, and the others just less than one-half of one percent. These other leading groups included Presbyterians, Methodists, Episcopalians, Congregationalists, Baptists, and members of the Reorganized Church of Jesus Christ of Latter Day Saints. About 25 percent of the people declined to tell the census reporters to which church, if any, they belonged.

The original Salt Palace, Salt Lake City (top), and the arena and bicycle race track (below).

The large increase in Utah population required more farm lands and more business opportunities. More farms required more water, for crop lands had reached the limit of available water supplies. Mining had taken the most accessible ores, and to extract the deeper ores would require deep-shaft mining, demanding heavy investments. Utahns needed to develop enterprises which could export products for sale outside the state and thus enable the people to buy goods which could be imported more cheaply than they could be produced locally. Utahns turned to the solution of some of these problems.

Business. The occupational structure of Utah in 1914 is illustrated by the following table showing the percentage of the working force in various occupations:

28.4% agriculture, forestry, animal husbandry
23.7% manufacturing and mechanical industries
9.9% trade
9.4% transportation
8.2% domestic and personal
7.6% mining
6.0% professional
4.9% clerical
1.9% public service

Agriculture. A major revolution took place in agriculture in Utah after 1890. Between 1890 and 1900 the number of farms and the total number of acres of improved farm land doubled. By 1920 the number of farms had increased to over 25,000 and the acreage of improved land to 1,715,380 acres. From 1900 to 1920 the comparative value of farms in Utah increased from $2,619 per farm to $9,499. By 1920 the available land for cultivation had been largely taken up. Utah acreage in farm land reached its peak about that year.

The major field crops were wheat, oats,

A Utah landscape near Draper, Salt Lake Valley.

place of dry farming in the United States. Dry farming was first tried in Utah in 1863 by farmers who tried plowing and planting good lands "above the ditch," without irrigation water. Few of these attempts succeeded. Later, methods were developed which proved successful. One of the leaders in this movement was Dr. John A. Widtsoe, director of the Agricultural Experiment Station, Utah Agricultural College, Logan. Dr. Widtsoe and his associates developed the theory that grains could be grown without irrigation in the areas of deep soil and ten inches of rainfall a year. With funds from the 1903 legislature, the Agricultural Experiment Station established experimental farms in Iron, Juab, San Juan, Sevier, Tooele, and Washington counties.

By 1905 experiments proved that by following a few basic rules dry farming could be successful. Deep soil must be cultivated on contours so as to retain moisture in the soil; seeds must be planted scantily; and the land

John A. Widtsoe, as director of the Agricultural Experiment Station, Utah Agricultural College, led studies which discovered techniques of successful dry farming in Utah. He also served as president of the college and of the University of Utah, was a leader in conservation and reclamation and scientific agriculture, and became a Mormon apostle.

barley, and rye; potatoes, alfalfa, and alfalfa seed were also important. During these years Utah became an important sugar beet producing state. There was a great expansion in fruit orchards. Dairy farming came into its own as did poultry farming. Sheep and cattle ranching remained important enterprises.

Many factors contributed to the agricultural expansion of these years. Government land policies were liberalized, giving farmers easier access to larger tracts of land from the public domain. (See chapter 20, section 4.) The building of dams, reservoirs, and irrigation systems made it possible to put more land under cultivation. Improvements in farm machinery made it possible for farmers to farm greater areas with fewer farm hands and less effort.

Dry farming. Utah is known as the birth-

A portion of the Delta canal system near Sutherland. Reclamation projects made possible the irrigation of new lands in Utah.

Sugar beet field and the Utah-Idaho Sugar Company's refinery, Garland.

must be left idle or fallow every other year to allow the soil to absorb moisture and to break down organic material. By 1910 dry farming was no longer experimental. Between 1912 and 1921 there was a great expansion of dry farming, increasing Utah's crop land by one-fourth. These lands produced crops of wheat, oats, rye, barley, and alfalfa.

The irrigation of additional lands was made possible by reclamation projects. Thousands of acres of land were brought into use by the application of water from reservoirs made possible by dams on the water courses. Under the Carey Act various projects were begun in Utah. Among the important federal projects were those at Delta and Hinckley, Millard County; Moab, Grand County; Woodside, Huntington, and Green River town, Emery County; Myton, Duchesne County; on the Dry Creek, Uintah County; on the Virgin River, Washington County; and on the Bear River, Rich County. Some projects, such as the Strawberry and Newton projects, were built under the National Reclamation Act (Newlands Act, 1902). The state also supported reclamation projects. There were the Hatchtown Project on the Sevier River in Garfield County and the Piute Project on the Sevier River near Marysvale.

The beet sugar industry was a major agricultural development in the twentieth century. Not only were Utahns supplied locally processed sugar, but Utah farmers were provided with a new major cash crop. After the failure to produce sugar in the 1850s it was not until the 1880s that new attempts were made, and then with state government and Mormon church financial support. Improvements had been made in the chemical process of extracting sugar from the sugar beet in Nebraska and California factories. The first successful attempt to produce sugar in Utah was at the Lehi factory of the Utah Sugar Company in 1891. Auxiliary plants were soon operating at Springville, Provo, and Bingham Junction. The Ogden Sugar Company factory, during 1898, its first year of operation, produced three million pounds of sugar, made from sugar beets grown within a hundred miles of Ogden. By 1900 these two companies were producing sufficient sugar for Utah's needs and were looking for markets for the surplus.

Other companies soon had plants in operation in the major valleys of the state. By 1903 the Amalgamated Sugar Company had factories in Ogden, Logan, and LaGrande, Oregon. The Lewiston Sugar Company had a factory at Lewiston in central Cache Valley. By 1912 the Utah-Idaho Sugar Company had consolidated various holdings and was operating factories from Blackfoot, Idaho, to Sevier County, Utah. The company was church promoted and controlled, but financed by eastern backers. By 1913 seven thousand farms furnished beets to the company's factories. In 1913-14 Utah ranked fourth in the United States in the production of sugar and the number of factories. By 1917 six sugar companies were in successful operation. Combined, they purchased 1,126,000 tons of beets, for which they paid the farmers $7,882,000, and from which they produced 274,500,000 pounds of sugar.

Dairying became a business during these years, especially in Box Elder and Cache counties. In the forty years from 1880 to 1920 the number of milk cows doubled. Excellent feed in alfalfa and silage made from corn stalks helped this growth. Professor George B. Caine of Utah State Agricultural College contributed to the dairy industry by bringing in purebred bulls from the East to improve the dairy herds. Holsteins became favorites. Dairymen from throughout northern Utah took their prize stock to Richmond for the annual Black and White Days, where cattle were judged and prizes awarded for quality and production.

Important to the dairy industry was the establishment of creameries, and butter, cheese, and *evaporated milk plants*. The first *cheese factories* and condensed milk plants were established in Cache Valley just after the turn of the century.

Though the foundations of a dairy industry were well laid in these years, Utah was still importing butter and cheese in large quantities.

Utah was also dependent upon other states for its *poultry*. In fact, the entire West was importing poultry and eggs at this time. Utah farmers began turning to poultry raising to supply this demand.

The processing of agricultural products is an important aspect of agriculture and industry. The Utah *canning industry* began in 1888 when Isaac N. Pierce moved from Colorado to Ogden, built a small factory and began canning tomatoes. That year the Utah Canning Company preserved three hundred cans of tomatoes. Soon the little factory was canning catsup, puree, tomato juice, beets, carrots, peas, kidney beans, stringless beans, pork and beans, and other foods.

In 1892 the Woods Cross Canning Company was formed. From tomatoes, this company turned also to canning vegetables and other fruits. Canning factories multiplied until there were twenty in 1910 and thirty-two in 1914 with an output of 1,338,497 cases of fruits and vegetables. Factories were located near farming centers ranging from Brigham City to southern Utah Valley. Farmers were being paid a half-million dollars for their produce, and factories employed 1,500 workers who received one-third of a million dollars in wages. By 1914 Utah ranked fifth in the canning industry among the United States. Utah canned products sold throughout the West and Midwest.

Preservation of food by canning greatly enlarged the market for Utah farm products.

The cowboy is indispensable on large cattle ranches.

The history of the *cattle industry* in Utah has gone through three periods. (1) In the pioneer period Utah farmers had a few cattle, which they put out to graze on the common field, in valley pasture lands, or on the hills and in the mountains. Improvement in the quality of the stock was achieved mainly by Utahns trading their well-fed cattle to overland emigrants who had good but tired stock, and by acquiring good stock from cattle drives from the Great Plains coming through Utah on their way to California. (2) Toward the end of the century cattle raising became a major occupation for many ranchers in Utah. At about the same time (1880s), the American cattle frontier came into Utah as ranchers from Texas and other Great Plains states moved their herds into southeastern Utah. These ranchers put their cattle on forested lands in the summer and moved them to the open range during the winter. (3) With the coming of national forests to Utah at the beginning of this century the period of free range began to end. It became necessary for cattlemen to pay a fee for a permit to graze cattle on most summer ranges. This reduced somewhat the number of cattle grazed, but it preserved the forests and their capacity as watersheds. Besides using forest permits, some cattle ranchers purchased land or leased land from the government on which to graze their herds.

The Utah Cattle and Horse Growers Association was organized in 1916 to help improve the livestock by allowing only pure-bred, inspected bulls to be used for breeding. The association also established a vaccination program to control disease. Although other breeds of cattle were used, the Hereford seemed best suited to Utah range conditions. San Juan County became the largest cattle-producing county in Utah, with Box Elder, Utah, Sanpete, and Sevier counties also leaders. In 1914 there were 237,543 cattle in the state valued at $4,042,911.

Sheep grazing increased greatly around the turn of the century. In 1889 there were about one million sheep grazing on Utah lands. During the next ten years the number increased four times. Wool production increased equally—from five million pounds in 1889 to more than seventeen million pounds ten years later. Two breeds of sheep were important to the industry—the Spanish Marino and the French Rambouillet. The excellence of these breeds improved production of wool and meat. Much of the grazing was on the forested slopes of the mountains. The establishment of national forest reserves led to the curtailment of grazing on those lands and the subsequent decline in the number of sheep grazing on them. (See chapter 20.) By 1914 it was estimated that there were 2,100,000 sheep in Utah, valued at $10 million and producing wool valued at $2,250,000. Utah sheepmen sent to eastern markets that year sheep valued at $3,250,000. In 1920 the Utah Wool Growers Association was organized to help make the industry more stable.

Processing cattle and sheep for market was an equally important part of the livestock industry. Salt Lake City and Ogden became centers for stockyards and meat packing, taking advantage of locations at the center of Utah's railroad system. Livestock were driven from the ranges to railroad loading stations and carried by railcar to stockyards. There the cattle were purchased by packing companies and moved to the slaughterhouses or meat-packing plants or were shipped to other centers for processing. The dressed meat was sold to local butcher shops or put into refrigerated railcars and shipped to distant cities.

The first public livestock yards in Utah were opened in 1891 on the northern outskirts of Salt Lake City. In 1906 a packing plant was opened in Ogden. The industry grew until in 1916 a general reorganization of companies took place. The Salt Lake Union Stock Yards, the Ogden Union Stock Yards, and packing companies emerged in 1917. The increased demands for food during World War I led to a rapid expansion of the industry. Ogden soon became the largest center for shipping, feeding, and marketing of livestock west of Omaha, Nebraska.

Mining. The story of mining during the period from 1896 to 1920 is mainly the story of copper, coal, and gold. Gold was successfully mined at Mercur and separated by a cyanide process which helped establish several wealthy mining families. However, the big story is in *copper*, and the story is of two men who made copper mining a success —*Samuel Newhouse* and *Daniel C. Jackling*. Newhouse and his partner, Thomas Wier, purchased claims in the Bingham Canyon area hoping to make money by extracting gold. Their Highland Boy Mine, however, turned out a high grade copper ore. This interested Newhouse, and he went to England and obtained financial support to mine copper. For his operation he set up a smelter in Murray. Word of this success brought other mining companies into the area, and soon there were

Miners, probably from Tintic district, about 1905.

Workers shoveling coal into boilers at Sunnyside, Utah, 1903.

three copper smelters and one lead smelter in operation between Murray and Midvale. Gold, silver, lead, and zinc were extracted from the ore as well as a crude copper which was sent east for refining.

By 1904 the smelters were in trouble because of the smoke belt that polluted the air and damaged crops and animals. The farmers joined forces and took the smelter owners to court, winning their case in 1905. This action closed all but the Murray smelter which stayed open after the owners agreed to pay $60,000 damages and to stop the harmful gas from escaping in the smoke.

Daniel C. Jackling, who had made money at Mercur, began his exciting chapter in the history of Utah mining in 1905. He is called the father of Utah copper because of his dream and success in the development of open-pit mining of low-grade porphyry copper ore. He and his backers purchased claims in Bingham Canyon region and designed and built a system of crushing plants, flotation mills, and smelters in Magna, Arthur, and

Tooele. Success was based not on the richness of the ores, but in the vast tonnage of copper ores handled. Immense steam shovels, moving seven tons of earth at a scoop, began clawing away at the mountain to create a great open pit. Railroad tracks were laid in the mine to receive ore from the shovels. Money was made by processing large quanti-

Daniel C. Jackling, the father of Utah copper mining, developed open-pit mining of low-grade ores.

380

ties of ore each day, and in addition to copper, gold, silver, lead, and zinc were extracted. This method of copper mining has been followed in other copper mines in both North and South America. By 1910 Utah mines were producing over $16 million worth of copper a year.

Coal mining was made profitable with the coming of the railroad to coal mining regions. Utah Fuel Supply, owned by the Denver and Rio Grande Western Railroad, built the company towns of Sunnyside, Castle Gate, Clear Creek, Winter Quarters, Black Hawk, and Mohrland. By 1910 twenty-two coal mines were in operation, and that number increased to forty-six by 1920. Production rose from 521,560 tons in 1897 to 6,005,199 tons in 1920. Through these years there was an average of about 2,500 men employed in the mines, each man mining between three and four tons a day. Part of this coal was converted into coke for use in Utah's smelters, though half of the coke produced in the state was shipped out. As coal became less expensive, it was used more and more to heat homes, offices, and factories.

Oil production in Utah had its beginning in this period. The first important exploration in Utah was in the San Juan area in 1907 when fifteen drilling outfits went to work. By 1909 oil production and refining in Utah were begun. Major uses of oil in those years were for kerosene, greases, and lubricating oils.

Labor. Utah labor history follows the general pattern of labor history in the United States. The Utah territorial legislature recognized the right of workers to organize and negotiate with their employers for better wages and working conditions. In 1852 the legislative assembly established a system whereby the mechanics of each county could elect twelve selectmen as referees to resolve disputes brought to them by mutual consent. Perhaps the oldest labor organization in Utah was the Salt Lake Typographical Union, organized August 3, 1868. During the 1870s railroad workers formed craft-oriented unions and the miners organized industrial-type unions. In February 1888 most of the local unions in Salt Lake City affiliated with the newly formed Utah Federated Trades and Labor Council, the first city central labor organization in Utah. In 1893 men in the building trades attempted to establish a limited and exclusive central organization of

Open-pit mining at Bingham Canyon consisted of cutting away the mountain in terraces on which steam shovels loaded ore into railroad cars headed for the smelter. At the smelter the ore was reduced to separate metals.

Each year on June 13 the miners' union at Park City held a parade. A parade before the turn of the century.

were usually restricted to improving working conditions and bettering wages. But the new mine workers' unions were radical in their goals. Some called for changing the economic system so that the miners could control the mines. The mine labor strikes of the period showed the changing economic structure of Utah and America. On one hand there were united and militant labor unions, and opposing them were the newly emerging large corporations and trusts which were gaining control of the mines as well as many other areas of the nation's economic life.

During the same years, the Utah legislature wrote laws to benefit laborers. The first legislature (1896) passed an eight-hour-workday law for certain workers. This act made history when the United States Supreme Court upheld the Utah law in a famous case, *Holden* v. *Hardy* (1898). Other important laws provided for the health and safety of miners, prohibited child labor, provided minimum wage laws for female workers, and workmen's compensation laws. The Utah State Bureau of Labor and the Utah State Industrial Commission attempted to recognize and remedy labor problems.

The Joe Hill case. A famous episode of American labor history occurred in Utah in 1915. Joe Hill, a member of the IWW, was executed for the murder of a Salt Lake City grocer and his son. There is some evidence indicating Joe Hill actually committed the murders, but there is also some reason to believe he was innocent. Because of this doubt, thousands of letters and even two requests by President Woodrow Wilson were sent to Utah's Governor Spry asking that Joe Hill be saved.

During the years before his arrest and while he was in jail, Joe Hill wrote songs about the experiences of working men and women telling of their hardships and their

building trade unions. But union efforts fell upon hard times. The depression of the 1890s put many men out of work, and employers had their pick of the laborers for small wages, bypassing the unions and their attempts to improve wages and working conditions. Utah was never an important base of operations for unionism. Generally, Mormon church leaders opposed compulsory unionism and were distrustful of strikes which usually ended, in those days, in violence and destruction.

In Utah's early mining camps, labor organized as in other western mining towns. Salt Lake City, in the center of the mining West, played an occasional important role. For three years (1898-1901) the Western Federation of Miners had its headquarters in Salt Lake City.

The first two decades of the century witnessed active and revolutionary unionism in Utah among the mining and smelter workers through such nationally known organizations as the Western Federation of Miners, the Industrial Workers of the World (IWW), and the Workers', Soldiers' and Sailors' Council. The purposes of the early labor unions

A photograph of Joe Hill, legendary I.W.W. worker and songwriter, taken shortly after his arrest in 1914. The charge of murder, for which Hill was executed in 1915, still leaves room for reasonable doubt as to his guilt.

hopes for a better life. His songs were printed in IWW song books and were sung by workers throughout the world. Today Joe Hill lives as a legend and many of his songs have become folk songs.

2. ELECTRICITY BROUGHT ABOUT A REVOLUTION IN COMMUNICATION, LIGHTING, AND POWER

The discovery of electricity and the applications of electrical energy caused a complete revolution in man's way of life. While the beginning of this revolution came in the nineteenth century the greatest changes came during the first half of the twentieth century.

Slowly the multitude of labor-saving devices, conveniences, and miracles of communication came to Utah. It will help us understand these changes if we keep before us a mental picture of Utah in the nineteenth century and add the inventions dependent upon electricity and witness the changes they brought to society.

The telephone. One of the early applications of electricity was the creation of the telephone. On March 10, 1876, Alexander Graham Bell first transmitted speech over his telephone. Less than two years later the telephone was introduced in Utah by A. Milton Musser, who had been a leading figure in the development of Utah's Deseret Telegraph Company in the 1860s. (He also brought the phonograph to Utah.) He established several small telephone circuits in Salt Lake City and temporarily connected Salt Lake City and Ogden. In 1879 an Ogden merchant installed a telephone line between his store and his warehouse. Soon several other private lines were installed in Salt Lake City and Ogden. In 1880 Utah's first telephone exchange was operated in Ogden, with twenty-four lines and approximately thirty telephones. Most of the

A confusing network of wires and poles characterized downtown Salt Lake City when electric companies competed for business. This was before companies were consolidated and lines were put underground.

early subscribers were business houses. Soon telephone exchanges were in Salt Lake City, Park City, Logan, and Provo. Lines were strung between towns for long distance calls. By 1890 communities between Nephi and Preston, Idaho, were linked by telephone.

Utah holds the distinction of having the transcontinental railroad, the telegraph, and the transcontinental telephone wires united in Utah. On June 17, 1914, four copper wires were spliced at Wendover to complete a 3,400-mile telephone circuit from New York City to San Francisco. The first call on the line was made by Mr. Bell in New York City to his assistant, Mr. Watson, in San Francisco, in memory of the first transmission of speech between them in 1876.

As many as sixteen different telephone companies incorporated in Utah. Some are still in operation as independent companies, though most have become part of the Mountain States Telephone Company, now Mountain Bell. A second transcontinental connection was also made at Wendover when an underground cable was completed in 1942. The new cable made it possible to carry six hundred conversations at one time.

Electricity for lights and power. As elsewhere, gas provided an intermediary stage of lighting between pioneer candles and modern electricity. Street lamps were first used in Salt Lake City in 1869, but it was not until 1873 that the city was first lighted with gas. It was years before other Utah cities had gas lights.

Shortly after Thomas A. Edison in 1879 introduced improvements that made possible the commercial production of the incandescent electric lamp, the people of Utah witnessed electricity in action. Exhibitions of the arc light were given on the streets of Salt Lake City in 1880 and of Ogden in 1881. Electric light and power companies were organized at once. Steam engines were first used to generate the electricity, and then producers looked to water power in the neighboring canyons. An electric power plant was built in Big Cottonwood Canyon in 1894; the Pioneer Power Plant was built in Ogden Canyon in 1897; and the Telluride Power Company built a power plant in Provo Canyon in 1897 and another in Logan Canyon in 1901. Soon a score of companies offered electricity to the Wasatch Front communities. Some businesses built their own plants to supply their electrical needs.

A remarkable advance came to the electric utility business when Lucien L. Nunn, a lawyer and mining man from Telluride mining district of southwestern Colorado, developed long-distance, high-voltage transmission of electrical energy by alternating current. His Ames, Colorado, plant was the first power station to transmit alternating current at high voltage for power purposes. Previously direct current had been used; small quantities of power were transmitted but short distances. In the summer of 1897 Nunn came to Utah because he saw the possibility of using water power to generate electricity and transmit it to mining operations. Nunn built his first station in Provo Canyon and operated one of the world's first 40,000-volt transmission lines. The lines went to the gold-mining town of Mercur. While Nunn's first objective was to supply the need of mining operations for electrical energy, he and his associates also saw the possibilities of selling electrical power, not only to mining operations, but to cities for light and power. To help train persons in the field of electricity, he set up the

Telluride Institute near his plant in Provo Canyon.

There was great competition among the power plants with price wars similar to those used by service stations today. On January 1, 1913, eighteen electric light and power companies were consolidated under the name of Utah Power and Light Company. This company was soon supplying about 90 percent of the power used, while small municipal and private plants supplied the other 10 percent.

Each community in Utah has stories of the coming of the electric light. Often a main street demonstration took place where a single bulb was lighted. First there were street lights, and then lights were put into homes. For years some municipal companies charged the homeowner a fixed amount based on the number of bulbs used in the house. Electricity was soon taken to the mines for light and power, though electricity arrived late in many parts of Utah. It was not until the 1906-07 school year that electric lights were installed in the school buildings of Salt Lake City. In

Mr. Malmstrom has just recently installed electric lights in his M & M General Store in Midvale.

Salt Lake streetcars operated out of the old car barns.

December 1920 a newspaper announced that Logan was then creating its "white way" with street lights along Center Street, Main Street, and First North Street—about three blocks of street lights. Some parts of Salt Lake Valley were without electricity until the 1930s, and parts of rural Utah did not get electricity until the 1950s.

3. STREETCARS, INTERURBAN RAILROADS, AND AUTOMOBILES EFFECTED A TRANSPORTATION REVOLUTION

At the beginning of the 1800s, man depended upon the speed of his horse for travel. Prior to the telegraph, mail service was dependent upon the speed of the horse. The application of steam made possible the railroad, and man could expect to travel as many miles in an hour as he formerly covered in a day by horse. The application of electrical power to transportation effected another revolution for man in the twentieth century.

Streetcars and interurban railroads. Electricity was applied to motor transportation in two major ways: the streetcar and the interurban railroad. Cars or trains ran on railroad tracks and picked up electricity by way of a trolley which rolled against an overhead power line. Streetcars were known in the major cities. Interurbans, as the name implies, ran between cities. They provided convenient mass transportation over short distances, at little cost, for passengers and freight.

Streetcars. The Salt Lake City Street Railway Company was organized in 1872 and operated as a horse-drawn car line over fourteen miles of track. Twenty-one cars served the system, and patrons paid ten cents a ride. In August 1899 the streetcar system was electrified. In 1891 an electric street railway began operating between Salt Lake City and Fort Douglas. Other companies entered the field and for a time an intense rivalry existed among competing companies. By 1903 the Utah Light and Railway Company had brought the different lines under one management. The system covered Salt Lake City and served Fort Douglas, Murray, and other suburban points. The railroad line from Salt Lake City to Saltair was electrified in 1917. The Salt Lake City transit system charged patrons seven cents fare, and they could transfer from one line to another. By 1916 Ogden (with a line up Ogden Canyon), Provo, Logan, and Brigham City had electric streetcar systems.

Interurban transportation. To answer the demand for local railroad freight and passen-

The Bamberger terminal, Salt Lake City, 1950.

The Bamberger interurban line operated, summer and winter, between Salt Lake and Ogden. The Orem line operated from Salt Lake to Payson.

ger service between the cities of the Wasatch Front, the *Bamberger railroad* was founded in January 1891. It built north to Hot Springs, Bountiful, Centerville, and Farmington. North of Farmington the company drained a large swamp, made an artificial lake, and established an amusement park. Lagoon, as the park was named, became a popular resort for swimming, dancing, and horse racing. By 1909 the railroad reached Ogden's Thirty-first Street.

The Salt Lake and Ogden Railway, or Bamberger line as it was popularly called, was converted from steam to electricity in 1910. Terminal stations were constructed in Ogden and Salt Lake, and double tracking was completed in 1913. The line soon won a place in the transportation business of Utah. Up to twelve trains a day ran the route taking about an hour for the trip.

Utah's second important interurban line was the Salt Lake and Utah Railroad, serving between Salt Lake City and Utah Valley. It was popularly called the Orem line, from its chief owner. Service was open between Salt Lake City and Payson by May 1916. The Orem line moved passengers and freight a maximum distance of 66.9 miles between Payson and Salt Lake. As many as twenty-six

trains a day were scheduled on the run, which took about two and a half hours.

City lines were built to serve cities and to connect to interurbans. The Ogden Rapid Transit Company began operating in 1900. The Logan Rapid Transit Company operated from 1910. In time, lines expanded their services, and consolidations took place. The Utah Idaho Central Railroad, popularly called the UIC, extended services from Ogden to Brigham City, to Collinston, and into Cache Valley with stops at Mendon, Wellsville, Hyrum, and Logan, and north to Preston, Idaho. The UIC also operated city systems in Logan, Ogden, and Weber County.

The automobile. The automobile first appeared in Utah at the turn of the century and gradually replaced the horse and buggy. During the 1800s men experimented with steam, electricity, and gasoline to make a self-propelled vehicle. By the 1890s Europeans and Americans were producing machines using these forms of power. In America, the first successful gasoline engine automobile was built by Charles E. and J. Frank Duryea in 1893. Others soon followed until several were in use by 1900.

About 1896 two steam "locomobiles" arrived in Utah for the brothers John and Hyrum Silver. One of the first to take a ride was Mormon church President Lorenzo Snow. After thirty minutes of riding in Salt Lake City, the president gave his excited reaction: "Oh, my, it is as wonderful as it is glorious." He said he had traveled the same roads in 1849 at the rate of a hundred miles per week by ox cart and believed that if the city roads were in good shape, this steam vehicle would have no difficulty in traveling thirty-five miles an hour.

A Lehi resident built his own vehicle in 1899-1900—a one-cylinder gasoline engine with a chain drive. However, the age of the automobile in Utah came with the arrival of automobiles manufactured in the East. In 1900 there may have been twenty gasoline-powered automobiles in the state. Twenty were counted in Salt Lake City in 1903 and between sixty and seventy in 1904. By 1909 a state law required the registration of motor

The popularity of the automobile and the determination of automobile drivers created a demand for better roads.

Driving on the Old Stone Road, Ogden, 1914, this motorist can drive much farther in an hour than he could with horse and wagon in a day.

vehicles. That year 873 cars and trucks were registered. Of these, 39 were electric cars, 13 were steam vehicles, and the remaining 821 were gasoline powered.

In early advertising to promote automobile sales, special pleas were made to doctors and merchants. "If you are a doctor, how can you get along without an automobile physician's car? It can be entirely closed in bad weather, has a physician's cabinet, and can do your work in one-fourth the time you can now with your horse and buggy, and will add many times to your comfort. It is sure to increase your practice; try it." Real estate agents could take prospective buyers great distances to see property, and "If you have a laundry, a bakery, a meat-market or any other kind of business you need an automobile to deliver your goods, to solicit trade, and to advertise your business."

While a primary appeal was made to the businessman, the pleasure driver was not forgotten. "It makes no difference who you are, you ought to get an automobile." "There is no out-door sport on earth that is nearly as healthful or enjoyable as that of controlling a powerful motor car and gliding along at almost any speed you desire, and gives one the sensation of flying or floating through space."

Notwithstanding the advertisements, there were many problems for the motorist in those first years. Acceptable roads existed in some parts of the city, but outside the city, roads were considered non-existent. They were usually unsurfaced, ungraded, dusty (except in the wet seasons when they turned into mud), narrow, with few if any signs to direct the motorist. Motorists prepared for any situation by carrying tools for the engine, body, and tires, and shovels for the road. Repairs were a problem. The motorist, when in trouble, sought the nearest blacksmith. Filling stations were few and far between. While gas-

oline sold for only four or five cents a gallon, the cars traveled only about three miles on a gallon. Oil was not expensive, but cars used it rapidly.

By popular demand state government was asked to provide better roads. In 1909 the State Road Commission was created by the legislature. During its first four years, the commission spent $1 million on roads, bridges, and culverts. The commission planned to take care of Salt Lake City first, link together the most important cities, then add branch roads. In 1913 the backbone of the road system was from Salt Lake City to Brigham City on the north and to Provo on the south. Near Spanish Fork, branches led to Payson and Nephi, Thistle and Price, and through Sanpete Valley south toward Kanab. From Brigham City one branch led into Cache Valley and another northward to communities in the Bear River Valley. Soon branch roads led to neighboring communities, and others followed the major wagon routes in and out of the state. In 1919 there was automobile passenger service from Salt Lake City to Vernal by way of Heber.

The Federal Highways Act of 1916 provided federal funds to be matched by state funds for the construction of major highway systems. The Lincoln Highway, a coast-to-coast route, passed through Utah.

The demands of World War I led to increased use of the automobile and stimulated road building. Until that time some members of the State Road Commission argued about whether to spend money for road improvements for fear the automobile was a fad. Prior to 1918 a total of about thirty-four miles of pavement, most of it within city limits, had been constructed in the state. In 1918 the nation, including Utah, turned to construction of permanent highways. That year the state spent about $1 million on construction, doubled the figure in 1919, and spent over $3 million in 1920, a level of support maintained for the next twenty-five years. By our standards the miles of highway construction seem very little, but to that generation it represented a major accomplishment. Significant progress in road making was to take place during the 1920s, and by the end of the decade Utah was on its way to having surfaced roads (gravel graded) along the main routes.

4. THE NEW IMMIGRATION ADDED A NEW DIMENSION TO UTAH

From the time of the pioneer settlements, Utah has been a home for various nationalities. In the Mormon migration many nationalities were represented. The coming of the railroad and mining to Utah led to additional waves of immigrants. Irish and Chinese came as workers on the railroad, and some stayed to work in the mines or to go into business. In 1870 most of the miners in Bingham were Irish, but by 1880 the Irish were leaving and being replaced by "Cousin Jacks"—a nickname for professional miners from Cornwall, England. Finns and Swedes followed.

A new immigration came to Utah during the 1890s, this time from southern and eastern Europe. The expansion of mining and smelting drew these laborers. As a result, Utah mining towns gained a colorful international flavor as Italians, Slovenes, Croatians, Serbs, Greeks, Armenians, and Montenegrins came. Later came Japanese and Koreans. By 1912 the Bingham population, for example, included 1,210 Greeks, 639 Italians, 564 Austrians, 254 Japanese, 217 Finns, 161 English, 60 Bulgarians, 59 Swedes, 52 Irish, and 23 Germans. For the most part each group had its own section of town and was known for the special skills it could contrib-

Rich in cultural traditions, the Greeks brought a new contribution to Utah's heritage. The wedding of Mr. and Mrs. Angelo Heleotes of Magna at the first Greek Church in Salt Lake City, 1915.

ute to the mining process.

The new immigrant was very important to mining and related industries, and, of course, work in the mines was equally important to the immigrant who had come to Utah without money. The new immigrants had a language barrier which led them to associate with fellow countrymen, making them seem clanish. The Catholics found churches and priests in Utah; however, those belonging to the Greek Orthodox Church had to wait for visiting priests to perform sacred rites. In 1905 a small Greek Orthodox church was built in Salt Lake City. By 1916 the Assumption, a traditional Byzantine church, was built in Price. The Holy Trinity Greek Orthodox church was consecrated in Salt Lake City in 1925. These churches brought permanent clergymen to Utah.

The *Greek immigrants*, to take one group as an example, had a difficult time during their first years in Utah. They were brought in to the coal mines during a strike.

As more countrymen came, they also worked in the mines. Working and living conditions were harsh. Unable to speak English, these laborers were taken advantage of by their employers and their own countrymen. Greek labor agents charged large sums for getting them jobs and some of the interpreters cheated the men as they did business for them. Until brides arrived from the old country, the men spent their free time in the coffeehouses with fellow Greeks, playing cards, reading newspapers, or talking. With the arrival of brides, homelife began. In time, Greek boarding houses were established, and the unmarried men could eat Greek cooking.

The Greeks were proud of their heritage and did all they could to preserve it. Schools were established after 1920 where the children were taught to read and speak Greek. Fraternal organizations helped keep alive Greek traditions. Feast days were celebrated annually; the Greek folk dances and colorful costumes brought a special excitement to those occasions. Traditional foods were always served—barbecued lamb, chicken, goat cheese, and delicious pastries made with imported nuts, fruit, and spices.

Children of immigrants had a tendency to acquire American speech and customs, and in time many of the wonderful old world traditions were neglected and lost.

As time passed and mining became more mechanized, miners had to find work in other industries. The new immigrants now turned to establishing their own businesses or to developing new trades.

Utah invited continued immigration. While Mormon immigration, as a policy and general practice, began declining in the 1890s, the state of Utah encouraged and invited immigration from other sources. The Utah Bureau of Immigration, Labor, and Statistics and the newspapers did all they could to promote immigration. There were some land speculation schemes and some genuine colonizing efforts.

The Jewish colony of Clarion. In 1911 a group of Jews in New York and Philadelphia selected a site near Gunnison for a colony of displaced Jews. A group of fifty-two families, under the leadership of Benjamin Brown, established the small community of Clarion. Over 6,000 acres of land were included. Contributions from Jews all over the United States went to support the colony. Notwithstanding the support, leadership, and fine people involved, the colony did not succeed. Poor land and lack of water were part of the problem. By 1915 the colony had broken up. However, Brown, his brother Nathan, and some twelve families remained on the land. They became successful poultry producers and in 1967 had a $9 million business incorporated as the Utah Poultry Producers Cooperative Association.

Iosepa, the colony of Mormon Hawaiians. Since the 1850s when Mormon missionaries in the Society Islands became concerned about the gathering of Polynesian Mormons to their American Zion, there had been interest in setting up a place for these people. Nothing came of the hope, but on August 28, 1889, a company of fifty Hawaiian Mormons arrived at the Quincy Ranch in Skull Valley, which had been purchased by the church as a gathering place for Polynesians. A townsite was surveyed and given the name Iosepa (Hawaiian for Joseph). Grants of land were given to each family, and the settlers then engaged in farming and livestock raising. Mormon church organizations and schools were established. They celebrated August 28 as their "Pioneer Day." The colony was presided over, in turn, by mission presidents recently returned from the islands. But the mortality rate was high among these people, and when they were promised a temple in Hawaii, the colony dissolved and the colonists returned to the Hawaiian Islands. The Mormon Hawaiian Temple was dedicated November 27, 1919.

5. A MODERN EDUCATIONAL SYSTEM EMERGED

Since Utah did not get the benefit of federal support to education through land grants until statehood, individual communities answered their problems of financing schools as best they could. Some communities passed a law calling for a *tax-supported school system*. Attendance of school-age children increased from an average of 36 percent to an average of 59 percent in 1891. The constitution of 1896 established a state educational organization which eventually led to a full-fledged secondary school program. School attendance was compulsory for twenty weeks each year in rural districts and for thirty weeks each year in cities for all children between eight and sixteen years. In 1910 and 1911 steps were taken to set up state tax-supported high schools. School districts in-

creased their support of public education between 1896 and 1914 by two to three times. The construction of new school buildings marked these years also.

A major achievement in education in Utah came in 1915 with the *consolidation of school districts* on a county and on a city basis. As early as 1875 Governor George W. Emery recommended consolidating the 236 school districts to save money and improve education. Although educators favored consolidation, it was not until 1904 that Salt Lake County set an example by organizing the Granite and Jordan school districts. The following year the legislature passed a law giving people in the counties the option of consolidating. Weber, Box Elder, and Cache counties soon set up county school districts. However, some counties had bitter fights as townspeople did not want to give up control of schools to a county board of education and superintendent. By 1915 consolidation had been effected throughout the state.

Even with the coming of free public schools to Utah, *Mormons, Protestants, and Catholics continued to operate their separate*

Mrs. C. I. Goff's classroom, Midvale, was typical of many elementary schools during the first decade of the twentieth century.

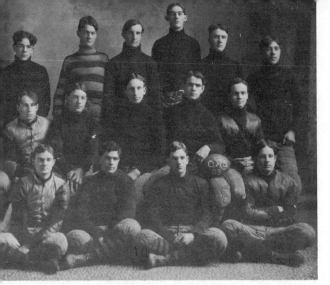

Ogden High School football team, 1903.

Rowland Hall basketball team.

school systems which now paralleled the expanding public school system. The Mormons had established Brigham Young Academy at Provo in 1875, the Brigham Young College at Logan in 1877, and the Latter-day Saint College in Salt Lake City in 1886. Between 1888 and 1911 they founded eight *academies* or high schools in Utah: Sanpete Stake Academy, Ephraim, (1888, named Snow College in 1902); Uintah Academy, Vernal (1891-1923); Weber Academy, Ogden (1889, named Weber College in 1922); Emery Stake Academy, Castle Dale (1890-1922); Murdock Academy, Beaver (1889-1922); Summit Stake Academy, Coalville (1906-12); Millard Stake Academy, Hinckley (1890, 1910-22); and Saint George Stake Academy, Saint George, (1911, named Dixie College in 1923). Brigham Young Academy offered courses leading to a four-year degree while Brigham Young College was a two-year college. Some of these academies became state-controlled colleges at a later date, chiefly between 1921 and 1923. Brigham Young College was transferred to the state in 1926. Brigham Young Academy became Brigham Young University.

The academies established a remarkable tradition for excellence in education, each institution being guided by outstanding educators who, in many instances, moved on to become leading figures in the universities in the state.

The Catholics continued to maintain Saint Mary's Academy, Salt Lake City (1875); the Sacred Heart Academy, Ogden (1878); All Hallows College, Salt Lake City (1885); Saint Ann's Orphanage, Salt Lake City (1891); and parochial schools at Park City and Eureka.

Westminster College, so named in 1902, was a continuation of the Salt Lake Collegiate Institute and the Sheldon Jackson College, Salt Lake City, founded by the Presbyterians. The Presbyterians also operated the Wasatch Academy, Mount Pleasant (after October 1891), and the New Jersey Academy, Logan (1878). The Methodists operated Price Academy in Price, the Congregationalists maintained the Proctor Academy in Provo, and the Episcopal Church operated Rowland Hall-Saint Marks in Salt Lake City.

The state-controlled and tax-supported school program gradually gained the confidence of the people, and the Mormons began in 1913 to withdraw from full-time instructional programs and to establish seminaries for religious instruction.

Farmers went to school, too, to learn the latest information on scientific agriculture and farm management.

Universities. Utah's major universities made remarkable gains during the first decades of the twentieth century. The name of the University of Deseret was changed in 1902 to the University of Utah, two years after the university moved from downtown to grounds on the western section of the Fort Douglas reservation. By 1913-14 there were 1,300 students enrolled in the following schools and departments: School of Arts and Sciences, School of Education, School of Mines, School of Medicine, School of Law, and Department of Extension Work.

The Utah Agricultural College at Logan had about 500 students enrolled in college work, while continuing to offer high school studies until 1915. Founded as Utah's land-grant college, its special emphasis was in agriculture, domestic science and arts, and industrial education. The Extension Division conducted farmers' round-ups, housekeepers' conferences, lectures, demonstration work, club work, and correspondence work. By these means the activities and offerings of the

school reached all parts of the state. The Experiment Station conducted scientific experiments in agriculture and related fields and made the results available to Utah farmers. County agricultural agents worked closely with farmers and ranchers applying the latest scientific knowledge to their work.

6. WHAT HAPPENED TO UTAH INDIANS AFTER THEY WERE MOVED TO RESERVATIONS

Following the removal of Utah Indians to the Uintah Indian Reservation in the late 1860s, the Indians did what they could to adjust to their new home. (Chapter 16, section 5.) They appreciated the Uinta Mountains and Basin. They attempted to keep their traditional ways and resisted efforts of the white man to force them to farm.

In 1887 Congress yielded to pressures from whites who sought more of the Indians' lands and passed the *Dawes General Allotment Act.* Under the provisions of this act the president was authorized to have surveyed

Ute tribal leaders photographed in Washington, 1868. Left to right: Ankatosh, Wa-rets, Ouray, Shavano, and Guero.

reservation land alloted to resident Indians. Each head of a family was to receive 160 acres of land, each single person over eighteen years of age was to receive 80 acres of land, and each minor was to receive 40 acres of land. Heretofore, reservation lands were held by the tribe for all Indians of that tribe. Now Indians were to be settled on their own pieces of land and were expected to become farmers or maintain small herds of cattle. The lands not allotted to Indians were to be made available to white settlers. By this general allotment, American Indians lost two-thirds of the lands given to them by treaty for reservations. The allotment program was put into effect for the White River and the Uintah Ute in 1897. In 1902 Congress passed a law to allot the Ute lands; surveys were made. Soon the unallotted lands were made available for white settlement.

The Uintah Indian Reservation was opened for white settlement in 1905. Pressures were on the government from people who wanted to farm, graze livestock, and mine the area. Conservation ideas were also present. In 1905 President Theodore Roosevelt set aside 1,010,000 acres of the reservation as a forest reserve, 2,100 acres as townsite land, 1,004,285 acres for homestead entry, 2,140 acres in mining claims, and 60,160 acres under reclamation projects. The residue, 282,460 acres, was set aside as unallotted tribal lands. This action led to a land rush in the Uinta Basin, one of the major stories in the settlement and economic development of Utah.

The opening of the reservation to homesteading was a betrayal of the government's agreement with the Indians, who had accepted the guarantee of those lands as their permanent home. According to earlier agreements, the reservation could be opened to white settlement only by an affirmative vote of two-thirds of the male tribal members. The government acted without such a vote from the Indians.

After August 1905 when lands were opened for homesteading, settlement proceeded quickly. The following communities were founded in 1905: Duchesne, Lapoint, Midview, Myton, Randlett, Roosevelt, Strawberry, and Tridell. The next year Altonah, Boneta, Hayden, Ioka, Mount Emmons, Neola, Redcliff, and Tabiona were established. In 1907 Arcadia, Bluebell, and Upalco were settled. Mountain Home was settled in 1908, and Talmage in 1909.

To meet the governmental needs of these people, Duchesne County was created in January 1915, from that portion of Wasatch County lying east of the main range of the Wasatch Mountains. The new county was made up almost entirely of the Uintah Indian Reservation lands.

Many Ute Indians, distressed by white occupation of their lands, fled for the Great Plains, hoping for an alliance with the Sioux against further white land grabbing. The 1906-8 trek to the plains ended in failure, and the Ute returned with government assistance to the Uinta Basin. Their sense of failure and loss of hope deepened.

Indian relations in southeastern Utah, 1880-1925. Southern Ute were brought together on a reservation established for them in 1868 in southwestern Colorado. At the same time, a reservation was established for the Navajo, including lands in Utah south of the San Juan River. It was in this area of southeastern Utah that there were occasional conflicts between Indians and whites until about 1925.

Conflicts arose between different groups of whites as well as between whites and Indians. Two groups of white settlers—Mormons from the central valleys of Utah, and miners and ranchers from Colorado and New Mexico—began to move into what became Grand and San Juan counties in the years following 1877. The Mormons, generally, sought peaceful coexistence with the Indians. The other whites thought of the Indian as a natural enemy and considered "a dead Indian a good Indian." The Mormons discouraged calling in the army during Indian troubles, but the non-Mormons favored quick military action to avenge any so-called Indian wrongdoing.

During the 1880s there were several armed conflicts. In 1880, two whites were killed and several wounded. In 1881 ten whites and at least seven Indians lost their lives in the Pinhook Battle east of Moab. Relations improved somewhat during the 1890s except for an attempt to transfer the Southern Ute reservation from Colorado to San Juan County in Utah. The entire Ute tribe made a brief exodus from Colorado to Utah in the winter of 1894-95. A war was avoided when the Indians were forced to return to their reservation in Colorado.

During the early twentieth century there were three major periods of white-Indian conflicts—1907-8, 1913-15, and 1923. The problem in 1907-8 grew out of a controversy over grazing grounds in Montezuma Canyon, where a Ute band claimed part of the public domain for its goats and horses. A more serious problem developed in 1913 over the murder of a sheepherder, allegedly by *Tesnegat*, the son of the Ute subchief Polk. Unsuccessful

efforts to capture Tesnegat resulted in an unfortunate shooting affair between a local posse of whites and Paiute and Ute camps near Bluff. Indians and whites were killed. Further killing seemed likely until General Hugh L. Scott, chief of staff of the United States Army, came to San Juan County and persuaded Tesnegat to surrender for trial. In a sensational trial the accused Indian was found innocent and released.

Friction between whites and Indians came to a head in 1923 in the *Posey War*. Posey and two Indian boys accused of robbing a sheep camp escaped from custody during their trial at Blanding. Correctly sensing the anger of the whites, most of the Ute and Paiute living near Blanding fled. A running battle took place in which several whites had close calls and in which one of the Indian boys accused of theft was killed and Posey badly wounded. Posey escaped. The remaining Paiute were imprisoned. After several days the imprisoned Indians learned Posey had died. Indians refused to take local officers to his body but did take a United States marshal who found Posey's remains and buried him. Later, Blanding residents dug up the old warrior to make sure it was Posey and reburied him.

As a result of the Posey War, arrangements were made to give San Juan County Indians about twelve sections of land on the Blue Mountains division of the La Sal Forest. With this help the acute need behind much of the trouble was reduced, and relations gradually improved.

The Indians of Utah, the original occupants of the land, within a half century had been dispossessed of their lands, defeated in battle, removed to and confined on reservations, and encouraged to adopt white man's ways and beliefs. They remained a forgotten people until mid-twentieth century.

UNIT SEVEN
PROSPERITY AND DEPRESSION

Utah emerged from her pioneer period at about the same time the United States emerged as a world power. The end of World War I brought a new position for the United States in world affairs, and by this time Utah was in line with American political, economic, and social developments. The history of Utah at this point partakes of the major movements in the history of the United States.

After 1920 there is little uniqueness to Utah history. Its role was part of the general history of the United States. Even so, it is interesting to learn what life was like in the new age. One of the most important themes in our history during the twentieth century is the relationship between the federal government and Utah state government. We have seen that Utah has benefited from the relationship. During the next period the federal government played a more dominant role in state affairs.

The generation of Utahns that lived between 1915 and 1945 witnessed participation by Utahns in two world wars and an intervening period of rapid and revolutionary change. The period between World War I (1917-18) and World War II (1941-45) was marked by a mixture of prosperity and depression in the 1920s and universal depression in the 1930s. During periods of prosperity there is expansion of business, production of goods, employment, and money in hand to buy goods. Periods of depression are marked by unemployment, lack of money, and reduction of business activities. America and Utah had experienced periods of depression before, but none so long or so serious. The coming of World War II and the forced economic activity of that war effort brought the United States, and Utah with it, out of the depression.

"Winter in Farmington," a painting by Utah artist LeConte Stewart.

THE TWENTIES: PROSPERITY AND DEPRESSION

The 1920s were years of prosperity for most Americans. In Utah almost all lines of business activity were prosperous except agriculture and mining, which were seriously depressed. There was great expansion, however, in other fields. The transportation revolution continued as railroads, interurbans, streetcars, automobiles, trucks, and buses expanded in numbers and services. The application of electricity to motors for industrial and home use, for lighting, phonographs, radio, and appliances spurred on a revolution already begun. The automobile, airplane, radio, movies, and refrigeration were among the most significant advances in modern life that reached many people during the 1920s. This meant expansion of businesses, employment, and production of goods and services, and money in the pockets of many people.

On the other hand, while agriculture and mining had earlier profited from filling contracts for the World War I effort, with the cancellation of these contracts, there was not only a surplus production but a declining market. The people who engaged in these activities were faced with a serious economic condition.

In a good economic system there is a high rate of employment, a high production of goods, fruitful competition, economic stability, and a fair distribution of wealth and income. Private ownership of property, free enterprise, and a free market are parts of our economic system. But the economy was obviously failing the farmers and miners. What was the role of government in the economy? It was generally believed that government was to keep hands off the economic system. In the early years of the century, Presidents Theodore Roosevelt, William Howard Taft, and Woodrow Wilson believed the economy was best served when government took the role of watchdog, to watch and take action only when necessary. As a result, during the 1920s, people did not look to government for a solution to their problems. There was unbounded faith in free competition. What of those hurt by depression? It was expected that every man would look after his own needs. There was little help from group, community, state, or national government. The depressed conditions of agriculture and mining were not relieved for twenty years. The great expansion in other areas of the economy reached a high level by the end of the 1920s which was one factor that led to the general depression in all areas of the economy in the 1930s.

IN THIS CHAPTER WE WILL LEARN

1. The period of the 1920s was fast moving with many changes for Utah.

2. Prosperity was a chief characteristic of the twenties.

3. There was depression in agriculture and mining during the twenties.

1. THE PERIOD OF THE 1920s WAS FAST MOVING WITH MANY CHANGES FOR UTAH

Americans had entered World War I with a simple faith that they were making the world "safe for democracy," and that this was "a war to end all wars." At the end of the war, enthusiasm was changed to pessimism and realism as Americans became disillusioned about the war aims. They wanted to return to the isolation and carefree days before the war. President Wilson staked his dreams on the establishment of the League of Nations, but the United States refused to join. In Utah, prominent Republicans fought against the league in the belief that the United States should not be involved in the affairs of other nations. Other Utahns held that we could not withdraw from the world and that peace had a better chance through cooperation. But most Utahns, like most Americans, chose to turn their backs on the world. Besides, they had problems of their own.

In American history, a period of radical change in the attitudes and practices of the people always seems to follow a war. Old standards and ideals are pushed aside. There is a rise in crime. Corruption in high office is likely. These developments were characteristic of the nation, and Utah participated in some of them.

The 1920s was the prohibition decade. The Eighteenth Amendment to the United States Constitution, prohibiting the manufacture, sale, or transportation of alcoholic liquors, went into operation January 16, 1920. Utah had earlier allowed towns to de-

Emma Lucy Gates (later Mrs. Albert E. Bowen), famed Utah singer, winds her phonograph to hear a recording. Late in the 1920s the phonograph was motorized.

cide whether or not they would allow the sale of liquor. In 1914 there were twenty-seven towns with a total of 334 saloons. Salt Lake City had 138 and Ogden 45. Most of the remaining saloons were in the mining and smelter towns of the state. During prohibition, most Utahns observed the law, but there were violations in Utah as elsewhere. There were bootleggers (illegal manufacturers) who set up distilleries ("stills") and then sold the illegal liquor. Federal and state revenue officers were kept busy policing illegal traffic in and through the state. In the United States there was widespread evasion of the law, and criminals gained control of organized distilling and distribution of the illegal liquor. By the end of the 1920s most Americans had decided that the prohibition experiment had failed. By 1932 the Democrats and the Republicans recommended that the question be submitted to the people. The Twenty-first Amendment, repealing the Eighteenth Amendment, was ratified on December 5, 1933, Utah being the thirty-sixth state to approve the amendment. The problem of controlling the manufacture and distribution of alcoholic drinks was turned back to the states.

The decade of the twenties was the Jazz Age, the age of the Ford car, and the Model T flivver. It was an age of fads, and of the "new woman"—the flapper. Marjorie Rambeau, a former Salt Laker and a stage star, commented on the flapper: "It's all bosh to say that our girls and boys of today have degenerated and are headed for perdition; that short skirts, bobbed hair and the rest are signs that the devil has them in tow." Hair and dress styles were changing radically for women and for men, too. During the territorial period, the Mormon men had distinguished themselves from their non-Mormon neighbors by wearing long beards. At the turn of the century, the style was changed, and

most Mormons became clean-shaven and trimmed.

401

Members of the Wasatch Mountain Club prepared to set out on an expedition.

Toward the end of the 1920's Henry Ford shifted from his Model T to a new Model A Ford, complete with rumble seat. Except for the rumble seat, popular with the young set, automobiles became completely enclosed.

2. PROSPERITY WAS A CHIEF CHARACTERISTIC OF THE TWENTIES

Throughout the decade nearly everyone had the word *prosperity* on his lips. The December 29, 1923, *Deseret News* carried a report of "The Business Picture": "The United States in 1923 had one of the most remarkable periods of prosperity in the memory of the present generation. Production was of tremendous volume and consumption kept pace throughout. Employment generally was steady at high wages and labor disputes were infrequent. Buying power increased over two billion dollars from enhanced crops, high wages, and improved incomes resulting from the return of industrial corporations to a dividend basis. Only a few basic industries failed to show adequate return on the investment. ... Agricultural conditions give promise of improvement." Similar announcements were made throughout the 1920s.

In Utah, the labor force stayed at about the same level though there was an increase in population. Throughout the 1920s and 1930s the labor force was about 45 percent of the population ten years of age and older.

This percentage was about 5.5 percent lower than that of the United States.

The automobile. By 1920 there was no doubt that the automobile was here to stay. The number of motor vehicle registrations increased over two and a half times from 1920 to 1929 (43,530 vehicles to 112,661 vehicles). About 85 percent of the vehicles were passenger cars. Utah was on the move. The number of automobiles alone is only a small part of the whole story of the influence of the coming of the automobile on business and industry and on the lives of the people.

The manufacture, sales, and servicing of automobiles revolutionized American business. Many new industries were necessary to produce the automobile in all its parts and thousands of people were employed in the process. Sales and servicing opened up a new line for many businessmen and salesmen. Formerly, there had been the blacksmith shop and a livery stable. With the coming of the automobile, the livery stable disappeared and the blacksmith shop was perhaps turned into a garage. The impact of the automobile can be seen by imagining main street without any business or activity that is identified with or dependent upon the automobile. This would eliminate automobile sales agencies, service stations, garages, auto parts stores, tire sales and repairs, body repair shops, drive-ins (of all sorts), motels, shopping centers, and parking lots.

The automobile meant mobility—the capacity to travel longer distances in a shorter time. Leisure time could be used in driving. For the businessman, it meant greatly expanding the number of contacts he could make, people he could serve. The automobile soon became a business necessity, and as cars improved and were closed in to make them more comfortable, they were put in operation year round.

Buses. The gasoline motor was soon adapted to vehicles designed to carry large passenger loads. During the 1920s bus transportation became a major business as companies established lines to transport large numbers of passengers from city to city. In Salt Lake City street motor buses came in 1933, after electrically operated trolleys had been in service a few years.

Trucking. An important use of the gasoline motor vehicle was in the truck. In 1909, when five trucks were registered in the state, it was necessary for the owner to obtain a chauffeur's license by making application, endorsed by three responsible owners of motor vehicles. He was then given his chauffeur's badge to wear.

It was a fine move for the peddler, who had been making his rounds in his horse-drawn wagon, to step into a motor truck. He could make his rounds more quickly and his produce had less chance of spoilage. But peddling was also hurt by improvements in transportation. People with cars could get to the stores more easily, and the stores could stock a greater variety of goods.

Most of the trucking in Utah took over from old freighting companies. By 1919 there were 108 trucking companies in the state. Trucking became big business in Utah as farm produce was hauled throughout the state and

The day was passing when only the well-to-do people could afford an automobile. The automobile soon replaced horse-drawn vehicles altogether. Main Street, Salt Lake City, 1916, daytime.

By the 1920s concrete highways were being laid along main lines of traffic.

This Utah touring party, en route to Yellowstone in 1918, detoured around a culvert repair only to get stuck in the stream. The interest in visiting distant places led to demands for better roads.

Near Cedar City, en route from Payson to Los Angeles, 1922. The road, most of the way, was the old wagon road. Bed rolls and camping equipment are tied to the side of the car.

to California, where more food was needed than was being produced locally. Later with refrigerated trucks even more fruit, vegetables, and dairy products were trucked to California.

Railroads. The use of the automobile and the truck in hauling goods and passengers cut into the business of the railroads enough to make them respond with competition. Railroads formed their own trucking and railway express companies.

The Union Pacific Railroad was an important agent in promoting tourism to the southern Utah parks and advertising the scenic attractions of Utah to the nation. On June 27, 1923, the Union Pacific completed a thirty-three mile extension of its system from Lund to Cedar City. President and Mrs. Warren G. Harding were the first to take the train trip. The formal dedication took place September 12 when a golden rail was fastened in place with four iron spikes made at the old iron works in Iron County sixty years before. This spur served to take tourists to the southern Utah parks and also to haul iron ore from near Cedar City to the smelter at Springville. The Utah Parks Company, a subsidiary of the Union Pacific, built and operated El Escalante Hotel at Cedar City, and food and lodging facilities at Zion, Bryce Canyon, and Cedar Breaks, and later (September 1928) at the north rim of the Grand Canyon. Motor buses operated from Cedar City to the parks, providing transportation and tours. The Union Pacific sent agents throughout the country with color-slide lectures on Utah's southern parks to stimulate tourism.

Aviation. Air transportation has changed our lives almost as much as the automobile. The first airplane flight in Utah took place in Salt Lake City, January 30, 1910, when Louis Paulhan, a Frenchman, flew over the fairgrounds at about 300 feet above the ground. His flight lasted ten minutes and thirty seconds and reached the speed of forty miles an hour.

The use of the airplane in World War I stimulated the use of air travel for private and commercial purposes after the war. One of the first applications of air travel was for carrying mail across the country. Salt Lake City became an important stop on the transcontinental air mail route. The pioneering of the air mail route was done by the United States Post Office Department under a grant from Congress in 1918. World War I airplanes and pilots were used in what proved to be a successful experiment. The first test flight from New York to San Francisco was begun on September 8, 1920. The airplane carried 16,000 letters. Although the pilot flew only during daylight, the train time for carrying letters the same distance was cut by twenty-two hours. On December 16, 1920, a mail pilot, James F. Moore, flew round trip from Cheyenne, Wyoming, to Salt Lake City in one

First passengers J. A. Tomlinson (left) and Ben Redman pose at Salt Lake City before boarding Western Airlines' first passenger flight on May 23, 1926.

A Boeing 40B, which traveled 110 miles per hour carrying four passengers.

day with 400 pounds of mail. Night flying was begun between Chicago and Cheyenne in 1924 after 289 flashing gas beacons had been set on the ground and thirty-four emergency landing fields had been rented.

By 1925 Salt Lake City was the center of the expanding air mail service. In 1926 the Post Office Department offered public bids for air mail service and turned over its airfields, beacons, and radio control systems to the Commerce Department. The Chicago-to-San Francisco portion of the route was contracted by Boeing Airplane Company and Edward Hubbard of Seattle, Washington. The first air mail service between Salt Lake City and Los Angeles was begun in April 1926 when pilot Jimmy James, in a Douglas M-2 biplane, flew for Western Air Express. It took him eight hours. A month later he carried the first passengers between the cities.

Commercial air travel began in 1927. Though it was expensive and very uncertain, people did want to travel by air. A passenger paid $404 for a thirty-two hour flight across the United States with fifteen stops en route. When there was more mail than expected, the passenger had to wait for another flight. That year 168 passengers, dressed in flying suits, helmets, goggles, and parachutes, riding with the mail, flew between Chicago and New York. The passenger took his own lunch or went without. Service between Chicago and the West Coast carried 445 passengers that same year as Boeing Airplane Company, more anxious for passenger business, equipped mail planes to carry two passengers.

Electricity. The decade of the twenties was an age of electricity. Besides lighting homes, streets, schools, factories, mills, and mines, electricity was applied through electric motors to produce power for everything from kitchen mixers to interurban electric trains. Besides light and power, the most important

Main Street, Salt Lake City, 1916, nighttime. The new carbon street lights were first turned on in 1916, making the street the "brightest lighted street in the world."

applications were to refrigeration, the phonograph, radio, and motion pictures. The use of electrical energy nearly doubled in the period from 1920 to 1929 (from 470,685,000 kilowatt-hours to 857,791,000 kilowatt-hours).

The major electrical power plants were located on the canyon streams near the major cities of the Wasatch Front. Obviously the nearby communities benefited first from the magical energy. First, streets were lighted; sometimes it was a single bulb hung from the power pole at a street intersection. As power lines were extended through the streets, services extended from street lighting to interior lighting, and businesses and homes knew a measure of light never experienced before.

The age of electricity came rapidly for some Utahns but slowly for others. Some homes in south Salt Lake Valley were not lighted until the 1930s. In 1923, 3,330 farms were connected to power lines (13 percent of the farms in Utah), while in 1930, 15,062 farms had electricity (55.5 percent). In 1935 the federal government, under the Rural Electrification Administration, promoted the extension of electricity to rural areas of the country (chapter 23, section 4). Electricity and power were available to most of the people by the end of the 1930s.

Refrigeration of food in the home was by ice until the 1920s. The ice truck, was a common sight in urban centers until the electric refrigerator came into general use by the 1930s.

Refrigeration. Prior to using electricity for refrigeration, people depended upon ice. During winter months blocks of ice were cut from ponds and lakes and stored in ice houses—underground pits insulated preferably by sawdust. Ice was then used in the warm season to cool the icebox. In cities ice was available from commercial ice companies which sent horse-drawn ice trucks throughout the city delivering ice to customers who would place an ice card sign in the window indicating the quantity of ice desired that day. Ice peddling lasted until replaced by the electric refrigerator.

The use of the new refrigeration units meant much to food processors as they could now store fresh meat and fish, fruit, and vegetables. Dairy products became more widely used because of refrigeration. Notice in a grocery store how many items are available because of refrigeration.

Radio. Perhaps the most exciting, the most talked about, and one of the most influential inventions to hit America in the twenties was the radio. Radio broadcasting is said to have begun in the United States in 1920 when radio station KDKA in Pittsburgh

407

On May 6, 1922, Heber J. Grant, president of the Mormon church, spoke the first words over radio in Utah. At KZN's first broadcast were, left to right: Nathan O. Fullmer, George Albert Smith, Mrs. Heber J. Grant, President Grant, C. Clarence Neslen (mayor of Salt Lake), and George J. Cannon. In the doorway at the left is Anthony W. Ivins.

broadcast the election returns of that year. In 1922 it was estimated that there were some 60,000 radio receiving sets. By 1927, five years later, the number had rocketed to 17,000,000 sets. In 1926 the coast-to-coast network of the National Broadcasting Company (NBC) was established; the following year the Columbia Broadcasting System (CBS) was established. By 1927 there were so many broadcasting stations that the federal government stepped in and assigned frequencies on which stations could broadcast.

While Utahns listened over their sets to stations outside the state from the beginning of American broadcasting, radio broadcasting began in Utah in 1922. Elias S. Woodruff, general manager of the Deseret News, and Nathan O. Fullmer, business manager, planned a radio station in Salt Lake City to receive and broadcast news. With the help of Harry Wilson, an engineer, a successful broadcasting

set was put together. A three-room studio was built on the roof of the Deseret News Building. On May 6, 1922, the first broadcast was made in Utah, by station KZN, owned and operated by the Deseret News. Station KZN was on the air each evening from 8:00 to 8:30; then the program time was lengthened to an hour and a half. Early programs combined live music from the studio orchestra and the playing of Victor records on a Victrola. Live concerts were sent by wire from the McCune School of Music to the station and put on the air. President Warren G. Harding's speech in the Tabernacle in June 1923 was broadcast. Programs were reported heard from as far away as Los Angeles.

In June 1924 the Deseret News sold its interest in KZN. The call letters were changed to KEPT. One year later the call letters were changed to KSL and the power was increased to 1,000 watts. In 1929 the power was in-

Earl J. Glade, leader in radio and cultural affairs in Salt Lake City, and later mayor of the capital city.

creased to 5,000 watts, and in 1932 to 50,000 watts. In 1932 KSL joined the National Broadcasting Company but later in the year switched to the Columbia Broadcasting System.

One of the more significant figures in radio in Utah was Earl J. Glade, who joined KEPT (KSL) in November 1924. Mr. Glade supervised the programs, managed the sales and accounts, announced programs, and took leadership for quality radio entertainment. He brought musical groups, vocalists, dramatic players, comedy teams, special speakers, special events, such as a report of the Dempsey-Tunney fight, and many other outstanding radio programs to KSL.

Glade was chiefly responsible for the launching of the broadcasts of the Tabernacle Choir and Organ. On July 15, 1929, the first broadcast of the Tabernacle Choir took place. In June 1930 Richard L. Evans became the announcer and served over forty years until his death in 1971. The program was not sponsored by the Mormon church but was produced and presented as a sustaining program of cultural value. As such it has continued through the years and is considered the oldest continuously presented nationwide program in the history of American radio. It is heard each week worldwide, through CBS, the Armed Forces network, shortwave, and scores of independent stations.

Other Utah radio stations have a similar history and have made similar contributions. KDYL began broadcasting in Salt Lake City in 1922, KLO in Ogden in 1924, KEUB in Price in 1936, KSUB in Cedar City in 1937, KVNU in Logan in 1938, KUTA in Salt Lake City in 1938, and KOVO in Provo in 1939.

Radio had a significant impact on the people's way of life. Young and old alike spent hours tuning the radio to find the most-distant stations. Families listened regularly to favorite programs. Businessmen were quick to take advantage of radio advertising. It is financial support from advertisers that makes private commercial radio possible. Some people thought there were so many ads that the word should be pronounced rADio. Besides influencing the people by way of entertainment and advertising, radio had a tendency to set a standard for music, humor, and language, and unified the nation as never before.

Motion pictures. The commercial motion picture came to Utah shortly after the turn of the century, and by World War I there were motion picture theaters in the major cities. During the 1920s theaters multiplied in number as they showed the variety of films or "flicks" available at that time—comedy, cartoons, and romances. Vaudeville, using live stage acts, continued as a major co-feature in the larger theaters until the 1930s. Favorite early stars include Tom Mix, the Keystone Cops, Our Gang, Charlie Chaplin, and Mary

At the American Theater, Ronald Coleman and Vilma Banky are playing in "Two Lovers." Main Street, Salt Lake City.

The new motion picture theaters were characterized by grand designs and elaborate ornamentation. The Princess Theater, Ogden.

Pickford. Toward the end of the 1920s "talkies" or sound movies came in, and movies then featured musicals with popular singing stars.

The motion picture theater hurt attendance at the stage plays at the Salt Lake Theatre, and by 1925 that pioneer theater was losing money. Three years later the historic theater was torn down to make way for a service station, then a telephone exchange building.

While the motion picture theater was important for entertainment and as a local business, the motion picture industry had a special interest in Utah—scenery. Three Parry brothers of Kanab promoted southern Utah as an outdoor studio for Hollywood movies. They convinced the movie makers of Utah's attractions and in 1922 Tom Mix made *Deadwood Gulch* near Kanab, the first picture using Utah scenery. *Covered Wagon* was filmed in 1922 near Garrison in western Millard County. The director, James Cruze, and the female leading star, Betty Compson, were both native Utahns. *Union Pacific* was filmed west of Cedar City, near Iron Springs. Many others followed. *In Old Arizona*, the first outdoor talking picture, was made by Warner Baxter in the Zion Park region in 1926. When Harry Goulding, owner of a trading post in the Navajo Indian Reservation in southeastern Utah, heard that John Ford was going to make a western movie, he went to Hollywood and induced him to film it in the Navajo country. The picture was *Stagecoach*, directed by John Ford in 1939 and starred John Wayne and Clair Trevor. It was John Wayne's big break in movies.

Cedar City and Kanab became movie-making centers, though other locations have been used frequently. The studios have hired hundreds of Utahns to act in the pictures as extras, rented their livestock, wagons, and other implements.

Utah became important to the movie industry in another way. Salt Lake City became the distribution center for films from all major producers. This center receives films from the producers and distributes them to several hundred theaters in the western states.

While the movie industry is of some local financial importance, the coming of motion pictures has changed the lives of the people greatly. While furnishing entertainment, it has been influential in standardizing tastes, habits, and ways of thinking.

3. THERE WAS DEPRESSION IN AGRICULTURE AND MINING DURING THE TWENTIES

However prosperous most businesses were in the twenties, some elements of the economy were depressed. Agriculture and mining were in depression throughout the 1920s and 1930s.

To meet the demands of war, the people of the United States made every effort to supply the materials of war and to feed our troops and allies in Europe. Industry expanded production, and farmers took up new land and expanded their operations to meet the demands for food. With the armistice of November 11, 1918, the demand for war goods ceased. Europeans were soon producing their own food again and rebuilding their torn countries. The United States government cancelled its orders for goods used in the war. Utah, as other states, had expanded its production to meet a demand and now the demand ceased. Utah producers were left with surplus products on hand and no market for their products, with debts incurred from expansion. While most businesses were adversely affected at the war's end, agriculture and mining were hardest hit.

Governor Charles R. Mabey in January 1921 described the postwar mood of the people: "With you the hour of exaltation has passed, and the inevitable reaction has set in. The blare of trumpets has ceased. There is less of glory and more of gloom. The nation is suffering from the lassitude of the athlete after a trying contest. Men's nerves are unstrung and they are given to complaint and criticism. There is not the incentive to take up the daily way and walk in it again." The *Deseret News*, December 17, 1921, described conditions in these words: "During the latter part of 1920 and through the greater part of 1921 Salt Lake and the intermountain country faced the greatest crisis in their history. ... Copper, cattle, sheep, and agricultural products had gone to their lowest price levels. Clouds of financial difficulties banked the horizon on every side."

In agriculture the depression was immediate and continued with little letup. Farmers had overexpanded and continued to produce though markets were closing. Farm products lost their value on the market. Some farmers who had diversified were a little better off, for while one product might not sell, another would. Utah farms produced fruits in abundance, but other states did too. There was an abundance of fruit compared to the demand for it, and the prices fell. During the late 1920s Utah suffered repeated annual drought, and many crops suffered for need of water at crucial periods.

Farmers learned that it was just as important to sell their products as it was to grow them. There were major efforts to sell Utah products outside the state. During the 1920s Utah celery brought Utah a reputation from New York to San Francisco. Utah became known also for its Spanish onion, cauliflower, lettuce, strawberries, grapes, melons, cucumbers, cabbage, and especially peaches, pears, apples, and cherries.

Since 1920 there has been little expansion in the acreage of harvested crops. Early in the 1920s cash farm income dropped about one half, and that 1920 level of cash income was not to be reached again until World War II. This halving of farm income was largely the result of (1) unusually low precipitation, (2) low prices of farm products, (3) the increase in the number of farms and the decrease in the size (hence production) of farms, and (4) the failure to increase or maintain yields and intensify crop and livestock production.

In January 1929, Governor George H. Dern reported that "the past two years have been anything but prosperous [for the farmer], and fully justify our citizens in their cry for 'farm relief'." The beet sugar industry had ups and downs but by 1929 had "suffered a relapse and is now languishing." The canning industry suffered severely following the war but showed signs of reasonable success toward the end of the decade.

Mining prospered with the war effort. In 1915 the needs of World War I led to the organization of the Utah Iron and Steel Company, later incorporated as the Utah Steel

This meeting in Bingham is probably either a political rally or a union organizing rally.

Bingham Canyon in the 1920s.

The area of the Highland Boy mine in Bingham Canyon.

412

Corporation. The company's plant at Midvale had a single open-hearth furnace with a daily capacity of 150 tons of steel. Later a second furnace was added. Utah's copper industry was also greatly stimulated, and with it many other industries.

At war's end, the cancellation of government contracts brought *financial ruin* to the new iron and steel industry; it was not salvaged until 1924. The copper industry in the West went into rapid decline. In 1919 Utah's production of leading metals was only half that of 1918. Companies were forced to curtail operations—men were laid off, plants were shut down. The Utah Copper Company closed its mill at Magna in February 1919. During 1920 the company operated on a 50 percent basis. With Utah Copper's total shutdown in April 1921, Bingham shriveled up as the 6,000 men who were working at the mine during the peak production of 1918 moved to other mining camps and other occupations. The towns of Arthur, Magna, and Garfield lost more than half their populations. Empty houses were boarded up.

The copper shutdown affected other industries. The shipments of coal out of Carbon County to the mines stopped. The Hercules Powder Company plant at Bacchus closed. The Utah Power & Light Company lost the major market for its electrical energy. The Bingham & Garfield Railroad that carried ore from the canyon to the mills idled its engines.

Past production had created large stockpiles of metals. As there was little sale of the metals, prices fell below the cost of production. However, as the stockpiles dwindled through new uses, orders were placed for more metals. By April 1922 the economic signs were good enough that *Utah Copper* began working back to a normal production rate. By the year's end production was about 40 percent of normal. As rapidly as suitable workmen could be found, mines, mills, and smelters were brought to normal operation. The recovery was fairly quick, but mining production and employment had its ups and downs through the rest of the 1920s and 1930s and was often in a depressed condition.

The steel industry was revived in 1924 when the efforts of the Utah Steel Corporation attracted the attention of the Columbia Steel Company in California. A new company, the *Columbia Steel Corporation*, was organized; coal deposits in Carbon County and iron ore deposits near Cedar City were purchased, and a plant erected at Ironton, south of Provo. The coke ovens and blast furnace at Ironton began producing pig iron (crude iron) on April 30, 1924. It was reported that an iron bell cast at Cedar City in 1855 announced the official dedication of the plant. This was the first financially successful iron-making effort in Utah, and the iron and steel industry was begun.

Mining iron for the Columbia Steel Company.

Tapping a heat of iron in the cast house of the blast furnace. Ironton plant, Provo, 1942.

The Ironton plant of the Columbia Steel Corporation, Provo, 1925. The mining industry was in depression for much of the 1920s.

The Ironton plant produced pig iron from ore mined at Desert Mound and Iron Mountain southwest of Cedar City. The iron ore was dug out of open pit mines and shipped by rail to the plant. The location for the plant was excellent because the ore and coal needed in the process were nearby. There were railroads from Iron, Carbon, and Emery counties. Water needed in the manufacturing process was in good supply, and there was a good work force living in the area. The pig iron made here was shipped to steel mills out of the state.

Manufacturing was still in its infancy and one of the major problems of the time is illustrated in mining. Utah had become a great smelting center, but she shipped only crude or partially refined ore concentrates. The refining of these concentrates and the manufacture of finished goods from the refined metals were done elsewhere. If Utah could refine the concentrates and manufacture finished products, many more people would be put to work, and the value added to the concentrates would appear as income to Utah workers. Governor Dern, in January 1927, pointed out this problem in Utah's economy. He said: "Financial prosperity, whether of the individual, the State or the nation, depends upon having money coming in faster than it is going out. The State of Utah as a whole cannot be prosperous unless it produces and sells more goods than it buys and pays for. Utah is primarily a producer of raw materials and food products, and is not one of the great manufacturing states, hence most of the things we use are imported and the bulk of our state income goes out of the state to pay for these imports. It is, therefore, essential for us to keep production up to the highest possible point and to encourage new sources of production in order to maintain a favorable balance of trade."

Effects of the economic depression were felt by many businesses and people. As opportunities for making a living decreased, people had few alternatives but to *seek a living outside the state*. Most of the land easy to obtain was taken up by 1920. Between 1910 and 1940 more people left Utah than entered it. The census of 1940 indicates that there were over 165,000 Utahns (by birth) living outside Utah. Where did they go? Utahns were in California, 75,027; Idaho, 35,216; Nevada, 10,992; Oregon, 6,748; Washington, 6,565; Wyoming, 6,444; Colorado, 5,639; Arizona, 4,342; and Montana, 3,838. As many as 10,000 were scattered among New York, Illinois, Missouri, Texas, Washington, D.C., Michigan, Ohio, and Pennsylvania.

For those who stayed in Utah and who were adversely affected by the depression, life became rather difficult. One indication is in the list of delinquent taxpayers appearing in the newspaper. The December 14, 1923, *Deseret News* devoted twenty-eight pages to listing about 7,000 businesses and persons who were delinquent in paying their personal or real estate taxes for 1923. The same newspaper, December 15, 1927, devoted forty-four pages to lists of delinquent taxpayers in Salt Lake County.

Bank failures were not uncommon in the first half of the 1920s. Farmers had borrowed heavily to buy machinery and land in the rush to produce more food crops. Much of the general expansion was on borrowed money. When the depression hit, borrowers were unable to pay off their obligations. Many old and well-managed banks were forced to close their doors.

The attitude of most people and of government was that America had suffered depressions before and had come out of it, and this depression could be weathered. The attitude of the state government was that its chief concern would be to reduce government expenses to save the people the expense of additional taxes. Rigid economy was practiced throughout the 1920s. Attempts were made to reorganize the state government to promote efficiency and reduce operating costs. Little help was offered beyond the axiom, "the Lord helps those who help themselves." As late as 1940 a government agricultural publication, after describing the depressed agricultural conditions of Utah in some detail, said, "The operation of physical and economic forces will eventually remove some causes of distress but the correction of others lies ultimately in the hands of Utah's farmers." No suggestions were given.

In the meantime there was a serious attempt on the part of the newspapers to print "boost stories" and optimistic reports. Only toward the end of the twenties did the newspapers print accurate reports on the effects of the depression.

Bingham in the 1920s. The depressed condition of mining in the twenties left many without work.

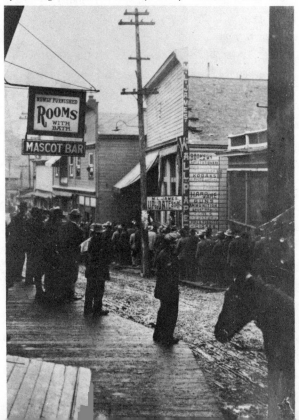

5. *Charles R. Mabey (R) 1921-1925*

- b. October 4, 1877, Bountiful, Utah
- d. April 26, 1959, Bountiful, Utah
- U.S. Army (Spanish American War) received silver star
- Instructor in artillery during WWI
- Taught school in Cedar City
- Organized Bountiful State Bank
- Justice of the Peace, town councilman, mayor — Bountiful
- State House of Representatives, 1912 and 1914

Major events or accomplishments during the administration:

- reorganized state administrative system
- worked for gasoline tax for highway construction
- participated in framing of the Colorado River Pact
- promoted tourism within state
- prompted surveying of previously ignored areas

6. *George H. Dern (D) 1925-1933*

- b. September 8, 1872, Dodge County, Nebraska
  To Utah in 1897 with family
- d. August 28, 1936, Washington, D.C.
- Initially hired as a bookkeeper, progressed through many business ventures in various capacities
- Member of State Senate in 1915, following merger of Progressives and Democrats in 1914. Reelected in 1916. Elected governor in 1924 in an otherwise Republican landslide. Reelected (30,000 margin) although Hoover won presidential race
- Appointed Secretary of War under F. D. Roosevelt in 1935

Major events or accomplishments during the administration:

- "father" of Utah workman's compensation act while state senator
- laid foundations for tax reforms, taking burden from tangible property tax. Not passed until Governor Blood in office.
- 1930 special session passed tax revision amendments to the state constitution providing for the State Tax Commission to have centralized control over all taxes
- responsible for six-state pact providing for sharing of benefits from construction of Boulder Dam
- organized Western Governor's Conference in 1931
- responsible for several acts, local and national, protecting states' rights to sub-surface mineral resources
- on national level, as Secretary of War, he was responsible for expanding the army and navy after a decade of neglect and reductions

The town of Bingham in the area of the Highland Boy mine.

LeConte Stewart, distinguished Utah artist, caught a typical scene of the depression—hoboes on the move.

UTAH IN THE DEPRESSION OF THE THIRTIES

In one of the most dramatic turns of events in American history, the general prosperity of the twenties changed suddenly to depression that deepened for years. There was widespread unemployment. Factories were idle. Business activity was slow. For many people there was little or no work, little or no income, and the necessities of food, clothing, fuel, and shelter were hard to obtain. The poor economic condition of agriculture and mining in the twenties was now extended to all phases of economic life. No depression in American history had struck so hard or remained so long.

What caused the depression has puzzled the best minds for years, but how to overcome the depressed business conditions was a great and immediate problem for everyone in the nation. The depression was so severe that some people challenged the capitalistic system, while everyone wondered what went wrong. Until this time most Americans believed that government should have little to do with the economy, that business affairs should be left entirely to businessmen, and government should keep hands off. A truly revolutionary change took place in attitudes during the first four years of the depression as many people came to agree that the government should take an active role in finding solutions to the terrible economic conditions of the time.

In Utah, the depression struck especially hard, yet without some of the more serious effects found in the urban East. To improve their economic life, some Utahns left the state. Others tightened their belts and stayed on, living on such scanty resources as were close at hand. Private groups, churches, and state and national governments waged war on the depression in Utah. Despite the persistence of depressed financial conditions through the thirties, the morale of the people was saved along with our capitalistic system of economic organization and our democratic form of government.

IN THIS CHAPTER WE WILL LEARN

1. The depression of the thirties was worldwide.

2. Utah was among the states hardest hit by the depression.

3. The burden of relief was on local programs during 1929-33.

4. The New Deal was a national effort to overcome the depression.

5. Federal, state, and local agencies worked in Utah to combat the depression, 1933-41.

6. The depression left an important heritage for Utah.

23

As the plant cover on the mountains diminished due to overgrazing and drought, flooding took place causing great damage.

1. THE DEPRESSION OF THE THIRTIES WAS WORLDWIDE

The depression of the thirties was state-wide, nationwide, and worldwide. While America had experienced depressions before, none was so severe or lasted so long. This depression affected so many people for so long that it shook the foundations of government and capitalism almost to the crumbling point.

Many factors contributed to the depression. The prosperity of the twenties resulted in numerous imbalances and bad adjustments in the economic system. The increases in profits to business owners were not passed on to the buyers, resulting in a *poor distribution of wealth* in the country. In 1929 it is said that the top twenty-four thousand families had three times the income of the six million poorest families. The optimism of the twenties led to excessive *borrowing and installment buying*. People purchased goods with a promise to pay the bill by monthly installments. Many people, wanting to share in the profits of leading companies, purchased stocks. But there was extensive buying of stocks for sheer *speculation*, using hoped-for earnings or credit to buy more stocks. To illustrate: Using his credit, a man with $1,000 could buy $10,000 worth of stocks. A 10 percent gain in stock prices meant he could sell for $11,000 and have a $1,000 profit, equal to 100 percent on his original investment. But a small decline in the market to $9,000 would wipe out the $1,000 investment. From 1923-28 wages advanced only 13 percent while speculative gains advanced 410 percent. This unrestrained speculation culminated in the Wall Street stock market crash of October-November 1929 and signaled the worldwide Great Depression. With little sale for goods, manufacturers cut back production. From 1929 to 1933 the total value of our national output declined by almost one-half. Workers were laid off. People out of work stopped buying. Banks failed as their customers were unable to repay loans. Disaster struck not only the business community but every segment of the country.

President Herbert Hoover, inaugurated in March 1929, at the peak of prosperity, was faced six months later with *the most serious and demoralizing depression the country had witnessed*. Early in 1930 three million people were unemployed. A year later the number had doubled, and by 1932 there were from fourteen to fifteen million people out of work. Many families faced starvation. Despite many signs to the contrary, most of the country's leaders and people believed the depression would soon be over. The thinking of the time is illustrated by the Smoot-Hawley Tariff Act, signed June 17, 1930, cosponsored by Utah's distinguished Senator Reed Smoot. Tariff acts set a schedule of duties (taxes) on imports from other countries. Duties were increased on agricultural raw materials from 38 to 49 percent, on other commodities from 31 to 100 percent higher than the 1922 schedules. America wished to protect her industries from foreign competition by taxing foreign goods to the point of making it unprofitable for foreign producers to sell goods in the United States. This schedule of duties was the highest in our history. By the end of 1931, twenty-five countries had taken steps to protect their own markets by increasing their duties on American goods. Since they could not sell their goods in the United States, they could not or would not buy American goods

in return. All this led to a rapid decline in world trade. In the United States the Smoot-Hawley Tariff Act helped to worsen the depression, and it had serious effects on the economies of other countries, particularly those in Europe.

President Hoover's attitude toward the role of government was that government was an arbiter, a judge, not a meddler, that state and local agencies and charities should take care of relief, and that there should be no direct federal relief for unemployed persons. He advocated local work relief programs and encouraged state and local communities to set up self-help programs. Nevertheless, as the depression worsened, he asked Congress for money for construction of public works, to employ people and thus put money into circulation. Some $600 million was spent on public works projects in the nation. In 1932 Congress set up the Reconstruction Finance Corporation (RFC), a lending agency to provide emergency financing for banking institutions, life insurance companies, building and loan associations, railroads, and farm mortgage associations. Hoover believed that if money was poured in at the top of the country's financial structure, it would filter down to the unemployed, and everyone would benefit. RFC loans benefited financial institutions but very few people.

2. UTAH WAS AMONG THE STATES HARDEST HIT BY THE DEPRESSION

Utah, with a high unemployment rate, was one of the states most severely hit by the depression. The depressed condition of mining and agriculture and other businesses such as manufacturing and the processing of dairy and mineral products had an adverse influence on other elements of the economy.

Utah was hit hard because of many factors. Utah depended to a high degree on her

Mining families were especially hard hit by the depression. Consumers, Utah, March 1936.

The effects of erosion are shown in these two photos, before and after. This destruction of the land led to demands for soil conservation.

mining resources. The *mining industry* in Utah followed the business trends of the nation. When mines were operating, wages were paid to workers in the state, but major profits went outside the state to the mine owners. Utah's location at long distances from markets and high freight rates discouraged expansion in *manufacturing*. Labor had little bargaining power, and there was a strong anti-union attitude.

Compared to the nation, Utah had an unusually high *birthrate*. The population increase was not being matched by increases in opportunities to earn a living. Utah was paying the cost of rearing and educating her people, but many were leaving the state and Utah received little in return.

Utah's limited *land resources* were a contributing factor. By about 1920, the opportunities for expanding farm and livestock production were limited. Utah's small farms were also a restricting factor. In 1931 the western states suffered a severe *drought* which reduced production in the fields, dried pastures and range lands, and reduced the weight of lambs and beef for marketing. The drought led to a falling off of milk, egg, and poultry production.

Utah suffered a more devastating drought in 1934. Livestock men were forced to reduce sharply the number of head grazed in order to conserve feed. The federal government established a program of purchasing sheep and cattle, thus averting an even greater disaster. Cash crops were complete losses in some localities. Some farmers, unable to meet monetary obligations, were economically wiped out by this drought.

As a result of the reduced production of mine, mill, factory, farm and range, and the heavy losses of businessmen, rich men became poor men, and poor men went unemployed.

A look at *unemployment* helps to show the **severity of the depression in Utah.** Of the total work force of 170,000 in 1930, 8,712 persons were unemployed. This meant that one in five families in Utah was likely without income for food, rent, clothing, and other necessities. But the situation worsened. In 1931, 36,000 persons were unemployed. In 1932 the highest figure of unemployment was reached: 61,500 persons—35.8 percent of the work force—or one out of every three working men was out of work.

Income per person fell sharply as a result of the decline in employment and reductions in wages. In 1929 the annual per capita income in Utah was $537 ($680 for the U.S.), but in 1932 it had dropped to $276 ($380 for the U.S.), and in 1933, the low point, it stood at $275 ($368 for the U.S.). By 1940 the annual per capita income for Utah had risen to only $480.

The *out-migration* from Utah, begun a decade or so earlier, increased in the thirties. With few employment opportunities and low income, it was not unusual for many Utahns, including entire families, to leave the state in hopes of finding work elsewhere. Sons took

to the road in hopes of finding a job and at least cutting down on the demand for the limited food in the house. Fathers also moved in search of work. During the 1930s, there were about 3,000 Utah homes in which fathers were absent. The children (two or three to a family) were dependent upon the ability of the mother to provide the necessities, or the family had to accept public assistance of some type.

There were so many *hoboes* (migratory workers) throughout America that most communities arranged somehow to give the hobo a meal and send him on his way again. In some towns, hobo shacks were erected on the outskirts of town, near railroads, where hoboes rested while searching for work.

Utah's families in all walks of life were affected by the depression. *Farm families* that had a garden, chickens, a cow, and pigs got along well so far as food was concerned. A real problem was finding enough cash to pay rent, mortgages, taxes, and to buy shoes, for example. Farmers who did not own their own farms were hard pressed to keep up payments. Many farmers who owned farms were unable to pay taxes, and so became tenants (who worked the land for the owner) or left the farm and joined the unemployed in cities. City dwellers without gardens were dependent entirely upon cash for their livelihood. These people suffered the most during the depression.

The *low-income families* were especially hard hit. When the worker was laid off, the family had to make many adjustments. *Savings* might be used but rarely lasted more than a short time. It is estimated that over half of the families in the United States had no savings, and those with savings had an average of only $339, which was the equivalent of a little more than two months' wages. Many people had "saved" in the form of buying a car, or home, or insurance. If the family was unable to make payments on these obligations, it lost car, home, and insurance. Families had to learn to reduce their wants and get along without unnecessary items such as the telephone, extra riding in the car, new clothes, and out-of-the-home entertainment. What fuel and food they had or could buy they used sparingly.

Food was one item difficult to cut down. Many grocers set up charge accounts for old customers. They needed the business, but for how much and for how long could a grocer allow his customers to charge? Merchants' losses through unpaid bills were a form of private relief to the needy.

Food prices give indication of the plight of the farmer and the lack of cash in the hands of the consumer. According to newspaper advertisements, in November 1930, potatoes sold ten pounds for 13 cents, carrots four pounds for 5 cents, and sirloin steak 21 cents a pound. By the end of December, sirloin steak had dropped to 12 cents a pound. By 1934 meat prices began to rise, but the price of potatoes remained low. In 1940 potatoes were selling for 1/2 cent a pound, while sirloin steak was up to 30 cents a pound, and carrots held at four pounds for 5 cents. Not until 1941 did potatoes come up to 1 1/2 cents a pound and sirloin steak to 33 cents a pound. In advertising foods during the depression years, roasts and hamburger began to be important. In 1932 a rump roast sold for 10 cents a pound and ground beef was two pounds for 19 cents. By 1940 a rump roast cost 27 cents a pound. In comparing these prices with today's prices, it is necessary to keep in mind the difference in salaries for the years involved.

Paying the rent or the mortgage on a home was often a major problem. Even with an income, it was difficult to keep up the

Families worked together in harvesting crops. Springdale, Utah.

payments. Out of work, a father would not know from where next month's rent was coming. It was such a good feeling when the mother knew the rent was paid and there was coal in the bin. Many people just could not pay the rent. Many landlords proved they were not the greedy persons often imagined. If the landlord could not collect, he seldom evicted the family. Rent forgiveness was an important form of relief given by private persons to destitute families.

Families sought ways to save. Most poverty-stricken families just stopped buying. Old clothes were remade. Mending became an important task in every household. Houses were sometimes allowed to run down. Cutting back on food led to malnutrition among some children. General health suffered, and teeth went without repair. Entertainment centered in the home. Working jigsaw puzzles, playing cards, and other games became common forms of entertainment. Listening to the radio was perhaps the most popular indoor

THE LOGAN GARMENT CO.
EXCLUSIVE MAKERS OF LOGAN GARMENT KNIT
presents the
**K·S·L PLAYERS IN
THE RADIO - PLAYHOUSE**

THE LADIES OF THE CAST OF K·S·L PLAYERS ARE WEARING LOGAN GARMENT KNIT

*Radio dramas were produced in Salt Lake City
and broadcast live.*

sport of the decade. Music, soap operas, plays, and comedians gave entertainment which lightened many hearts and helped keep the human spirit alive.

Neighbors performed many acts of kindness to needy families. Persons with gardens often shared their produce with neighbors lacking those items. Others shared their shelter, warmth, sometimes small loans, and always encouragement.

When there was no food to eat and no fuel to keep the family warm, and little or no help from neighbors (who likely as not were as bad off), relief had to be found. A family might turn to private charities, churches, or to county, state, or federal relief as it became available.

The destitute condition of people and the extent of the depression in Utah can be shown by the fact that in March 1933 there were over 161,000 persons in Utah receiving all or part of their food, clothing, shelter, and other care from relief funds. This was

almost 32 percent of the entire population. Fortunately, there was a change for the better. In October 1933, the number on relief had dropped to 71,558, or 14 percent of the total population. But by November a year later, the number was up to 110,000, or 22 percent of the population. In January 1933 Governor Blood estimated that "probably 12,000 families in Salt Lake County alone are now receiving some form of assistance from public or private sources. The situation is such all over the State that private charity and county poor funds have not been able to carry the load."

The droughts and the depression produced in the minds of the people a third calamity, a spirit of pessimism and self-pity which threatened more havoc than drought and depression.

3. THE BURDEN OF RELIEF WAS ON LOCAL PROGRAMS DURING 1929-33

No people were better equipped by tradition to help themselves out of the depression than the people of Utah. Cooperation, self-sufficiency, self-reliance, and mutual sacrifice were strong Utah traditions, still alive in the memories and lives of the people. Persons shared what they could and gave encouragement. The pioneer practices of "make it over," "make it do," "wear it out," and "eat it up," were repeated in many households. It was generally expected that families would take care of their own problems. Few looked to government for any aid.

President Hoover said that private institutions in the local communities were the front line of attack upon the depression. Utahns agreed. Governor George H. Dern believed that there was no state machinery to deal with the problem of unemployment, and that if action were to be taken, the legislature would have to take it. When the legislature met, he made no recommendations for positive action of any sort. Rather, he gave advice and encouragement to cities and counties in their efforts. Utah law prevented towns from appropriating money or levying taxes for unemployment or relief, but counties were permitted to levy taxes for relief of their "poor and indigent" residents. However, with people having little money to pay taxes, funds were extremely limited. Furthermore, most people were against anything like the dole—"something for nothing." General attitudes were equally against deficit spending (borrowing from citizens by selling bonds to them, to be redeemed later).

At the outset of the depression, there was no way of knowing how long it would last or how severe it was going to be. The optimism of the 1920s carried over into the first year of the depression. One of Utah's distinguished economists, in a *Deseret News* prize-winning essay December 1931, pointed out that the business cycle showed that depressions came periodically and lasted one to three years. Stating that this depression "ranks among the most severe," he allowed it would take longer to recover. But he fully expected business conditions to improve during the next twelve or fifteen months, "approaching normal sometime in 1933." As events were to prove, the depression hit rock bottom in 1933, and the country was years from recovery.

Most relief from 1929 to 1932 was provided by *private charities* and *the counties.* The assistance was limited and often disorganized. The most significant private charities were provided by the churches: the Mormon church (with its Relief Society), the Salvation Army, the Jewish Relief, the Catholic Women's League, and the Protestant Ladies Aid Society. The Red Cross also performed essential services.

City and community groups cooperated to combat the effects of the depression. As the shock of the depression was felt in Salt Lake City in 1930, the Salt Lake Mayor's Advisory Committee effected a work relief program which operated between November 1930 and March 1931. The city spent $104,736 in providing 10,241 jobs for unemployed in the city. Salt Lake City also voted a bond issue of $600,000 to be spent to construct a storm sewer and other drainage projects.

Some communities put on charity shows, charged admission, and used the proceeds to help families in need. Such a charity show in Panguitch, December 1930, benefited forty homes. In Logan, on Christmas that year, cheer boxes were taken to needy families representing 1,200 persons (or about 12 percent of the population). In this gesture the Relief Societies and the Elks cooperated, with the help of junior high school students. Boxes of food, clothing, and toys, estimated to be worth five dollars, were given to the families. In Ogden, an aid fund benefited 1,800 persons. Other communities undertook similar charities.

By August 1931, Mormon stake and ward units were organizing to help their members. Using tithing and fast offering money, stores and storehouses were set up. At stores, goods were sold at cost. At storehouses, the unemployed could get items by performing work for the church, at a respectable wage of two dollars a day, or a person could promise to pay for items with work, the work to be done in and on church buildings. During the early years of the depression, the Mormon church spent in the state of Utah an average of over one-quarter of a million dollars annually for "church relief." The high was 1932 when $307,222 was spent, the low was in 1933 when $189,513 was spent.

In August 1931 Governor Dern organized a statewide *Unemployment Committee of One Hundred*, with representation from each county, the major cities, business, and welfare workers. Chairman was Sylvester Q. Cannon, presiding bishop of the Mormon church. The committee made recommendations for easing unemployment, but the suggested measures promised little prospects of real help. That September, the Salt Lake County Commission, the Salt Lake Community Chest, and the Presiding Bishop's Office of the Mormon church cooperated in relief work through a central warehouse: donations of food, clothing, and coal would be received, and then given to the needy.

Under the Agricultural Marketing Act of 1929, the government tried to help the farmers of the country by buying up surplus wheat. In the winter of 1931-32, the Red Cross distributed wheat from that program. By November 1932, some 70,000 families in Utah had received 58,000 barrels of flour.

As family incomes diminished, contributions to churches and charities also dropped. The resources of these private charitable organizations dwindled. Organizations set up to care for a few hundred persons obviously could not care for the thousands of families without incomes. The relief load in Utah had grown by 1932 to almost 29,000 families. By April of that year, county storehouses for relief were closing their doors. They had no more to give, except for the distribution of Red Cross flour.

Self-help efforts. The first years of the depression were also marked by relief programs started by individuals. One of the most interesting was that begun by Benjamin B. Stringham in the summer of 1931, and later known as the *Natural Development Association*. Stringham's idea was simply to create a situation in which the unused labor of the unemployed could be exchanged for surplus products of the farm, thus trading work for foodstuff. With this in mind, he took several truck loads of potatoes from Idaho to Salt Lake City to barter for other goods and services. He was so successful in this that he transported daily a group of unemployed to nearby farms. There fruit, vegetables, eggs, and other products were secured in return for labor. By the spring of 1933 he was operating fifteen units in four states (nine units in Utah) with an estimated total membership of 2,000 families. A later estimate suggests a membership of 7,500 families. Scrip was used as a medium of exchanging commodities for labor and labor for commodities. Sometimes retail stores accepted the scrip in exchange for goods, but most merchants were reluctant to accept it as a general practice, and opposed the association. An association store was maintained at which members could redeem the scrip for goods. The system did not supply all needs, but it was a major effort in putting people to work and helping farmers and other producers move their goods. Stringham's program continued until the summer of 1934, when it was closed because of the loss of value of the scrip and other problems.

Utah was a center for self-help programs. Utah became the first state to appropriate funds for self-help production when in March 1935 the legislature created the Utah Self-Help Cooperative Board. Many self-help groups were organized and operated under the direction of this board. More than sixty groups were formed the first year, but that number later declined. Each self-help unit was built around a single activity. Goods produced were either consumed by the group or traded with other groups. A warehouse was operated to help exchange goods between the units. Out of this experience, the board began to develop consumer cooperatives as outlets for

Woodcutting provided work for men during the depression.

self-help products. With this background, the Utah Cooperative Association was incorporated in August 1936. The following cooperative projects were conducted between 1935 and 1938: canning, coal mining, farming and gardening, flour milling, sawmilling, sewing, soapmaking, stonecutting, woodcutting, and woodworking. A lime kiln, machine shop, and retail wood and coal yard were established. Although the self-help cooperative program was not a substitute for relief, it made it possible for some men and women to supplement their low and irregular incomes, thus keeping them from being on relief.

State and local government programs (1929-1933). During the first years of the depression, state government believed the best thing it could do was to keep down its expenses and make government as efficient as possible, thus reducing the tax load. Legislatures were asked not to multiply services. Reorganization of government, for efficient operation, was urged. In 1931 the State Tax Commission was organized to bring under one agency the collection of all taxes and revenues to the state.

During Governor Dern's administration (the Hoover years), *little was done* to ease unemployment or give relief. The governor did recommend that the state adopt a five-day work week and a six-hour day so that more could be employed. It was not followed. When Governor Dern addressed the legislature in January 1931, fourteen months after the stock market crash, he admitted that the state had no agency that collected unemployment statistics, nor was there any agency charged with the duty of taking steps to relieve unemployment. The governor thought that one means of relieving unemployment was "advance planning of public works." The Eighteenth Legislature (1929, meeting before the stock market crash) had provided $1,115,000 for needed construction. That program provided some employment. Also, the State Road Commission was spreading out its road work so more men could have jobs.

Not all Utahns agreed with this policy of inaction. Perhaps the most radical exercise of opposition occurred on January 30, 1931, while the legislature was in session. A march was made to protest government inaction. About 1,500 men and women marched from Temple Square to the Capitol Building steps. The march was led by leaders of the Communist party in Utah who presented their demands to the administration: unemployment insurance, ten dollars a week for a single man, fifteen dollars a week for a married man, and two dollars a week for each child. The administration said it would consider the proposals, but nothing was done. Some of the placards carried in the march read: "Organize or Starve, Workers," "Milk for the Kiddies," "Welcome to Our Ranks," and "No More Stalling."

Under President Hoover's administration, the Emergency Relief and Construction Act of July 1932 made federal money available, on loan, to the states through the Reconstruction Finance Corporation. Utah's portion was made available to the counties through Governor Dern's *Committee on Emergency Relief for Utah*, appointed August 24, 1932. During the next seven months, several million dollars were spent in direct relief with only a limited amount of work relief. The direct relief was mostly in the form of food, clothing, and fuel. The money went directly to the counties for needy families. By March 1933, about 30 percent of the total population of Utah was receiving government assistance from this source.

County welfare committees shouldered the primary burden of providing relief in the early years of the depression. The committees represented local government, churches, and other charitable organizations. County storehouses were stocked with surplus food, clothing, and bedding, donated for needy people, collected by Boy Scouts and other school children. Surplus food, including meat, was canned and made available for the poor. Flour, sugar, potatoes, and cereal were in greatest demand. Sheep lost in the 1934 drought furnished wool from which mattresses and quilts were made at relief centers. Needy men could work for the city, for example, for two dollars a day in credit which could be drawn on at the storehouse for goods. Work preference was given to heads of families. Mormon ward bishops often acted as survey committees listing heads of families in need of work. As early as 1931 every county in the state was giving aid to the jobless.

4. THE NEW DEAL WAS A NATIONAL EFFORT TO OVERCOME THE DEPRESSION

Despite piecemeal local programs and Hoover's efforts, the depression continued to deepen throughout the nation, reaching its low point in 1932 and 1933. The industrial output of America was half its 1929 level. Fifteen million people, or about one of every four workers, were unemployed. One third of the nation's railroad mileage was idled due to bankruptcy of the railroad companies. Many farmers lost their farms due to loaning agencies foreclosing on their loans. Banks throughout the country failed.

The election of 1932 pitted President Hoover (R) against Franklin D. Roosevelt (D), governor of New York. Hoover campaigned on his record in office and saw the contest as between individualism and state control. Roosevelt saw the contest as between his and Hoover's theories of achieving prosperity. He stated that Hoover's theory was that if the rich and the financial institutions were supported, the common man would gain. Roosevelt's theory was that if the masses, the poor, were supported, everyone would profit. Roosevelt won the election with over 57 percent of the popular vote in the nation. It was a Democratic landslide in the nation and in Utah. The voters of Utah gave Roosevelt 56.5 percent of their votes. Veteran Reed Smoot (R), dean of the United States Senate after thirty years of service, lost to Elbert D. Thomas (D), a University of Utah professor, who won 57.5 percent of the votes. Governor Dern (D) did not stand for re-election. He supported Henry H. Blood (D) for the governorship, who won 57 percent of the votes. Discontent showed up in the heavy Democratic vote and in the fact that 4,080 Utahns voted for the Socialist presidential candidate, and 935 voted Communist. Hoover received but 41 percent of the popular vote in Utah; his fellow Republicans did only a little better. "Hard times" had a significant influence on political decisions.

Between the November elections and the

Henry H. Blood, governor of Utah, 1933-41, was one of Utah's most effective governors. As governor during the depression he took energetic steps to meet the needs of the people, making full use of state government and cooperating with the federal government programs.

March 1933 inaugural of the new president, little was done, and the depression worsened. The banking crisis was most critical. Immediately upon assuming office, President Roosevelt declared a national bank holiday, closing all the banks in the country. Banks were given time to regulate their affairs and prove to examiners that they were financially able to reopen before they were permitted to do so. Roosevelt then called a special session of Congress. During the next hundred days, the president presented legislation which was, for the most part, passed. It is called the New Deal. The president appealed to the "common man," the unemployed, the small businessman. Believing the little men had been dealt with poorly, the president proposed "a new deal" of the cards.

The New Deal was an attempt on the part of the federal government to adjust to an economic collapse that threatened the American way of life. Roosevelt was criticized

from many sides. But he did something; in fact, he tried everything. If one program did not work, he tried another. The Republicans feared violation of the Constitution of the United States and criticized him for going as far as he did. The Socialists and Communists criticized him for failing to go far enough. Actually, our democratic form of government and our economic system of capitalism were saved. Many of the New Deal programs are gone, but some are still with us and those that remain are supported almost universally by Democrats and Republicans alike.

The New Deal created many agencies, each of which was to play a special role in helping to overcome the depression. Its programs were aimed at three general purposes: *relief, recovery*, or *reform*. These were known as the three Rs of the New Deal. Relief legislation aimed to give immediate relief to the unemployed and the starving, sometimes in an outright dole; work might or might not be involved. Recovery legislation usually proposed putting people to work, but on jobs or in programs which aimed at the long-term solution of depression problems. Reform legislation aimed to correct those abuses of the American capitalistic system which had led directly to the depression.

Legislation, New Deal agencies, and President Roosevelt's messages did much to restore the confidence and morale of the people. The Federal Deposit Insurance Corporation (FDIC), which insured bank deposits up to $5,000, gave a government guarantee that a depositor would not lose his savings or deposits as a result of a bank failure. The Securities and Exchange Commission (SEC) sought to prevent another stock market crash by putting controls on the buying and selling of stocks.

The Social Security Act of 1935 established an old-age insurance system to help

It was difficult for people accustomed to taking care of themselves to receive welfare assistance. This Danish woman receives her first old-age assistance check, Widtsoe, Utah, April 1936.

older people. Employees and employers contributed to a retirement fund, and at age 65, the employee would draw monthly payments the rest of his life. This program gave retired people some income, and forced others to prepare for their retirement years. It also helped the employment picture by taking people over 65 off some jobs.

Direct relief and work relief were made available through a variety of agencies. The government put money into thousands of construction projects. The National Recovery Administration (NRA) set minimum wages and provided other benefits to labor. The NRA affected 500 job categories and a total of 22 million employees. The Public Works Administration (PWA) provided funds for the construction of roads and public buildings.

Some projects combined construction of civil works and direct relief. One agency that combined purposes was the Works Progress Administration (WPA). The control and prevention of soil erosion was given to the Soil Conservation Service. The Civilian Conserva-

tion Corps (CCC) was set up to prevent soil erosion, construct roads, and pursue a reforestation program.

Special attention was given to the plight of the farmer. It was believed by many that his problem was overproduction. But the basic problem was that unemployed workers had little or no money with which to purchase foodstuffs; the purchasing power of the nation was drying up, and farmers were unable to market even normal production.

To help the farmer the New Deal attempted various programs. The Agricultural Adjustment Act (AAA) aimed to remove the agricultural surplus by getting farmers to reduce their production. Credit was given farmers who had lost their farms through foreclosures. Although the AAA was declared unconstitutional by the United States Supreme Court, many of the act's constitutional features were taken over by other agencies.

Rural Americans were benefited by the Rural Electrification Administration (REA), which encouraged programs for generating and

A cooperative specialist is talking three Ericson brothers into forming a cooperative to buy a tractor to replace horses. Box Elder County, 1940.

distributing electricity to isolated areas not served by private utilities.

Young people who wanted to go to school but did not have necessary funds were helped by the National Youth Administration (NYA), which provided part-time employment for high school and college students to help them continue their education.

Anticipating the repeal of prohibition (see chapter 22, section 1), Congress passed in 1933 the Beer-Wine Revenue Act which legalized beer with a content of 3.2 percent alcohol. A tax was placed on beer and wine, though states were left in control of the sale and distribution of liquor. The taxes on beer and wine went into relief funds.

There were many other acts and agencies of the New Deal, but these were the most important as they related to Utah. The effect of these programs was to put many people to work, increase business activity, and raise prices. There were signs of overcoming the depression, but in 1937 the business recovery was interrupted by a brief, but acute, recession. Increased spending contributed to a recovery from this recession, and it seemed that the depression might be defeated. Even so, in August 1939, there were about ten million persons in the nation still unemployed.

Reaction to the New Deal in Utah was mixed. Many people were grateful for some action being taken. Even so, there was a reluctant acceptance of New Deal measures. Although the *Deseret News* and the *Salt Lake Tribune* took strong stands against the reelection of Roosevelt in 1936 and supported his opponent, the Utah voters gave Roosevelt 70 percent of their vote. Roosevelt carried the nation by a similar vote.

Roosevelt And Blood Gain Sweeping Victory

5. FEDERAL AND STATE GOVERNMENTS AND LOCAL AGENCIES WORKED IN UTAH TO COMBAT THE DEPRESSION, 1933-41

New Deal programs in Utah were of two kinds: direct relief and work relief. *Direct relief* was the outright payment of money to unemployed or to fatherless families. *Work relief* meant not only a small income for the jobless family, it meant that money was spent for construction materials, and the demand for construction materials in turn stimulated many other industries. Work relief prevailed in Utah. The fact of employment and some income provided necessities and lifted the spirits of a large percentage of the families in Utah.

One of Roosevelt's first attempts to relieve the distress of the unemployed was the *Federal Emergency Relief Administration* (FERA). The FERA combined direct relief with work relief and the use of federal money with state money. It functioned under state management. To help administer the FERA in Utah, Governor Blood appointed a committee, May 16, 1933, known as the *State Advisory Committee on Public Welfare and Emergency Relief.* The FERA continued until March 1934 during which time it employed teachers, distributed surplus commodities provided by the federal government, furnished lunches to school children, gave part-time employment to college students, and undertook to relieve drought victims. The governor's advisory committee administered relief programs until 1935.

To get in line with the federal government, the Utah legislature passed the Emergency Revenue Act of 1933, which provided a *2 percent sales tax* for the sole purpose of relief. The tax brought in about $115,000 a month while the federal government contributed $1 million a month. The combined sum was spread among the 120,000 or more men, women, and children receiving their subsistence from relief agencies in Utah.

The Civil Works Administration (CWA) was one of the first federal work relief programs in Utah. It began operating November 19, 1933, and by the second week 10,788 persons were working for their paychecks. The CWA operated only until March 31, 1934, when its responsibilities were taken over by Utah's Emergency Relief Administration. During those four months, the CWA employed between 13,000 and 20,000 persons in the construction of highways, roads, city streets and sidewalks; building hospitals; construction and repair of school buildings and other public buildings; the development of parks and playgrounds; and improvements to waterways, municipal water supply units, sewers, and drainage systems. The total amount spent under the program in Utah was $5,228,952, of which 13.6 percent came from state and local funds.

The Utah Emergency Relief Administration (UERA) began in April 1934 and lasted until December 1935. It continued the work of the CWA. The action was on the county level. The program was administered by public-spirited social workers. Relief was granted on the basis of need. A family budget was determined, and the man was given work to make up the deficiency in his budget. During 1934 the UERA administered $11,488,005 to needy families. Of that sum 81.67 percent came from federal funds, 11.83 from state, and 6.5 from local. Reports indicate that the typical citizen preferred an "honorable means of caring for himself and his family through his own exertion, to any dole." Only 5 percent of the 30,000 families on the relief rolls preferred food orders to employment.

The projects undertaken by the UERA

The prevention of soil erosion on Utah's mountains was a lasting contribution of the federal Soil Conservation Service and the CCCs. Mountain sides were terraced to reduce the possibility of soil erosion and flooding.

were similar to those of the CWA, except that they went farther and were more diverse. For example, trees and shrubs were planted in parks and around public buildings. To protect big game, furbearing animals, upland game birds, and livestock, over five thousand predatory animals were destroyed. The pelts were sold and the returns placed in the FERA fund. Over a hundred canning centers were established, and hundreds of thousands of cans of meat, vegetables, and fruit were preserved. Over two million pounds of fresh meat were cut and distributed to the needy.

School lunches were served students. Classes were conducted by dieticians who taught mothers the principles of nutrition and how best to feed their families. Employment was given to artists (to "increase the cultural assets of the state"). People from all walks of life cooperated in educational programs to help each other make the most of their resources.

One of the most popular federal work relief programs was the *Civilian Conservation Corps*. The CCC employed young men in their late teens and early twenties, selected by their local unemployment agencies, and placed in camps away from home. Young men from across the nation—New Jersey, Ohio, the South—were in CCC camps in Utah. In the camps of tents or barracks, the boys were under army discipline and forest service direction, with educational and recreational leaders. The pay was one dollar a day plus food, clothing, and shelter. Most boys sent their pay back home. Educational directors helped the young men continue their education. Books were brought to camps by traveling libraries. The boys lived in the out-of-doors, worked hard, and gained in health and self-respect. Camps were located throughout the forest areas of Utah. In the winter months, the northern Utah camps were closed and the boys went to Utah's Dixie to work until summer.

It is estimated that the CCC spent $52,756,183 in Utah. The program operated from September 1933, beginning with about 1,100 young men, until the end of 1941. On the average, there were about 2,000 young men employed all the time, though the high of 4,500 enrollees was reached in June 1935.

The CCC was given tasks related to reclamation and conservation in forest areas. Roads and trails were built, forest fires checked or prevented, and measures taken to

Ford Creek Flood Control, a pastel drawing by Utah artist Ranch Kimball.

Woods Cross CCC Winter Camp, by Ranch Kimball.

prevent erosion and floods by building retaining walls, terracing, and planting trees. Springs were cleaned and water holes opened. The CCC boys fought crickets in Millard County, killed rodents in range lands, reseeded grasses in eroded areas, and planted trees where the forests had been too heavily cut. They riprapped portions of the Virgin River to control its course, built bridges in various places in the state, created campgrounds and recreational facilities in canyons, built the rodeo grounds at Tooele, worked on the Bear River Bird Refuge, helped build scores of dams and reservoirs, and did the terracing above and overlooking Willard and Bountiful, thus preventing a repetition of the terrible flash floods of the years immediately before when tons and tons of sand, earth, and gravel were washed down upon those communities.

The popularity of the CCC is shown by the fact that four out of every five Americans, according to a 1936 poll, supported the CCC. The *Deseret News*, which had little good to say for the New Deal, reflected popular belief when on December 11, 1934, it editorialized that many mothers knew the benefit the CCC had been to their sons. The benefits derived through their projects, it was believed, more than repaid costs.

The National Youth Administration (NYA) was a work relief program for young people who were eager to complete their schooling but needed financial help. The student aid program in Utah began in December 1933 and did not end until March 1943. While there was an average of 2,232 Utah students receiving help over the ten-year period, during the years of its greatest numbers, it was enrolling 3,000 to 4,000 persons. The hourly wage was small, but the work helped many students complete their education. NYA students worked at mending and cataloguing library books, servicing library patrons, typing for teachers, and assisting in campus repairs and maintenance.

In March 1936 the NYA began work projects. The employment of young people on work projects, from 1,500 to 2,900 a year, lasted until June 1942. NYA work project people made and lettered street signs, repaired discarded toys for poor children, built

CCC work projects helped prevent slides such as this due to heavy rains.

school furniture, constructed footbridges for rural school paths, to name but a few of their activities.

The New Deal entered a new phase in 1935. The federal government moved out of direct relief, leaving that to the states and local communities. In May 1935 the Utah State Department of Public Welfare was created and began to absorb the functions of the Utah Emergency Relief Administration that related to the relief of the unemployable. People who could not work were now taken care of by either Social Security or the Utah State Department of Public Welfare.

As the federal government moved out of direct relief, it provided funds for a large-scale national works program. The major agency of this works program was the *Works Progress Administration (WPA), later (1939) called the Works Projects Administration*. The primary task of the WPA was to put 3,500,000 persons in the nation to work. In Utah, Darrell J. Greenwell was appointed state administrator of the WPA and director of the State Department of Public Welfare.

The WPA operated in Utah from September 1935 to the end of 1942. During the first years, an average of over 13,000 persons was employed; overall during its years of operation in Utah, the WPA employed a yearly average of 10,655 persons. During the quarter ending September 1936, the peak figure of 17,672 was reached. Altogether more than $55 million of federal and local funds were spent on WPA projects. Laborers received 70 percent of the money spent, the rest was spent on materials and related expenses.

The WPA had a poor image among many people. Some thought of WPA workers as "leaning on a shovel" all day. The WPA did not necessarily train people in new jobs; its primary purpose was to give unemployment relief—the work accomplished was secondary. Even so, the accomplishments of the WPA for Utah were diverse and significant and the record of constructions is impressive.

Some of the major construction accomplishments include construction on the ordnance depot near Ogden, improvements at Fort Douglas; construction of armories at Logan, American Fork, Nephi, Mount Pleasant, Fillmore, and Cedar City; construction of the Salt Lake City School Administration Building; and remodeling of many Salt Lake City schools.

Construction in the counties illustrates local needs and the variety of projects. In Uintah County emphasis was on reservoirs, with the construction of the Oak Park and Montez Creek dam and the Long Park reservoir. In Summit County, it was highway and roadwork that was most needed. The O'Driscoll dugway improvement provided a connection to the main highway, and "a year-round outlet to the whole area of the Kamas Valley." A building program benefited the people of Sanpete County with the completion of a

CONSTRUCTION UNDER THE WPA

Highways, roads, and streets

4,796 miles, new and improved
1,206 bridges and viaducts, new and improved
12,494 culverts, new and improved

Public buildings

36 new schools or additions
209 schools underwent reconstruction or
    improvements
385 other new construction and additions
537 other reconstruction or improvement

Outdoor recreational facilities

30 parks
161 playgrounds and athletic fields
23 swimming and wading pools

Public utilities and sanitation

29 utility plants new and improved
343 miles of storm and sanitary sewers,
    new and improved
487 miles of water mains and distribution
    lines, new and improved
28,775 new sanitary privies

Airport facilities

6 new landing fields
77,130 linear feet of runway, new
    construction
15,288 linear feet of runway, reconstruction
    or improvement including surfacing

Airport buildings

5 new
6 reconstruction or improvement

---

new county courthouse, an armory at Manti, a municipal building and a mechanical arts building at Ephraim. Cache County used the WPA on road construction, erecting buildings at Utah State Agricultural College, and major improvements at the airport.

Reclamation projects. Closely related to the New Deal agencies in Utah were federal reclamation projects. Utah's agriculture, industry, and communities benefited from seven

The Salt Lake City Municipal Airport was improved by WPA labor.

Deer Creek Reservoir, Heber Valley.

These Utah Valley lands were brought under irrigation by the Deer Creek reservoir on the Provo River.

projects authorized by President Roosevelt between 1935 and 1943. Dams, reservoirs, and related water distribution systems were constructed. Water users agreed to pay back to the federal government the cost of construction and have since done so.

The Hyrum Project created Hyrum Dam and reservoir in southern Cache County. The Moon Lake Project constructed the Moon Lake Dam and reservoir in Duchesne County. The Sanpete Project, with units at Ephraim and Spring City, furnished water to lands under local irrigation companies. The Ogden River Project, which extends into Weber and Box Elder counties, built the Pine View Dam and reservoir and related distribution systems. The Provo River Project, extending into Utah, Salt Lake, Summit, and Wasatch counties, built the Deer Creek Dam and reservoir and related tunnels, reservoirs, and canals. The Newton Project built the Newton Dam and reservoir in northern Cache County to replace an old dam built in 1871. The Scofield Project, in Carbon County, replaced the deteriorated Scofield Dam. At a total cost of about $22 million, these seven projects have brought water to about 750,000 acres of land. These lands yield a gross crop value each year of over $12 million.

Cultural programs of the WPA. While artists had been employed in 1934 under the FERA, in 1935 the WPA set up programs for artists, musicians, and writers. These programs kept skilled and talented people in the state, recognized the necessity of keeping the creative arts alive, and helped take art throughout the state to the people.

The Utah WPA Art Project was directed by Mr. Elzy J. Bird. In 1937 the legislature reorganized the Utah Art Institute (created in 1899), changed its name to the Utah State Institute of Fine Arts, and authorized it to cooperate in federal programs. Under such

437

An artist prepares to make sketches of petroglyphs in Barrier Canyon under a WPA project.

Lynn Fausett creates a mural of petroglyphs from Barrier Canyon.

programs, artists were employed at $80 a month to create works of art and to teach others. Art project centers were established at Salt Lake City, Provo, Helper, and Price. Artists created murals for communities that could not otherwise have afforded them. It cost the WPA about $1,600 for Lynn Fausett to paint the mural in the Price City Hall; the mural was recently insured for $40,000.

One especially interesting project was reproducing on canvas the petroglyphs in southern Utah's Barrier Canyon, which were threatened with destruction by an oil company operating in the area. A team of WPA workers under Fausett recreated the Indian work on a canvas eleven feet by eighty feet. Today, the canvas hangs in the University of Utah Museum of Natural History.

Sketches and watercolor paintings of Utah pioneer handicrafts, including clothing, furniture, and tools, were made for inclusion in the National Index of American Design.

The Springville Art Gallery was built by the WPA in 1937. The Springville Art Association, one of Utah's most distinguished art groups, was formed out of a movement among students of the Springville High School. The noted Utah painter John Hafen helped start the collection by giving one of his paintings, and since that time the community has assembled by gifts and purchases a most notable collection of art, worth hundreds of thousands of dollars. Portraits of historic Utah figures now in the Capitol Building dome were done, under the WPA, by painters directed by Lee Greene Richards.

Among the notable artists in the WPA program were Elzy J. Bird, Lynn Fausett, Gordon Cope, William J. Parkinson, Howell Rosenbaum, W. H. Shurtliff, Paul Smith, Henry Rasmussen, Edwin Evans, Everett Thorpe, Carlos Anderson, Ranch Kimball, Florence Ware, Calvin Fletcher, Irene Fletcher, and others. There were in all about twenty Utah artists producing artwork in the program.

Although this part of the WPA program was expensive, it saved the artists from loss of creative talent, gave the people of Utah the experience of seeing art exhibits, and trained many young artists.

The WPA music program came at a time when musicians were struggling against the inroads being made by the motion picture theater. The Salt Lake Theatre, the primary supporter of legitimate theater and music drama, was torn down in 1929. While the Mormon church subsidized its own music program, operatic and orchestral works were neglected. The WPA Music Project gave renewed support for orchestra music in Utah. Under the WPA, a Utah State Symphony Orchestra was begun. Local musicians contributed their talents to the orchestra and taught music to thousands of receptive school children and adults. Programs of symphonic music were presented throughout the state in parks, public halls, and before public school children.

Writers were also included in the WPA work relief programs. The Federal Writers' Project in Utah (known after 1939 as the Utah Writers' Project) put historically inclined people to work preserving and writing a record of Utah's history. Out of the experiences of Mrs. Juanita Brooks of Saint George in making typewritten copies of pioneer diaries and records, there emerged a federally sponsored program called the Historical Records Survey. Pioneer diaries, journals, memoirs, and interviews were collected from pioneer residents of the state. Inventories of county and church archives were made. A history of Provo, *Provo: Pioneer Mormon City*, was written, also a pamphlet *History of Ogden*. Very important was the monumental task of putting together a basic collection of information on Utah, called *Utah, a Guide to*

The establishment of the WPA Symphony Orchestra in 1940 was a big step forward in the cultural life of Utah.

A significant step in the preservation of historical sources and writing Utah history was taken by these three leaders.

Dale L. Morgan

Juanita Brooks

Mabel Jarvis

Center of Mormon church welfare activities was Welfare Square in Salt Lake City where there was built a large grocery and meat department, a flour mill, and a canning factory.

the State. This was compiled mainly through the efforts of Dale L. Morgan, a supervisor and writer in the program, later to become one of America's leading historians of the West. Utah can be justly proud of this excellent work. The inventories, collections of pioneer records, and the large number of historical essays produced all add up to a significant effort in preserving Utah's history, unmatched since that time. Most of the materials collected are now in the Utah State Historical Society, Salt Lake City.

Mormon Church Security Program. The Mormon church had a tradition of charitable services for its people, and the Relief Society organization had a specific responsibility to care for the poor. A Relief Society report shows that from 1929 to 1933, the Mormon church spent in Utah an average of over one-quarter of a million dollars annually for "church relief." In 1936 when the church learned that over 7 percent of its members were on relief rolls, it moved in a more direct way to take them off relief. A program, later called the Church Welfare Plan, was an-

nounced in May 1936. Proceeds from fast offerings and tithing were used to help the poor. Surplus commodities and donated goods were placed in church storehouses, from which the unemployed were aided according to their need. Whenever possible the policy of work relief prevailed. Projects were created to make work for those who would then receive relief in the form of goods.

Emergency and permanent projects were undertaken. Sewing, farming, and canning projects were among the first. Cooperative farms were established, crops harvested, and storage bins erected. The sick were assisted, and for some destitute families, houses were built. A beautification program for church buildings was begun. Regional storehouses were erected and exchange programs put in operation. The construction of a reservoir in the Uinta Mountains illustrates a permanent aspect of the program.

Despite all the efforts by federal, state, and local governments and private organizations, the depression hung on. From 1932 to 1940 the total number of unemployed was reduced by only half. In 1940, 7.8 percent of Utah's labor force was on public work projects, and 10 percent was unemployed. A 1938 study shows that Utah was far above the national average in the percentage of workers on federal work relief projects. According to the study, Utah had 32 percent more workers on WPA projects, 45 percent more on CCC projects, 50 percent more in the NYA, 175 percent more students receiving student aid, and 60 percent more workers on the PWA than the national average. The united effort of all agencies had taken care of tens of thousands of unemployed, and that was a great achievement. Through employment, people were saved. As a by-product, many physical improvements were made in Utah's communities.

6. THE DEPRESSION LEFT AN IMPORTANT HERITAGE FOR UTAH

President Hoover should not be blamed for the depression, nor should President Roosevelt be credited with solving the problems of the depression. The depression was a product of forces operating for years before, climaxing the so-called prosperity of the twenties. The depression was worldwide. The United States contributed to it and participated in it. The droughts which brought untold suffering to many people may be charged to nature.

It was not the three Rs of the New Deal which brought the United States out of the depression. Rather, the depression was ended by a fourth R—Rearmament. The outbreak of war in Europe in September 1939 led to demands for United States goods, and there followed a sudden increase in economic activity. By December 1939, unemployment in the United States had dropped 10 percent. As the United States developed its military program, government expenditures, industrial production, and national income increased.

The New Deal did represent an attempt of the federal government to meet the problems of economic collapse that threatened the American way of life. The government did not want to control the economy, neither did it want all programs of the New Deal to become permanent programs. But the American people came to accept the position that government should have an active role in helping keep the economic life of the country healthy and being responsive to the public welfare.

For Utah, many aspects of the New Deal program were of lasting value. This is true for most of the construction projects. Conservation was given a big boost by the CCC, WPA, and the reclamation projects. Farmers and ranchers became more interested in learning the science of agriculture.

Utahns came to place a higher value on education as it was realized that most of the men on relief projects were unskilled or semi-skilled laborers.

Families learned to make the fullest use of every article in their possession. People learned it was good economy to stay healthy. They continued to grow gardens and experienced the delight and food value of fresh and home-canned fruits and vegetables.

Individuals learned the value of having a job, a regular income, and some security for the future. They talked a great deal of personal initiative, self-reliance, and hard work. While some people came to place unusual value on material goods, others looked anew at religious and spiritual values. For many who worked in the belief that America could and would survive the depression, there was a developing sense of social responsibility within the framework of the American system of democratic capitalism.

Salt Lake City, from the State Capitol Building, looking south, 1931.

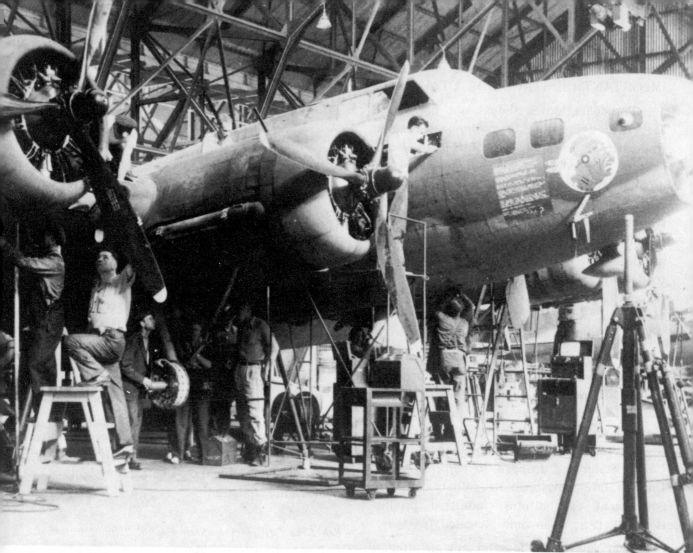

The "Suzy Q," a B-17 bomber aircraft, was the first to come to Hill Field for repair.

A Salt Lake City street scene during the war. Can you identify the war leaders and date this picture?

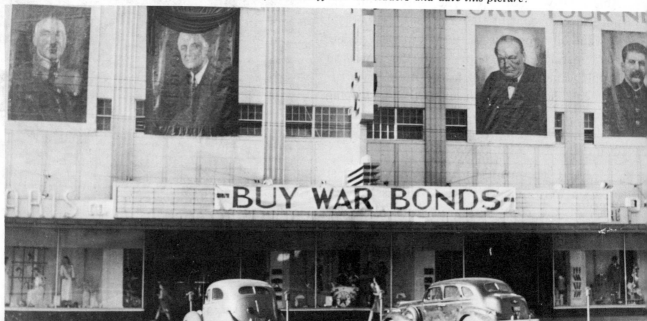

EXTRA!

The Deseret News

Vol. 361. No. 62. 92nd Year

Salt Lake City, Utah, Thursday, December 11, 1941

Price: Five Cents

XTRA!

U.S. DECLARES WAR ON GERMANY, ITALY

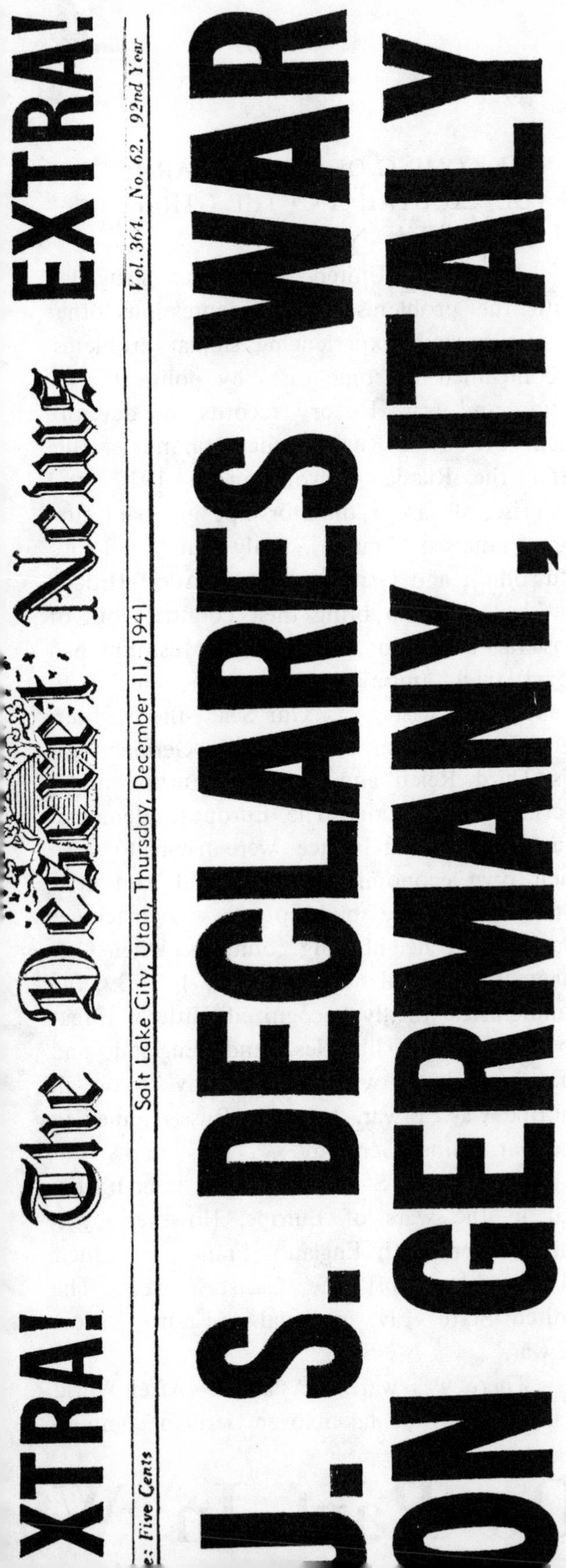

UTAH DURING WORLD WAR II

World War II has influenced the twentieth century more than any other single event to date. The causes of that war are very complex and come from conflicts and forces developing decades before. Many of the conditions of the world today stem directly from the war and the arrangements between nations following the war.

Utah, like other states in the Union, participated fully in the national war effort. In turn, Utah was affected by the war. Family life was disrupted. Employment patterns were changed. Utah was called upon to furnish men and women for the armed forces as well as to furnish war materiel. Defense plants and training centers brought many people into the state. The expenditures of large sums of money by the federal government for these services led to full employment and a prosperity Utah had not known before. Utah's economic and social patterns of life were changed. No other single event has changed Utah so much or so quickly as World War II. Modern Utah came fully into being as a result.

IN THIS CHAPTER WE WILL LEARN

1. The coming of World War II involved Utah and the other states in the nation.

2. Life on the home front was changed.

3. Utah made a significant contribution to winning the war.

4. Utah life was greatly changed by the war.

24

Men on the street listen to the world series over the radio at a shop in Saint George, 1940. The war in Europe soon changed their lives as many were called up to military duty.

1. THE COMING OF WORLD WAR II INVOLVED UTAH AND THE OTHER STATES IN THE NATION

While the United States was struggling with the problems of the depression, other countries were experiencing similar problems, accompanied in some cases by political revolution and war. History records the development of Soviet Russia under communist rule after the Russian Revolution of 1917, and the rise of fascist dictatorships in Spain (under Francisco Franco), Italy (under Benito Mussolini), and Germany (under Adolf Hitler). Besides trying to bring their countries out of postwar depression, Hitler and Mussolini had territorial ambitions. Mussolini sought to make Italy master of "Our Sea"—the Mediterranean—and Hitler to unify all "Germans" in his Third Reich and place all Europe under German domination. The European democracies—England and France—were trying to solve their own economic problems and paid little attention to the buildup of war machines among their neighboring countries. When Germany invaded Poland, September 1, 1939, the democracies finally recognized Hitler's threat to their own liberties, and England and France declared war on Germany. Soon all Europe was at war. In time, Russia joined in the war against Germany.

The United States wanted to remain neutral in the wars of Europe. However, sympathies were with England, France, and their allies, and against the fascist powers. The United States gave material assistance "short of war."

There was war in Asia also. After World War I, Japan had taken over German commer-

Utah Prepares To Do Part In Wa

cial interests in eastern Asia and in general asserted an aggressive trade policy in the Orient. Japan built up her military power too. Incidents occurred between Japan and China during the 1920s, but in 1931 open warfare broke out when the Japanese occupied Manchuria, a northern Chinese province. From there the war spread, continuing during the 1930s.

The expansion of Japan in eastern Asia was a threat to the interests of the United States in the Orient. After the European war broke out in 1939, the United States was virtually the only power standing in the way of Japan's expansion. Friction increased, and on December 7, 1941, Japanese forces made simultaneous attacks upon our Pacific Ocean territories—Pearl Harbor in the Hawaiian Islands, the Philippine Islands, Wake, and Guam. The next day Congress declared that a state of war existed between the United States and Japan. Three days later, Germany and Italy declared war on the United States. Most of the world was soon lined up in a gigantic military struggle.

For the United States, the war lasted from December 7, 1941 until 1945 when fighting ended in Europe on May 8 and in Asia on September 2. It is impossible to tell the human misery caused by the war, or the destruction to life, property, human values and relations, and governments.

Utah, like all other states in the Union, was involved at once in the war—supplying manpower for the armed forces, contributing dollars by buying war bonds, and working in a united effort to win the war.

2. LIFE ON THE HOME FRONT WAS CHANGED

The Japanese attack on Pearl Harbor united the nation in an immense effort to win the war in the Pacific and in Europe.

Work speeded up. Everyone wanted to do his part. There was not the naive enthusiasm for war there had been in 1917. People went realistically about their jobs with a determination to make their efforts count to win the war as quickly as possible.

Fear of enemy attack was real. If the enemy could make such a successful surprise attack on Pearl Harbor, it was believed that attacks could be made on the West Coast states. Aircraft carriers made it possible for enemy planes to be within striking distance of important targets. Many measures were taken in the name of *civil defense*.

The State Council of Defense was set up by the Utah legislature in 1941. Governor Maw served as chairman, and Gus P. Backman, who directed civilian defense activities in the mountain states, was vice-chairman. Council members coordinated state and federal civil defense efforts. Committees supervised special activities which might become necessary in time of emergency. Subcommittees dealt with the problems of housing, consumer goods, mining and smelting, agriculture and livestock, civil protection, health and welfare, transportation, utilities, industry, publicity, personnel and labor, supplies and maintenance, and aeronautics. The law provided also for the appointment of special police, a state guard, regulation of explosives, sabotage prevention, and the construction of defense highways. Throughout the war period this council directed many affairs which helped make Utah's effort a successful contribution to winning the war and preparedness for defending ourselves in emergencies.

Civil defense took many forms. Fear of sabotage led to setting up guards to protect bridges, highways, dams, and culinary water systems. Other civilians were called to watch the skies and alert the population to possible enemy air raids. The enemy did not attack

n Japan

our shores, and by December 1943 the battle line of the Pacific was well to the west of our coast. The services of the air-raid watchers were suspended and the dimout (minimum lights at night) was lifted. Eight hundred Utah adults served in the Civil Air Patrol, an official auxiliary of the Army Air Force. The patrol was placed in charge of many emergency wartime programs, including the enlistment and training of cadets. Some 1,100 cadets, ages fifteen to seventeen, trained in navigation, meteorology, aircraft instruments, radio, and intelligence. Many if not most of these people served without pay or expense money.

Utah men served on many war fronts. Over 65,000 Utah men and women served in the armed forces during World War II. Servicemen went into the army, the navy, the marines, and the air force, and served in military activities including battles in the Pacific, North Africa, and Europe. A number of Utah women served in the auxiliary branches of the military, performing services that freed men for combat duty. Of the Utah men and women serving, 1,450 were killed.

All families, to some degree, sooner or later, were involved in the selective service, or draft, of young men for military service. By 1945, approximately half of the families in Utah had someone in the service. Over one-third of Utah's servicemen enlisted for a specific service; they did not wait for the draft. The services attempted to classify servicemen for the jobs that best used their talents, but this was not always possible. However, many servicemen learned new trades and job skills, or gained special education which opened up new careers for them after the war. Some servicemen were stationed in the states for the duration of the war, but most went through training camps and were then sent overseas. The postal service and the telephone became very important in keeping communications open between servicemen and their families. To some children a father was just a picture of a person heard about but never seen.

Life on the home front. Those who remained home were soon caught in a series of changes. *Men* not in the service were expected to take jobs in one of the essential industries. Work shifts in some industries and businesses went beyond the eight-hour day. Most industries operated around the clock to produce the goods, materials, and supplies essential to the armed forces.

To help fill the labor shortage, thousands of *women* went to work outside the home. The women who remained home often took care of the children of mothers who worked. Women at home knitted sweaters for servicemen, helped with Red Cross projects, and where possible had a garden to supplement the food supply of the family. Many worked with the United Service Organization (USO), centers established in towns near military bases where servicemen might go for entertainment, to meet civilians and make new friends, and to keep up or develop hobbies and interests.

During World War II women joined men in jobs. Here they are working on aircraft engines.

Farmers were encouraged to grow as much as possible for use on the home front and by the United States allied countries.

Children helped with the war effort too. They collected scrap metal, tin cans, newspapers, and other materials to contribute to the war effort. Some attended schools in shifts, either early or late in the day. This double use of a building was especially needed in communities where large employment at defense plants and installations brought large increases in the number of students.

Because of the heavy demands on food and supplies for the war effort, there was *rationing* of certain foods, gasoline, and automobile tires. The federal Office of Price Administration (OPA) was charged with the responsibility of ensuring that each civilian had a fair share of the goods available. To accomplish this, many goods were rationed. Citizens were registered with the OPA and issued stamp books for food and gasoline. Rationed goods could not be purchased without stamps. It was a chore for a housewife to budget her food stamps to obtain the best value from them especially as meat, sugar, and canned goods were scarce. The gasoline shortage cut down driving for pleasure, and induced many workers to form car pools and ride to work together. Since the gasoline and tire mileages are increased at slow speeds, speed limits were lowered to save on gas and tires. Rationing was an inconvenience, but it did keep those who had money from buying and hoarding the available stocks of food and other essential goods. It also forced some people to return to pioneer resourcefulness and make their own things or do without.

The housing problem was acute. Efforts were made to put every available lodging place into use at a reasonable price.

The unemployment problem was solved to a degree when tens of thousands of men went into military service, leaving their jobs for others. Pre-draft-age boys worked at many jobs. The draft and the job had an effect on attendance at the universities in the state. Enrollments dropped about 20 percent each year after 1941. By 1945 enrollments were down as much as 70 percent from the prewar level.

The state university campuses, however, became the scene of military training as the armed forces made use of the technical knowledge and skills in the faculties for the specialized training of thousands of selected servicemen. Army, navy, and air force training programs were conducted. Enrollees were given special instruction in mathematics, physics, meteorology, photography, radio and electronics, chemistry, psychology, and foreign languages. Nurses and social workers were trained for work in the Red Cross. For these training programs, the universities devised accelerated courses and operated on a year-round basis.

With industry geared to war production, few consumer goods were available and *peo-*

ple were encouraged to save their earnings. More important, they were urged to *invest* their money in United States War Bonds. In effect this was a system by which the federal government borrowed money from the citizens to help finance the war. The promotion of savings bond drives was everybody's business. Entertainments promoted sales. Businesses competed in getting employees to buy bonds. School children bought savings stamps which could be turned in for bonds. Between 1942 and 1945, Utahns purchased over $500 million worth of bonds.

Life during wartime was difficult for almost everyone. *Businessmen* had a difficult time getting merchandise, since the production of war-related supplies had priority. Anything made of metal or rubber was hard to get and keep in stock. Clothing was also in short supply due to the demand for uniforms and other clothing for servicemen. Many businesses had to take on younger, inexperienced workers to perform the jobs of those who had joined the military or gone to work at better paying defense jobs.

The wartime demand for food helped bring Utah's agriculture out of depression.

Utah *farmers* were free to grow as much as their land would produce because of the great demand for food by the armed forces, the people at home, and our allies in war-torn countries. However, farmers worked under the hardship of a shortage of labor and machinery, thus they had to work long hours to produce record crops.

There was a shortage of *school teachers* as many went into the service, or went to work at higher paying jobs in defense plants and military installations. Many teaching positions were filled by teachers with temporary certificates. Many schools were handicapped for lack of funds and teachers. The wartime experiences made the public more teacher-conscious and interested in improving schools.

Utah also experienced a shortage of *doctors and nurses* because many volunteered for war service. People at home had to become more resourceful in caring for their health problems.

Recreation for those in the service and for those at home centered around movies, dances, and listening to the radio. Motion pictures were an important form of recreation during the war. The same movies shown at home were seen by the servicemen throughout the United States and overseas. The demand for movies and the need for morale-building stories resulted in a great variety of excellent motion pictures.

Social dancing had been a traditional form of recreation in Utah. Wartime seemed to make it even more important. There were dances at the USOs, hotel ballrooms, Lagoon, Saltair, and in church recreation halls.

Radio programs were important. The comedy programs of such stars as Jack Benny, Bob Hope, Fred Allen, and George Burns and Gracie Allen brought laughter into the lives of everyone. Classical and popular music was heard. The songs of the various branches of the service were very popular. "Anchors Aweigh," "From the Halls of Montezuma," and "Off We Go into the Wild Blue Yonder" were almost as popular as "I'm Dreaming of a White Christmas."

3. UTAH MADE A SIGNIFICANT CONTRIBUTION TO WINNING THE WAR

Even before the attack on Pearl Harbor, steps were being taken to make Utah a defense center. Utah's geographical location made her ideally located to play an important part in the war effort. The Salt Lake-Ogden area was the center of a great system of highways, railroad lines, and air lanes. The area was out of range of probable attack and equidistant to all points on the West Coast. There were railroad and highway connections with centers of population and production in the East.

Utah already had some facilities which could be used at once as well as expanded. These included Fort Douglas, Hill Field, and the Ogden Ordnance Depot. There was unused land for additional depots, airfields, and practice bombing ranges. The number of clear days made a base for flight training possible.

Utah's political and business leaders were quick to draw the attention of federal officials to the possibilities of locating defense industries and military installations in Utah. Their efforts were to prove successful. Utah also needed the payrolls, for she still had many people out of work due to the depression.

The twenty-fourth Utah legislature, meeting early in 1941, set up a Department of Publicity and Industrial Development to advertise the attractions of Utah and make efforts to bring in new payrolls.

Promoters of Utah stressed that Utah was the major commercial source for coal

Herbert B. Maw, governor from 1941 to 1949, led Utah through the war years and after.

west of the Rocky Mountains, that Utah had the only blast furnace in the West at the Columbia Steel Company plant in Provo, and that Utah had great mineral wealth near the population centers. They pointed out that Utah had other essentials to successful industrial development: necessary water, electric power, natural gas, and a dependable labor force.

Governor Herbert B. Maw, Senators Elbert D. Thomas and Abe Murdock, Congressmen Walter K. Granger and J. W. Robinson worked closely with Gus P. Backman, secretary of the Salt Lake Chamber of Com-

Gus P. Backman, Utah civic leader before, during, and after the war.

At Hill Field bombers were repaired for return to the fighting front. B-24 aircraft are shown here.

During the war Utah became a center for producing, storing, and shipping war materiel.

merce, members of the Ogden Chamber of Commerce, particularly Frank M. Browning, and administration leaders in Washington to advance Utah's claim for new industries. President Roosevelt told Governor Maw and Utah's congressional delegation in mid-April 1941 that it was probable that a munitions plant would be located in the Salt Lake City area and that a steel mill would be built near Provo to ensure the production of steel in case the West Coast steel mills were destroyed by the enemy.

Existing installations helped the war effort at once. Since the Utah War of 1857-58, military forts had existed in Utah. Fort Douglas had served army needs for over seventy-five years, and since World War I the War Department had stored surplus ammunition at an arsenal near Ogden. During the later years of the depression, Hill Field was begun. As war approached, these facilities were ready to serve.

Fort Douglas became a center of significant activities as early as September 3, 1940, with the arrival of bombers and men of the Seventh Bombardment Group, the Eighty-eighth Reconnaissance Squadron, and the Fifth Air Base Squadron from Hamilton Field, California. The bombers roared in formation through the skies over Salt Lake City before landing at the Salt Lake Municipal Airport. Officers were given an official welcome by Governor Blood, Mayor Jenkins, and other political and business leaders, before a crowd of 5,000 spectators. About 250 officers and 1,050 men were attached to the units stationed at Fort Douglas.

Less than a month after Pearl Harbor the Ninth Service Command moved from San Francisco to Fort Douglas. This headquarters directed army operations for the Rocky Mountain and Pacific Coast states. Men drafted or enlisted from the eleven western states were initiated into military service at Fort Douglas. As they passed through the induction center, they were given physical and mental examinations, interviewed, and assigned to a branch of the army for training programs to prepare them for active duty. Fort Douglas became a repair and salvage center for military vehicles and equipment. The Army Finance Office at the fort handled the financial matters of a dozen military installations in Utah, paying out as much as $97 million in fiscal year 1942. As the tide of the war changed, the fort served also as a separation center for men leaving the service.

The Ogden Arsenal (first named the Ogden Ordnance Depot) had been established in 1920 when the War Department moved surplus World War I ammunition from the east coast for storage. South of Ogden and west of Weber Canyon, the depot was situated on 1,200 acres of land. Later, the land area was increased and during the depression, under army direction, the facilities were repaired and new buildings constructed, much of the work being done by the WPA and the CCC. With the coming of the war the depot served as a manufacturing center, producing bombs and artillery shells, and linking cartridges into machine gun belts. Later the depot became a distribution depot to handle supplies for the Ordnance Corps for West Coast export centers. At peak times the arsenal employed more than 6,000 persons, though by December 1945 the number was reduced to about 3,000.

Hill Field contributed significantly to the war effort. In 1935 the War Department, with an eye on war developments in the Pacific, decided to locate an "air defense, supply and training base for the Pacific coast" in the Rocky Mountain area. Through the efforts of the Ogden Chamber of Commerce and political leaders, Ogden was chosen as the

Fighter aircraft being repaired at Hill Field.

site for the air depot. In 1936 the Ogden Chamber of Commerce obtained and donated to the United States government about 400 acres of land in Davis County. In November 1938 WPA workmen started the first construction project: six temporary buildings and the grading for 7,500-foot runways. Between 1936 and 1938 the chamber of commerce went farther and obtained over 4,200 acres of land in Davis County and held it for the government for a depot, saving the government large sums of money. In August 1939 President Roosevelt signed an appropriations bill authorizing $8 million for the construction of an army air base at a location adjoining the Ogden Arsenal. On December 1, 1939, the new base of the Ogden Air Depot was given the official name of Hill Field, in honor of Captain Ployer P. Hill, a test pilot killed in a crash while testing a bomber in Ohio in 1935. The first phases of the new construction began January 12, 1940, and on November 7, 1940, Hill Field was activated.

From these beginnings Hill Field soon evolved into one of America's important units in the national defense system. The growth in

the year 1941 illustrates the rapid expansion of the base in wartime. With no more than a dozen employees on the payroll in January, by October the civilian force was up to 417. By December 31, there were 1,639 civilians on the payroll earning an average annual wage of $1,540. The total payroll for that year was $150,000. A dozen buildings housed the activities. The initial assignment was aircraft repair and maintenance. The huge hangers were completed in 1941 and the first of thousands of aircraft were put through its lines for repairs. During World War II Hill Field handled the repair and maintenance of B-17 and P-47 aircraft. Parachutes were repaired and scarce aircraft parts were manufactured. Aircraft destined for action in the Alaskan area were repaired and winterized. The expanded assignments required increased manpower. Employment reached its peak in May 1943 with 15,780 civilians and over 6,000 military personnel on the base. Many of these employees required special training in needed skills, a service provided by local schools.

New installations. Existing federal installations helped induce the federal government to place other facilities in Utah.

Geneva Steel Plant. The government was concerned that if the enemy closed the Panama Canal, it would be difficult to get steel from eastern mills to shipping centers on the West Coast. By February 1942, through the efforts of Utah leaders, it was decided that a new steel plant would be built in Utah near the eastern shore of Utah Lake, west of Orem at a point where the Denver and Rio Grande Western and the Union Pacific railroad lines met. The area included the resort of Geneva and the plant was immediately known as the Geneva works. Essential resources were nearby. At such a favorable location the cost of assembling raw materials would be less per ton than for any other major steel manufacturing center in the nation.

The Geneva mill was designed by United States Steel engineers and built by Columbia Steel Corporation, a company purchased by United States Steel in 1930. A crew which ultimately numbered some 10,000 men began construction in March 1942 and completed the job by the end of 1943. Total cost to the government was about $200 million. In 1943 the Geneva Steel Company, a United States Steel subsidiary, was organized and immediately began operating the new plant for the government. The first pig iron was smelted in January 1944, and the first open hearth steel was produced in February. The first production of steel plate (five carloads totaling 600 tons) was sent from the plant in April to West Coast shipbuilders.

The number of men employed in the operation of the mill began at 1,500 and reached a high of 4,200 in January 1945. Iron ore was brought from the Iron Mountain mines west of Cedar City. A new coal mine was opened at Horse Canyon in Carbon County, about 120 miles southeast of the

Construction of the Geneva steel plant was rapidly completed by working day and night.

The Geneva steel plant produced steel for west coast shipbuilding centers.

Iron ore is being loaded at open-pit mines in southern Utah for the Geneva steel plant near Provo.

The Utah General Depot on West Second Street in Ogden was a major storage and distribution point for army equipment.

Geneva plant. Limestone and dolomite, necessary in the milling process, were quarried about 35 miles from the plant, near Payson.

While Hill Field and the Geneva steel mill were the two major installations developed during the war, there were many other facilities that contributed to the war effort.

A small arms ammunition plant was built by the War Department in western Salt Lake City for the production of ammunition. The plant was operated under the supervision of the Army Ordnance Division, with the Remington Arms Company as the contractor. The *Utah General Depot* (now called Defense Depot Ogden), on West Second Street, Ogden, was built as a major storage and distribution point for army equipment other than weapons and ammunition. On the 1,600 acres of land, over forty buildings were constructed, including thirteen large brick warehouses, magazines, garage buildings, and shops. The depot received and distributed the necessary

supplies for army units stationed in the states north and west of Utah. The *U.S. Naval Supply Depot*, at Clearfield, served the navy like the Utah General Depot served the army. The navy needed an inland storage facility from which equipment and supplies could be shipped to West Coast supply points and advance bases in the Pacific.

Kearns Army Air Base was established on dry-farm lands west of Salt Lake City as a basic training center for army air corps personnel and for training ground crews and air corps gunners. At this typical air force training base, troops were put through basic military training. By October 1943 some 90,000 airmen had been trained at Kearns. *Wendover Air Force Base* was used as an air gunnery range, a bombing range, and for bomb storage. Air crewmen were trained in B-17s, B-24s, and B-29s to fly group formation in preparation for active duty. For much of the war this base provided the air force's only

The "Enola Gay," a Boeing B-29 superfortress. Her crew trained at Wendover Air Force Base, and from this plane dropped the atomic bomb on Hiroshima, Japan, August 6, 1945.

The crew of the "Enola Gay" before a takeoff.

bombing and gunnery range. For practice, mock cities and battleships were fashioned. War exercises were carried out in high-altitude flying, long-range navigation, target identification, and simulated combat missions. Altogether, twenty-one heavy bombardment groups trained at Wendover, forming complete combat units, thoroughly trained for overseas duty. The crew which dropped the atomic bomb on Hiroshima, Japan, trained here.

Tooele Ordnance Depot, in Tooele Valley, expanded the facilities and services of the Ogden Arsenal. The original mission of the Tooele Ordnance Depot was to receive, store, repair, and ship combat vehicles, small arms, and fire equipment; and to overhaul and modify tanks, track vehicles, and their armament. The depot utilized about 25,000 acres of land. Over a thousand buildings and storage areas were built—warehouses, repair shops, magazines, igloos, administration buildings, barracks, a hospital, an elementary school, and a shopping center.

Dugway Proving Grounds, south of Skull Valley and the Cedar Mountains, was operated by the Chemical Warfare Service for the purpose of experimenting with chemicals in warfare—poison gases, flame-throwers, incendiary bombs, and chemical sprays. The installation covered 264,900 acres of land. Chemicals and chemical weapons were tested, and studies were made on how to protect man and animals against their effects. Weapons which were proven effective here were used in the European and Pacific theaters of war. The *Desert Chemical Depot*, located in Rush Valley, about twenty miles south of Tooele, was a storage and shipping center for chemical warfare materials. The site was so isolated that to meet the needs of the workers a new

Tooele Ordnance Depot workers are clearing a bomb storage area.

town was built, complete with dormitories and houses, theaters, shops, stores, laundries, and cafes.

The primary purpose of the federal defense installations was to help win the war. This goal was reached. However, for Utah, there were additional benefits. Utah's economic life was strengthened. Most of these installations were built in 1942-43. It required tens of thousands of construction workers to build them and thousands of civilians to help run them. Money spent in Utah for construction materials and labor helped bring Utah out of the depression. Hundreds of millions of dollars were spent in construction; annual payrolls reached tens of millions of dollars. Utah has not been the same since.

Utah industries and businesses made significant contributions. The war effort made use of more than Utah's location and transportation facilities. It made good use of her natural resources and her business and industrial know-how. Utah's mining industry contributed significantly to the war effort through expansion and new developments. A tungsten concentrating plant was operated by the United States Vanadium Corporation of America, employing from 70 to 90 persons. The Kalunite Plant in south Salt Lake produced aluminum oxide and potassium sul-

phate from alunite ores mined near Marysvale. Operating between 1942 and 1945, this plant employed about 165 persons. The demands for vanadium were partly met through the milling of vanadium at Monticello and Moab. The Eitel-McCullough radio tube plant employed up to 1,700 persons in making radio tubes and related parts essential for radio communications in the war. The Standard Parachute Company at Manti employed up to 450 persons from June 1942 to May 1944, making and repairing parachutes. Gasoline refineries expanded their production. Communities built up their airports in the interest of civil defense.

Utah's small businesses contributed directly to the war effort. From Utah's air, water, and earth a steady stream of goods flowed to the armed forces. Pure oxygen from Utah's high mountain areas was compressed into metal bottles for use by pilots and their crews. Oxygen was also used in welding and cutting metals on construction jobs. Local industries also produced acetylene gas for welding. Hospitals around the world used many pounds of Utah-produced oxygen. Gilsonite from eastern Utah was used in waterproofing ships. As Utah copper was used in greater quantities than ever, mines reached new high levels of production. Many items manufactured in Utah went directly to the battle front, others were used nearer home.

The wounded and prisoners. Besides contributing to the war effort through its industry, Utah was also the scene of wartime activities associated with the wounded and with prisoners.

Bushnell Hospital, at Brigham City, completed by October 1, 1942, served as a treatment center for American soldiers wounded in the war. The first group of patients arrived October 10, 1942. It is estimated that as many as 13,000 soldiers were treated at the hospital. The staff, consisting of 200, pioneered the use of penicillin in April 1943. The hospital was closed after the war on June 3, 1946. It remained unoccupied for three years before the buildings came to a new use as the home of the Intermountain Indian School.

Prisoner-of-war camps. German and Italian prisoners of war were brought to the United States to remain until the war was over. Camps were set up in Utah near Bushnell General Hospital, Clearfield, Deseret Chemical Warfare Depot, Fort Douglas, Dugway Proving Ground, Hill Field, Logan, Orem, Salina, Tooele, Tremonton, and Ogden Utah Army Service Forces Depot. The prisoners were kept under guard and generally given the same food and facilities American soldiers had in their camps. Educational classes were conducted, and for recreation the prisoners saw motion pictures, played musical instruments, played soccer and other games, heard lectures, and read. Utahns remember the prisoners as laborers in the fields of nearby farms, for the prisoners were allowed to work at various types of jobs. Some prisoners were also employed at some of the military installations. When Italy surrendered in September 1943, Italian prisoners of war were given options for freedom. Those who were anti-Mussolini were given special privileges upon signing a parole agreement. Prisoners generally felt they were given fair treatment. Some remained in Utah or returned to live at a later time.

The Japanese relocation center at Topaz. One of the sad experiences of the war and a serious mistake of the government was the separation of American citizens of Japanese ancestry into camps called relocation centers. The action illustrates the prejudices and hatreds war promotes. In 1942 President Roosevelt, yielding to widespread feelings of

From the west coast, Japanese-Americans were brought to the desert camp at Topaz and put into new barracks to live.

Families, under the most crowded conditions, attempted to maintain some customs and traditions.

suspicion and fear, gave the army responsibility to deal with the possible problem of Japanese-Americans assisting the Japanese war effort. The army declared the western half of the Pacific Coast states a military zone and ordered all Japanese removed inland. Japanese-Americans lost most of their property, since they were permitted to take with them only what they could carry. Their destination was the relocation centers that were very similar to prisoner-of-war camps.

One of the ten relocation centers was placed in Utah, at Topaz, Millard County, about ten miles northwest of Delta in the Pavant Valley of the Sevier Desert. The center was opened September 11, 1942, and operated until October 31, 1945. During that time, up to 8,000 American citizens and resident aliens were retained there.

Topaz was a mile-square city of barracks grouped into blocks. Each block included a mess hall, recreation hall, and a combination washroom-toilet-laundry building. Each barrack was divided into rooms, one family to a room. For the community there were general facilities—an auditorium, gymnasium, canteens, schools, libraries, churches, athletic fields, post office, fire station, and a cemetery. Altogether there were 623 buildings, all of frame construction and covered with black tar paper, with the exceptions of the administration building and hospital that were painted white. One child, upon arrival with his parents, said: "I don't like it here. When are we going back to America?"

Most of the people at Topaz came from the San Francisco Bay area. Sixty-five percent were native-born American citizens; the others had been born in Japan. Many distinguished Japanese-Americans were among the Topaz residents. From the beginning the Japanese followed the principle of "realistic resignation." Chiura Obata, professor of art at the University of California at Berkeley, said, "We will survive, if we forget the sands at our feet and look at the mountains for inspiration."

Employment outside the camp was permitted. Many worked in the sugar beet fields of Utah farms. Some took up camp farming projects. The government obtained land and water rights for thousands of acres which the Japanese put to crops. Their experiences were just as trying as those of the Utah pioneers. Those of college age were permitted to attend college. But the governor recommended against the University of Utah taking them, and Utah State Agricultural College declined their applications for fear of popular disfavor against them. Some of the Topaz young men enlisted in the United States armed forces and distinguished themselves in combat in Europe.

War-born prejudices showed themselves in many ways. In March 1943 the Utah legislature showed popular feelings by passing a bill barring Japanese-Americans from purchasing or leasing real estate in Utah. The governor vetoed the bill. (It is possible that if the bill had become law, the government would have prohibited the evacuees from working for Utah farmers.) The legislature was later able to pass a law stating that Japanese-Americans could not own or make long-term leases of lands in Utah, but permitted farmers to employ them or lease land to them for a period of one year. When the war was over some people tried to keep the Japanese from taking up land. A *Deseret News* editorial, December 4, 1945, denounced such practices, calling on the people "to banish this foolish prejudice from our natures, and let us attempt to see that all good and loyal Americans are treated as such."

At the close of the war the Topaz people were permitted to find new homes. Less than half returned to California and the West

Crowds in Salt Lake City gave way to joyful celebration at news of the war's end.

Coast. Some stayed in Utah. The camp was abandoned and its buildings sold.

4. UTAH LIFE WAS GREATLY CHANGED BY THE WAR

State political leaders, as we have seen, were active in getting federal defense installations in Utah. Along with taking care of civilian defense needs, the state officials saw that all functions of state government were carried out. State indebtedness was paid off, highways were kept in good condition, the educational system supported, and persons on welfare received help.

Utah reversed her *population movement patterns* of the preceding thirty years. During the war years Utah began to receive more people than she lost through out-migration. Her rate of population growth was faster than that of the United States. Defense spending was responsible for creating 49,500 new jobs

With the surrender of Japan, August 1945, the war was over.

459

in Utah during the first three years of the war. While many workers left the state just as soon as the construction jobs were completed, Utah had a net in-migration of 18,400 persons during the war years.

The greatest changes took place in the six counties along the Wasatch Front—Box Elder, Weber, Davis, Tooele, Salt Lake, and Utah. Population of these counties increased about 50,000. Almost all of Utah's defense installations were located in these counties.

Two of the major problems Utah faced with the rapid expansion of population and industry were a sufficient water supply and adequate sanitation facilities. New sources of water supply were tapped. Sewer systems were extended and enlarged, and other provisions were made for health protection.

Utah's economy during World War II underwent sweeping changes. Economic activity which had been in decline for the past couple of decades now became dynamic. The major factor contributing to the changes in economic life was the increase in the number of manufacturing and defense installations. The Geneva Steel plant, Hill Air Force Base (formerly Hill Field), army and navy warehouses, depots, and repair centers, all had a great impact on Utah's economic life.

Private business was as energetic in doing its part as were the state and federal governments. Some of the federal contracts, subcontracts, and orders for materials were placed with Utah businesses. Construction firms provided the new buildings for the defense installations; new housing was provided as quickly as possible. Many businesses worked under the difficulties of the scarcity of help and of getting materials and goods. With the quickening of economic life, particularly through federal spending and construction, most businesses throughout the state experienced expansion and better times. Utah came out of

depression into prosperity during the war years.

Per capita personal income of Utahns increased 124.6 percent. This was a greater percentage increase than the average for the United States and the other western states (109.9). This new and added income helped the financial condition of the people. Families were able to pay off farm and home mortgages and installment debts and began to save and invest. A soldier's family might receive part of his monthly salary; many took this as an opportunity to save for schooling, a new home, or to start a new business when the war was over.

Utah became more *cosmopolitan* as a result of the war. New people came into the state to work. Native Utahns returned to the state to work. Servicemen and servicewomen returned after living in widely different parts of the world. These people with worldwide experiences added a new dimension to life in Utah and gave her a little different character.

At the close of the war, Utah's servicemen were welcomed home. Servicemen's centers were set up to help find employment for the returning veterans, and to help them take advantage of various federal programs in operation for them, such as the so-called GI Bill of Rights. Under the GI Bill of Rights, signed June 22, 1944, discharged veterans were entitled to unemployment compensation, government-guaranteed loans, or financial support for college training up to four years. Everything was done to help the veteran make a successful adjustment from military life to civilian life.

Just how business and the rest of society would adjust to peacetime was a concern to everyone. Obviously, most wartime efforts would cease, but would there be a continuation of prosperity or would the economy slump back into depression?

UNIT EIGHT
CONTEMPORARY UTAH

Our study of Utah's heritage now brings us to the contemporary age—the time since the end of World War II in 1945.

The world has undergone rapid and revolutionary change since the end of World War II. There has been conflict between the United States, other democracies and capitalistic countries on the one hand, and the Soviet Union and communist countries on the other. There has been a strong movement toward international cooperation, as evidenced by the United Nations and other organizations. At the same time individual countries have experienced the feeling of nationalism and have declared and won their independence.

At home, the nation has experienced a period of prosperity unknown before. Utah has shared in that prosperity. Utah's population has grown at a rapid rate. Family income has risen. Business and industry have expanded. Television has supplemented radio. Air travel has become common. There is more time for recreation and there are many recreational facilities available. The expansion of the population, business, and industry, have led to the urbanization of the Wasatch Front and a slight decline of population in some rural counties.

Notwithstanding the general prosperity, many Utahns suffer from poverty, the lack of adequate civil rights, and the lack of economic and social opportunities. One of the major movements of recent times has been concerned with the advancement of and equal opportunities for Spanish-speaking Americans, Negroes, Orientals, and Indians.

A significant concern of recent times is the preservation and renewal of Utah's natural resources and the natural environment through various conservation and reclamation projects, state and federal programs, and education of the public.

Utah's educational system has advanced in the number of students and physical plants, and in quality. There have been significant advances in the arts. Prosperity and leisure give promise of further advancements.

Notwithstanding Utah's remarkable achievements during this period, she still faces many problems. However, Utah has equally as many opportunities. The challenge of the present is to build solidly on Utah's heritage for a future of equal self-realization for all people.

Aerial view of Salt Lake City today.

UTAH SINCE WORLD WAR II

What are the sources for the study of the recent past? Many sources we will have later are not yet available—many persons and businesses have not placed their papers in archives for public use. On the other hand, many sources are available to us that will not be available later—living persons can be interviewed, and current publications may be had from issuing agencies. Newspapers are a valuable source of information, but we must be aware of the fact that complete and accurate coverage of all events is impossible.

A greater problem faces the student of the recent past. It is difficult for us right now to distinguish between the important and the unimportant. We are still keenly involved in the controversial issues. We have not had time to see ourselves in relation to other events of our times or to the past.

It is a challenge to us to think about the present in relation to the past and the future, to see ourselves in relation to others, and to try to understand the different points of view represented in the issues of our day.

Increasingly during the twentieth century life in Utah has become influenced by and closely tied to national and international developments. America's international commitments are Utah's commitments. National economic developments determine much of Utah's economic development. Yet these influences mainly set the stage; the human action is Utah's own. Civilizations are known to have risen and fallen depending upon their response to the conditions they faced.

IN THIS CHAPTER WE WILL LEARN

1. Utah affairs were greatly influenced by national and international developments.

2. Government attempted to keep pace with the new age.

3. Population growth led to expansion in other areas of life.

4. Economic prosperity was a dominant feature of life in Utah after World War II.

5. Minority groups strived for identity and equal opportunity in Utah.

6. There was a major movement for reclamation and conservation of natural resources.

7. Utah achieved a new high in her cultural tradition.

25

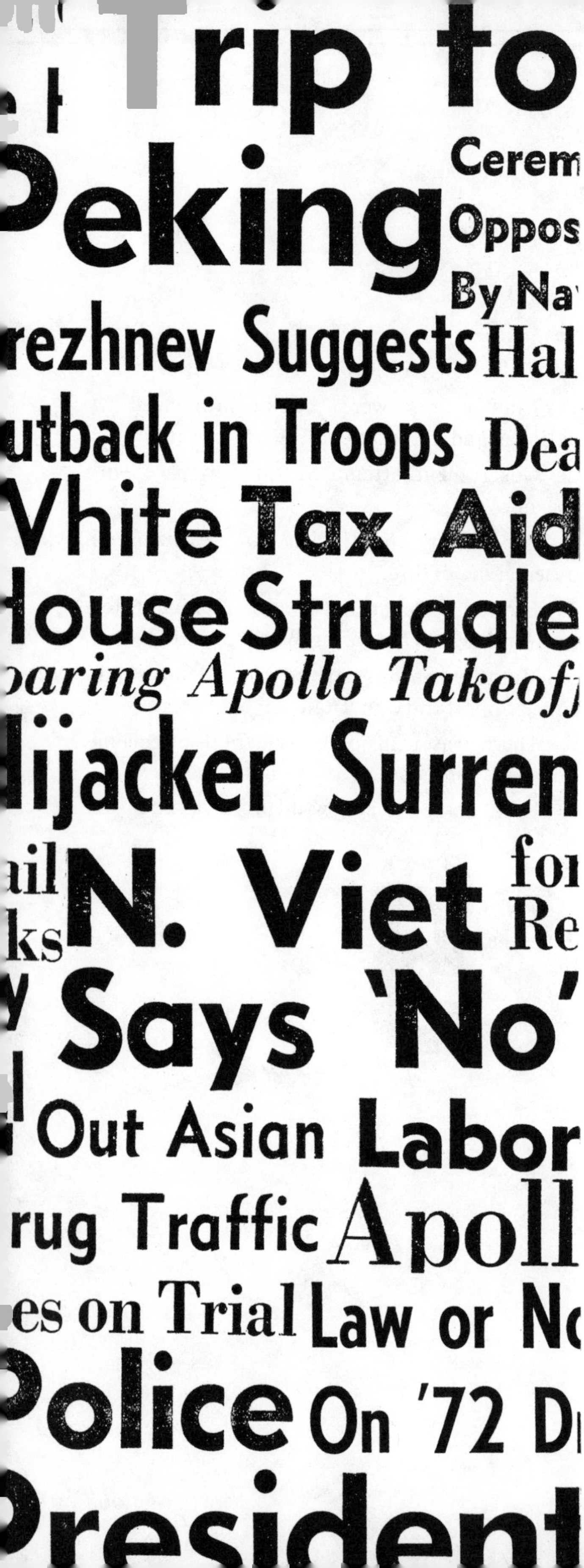

Trip to Peking

Cerem
Oppos
By Na

rezhnev Suggests Hal

utback in Troops Dea

Vhite Tax Aid

House Struggle

paring Apollo Takeoff

Hijacker Surren

ail

N. Viet for
ks Re

Says 'No'

Out Asian Labor

rug Traffic *Apoll*

es on Trial **Law or No**

Police On '72 D

President

1. UTAH AFFAIRS WERE GREATLY INFLUENCED BY NATIONAL AND INTERNATIONAL DEVELOPMENTS

With the surrender of Japan in August 1945, World War II was over. During the following year or two there was a hasty demobilization of nearly nine million men. Everyone wanted to return to normal living, but as events were to prove, that was not possible. The war had been terribly destructive. Both allied and enemy countries suffered untold loss of lives and property. It was going to take time to rebuild personal lives and re-establish governments.

Many people placed their hopes for future world peace and security in the *United Nations Organization* (UN) whose charter had been written at San Francisco in June 1945 and whose headquarters were located in New York City. The United States took a leading role in the formation and support of the United Nations.

One of the major results of the war was a new alignment of political power in the world. **Two super powers emerged**—the United States and Russia (the Union of Soviet Socialist Republics). Russia's commitment to communism and America's commitment to capitalism (two opposing economic systems) set the two powers in opposition to each other. Russian imperialistic expansion led Americans to fear the forced spread of communism in the world, including the United States. Communism seemed to take hold where people had been exploited by colonial powers or in economically underdeveloped countries. To check the spread of communism in the world, the United States became involved in a variety of activities. Economic and military aid was given to countries threatened by communism (the Truman Doctrine, March 1947). The Marshall Plan (June 1947) offered American aid for a European Recovery Program. Since that time the United States has continued such aid and in addition has taken an active part in the formation of alliances with groups of countries in an effort to keep the Soviet Union in check.

American military and economic aid to foreign countries met similar efforts by the Soviet Union. Conflicts resulted in various parts of the world. The condition was referred to as the *Cold War*—not a shooting war but a war of political and economic influences. To meet the demands of its foreign policy, the United States government spent enormous sums of money for defense and foreign aid. These expenditures stimulated the economy of this country. Utah shared significantly in the prosperity which came to the nation.

The fact that the United States had exploded atomic bombs in a military operation led other people to believe it could happen again. Other nations developed atomic weapons. The expansion of atomic (nuclear) weapons led to widespread fear among the people of the world of a nuclear war in which human life on the earth would be destroyed. The people of the world still live in that fear.

The Korean War. On June 25, 1950, North Korean armies invaded South Korea. The United Nations Security Council asked UN members to furnish military assistance to South Korea. Some fifty-three nations supported the UN action, many contributing military and economic aid. The United States responded with troops, as did other countries.

The outbreak of this war led Congress to revive the selective service draft, and American young men again were called for military service. Utah men were drafted and six Utah units of the National Guard were called up for active duty. The Korean War lasted over three years before an armistice was signed. Even so, there is still action there, with American and Utah soldiers serving.

Vietnam. One of the trouble spots in which the United States became involved was Southeast Asia. At the end of World War II, the Vietnam Republic declared its independence from France. But Vietnam was soon divided between communist and national parties. Armed conflict between the two parties attracted international support. In an effort to end civil war in Vietnam, an international conference in Geneva in 1954 divided Vietnam at the Seventeenth parallel, between the communist north and the nationalist south governments. But the civil war continued. In June 1961 the United States agreed to assist South Vietnam further by increasing its number of military advisors and observers, and to send 20,000 American troops. From that time, additional troops, observers, and advisors have been sent, along with military equipment. The war has continued.

American (including Utah) soldiers have served in Vietnam since 1961. The Vietnam war has become one of America's most controversial wars; stemming from this are many contemporary problems in America.

The period after World War II was marked by peace and war, peace movements at home and conflicts abroad. There were technological advances (including atomic energy and space exploration), international cooperation and the rise of new national states, the spread of communism and capitalist influences in the world, and national resistance to one or the other.

It was a period of prosperity at home. The expansion of the national economy swept away fears that the United States would slip back into depression.

Many factors contributed to postwar prosperity. By 1945 the American people had endured economic hardships (the scarcity of goods) for nearly twenty-five years—through the depression and war years. People had put away *savings* during the war and they were ready to spend it. *American industry* was capable of supplying the goods to meet consumer demands. American industry had grown during the war under government prodding and patronage. It was now ready to put that same industrial power into the production of civilian goods. *Farm production* was at a high level due to the demands of war, improved farm implements, improved husbandry, and numerous irrigation projects. *Credit* was available for those who did not have cash or savings. Veterans were given special credit treatment. Stores offered credit by handling customers' accounts. Banks were in a position to offer long-term credit for persons buying homes and starting businesses. At the same time, there was a *population boom* as veterans began their families, long postponed. The birthrate soared. New families demanded new homes and all that went into a home. Thus there was an increasing *demand for goods*. All these factors worked to give the United States the world's strongest economy in the postwar world.

But as time went on, an additional factor contributed to prosperity: defense spending. The *defense and military installations* constructed and operated in Utah during the war continued to operate, creating new jobs and pouring hundreds of millions of dollars into the economy.

2. GOVERNMENT ATTEMPTED TO KEEP PACE WITH THE NEW AGE

The experience of the people with the depression and the New Deal led them to demand more from their governments, and to expect governments to be more responsive to their needs. Yet, with the end of the war there was a reaction against "too much government," taxes, the "welfare state," and governmental controls. The two traditions conflicted in Utah during the years following the war. The Democrats seemed to represent the tradition of concern for the well-being of the individual citizen himself, while the Republicans seemed to represent the reaction to the New Deal days and pleaded the special cause of the business community. In reality the two parties, in Utah, are not as different as they are in some states. In Utah both are conservative and both are concerned about human freedoms.

Politics. During the years of the New Deal and World War II, the Democrats held control of the governorship, the two senatorial seats, and the two congressional seats. With the end of the war, when reaction against Democratic leadership set in, the Republicans gained the governorship (J. Bracken Lee). Two years later the Republicans gained the other senatorial seat (Wallace F. Bennett) and in 1952, with the election of Eisenhower as president, the Republicans swept all these offices in Utah. The Republicans held all these offices from 1953 to 1959, when the Democrats began to take some of them back. In 1958 Frank E. Moss won the senatorial seat of Arther V. Watkins and has been re-elected twice since. That year David S. King won the second congressional district seat.

Since the end of World War II the political leadership of the state has been in the hands of the following men. Our senators have been Arthur V. Watkins (R), 1947-59; Wallace F. Bennett (R), 1951-present; and Frank E. Moss (D), 1959-present. Our congressmen have been Walter K. Granger (D), 1949-53; William A. Dawson (R), four terms; Reva Beck Bosone (D), two terms; David S. King (D) three terms; Laurence J. Burton (R), four terms; Sherman P. Lloyd (R), four terms; and Gunn McKay (D), one term. Douglas R. Stringfellow (R) won election to the first congressional district seat in the 1952 sweep, as a war hero. During his campaign for reelection in 1954 it became known that many of his stories of alleged heroism were false. The Republicans replaced him on the ticket with Henry Aldous Dixon. Dixon, who had served ably as president of Weber College and Utah State Agricultural College, won easily and served for three terms in the House.

The governorship through these years has been held by three men. J. Bracken Lee (R) served two terms, 1949-57, and was succeeded by George Dewey Clyde (R), who served two terms until 1965. In 1964 the Democrats won the governor's chair with Calvin L. Rampton, who has served since 1965.

Finances. Since 1945 state revenues have increased from $55 million to $473 million in 1971. Expenditures have increased proportionately. The chief sources of revenue during the

J. Bracken Lee, a political leader during the postwar years, was mayor of Price before he served as governor, 1949-57. Thereafter he served as mayor of Salt Lake City until 1972.

George Dewey Clyde, governor from 1957 to 1965, was also a distinguished engineer and educator.

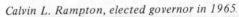

Calvin L. Rampton, elected governor in 1965.

period have been from taxes (about 45 percent) and federal grants (about 20 percent). The federal grants are in support of education, road construction, and public health and welfare. The chief expenditures have been for education (about 35 percent), roads and aeronautics (about 20 percent), and public health and welfare (about 10 percent).

Since 1936 the Public Welfare Commission has had major responsibility for public welfare, which includes such assistance programs as Old Age Assistance, Aid to Families with Dependent Children, Aid to the Blind, Aid to the Disabled, Medical Assistance for the Aged, and General Assistance and Foster Care. Welfare services include Child Welfare, Committee on Youth, Committee on Aging, Day Care Centers for handicapped children, and Child Welfare Services. Toward the cost of public welfare the federal government contributes about 60 percent and the state about 40 percent. Counties also make contributions to public welfare in their jurisdictions.

Needs and responses. After World War II, Utah found itself with an enormous backlog of needed improvements such as buildings and highways. During the depression and World War II there was little construction in these areas. With the end of the war there was an increased attendance at universities and colleges as veterans returned from war and returned to school. A population explosion meant there were more youth to be educated, hence a need for school buildings and teachers. There were also more aged to be cared for. Government had the problem of trying to keep salaries somewhat in line with those of private business.

Rather than looking to future needs and planning to meet those needs, for nearly two decades after the war there was little planning. Problems were met on a crisis basis, and the general attitude of state government was to postpone building until money was available. In the meantime, the increases in construction costs far exceeded the cost of borrowing money and the state ended up not getting buildings and highways as soon as they were needed and paying much more for them in the end.

Since 1930 the state has relied proportionately less on property taxes than other taxes. In 1930, 82 percent of the revenues were from property taxes. In the 1960s, 40 percent of the revenues came from property taxes. Increasing reliance has been placed on sales taxes and income taxes.

To improve the efficiency of state government in performing services, there have been attempts to reorganize the executive branch. Under the leadership of Governor Maw there was a significant reorganization in 1941. The next attempt came in 1966 under Governor Rampton. A special Commission on the Organization of the Executive Branch of Government (called the Little Hoover Commission) made serious studies and recommendations to the legislature. While some of the commission's recommendations were adopted, the governor was left to experiment in the grouping of departments, commissions, and boards.

The twenty-nine counties of Utah have had to expand their functions during the past quarter century. Like state government, county governments are also concerned with highways, public welfare, and local problems.

Government of cities has changed some in recent years. Utah has 215 cities and towns. Salt Lake City, with a population of about 176,000, is the only city of the first class (according to the definition of the law). There are four cities of the second class: Murray (population, 21,206), Ogden (69,478), Provo (53,131), and Logan (22,333). There are 106 cities of the third class and 104

The population boom showed itself on the landscape with the spread of towns and cities including the familiar tract housing projects.

towns. Twenty-six communities have taken the option to have city managers.

3. POPULATION GROWTH LED TO EXPANSION IN OTHER AREAS OF LIFE

Soon after the end of the war fears of depression were put to rest, and Utah and the nation moved into a period of prosperity characterized by growth in population, higher personal income, a higher standard of living, increased capacity of the people to buy new homes and a wide range of material goods, and the expansion of schools.

The population. From 1940 to 1970 Utah's population doubled, increasing from 550,310 to 1,059,273. The 1940s witnessed a 25 percent increase, while the 1950s witnessed an increase of nearly 30 percent. During the 1960s the total population increased 19 percent. This increase was due to natural increase (births) and to in-migration. Utah did not absorb in employment in the 1960s all of her natural increase. Utah had a loss of population by 1970 of minus 1.2 percent of the 1960 population number.

The increase in population meant increased demand for housing, food, clothing, furniture, automobiles, and other conveniences. It meant the coming of suburbs with new homes, tract houses, shopping centers, and improved roads.

Most of the increase in population centered in the six counties of the Wasatch Front: Box Elder, Weber, Davis, Salt Lake, Tooele, and Utah. In 1940 these counties held 67 percent of the total population; in 1970 they held over 80 percent. In 1960 Utah was the tenth most urbanized state in the nation. During the 1960s Utah became even more urbanized. The urban centers absorbed the increases in population while there was an out-migration from some of the rural counties. The following counties lost population during the 1950s or 1960s: Beaver, Duchesne, Emery, Garfield, Juab, Millard, Piute, Rich, Sanpete, Sevier, Summit, and Wayne.

This **urbanization** of the Wasatch Front, a movement begun in pioneer times, has concentrated in *three metropolitan areas*: (1) Salt Lake City, Salt Lake County, and the southern part of Davis County; (2) Ogden City,

Fishing in Utah's reservoirs, lakes, and streams is a favorite summer acitivity.

Weber County, and the northern part of Davis County; and (3) Provo City and Utah County. In these areas manufacturing and processing plants, receiving and distribution centers, and residential areas are heavily concentrated.

Urbanization is well illustrated in Davis County. Between 1940 and 1950 the population of the county doubled. The population of Layton increased 435 percent, Clearfield 348 percent, and Sunset 259 percent, while Bountiful, Centerville, West Point, and East Layton nearly doubled in population. The increase resulted from the general industrial expansion of Utah and more specifically from the establishment of military and defense in-

stallations in northern Davis County. Farm-oriented workers and farm-oriented businesses continued at the same level, while the number of industrial workers, professional and business people increased. The number of businesses doubled; there was still the small fruit stand, but there were now the big businesses and shopping centers with specialized stores. The standard of living rose for most people. Women began to work outside the home in greater numbers.

The creation of urban centers in Utah put heavy demands upon the construction industry. The increase in population and housing is illustrated by the statistic that 32 percent of all housing units occupied in 1960 were built in the years 1950-60. Improvement in the standard of living is shown by the statistic that 83 percent of all housing units in 1960 were well constructed and had all the plumbing facilities.

Notwithstanding urbanization in these Wasatch Front counties, it is important to keep in mind that many people there live in rural conditions and that agriculture in these counties is important to them and important to the economic life of Utah.

Income levels. During the last twenty-five years the personal income of Utah families has increased. During World War II, per capita personal income more than doubled. During the next twenty years, 1945-65, it doubled again, reaching $2,362. However, Utah ranks below the national average, usually by 10 to 15 percent, and she ranks low among the neighboring western states in per capita personal income. In 1970 the average family income in Utah was $9,320.

Recently the United States Office of Economic Opportunity set poverty level income figures for families. On the basis of their studies 22,082 Utah familes (9 percent of all Utah families) had less than what is

A wide range of recreational activities is available to Utahns.

The Utah Stars brought professional basketball to Utah.

considered minimum-level family income. Nearly 75 percent of these families were in the relatively prosperous counties of Cache, Weber, Davis, Salt Lake, and Utah. The rural counties had comparatively few families in this group.

Recreation has become more important as people perform less physical activity in their work and as they have more free time and more money to spend. Camping, hunting, and fishing continue to be popular outdoor sports in summer. Skiing has boomed since World War II. Brighton, Snow Basin, Alta, Park City, Brian Head, and Beaver Mountain are the major skiing centers. Alta and Park City, old mining towns, have resort centers and are attracting skiers from all over the United States. Snowmobiling is gaining interest. Although snowmobiling gets people out in nature, it does not provide the exertion of other sports. There are many questions as to the damage done by this activity. A great number of people follow the spectator sports: baseball, high school and college football and basketball, and Utah's own professional hockey team, "Golden Eagles," and basketball team, "Utah Stars."

Utah's canyons offer quiet retreats from urban life.

Utahns enjoy the Golden Eagles and professional hockey.

A news program being televised from the KUTV studios.

Television was invented by a Utah scientist, Philo T. Farnsworth. He was interested in invention from early youth and by the age of eighteen had worked out the fundamental concept of television. After working in radio in Salt Lake City, he went to San Francisco to work as a research scholar. In 1934 he gave the first public demonstration of television at the Franklin Institute, Philadelphia.

Utah's first television station, KTVT, began broadcasting in 1948. Soon others were in the field. KCPX, channel 4 (ABC), began broadcasting in 1948; KSL, channel 5 (CBS), began in 1949; and KUTV, channel 2 (NBC), began in 1954. Utah's educational television station, KUED, channel 12, is in Salt Lake City. Brigham Young University also operates an educational television station.

Television has made great changes in Utah's social and economic life. Motion picture theaters have felt television's impact with fewer customers at the box office and the quality of radio programs declined as television continued to develop. Television has furthered the tendency toward one culture of all the people, aiming at or below the average intelligence. Yet, through television, the world has been opened to people in their own homes. Instantaneous pictorial reports from around the world and even the moon are common events. One may pick and choose between old movies, new shows, news, sports events, or educational features.

Radio broadcasting today in Utah is handled by forty-six stations in sixteen communities. Fifteen stations broadcast on FM frequencies.

Education. The population boom has had tremendous impact on education in Utah, both in the public schools and in the colleges and universities.

The *colleges and universities* came fully of age in the postwar period. During the 1920s Utah colleges and universities came to university status. During that decade many young Utahns went to the great universities of the United States and Europe for their advanced degrees and returned to help upgrade Utah institutions. The professionalizing of these institutions continued, until by World War II they were fully ready to perform the demanding tasks required of them. After the war they were ready for the great influx of students.

Traditionally, American war veterans have been given bonuses in the form of land for their services. With available land very nearly gone by 1945, Congress passed the GI

The University of Utah campus witnessed extensive expansion during the postwar years, paralleling its growth in enrollment. The new medical center is at the upper left.

Utah State University campus.

Brigham Young University at Provo, under the presidency of Ernest L. Wilkinson (1950s and 1960s), became the world's largest denominational university. Its enrollment exceeded 20,000 students; its campus spread to meet their needs.

Weber State College, the new upper campus.

Bill of Rights giving each veteran choices of benefits. This included the payment to him and the college of his choice for a four-year college education. Many veterans took advantage of this education option and went to school. Enrollment in Utah colleges and universities rose at once, doubling and quadrupling in some instances in a few years. Increased enrollments put a heavy demand on teachers, classroom space, buildings, and administrations. Some veterans who already had their bachelor's degrees used their GI benefits to obtain advanced degrees. The growth in enrollments continued through the 1960s when enrollments began to level off.

The achievement of Utah colleges and universities by the 1950s and 1960s is reflected in the changed status of some of them. In 1957 Utah's land-grant college's name was changed from Utah State Agricultural College to Utah State University in token of its already broadened curriculum and stature among American colleges. In 1959 Weber Junior College was made a four-year institution and renamed Weber State College. The first senior class graduated in 1964. The Branch Agricultural College at Cedar City gained independent status in 1965 and is now named Southern Utah State College. Carbon College was named the College of Eastern Utah. Dixie College at Saint George has retained its name. Like others, Westminster College has grown in stature, student body, and physical plant.

Greater interest in adult education developed in the 1960s. Utah State University established extension centers in Logan, Provo, the Uinta Basin, and Richfield. The University of Utah enlarged its night school and extension class offerings. Brigham Young University set up its center of Adult Education in Salt Lake City in the church-owned McCune School of Music.

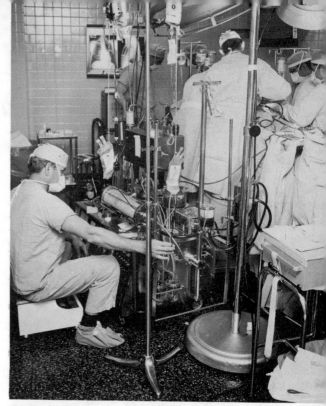

The Medical Center at the University of Utah is dedicated to medical service and scientific research.

The University of Utah's new medical center was completed in 1958. The medical school, started in 1942, has grown steadily and become one of the fine medical schools in the nation.

Elementary and secondary schools witnessed a similar growth during the postwar years. "War babies," born during and shortly after the war, were soon entering kindergarten and the early grades. The public schools felt the flood of children. The number of schools increased from about 440 in 1945 to 579 in 1971, the number of teachers increased from about 4,000 to about 10,000, and the number of students from 122,414 to 312,157. New schools were built, many were enlarged.

Utah is noted for its educational achievement. Utah usually ranks high in student enrollment, attendance, and achievement, low in teachers' salaries and classroom space, and high in effort to finance her educational system. Utah is noted for the achievement of her native sons and daughters—in the arts, science, business, education, government, and public service.

4. ECONOMIC PROSPERITY WAS A DOMINANT FEATURE OF LIFE IN UTAH AFTER WORLD WAR II

Business activity associated with World War II brought Utah a degree of prosperity not known before. With the end of the war there was a letdown that was cut short, however, by the demands of the Cold War. As the country responded to national defense demands, Utah participated in the general prosperity. The standard of living in Utah was raised to a new high, and Utah's economy developed in a more balanced manner.

Four basic industries form the foundation of the general economy of Utah—government (defense installations and industries), mining, manufacturing, and agriculture. In each of these areas there were developments of special interest during the postwar period.

Defense installations in Utah (see chapter 24, section 3) showed a slowdown of activity just before and after the end of the war. Depots which had funneled materiel to the war front served to receive it back for storage, reuse, repair, or sale. Some installations were threatened with closing, but the Cold War brought the United States back to a war footing and kept most of the installations in demand.

Hill Air Force Base served a variety of missions after the war. The most significant new mission came in 1957 when the base was chosen as a center for the repair and storage of a variety of missiles. Hill Air Force Base is now one of the most important air bases in the United States and has world importance. It is Utah's largest single employer with the largest single payroll.

At Fort Douglas activity slowed as the

The Ramjet engine developed by Marquardt Corporation with research laboratories near Ogden.

Ninth Service Command moved back to San Francisco. The arsenals, depots, and proving grounds fluctuated in their activity according to the demands of war.

Some defense installations were deactivated. Kearns Army Air Base was declared surplus in 1947. A private company bought the area (a ready-made housing development) and built the community of Kearns on its foundation (1970 population, 17,071). The Naval Supply Depot at Clearfield was deactivated in the early 1960s. Half the land and buildings was sold to a firm which established a Freeport Center. The Utah legislature had passed a law declaring that goods held in Utah for shipment out of the state should not be taxed as inventory. This made it profitable to use these buildings for storage for transcontinental shipment of goods. Wendover Air Force Base, used occasionally after the war, was put on caretaker status in 1961.

Plants built during the war for the manufacture of goods and materiel directly related to the war effort were sold to private businesses, and their functions were either taken over and continued or the buildings put to other uses. The Geneva Steel plant was sold in May 1946 to the United States Steel Corporation on condition it reconvert the plant to peacetime production. Geneva Steel

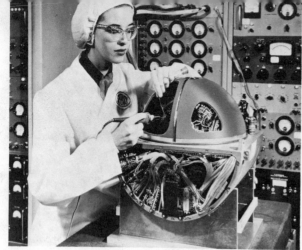

The finishing touches are being put on a unit of the Sergeant missile in the "Clean Room" at Sperry Utah Company.

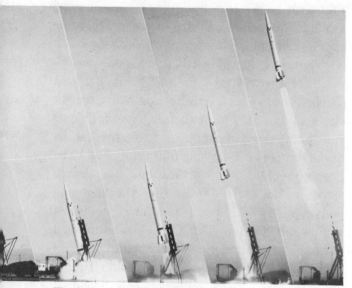

The Sergeant missile being launched.

The Athena missile ready for a test launch at the Green River test complex.

continues to have an enormous influence on Utah's economy.

Missiles. In the mid-1950s, when the United States discovered it was behind the Soviet Union in the development of missiles, it contracted with companies to develop and manufacture missiles. Several companies receiving contracts chose Utah for their operation. Sperry Utah Company, which located in Salt Lake City in 1956, conducted research and produced the Sergeant missile, antiaircraft weapons systems, and radar systems. The Marquardt Corporation built a plant in 1956 southwest of Ogden where advanced space research was conducted in connection with their famous ramjet engine. This engine was adapted to the Bomarc missile.

In 1956-57 the Thiokol Chemical Corporation constructed a $15 million research and development center west of Brigham City for the development of solid-fuel rocket propulsion engines. During the next two years the corporation spent $77 million on the propulsion phase of the Minuteman missile. In 1961 Thiokol built an Aerospace Center in Ogden from which to coordinate the firm's missile activities. The Hercules Powder Company, near Salt Lake City since 1914, contracted to build the third stage of the Minuteman missile. The U.S. Air Force built three plants in Utah, each associated with the Minuteman missile. Two plants built stages while a third plant assembled all stages and checked the completed Minuteman before the missiles were sent to launching sites. The latter plant, operated by Boeing Company, took over the old Ogden Arsenal facilities near Ogden.

Litton, Inc., a manufacturer of microwave electron tubes, built a plant in Salt Lake City, produced tubes, then began building electronic data processing systems.

All these installations and industries

brought hundreds of millions of dollars to Utah in the form of construction contracts, payrolls, and purchases from local businesses. Defense became a very significant part of Utah's postwar economy. Over 20 percent of personal income in Utah derived from and over 20 percent of the work force were employed in these activities. They helped boom Utah's population. Many of the defense installations brought their own management, supervisory, and research people with them. But many native Utahns were employed too.

Mining. Utah's mining industry has witnessed a remarkable growth during the past decades. From the outbreak of the war in Europe in 1939 until its end in 1945 the value of Utah mineral production more than doubled, and in the period since 1945 it has tripled. In 1969 the total value of Utah's mineral production was $542,489,000. More than half of this was in copper. Other leading products were petroleum (crude oil), coal, gold, sand and gravel, iron, lead, silver, and zinc.

Uranium mining had a dramatic life during the 1950s. From 1951 to 1958 the Atomic Energy Commission guaranteed the price of uranium to encourage uranium prospecting because the federal government wanted to build a stockpile of uranium to be used as a source of atomic energy. The uranium boom was compared to earlier gold rushes, but it was different. Instead of the miner having a mule, a pick, and a pan, the

The oil refining center of Utah is located in the northwest section of Salt Lake City. Utah Oil Refining Company's plant has a total capacity of over 35,000 barrels of crude oil per day, with more than a dozen major processing, treating, blending, and utility units.

Drilling for new oil wells yielded important oil discoveries in San Juan County and the Uinta Basin.

Copper mining continues to be the most important element in Utah's mining industry. The recent expansion of the world-famous open-pit mine took the mining town of Bingham.

Potash mining is one of many phases of Utah's important mining industry.

prospector of the 1950s was equipped with a jeep and a Geiger counter. Some prospectors spent only weekends or vacation time, sometimes using a scintillometer in a low-flying airplane to detect the presence of ores with high radioactivity. Successful prospectors often sold their claims; others took to mining.

Charlie Steen is the best known of the "make it rich with uranium" miners. He was ready to quit when some cores he had taken showed a high concentration of uranium. He staked a claim and raised money to put in his own processing plant. His mine and his name became world famous.

Uranium mining in Utah centered in San Juan County, although there was activity in Emery, Grand, Wayne, and other counties. The valuation of property in San Juan County, from 1954 to 1959, jumped from less than $4 million to over $37 million.

By 1958 the Atomic Energy Commission withdrew its support for new prospecting and mining operations. Further expansion was halted; however, the commission continued to buy uranium from plants operating before this action was taken.

The mining and processing of the "Cinderella minerals" (those which seem to have little value) has become an important part of Utah's economy. These nonmetallics—gypsum, cement rock, clay, limestone, sand and gravel, Gilsonite, fluorspar, salt, sulphur, potash, and phosphate—are used extensively in building and construction and in other industries.

The *petroleum* industry also experienced a boom in the postwar years. In 1948 a successful oil well drilled in Ashley Valley southeast of Vernal set off a boom in oil exploration and development. At Aneth, on the San Juan River, a boom began in 1955. Now 500 wells in the Aneth area produce 75 percent of Utah's crude oil. Recently new oil discoveries have been made in Duchesne County. Pipelines carry the crude oil from the oil fields to refineries north of Salt Lake City. The refined products are then carried by pipelines to points in Utah, Idaho, Oregon, and Washington.

Manufacturing. The expansion of defense installations, mining, and related activities was paralleled by expansion in manufacturing. Until recently Utah had produced raw materials and shipped them out of the state for processing. Utah now moved more and more to processing raw materials and manufacturing goods from her minerals. The demand for finished goods came from the western states, chiefly California. The Pacific Coast states had experienced an expansion of population beyond their capacity to supply. Utah had the raw materials, the know-how, and the transportation system necessary to increase her role as a manufacturing state.

From 1939 to 1963 the number of manufacturing establishments doubled, the number of persons employed tripled, the amount of payroll increased seventeen times, and the value added to materials by manufacturing increased sixteen times. Most of the increase came in refining, smelting, processing, and fabricating Utah's metals and other mineral resources. Increase also came from processing food. There was expansion in meat-packing plants, poultry-processing plants, canning factories, and frozen food plants. Processing of dairy products increased.

Utah expanded manufacturing in other lines, such as candy making, milling, wearing apparel, printing and publishing, chemicals, paints, and tools.

Agriculture has undergone several changes in the postwar period. The number of farms decreased (from 28,500 in 1940 to 14,500 in 1971) while the size of farms increased (from an average of 354 acres in 1940 to 924 acres in 1971). The total number of acres of land in farms in Utah has increased only slightly. Today, Utah's cropland amounts to 4.1 percent of the total land area of the state, with 2.6 percent irrigated and 1.5 percent non-irrigated.

Farm income reached new highs. In 1970 farmers received $216,900,000 from sales of crops, livestock, and livestock products. This is the highest figure in Utah's agricultural history. Farmers received 31 percent of their income from cattle, 10 percent from sheep and wool, and about 20 percent from milk. This means that about 60 percent of farm income was from cattle, sheep, and dairying. About 80 percent of farm income was derived from livestock and livestock products: cattle, sheep and wool, milk, turkeys, chickens and eggs, and hogs. About 20 percent of farm income is derived from crops: grains, hay, sugar beets, vegetables, and fruits.

There has been a trend away from planting sugar beets and toward putting that land into feed crops for livestock.

A decline in the production of fruits

Urbanization and the expansion of industry required increased output of electric power.

since the 1930s has been partly due to urban expansion taking over orchard areas, but is also due to repeated killing frosts.

Electric power. Postwar expansion in business, industry, and urbanization required electric power production to keep pace. Most of the power used in Utah today is interconnected and furnished by over forty plants owned by a variety of utilities companies: private, municipal, cooperative, and federal. Increased power was furnished by expansion of the plants of private utilities, but also by reclamation projects under the Colorado River Storage Project (section 6). About 75 percent of the power is produced by steam (coal being used for heat), 20 percent by water power, and about 5 percent by internal combustion engines.

Transportation has undergone revolutionary changes in the past quarter century. The number of passenger cars approaches a half million. Trucking has become a major transportation business along with railroading and air freight transportation. Developments in aviation were advanced by the war. Today Utahns think nothing of flying great distances as a part of their normal business activities. The Salt Lake International Airport has expanded to keep up with its traffic and is a major link in national and international airways.

Increased mobility of people and urbanization have required the building of more and better highways in cities and between cities. The Federal Highways Act of 1958 provided for the construction of an interstate system of highways, 90 percent of the cost to be borne by the federal government. Governor Clyde took special interest in the system and put priority on those sections along the Wasatch Front. The system, when completed, will connect the communities of the state with north-south and east-west highways.

Railroading continued to be an essential part of Utah's transportation system with Ogden the rail center of Utah and much of the Mountain West.

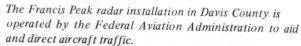

Jet aircraft increasingly took over passenger traffic and helped set the fast-moving pace of the postwar era.

Cloverleaf patterns of highways in the interstate system help keep a non-stop and even flow of traffic.

The Francis Peak radar installation in Davis County is operated by the Federal Aviation Administration to aid and direct aircraft traffic.

Interstate highway system in Utah.

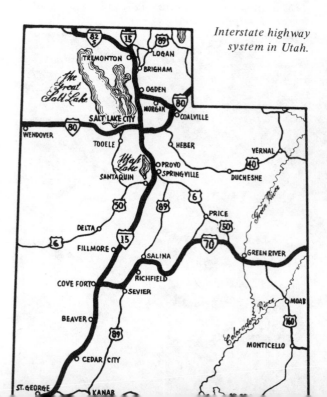

The Japanese Obon Festival, held annually in Salt Lake City.

5. MINORITY GROUPS STRIVED FOR IDENTITY AND EQUAL OPPORTUNITY IN UTAH

Utah has been built by people from many countries and of different backgrounds. While settlers from the British Isles and northern Europe have predominated, many from southern Europe and other countries of the world have come to Utah, made their homes, and added their skills and knowledge to making Utah what it is today. During the nineteenth century there was a general fusion of these peoples and their cultures. Utah was referred to as a "melting pot" by Utahns.

After World War II it became apparent that possibly four minority groups in Utah—the Spanish-speaking Americans, the Negroes, orientals, and Indians—had not "melted" and that they were being denied civil rights and equal opportunities for employment, housing, and entertainment, for example.

During the 1960s strong movements began among these minority groups for equal opportunities and the full exercise of the rights of citizenship. They wanted their group identity recognized. They wanted to preserve their own culture and their way of life. At the same time, they wanted to have equal opportunity for an education, for employment, and for building their own lives as citizens of Utah and the United States.

Spanish-speaking Americans (some use the name Chicano) make up the largest minority group in Utah today. The 1970 census estimated 43,550 people in this group, of which 29,629 have Spanish as a mother tongue. Of the nearly 9,000 families, 88 percent live in the urban areas of Weber, Davis, and Salt Lake counties with largest populations in Salt Lake City, Ogden, Provo-Orem, Tooele, and Brigham City. Many of these people came to the United States from Mexico, and to Utah from New Mexico, Colorado, and Texas. Some were brought into the United States to work for railroads, on farms, and in mines. Others came during World War II to work in defense industries. Nearly two-thirds of them have come to Utah since 1960. Notwithstanding the success of many in finding employment in a variety of occupations and in establishing homes, 14 percent of all the Spanish-speaking American families receive public assistance. In 1970 it was estimated that 18 percent of all families earn less than a poverty level income, and 41 percent of these families receive public assistance income.

These citizens are working to establish their own identity, maintaining some customs and features of their cultural background. They are working for equal opportunity in

A volunteer tutor from the University of Utah teaching English as a second language at the Guadalupe Center, Salt Lake City.

employment, education, social life, and civil rights.

Negroes have been in Utah since the days of the Mountain Men and the Pioneer Company of 1847. Negroes who came in 1847 were slaves. During the Civil War these slaves were freed, though some Utah slaveholders had freed their slaves before this time. Some freedmen moved on to California; others remained in Utah, where their descendants live today. Railroading and mining attracted other black workmen, until toward the end of the century there were about a thousand Negroes living in Utah.

From 1910-40 the Negro population averaged 1,233 persons. With World War II there was a rapid in-migration, but many of these left after the war. However, during the 1950s and 1960s the population increased until by 1970 the black population had increased to 6,617. Almost all of these families (92 percent) live in urban areas, the greatest numbers in Salt Lake City and Ogden. Black

citizens have met the same difficulties in Utah as they have in other states. They have been denied equal opportunities and have been confined, for the most part, to the poorer sections of cities. While blacks find employment in a variety of occupations, many are employed in the lower paying jobs. Of the black families as a whole, 18 percent receive public assistance. As many as 26 percent of all black families have an income less than that considered poverty level. Of these 42 percent receive public assistance.

Unfortunately, black citizens are discriminated against in Utah, legally, economically, and socially. While the Civil Rights movement has done much to effect actions which may correct some of these injustices, one of the major challenges of our time is to overcome prejudices and to establish attitudes and actions which will guarantee to all people equal rights and opportunities.

Orientals. The Chinese and Japanese came to Utah at various times in Utah's history. Their coming has been related in earlier chapters. While individual families may strive to maintain cultural identity, there is today a lessening of these cultural traditions, and ways are opening for orientals to participate more fully in all phases of American life.

The Indians of Utah in the twentieth century. (See chapter 21, section 6.) While the Dawes General Allotment Act of 1887 anticipated the end of the reservation system, the Indians found the reservations their main, if not their only means of retaining cultural identity and unity. Close groupings, as reservations or as settlements, persisted even when reservation lands were broken up and occupied in part by whites.

Reservation life was hard, at best. The allotment act hurt the Indians seriously. The act itself anticipated that in three generations the Indians would be landless, presumably assimilated into white society. The majority of Indians had little disposition to become farmers, even if they had the training. Much of the land allotted to them was poor and incapable of producing enough to support the family. Under these conditions some Indians leased or sold their lands to whites. Reservations were governed by agents appointed by the federal government. Indians had few freedoms, were often confined to the reservation, and forbidden the exercise of their native religious rituals and ceremonies. Their old traditions, dances, games, the telling of myths, legends, and folktales, were frowned upon.

The Indians were almost entirely forgotten until the 1920s when reform movements called national attention to their problems. Since that time the following *major developments* have taken place: (1) citizenship was granted to all Indians in 1924, though some had received it earlier under treaties; (2) the Indian Reorganization Act of 1934; (3) the establishment of the Indian Claims Commission in 1946; (4) the policy of termination of federal responsibility from about 1953 to about 1958; (5) the relocation of Indians from reservations to urban areas; and (6) the policy of self-determination and its implementation. These developments in national policy had their influence among Utah tribes though there were variations in how policies were effected, each band or tribe being different.

Reform movements called for a study of the conditions of Indian life. In 1928 the Meriam report detailed the serious conditions under which the American Indians lived. The poverty of the Indians, their poor health, education, and economic conditions shocked the nation. Some attempts were made to help the Indians at that time, but the United States was soon in an economic depression and there was little help. However, in 1934 Congress passed the Wheeler-Howard Act,

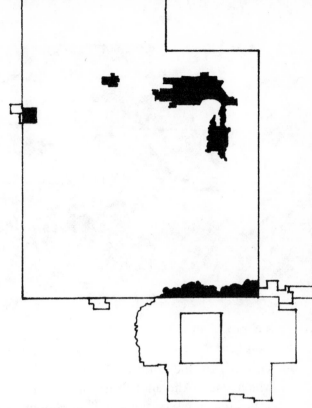

Indian lands operating under some degree of federal responsibility are shown on this map. Much of the northern portion of the Uintah and Ouray Indian Reservation has been allotted and opened to settlement.

The Ute Tribal Business Committee, 1969. Standing, left to right: Gary Poowegup, Fred Conetah, Wilbur Cuch. Sitting, left to right: Homey Secakuku, Francis Wyasket, Chairman, and Irene Cesspooch Cuch.

483

A Navajo family in Monument Valley.

Rug weaving continues as a Navajo art.

known as the *Indian Reorganization Act*, which ended the allotment policy and encouraged the conservation and development of Indian lands and resources. The act granted the Indians the right of self-government through written constitutions and elected tribal councils. Financial credit was extended to the tribes. Provisions were made for vocational education. Indians were given the right to form businesses and other organizations. Freedom of religion was restored, and Indians were encouraged to revive native customs and culture traits and activities. The allotment of land to individual Indians was forbidden; surplus lands remaining were to be restored to tribal ownership. Indian response was slow, but some economic gains were made.

Utah Indians served in World War II and had close contacts with the non-Indian world. Some of these Indians returned to the reservations determined to help their people gain some of the advantages of white technology. Others moved from the reservations to towns and cities.

In August 1946 the government set up the *Indian Claims Commission* to hear all Indian claims of unjust land dealings with the view to compensating the Indians for lands taken from them illegally or for less than proper payment. In cases presented by Utah Indians before the commission, Utah Indians have received millions of dollars in payment for lands they lost to the white man. Since 1950 over $38 million has been awarded to the Ute Tribe of Utah and Colorado. The money received from these court decisions has been divided among the tribes and members of the tribes.

In the meantime, Senator Arthur V. Watkins of Utah and many others believed it was time for the government to terminate its stewardship over the Indians, that Indians should no longer be wards of the government, that they should be free from the reservations, and should step out into full, equal, and responsible participation in American life. *Termination* of federal supervision was thought of as removing restrictions over Indian property and persons. In 1953 termination was applied as government policy. Federal responsibility for Paiute Indians on five reservations or settlements in Utah was terminated in 1956: Cedar City, Indian Peaks, Kanosh, Koosharem, and Shivwits.

A second government program of the 1950s was the *relocation* of Indians from reservations to towns and cities where homes and jobs were to be found for them. Many Indians relocated and became successful residents in the cities. Hundreds of "urban Indians" are found in Utah towns and cities today. But many "relocated" Indians were not happy and returned to the reservations.

The receipt of money from the Indian Claims Commission and from the development of gas and oil led Ute Indians of mixed ancestry to request termination. Many Ute, however, elected to remain on the reservation and retain their special relationship with the government. The Ute Partition Act of August 27, 1954, formally separated the two groups. In 1961 the secretary of the interior terminated federal supervision over the affairs of the withdrawing mixed-blood Ute.

By 1958 it was seen that termination was not working as planned. Bands of Paiute and some Ute Indians were brought close to economic and social chaos by the withdrawal of the services of the Bureau of Indian Affairs. Gradually termination as a policy has been replaced for many Indians. Since 1968 various programs of the federal government have been applied to the Indians. The Office of Economic Opportunity early provided funds for programs the Indians would run themselves. This was perhaps the first time Indians had been permitted to assume full responsibility for the management of funds for reservation programs. The success of this program prompted a new national Indian policy of *self-determination*, something the Indians had been advocating for years. President Richard M. Nixon, in a special message to Congress on Indian affairs, July 8, 1970, stated: "We must begin to act on the basis of

what the Indians have long been telling us. The time has come to break decisively with the past and to create the conditions for a new era in which the Indian future is determined by Indian acts and Indian decisions." Today many programs are suggested by Indians, financed by the federal government, and managed and controlled by the Indians themselves. Self-determination is the key word in American Indian policy today. It finds expression in educational, medical, social, and economic programs on the reservations.

Today in Utah there are over eleven thousand Indians on reservations, in settlements, and in towns and cities. There are two major tribes and reservations: the Navajo Tribe on the Navajo Indian Reservation (Utah, Arizona, and New Mexico) and the Ute Tribe on the Uintah and Ouray Indian Reservation in the Uinta Basin. Tribes are largely in charge of their own affairs.

The *Navajo Tribal Council*, with headquarters at Window Rock, Arizona, manages affairs for the Navajo Tribe on the Navajo Reservation. The *Navajo Times*, published weekly for and owned by the Navajo people since 1959, is the official newspaper of the Navajo Tribe. Schools, hospitals, and other services are being provided with federal assistance through community action. The Seventh-Day Adventists have established a medical mission in Monument Valley. Navajo children are being taught an understanding of and an appreciation for their native culture as well as the white culture. In 1964 there were 1,177 children between the ages of six and eighteen among the Navajo living in Utah. Of these 582 attended school in federal boarding schools, 241 were attending public schools, and 24 attended mission schools. At Aneth boarding school, 65 students are enrolled. Many of the Navajo children from the reservation attend the Intermountain School in

Brigham City. This federal boarding school, started in 1949, enrolls over two thousand Navajo students. Increasingly it is a school administered by and for the Navajo.

The Ute Indian Tribe, a chartered corporation under the provisions of the Indian Reorganization Act, comprises three bands: The Uintah (about 44 percent of the total population), the White River (18 percent), and the Uncompahgre (38 percent). The tribe is governed by a Business Committee of six members. In addition to this committee, each band has its traditional "council of old men."

Under the self-determination program the Ute have taken advantage of many government programs since 1967. Funds have come through the Office of Economic Opportunity, the Department of Health, Education, and Welfare, and the Bureau of Indian Affairs. The Ute Indian Tribe set up an Advanced Action Agency to promote these community action programs on a reservation-wide basis. Educational programs include meeting needs of preschool children (Head Start and Day Care), potential college students (Project Upward Bound), adults who want to continue their education (Career Development program), and the elderly who wish to participate in social, recreation, and craft programs. A program exists to help alcoholics. The Advanced Action Agency has been especially active recently in sponsoring economic development programs. Now under construction is the multi-million dollar motel-resort complex for the Bottle Hollow Reservoir area. This is part of a master plan for the development of recreation on the reservation. Other lodges are being built and recreation facilities constructed for year-round recreation for visitors. Tribally owned and operated businesses include Utefab Ltd. and the Ute Crafting Company, which provide jobs in furniture manufacturing and craftwork.

In addition to the money received from the Indian Claims Commission, the tribe has income from 15,000 acres of commercial timberlands, Utah's only reservation with significant timber resources. There are many irrigation projects, the most notable being the Uintah irrigation project, which provides water to irrigate 79,000 acres of land. Ranching is a significant aspect of Ute economic life. In the years ahead the Ute plan to capitalize on the scenic attractions of their land and provide recreational facilities and opportunities for vacationers.

The typical Ute today has completed nine years of formal schooling, including some vocational training. He lives in a community of less than 250 people. His house, usually more than fifteen years old and overcrowded, is equipped with electric lights, television, radio, a refrigerator, a washing machine, and a gas or electric stove in the kitchen. Many live in modern homes, but 40 percent of the houses are judged substandard. Fifty-eight percent of the families have incomes less than $3,000 a year.

School enrollment among the children on the Uintah and Ouray Reservation is high. In 1964, of 520 children between the ages six to eighteen, 510 were in school: 471 in public schools, 37 in federal boarding schools, and 2 in mission schools. Taking special work were 151 persons over eighteen.

The majority of Utah Indian children, generally, have been attending public schools since 1952. In addition to the schools named above, a small day school is maintained at Ibapah to serve the Gosiute Tribe. There is a Bureau of Indian Affairs dormitory at Richfield; students attend the Richfield public schools. Higher education grants and scholarships are available for qualified students.

Today, Indian birthrates are almost double the United States rate as a whole.

INDIAN RESERVATIONS AND SETTLEMENTS IN UTAH

	Band or Tribe	Estimated Population	Location
Reservations			
Uintah and Ouray	Ute	1,600 (1971)	Duchesne and Uintah counties. Settlements: Fort Duchesne, Ouray, Randlett, Whiterocks, and others. 852,500 acres.
Skull Valley	Gosiute	30 (1969)	Tooele County. Most live in Grantsville. 17,400 acres.
Goshute	Gosiute	100 (1959)	In Utah and Nevada; Juab County, Utah. 38,800 acres in Utah
Navajo	Navajo	4,485 (1963)	In Utah, Arizona, and New Mexico. San Juan County, Utah. 1,194,800 acres in Utah.
Settlements			
Cedar City (termination, 1956)	Paiute	28 (1955)	Northeast edge of Cedar City. A few acres.
Gandy Homestead	Paiute		South of Goshute, Millard County. 160 acres.
Indian Peaks (termination 1956)	Paiute	26 (1955)	Southwestern Utah.
Kanosh (termination 1956)	Paiute	42 (1955)	Southeast of Fillmore, in central Utah.
Koosharem (termination 1956)	Paiute	34 (1955)	Southwest of Koosharem, in southcentral Utah.
Shivwits (termination 1956)	Paiute	130 (1955)	West of Saint George in southwestern corner of Utah.
Washakie	Shoshoni		Box Elder County near Idaho boundary line. Farm owned and operated by the LDS Church Welfare Program.
Paiute	Paiute		Beaver County.

During the 1940s the Indian population in the United States increased 20 percent, during the 1950s 40 percent, and during the 1960s 50 percent.

While the Indian is learning from the white man the white man can learn much from the Indian—the values of group identity, respect for nature, and reverence for life, for example. It is now a century since the reservation system was established. Many things have changed, many others have not. Today the reservation is "the last stronghold of Indian culture and of an emerging Indian nationalism."

6. THERE WAS A MAJOR MOVEMENT FOR RECLAMATION AND CONSERVATION OF NATURAL RESOURCES

Water, so essential to life in Utah, continued to be one of our most precious resources. Cities, industries, and farms increased their demands on the short supply of available water. Utah's future development, it was believed, was tied closely to the development of water resources. Leaders in Utah and other western states years ago saw the need to make fullest use of our water resources when they looked to the Colorado River as an additional source for water.

The Colorado River. Waters of the Colorado River drainage area have been used from the beginning of settlement along the tributaries of the river. Under the Reclamation Act of 1902 Utah's first major reclamation project involving Colorado River waters, the Strawberry Valley Project, was completed. (See chapter 20, section 4.) Other projects followed. In time, states sharing the Colorado River came to have similar interests in the waters flowing into the river. The upper Colorado River states wanted to use its waters for irrigation and electric power production. The lower Colorado River states had these same interests as well as flood control. In January 1922 the *Colorado River Commission* was organized. Out of the work of that commission the *Colorado River Compact* was signed November 24, 1922. Governors, state legislatures, and Congress approved the compact. Its tasks were to define the purpose for which water could be used beneficially, set priorities, and provide for an equitable distribution of the water supply. Under the compact, the water resources were to be developed for the entire Colorado River basin. The history of the efforts to achieve the goals of the compact has been long and stormy. Nevertheless some important achievements have been made. It was under this compact and federal legislation that the Hoover (Boulder) Dam and other lower basin projects and canals were constructed.

It was not until 1948 that the upper basin states agreed on the amount of Colorado River water to be apportioned to the several states. Under the *Upper Colorado River Basin Compact* of 1948 waters were apportioned as follows: Colorado, 51.75 percent; New Mexico, 11.25 percent; Utah, 23 percent; Wyoming, 14 percent; and Arizona, an amount not to exceed 50,000 acre-feet per year. In 1952 a master plan was developed

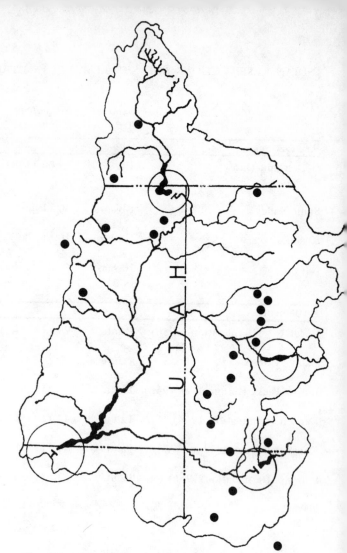

The Colorado River Storage Project features four storage units and many participating projects.

for the construction of dams and reservoirs which would provide Colorado River water to farm lands. The plan was called the *Colorado River Storage Project and Participating Projects*. It was signed into law on April 11, 1956, by President Eisenhower. Two major projects were to come to Utah at once—Glen Canyon and Flaming Gorge.

Flaming Gorge Dam was completed in the fall of 1963. The generation of electric power began in November, and the Flaming Gorge Dam and Recreation Area was dedicated by Mrs. Lyndon B. Johnson in August 1964. The dam, on the Green River in the

Flaming Gorge Dam provides water power for generating electricity and backs waters up the canyons of the Green River, providing recreational opportunities.

A major purpose of Flaming Gorge Dam is the generation of electric power. These men are lowering the 120-ton rotor into the stator ring of a generator. The rotor will spin at 240 revolutions per minute and generate 36,000 kilowatts of electricity at full capacity.

The Glen Canyon Dam provides waterpower for the generation of electricity and creates Lake Powell, center of boating and fishing.

Lake Powell, the reservoir behind Glen Canyon Dam, is in colorful contrast to the rugged character of the canyonlands of southeastern Utah.

Construction of the Glen Canyon Dam began in 1960 and was completed in 1964.

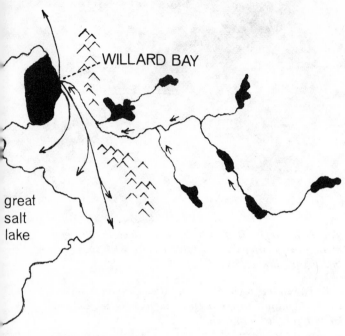

WILLARD BAY

great
salt
lake

The Weber Basin Project will control waters of the Weber and Ogden river systems by conserving them in Willard Bay. When needed the waters are pumped from the bay into a system of canals leading to farm lands.

The Bonneville unit of the Central Utah Project is designed to take waters from the Colorado River drainage area and move them into the Bonneville drainage area to the west of the Wasatch Mountains.

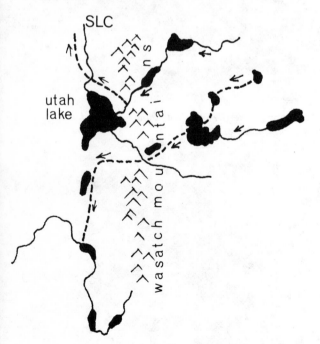

SLC

utah
lake

wasatch mountains

Uinta Mountains, rises 495 feet above its foundation. Water is backed up through the canyons of the Green River and into Wyoming.

Glen Canyon Dam was completed in 1964. The dam, situated on the Colorado River in Arizona about twelve miles downstream from the Utah-Arizona state line, impounds waters upstream into the far reaches of the canyons of the Colorado River in Utah.

The main functions of these two major storage units are storing water, flood control, and generating electric power. Associated with these units are participating projects that distribute water to new land, which supplements existing irrigation water supplies and furnishes water to communities for industrial and domestic use. Projects for the recreational use of the waters are also underway.

The *Emery County Project*, west of Castle Dale and completed in 1966, consists of the Joes Valley Dam, diversion dams, and canals. Waters stored in the reservoir are used to irrigate over 18,000 acres.

The *Central Utah Project* will divert water which would otherwise flow into the Colorado River for use in the Uinta and Bonneville basins. The water will be used for irrigation, municipal and industrial purposes, and the production of hydroelectric power. The plan is to intercept waters flowing down the south slope of the Uinta Mountains and convey them westward by gravity flow to the Strawberry Reservoir and thence into the Bonneville Basin, benefiting communities, industry, and farms in Salt Lake, Utah, and Juab counties. Bays of Utah Lake are to be isolated and used to store fresh water for diversion by canals to irrigated and new lands. Units of the project will increase water to the Uinta Basin as well as replace waters diverted westward. The project is in its initial phase only, some units are under construction, other units have not been approved. The Vernal unit has been completed: The Steinaker Reservoir, north of Vernal, stores and distributes the excess flow of Ashley Creek.

Other reclamation projects.

The *Dixie Reclamation Project* was authorized by Congress in 1964 for the Virgin and Santa Clara rivers. Its purposes include flood control, irrigation, providing municipal water, electric power, and new recreation areas.

The *Weber Basin Project* was authorized by Congress in 1949 and funds were appropriated in 1952. When the various projects are completed the water supply for the area will be doubled. A few of the units have been completed; others are under construction. Besides the usual water development projects such as building dams to store and control the flow of water, this project looks to the reclamation of low-lying lands near the shores of Great Salt Lake through drainage. Completed is the Willard Bay unit, a fresh water bay on the bed of Great Salt Lake. Fresh water is stored there in runoff seasons and during dry months its waters are pumped into canal systems which carry the water to farm lands.

These reclamation projects not only provide more water for Utahns for irrigation, industries, and municipalities, but also recreation facilities. The federal Bureau of Reclamation and the Utah State Water and Power Board are the two agencies responsible for the reclamation program in Utah. They are planning for the future water and power needs of Utah.

Concern for the environment. With the expansion of population and increased leisure time for recreation, many people "took to the hills." There were demands to increase accommodations in the national parks and monuments and an equally strong demand to preserve the environment from destruction due to the number of visitors. There were two major movements during the 1950s and 1960s with regard to natural resources and the environment: (1) make scenic attractions of Utah available to visitors through good roads and accommodations for eating and sleeping; (2) preserve the scenic wonders from destruction by putting these areas under national or state protection and opening them to the public on a limited basis.

Members of the business community saw the issue in different ways. There were those who wanted to encourage out-of-state visitors to come to Utah for vacations in order to bring more money into Utah. On the other hand there were persons with mining and livestock interests who saw the enclosing of lands into reserves as hurting their interests. The problems are complex; the answers are not easy. There have been, and there continue to be, accommodations on all sides.

National parks, monuments, and reserves. The conservation movement of the 1960s found expression in Utah in the addition of natural reserves for the enjoyment of the people. Utah had already made considerable strides in the establishment of national parks and monuments. (Chapter 20, section 6.) In September 1964 *Canyonlands National Park* was added to Utah's list, and in 1971 two national monuments were made national parks: Arches National Park and Capitol Reef National Park. Some reserves were increased in size.

Upon completion of the Glen Canyon Dam and with the creation of Lake Powell, 1,196,545 acres in Utah and Arizona consisting of Lake Powell were set aside as the *Glen Canyon National Recreation Area*. Similarly, when Flaming Gorge Dam was completed, *Flaming Gorge National Recreation*

Area was created. These additions have given Utah a total of five national parks, six national monuments, and two national recreation areas.

Utah also has four national wildlife refuge areas: Locomotive Springs National Wildlife Refuge, Bear River Migratory Bird Refuge, Ouray National Wildlife Refuge, and Fish Springs National Wildlife Refuge. In addition to these refuge areas there are several waterfowl management areas: Stewart Lake, Clear Lake, Powell Slough, Farmington Bay, Howard Slough, Ogden Bay, and Salt Creek.

The *High Uintas Primitive Area*, another national reserve, was set aside by the United States Forest Service in 1931 for the purpose of protecting a unique wilderness area.

In 1965, largely through the efforts of Bernice Gibbs Anderson of Corinne, and in anticipation of the centennial of the completion of the transcontinental railroad at Promontory Summit, May 10, 1869, Congress established the *Golden Spike National Historic Site*, consisting of 2,172 acres at the site of the union of the rails.

In the decade after the end of World War II the number of visitors to the national parks and monuments doubled; the National Park Service and the Department of the Interior became alarmed at the threat of overcrowding and the lack of facilities. The National Park Service renewed its efforts to achieve the purposes of the reserves by establishing *Mission 66*—a set of objectives to be accomplished by 1966, the fiftieth anniversary of the National Park Service. The program was "*to conserve* the scenery and the natural and historic objects and the wildlife therein, and *to provide for the enjoyment* of the same in such manner and by such means as will *leave them unimpaired* for the enjoyment of future generations." The mission was accomplished and these national reserves are being protected as well as possible against heavy use. Nearly two million people visited Utah's national parks and monuments in 1966. The number of visitors continues in ever-increasing numbers.

State parks movement. In 1957 the legislature created the State Park and Recreation Commission and charged it with the responsibility of putting into effect a broad state park program. Three existing state parks were put under the supervision of the commission. Today there are over forty state parks. Included in the state park and recreation system are museums, recreational areas, historic and geologic sites.

7. UTAH ACHIEVED A NEW HIGH IN HER CULTURAL TRADITION

The fine arts in Utah in recent years have developed from **well established traditions**. *College and university* departments of music, art, and drama continued these traditions. Each season might witness the performance of a symphony, oratorio, and opera, as well as Greek, Shakespearean, or contemporary plays. Art exhibits of faculty and students were regular features.

The *McCune L.D.S. School of Music* was an important music center from the early 1920s to the mid-1950s. Mr. and Mrs. Alfred W. McCune gave their magnificent home on North Main Street in Salt Lake City to the Mormon church for its use, and the school of music came into being. Through the years over forty thousand students studied vocal and instrumental music under some of Utah's finest musicians. Anthony C. Lund, Tracy Y. Cannon, N. Lorenzo Mitchell, and B. Cecil Gates were among the leaders through the years.

The *Utah Art Institute* (created by the legislature in 1937 as the Institute of Fine Arts) has been a leading force in encouraging

The Utah Symphony Orchestra, with Maurice Abravanel conducting, is shown here on tour, giving a concert in Athens, Greece.

the development of the arts in Utah. The *Salt Lake Art Center*, founded in 1933 as the Art Barn, has provided artists a place to show their work. From September to June each year the center has a traveling exhibit which shows to the public schools in the state.

The *Utah Symphony* grew out of the Utah WPA Orchestra, organized in 1935 under the direction of Reginald Beales. Wartime problems plagued the symphony. In 1947 Maurice Abravanel came as director and he has since built a symphony with a national reputation. Besides annual concerts in Utah, the symphony has given concerts throughout the United States, Europe, and South America. Recordings have been well received. Concerts in Utah have featured national artists as well as talented young Utahns.

Prosperity, the expansion of universities, increased leisure time, and a higher educa-

tional level of the people contributed to the growth of the fine arts in Utah in the postwar period.

The **universities and colleges** emerged as important centers for the development of the arts. The construction of fine arts buildings during the 1960s added considerably to the cultural enjoyment of Utahns. These centers provide theaters and concert halls where audiences may enjoy dramatic and comic stage plays, operas, ballet and modern dances, symphonies, choral groups, small groups of musicians, and solo artists. These centers have hosted America's great performing artists and have given Utah performing groups a setting for their concerts. Art galleries have provided opportunity for faculty and students to display their works in the visual arts. Many of the leading artists working in painting, ceramics, sculpture, fabric sculpture (weaving),

Ballet West, Utah's distinguished ballet group, has won wide praise.

and design are connected with the universities. Their instruction has inspired many students to become professionals themselves and has lifted the level of appreciation of Utahns for works of art. In recent years the universities and colleges have experimented with new art forms. The late Calvin Fletcher at Utah State University had considerable influence in redirecting painters from stereotype portrayals and traditional media toward *experimentation*.

Elsewhere in the state new art forms developed. Ballet is Utah's newest performing art, largely through the work of Willam Christensen at the University of Utah. Today, *Ballet West*, under his direction, is an outstanding group. Virginia Tanner has achieved national recognition for her Children's Dance Theater. The *International Folk Dancers* of Brigham Young University are famous. The Southern Utah State College at Cedar City has developed an excellent *Shakespeare theater* which produces a festival of three plays each summer.

Music continues to have an important place in Utah's cultural tradition. In 1965 the Salt Lake Oratorio Society presented its fiftieth annual rendition of Handel's *Messiah*. For the Utah centennial celebration in 1947, *Promised Valley* was written by Arnold Sundgaard and Crawford Gates. This musical, themed to the Mormon migration in Utah, has been repeated as an annual summer presentation. *All Faces West*, a successful musical with a similar theme, is produced in Ogden.

The Tabernacle Choir continues to be Utah's best-known performing group. The choir became better known when it made a European tour in 1955 and a tour of the United States in 1958. The choir has also sung at recent presidential inaugurals. Recordings of its songs, sometimes with accompaniment by symphony orchestras, have been popular nationally. The Sunday morning broadcasts are heard and seen through much of the world.

Utah is also honored by such talented people as Leroy J. Robertson of the Univer-

sity of Utah, whose musical compositions have been performed widely and recorded by soloists and groups. Alexander Schreiner, Tabernacle organist, is one of America's finest organists. A Utah pianist, Grant Johannesen, resident in New York City, is a nationally recognized concert artist.

Utahns have also achieved eminence in *sculpture*. Cyrus E. Dallin achieved a place in American art as a sculptor of the Indian. He also did the Paul Revere statue near the Old North Church in Boston. Perhaps Utah's most distinguished sculptor was Mahonri Young, a grandson of Brigham Young. His Seagull monument on Temple Square was his best-known work in Utah until 1947 when his bronze figures and dramatic friezes were unveiled on the This is the Place monument.

As prosperity continues and leisure is available, no doubt the arts and literature will continue to flourish. While a great deal of writing has been done on Utah's history and culture in the past generation, still there has not been written the great history, novel, poem, play, or musical catching the full spirit of Utah's heritage.

Performers from the Repertory Dance Theatre Company create a modern dance number.

A scene from a play at the Pioneer Memorial Theatre.

UTAH'S HERITAGE TODAY

Our study of Utah's heritage may be said to have come to a close with chapter 25. Heretofore the author has selected and organized those facts and judgments he thought were important for an appreciation and understanding of Utah and her heritage. In this chapter the author comments on contemporary developments and future prospects for Utah. You will want to think about the issues raised and the problems discussed. The future of Utah will depend partially on how you respond to the challenges this age presents.

IN THIS CHAPTER
THE AUTHOR COMMENTS ON

1. Utah's challenges and opportunities in government and finance.

2. The gains and losses of urbanization.

3. Utah's heritage through historical study and preservation.

4. Utah's heritage and you.

26

1. UTAH'S CHALLENGES AND OPPORTUNITIES IN GOVERNMENT AND FINANCE

Throughout Utah's history, there have been problems to live with and work through. Each generation meets problems, solves some, and leaves unsolved ones for the next generation. No generation ever "had it made" for them. We have inherited a world not of our making—of good things and bad things. The bad things we should accept as challenges and opportunities. From our study of the recent past in Utah's history, here are some of the problems you will have to live with, big problems you will have to help solve.

Utah is economically dependent on other regions. Despite the energies of her people through the years, Utah has not developed an economy that produces more than it brings in. In other words, we buy more than we sell. We are somewhat balanced in our economy now because of the money the federal government spends in Utah. If it were not for federal spending in Utah—military installations, defense industries, reclamation projects, and similar businesses—Utah's economy might be in a depression.

The United States enjoys a high degree of prosperity at this time, but this prosperity is built largely on American spending for war and foreign aid. A major challenge of our time is to *create a society and economy on the foundation of peace, not war.*

Utah state expenditures go mainly for education, roads and highways, and public welfare. Each area is also supported by federal grants. In financing public education, Utah has a special problem. Utah has a high birthrate and ranks high among the states as to the number of school-age children and the percent who attend school. Since Utah has comparatively few private schools, the children go to public schools that depend on tax money for support. Utah also ranks very high in the nation in the proportion of its college-age youth attending colleges and universities. While the demand for education is high, our ability to pay is less than average in the nation. But people spend their money for what they value most. It is a tribute to the people of Utah that they support education as they do, but the needs are still great.

Public welfare is one of man's opportunities to show his humanity to his fellow man in an anonymous manner. But the expenditures for public welfare to the *unemployed* is a problem worthy of study. There is a growing interest in having employables work for their checks, as in WPA days. This would reduce unemployment and welfare and at the same time provide the manpower for needed and desired community and state projects.

Taxes and services.

One of the major problems Utah faces today is the financing of services performed by state and local government. Our needs are many. We make many demands on government. But our income is comparatively small, hence our ability to pay is less than average. The state has increasingly relied on sales and income taxes and less on property taxes. Utahns pay a higher percentage of their personal income in state sales tax and individual income tax than do people in any other western state. On the other hand Utah taxes corporate income less than other western states with such a tax. Utah business and industrial owners pay a larger portion of the property taxes than residential and agricultural owners, compared to most other states.

Many people are opposed to taxation in any form and for any purpose, but any system of government can only be kept alive by taxation. Citizens must be willing to pay for services rendered. The essential point is: Citizens, through their representatives, should determine the services they want of state and local government and then be willing to be taxed sufficiently to pay for those services. Too frequently, in an effort to save tax dollars, a service is poorly financed and can do little of the business it was created to do beyond "keeping the shop open." But citizens should insist that government exercise economy and provide efficient service. We should insist that local, state, and federal governments engage in long-term planning of programs.

What services should local governments perform? Local government must be the servant of the people and serve the needs of the people. It is a general observation of students of government that if state and local governments do not provide essential services, the people will demand that the federal government provide them.

Many people feel the federal government has increased its powers. The central government has always been strong, and we should not want it otherwise. However, some feel that state government should be stronger. We can make state government stronger by our greater participation in it. When local governments fail to do essential tasks, to provide proper and essential services for the people, the people seek a solution to their problems by going to that level of government which will help them.

It is important that we respect each level of government for the work it should perform. It is equally important that we exercise our influence on each level of government, by voting, by writing letters to our mayors, commissioners, representatives, and others, and by attending public meetings.

The national government has become big government, but it should not be distrusted any more than small or state government should be despised. In this age of rapid communication, Washington, D.C., is closer to us than south Salt Lake City was to Brigham Young in the 1850s. Time and distance are no problem to us today; it is simply a matter of our taking time to let our governments know how we feel about things. Big government need not be feared any more than big church, or big bank, or big company. It is important that governments, churches, banks, and companies tell the people about their activities and that the people make it their business to know what is going on. It is important to have respect for elected representatives—on the city, county, state, and national level—and that we let them know how we feel and think about issues. It is equally important that they keep us fully informed about the affairs of government.

The success of a democracy depends largely on the people exercising the right to vote. In many states in recent years as few as 50 percent of the eligible voters actually voted in an election. However, Utah has ranked high, and recently 80 percent of Utah's voters went to the polls, making Utah the state with the highest percentage of people voting.

2. THE GAINS AND LOSSES OF URBANIZATION

The pioneers of Utah came with the dream of establishing villages patterned after their prophet's City of Zion. While the pioneer villages were laid out in that pattern, and the physical evidence remains in our street plans, the concept seems to have been forgotten. Our capacity to build beautiful cities far exceeds that of the pioneers; the pioneer vision of beautiful cities far exceeds our will to create.

The rapid urbanization of the Wasatch Front has made it possible for citizens to have many comforts and conveniences of city-dwelling. However, urbanization has brought many problems.

Urban growth is often new growth, leaving the old center of town or city to decay from disuse and become an empty shell. *Slums* exist in some Utah communities, and in many more there are dying centers while new growth expands on the outskirts, taking agricultural land and requiring additional services in electricity, water supply, and sewage disposal. Salt Lake City has had the problem of urban decay for decades. In the 1960s steps were taken toward *urban renewal* through such actions as the demolition of old buildings and in the erection of the Salt Palace complex, the Metropolitan Hall of Justice and Service Center, the Central Public Library, storm sewers for protection against flood damage, and sewage treatment plants.

In metropolitan areas there is emerging the problem of multiple and overlapping units of government between cities and county. Studies must be made and firm actions taken. This may include consolidation or the elimination of overlapping functions and services.

The spread of suburbs has taken some of Utah's better agricultural lands. Expansion and building of airports and interstate highways has added to this problem. It is estimated that each year one million acres of top grade farming land is lost to building programs and that one-quarter million acres is lost to erosion. Land use studies and planning of urban developments could save not only important farming areas but the beauty of the Utah landscape.

Some communities have grown without regard for the available water supply; some communities cannot grow larger because there is no water for expansion. Although farming takes about the same amount of water it has in past years, industry is using much more water than in the past. As new industries come to the state, the need for more water becomes important. More water is also being used in the home. We have water-using appliances—automatic washers, dishwashers, and air conditioners. Frequent showers or baths and fresh clothes are taken for granted. Some homeowners have swimming pools.

Better care must be taken of our existing water supply. We can keep our streams and lakes clean. We have the technology to develop better ways of recycling water. Water can be stored through use of antievaporation aids and through use of underground water storage. Multiple use of water can be improved.

Utah faces serious problems in waste disposal—garbage dumps and sewage. Lakes and streams, once the place of refuse, are becoming polluted to a dangerous degree, not only to the life of the waters, but to the health of man. Water is perhaps Utah's most essential natural resource. With our limited supply, it must be safeguarded and utilized with the greatest frugality.

Utah's industries and heating plants are contributing to an air pollution problem. The geographic situation of Salt Lake City is such that the valley easily retains smoke in the air. The valley has been known for its smoke since the days of coal heating. The multiplication of the use of automobiles also presents metropolitan Utah with a problem. Formerly, electric interurbans and streetcars carried many people great distances at little expense. The automobile is more individualistic, more convenient, faster, and each driver can take his own route at his own time. But traffic congestion and a degree of air pollution are among the results. The possibility of municipal rapid transit systems must be studied more thoroughly and the alternatives considered.

Pollution does not stop with air and water. There is also visual pollution. Commercial signs along our roads block our view of the scenery. Litter is not an uncommon sight. Housing and recreation projects sometimes are built without regard to the natural landscape. Power lines, television antennas, wrecked automobile yards, and garbage dumps are other examples of visual pollution.

For some, the solution to these and similar problems is the reduction of the number of people. This may be so, for sheer numbers can be a major problem. A greater problem, though, is *what* people do. Already most of our cities and communities are cleaner than they were at an earlier age. Man needs to put forth his best efforts to solving these problems. Part of the solution will require people to adjust to changes for the good of all the people and for our total environment.

3. UTAH'S HERITAGE THROUGH HISTORICAL STUDY AND PRESERVATION

The study of the past is impossible without records. Our study has been possible because individuals, government agents and agencies, churches, businesses, and other organizations kept records and have made them available for use. We know something of the early historic Indian tribes in Utah because travelers described them in writing. We know of the Mountain Men because some wrote diaries, or recorded their memories. The Mormons are known for record-keeping. From the beginning of their movement they kept official and personal records—their story can be told quite fully. Miners and railroaders rarely kept records—we know comparatively little of them. Much of what happened in our past can never be known because records were not made or preserved. Personal records for the twentieth century are particularly lacking. Only as the records of all the people who have built Utah are brought together can the story of all the people be told.

This points to one of the needs of our time—*the collection, preservation, and publication of the sources for Utah's history*. Much has already been done; much remains to be done. Many of the sources are in Utah, preserved and available for use, while others are scattered, unorganized, and in personal possession. Some of the sources are outside Utah and need to be microfilmed and brought to Utah. Before we can know more of our history, we must have more sources for study. The scattered materials must be collected, arranged, preserved, and housed so they can be used safely in generations to come.

There are diaries, journals, and bundles of letters in most homes in Utah. Old business records are in most offices. To guard against accidental loss or destruction, persons should consider having these records placed in public libraries and archives where they will be protected against loss by theft, fire, heat, moisture, or accident. Not every library is prepared to preserve and service important collections of papers. The best places to deposit personal and business records in the state are in the following libraries and archives: Utah State Historical Society, Salt Lake City; Western Americana Collection, University of Utah Library, Salt Lake City; the Historical Department (Archives), the Church of Jesus Christ of Latter-day Saints, Salt Lake City; Special Collections, The Library, Brigham Young University, Provo; and Special Collections, The Library, Utah State University, Logan.

The official records of the Territory of Utah and the State of Utah are in the *State Archives* in the State Capitol Building. But the space allotted to the archives is small and the records are subject to heat and possible damage by moisture. One of the great needs

of the state is a home for the archives of the state.

Some agencies have done well in preserving our history. The Utah State Historical Society collects historical source materials and publishes interesting selections from the sources and articles about our past in the *Utah Historical Quarterly*. The Daughters of Utah Pioneers also collect sources and have published, under the general editorship of Kate B. Carter, these series of volumes: *Heart Throbs of the West, Treasures of Pioneer History,* and *Our Pioneer Heritage*. The Historical Department (formerly the Church Historian's Office) of the Mormon church has one of the greatest collections of material on the settlement and early history of Utah and the Mountain West in existence. These public and private agencies should receive our support as they attempt to serve all the people.

The sources from which history is created, however, are not restricted to written records. Paintings, photographs, and maps, for example, are also studied by the student of the past. Just as important are the larger objects and remains: houses, churches, and other buildings, art and craft objects, tools, and machines. Thus, historical preservation includes more than saving the written records.

One of the major movements of recent times has been the realization by many people of the value of the *preservation of historic buildings, sites, and objects*. The Utah Heritage Foundation is the Utah part of a national effort to preserve the most significant of the historical remains of our past. The Utah Heritage Foundation, with other groups, has been influential in having buildings preserved which otherwise would have been destroyed.

In addition to this private movement, Governor Rampton created a Committee on Historic Preservation in 1969. Its purpose is to survey historic sites and choose significant examples to be included in the National Park Services register of historic places.

4. UTAH'S HERITAGE AND YOU

Our study of Utah's past should give us an appreciation for the lives and accomplishments of the many different people who made contributions to Utah's heritage. Indians, explorers, overland emigrants, Mormon pioneers, non-Mormon pioneers, merchants, miners, railroaders, ministers, teachers, government officials, soldiers, and explorers—all contributed to make Utah what it is. We have seen the influence of the lives of great men and women. But outside influences have shaped Utah's heritage, too. We have seen the impact of events in the nation and the world on affairs in Utah. The impact of scientific inventions and a variety of political, economic, and social ideas have been great in shaping our lives.

We all share in the material aspects of Utah's heritage, to a varying degree. Government strives to protect our liberties and freedoms, our lives and property, and performs many essential services. Schools and churches have been built for us. Parks and recreation areas have been established where we can refresh and enjoy ourselves. All these, and many more, have been established for us by someone else.

Utah's greatest heritage is her people— their ways of life, their beliefs and attitudes, their habits, their hopes for the future, and their abilities to achieve for themselves and for society. Our study of Utah's heritage has given us some of the values of those who have gone before.

Utah's heritage to us, individually, depends on what we will accept from that which people have valued most and passed on to us. There is the courage and daring of the

Mountain Men. The Mormon pioneer tradition points to the necessity of religious freedom and the opportunity to attempt to establish a new society on new foundations should the people be willing. That pioneering generation lived by dreams and visions for the future, yet they were practical, self-reliant, hard-working, and resourceful. While they respected the individual's freedom, they believed in cooperation and sacrificing for the common good. They valued education and service. Out of all this came the tradition of learning, of understanding wide fields of knowledge, of interest in the arts and sciences, and seeking excellence.

Utah's heritage includes a tradition of progressive reforms, a spirit of progress, a search for the beautiful in surroundings. There is a heritage of cooperation and helpfulness. Each generation has faced problems and has regarded them as opportunities.

This heritage has been instilled into the

people of Utah and shows itself in their accomplishments. Some have left the state to perform services for community and nation. Utahns have served on the Supreme Court of the United States, as governors of other states, as members of the cabinets of presidents of the United States, as chairmen of important national and international boards, as servants in high places in the Department of State, and in many other branches of federal government. During World War II a study showed that Utah produced more noted scientists in proportion to her total population than any other state in the Union. Utahns have also made names in education, literature, and arts, and various fields of entertainment.

More important, Utahns have contributed significantly at home in building Utah's society. These citizens who have chosen to give Utah their dedicated services deserve our praise and appreciation.

What will we do with our Utah heritage?

Governor Calvin L. Rampton gave us a challenge at ceremonies marking Utah's seventy-fourth birthday in January 1970. "The generations of Utahns living today have a commitment to the future of this state ... which was left to them by our pioneer fathers who provided our children with more than mere pages in history, but with a heritage of accomplishments and promises. ... Young and old—black, brown, yellow, or white—protestant, Jew, Mormon, or Catholic— no matter what our faith, color or creed, we must be willing to achieve progress without strife."

Our ability to see ahead is determined in part by our ability to see where we have been and what has been accomplished in the past. Knowing what people have accomplished in the past gives us courage and strength to achieve in the future.

CITATIONS ACKNOWLEDGEMENTS

Page 67. J. H. Simpson, *Report of Explorations across the Great Basin of the Territory of Utah; for a Direct Wagon-Route from Camp Floyd to Genoa, in Carson Valley, in 1859* (Washington, 1876), 52-57.

Page 87. Herbert E. Bolton, *Pageant in the Wilderness: The Story of the Escalante Expedition to the Interior Basin 1776; Including the Diary* . . . (Salt Lake City: Utah State Historical Society, 1950); *Utah Historical Quarterly*, XVIII, 184-186.

Page 90. Herbert E. Bolton, *ibid.*, 127.

Page 98. Charles L. Camp (ed.), *James Clyman, American Frontiersman, 1792-1881: The Adventures of a Trapper and Covered Wagon Emigrant as Told in his own Reminiscences and Diaries* (San Francisco, 1928), 25-26.

Page 100. Osborne Russell, *Journal of a Trapper, Or Nine Years in the Rocky Mountains, 1834-1843* (Boise, Idaho: Syms-York Co., 1921), cited by LeRoy R. Hafen, "Mountain Men before the Mormons," *Utah Historical Quarterly*, XXVI (October 1958), 324.

Page 109. Dale L. Morgan, *Jedediah Smith and the Opening of the West* (Indianapolis and New York: Bobbs-Merrill Company, Inc., c1953), 213-14; reprinted by University of Nebraska Press, Lincoln, 1964.

Page 119. John C. Frémont, *Report of the Exploring Expedition to the Rocky Mountains in the Year 1842, and to Oregon and North California in the Years 1843-'44* (Washington, 1845), 160.

Page 121. John C. Frémont, *ibid.*, 277.

Page 127. "The Journal of Heinrich Lienhard," *Utah Historical Quarterly*, XIX (1951), 134.

Page 144. *William Clayton's Journal: A Daily Record of the Journey of the Original Company of "Mormon" Pioneers from Nauvoo, Illinois, to the Valley of the Great Salt Lake* (Salt Lake City, 1921), April 18, 1847.

Page 146. Journal of Orson Pratt, *The Latterday Saints' Millennial Star*, XII (June 15, 1850), 178.

Page 147. *Ibid.*, 178.

Page 178. Howard Stansbury, *Exploration and Survey of the Valley of the Great Salt Lake of Utah* . . . (Philadelphia, 1852), 223.

Page 178. "The Handcart Song," *Pioneer Songs*, Compiled by Daughters of Utah Pioneers, Arranged by Alfred M. Durham (Salt Lake City: Daughters of Utah Pioneers, 1932), 21. Used by permission.

Page 199. Stansbury, 146-7.

Page 254. "Echo Canyon," *Pioneer Songs*, 196-7. Used by permission.

Page 283. "Once I Lived in Cottonwood," *Pioneer Songs*, 194. Used by permission.

Gratitude is expressed to the great number of friends, students, teachers, and colleagues who have given me assistance and encouragement in the preparation of this work.

I am indebted to my colleagues and students who have taught me a great deal and helped me refine ideas. Like all historians, I owe much to those who left primary sources and records from which the history of Utah can be written. Many writers have made significant contributions in secondary literature—general histories, reference works, monographs, theses, dissertations, and articles. These have been used with appreciation and are listed in the Teacher's Guide.

The library staff at Utah State University has been cooperative and helpful to the point of indulgence. For expert assistance from them and other librarians in Utah and elsewhere, I express my sincere thanks.

I am in a particular great debt to three persons. Pearl F. Jacobsen of Richfield read early drafts of the first eighteen chapters and gave invaluable assistance and encouragement when needed most. Everett L. Cooley, curator of Western Americana, University of Utah Library, and a former director of the Utah State Historical Society, and Charles S. Peterson, my colleague at Utah State University and former director of the Utah State Historical Society, each read the entire manuscript, offered suggestions, and saved me from many errors. I am deeply grateful for their help and encouragement.

Sheryl S. White, Evelyn Lawrence, and Mary Turner Adams have performed editorial services. Mary Turner has expedited the management of the project and simplified tasks considerably by handling many details. She prepared the index. Maria S. Ellsworth, my wife, has been most helpful through the years of preparation. Her expertise in elementary education, keen interest in the subject, and extensive reading and discussions with me have resulted in a much better book. The assistance of Marlowe C. Adkins, Jr., has been appreciated.

In acknowledging these contributions I must say that all errors in fact and interpretation in the text are my responsibility.

Appreciation is expressed to Gibbs M. Smith and Catherine Smith of Peregrine Smith, Inc. for taking on the project. Their patient persistence has paid off in the early publication of the book.

I am deeply grateful to Dale Bryner for designing the book, to Margaret D. Lester for her services in helping select photographs, and for the courtesies extended by her and the Utah State Historical Society for this project.

PICTURE CREDITS

Bert V. Allen, Utah State University, 15, 45.

Art Work of Utah (2 vols., Chicago, 1896), 276, 312, 313.

M. D. Baer, Salt Lake City, 387.

Ballet West, Salt Lake City, 494.

Bancroft Library, Berkeley, California, 81.

Brigham Young University, 473; College of Fine Arts for use of the C. C. A. Christensen paintings, 132-33, 142, 145, 148.

Dale Bryner, Weber State College, 26-27, 36, 53, 80, 92, 94, 97, 114, 154, 166, 174, 181, 211, 226, 293, 318, 365, 396, 401, 410, 483, 488, 490.

Olive Burt, courtesy of, Salt Lake City, 383.

Richard F. Burton, *The City of the Saints, . . .* (New York, 1862), 161, 202.

Deseret News, 407, 493.

Dale Fletcher, Brigham Young University, 280.

G. K. Gilbert, *Lake Bonneville*, U.S.G.S. Monograph No. 1 (Washington: G.P.O., 1890), 18, 19.

Thomas Gilcrease Institute of American History and Art, 163.

Earl J. Glade family, courtesy of, Salt Lake City, 409.

Guadalupe Center, Salt Lake City, 482.

Harper's Weekly, 214 (April 24, 1858), 219 (October 9, 1858), 322 (June 20, 1885).

Hill Air Force Base, Ogden, 442, 446, 450.

Historical Department (Church Historian's Office), Church of Jesus Christ of Latter-day Saints, and the courtesy of Leonard J. Arrington, church historian, 178, 277, 279, 280, 293, 294, 308, 309, 322, 334, 428, 440, 457.

Flora Belle Houston, "When the Mormons Settled San Bernardino," *Touring Topics*, April 1930, 185.

Index of American Design, National Gallery of Art, Washington D. C., 196, 197, 198.

Pearl F. Jacobson, courtesy of, Richfield, 284, 371.

Joslyn Art Museum, Omaha, Nebraska, 98, 111.

Thomas Koseki, Salt Lake City, 481.

KUTV, Salt Lake City, 472.

LeConte Stewart Art Museum, Kaysville, 398, 418.

Library of Congress, Washington, D. C., 118, 119, 214, 290, 414, 422, 424, 431, 444, 447, 453.

Gaell Lindstrom, Utah State University, 12-13, 29, 50, 82, 85, 288, 289, 366, 464.

James Linforth (ed.), *Route from Liverpool to Great Salt Lake City, illustrated with steel engravings and wood cuts from sketches made by Frederick Piercy . . .* (Liverpool, 1855), 126, 190.

Mesa Verde National Park, 50, 52, 55, 56.

Ogden Standard-Examiner, 465.

Orderville L.D.S. Ward, Orderville, painting by Elbert Porter, photographed by R. D. Adams, 297.

Oregon Historical Society, Portland, 106.

H. Reuben Reynolds, Utah State University, 473.

Hal Rumel, photographer, Salt Lake City, 462, 469.

Salt Lake Tribune, 442, 450, 452, 459, 503.

Roland Seigrist, Salt Lake City, and Utah State Historical Society, 50, 51.

Howard Stansbury, *Exploration and Survey of the Valley of the Great Salt Lake of Utah . . .* (Philadelphia, 1852), 116, 126, 149, 164.

Smithsonian Institution (U. S. National Museum), Washington, D. C., 122, 394, 502.

Leo Thorne, photographer, Vernal, 16.

Uintah School District, June Lyman and Norma Denver, *Ute People . . .* (Salt Lake City, 1970), 483.

Union Pacific Railroad, Omaha, Nebraska, and Salt Lake City, 125, 244, 253, 257, 308, 372, 480, 496.

United Air Lines, Salt Lake City and Chicago, 405, 480.

United States. Forest Service, 19, 24, 30, 31, 34, 46, 47, 420, 422, 433, 435. Bureau of American Ethnology (Smithsonian Institution), 15, 16, 64, 66, 67, 69, 70, 71, 72, 73, 74, 86, 224, 243, 394. Bureau of Reclamation, 88, 241, 489. Fish and Wildlife Service, 28, 42, 96. Geological Survey, 226, 239, 240, 241, 242, 243, 256. Federal Aviation Administration, 480. National Archives and Records Service, 368, 457. National Park Service, 255.

Ernest Untermann, Vernal, 17.

Utah. Department of Highways, 370, 388, 404, 480. Governor's Office, 467. Travel Development Division (Utah Tourist and Publicity Council), 12-13, 21, 24, 37, 470, 471. Utah Water and Power Board, 437. Wildlife Resources Division (Utah Department of Fish and Game), 96.

Utah Heritage Foundation, 266, 306, 307.

Utah State Historical Society, 16 (National Park Service), 22 (Inglesby collection), 23, 31, 48, 54, 58, 67 (Von Breckh, Simpson expedition, National Archives), 83, 84, 86 (Paul Salisbury), 89, 96, 99 (William H. Jackson), 112, 116 (William H. Jackson), 122, 126, 128, 130 (Ogden Chamber of Commerce), 134, 135, 140, 144, 148, 149 (Howard Stansbury), 150 (*Salt Lake Tribune*), 153, 155 (*Salt Lake Tribune*), 160, 168, 172-73 (T. B. H. Stenhouse), 176, 185 (Von Breckh, Simpson expedition, National Archives), 187, 188-89, 190, 191, 192, 193, 194, 200, 201, 202, 204, 206-7, 208, 209, 211, 212, 215, 217, 218, 219, 220, 221, 225, 228, 229, 230,

INDEX

PICTURE CREDITS